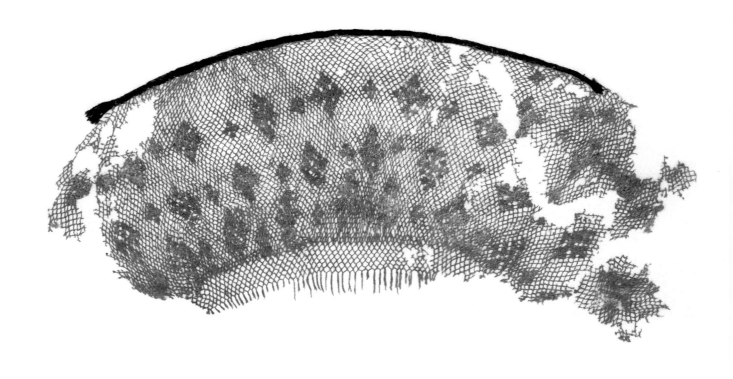

Hair-covering of embroidered silk net with braid edging.
Cat Nos 351 and 352/A7577a, b.

PERTH HIGH STREET

ARCHAEOLOGICAL EXCAVATION
1975–1977

Fascicule 3
The textiles and the leather

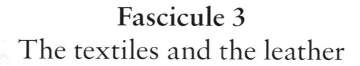

The textiles
P Z Dransart, H Bennett
and the late N Q Bogdan
with M L Ryder

The leather
Clare Thomas and the late N Q Bogdan
with an Appendix by Tom Bryce

Illustrations by Dave Munro and Tamlin Barton

TAYSIDE AND FIFE ARCHAEOLOGICAL COMMITTEE
PERTH
2012

This fascicule is one of four in a special series and is available by post from
John Sherriff, Hon Treasurer TAFAC, 21 Burleigh Crescent, Inverkeithing, Fife, KY11 1DQ
www.tafac.org.uk

Monograph One
Excavations in St Andrews 1980–89 A decade of archaeology in a historic Scottish Burgh

Monograph Two
The salt and coal industries at St Monans, Fife in the 18th and 19th centuries

Monograph Three
Perth: the archaeology and development of a Scottish burgh

Monograph Four
Dundee rediscovered: the archaeology of Dundee reconsidered

Monograph Five
Excavations at Brown Caterthun and White Caterthun hillforts, Angus, 1995–1997

Monograph Six
Excavations at St Ethernan's Monastery, Isle of May, Fife 1992–7

Monograph Seven
First Contact: Rome and Northern Britain

Submission of potential monographs
Offers of monographs are welcomed, and intending contributors should first contact the Assistant Editor,
34 Glenfarg Terrace, Perth PH2 0AP.

Front cover Artist's impression of medieval interior and leatherworkers by Maureen Rooney Mitchell.
(© Maureen Rooney Mitchell)

Back cover Decorated leather sheaths from Perth High Street.
(© Dave Munro)

Editor's note
TAFAC would like to acknowledge the support of Historic Scotland, Perth and Kinross Heritage Trust, the Guildry Incorporation of Perth, The Strathmartine Trust and Perth Museum and Art Gallery.

Published with assistance from the Perth Common Good Fund

ISBN 978 0 9561783 6 7

Copy edited by Lisbeth Thoms

Typeset by Christina Unwin *e-mail* christina@wave.demon.co.uk

Printed and bound by Farquhar and Son Ltd, Perth

Contents

THE LEATHER

Illustrations

Textiles

Tables

Textiles

Leather

Appendix 3

Foreword

It was in Perth in the mid 1970s that we saw, for the first time in Scotland, just how rich the urban archaeological resource might be. Perth is still the jewel in our urban archaeological crown, unique amongst Scottish towns for the depth, importance and consistently high quality of its archaeological remains. On the High Street, a depth of four metres of deposits is not unusual: layer upon layer of floors, occupation levels, yards and rubbish pits, which together represent the remains of successive buildings – workshops, storehouses, byres and dwellings – their load-bearing timbers made of oak or ash, and their walls of birch wattle.

The Perth High Street 1975–77 excavation was extraordinarily rich in artefacts and environmental evidence, providing a remarkably detailed picture of domestic and commercial life within a 12th- to 13th-century Scottish burgh. The soil conditions were often waterlogged and large quantities of organic material survived: over 6,000 pieces of leather alone; a wide range of wooden artefacts, including a French wine barrel; and the textiles included silk and hair. Over 50,000 sherds of pottery were recovered – probably the largest assemblage from a single site anywhere in Scotland. Numerous excavations in Perth through the 1980s and 90s have continued to furnish a wealth of evidence and opened windows on the past in sometimes surprising ways.

And yet, when Nick Bogdan and his team began their work at Perth High Street in 1975, they could not have foreseen the riches they would unearth – or that it would become Nick's life's work. In many ways Nick was ahead of his time. He surveyed the standing buildings on the site in meticulous detail, long before it was generally realised that this was an important aspect of urban archaeological work. He pioneered the use of job creation schemes in Scotland, seeing the potential they offered in enabling large-scale excavations to take place, while also offering youngsters the opportunity for employment. He recognised the impact that the natural topography had on the history and growth of the burgh. His love of technology led him to embrace the use of computers in innovative ways long before this had become commonplace. He recognised early on that the results of his excavations warranted publication in a series of fascicules, which was not usual in Scotland in those days.

The Nick I knew was an entertaining companion, an unfailingly kind and considerate man, always enthusiastic, hugely knowledgeable in many areas, generous with both his time and knowledge, immensely loyal to his family and friends and, above all, a man fascinated by history and archaeology, and utterly dedicated to completion of the important work he started. In his latter years Nick found personal happiness when he embarked on a new project at the Bishop's Palace, Fetternear, with his partner Penny Dransart, and brought to it his customary scholarship and passion. But his commitment to Perth High Street never wavered. I never doubted that this project would be completed, and I have no doubt that Nick would have led its completion but for his untimely death at the age of 55.

It is a source of great sadness that Nick is not here to see these volumes in print. He would have been thrilled. He would also have been very aware of the great debt owed to all those volunteers, young people, archaeologists and specialists who worked with him, and those who have laboured long and hard in more recent years to bring the project to a successful conclusion.

I am delighted to welcome this third volume in the publication of Perth High Street 1975–77 archaeological excavations. The completion of this important project is not only a credit to everyone who has been involved, but also a fitting tribute to Nick's memory.

Olwyn Owen
Historic Scotland

Obituary
Nicholas Quentin Bogdan 18 June 1947 to 15 August 2002

The life story of Nicholas Q Bogdan is intimately entwined with that of the Perth High Street excavation. An energetic and forceful personality, Nick, as he was known to his digging team, came to prominence in Scottish archaeology as the director of these explorations in rescue archaeology in 1975, having previously excavated with Professor Nicholas Brooks in St Andrews. His academic career had begun at Gordonstoun in Moray, then took him to Queen's University of Belfast, where he read archaeology, thence to St Andrews where his postgraduate research on the origins of castles became part of a lifelong passion. Nick's enthusiasms crossed the boundaries of history, archaeology, architecture, genealogy and many other '-ologies' besides: he was not limited by mere geography and always looked beyond, keen to place medieval Scotland in its wider European setting.

He was involved in the formation of a number of archaeological bodies, among them the Scottish Castle Survey and the Scottish Episcopal Palaces Project. From 1976 until 1982 he was a founder member of the Tayside and Fife Archaeological Committee (TAFAC), the group which brought together those involved in and supporting archaeology in Tayside and Fife.

Nick, though with one foot firmly in the past, had an ability to spot trends which he could usefully exploit in his work and was therefore always an enthusiastic user of new technology. 'New' in the 1970s meant the use of computers which utilised punch cards; by the 1990s he had advanced so far as to set up his own archaeological website. Publication however always seemed to lie somewhere just out of reach and although several interim reports of his work at Perth High Street were intermittently produced, the final drawing together of the great work was forever 'in progress' or 'forthcoming'.

In later years, his major post-Perth project was at Fetternear Bishop's Palace, where with boundless enthusiasm and the help of his collaborator and partner Dr Penny Dransart, through the auspices of the University of Wales, Lampeter, he excavated and researched until his untimely and sudden death, of a heart attack, at the age of 55.

A newspaper obituary (*Guardian*, 28 August 2002) described Nick's 'cheerful disdain for administration'. Perhaps so, but it is despite this, and all the vicissitudes of fortune of the last three decades, that the present volume is now offered as a tribute to his memory.

THE TEXTILES

Summary

P Z Dransart

Between 1975 and 1977, 411 samples of textiles, fabrics, yarns and cordage were excavated from medieval deposits at the High Street, Perth. Most of this material was recovered from levels dating between the early 12th and the later 14th centuries; only seven samples came from unstratified contexts.

In addition to wool (the most commonly represented fibre), goat hair and probably horse hair were detected. A total of 31 items are of silk. The absence of linen is attributed to the acidic soil conditions, which do not favour the preservation of bast fibres.

The largest group consists of loom-woven textiles. Under this heading, 2/1 Twill without nap, ZS is the most abundant type of weave. Also well represented are the categories 2/1 Twill with nap, ZS and 2/1 Twill without nap, ZZ. 2/2 twills are present in much lower numbers, but they maintain a much more consistent presence throughout all five periods. In contrast, there is a tendency for the 2/1 twills to undergo a marked increase from the first half of the 12th century onwards.

Most of the textiles are woollen and monochrome in colour. It is estimated that approximately 30% of the cloths were dyed. Madder and kermes were identified among the red dyestuffs, the former being more common. Indigotin and a further, unidentified blue dye were also recognised. The yellows identified in the textiles were kaempferol, quercitin and rhamnetin, perhaps from residues of plant crops such as onion skins. *Reseda luteola*, or weld (Dyer's Rocket), was not detected, but some of its seeds were recovered from the site. Patterned weaves are rare in the Perth textiles. Examples of patterning include a 2/1 twill check, which employs yarns of different weight and colour (Cat No 93/A10193c). This is notable as the only recorded check fabric in Scotland between a check from Falkirk, belonging to the mid-third century AD and another from the Dava Moor burial dated c1600. High Street 2/2 twills with pattern effects are a diamond twill (Cat No 18/A12340a), and a fragmentary fabric with a single reverse in the direction of the line of the weave (Cat No 105/A10057). In a further 2/2 twill, the diagonal line of the weave is emphasised by using a dark warp and a light weft (Cat No 82/A12553b). This cloth has been identified as wadmal (*vaðmál*); it is probably an import from Scandinavia.

Another characteristic exploited in a few textiles is the use of yarns with different spin directions in the same system (either warp or weft), as in Cat Nos 259/A09-0104 and 337/A09-0041, both 2/1 twills. A homogeneous group of textiles consists of tabbies woven from two ply yarns. They occur in all periods of the site, but with a concentration in Period II (1150–1200). These textiles, with a low warp and weft count, are similar to examples found at many other European sites. At the High Street, there are tabbies with 2S ply yarn and tabbies with 2Z ply yarn; the former occur in greatest numbers.

Positive evidence for the use of the warp-weighted loom has been noted among the High Street material. This includes textiles with a starting edge and pin beaters. In contrast, no parts of horizontal looms appear to have been found.

Eleven of the loom-woven textiles are of silk, and a further tablet-woven fabric is a composite piece which incorporates two sections of tabby ribbon (Cat No 271/A09-0097). While most of the silk textiles are of tabby weave, four of the samples are twill weaves. The latter comprise weft-faced compound twill (three samples), and a 2/2 lozenge twill which may have been manufactured in 13th-century Spain (Cat No 233/A09-0122).

Among the non loom-woven fabrics are tablet-weaves, felt, sprang, knotted net and braids. The sprang (Cat No 227/A09-0121), belonging to Period V (1300-1350), is notable as the technique is extremely rare at medieval sites in Britain. Three examples of knotted net, constructed from two ply silk yarn, were obtained from levels also dated to Period V. Two of these nets have embroidered designs executed in varieties of darning (*lacis*). They are comparable with cushion covers from the royal burials at the convent of Las Huelgas, near Burgos, Spain, and with hair-coverings from Germany. These nets contribute to the evidence obtained from other finds represented among the High Street finds for trading links with the Continent.

Many of the High Street loom-woven textiles have cut edges; they are probably discarded offcuts. Confirmation for tailoring activities was found at the site in the form of shears, scissors and needles. From an examination of different categories of finds from the site, including metalwork, illustrations depicting clothed personages, and other contemporary material in Scotland, it is suggested that the inhabitants of 12th- to early 14th-century Perth wore long woollen garments with soft, loose folds. The basic garments adopted by women and men were similar. Differences may be observed in the variable length of men's tunics, while women's garments always reached the ground. It is assumed that the wealthier inhabitants of Perth would have worn dyed clothing and the finer qualities of cloth, but most people would have worn natural shades of brown.

Despite the apparent homogeneity in colour, a closer study of clothing in Perth, considered in the light of what is known of the history of the burgh, shows that the outward forms of dress reveal the articulation of more complex internal social organisation.

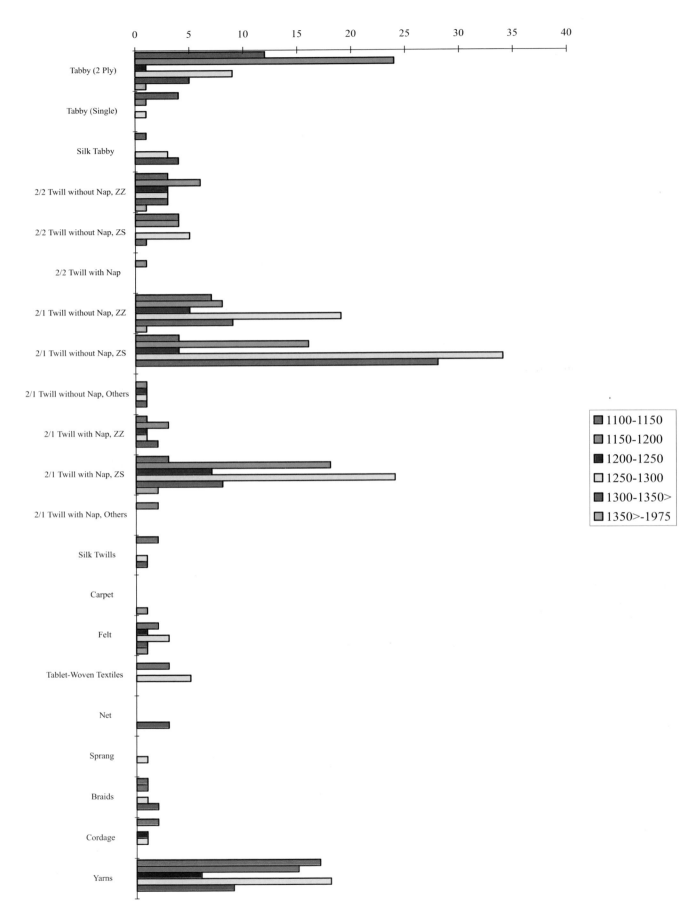

Illus 1 *Bar diagram showing frequencies of the different categories of textiles, fabrics and yarns from the Perth High Street Archaeological Excavation.*

Introduction

P Z Dransart, H Bennett and the late N Q Bogdan

The High Street excavation recovered 411 samples of textiles and fabrics, 403 of which were found within deposits that had been laid down within a period of little more than two and a half centuries dating between c AD 1100 and c1350 . They were present in significant numbers in all periods, preserved by the damp and slightly acid environment. Over 7.5% (31) are of silk, the remaining 380 being animal hair, usually sheep's wool. There are, however, also at least two examples of goat hair in addition to what could be a number of specimens of yarns and cordage of horse hair.

Of these samples, 318 are of loom-woven cloth, varying in quality from fine, often highly-finished fabrics suitable for the clothing of the wealthy, to coarse, heavy weight pieces which may have served as matting and packaging. In addition non loom-woven fabrics such as felt, tablet weaving, net, sprang, braids, yarns and cordage are also well represented.

Textiles are rarely durable, and for a piece to survive over several centuries, either above or below ground, special conditions are required. Consequently, examples of medieval clothing and soft furnishings, or the materials used in making them, were very rare in Scotland before the High Street discoveries. Of all medieval textiles it was those which had been used as vestments, or for other ecclesiastical purposes such as wrapping relics, which were most often preserved, usually in the safe-keeping of church treasuries. Nevertheless in Scotland there are barely half a dozen such pieces which can safely be said to pre-date the Reformation. These, of which the so-called Fetternear Banner of c1520 is the best known (McRoberts 1956), all belong to the late Middle Ages and appear to be the sole survivors of the wholesale destruction of vestments which took place during the Scottish Reformation. Amongst the few medieval vestments to have survived are remounted orpreys (embroidered bands) which were kept clandestinely by Catholic families (Dransart and Bogdan 2004, 465–6).

Until the High Street excavation, textile material from archaeological sources had scarcely been more plentiful. When, in the 1950s, Audrey Henshall (1952; et al 1956) examined the early textile finds from Scotland, those of possible native production which could be placed between the 10th century and the middle of the 16th century were limited to six. These consisted of scraps of woven wool or linen, mostly preserved by contact with metal, and the enigmatic woollen shirt of possible 14th-century date from Rogart, Sutherland, which had been buried with its owner in peat (Henshall 1952, 17–21). Fragments of silk from a grave at Dunfermline attributed to Robert I (the Bruce, d 1329), and the tombs of Archbishop

Gavin Dunbar (d 1547), in Glasgow Cathedral, and an unknown early or mid-16th century bishop in Fortrose Cathedral, were all that remained of imported goods (Henshall et al 1956).

Since the High Street excavation, work in other Scottish burghs – Aberdeen (Bennett 1982; Gabra-Sanders 2001a), Elgin (Bennett nd a), Leith (Bennett and Habib 1985) and elsewhere in Perth (Bennett 1987; Bennett 1995; Harrison and Janaway 1997) – have produced further examples of woollen and silk fabrics. They have been found on a few other medieval sites: Fast Castle, Berwickshire (Ryder and Gabra-Sanders 1992; Gabra-Sanders and Ryder 2001), Threave Castle, Kirkcudbrightshire (Bennett nd b), Sillerholes, West Lothian (Gabra-Sanders 1997), Dairsie, Fife (Dransart forthcoming), and The Biggings, Papa Stour, Shetland, which produced a few textile finds from medieval phases and a greater quantity from more recent phases (Bennett nd c; Walton Rogers 1999). In addition, the remains of a leather shroud and wool cloth wrappings were recovered from a grave at Coldingham Priory, Berwickshire in 1972 and are now in the National Museum of Scotland. The grave was covered with a slab inscribed with the name of a prior of Coldingham who died c1198, but the interment may not be the original. The main fabric is a fine 2/1 diamond twill of high quality, woven from very firm, combined Z spun yarn, with a count of 33 by 10 threads per 10mm. Apart from Sillerholes, most of these medieval fabrics are present in relatively small quantities.

The finds from the High Street, therefore, remain by far the largest corpus of medieval textiles from Scotland. Indeed they are still one of the largest assemblages recovered from a single site in the British Isles. Dating in the main from the early 12th to the first quarter of the 14th century, they bridge the important period between the major collections from Anglo–Scandinavian York (Hedges 1982; Walton 1989), the predominantly 14th-century material from various sites in London (Crowfoot et al 1992) and the 15th- and 16th-century textiles from the Castle Ditch in Newcastle upon Tyne (Walton 1981).

While our knowledge of textile use and production in Scottish medieval burghs on the basis of documentary sources has been extremely patchy, the High Street assemblage presents detailed information. The High Street finds take the form of offcuts, rags and scraps. A few finds – Cat Nos 351/A7577a and 370/A10112, both recognisable as decorative hair-coverings, and 406/A9821, the felt lining of a boot – are identifiable entities (see Net and Felt below). In view of this lack of complete objects, the finds are considered according to their method of manufacture. The fragments of loom-woven textiles are considered first, divided according to the fibre, type of yarn used, the weave, and the method of finishing. They are followed by the non-woven fabrics, again divided according to structure but with no distinction as to fibre. Finally there is a General discussion and sections on the Hair and wool, Textile tools and Dress in medieval Perth: the evidence from the site.

In general, to assist non-specialists, technical terms have been explained (see also the Glossary of textile terms). For further elucidation of terms relating to fabrics and, more specifically, textiles the reader is directed to Burnham (1980), CIETA (1964) and Emery (1980). Technical works on the non-woven fabrics are mentioned in the relevant sections.

Loom-woven textiles

H Bennett, P Z Dransart and the late N Q Bogdan

Fibres

Of the 318 samples of loom-woven textiles, all but 13 appear to be of wool or hair. Twelve of the exceptions are silk. The thirteenth, Cat No 403/A11083, a piece of carpet, has a base of jute or sisal, but is certainly modern (see Carpet, below). From the remaining 305 cloths a number were selected at random for fibre analysis, and generally samples were taken from both warp and weft. As expected, most were found to be sheep's wool, but the fibres of two exceptionally coarse textiles, Cat Nos 63/A9993a and 64/A9993b, were identified as goat hair. Full details are given in Dr Ryder's report below. It may also be mentioned that one of the leather shoes proved to have been sewn with cow hair, and another with cow or goat hair (see The leatherwork, this fascicule), and that two of the non-woven textiles, Cat Nos 15/A11080c and 174/A09–0141, are probably made of horse hair (see Yarns and cords, below).

Like wool and animal hair, silk is a protein fibre. However, if it is to be produced on a large scale, special conditions are required. Silk is actually a very long filament secreted in two parallel strands by pupating silkworms. These silkworm chrysalids also secrete a substance known as sericin, which gums the strands together as the cocoon is formed. In order to unreel a cocoon, the chrysalid must be killed to prevent the secretion of another substance which would dissolve the sericin and damage the silk strands. Reeled silk is still hard when wound off the cocoon, although it may be woven in such a condition. On removing the sericin, by washing either the yarn or the woven fabric in warm water, the silk is both soft and shiny. In the wild, silkworm larvae emerge as silkmoths, breaking through the cocoon. The broken sections of silk filament may be carded and spun like wool, and the final product is termed 'spun' or 'wild' silk. However, the production of 'cultivated' silk involves using domesticated silkworms, the most important of which is *Bombyx mori*, which feeds on the leaves of cultivated 'white' mulberry trees. Sericulture (silk production) and silk weaving were first undertaken in China, where the reeling of silk has been practised for at least 4,600 years (for further information, see Geijer 1979, 4–6 and chapter VII).

With the exception of the modern piece mentioned above, and possible fragments of linen, caught in a seam on one of the silks (Cat No 346/A09–0044), there is a total absence of bast fibres. This is not unexpected, for the damp, acid conditions which have allowed the survival of the wools and silks are much less favourable to the products of flax, hemp and the like. That such products were available in Scotland during the period under consideration, if only to a limited extent, is not in doubt (see General discussion, below). Indeed the presence on some samples of seam lines and needle holes but without traces of sewing yarn, strongly suggests the use of linen thread, or similar, which has proved more susceptible to the conditions in which the fabrics were buried.

Spinning

Yarn is described as Z or S spun; this convention indicates whether the twist of the constituent fibres follows the direction of the central bar of the letter Z, or that of the letter S (Illus 2). If a yarn is then plyed (twisted together) with one or more others, it is usually twisted in the opposite direction to that in which it was spun – thus, for example, Z spun yarns are plyed together in S direction. In most of the cloths single thicknesses alone have been used, but in one group, consisting of 53 samples of coarse tabby, 2 ply yarns have been used throughout; in one sample only, Cat No 157/A8366, 2 ply yarn (in the warp) and single ply (in the weft) are combined. Among the 251 woollen cloths made entirely from single ply yarns, the majority are either Z spun in both systems (81), or Z spun in one and S spun in the other (164). In the latter group the Z spun yarn, which tends to be the normal product of

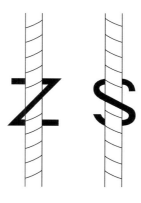

Illus 2 *Z and S directions of spinning.*

a right-handed person spinning with a spindle (Illus 3 and 4), is often of better quality, more firmly spun and evenly made. Further, where the existence of a selvedge allows warp and weft to be identified, the Z spun yarn is generally the warp; it also tends to have the higher count – that is, the density of threads per unit measurement, which in part determines the quality of the cloth. The use of Z and S yarn together in one system is unusual, and is found here in only four fabrics – Cat Nos 93/A10193c (Illus 9), 168/A9057a, 259/A09–0104 (Illus 38) and 337/A09–0041 (Illus 37).

On medieval sites elsewhere it has been noted that cloths made solely from S spun singles, although popular earlier and later, are rare among 12th- and 13th-century material (Endrei 1968, 19; Lindström 1982, 182). Only one textile, a 2/1 twill, is listed with S spun warp and weft from 12th- and 13th-century contexts in London (Crowfoot et al 1992, 27). The High Street site has produced just two – Cat Nos 142/A9536b and 204/A09–0133a (Illus 21). It might be argued that Cat No 204/A09–0133a represents a selvedge, all that remains of a larger fabric, in which case the rest of the textile might not have been woven from S spun warp. This would still leave Cat No 142/A9536b, which dates from the late 12th century, unexplained. It is a 2/1 twill, as is Catalogue No 15 from Kirk Close, Perth, probably dating from the 14th century (Bennett 1987, 164). A further 2/1 twill with S spinning throughout should be noted from 30–46 Upperkirkgate, Aberdeen, but it belongs to the 15th century (Gabra-Sanders 2001a, 232). Textiles with S spun warp and weft predominated at Fast Castle, Berwickshire, in the second half of the 15th century, but these were all woven in tabby (Ryder and Gabra-Sanders 1992, 8; Gabra-Sanders and Ryder 2001, 126). In addition, S spinning in warp and weft prevailed over other combinations amongst the 15th- and 16th- century textiles excavated from the Castle Ditch, Newcastle upon Tyne; several weave types were present, but the 2/1 binding was absent (Walton 1981, 193). In sum, it may be stated that although they are rare, post-11th-century and pre-15th-century textiles with S spinning throughout are sometimes present on archaeological sites. It may be suggested that some of these textiles were quite unusual, such as the high quality, light weight 2/2 cloth from a 13th-century pit in the Queen Street Midden Area, Aberdeen (Catalogue No 155 in Bennett 1982, 199). It should also be noted that the 2/1 fabric with an added unspun pile from Lund has S spinning in both warp and weft (Lindström 1982, 182).

There is plentiful evidence that yarn was being prepared on the site throughout the period under discussion. Two wooden spindles have survived (see Fascicule 2, The wood), as have 41 whorls which were used to weight spindles. The whorls, in wood, bone and stone, vary considerably in weight, suggesting that a range of different thicknesses of yarn was being produced.

Illus 3 *Eve spinning with a spindle. Detail from the Hunterian Psalter, Glasgow University Library, MS Hunter 229 (U.3.2), folio 8r. (© Bridgman Art Library)*

Illus 4 *Eve spinning with a spindle, from the Taymouth Hours, f.23v (British Library, Yates Thompson 13). (© The British Library Board)*

Illus 5 *Spinning and carding wool, from the Luttrell Psalter, East Anglia c1335–40 (British Library, Add 42130 f.193). (© The British Library Board).*

There is, however, no means of knowing whether this activity was associated with the professional cloth industry in the burgh (see General discussion below), or was purely for domestic purposes. During the Middle Ages an additional method of spinning was introduced, namely, the wheel. This was the spindle wheel, later known in Scotland as the muckle wheel to distinguish it from the newer and smaller flyer wheel. The spindle wheel was in use in England by the 1330s (Illus 5), but how soon it was adopted in Scotland is uncertain. References to the spindle wheel are difficult to trace in Scottish documents before the 16th century, and as yet no parts of spinning wheels have been recognised on medieval sites. Nor may anything be deduced from the High Street cloths – unless, that is, the somewhat irregular and lumpy S spun noted in the ZS twills may be taken as an indication of experiments with the new method of spinning. Carole Morris identified a component of a spindle wheel, a wooden drive-whorl, amongst material from a layer dated to the 17th century at 16–22 Coppergate, York (Walton Rogers 1997, 1745, Catalogue No 6650).

Wool yarn is normally designated worsted or woollen, according to the manner in which it has been prepared. For worsteds, the fibres are laid parallel before spinning, generally by combing. The result is a smooth, often firm and lustrous thread; a cloth woven from worsted yarn is characteristically hard to the touch, and the pattern of the weave is clearly visible. For woollens, the fibres are worked into a loose, airy mass with the aid of pairs of hand cards – flat wooden tools with fine metal hooks set in the faces (Illus 5). This process results in yarns which are softer and fluffier than the worsted, and the made-up cloth is less crisp in appearance. It is particularly suitable for use where the surface of the cloth is to be napped (see Finishing, below), a popular treatment during the medieval period. However, there is virtually no evidence for hand cards in Scotland until 1349, when a ship was seized on its way to Scotland from France, where cards with metal teeth have been made since the 13th century. Wool carding combs were one of the items listed in a varied cargo on board the ship (*CDS*, iv, no 462). Combs and cards are both mentioned in the Black Book of Taymouth; in an inventory of 1600 of the 'woman hours' at Finlarg, four pairs of old 'stok cardis' and two pairs of wool combs or 'woll kaims' were listed (Grierson 1985, 6).

Weaves and patterns

Each of the 305 cloths of wool or other animal hair is constructed in one of three basic weaves: tabby, 2/2 twill and 2/1 twill. On some medieval sites (eg Kjellberg 1979, 84–5) tabby – the simplest of all weaves, in which each warp passes alternately over one weft and under the next (Illus 6, 16) – predominates. Here, though, with 59 examples (19.34%), it occupies a secondary place. The remaining fabrics are all twills,

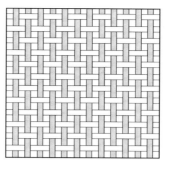

Illus 6 *Tabby weave.*

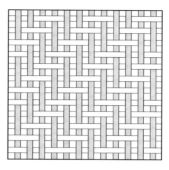

Illus 7 *2/2 twill.*

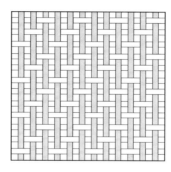

Illus 8 2/1 twill.

that is, each warp passes over two or more weft threads and under the next one or more, or under two or more weft threads and over the next one or more; the binding points are moved one thread sideways on each successive throw of weft, forming the diagonal lines which are a distinctive feature of twill weaves. Thirty-four of the cloths (11.14%) are in 2/2 twill – in which each warp passes alternately over two weft threads and under two (Illus 7). By far the largest number of fabrics, 212 (69.5%), are 2/1 twills. Here, each warp passes over two weft threads and under one (Illus 8). This weave is not reversible, of course, and viewed from the other side the warp ends are seen to travel under two weft threads and over one – in which case it is described as 1/2 twill. When dealing with an excavated fragment, however, it is often difficult to determine which surface was intended to be the main face, so, for convenience, all examples of this structure are described here as 2/1 twill.

As is common among medieval material, plain cloths are in the large majority. There is a marked shortage both of patterned twills prominent during the Viking period, and of the checks familiar from post-medieval Scotland, and only twelve of the fabrics show any

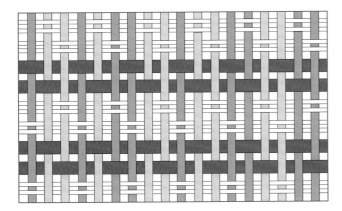

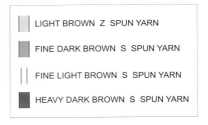

Illus 9 2/1 twill with checked pattern, incorporating yarns of different weight and colour. Cat No 93/A10193c.

deliberate variation in weave, colour or yarn. Four are extended weaves, that is, some elements are duplicated and consist of two threads running side-by-side in the same course; in all four cases this duplication is found in one system only. In Cat Nos 204/A09–0133a, a warp-faced tabby with a weft-wise rib (Illus 21), and 157/A8366, a heavily napped fabric, probably 2/1 twill, the weft threads are paired, while in Cat No 168/A9057a, a heavy weight 2/1 twill (Illus 39), each pair in one system, again probably the weft, consists of one Z spun and one S spun thread; in the fourth sample, Cat No 93/A10193c (Illus 9), the weave is only partially extended, two pairs of threads alternating with two single threads. This last is also notable as the only example of a check in Scotland between the Falkirk piece of the mid-third century AD and those from a burial of c1600 from Dava Moor, Moray (Henshall 1952, 8, 21–4). A 2/1 twill, it might be termed a fancy weave, for it incorporates yarns of different thicknesses as well as of different colours (unlike tartan, it may be noted, which is usually manufactured from yarns of the same weight, and for which the classic weave is 2/2 twill).

Three other samples make use of yarns of different colours. Cat No 20/A12340c, a tabby (Illus 22), is striped in one system, probably the warp. A 2/1 twill (Cat No 22/A12340e) has an irregular banded effect in system 2, achieved by alternating a light beige colour with either mid brown or dark brown. The striping is most conspicuous on the face of the fabric in which these coloured threads float, but the clarity of the design would have been obscured by the raising of the nap. In Cat No 82/A12553b, a 2/2 twill identified as *vaðmal* (Illus 31), the diagonal lines of the weave have been emphasised by combining a dark warp with a pale weft. Cat No 283/A09–0077b, a 2/1 twill in very poor condition (Illus 42), may have been a weft-striped fabric: in this case the bands would have been formed by using a finer yarn than that used for the ground; it is no longer apparent whether this yarn was originally of a different colour. In Cat No 259/A09–0104 (Illus 38), an unfulled 2/1 twill, a change in texture has been achieved simply by substituting a yarn spun in the opposite direction: thus, in one system a block of Z spun threads is followed by a block of threads of

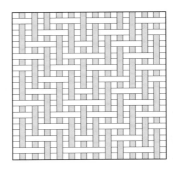

Illus 10 *2/2 twill with reverse. Cat No 104/A9975.*

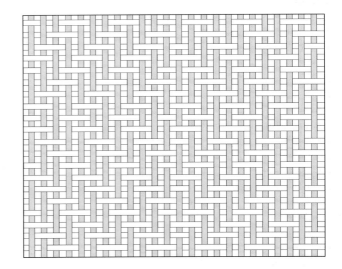

Illus 11 *2/2 diamond twill. Cat No 18/A12340a.*

similar weight, but S spun. Insufficient of the fabric remains to show whether this spinning pattern was repeated. Among the large number of twills present there are only three, all 2/2 twills, in which use is made of the possibility of patterning the fabric by reversing the direction of the diagonals. Cat Nos 104/A9975 (Illus 10, 29) and 105/A10057 have a single reverse which, if repeated across the width or down the length of the web would have produced a chevron twill. Cat No 18/A12340a (Illus 11) has reverses with axes in the directions of both the warp and the weft, creating a diamond pattern.

Selvedges and evidence for loom types

There is a closed edge, which in most cases may be
regarded as a side selvedge, on 38 samples. Although
there are examples of each of the basic weaves with a
length of selvedge intact, a disproportionate number
of those surviving, 15 (39.47%), are on coarse tabby
fabrics made from 2 ply yarns. The same feature has
been noted on similar material from Dutch sites, leading
Sandra Vons-Comis (1982a, 155) to suggest that either
they were used for some purpose such as blankets which
did not require much cutting and shaping of the web, or
they were woven in narrow widths. As yet though, no
complete loom-width has come to light. Twenty-eight of
the selvedges are simple constructions in which the weft
turns directly back into the fabric at the end of its course,
and there are no additional warp threads or other special
arrangements (Illus 12). In other samples, measures have
been taken to strengthen the edge of the web: in Cat No
92/A10193b, a 2/2 twill, the outermost three threads
act as one. In Cat Nos 74/A11154 and 145/A10409b,
both 2/1 twills with nap, the warp ends are paired for a
width of 7mm and 10mm respectively. Another means
for strengthening the selvedge is found in Cat Nos 32/
A11567c and 181/A8085, both twills woven from Z spun
yarns, which have tubular selvedges (Illus 13). Tubular
selvedges are present on a textile identified as a blanket
from a chieftain's grave at Evebø/Eide in Norway, dating
from the Migration Period (Raknes Pederson 1982, 75–6,
Figs 1 and 2), indicating that this selvedge arrangement
was long lived. Hollow selvedges date from the Bronze
Age, at least; they were used preferentially in the Gallo–
Roman period, as in the rest of Iron Age Europe (Wild
and Bender Jørgensen 1988, 78). An unusual border
treatment is represented by Cat No 157/A8366, where Z
and S plied yarns form a heavily reinforced edge. This
may have been designed to provide a robust selvedge to
enable the wet cloth to be stretched on a frame to dry
after fulling, as part of the finishing process (see below),
but it is a particularly early example of such a border
(Walton 1981, 195–7). One further strengthened closed
edge, that on Cat No 64/A9993b, a tabby made from 2
ply yarn of goat hair, requires comment. Whereas, as
has been noted above, the closed edges on other fabrics
of this type are simple, in this case the two outermost
threads act as one, and the three in the next place act as
one (Illus 14). It seems strange that such pains should
have been taken with an otherwise exceptionally coarse
and makeshift fabric – unless, perhaps, the brittle nature
of the goat hair made it essential. It is just possible that
this is a starting edge, examples of which have been
found on coarse textiles of this kind elsewhere (Kjellberg
1982, 142; Pritchard pers comm).

While the majority of the selvedges undoubtedly
come from the longitudinal edges of the cloth, there is
at least one example of a transverse selvedge, that is, the
closed edge from the beginning (or sometimes the end)
of the web found on fabrics made on vertical looms. The
certain example is the looped and twisted edge on Cat
No 84/A12553d, a 2/2 twill (Illus 15 and 32): no exact

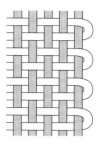

Illus 12 *Simple selvedge.*

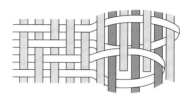

Illus 13 *Tubular selvedge. Cat No 181/A8085.*

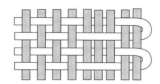

Illus 14 *Strengthened selvedge. Cat No 64/A9993b.*

Illus 15 *Looped and twisted starting edge. Cat No 84/ A12553d.*

parallel is known, but it is probably a variant of the
corded starting edges found on some products of the
warp-weighted loom (see 2/2 Twill with nap below).
One other closed edge, that on Cat No 282/A09–0077a,
a 2/1 twill (Illus 35), is a possible starting edge with
heading cords. Since the appearance of Dr Hoffman's
monumental study (1964) of the warp-weighted loom,
it has generally been held that 2/1 twill was not a
typical product of that loom type. The subsequent
reporting of more examples of 2/1 twill with closed
starting edges (eg Kjellberg 1979, 86–7; Lindström
1982, 182–3) reopened the question, suggesting the
possibility that 2/1 twill was made on the warp-
weighted loom more often than has been supposed.
Not only have Batzer and Dokkedal (1992, 234)
demonstrated that it is possible to weave 2/1 and other
twills on the warp-weighted loom, it is also possible

that on occasions, the use of a starting edge might have been transferred to the newer horizontal loom. In view of this suggestion, it is particularly unfortunate that the Perth piece is poorly preserved, with the putative warp threads so deteriorated as to prevent proper analysis. It is difficult to arrive at any conclusions concerning the looms in use either in Perth or in medieval Scotland as a whole. It has been suggested that the change from domestic cloth production by women to professional manufacture by men, and with it the change from vertical to horizontal looms, began about AD 1000 in Western Europe (Hoffman 1964, 258–65). On this basis, since there is known to have been a craftsman-based cloth industry in Perth, as in other burghs, by the 13th century, the horizontal loom should have been present in Scotland during the period covered by the excavation. As yet, though, there is no evidence either to confirm or disprove this supposition. Nor are the cloths from the High Street helpful on this point; although 2/1 twills predominate among the finds, for the reasons noted above, their presence cannot be taken as indicative of the use of the horizontal rather than the vertical loom.

For the use of vertical looms in Scotland at this period, there is some positive evidence. As has been noted above, a few of the fabrics from the High Street, by reason of the presence of the starting edge, may be said to have been manufactured on a vertical, more particularly the warp-weighted, loom. The two twills should not, perhaps, be cited as evidence that the warp-weighted loom was in use in Scotland, since as they are not typical of the general run of twills from the site they are more likely to be imports; Cat No 84/A12553d is close to Scandinavian material. On the other hand, Cat No 64/A9993b, the tabby made from coarse 2 ply yarn, is of a type well-represented on the site and which seems likely to be a local product - if only because such low grade cloth could scarcely have borne the cost of transport. If the strengthened edge on this piece may be taken as a starting edge, then it is a useful indicator of the survival in the area of some kind of vertical loom. This would not be surprising for, as Dr Hoffman has shown (1964, 51–2), in some areas the horizontal loom took centuries to supplant the older type – until the 18th century in the case of Orkney and Shetland, for example. Perforated stones from most phases of the excavation at The Biggings, Papa Stour were identified as loom weights (Ballin Smith 1999, 175–7).

The possibility that the vertical loom should have continued in use in eastern Scotland during the Middle Ages, at least on a domestic basis, has been strengthened by the discovery of artifacts associated with the warp-weighted loom. In Perth Museum there is a sword beater (used for beating up the weft) found in Watergate, Perth, in 1898. As this was a chance find it was not stratified, but another recently excavated in Aberdeen came from an early 14th-century context; in addition, the same site in Aberdeen yielded a pin beater and a possible loom weight from later levels (Murray 1982, 180, 182, 184). Pin beaters were also excavated

from Perth High Street (see Textile tools below). So far these are isolated finds and if the warp-weighted loom was in widespread use it is curious that more loom weights have not been recovered; the possible weight from Aberdeen appears to be the only recorded example from a medieval site in mainland Scotland. Dr Grant (1961, 226–7) stated that 'the weights for these upright looms, flat stones with holes through them, are found on old sites all over the Highlands . . .' but did not go on to substantiate the point with specific instances. One further clue to the question of the continued use of the vertical loom might be the presence of gores in the excavated cloths (see Henshall 1952, 3–4). None has been noted among the Perth textiles, but as gores are difficult to identify in fragmentary material it is possible that some have been overlooked.

Dyes

A selection of the cloths woven from wool were subjected to dye analysis in 1979 by Professor Whiting and Dr J Harvey of Bristol University's Department of Organic Chemistry. We are indebted to them for their comments, quoted below, and for the data set out in Table 1.

As is often the case with excavated textiles, the Perth fragments are almost all in shades of brown or black, with only occasional pieces showing obvious signs of having been dyed; among the latter it is generally a pink shade that is evident. Forty samples were selected at random, with a further one, Cat No 19/A12340b, selected by eye. In addition, a sample of pile from the fragment of carpet Cat No 403/A11083, was submitted: the discovery of a modern chemical dyestuff in the pile confirmed the opinion that this is of recent manufacture and not part of the medieval deposits.

The most striking aspect of the results is how few of the cloths examined can be said to have been dyed. Of the 41, only 14 gave positive indications, and even among these, the results for two, Cat Nos 119/A09–0136 and 204/A09–0133a, were extremely tentative. It may be added that Dr Ryder's work gave a similar impression (see The wool and hair, below); whereas about two-thirds of the fabrics subjected to microscopic examination were found to have at least some degree of natural pigmentation, only six showed evidence of dyeing. The two sets of results taken together suggest that barely 30% of the cloths were dyed. In contrast, all twelve samples taken from textiles excavated from 80–86 High Street, Perth yielded evidence for dye residue (Harrison and Janaway 1997, 758). The finding of undyed fabrics at the High Street was not entirely unexpected. The burgh laws of the 12th and 13th centuries single out dyed, fulled and sheared cloth, the manufacture of which was the prerogative of craftsmen burgesses in the towns (*Ancient Burgh Laws*, 11, 97–8). This suggests, by implication, the existence of another class of fabrics, undyed and with little or no finishing, which were presumably those in general use

Table 1 *Results of dye tests carried out on the wool cloths.*

Cat/accession	phase	weave	no dye *	indigotin	madder	P/A ratio	kermes	others
South Sector								
19/A12340b	(Ia–)Id	2/1 twill	–	–	–	–	2,100	–
23/A11551a	(Ia–)Id	tabby	*	–	–	–	–	–
24/A11551b	(Ia–)Id	2/2 twill	*	–	–	–	–	–
31/A11567b	Ia–Ie	2/2 twill	*	–	–	–	–	–
35/A11567f	Ia–Ie	tabby	*	–	–	–	–	–
38/A11567i	Ia–Ie	2/1 twill	–	–	400	2/3	–	minute trace unknown blue dye (?)
69/A11510b	If,IIa	2/1 twill	–	–	–	–	–	Q, R, unknown (?)
95/A10624a	IId	2/2 twill	–	–	–	–	–	Q, K, R, unknown (?)
98/A10332	IId	2/1 twill	*	–	–	–	–	–
103/A12650	IId,IIe	tabby	*	–	–	–	–	–
105/A10057	IId,IIe	2/2 twill	*	–	–	–	–	–
109/A9907	IId–IIf	tabby	*	–	–	–	–	–
114/A8863b	IIa–IIff	2/1 twill?	*	–	–	–	–	–
119/A09–0136	<IIc–IIff	tabby	–	–	–	–	–	minute trace unknown blue dye (?)
127/A9478c	IIe–IIg	2/1 twill	*	–	–	–	–	–
134/A9271	<IIg(IIh)	2/1 twill	*	–	–	–	–	–
139/A9506	<IIg(IIh)	2/1 twill	*	–	–	–	–	–
167/A9056	IIi	2/2 twill	*	–	–	–	–	–
177/A09–0108	IIIb	2/1 twill	–	90	–	–	–	–
180/A09–0138	IIg–IIIb	tabby	*	–	–	–	–	–
187/A09–0091	IIIc	2/1 twill	*	–	–	–	–	–
196/A09–0123	IIId	2/1 twill	*	–	–	–	–	–
197/A8520	IIg–IIId	2/2 twill	*	–	–	–	–	–
204/A09–0133a	<IIIc–IVa	tabby	–	–	–	–	–	minute trace unknown blue dye (?)
213/A9905	IVa	2/1 twill	–	–	500	2/1	–	–
230/A6124c	IVb	2/1 twill	–	–	220	1/1	–	–
272/A09–0147	IVb	tabby	–	–	Trace	–	–	–
279/A09–0056a	IVb	2/1 twill	–	–	–	–	–	Q, unknown (?)
297/A8101	IVb,IVc	2/1 twill	–	–	600	1/1	–	–
301/A8097a	IVb,IVc	2/1 twill	–	9	2	high	–	–
309/A6653a	IIIa–IVcc	2/1 twill	*	–	–	–	–	–
333/A6652a	Va	2/1 twill	*	–	–	–	–	–
334/A6652b	Va	2/1 twill	*	–	–	–	–	–
357/A6127d	Va,Vaa(VI)	2/1 twill	*	–	–	–	–	–
364/A6626	Va,Vaa(VI)	2/1 twill	*	–	–	–	–	–
365/A6627	Va,Vaa(VI)	2/1 twill?	*	–	–	–	–	–
372/A8880	Va,Vaa	2/1 twill	–	–	–	–	–	Q, K, R?
374/A09–0019	Vaa	2/1 twill	*	–	–	–	–	–
386/A09–0036	Va,Vaa	2/1 twill	*	–	–	–	–	–
North Sector								
410/A7336	(1)2	2/1 twill	*	–	–	–	–	–
411/A6147	G	tabby	*	–	–	–	–	–

All figures indicate parts per million
A = alizarin, K = kaempferol, P = purpurin + pseudopurpurin, Q = quercitin, R = rhamnetin

among poorer folk. Later, in the 15th century, there is surviving documentary evidence of attempts to restrict, through sumptuary legislation, the use of coloured cloths by the commons (Shaw 1979, 82–3). Further, finds in peat bogs of woollen clothing covering the period from about 1580 to 1715, little of which appears to have been made from artificially-coloured yarn (Henshall 1952; Henshall and Maxwell 1952; Bennett 1975), have suggested that even in more recent times many Scots must have been content with clothing in the natural whites, greys and browns of the native sheep. Even so, the high proportion of undyed cloths in the Perth samples is impressive.

The dye with the highest incidence in the Perth group is madder, which was identified in six samples. Professor Whiting notes for comparison that among the textiles excavated from Baynard's Castle, London – the site of docks filled in 1350 and 1499 with rubbish which

possibly included material derived from the adjacent Royal Wardrobe – madder was found in around 50% of all samples tested. The dye, which has a long history of use in Northern Europe (Brunello 1973, 14 *passim*), is derived from a plant which was widely cultivated in Europe during the Middle Ages but not, as far as is known, in Scotland. That it was available to Scottish dyers is clear from the Assize of Petty Customs which lists tolls for madder as well as for two other imported dyestuffs – woad and brazil – as well as the mordant 'alom' [alum] (*Ancient Burgh Laws*, 105); the list relates to the reign of Robert I (the Bruce) (1306–1329) and earlier. Depending on the mordant used, madder produces rose and various shades of red and brown. It is also known to have been used in combination with woad to produce black (Brunello 1973, 242). This may have been the intention in one cloth, Cat No 301/ A8097a, in which madder and indigotin (derived from woad or indigo) were found together, albeit in small quantities; alternatively, a shade of purple may have been aimed for. In another case, Cat No 38/A11567i, madder predominates, but is accompanied by a small amount of an unknown blue dye, not encountered in any other work, which could have been meant to give a wine-red shade similar to kermes.

Kermes, the other source of red met with in the group, is a greater rarity than madder in British medieval textiles. Like cochineal, its source is the dried bodies of insects, in this case the female of *Coccus ilicis* which is found in Southern Europe and North Africa. In the sample in which it was discovered, Cat No 19/A12340b (42), deposited during the first half of the 12th century, it is present in quantity; even after eight centuries and more in the ground it remains a strong bluish-red. Professor Whiting comments: 'I would imagine that if kermes were imported as a dyestuff and used locally, one would find it used sparingly and eked out with madder; in Baynard's Castle, as here, it is rare, but pure and abundant when found'. Kermes was expensive and, as might be expected, the fabric on which it has been used is of good (although not outstanding) quality – evenly spun and woven, with a fine, smooth finish: Professor Whiting suggests that it may have been a product of the highly skilled Venetian cloth industry. A similar fragment of kermes-dyed cloth, dating from the second quarter of the 14th century, was found at Baynard's Castle, London (Crowfoot et al 1992, Plate 2B and Figure 132, Cat No 50), although it is a tabby, rather than having the 2/1 twill binding of Cat No 19/A12340b. Walton Rogers (2001, 239) observed that two textiles recovered from a pit at 16–18 Netherkirkgate, Aberdeen, had a similar red appearance but analysis indicated that one was dyed with kermes and the other with madder.

Of the blue dyes present in the Perth samples, indigotin could have come, in theory, from either indigo or woad, the products of which are virtually indistinguishable. In practice, though, woad is the more likely candidate. It is thought that indigo was being imported to Europe by the 12th century, but references to its use in the West are not common until after the medieval period (Vetterli 1951, 3066–8). Likewise, indigo is difficult to trace in Scotland until the 17th century, when it appears on the import side of the 1612 customs list as 'Anneil of Barbarie for litsteris (dyers)' (*Halyburton's Ledger*, 288). Mentions of woad, by contrast, are moderately plentiful for the preceding three centuries. It appears that by the 14th century woad was sufficiently well known for the word to be used, on occasion, as a synonym for dyestuffs in general. As an illustration, the instructions issued to the Chamberlain as to the enquiries he was to make, when visiting the royal burghs on ayre, include an injunction to ask about 'litsters, burgesses, wha puttis their hands in the wadd' (*Ancient Burgh Laws*, 125); it should perhaps be explained that, at that time, the work of dyeing was considered to be incompatible with the dignity of burgess-ship, and a dyer who wished to

become or remain a burgess was required to delegate the practical aspects of his craft to servants. It is surprising that indigotin appears only twice in the dye samples (a minute quantity of blue dye, not indigotin, was present in three further samples). This relative absence may be due to chance, or possibly it indicates that the popularity of woad as a dyestuff in Scotland post-dates much of the Perth material. Alternatively it might be a reflection of the state of the cloth industry in Perth (see General discussion, below).

As for yellow dyes, Professor Whiting comments on the absence of luteolin, which was found in samples dating from the second quarter of the 14th century at Baynard's Castle, London (Walton 1992a, 201, BC72 Cat Nos 210 and 254). The usual source was weld, also known as Dyer's rocket (*Reseda luteola*), which was widely cultivated for this purpose. The plant also grows wild on waste ground, and it is interesting to note that seeds from the plant are present in soil samples from nine contexts at the High Street, if only in moderate quantities (see Fascicule 4, The botanical remains, 70). Remains of *R. luteola* were present in Phase 2a deposits (1250–1350) at 45–75 Gallowgate, Aberdeen (Kenward and Hall 2001, 286) and two *R. luteola* seeds were also identified by Fraser and Dickson (1982, 241) from Phase 1 pits (probably second half of the 13th century), at the Queen Street Midden Area in Aberdeen. While dyer's rocket is known to be a prolific seed producer (Kenward and Hall 2001, 286), Fraser and Dickson (1982, 242) cited Thurston's recommendation that *R. luteola* should be gathered before it seeds to obtain a strong colour. Such a practice might limit the occurrence of the seeds on archaeological sites.

In any case, yellow and brown dyes are not easily recognised in archaeological textiles (Walton 1992a, 201). The yellows that are present in the High Street textiles are kaempferol, quercitin and rhamnetin, which, as Professor Whiting explains, are regarded as inferior to luteolin: 'K, Q and R are the flavanols present in a huge number of plants, often residues from useful crops (pomegranate rind, onion skins, etc) and their use implies a less quality-conscious dyeing industry'. Other potential dye plants detected amongst the High Street botanical remains include bog myrtle (*Myrica gale*), which can be used to extract a yellow dye, gipsywort (*Lycopus europeus*), which produces a colour-fast black, bur-marigold (*Bidens tripartita*), used for producing a bright orange, and yellow flag (*Iris pseudacorus*), the roots of which have been used to produce grey-blue or black (see Fascicule 4, The botanical remains, 78–9). Traces of leaves and fruit from bog myrtle were also present on the 45–75 Gallowgate site in Aberdeen (Kenward and Hall 2001, 287).

Finishing

Rather less than one third of the wool cloths (98) appear to have been fulled, that is, pounded while wet to shrink and hence to thicken and condense the fabric. Burial in damp conditions might have a similar effect, and it is possible that the felting together of the fibres visible on some of these pieces may have occurred in the ground rather than at the time of manufacture. However, if heat and friction were not involved in the process of deposition, it is unlikely that secondary felting would have occurred (Ryder and Gabra-Sanders 1992, 6; Gabra-Sanders and Ryder 2001, 126). All 98 cloths are 2/1 twills and all but six are woven from a combination of Z and S yarns. Seventy of these fabrics have a nap; after fulling, the surface fibres have been raised. In most cases the nap has then been sheared to level it. Taken to extremes, napping and shearing totally obscure the structure of the cloth, but only a few of the pieces have the smooth, felt-like surface which became a popular finish during the Middle Ages. A further three fabrics – Cat Nos 84/A12553d, a 2/2 twill, and 37/A11567h and 126/A9478b, 2/1 twills woven from Z spun yarns – have a nap but do not appear to have been fulled. How this effect was achieved is not clear, for raising the nap without fulling might be expected to damage the cloth.

How many of these finished cloths were locally made is debatable, but, as mentioned above (see Dyes, above), fulled and sheared fabrics were undoubtedly being produced in Scotland at the time and by craftsmen, rather than on a domestic basis. In Perth itself there were professional fullers by the 13th century (*RRS*, ii, no 467), although it is not clear whether they had access to a fulling mill or relied on hands and feet alone. Mechanised fulling is thought to have been introduced to England in the late 12th century (Carus-Wilson 1954, 188–90), but the earliest fulling mill on record in Scotland seems to be one belonging to Coupar Angus Abbey (Perthshire) in c1260 (*Coupar Angus Chrs*, 131).

Specialist shearers too made an early appearance (Craigie 1925, 66) and there are indications of the import of teasles (or teasels) referred to as *cardones* (*Ancient Burgh Laws*, 107), which were used to raise the nap before shearing.

Sewing

The High Street site produced a number of needles – of bone, copper and iron and varying from fine to coarse – but there is a remarkable shortage of examples of needlework among the textiles. There are the obvious exceptions of the darned hair-coverings (see Net, below), and a few of the silks bear traces of stitching, but only 15 of the wool fabrics show signs of having been sewn. In twelve cases no thread remains, but lines of needles holes, marks in the cloth, or the felting together of two fragments serve to indicate the original presence of a seam; presumably the sewing was done with a vegetable fibre, such as linen, which has not survived prolonged burial. In the remaining three samples, wool yarn has been used. On Cat

No 98/A10332, a twill, a tear has been mended by oversewing with firm Z spun yarn used double. Cat No 95/A10624a, a twill, has a margin turned under and slip-stitched with fine 2 ply yarn. Cat No 78/A10724, a heavy tabby fabric woven from 2 ply yarn, has a length of similar yarn run through it. Stitching is also to be found on some of the silk fabrics: Cat Nos 267/A09–0127 and 346/A09–0044 (both tabbies); Cat Nos 6/A9500 and 46/A7323 (both tubular bands of compound twill); and 271/A09–0097 (tablet weaving).

Tabby weaves from two ply yarns

The tabby textiles woven entirely from two ply yarns, of which there are 53 drawn from all phases, but with a concentration in the second half of the 12th century, form the most homogeneous group from the site. They are exceptionally heavy, mainly in the range 1–5 threads per 10mm, and are so coarse and harsh to the touch as scarcely to be classifiable as cloths (Illus 17). In Audrey Henshall's (1952, 17) account of early textiles found in Scotland, the one fragment of this type then known was said to have 'a heavy rough appearance quite unlike any other in the Museum'.

Illus 16 *Tabby woven from 2 ply wool yarn. Cat No 272/A09–0147.*

Illus 17 *Tabby woven from 2 ply wool yarn, with simple selvedge. Cat No 29/A7439.*

Tabby weaves from two ply yarns.

Cat/Accession	Area	Rig	Feature	Phase
South Sector				
5/A10072	1	VI	MC010a, SA3829	Ib
11/A11506*	4	V, VI	MC017	Ia–Icc>
12/A11155	3	V	MC031, Pit 5096	Ia–Id
21/A12340d	3	V	MC025, Pit 5337	(Ia–)Id
25/A09–0006	3	V	MC025, Pit 5337	(Ia–)Id
29/A7439	2	VI	MC030b	Id,Ie
36/A11567g	3	VI	MC037a, Pit 5157	Ia–Ie
42/A12614	4	VI	B16 (Phase 1), Pit 4742	(Id)Ie
47/A7339	2	VI	M14b(b)	Ie
48/A7568	2	VI	M14b(b)	Ie
55/A09–0035	3	VI	P5.3a	If
61/A12381	3	VI	MC053c	If
62/A2828	1/2	VI	MC044b	If
63/A9993a*	4	VI	B16 (Phase 2), Destruction	If,IIa
64/A9993b*	4	VI	B16 (Phase 2), Destruction	If,IIa
66/A12534	4	VI	B16 (Phase 2), Destruction	If,IIa
68/A11510a	3	VI	P5.3b	If,IIa
73/A6625	2	VI	MC061	IIb
75/A11673a	3	VI	MC056, Pit 5155	Ia–IIc
76/A11673b	3	VI	MC056, Pit 5155	Ia–IIc
78/A10724	3	VI	B4, 'Courtyard'–Occupation	IIc
87/A8857	2	VI	MC069, Pit 3584	(IIc)IId
101/A12343	3	VI	M1.1c, Pit 5005	IId
103/A12650	4	VI	MC084	IId,IIe
106/A10668	3	VI	M1.1a	IId,IIe
107/A10784	3	VI	M1.1a	IId,IIe
109/A9907	2	VI	M1.1d & M1.1e	IId–IIf
118/A09–0007	3	V	B23, North Room–Occupation (1a)	IIb–IIff
119/A09–0136	9	VII	B27, North Room & South Room–Occupation (1a)	<IIc–IIff
120/A09–0137	9	VII	B27, North Room & South Room–Occupation (1a)	<IIc–IIff
123/A9891	4	VI	B12, Occupation (1b)	IIe–IIg
150/A10412	3	VI	M1.2, Pit 2648	<IIg(IIh)
151/A10427	3	VI	M1.2, Pit 2648	<IIg(IIh)
153/A11266	3	VI	M1.2, Pit 2648	<IIg(IIh)
156/A8497	4	V, VI	M11	IIh
159/A8505a	3	VI	M1.3	IIi
180/A09–0138	9	VII	M13	IIg–IIIb
221/A6126	3	VI	B2, WW2498	IVa,IVaa
246/A09–0101	7	VI	M1.4f	IVc
270/A09–0099b	7	VII	B18 (Phase 2b), North Room, Hall & Hall South–Occupation (10)	IVb
272/A09–0147	7	VII	B18 (Phase 2b), North Room, Hall & Hall South–Occupation (10)	IVb
274/A09–0032a	9	VII	B18 (Phase 2b), North Room, Hall & Hall South–Occupation (10)	IVb
292/A09–0029	9	VII	B18 (Phase 2b), Hall South–Occupation (13b)	IVb
299/A9904	3	VI	M1.4d	IVb,IVc
306/A6144	3	V, VI	M1.4c	IIIa–IVcc
313/A6701	3	V, VI	M1.4c	IIIa–IVcc
358/A6127e	3	V, VI	M1.5a	Va,Vaa (VI)
384/A09–0043	7	VII	M8a	Va,Vaa
393/A09–0008	7	VII	P8.5	Vb,Vbb
398/A8869	4	V, VI	M3a	Vb–Vc
400/A8858	4	V	M3c	Vd
407/A09–0005	7–10	VI–VIII	Unstratified	U/S
North sector				
410/A7336	5	–	Ditch	(1)2

* Goat hair

The description is equally applicable to the Perth group and these fabrics have a primitive appearance. The threads are often unevenly packed and of irregular tension; there is no finishing, and in 13 surviving selvedges the weft simply passes round the outermost warp and no measures have been taken to strengthen the edge (Illus 12, 18). In a mid-12th-century example, Cat No 64/A9993b, the closed edge is slightly more complex (Illus 14), but there is no means of determining whether this is a side selvedge or, as has been found on fabrics of this type elsewhere (see Selvedges, above), a starting edge. As regards colour, most of the fragments have an irregular mottled tone from the yarn having been spun from unsorted, naturally-pigmented fibres of varying shades. It is unlikely that the colour in these fabrics was ever reinforced by dyeing; of 12 samples from six fabrics examined by Dr Ryder, eight were found to be heavily pigmented, but none revealed any trace of dye. Further, the six samples analysed by Professor Whiting gave four negative results, and the remaining two contained traces so minute that the possibility of the complete web having been dyed is considered fairly remote. Perhaps these few dyed fibres are an indication that waste wool from other purposes was sometimes incorporated.

The harshness of these fabrics results in part from the use of yarn spun from coarse, hairy fibres. Generally these are from sheep, but on examination by Dr Ryder, two exceptionally coarse pieces, Cat Nos 63/A9993a (Illus 18) and 64/A9993b, proved to have been made from goat hair. With the exception of Cat No 398/A8869, which is made from both Z and S twisted yarn, the same yarn appears to have been used in both systems; 41 pieces are constructed from 2 ply yarn twisted in S direction (from Z spun components), and 10 from yarn twisted in Z direction (from S spun

components). (In Cat No 156/A8497, an unconserved piece, the identification of the spin and ply directions is not clear.) There is no obvious structural reason for the use of a yarn with a different twist in these latter fabrics, and in all other respects they are similar to those in the former group. Moreover, there is some variation in the looseness or firmness of the ply angle in both types of yarn. Nor has any chronological trend been detected; both are present in all five periods of the site, the Z plied yarn in consistently fewer numbers (Illus 38). This type of heavy tabby fabric is by no means unique to the High Street excavation, but has been found in medieval layers on other sites, both in Scotland and elsewhere. There are four pieces (all with S plied yarns) from an excavation in Kirk Close, Perth, on the opposite side of the High Street (Bennett 1987, 159), and one with Z plied warp and weft of 13th- or 14th-century date from Aberdeen (Bennett 1982, 199). As mentioned above, Audrey Henshall (1952, 17) described a similar textile with S plied yarns, which came from a long cist of probable medieval date found near Kelso Abbey, Roxburghshire. At the time of publication the yarn was thought to be of vegetable fibre, but it is now recognised as wool. Four 14th-century examples are known from the Quayside, Newcastle upon Tyne (Walton 1988, 52), two of which have S ply yarn (of cattle hair and goat hair, respectively), and two Z ply yarn (of goat hair and ?wool). There are parallels from London, including an 11th-century goat hair tabby from Milk Street (Pritchard 1984, 59), and 13 further samples, also apparently of goat hair, mainly from waterfront revetment dumps on the Thames, dating from the early 13th to late 14th centuries (Crowfoot et al 1992, Table 8). In contrast with the Perth two ply tabbies, only one of the London pieces has S ply warp and weft; all the others are of Z ply yarn.

0　　　　　　　3cm

Illus 18 *Tabby woven from 2 ply yarn of goat hair. Cat No 63/A9993a.*

Thread Densities of Tabby Weaves (2S Ply Yarn)

Thread Densities of Tabby Weaves (2Z Ply Yarn)

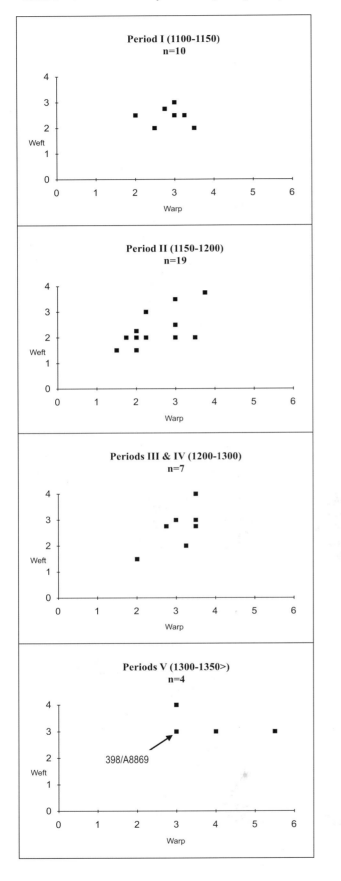

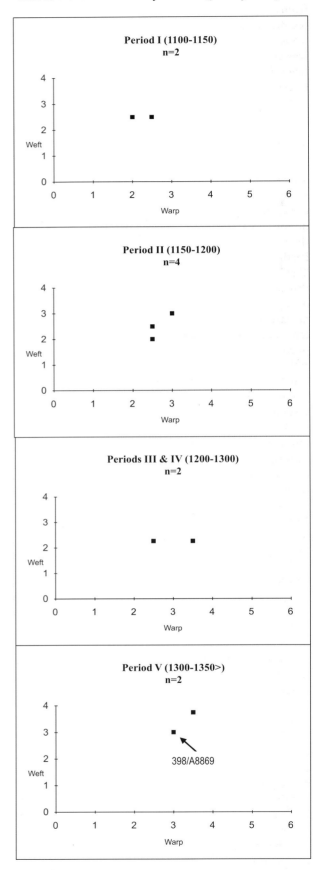

Illus 19 *Scatter diagrams of the South Sector stratified tabby weaves from 2 ply yarns, showing average thread counts per 10mm.*

Numerous examples of two ply tabbies are known from Scandinavia and elsewhere in northern Europe (eg Bender Jørgensen 1979, 3; Kjellberg 1982, 138; Vons-Comis 1982a, 155; Schjølberg 1984). Goat hair was encountered in comparable tabbies excavated from the site known as 'The Farm beneath the Sand' in Greenland (Østergård 2009, 75).

It has been suggested that the S plied tabbies represent a north German/Scandinavian type, and it has been further observed that they have a slightly denser thread count than tabbies of Z plied yarns (Schølberg 1984, 88; Walton 1988, 82). Although it might be argued that some of the Perth tabbies represent packaging which protected imports from the Baltic and north Germany (given the presence of imported wooden items and pottery from those areas in the High Street assemablge), the thread densities of the Perth pieces do not lend support to the observations. The Perth Z plied tabbies seem to have a fairly constant thread count through time, while more variety may be observed in the S plied tabbies, which occur in far larger numbers, especially in Period II. There is a tendency towards slightly higher thread counts in S plied tabbies in Periods III to V, but the numbers are rather low for any degree of confidence. In any case, Cat No 398/A8869 confounds proposed distinctions based on ply direction, since it has Z plied yarn in system 1 and S plied yarn in system 2.

Despite the considerable quantities in which this fabric has been recovered from the High Street site its purpose can only be conjectured. In addition to the piece from near Kelso Abbey, Roxburghshire, at Lund, Sweden and in late 14th-century Winchester it was used for shrouds (Lindström 1982, 181; Crowfoot 1990, 485), but the frequency with which it is found on habitation sites indicates that it was not confined to this purpose. Apart from the haircloth associated with ascetics (Østergård 2009, 75), such a coarse, harsh textile is unsuitable for clothing or bedding. In some cases the fragments are so inelastic, open-textured and generally ill-made, that it is difficult to imagine any use for them except perhaps as inferior horse-blankets, matting, or the like. One of the pieces from Newcastle Quayside was heavily tarred and another was associated with caulking material, leading to the suggestion that they might have played a role in the caulking of ships' timbers (Walton 1988, 82, 91). The majority at Perth, however, might well have served as sacking and packaging. The rectangular pad into which Cat No 11/A11506 was folded suggests such a use. It is usual for vegetable fibres to be used for this purpose, as being generally cheaper (and more robust) than wool. Yet this might not have been the case in medieval Perth. Little is known of the cultivation or availability of flax and hemp in Scotland before the 16th century, and the fact that a number of shoes from the excavation proved to have been sewn with sheep's wool or even cow hair (see The leather, this fascicule, for further details), both of which are ill-suited to the job, suggests that on occasions vegetable yarn may have been in short supply. If, at the same time, goat hair and coarse wool from native sheep, which was not ideal for clothing or furnishing purposes, was readily available, then to manufacture it into packaging may have been the more economical course.

Tabby weaves from single yarns

Unlike the examples of tabby woven from 2 ply yarn, those manufactured from the more usual single ply yarns are few and heterogeneous and do not form a coherent group. The only additional common factor is that all are without nap. This absence of napped tabby cloths is unexpected in view of Elisabeth Crowfoot's (1977, 374) comment that they are one of the commoner types of fabric found on English medieval sites. In the Perth group there is a wide variation in both weight and quality. Lightest, and best made, is a fine open-weave undyed fabric, Cat No 35/A11567f, from before 1150 (Illus 20). Now reduced to fragments, it is constructed from combed, firmly-spun yarn with Z spinning in both systems and, considering its open texture, is remarkably stiff; it might have served as a backing or interlining in a garment or other textile item. Similar, but even finer, cloths are known from late 12th-century Oslo (Kjellberg 1982, 138) and from a late 13th-century context in Trig Lane, London, (the latter is actually a fine worsted tabby; it is one of the few tabbies from London with a slightly open-textured balanced weave said to characterise many earlier textiles (Crowfoot et al 1992, 43 Cat No 397). Tiny fragments of another fine textile with Z spun warp and weft have been detected in the fill of a gully dated to the late 12th or 13th century beneath the medieval hall house at Tî Mawr, Castell Caereinion, Montgomeryshire (Dransart 2001, 110). However the yarn here may have been spun from bast fibres and it

0   3cm

Illus 20 *Tabby woven from firm worsted yarn. Cat No 35/A11567f.*

Tabby weaves from single yarns.

Cat/Accession	Area	Rig	Feature	Phase
South Sector				
20/A12340c	3	V	MC025, Pit 5337	(Ia–)Id
23/A11551a	3	V	MC025, Pit 5337	(Ia–)Id
34/A11567e	3	VI	MC037a, Pit 5157	Ia–Ie
35/A11567f	3	VI	MC037a, Pit 5157	Ia–Ie
133/A9130	3	VI	M1.2, Pit 2648	<IIg(IIh)
204/A09–0133a	7	VI	MC119, Pit 7390	<IIIc–IVa

is possible that the fine, open-weave textiles of wool imitated similar products of linen or other plant material.

Three of the other Perth pieces have a corded appearance resulting from the threads in one system being sufficiently closely packed to obscure those in the second. Cat No 204/A09–0133a (Illus 21) is heavy weight and consists of two pieces, both with a closed edge on one long margin. In the obscured system, which runs perpendicular to the closed edge, the threads run in pairs and the strips may be the remains of a starting edge. However, as the pairs of threads continue to run as one on reaching the edge, rather than separating into adjacent sheds (cf Hoffman 1964, Figure 75), it is more likely that they represent the weft, and the closed edge a side selvedge. Cat No 34/A11567e, which is lighter weight and has single threads in both systems, is fragmentary and in poor condition. Cat No 20/A12340c (Illus 22), which is lighter still, is one of the few patterned fabrics from the site; the predominant system is striped (?) yellow and brown. The fragment has no closed edge, but the obscured system, the threads of which are widely spaced and insubstantial, is more likely to have been the weft. If this is the case, the fragment may be the remains of a narrow textile, comparable with later examples which served as garters, straps or belts (Henshall 1952, 26; Henshall and Maxwell 1952, 35). In Scotland in more recent times such textiles were made on a variety of simple looms (Mitchell 1880, 11; Grant 1961, 237). Of the remaining tabby fabrics, Cat No 133/A9130 is coarse and too small for the identification of the weave to be certain, while Cat No 23/A11551a is medium weight, irregular and ill-made.

Tabby weaves of silk
P Z Dransart

Eight tabby woven silks were excavated from different areas of the site. One of these samples consists of two narrow ribbons stitched to sections of tablet-woven band (Cat No 271/A09–0097). This fabric is discussed more fully under the category of Tablet-woven textiles; only the tabby ribbons are considered in this section. Four further compound weave textiles are considered below (see Twill weaves of silk, below).

0   3cm

Illus 21 *Extended tabby with simple selvedge. Cat No 204/A09–0133a.*

0   3cm

Illus 22 *Tabby with striped ?warp. Cat No 20/ A12340c.*

Tabby weaves of silk.

Cat/Accession	Area	Rig	Feature	Phase
South Sector				
4/A9976	1	VI	MC006, T3852	Ib
267/A09–0127	7	VII	B18 (Phase 2a), External 1, Pit 7314	IVb
271/A09–0097	7	VII	B18 (Phase 2b), North Room, Hall & Hall South– Occupation (10))	IVb
323/A09–0059	7	VII	M9a	IVc,IVcc
343/A09–0046	7	VII	P8.4	Va
344/A09–0047a	7	VII	P8.4	Va
346/A09–0044	7	VII	P8.4	Va
362/A6149	3	V, VI	M1.5a	Va,Vaa(VI)

In the descriptions of the spin and ply directions in the sections of this fascicule relating to silk, the letters Z, S and I are used. The first two letters correspond to the spin directions of Illus 2, while the third denotes a thread with no appreciable spin direction. The technical term for twisting reeled silk is 'throwing' (that is, 'turning'), a term which can be traced from at least the 14th century. A silkwoman might be known as a 'silk throwster' and the yarn she produced 'throwen silk' (Lacey 1987, 196 n12).

Four of the silks, from deposits dating from the second half of the 13th or from the early 14th century, have similar characteristics (Cat Nos 267/A09–0127, 343/A09–0046, 344/A09–0047a, and 346/A09–0044). They are woven in a tabby weave which is close to balance; in other words they have a similar thread count in both systems. The threads in one system are Z thrown and the threads of the second system are untwisted (I). Since two of the pieces have a selvedge along one edge (Cat Nos 343/A09–0046 and 344/A09–0047a), it would seem that the warp consists of Z thrown silk yarn, and the weft of untwisted yarn. The warp tends to be of a finer, more consistent diameter than the weft, which is often slightly irregular. Three of these silk tabbies have a warp count which falls in the range of 33–38 threads per 10mm, and a weft count of 32–35 threads per 10mm. The fourth, Cat No 267/A09–0127, has a count of 42 warp threads and 38 weft threads per 10mm. It is further distinguished by its colour, which is now a dull crimson red. All four have been carefully cut into rectangular or trapezoidal shapes.

Traces of stitching remain on two of these ZI tabbies. Cat No 267/A09–0127 retains a few stitches of light brown, loosely S plied silk thread. More detail has been preserved in Cat No 346/A09–0044, since the piece was cut across a seam uniting two sections of fabric. The edges of the two pieces were turned under twice to form a hem, and a widely spaced, loose overcast stitch was executed through the folds, joining the two together. A straight running stitch holds down the hems, and a further section of running stitch survives, parallel to the hem on one side (Illus 23). A dark brown 2 ply yarn (Z thrown and S plied) was used for all the stitching.

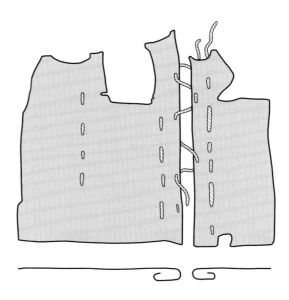

Illus 23 *Stitching on silk tabby. Cat No 346/A09–0044.*

While Cat No 323/A09–0059, recovered from deposits of the late 13th century, is an offcut, it is unlike the four ZI tabbies because it is cut on the bias. It is a tabby of full-bodied appearance with a similar thread count in both systems. There are 41–45 threads per 10mm in system 1; the yarn of this system is Z twisted. It is regular in diameter, save for an occasional thread which is more coarse. Two threads seem to have been used in broadly alternating blocks in system 2; an untwisted yarn with a count of 48–50 threads per 10mm, and a coarser yarn with a count of 19 per 5mm. This coarser yarn has a slight Z twist and it is visible at an upper and a lower angle of the offcut, which has the shape of an attenuated triangle.

The remaining three silk tabbies from the High Street display a greater variety of characteristics. Cat No 362/A6149, from a level dated to the early 14th century, has Z twisted yarn in both warp and weft. Although it has a high thread count (51–54 threads per 10mm in system 1 and 33 threads per 10mm in system 2), both warp and weft are widely spaced. Hence the

Illus 24 *Silk tabby. Cat No 362/A6149.*

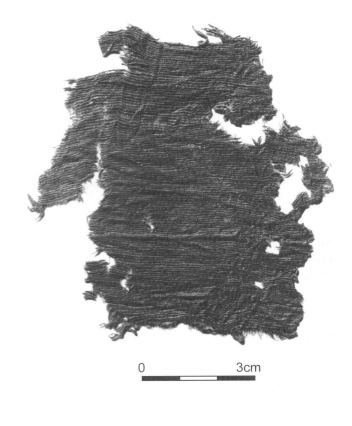

Illus 26 *Silk tabby, with grège weft. Cat No 4/A9976.*

Illus 25 *Detail of silk tabby. Cat No 362/A6149.*

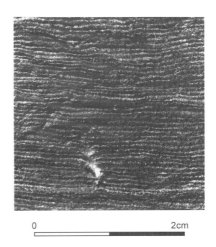

Illus 27 *Detail of silk tabby, with grège weft. Cat No 4/A9976.*

web has an open, delicate character (Illus 24, 25). It is of a donkey brown colour; the fragment has the shape of an irregular parallelogram with worn edges which were, perhaps, once cut. The overall regularity of the shape suggests that this textile was part of a length of bias binding which was reused, perhaps several times.

Another textile of irregular outline is Cat No 4/ A9976 (Illus 26, 27), of which three fragments have survived. The thread in both systems is yellow-brown in colour, but there is a striking difference between warp and weft. In system 1 the yarn is extremely fine and Z twisted; there are 32 threads per 10mm. In contrast the yarn in system 2 is much coarser and it has a matte appearance. This yarn has a very slight Z twist, and there are only 16–17 threads per 10mm. A preliminary inspection of the textile indicated the presence of traces of a metallic substance. However, further investigation by X-ray fluorescence gave negative results for silver in the Research Laboratory of the National Museum of Antiquities of Scotland

	Warp	Weft
4/A9976	32	16.5
267/A09-0127	42	38
271/A09-0097	44	30
323/A09-0059	43	49
343/A09-0046	36	33
344/A09-0047a	33	33
346/A09-0044	37	33
362/A6149	52.5	33

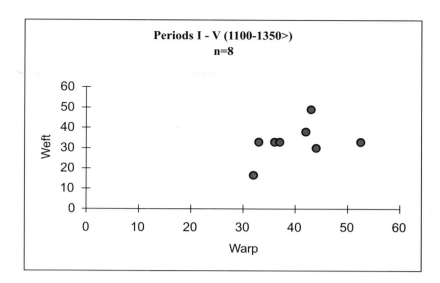

Illus 28 *Scatter diagram of the tabby weaves of silk showing average thread counts per 10mm.*

(now National Museums Scotland). Examination of one of the particles in polarised light at a magnification of x400 showed it to be both transparent and crystalline. The likelihood, therefore, is that the particles are not metallic, as originally thought, but some substance such as quartz or mica, presumably derived from the burial deposit. This textile was recovered from a deposit belonging to the early 12th century. Hence it belongs to a significantly earlier context than the other silk tabbies from the High Street site.

The final fabric considered in this section is actually a ribbon, of which two sections remain, interspersed between pieces of tablet-woven band (Cat No 271/A09–0097; Illus 53). In this tabby the warp is predominant, since the warp is more tightly spaced than the weft. Both warp and weft are light brown in colour. However, the warp is S thrown and the finer weft is Z thrown. The ribbon measures 4–5mm wide, and there are 22 warp ends in the complete width. This would be equivalent to at least 44 warp threads per 10mm. The picks of the weft are unevenly packed, and there are 26–31 threads per 10mm.

Silk textiles have been produced over an extremely long period of time – at least four thousand years in China (Geijer 1979, 75). Some general, broad scale chronological and geographical trends have been detected among surviving silk tabbies (ibid, 75–6; Muthesius 1982a, 133; Walton 1989, 374). In general, tabby weaves have received little attention from art historians (Geijer 1979, 63), hence they are often only given a broad chronological grouping. Most extant silks in Europe have been preserved in treasuries and tombs, where they lack the chronological contexts that archaeological excavations may provide. For instance, some silk tabbies in the treasury of St Servatius, Maastricht, in the Netherlands, have been attributed to a timespan which predates the eighth century continuing up to the 12th century (Muthesius 1974, 326–7). A rare example of a tabby bearing a Kufic inscription reveals that the textile (housed in the Bamberg Diocesan Museum) may be dated before 1047,

and that it was woven in an Islamic centre (Müller-Christensen 1960, 54). It has Z thrown elements, with a count of 26–29 warp threads and 31 weft threads per 10mm.

Most of the discussions concerning chronological and geographical trends in silk tabbies focus on two main characteristics: thread densities and the direction of twist in the constituent yarns. As far as the former is concerned, it has been demonstrated that thread counts made on silk tabbies from 9th- to 11th-century contexts at 16–22 Coppergate, York, fall within the middle to lower end of the range of the densities recorded for such textiles in European treasuries (Walton 1989, Figure 157). In other words, there is a tendency for greater numbers of finer fabrics to be represented in the treasuries. Although the Perth silk tabbies are considerably later than their York counterparts, they too belong to a somewhat similar range towards the middle and coarser end of the range (Illus 28). Nevertheless, comparisons between the High Street silk tabbies and material in treasuries may be made. A ZI tabby of dark violet colour found in a sarcophagus at Chur, Switzerland, has a warp count of 33–35 threads and a weft count of 35 threads per 10mm (Schmedding 1978, 79–80, Cat No 81). (For further examples, see Schmedding 1978, Cat Nos 35a, 35d, 35e and 37 from Beromünster, Nos 82a, 82b, 82d and 82i from Chur and No 228 from Sion.)

Differences in the combinations of yarns, whether Z, S or I, have been attributed to various geographical regions in which silks were produced. However, with the exception of silk tabbies in which both warp and weft are of untwisted yarn, often assigned to China or Central Asia (Schmedding 1978, no 8; Walton 1989, 374), the provenance of fabrics cannot be reliably identified on this basis alone. In any case, this combination is not present in the High Street silks. An early 13th-century silk tabby with warp and weft lacking 'any appreciable twist' is known from the Seal House site in London (Crowfoot et al 1992, 90). The ZI combination, with a Z thrown warp and untwisted weft, tends to be more commonly represented at sites and in western treasuries (Walton 1989, Figure 157c). This situation is reflected in the High Street sample, with four of the silk tabbies displaying the ZI combination.

The selvedges, where preserved, have greater potential for revealing differences in the tabbies. Silk tabbies dating from pre 11th-century levels at 5 Coppergate and 16–22 Coppergate, York, have paired warp ends for strengthening the selvedges (Muthesius 1982a, 133; Walton 1989, 363). In contrast, the High Street silk tabbies discussed above (Cat Nos 343/A09–0046 and 344/A09–0047a) have a selvedge which consists of an outermost bundle of threads and more tightly packed warp ends immediately adjacent to the bundle. This is a type which has also been reported among 13th- and 14th-century silk tabbies from London (Crowfoot et al 1992, Table 10). However, also present in the London silk tabbies of the second quarter of the 14th century, as well as of the last quarter of the 14th century, are tabbies in which the selvedge consists of several paired or grouped warp threads (Crowfoot et al 1992, Table 10).

Most of the silk tabbies from the High Street were cut down or represent worn fragments of larger pieces of cloth. Cat No 271/A09–0097 is an exception since it is a narrow ribbon. It has a warp with a slight S twist and a weft with a slight Z twist. This is an unusual combination. It has been suggested that S thrown silk yarn in both warp and weft, or S thrown warp and untwisted weft, are combinations often associated with narrow ribbons, on the basis of finds from Viking age and medieval sites in Dublin and York (Pritchard 1988, 157; Walton 1989, 374). However ribbons and tape from Saxon London have Z thrown or untwisted warp elements (Pritchard 1984, 60). Some variety has been reported in the literature, since 10th- and 11th-century silk ribbons from Winchester have an untwisted warp and S twisted weft (Crowfoot 1990, 481–2, Cat Nos 1017 and 1018). The nearest examples to the SZ combination in the Perth ribbon would seem to be a textile from Winchester, with a possible warp which is mostly untwisted (it displays an occasional S twist) and a Z twisted yarn in the second system (ibid, 482, Cat No 1019), and a narrow fragment from late 13th-century Southampton, with the thread of one system untwisted and that of the other system Z twisted (Crowfoot 1975, Cat No T2).

The silk tabbies found in treasuries were used for wrapping relics and as burial wrappings. They were also used in garments; on Viking sites (5 and 16–22 Coppergate, York, Saltergate, Lincoln, and Dublin), rectangular lengths of silk tabby have been found made into simple caps (Muthesius 1982a, 136; Walton 1990, 68–9; Heckett 1990). These caps predate the 11th century. However, silk tabby cloth continued to be associated with headgear. In 12th-century England, girls and women of high rank wore their hair in plaits encased in silk sheaths known as *fouriaux,* or more generally from the 12th to 14th centuries, women wore a wimple or gorget which was sometimes of silk (Cunnington and Cunnington 1952, 40). It is possible that some of the Perth silks may have originally formed neck coverings or headgear.

However the silks were employed, it is certain that silk cloth represents an import in Scotland. In addition to China, Persia, Byzantium and various Islamic countries all had flourishing silk weaving centres. The term tabby is derived from *attābī,* after a type of silk textile woven in the quarter of the same name in Baghdad (May 1957, 67); Dr Johnson (1785) regarded tabby as a 'kind of waved silk'. As the influence of the Byzantine empire waned in the 11th and 12th centuries, Islamic countries were increasingly in a position to export textiles to the west. Prior to this, Syria had been one of the first countries to establish its independence from the empire, and it was already one of the most highly esteemed producers of silks. With the expansion of Islam, the weaving of silk soon spread to other areas. Sericulture and silk weaving probably date from the eighth century in Spain, reaching a peak of production during the 13th century (May 1957, 3–10). Since the 'Miracle of the Silkworms', recorded as one of the *Cántigas de Santa María,* edited by Alfonso X, King of Castile and Léon, concerned a Christian woman of Segovia who was a weaver of silk headdresses, it can be seen that the craft was not only practised by Muslims.

Silk weaving was also established in Italy and France. In Paris, silkworkers might belong to one of several craft guilds whose statutes were compiled c1270 by Estienne Boileau (*Réglemens sur les arts et métiers de Paris;* Depping 1837). Typically these guild regulations forbade craftworkers from weaving at night when the light was poor. Members of the guild of workers in silk textiles were able to become 'a mistress' (*mestresse*) of the craft after fulfilling an apprenticeship of at least six years and after practising it for 'a year and a day' (ibid, 88). Another guild, that of the weavers of silk kerchiefs (cloths for covering the head) stipulated that people wishing to become members had to demonstrate that they knew well and truly (*bien et loialment*) its uses and customs; they had to accomplish an apprenticeship of at least seven years (ibid, 99–100). Another statute was inserted in Manuscript B of the *Réglemens*: 'No one may sell warped cards, if they are not worked in the craft' (ibid, 100 n1).

It is likely that the reputation deriving from the control over weaving such a prized material travelled with the silks that reached Perth. The condition of these remnants indicates that they were probably used in garments. Some had perhaps been recycled several times before being discarded and others seem to have been cut from larger, perhaps worn, textiles. The recycling of cloth is considered below, in the section on Dress in medieval Perth.

2/2 Twill without nap, ZZ

There are 20 samples in this group, all but a few of which have shared characteristics and are of roughly similar type. The majority are light or medium weight fabrics, moderately close-woven, with similar yarn used for warp and weft and the two systems close to balance; the counts range from 16 by 15–17 threads per 10mm in Cat No 239/A09–0069 to 8 by 8 threads in Cat No 31/A11567b. The constituent yarns may be classed as worsteds (see Spinning, above) and the texture of the weave is clearly visible. Even so, not all are firm to the touch, and Cat No 409/A09–0009 in particular is quite soft. The colour of the cloth is generally even, suggestive of careful sorting of the wool before spinning. Four samples (Cat Nos 31/A11567b, 105/A10057, 167/A9056 and 197/A8520) gave negative results when tested for dyes, while Cat Nos 167/A9056 and 181/A8085, examined by Dr Ryder, showed a substantial degree of natural pigmentation. With the exception of Cat No 381/A09–0042, which has numerous weaving errors, and 197/A8520, in which the threads are unevenly packed, spinning and weaving are mostly regular. While none of the cloths is of the highest quality, the best of them have a pleasant, even appearance. Among these are Cat Nos 104/A9975 (Illus 10, 29) and 105/A10057, which are probably part of the same fabric: the two are unusual among the Perth textiles in that the simple diagonal weave has been varied – in both cases by a reverse in the direction of the twill (Illus 10). This suggests that the cloth had an overall chevron pattern but, if so, the chevron stripes must have been comparatively wide, for on the large

Illus 29 *2/2 twill with reverse. Cat No 104/A9975.*

piece there are over 80 threads (65mm) beyond the turning point without a further reverse.

As yet there are no 2/2 twills woven entirely from Z spun yarn from other medieval sites in Scotland and only occasional examples from England. From sites in London, three from the second half of the 13th century, 27 from the first half of the 14th century and 37 from the second half of the 14th century are listed by Crowfoot et al (1992, 27). It should be noted that most of these were considered to be worsteds (ibid, 37). In Scotland, fabrics in this category are, however, known from earlier periods: these include three cloths from a cist of probably Viking date at Greenigoe, Orkney (Henshall 1952, 17); the loom-woven part of the undated Orkney hood is a chevron twill of this type (ibid, 10). The tubular selvedge on Cat No 181/A8085 (cf Illus 13) is a feature of ancient origin (although still in use today) recorded elsewhere as early as the Bronze Age (Hald 1950, 427–8).

2/2 Twill without nap, ZZ

Cat/Accession	Area	Rig	Feature	Phase
South Sector				
31/A11567b	3	VI	MC037a, Pit 5157	Ia–Ie
33/A11567d	3	VI	MC037a, Pit 5157	Ia–Ie
40/A12342	3	VI	MC037a, Pit 5157	Ia–Ie
89/A10075	4	VI	M1.1c	IId
92/A10193b	4	VI	M1.1c	IId
96/A10624b	4	VI	M1.1c	IId
104/A9975	3	VI	M1.1d	IId,IIe
105/A10057	3	VI	M1.1d	IId,IIe
140/A9522	3	VI	M1.2, Pit 2648	<IIg(IIh)
167/A9056	3	VI	M1.3	IIi
181/A8085	4	VI	M1.4a(a)	IIIa–IIIc
188/A09–0084	9	VII	P8.1c	IIIc
197/A8520	3	V	M6b	IIg–IIId
239/A09–0069	9	VII	B18 (Phase 1/2)	IVaa,IVb
243/A09–0034	9	VII	B18 (Phase 1/2), MF9194	IVaa,IVb
269/A09–0099a	7	VII	B18 (Phase 2b), North Room, Hall & Hall South–Occupation (10)	IVb
356/A6127c	3	V, VI	M1.5a	Va,Vaa(VI)
375/A09–0023a	7	VI, VII	M1.5b	Vaa
381/A09–0042	7	VI, VII	M1.5b	Vaa
409/A09–0009	7/9	VII	Modern, T7014	VI

Three fabrics stand apart from the general description given above. Cat No 89/A10075 is a heavy loose-woven mottled fabric, with a count of 4–5 threads per 10mm in both systems, made from yarn of irregular thickness spun from unsorted fibres. Cat No 96/A10624b is closer-textured and less coarse, but has a careless lumpy appearance, which results from the use of yarn of irregular thickness and tension. Cat No 92/A10193b, which has a closed edge and is probably a discarded selvedge strip, is light weight and moderately well spun and woven. In this case the yarn has a fluffy appearance and the texture is soft, with slight felting on both surfaces. Microscopic examination by Dr Ryder has revealed that the warp and weft yarns were dyed different colours, but too narrow a strip remains to indicate whether this was true of the main part of the fabric.

2/2 Twill without nap, ZS

Two fabrics in this group, Cat Nos 18/A12340a and 82/A12553b, have special characteristics and are considered individually below. The remaining 11 samples, which are drawn from all periods of the site, are of undistinguished appearance. In all cases the yarn in both systems has the appearance of having been combed, and there is no sign of fulling. Mostly the warp and weft are of similar quality (Illus 30), but in three cases (Cat Nos 24/A11551b, 121/A10496 and 205/A09–0133b) the S spun yarn is noticeably thicker and less firmly spun than the Z spun in the other system. Seven of the fabrics are approximately balanced, in the range 6–9 threads per 10mm, while the remainder range from 10–12 by 15 threads to 6–7 by 4–5 threads. All but Cat no 205/A09–0133b are uniform in colour. Of the two subjected to dye analysis, Cat No 24/A11551b was negative, and Cat no 95/A10624a proved to have been dyed with flavanols (see Dyes above); Cat No 361/A6148, examined by Dr Ryder, showed a high level of natural pigmentation.

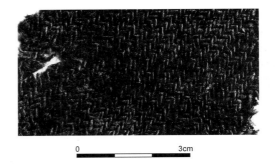

0   3cm

Illus 30 *2/2 twill without nap, ZS.*
Cat No 324/A09–0014.

Cat No 18/A12340a comes from a large pit which had been infilled before 1150, and is the one example in wool of diamond twill (Illus 11), a weave more familiar from earlier periods than the medieval. Composed of smooth lustrous yarn, and unfulled, the fabric is comparatively coarse with 6–7 threads per 10mm in both systems. Audrey Henshall (1952, 7, 17) records just two other diamond twills from Scotland – one of the first or second century AD, and the other of probable Viking date – both fine, and of a different pattern. Diamond twills with Z spun yarn in one system and S spun in the other have been found among 10th- to 11th-century material from York (Hedges 1982, 111–13, 126). Most are finer than the High Street piece, but one has a similar count (although a different pattern). In one case the existence of a selvedge has confirmed that the Z spun yarn is the warp. If the same is true of the Perth fragment, the diamonds are symmetrical in the warp but asymmetrical in the weft. By the same reasoning, an interruption of the pattern visible in one area of the fragment may be interpreted as the result of faults when threading the heddles.

Cat No 82/A12553b (Illus 31), deposited just after 1150 within the courtyard of a small backland wattle structure (B4), is notable among the High Street finds in that the warp and weft are of different colours,

2/2 Twill without nap, ZS.

Cat/Accession	Area	Rig	Feature	Phase
South Sector				
1/A09–0003	4	V, VI	MC004	Ia
9/A8086	1/2	V	B10, South Room–Floor (3)	Icc
18/A12340a	3	V	MC025, Pit 5337	(Ia–)Id
24/A11551b	3	V	MC025, Pit 5337	(Ia–)Id
77/A10417	3	VI	B4, Floor	IIc
82/A12553b	3	VI	B4, 'Courtyard'–Occupation	IIc
95/A10624a	4	VI	M1.1c	IId
121/A10496	4	V	M10	IId–IIg
205/A09–0133b	7	VI	MC119, Pit 7390	<IIIc–IVa
222/A9902	2	VI	B2, Late Occupation/Abandonment (2) & M1.4d	IVa–IVc
252/A09–0117b	7	VI	M1.4f	IVc
324/A09–0014	9	VII	M9a	IVc,IVcc
361/A6148	3	V, VI	M1.5a	Va,Vaa(VI)

emphasising the diagonal pattern of the weave (although readily visible to the naked eye, this does not show clearly in a black and white photograph). One system, probably the warp, is firmly Z spun dark brown yarn, 11-12 threads per 10mm, and the other a softer and thicker mid-brown S spun yarn, 8 threads per 10mm. No parallel is recorded from the mainland of Scotland, but fabrics of this type are well known in the Nordic sphere in Scandinavia (for example Kjellberg 1979, 89, 103) including, for example, from The Biggings, Papa Stour, Shetland (Walton Rogers 1999, 195) as well as the medieval cemetery at Herjolfsnæs, Greenland (Nørlund 1924, 89–90; Østergård 2009). There are a few fragments with similar characteristics from 14th- and 15th-century levels in London (Pritchard 1982, 199–200) and another, of late 13th-or early 14th-century date, from King's Lynn, Norfolk (Crowfoot 1977, 374–6). These Elisabeth Crowfoot identified as varieties of *vaðmal*, an imported fabric, originally made on the warp-weighted loom in the countries of the north, noticeably Iceland (Hoffmann 1964, 194–226 passim). The piece from King's Lynn, which is exceptionally coarse, is considered to be Icelandic *pakkavaðmál*, so-called because it was used for wrapping more expensive goods. Such a specific identification is not warranted for the Perth fragment, but Dr Hoffmann (pers comm) agreed that it comes under the general heading of *vaðmál*; she commented that although *vaðmál* was often fulled, records also mention unfulled cloth of this type. The Icelandic export of *vaðmál* is reported to have been at its height in the early Middle Ages (Hoffman 1964, 198) but the possibility exists that the Perth fragment may not have come from so far afield. *Vaðmál* is known to have been produced in both Orkney and Shetland (*SND* sv *wadmal*) and, as late as the end of the 18th century, the memory of weaving *vaðmál* on the warp-weighted loom was still alive in Orkney (*OSA*, xiv, 319, 324–6). The antiquity of making *vaðmál* in the Northern Isles is not known, but since it was used in payment of *skatt*, a land tax originally imposed during the five centuries of Norse occupation and payable to the earls on behalf of the Norwegian Crown, it must pre-date 1472, when the islands were annexed to the Scottish Crown.

2/2 Twill with nap

The only sample in this category, Cat No 84/A12553d (Illus 32), deposited just after 1150 within the courtyard of a small backland wattle house (B4), is an even, light weight, slightly open-textured cloth, woven from combed

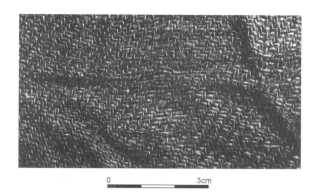

Illus 31 *2/2 twill without nap, ZS, vaðmal. Cat No 82/A12553b.*

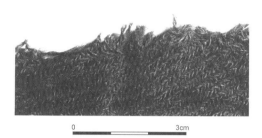

Illus 32 *2/2 twill with nap, with looped and twisted starting edge. Cat No 84/A12553d.*

Z spun yarn. It is remarkable for its shaggy surface, which is quite unlike that on any other textile from Perth. How this nap was formed is not clear. As the fabric does not appear to have been fulled, it is doubtful that it would have been brushed with teasles, a process likely to damage a raw fabric; the nap could perhaps be the result of using wool which has been combed, yet without the short fibres having been removed, or possibly of the conditions in which the piece was buried. An interesting feature, which links the fabric with vertical looms, is a looped and twisted closed edge – not a side selvedge but a transverse edge (Illus 15). Somewhat similar, although less complex edges remain on the body and sleeve fabrics of the coarse shirt from Rogart, Sutherland, which may be of medieval date (Henshall 1952, 18–21, Fig 6 and Plate 3); both cloths are tabbies and the sleeve fabric incorporates a pile. Henshall (ibid, 4) considered the possibility that these had been woven on a simple two-beam vertical loom of a type which produced a tubular web. As, however, examples of the latter from northern Europe belong to the prehistoric period, she concluded that the Rogart

2/2 Twill with nap.

Cat/Accession	Area	Rig	Feature	Phase
South Sector				
84/A12553d	3	VI	B4, 'Courtyard'–Occupation	IIc

pieces had more likely been woven on a warp-weighted loom: in this case, a heading cord or cords would have been passed through the loops and attached to the top beam of the loom, thus holding the warp ends in place; the cord(s) would have been removed when the finished web was taken from the loom. She commented that the division of the warp threads for the passage of the first weft on the Rogart pieces is haphazard and was presumably done manually after the warp was fixed in place. On the Perth piece, by contrast, the division and arrangement of the warp, although complicated, appears regular and is more likely to have been achieved during warping, although it is difficult to imagine how this was carried out. Dr Hoffmann (1964, 175–82) described and illustrated a number of fabrics begun with a heading cord but all are in tabby weave and, with the exception of a blanket from Thorshavn, in the Faroes, all have simple arrangements at the closed edge. The closest parallel to the Perth piece is a fragment of 2/2 twill from a 13th-century level in Oslo, Norway (Kjellberg 1982, 141), the edge of which is constructed as follows: 'Between two warp threads connected by a loop there are five single warp threads. These threads are again connected to other warp threads by loops'. The Perth edge is a more complex variation of this set up; the loops are apparently arranged in pairs, but while the two ends of one loop are separated by five other warp threads, those of the other loop have only one warp thread between them. It is understandable that the division of the warp should have been so arranged that the first weft passed through each loop, thus providing proper closure when the putative heading cord (or cords) was removed, but it is not clear why it was necessary to intertwine the warp in so complicated a manner. Such an arrangement might have been necessary when setting up the warp for a patterned cloth, such as a check but, as far as can be seen, Cat No 84/A12553d is monochrome. For the moment, therefore, the structure of this edge remains a puzzle.

2/1 Twill without nap, ZZ

Typically, the pieces in this group, which consists of 49 samples drawn from all periods, are closely woven from combed yarn and have not been fulled; most are hard or moderately firm to the touch. Cat No 38/A11567i is unusual for its loose texture, and Cat No 349/A6710b for its softness. In general, similar yarn was used for the two systems, and warp and weft counts are close to balance. A notable exception is Cat No 108/A6125 (Illus 33), deposited in a late 12th-century midden, which in continuation of an earlier tradition, is heavily warp-faced on one surface; a thicker yarn was used for the weft (the identification of which is confirmed by the existence of a selvedge),

Illus 33 *2/1 twill without nap, ZZ. Cat No 108/A6125.*

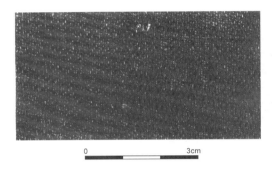

Illus 34 *2/1 twill without nap, ZZ. Cat No 264/A09–0105.*

and the count is 18 by 9 threads per 10mm. Another fabric, Cat No 376/A09–0023b, from an early 14th-century midden, has a similar count but it is too small to give an adequate impression of the appearance of the cloth. There are four heavy fabrics, with 4–7 threads per 10mm in both systems, but the majority are of light or light-medium weight, with a preponderance of fine cloths with counts in the range 12–24 threads per 10mm. Most are very competently executed, evenly spun and woven (for example Cat No 264/A09–0105, Illus 34) – more consistently well made, indeed, than any other group from the site. Six fabrics have selvedges remaining, all simple except that on Cat No 32/A11567c which is tubular (compare with Illus 13). Of three moderately fine fabrics tested for dyes Cat Nos 69/A11510b and 279/A09–0056a were positive for flavanols, but Cat No 196/A09–0123 was completely negative; Cat No 38/A11567i, the soft fabric mentioned above, which at 24 by 18–19 threads per 10mm had the highest thread count in the group, was positive for madder; Cat No 349/A6710b, similar but less fine, examined by Dr Ryder, showed signs of a dark red dye; while Cat No 98/A10332, one of the heaviest fabrics, with a count of 4–7 by 5–6 threads per 10mm, gave no indications of having been dyed.

2/1 Twill without nap, ZZ.

Cat/Accession	Area	Rig	Feature	Phase
South Sector				
†8/A12612B	1/2	V	B10, South Room–Occupation (2b)	Icc
27/A09–0026b	3	V	MC025, Pit 5337	(Ia–)Id
32/A11567c	3	VI	MC037a, Pit 5157	Ia–Ie
38/A11567i	3	VI	MC037a, Pit 5157	Ia–Ie
39/A11567j	3	VI	MC037a, Pit 5157	Ia–Ie
41/A11524	3	VI	MC037b, WW5121	Ib–If
59/A11142	3	VI	MC053c	If
69/A11510b	3	VI	P5.3b	If,IIa
91/A10193a	4	VI	M1.1c	IId
94/A10193d	4	VI	M1.1c	IId
98/A10332	3	VI	M1.1c, Pit 5005	IId
108/A6125	2	VI	M1.1d & M1.1e	IId–IIf
111/A6649	2	V	B5, North Room–Floor/Occupation (1)	IIa–IIff
113/A8863a	2	V	B5, North Room–Floor/Occupation (2)	IIa–IIff
144/A10409a	3	VI	M1.2, Pit 2648	<IIg(IIh)
170/A09–0142	9	VII	B19 (Phase 1), North Room–Occupation (4b)	IIIa
190/A09–0130	7	VI	M6a	IIg–IIId
191/A09–0058	9	VII	M15	IIId
193/A09–0081	9	VII	M15	IIId
196/A09–0123	7	VII	M15; Pit 9415	IIId
206/A09–0134a	7	VI	MC119, Pit 7390	<IIIc–IVa
207/A09–0134b	7	VI	MC119, Pit 7390	<IIIc–IVa
211/A9903a	3	V	P2.2b	IVa
224/A09–0075a	9	VII	B18 (Phase 1b), North Room–Floor	IVa,IVaa
225/A09–0075b	9	VII	B18 (Phase 1b), North Room–Floor	IVa,IVaa
226/A09–0120	7	VII	B18 (Phase 1b), North Room–Occupation (5b)	IVa,IVaa
253/A09–0126	7	VI	M1.4f	IVc
254/A09–0119a	7	VI	M1.4f	IVc
264/A09–0105	7	VII	B18 (Phase 2a), External 1, Pit 7314	IVb
276/A09–0045	9	VII	B18 (Phase 2b), North Room, Hall & Hall South–Occupation (10)	IVb
279/A09–0056a	9	VII	B18 (Phase 2b), North Room, Hall & Hall South–Occupation (10)	IVb
284/A09–0027	9	VII	B18 (Phase 2b), North Room, Hall & Hall South–Occupation (10)	IVb
286/A09–0022	9	VII	B18 (Phase 2b), Hall & Hall South–Occupation (12a)	IVb
287/A09–0039	9	VII	B18 (Phase 2b), Hall & Hall South–Occupation (12a)	IVb
288/A09–0092a	7	VII	B18 (Phase 2b), North Room & Hall–Floor (2)	IVb
314/A6708	3	V, VI	M1.4c	IIIa–IVcc
321/A09–0051	7	VII	M9a	IVc,IVcc
322/A09–0076	7	VII	M9a	IVc,IVcc
325/A09–0080	10	VIII	M9b(b)	IVc,IVcc
334/A6652b	3	VI	B34, Floor	Va
338/A09–0050	7	VI	B34–Courtyard	Va
340/A09–0054	7	VII	P8.4	Va
349/A6710b	3	V	B1(a), T2477	IVcc,Va
350/A6695	3	V	B1(a), Levelling	IVcc,Va
367/A6648	3	V, VI	M1.5a	Va,Vaa(VI)
371/A6146	3	V, VI	M1.5a	Va,Vaa
376/A09–0023b	7	VI, VII	M1.5b	Vaa
380/A09–0037	7	VI, VII	M1.5b	Vaa
404/A1268	2	V, VI	Unstratified	u/s

† indicates item is not listed in original site Finds Register

2/1 Twill without nap, ZS

With 87 samples this is the most numerous category from the site. About one third of the fabrics appear to have been fulled, although it may be that the felting together of the yarns is in some cases the result of the conditions in which they were buried (see Finishing, above). In a majority of the samples the S spun yarn is of a different quality to the Z spun; it is usually less firm and often less regular in thickness and tension. These characteristics are especially noticeable among the fulled fabrics, where in most pieces combed Z spun yarn in one system is combined with S spun yarn, which is woollen (or at least lacking the qualities of combed yarn), in the second. Most of the 2/1 twills from 14th-century deposits on archaeological sites in London have Z spun warp and S spun weft. Like the earlier Perth examples, the warp yarn was probably combed prior to spinning; it is smooth and fine. Equally, the weft often has less twist than the warp. Crowfoot, Pritchard and Staniland (1992, 31) comment that because of the longer weft spans on the face of the fabric with the weft floats, the cloth has become matted and woolly.

Only five PHSAE pieces in this category have closed edges, but in four – Cat Nos 14/A11080b, 97/A09–0001, 184/A09–0106 and 390/A09–0146 – the Z spun yarn runs parallel to the side selvedge and is, therefore, the warp; the Z spun is also the warp in the fifth sample, Cat No 282/A09–0077a (Illus 35), if the heavy threads at the closed edge may be interpreted as heading cords rather than side strengthening (see Selvedges, above).

There are a few fine unfulled cloths of good quality (for example Cat Nos 294/A6128, 310/A6653b, 311/A6653c and 332/A6151); they are closely woven from worsted yarn, in the range 15–20 threads per 10mm in one or both systems. There is a similar cloth, softer but also made entirely from combed yarn, among the fulled fabrics (Cat No 392/A09–0013). But the majority are heavier, many in the range 8–13 threads per 10mm, and of moderate or even poor quality. Whether unfulled (for example Cat No 100/A11550, Illus 36 or fulled (for example Cat No 337/A09–0041, Illus 37) – albeit 337/A09–0041 has mixed spinning – they have an undistinguished appearance and a tendency to irregularity in both spinning and weaving. The colour too is often uneven and few samples appear to have been dyed. Of twelve examined by Dr Whiting only two proved positive: Cat Nos 177/A09–0108 dyed with indigotin and 372/A8880 dyed with flavanols; Dr Ryder noticed a 'yellow discolour' in both the warp and the weft of Cat No 158/A8432, but its origin is unknown.

An unusual fabric in this group is Cat No 97/A09–0001, which was deposited in a Rig VI backland midden late in the 12th century. In this unfulled piece the hard combed warp is so closely packed as to cover the softer combed weft on both surfaces, giving the fabric an almost polished appearance. The use of fine worsted yarn, close weaving, and a high proportion of warp to weft threads (26 by 10) links the Perth

Illus 35 *2/1 twill without nap, ZS, with ?heading cords.* Cat No 282/A09–0077a.

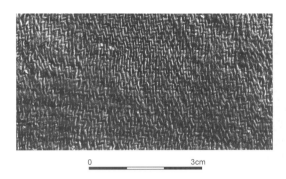

Illus 36 *2/1 twill without nap, ZS, not fulled.* Cat No 100/A11550.

piece with some earlier fabrics of exceptional quality, including a group, of the 9th to 10th centuries, from Birka, Sweden (Geijer 1938, 22–9), and another of the 9th to 11th centuries recently found in York (Hedges 1982, 102–4). These fabrics, which have been the subject of much discussion as to their origin (for example Hoffman 1964, 239–46; Geijer 1980, 211–13), are, however, mainly diamond twills and Z spun in both systems. A 2/1 diamond twill of comparable quality has been recovered from a grave of possible 12th-century date at Coldingham Priory, Berwickshire.

A coarser warp-faced diagonal twill, Cat No 108/A6125 (Illus 33), discussed among the 2/1 ZZ weaves from Perth, was deposited in the latter half of the 12th century. It also represents a continuity with previous tradition.

2/1 Twill without nap, others

Only one of the four fabrics has been fulled (Cat No 337/A09–0041). At first sight, this fulled textile appears to be a 2/1 twill without nap, ZS. However, a closer examination of the yarns used in system 1 shows that for every 12 to 14 Z spun elements, there are two S spun elements interspersed in fairly regular succession across the width (Illus 37).

Of the unfulled fabrics, Cat No 259/A09–0104 (Illus 38), from the second half of the 13th century, shares

2/1 Twill without nap, ZS.

Cat/Accession	Area	Rig	Feature	Phase
South Sector				
2/A9992	1	VI	MC006, T3852	Ib
13/A11080a	3	V	MC025, Pit 5337	(Ia–)Id
14/A11080b	3	V	MC025, Pit 5337	(Ia–)Id
60/A11143	3	VI	MC053c	If
81/A12553a	3	VI	B4, 'Courtyard'–Occupation	IIc
90/A10076	4	VI	M1.1c	IId
97/A09–0001	4	VI	M1.1c	IId
100/A11550	3	VI	M1.1c, Pit 5005	IId
127/A9478c	4	VI	B12, Pit 2345	IIe–IIg
130/A8833	4	VI	B12, Occupation (1/2)	IIe–IIg
132/A9129	3	VI	M1.2, Pit 2648	<IIg(IIh)
134/A9271	3	VI	M1.2, Pit 2648	<IIg(IIh)
139/A9506	3	VI	M1.2, Pit 2648	<IIg(IIh)
147/A10409d	3	VI	M1.2, Pit 2648	<IIg(IIh)
149/A10409f	3	VI	M1.2, Pit 2648	<IIg(IIh)
154/A9121	3	VI	M1.2, Pit 2648	<IIg(IIh)
158/A8432	3	VI	M1.3	IIi
160/A8505b	3	VI	M1.3	IIi
161/A8725	3	VI	M1.3	IIi
165/A9138	3	VI	M1.3	IIi
169/A9057b	3	VI	M1.3	IIi
177/A09–0108	9	VII	B19 (Phase 2a), North Room–Occupation (3c)	IIIb
184/A09–0106	9	VII	B19 (Phase 2b), North Room–Floor (1)	IIIc
192/A09–0078	9	VII	M15	IIId
198/A9497	3	VI	MC119, Pit 7390	<IIIc–IVa
199/A9766a	3	VI	MC119, Pit 7390	<IIIc–IVa
200/A9766b	3	VI	MC119, Pit 7390	<IIIc–IVa
201/A9766c	3	VI	MC119, Pit 7390	<IIIc–IVa
208/A09–0135a	7	VI	MC119, Pit 7390	<IIIc–IVa
210/A09–0135c	7	VI	MC119, Pit 7390	<IIIc–IVa
212/A9903b	3	V	P2.2b	IVa
218/A6634	1	VI	B20, Occupation (1a)	<IIId–IVaa
219/A11662	1	VI	B20, Occupation (2b)	<IIId–IVaa
220/A09–0139	7	VII	MC130	<IIIc–IVaa
229/A6124b	4	VI	MC160, Pit 2232	IVb
242/A09–0033	9	VII	B18 (Phase 1/2), MF9194	IVaa,IVb
244/A09–0062	9	VII	B18 (Phase 1/2), MF9194	IVaa,IVb
245/A09–0100	7	VI	M1.4f	IVc
247/A09–0113	7	VI	M1.4f	IVc
248/A09–0114	7	VI	M1.4f	IVc
249/A09–0115	7	VI	M1.4f	IVc
251/A09–0117a	7	VI	M1.4f	IVc
255/A09–0119b	7	VI	M1.4f	IVc
275/A09–0032b	9	VII	B18 (Phase 2b),North Room, Hall & Hall South–Occupation (10)	IVb
278/A09–0049b	9	VII	B18 (Phase 2b),North Room, Hall & Hall South–Occupation (10)	IVb
280/A09–0056b	9	VII	B18 (Phase 2b),North Room, Hall & Hall South–Occupation (10)	IVb
282/A09–0077a	9	VII	B18 (Phase 2b),North Room, Hall & Hall South–Occupation (10)	IVb
289/A09–0092b	7	VII	B18 (Phase 2b), North Room & Hall–Floor (2)	IVb

(continued)

2/1 Twill without nap, ZS (continued).

Cat/Accession	Area	Rig	Feature	Phase
291/A09–0038	9	VII	B18 (Phase 2b), Hall South–Occupation (13a)	IVb
293/A9127	3	V	MC155, Pit 2691	IVb,IVc
294/A6128	3	VI	M1.4d	IVb,IVc
304/A12372b	3	VI	M1.4d, Pit 2566	IVb,IVc
305/A03–0253	7	VI	M1.4h	IVc
309/A6653a	3	V, VI	M1.4c	IIIa–IVcc
310/A6653b	3	V, VI	M1.4c	IIIa–IVcc
311/A6653c	3	V, VI	M1.4c	IIIa–IVcc
319/A09–0010	9	VII	P8.3	IVc,IVcc
320/A09–0085	7	VII	M9a	IVc,IVcc
328/A6631	3	VI	M1.4e, Pit 2446	IVcc(Va)
331/A6152	2	VI	B34, MF2759	Va
332/A6151	3	VI	B34, Floor	Va
333/A6652a	3	VI	B34, Floor	Va
335/A09–0052	7	VI	B34–Courtyard	Va
348/A6710a	3	V	B1(a), T2477	IVcc,Va
354/A6127a	3	V, VI	M1.5a	Va,Vaa(VI)
357/A6127d	3	V, VI	M1.5a	Va,Vaa(VI)
359/A6145a	3	V, VI	M1.5a	Va,Vaa(VI)
360/A6145b	3	V, VI	M1.5a	Va,Vaa(VI)
363/A6150	3	V, VI	M1.5a	Va,Vaa(VI)
364/A6626	3	V, VI	M1.5a	Va,Vaa(VI)
368/A8861	3	V, VI	M1.5a	Va,Vaa(VI)
372/A8880	3	V, VI	M1.5a	Va,Vaa
373/A09–0017	7	VI, VII	M1.5b	Vaa
374/A09–0019	7	VI, VII	M1.5b	Vaa
378/A09–0072a	7	VI, VII	M1.5b	Vaa
379/A09–0072b	7	VI, VII	M1.5b	Vaa
382/A09–0064	7	VI, VII	M1.5b	Vaa
386/A09–0036	7	VII	M8a	Va,Vaa
388/A09–0015	9	VII	M8a	Va,Vaa
389/A09–0074	7	VII	M8a, T7206	Va,Vaa
390/A09–0146	7	VII	B53 (Phase 1), Central Area–Occupation (2a)	Vb
392/A09–0013	7	VII	B53 (Phase 1), North Area–Occupation (4)	Vb
394/A09–0016	7	VII	B53 (Phase 2), North Area–T7072	Vbb
395/A09–0025	7	VII	B53 (Phase 2), South Area–Occupation (6)	Vbb
396/A09–0012	7	VII	B53 (Phase 2), North Area–Occupation (15)	Vbb
399/A8910	2	VI	P1b	Vd
North Sector (Area 6)				
411/A6147	6	–	'Garden'	G

2/1 Twill without nap, others.

Cat/Accession	Area	Rig	Feature	Phase
South Sector				
93/A10193c	4	VI	M1.1c	IId
168/A9057a	3	VI	M1.3	IIi
259/A09–0104	7	VII	B18 (Phase 2a), North Room & Hall–Construction (1)	IVb
337/A09–0041	7	VI	B34–Courtyard	Va

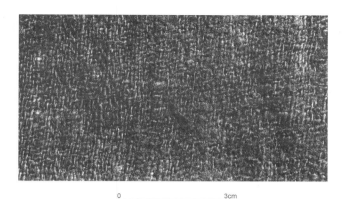

Illus 38 *2/1 twill without nap, others, with change in one system from Z to S yarn. Cat No 168/A9057a.*

Illus 37 *2/2 twill without nap, others (mixed spinning in the system with the vertical elements), fulled. Cat No 337/A09–0041.*

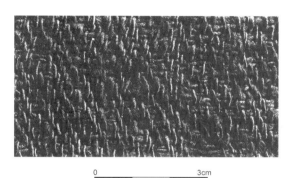

Illus 39 *Extended 2/1 twill without nap, others, with paired Z and S threads in ?weft. Cat No 168/A9057a.*

the characteristics of many of the three-shed twills woven from Z spun yarns. The cloth, which is harsh to the touch, is closely woven from well made worsted yarn; the thread count is 15–18 per 10mm in both warp and weft. The unusual feature is that whereas in one system Z spun yarn is used throughout, in the other it is used for only part of the fragment, the remainder being executed in similar S spun yarn. The change to a yarn spun in the opposite direction creates a noticeable difference in texture, but insufficient of the fabric remains to show whether this was part of a regular pattern. If the Z and S spun threads in this second system were originally of different colours, this is no longer evident, as the piece is a uniform dark brown. Cat No 168/A9057a (Illus 39), deposited c1200, is a heavy fabric in which the weave is extended in one system (see Weaves and patterns, above); each pair of threads consists of one Z spun and another similar, but S spun. Cat No 93/A10193c (Illus 9), from the second half of the 12th century, is also a partially extended weave, but in this case threads running in pairs and thicker single threads are used in the same system. The fragment is notable as being the only example of a check from the High Street site, although again too little remains to give an adequate impression of the pattern.

2/1 Twill with nap, ZZ

The eight fabrics in this category are heterogeneous. The two earliest samples, Cat Nos 37/A11567h and 126/A9478b, are made from combed yarn and have much in common with the un-napped 2/1 twills constructed from Z spun yarn; despite the presence of a light nap on one or both surfaces, they do not appear to have been fulled. In the remaining six cloths the yarn in one or both systems is comparatively soft and was probably not prepared by combing. All six have been fulled, although the degree of fulling varies from light in Cat No 185/A09–0096 to heavy in 273/A09–0024. In Cat No 365/A6627, the fabric with the highest count in the group, 18 by 17 threads per 10mm, the surface has been sufficiently heavily finished as to render the identification of the weave slightly doubtful.

2/1 Twill with nap, ZZ.

Cat/Accession	Area	Rig	Feature	Phase
South Sector				
37/A11567h	3	VI	MC037a, Pit 5157	Ia–Ie
126/A9478b	4	VI	B12, Pit 2345	IIe–IIg
148/A10409e	3	VI	M1.2, Pit 2648	<IIg(IIh)
162/A10070	3	VI	M1.3	IIi
185/A09–0096	9	VII	B19 (Phase 2b), North Room–Floor (2b)	IIIc
273/A09–0024	9	VII	B18 (Phase 2b), North Room, Hall & Hall South–Occupation (10)	IVb
355/A6127b	3	V, VI	M1.5a	Va,Vaa(VI)
365/A6627	3	V, VI	M1.5a	Va,Vaa(VI)

2/1 Twill with nap, ZS

All 62 samples in this group have been fulled. Like the
2/1 ZS weaves, without nap, there is often a disparity
in quality, texture, or both, between the Z and S yarns.
In any given fabric the Z spun yarn is usually, although
not invariably, the more firmly spun and with the higher
count. On only three pieces, Cat Nos 74/A11154, 145/
A10409b and 257/A09–0131, is the selvedge preserved,
but in all three cases the Z spun yarn is the warp. The
selvedge is simple in Cat No 257/A09–0131 but in Cat
No 74/A11154, the weave has been extended, that is,
the warp threads run in pairs, for a width of 7mm. In
Cat No 145/A10409b the weave is also extended, in
that the warp threads are grouped in pairs for a width
of 10mm, but the interlacing employed in the selvedge
is tabby.

The degree to which the nap has been raised varies
considerably. Eighteen of the pieces, the earliest of
which, Cat No 83/A12553c, comes from the courtyard
occupation of a backland house (B4) that dated from
after 1150, have been heavily napped on both surfaces,
often to the extent of totally obscuring the structure
of the cloth (for example Cat No 297/A8101; Illus
40). Where, as is often the case, fulling has also been
extensive, the texture of the fabric is very firm. On
those pieces where the nap has partially worn away,
allowing the threads to be examined, the count varies
from 10 by 6 to 14 by 12 threads per 10mm. About a
further dozen of the cloths are either napped on one
side only, or have been more heavily napped on one
surface than the other: in each case, (for example Cat
Nos 19/A12340b and 290/A09–0093; Illus 41, 43), the
nap is more prominent on the surface on which the S
threads predominate. The raising of the nap on this
surface in Cat No 22/A12340e converts the stripes
into a more indistinct and mottled effect. Thread
counts are in the range 8 by 8 to 17 by 13 per 10mm.

The remaining samples, constituting nearly half the
group, have a light nap on both surfaces; most have
between 8 and 14 threads per 10mm in both systems.
Cat No 128/A9481, with a count of 7–8 by 4 threads,
is unusual for its coarseness and mottled colouring. In
Cat No 283/A09–0077b (Illus 42), from the second half
of the 13th century, the main S spun yarn is replaced in
part by a group of considerably finer and very closely-
packed S spun threads. The sample is fragmentary
and in a poor state of preservation, but may have been
a weft striped fabric, analogous with the tabby and
twill cloths patterned with extended tabby stripes, of
the 13th to 15th centuries, known from England, the
Netherlands, and elsewhere (Crowfoot 1980, 112–13;
Pritchard 1982, 200 Fig 1; Vons-Comis 1982a, 156, Fig
1; Walton 1989, Fig 161a). In the Perth piece, however,
the basic three-shed construction seems to have been
retained for the stripe(s), the effect depending on the
change of yarn and the close packing of the threads;
the colour of both wefts is now the same.

Illus 40 *2/1 twill with nap (partially worn), ZS.
Cat No 297/A8101.*

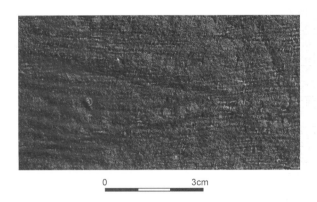

Illus 41 *2/1 twill with nap, ZS. Cat No 290/A09–0093.*

Illus 42 *2/1 twill with nap, ZS, with ?weft stripe
of finer yarn. Cat No 283/A09–0077b.*

2/1 Twill with nap, ZS.

Cat/Accession	Area	Rig	Feature	Phase
South Sector				
19/A12340b	3	V	MC025, Pit 5337	(Ia–)Id
22/A12340e	3	V	MC025, Pit 5337	(Ia–)Id
58/A09–0011	3	V	MC034a	Ie(If)
70/A11510c	3	VI	P5.3b	If,IIa
74/A11154	3	VI	MC048	(Ia–)IIa–IIc
83/A12553c	3	VI	B4, 'Courtyard'–Occupation	IIc
99/A10787	3	VI	M1.1c, Pit 5005	IId
110/A9901	3	VI	M1.1e	IIf
114/A8863b	2	V	B5, North Room–Floor/Occupation (2)	IIa–IIff
115/A8871	2	V	B5, North Room–Floor/Occupation (2)	IIa–IIff
116/A6716	2	V	B5, North Room–MW3587	IIa–IIff
125/A9478a	4	VI	B12, Pit 2345	IIe–IIg
128/A9481	4	VI	B12, Pit 2345	IIe–IIg
138/A9326	3	VI	M1.2, Pit 2648	<IIg(IIh)
141/A9536a	3	VI	M1.2, Pit 2648	<IIg(IIh)
143/A9536c	3	VI	M1.2, Pit 2648	<IIg(IIh)
145/A10409b	3	VI	M1.2, Pit 2648	<IIg(IIh)
146/A10409c	3	VI	M1.2, Pit 2648	<IIg(IIh)
155/A11288	3	VI	M1.2, Pit 2648	<IIg(IIh)
163/A8832	3	VI	M1.3	IIi
164/A9108	3	VI	M1.3	IIi
176/A09–0110	9	VII	B19 (Phase 2a), North Room–Occupation (3c)	IIIb
178/A09–0111	9	VII	B19 (Phase 2a), North Room–Occupation (3c)	IIIb
182/A09–0094	9	VII	P8.1b & B19 (Phase 2b), South Room–Occupation (1a)	IIIc
186/A09–0086	9	VII	B19 (Phase 2b), North Room–Occupation (3)	IIIc
187/A09–0091	9	VII	B19 (Phase 2b), South Room–Occupation (2a)	IIIc
189/A09–0089	9	VII	P8.1c	IIIc
195/A09–0083	9	VII	M15	IIId
209/A09–0135b	7	VI	MC119, Pit 7390	<IIIc–IVa
213/A9905	3	V	P2.2b	IVa
215/A09–0057	9	VII	B18 (Phase 1a), Middle Room/Hall–Occupation (1b)	IVa,IVaa
228/A6124a	4	VI	MC160, Pit 2232	IVb
230/A6124c	4	VI	MC160, Pit 2232	IVb
231/A9906	4	VI	MC160, Pit 2232	IVb
236/A09–0124c	7	VII	MC126, Pit 7402	IVaa,IVb
241/A09–0067	9	VII	B18 (Phase 1/2)	IVaa,IVb
257/A09–0131	7	VII	B18 (Phase 2a & 2b), T7385	IVb
258/A09–0103	7	VII	B18 (Phase 2a), North Room & Hall–Construction (1)	IVb
260/A09–0030	9	VII	B18 (Phase 2a), North Room & Hall–Construction (1)	IVb
263/A09–0102	7	VII	B18 (Phase 2a), North Room & Hall–Construction (2)	IVb
277/A09–0049a	9	VII	B18 (Phase 2b), North Room, Hall & Hall South–Occupation (10)	IVb
281/A09–0071	9	VII	B18 (Phase 2b), North Room, Hall & Hall South–Occupation (10)	IVb
283/A09–0077b	9	VII	B18 (Phase 2b), North Room, Hall & Hall South–Occupation (10)	IVb
290/A09–0093	7	VII	B18 (Phase 2b), North Room & Hall–Floor (2)	IVb
297/A8101	3	VI	M1.4d	IVb,IVc
298/A8515	3	VI	M1.4d	IVb,IVc
301/A8097a	3	VI	M1.4d, Pit 2566	IVb,IVc
302/A8097b	3	VI	M1.4d, Pit 2566	IVb,IVc

2/1 Twill with nap, ZS (continued).

Cat/Accession	Area	Rig	Feature	Phase
303/A12372a	3	VI	M1.4d, Pit 2566	IVb,IVc
315/A7352a	3	V, VI	M1.4c	IIIc–IVcc
316/A7352b	3	V, VI	M1.4c	IIIc–IVcc
318/A7424	3	V, VI	M1.4c	IIIc–IVcc
326/A7616	3	VI	M1.4e	IVcc(Va)
329/A6644	3	VI	P6	IVcc,Va
347/A8859	3	VI	P6 & B1(b), Destruction	IVcc,Va
369/A8911	3	V, VI	M1.5a	Va,Vaa(VI)
377/A09–0060	7	VI, VII	M1.5b	Vaa
385/A09–0040	7	VII	M8a	Va,Vaa
397/A6709	2	V, VI	M4a	Vaa–Vc(VI)
402/A09–0028	10	VIII	B51, T7008	Vd,Vdd
405/A2827	3/4	V, VI	Unstratified	u/s
408/A09–0066	7–10	VI–VIII	Unstratified	u/s

In general the quality of the cloths in this category is rather higher than that of the 2/1 ZS weaves without nap, especially among the more heavily finished fabrics. This particularly applies to colour, which is often rich and even, suggestive of dyeing; a number of the pieces have a distinct pink or red tinge. An offcut of a high quality fabric, Cat No 138/A9326, is characterised by its deep red colour and even spinning in both warp and weft. The fragment with the strongest and clearest colour, Cat No 19/A12340b (Illus 43), one of the earliest fabrics from the site, was found by Professor Whiting to have been dyed with kermes (see Dyes above). Three others (Cat Nos 213/A9905, 230/A6124c and 297/A8101) have been dyed with madder, and a fourth (Cat No 301/A8097a) with both madder and indigotin. In addition, Cat No 302/A8097b was noted by Dr Ryder to be pale yellow in both systems, and it is recorded that Cat No 397/A6709 ran red when being washed during conservation. Two other samples examined by Professor Whiting, Cat Nos 114/A8863b and 187/A09–0091, proved negative.

2/1 Twill with nap, others

These two fabrics are considered separately because of the unusual combinations of yarn used in their manufacture, but their general appearance is also unlike the other 2/1 twills with nap. Both are from late 12th century Rig VI middens. Cat No 142/A9536b, of which only a few square centimetres remain, is a fulled, medium weight fabric with eight threads per 10mm in both systems, and has a moderate nap on both surfaces. It is one of only two cloths from the site constructed entirely from S spun single ply yarn. The rarity of the SS combination among medieval wool cloths, at least before the 15th century, has been noted elsewhere; in a substantial collection of finds from Lund, Sweden, for example, it is reported to disappear entirely after the early 1100s (Lindström 1982, 182). However, post-11th-century and pre-15th-century 2/1 twills

0   3cm

Illus 43 2/1 twill with nap, ZS, dyed with kermes. Cat No 19/A12340b.

with S spun warp and weft do make rare appearances at archaeological sites as previously discussed (see Spinning, above).

Cat No 157/A8366 is a strip of stiff heavy weight fabric with one long edge closed. It has been so thoroughly finished that the analysis can only be tentative. As far as can be seen, it is an extended weave, the weft consisting of fine S spun threads used in pairs. The warp exhibits a curious combination of loosely twisted 2 ply yarns – some Z spun and S plied and others S spun and Z plied. The piece is narrow, no more than 25mm, and it is possible that this is special structure for a selvedge rather than that of the main fabric. Heavily reinforced edges with paired and plied warp elements were detected among fulled cloths from the Castle Ditch, Newcastle upon Tyne. These borders have been interpreted as strengthened selvedges for stretching the cloth on tenter frames to dry after fulling (Walton 1981, 195–7). However, it should be noted that there is a considerable lapse of time between Cat No 157/A8366, dating to the late 12th century, and the 15th- to 16th-century textile assemblage from Newcastle. Another 15th-century textile, 753C, a tabby felted on both sides, has a simple selvedge of four Z plied yarns at Fast Castle, Berwickshire (Ryder and Gabra-Sanders 1992, 6; Gabra-Sanders and Ryder 2001, 127).

Twill weaves of silk
P Z Dransart

Of the four silk twill weaves recovered from the High Street, the two earliest were recovered from deposits laid down shortly before 1150. The other two came from Rig VII contexts dating from the second half of the 13th century and first decade or so of the 14th century. Three of the silks in this category are weft-faced compound twills, while the fourth (Cat No 233/A09–0122) is a 2/2 lozenge twill (Illus 47, 48).

In their present condition, the High Street twill weaves are small and somewhat disparate in shape: Cat No 342/A09–0088 is a sample consisting of two small triangular fragments, Cat Nos 6/A9500 and 46/A7323 are similar narrow bands, while Cat No 233/A09–0122 is a larger piece of fabric, evidently very worn when it entered the archaeological deposits. They do, however, testify to the variety of silk fabrics imported into Scotland and complement finds from other medieval sites.

Weft-faced compound twill is a textile structure with a widespread geographical distribution; it occurs in three of the silk twill weaves from the High Street. It was also long lived, although less so than the tabby used in the silks discussed above (see Tabby weaves of silk). Often referred to by the medieval term samitum, weft-faced compound weaves were perhaps developed in Iran during the second and third centuries AD (Geijer 1979, 58). Compound weaves are woven with two warp sets which function, respectively, as a main warp and as a binding warp. The main warp may be used singly, in which case there is a proportion of one main warp end to each binding end. Alternatively, there may be one pair of main ends to each binding end. The existence of two functionally distinct warp systems in one fabric suggests that the drawloom was employed, with the figure harness controlling the main warp ends and the ground harness the binding ends (ibid, 58 and 101). Movements of the main warp ends determine the order in which different wefts appear on the surface, but these warp threads are largely obscured by the weft floats. Weft-faced compound weaves are ideally suited for executing complex designs and they formed the predominant technique for patterned silks in the first millennium AD (ibid, Plates 12–22). However, they were still current in the 12th to 14th centuries, to judge from textiles excavated from various medieval centres in Britain. In addition to Perth, they have been found at, for example, Southampton (Crowfoot 1975), Winchester (Crowfoot 1990) and London (Crowfoot et al 1992).

2/1 Twill with nap, others.

Cat/Accession	Area	Rig	Feature	Phase
South Sector				
142/A9536b	3	VI	M1.2, Pit 2648	<IIg(IIh)
157/A8366	4	VI	M1.3	IIi

Twill weaves of silk

Cat/Accession	Area	Rig	Feature	Phase
South Sector				
6/A9500	1	V, VI	B15(West/East), PH3792	Ic,Icc
46/A7323	2	VI	M14b(b)	Ie
233/A09–0122	7	VII	MC126, Pit 7402	IVaa,IVb
342/A09–0088	7	VII	P8.4	Va

Two of the High Street pieces, Cat Nos 6/A9500 and 46/A7323 (Illus 44), share similar characteristics. In these long strips of cloth, there are two wefts, one on each surface of the fabric. The weft travels under one and over two binding warp ends (that is, a 1/2 order of interlacing). Since the binding warp forms longer floats on one side of the fabric (the reverse), the two faces are not exactly the same. In this twill structure, the main warp is all but obscured (Illus 45). Closer examination indicates that there is a proportion of one main warp to each binding end in these two pieces. Both the warps in each piece are Z thrown, while the weft is untwisted and of a coarser diameter. However, slight differences in thread densities may be noted. Cat No 6/A9500 has a warp count of 16 binding warp ends and 16 main warp ends per 10mm, and a weft count of 24 threads per 10mm on each surface of the fabric. In contrast, Cat No 46/A7323 has a count of 14–15 warp threads of each type, and a weft count of 18 threads per 10mm on each surface.

Both pieces probably served a similar purpose as the binding or edging of a garment, or perhaps as tapes. One long margin on Cat No 6/A9500 is deteriorated and the constructional details of Cat No 46/A7323 are clearer (Illus 46).

The third weft-faced compound twill from the High Street (Cat No 343/A09–0088) is structurally similar to the other two. It differs in that the ridges formed by the twill weave constitute a Z diagonal. In the case of Cat Nos 6/A9500 and 46/A7323, the ridges form S diagonals. The colour is different too, being a dark golden yellow instead of the brighter yellow which characterises the two strips. It has a warp count of 17 binding warp ends and 17 main warp ends per 10mm. There are 24 weft passes per 10mm.

As mentioned above, weft-faced compound weaves constitute an ideal medium for complex patterning. A fragmentary silk fabric from Milk Street, London, was executed in a 1/2 weft-faced compound twill with red, white and blue weft threads, dating from the late 9th to 10th centuries (Pritchard 1984, 61–2). Unlike the Perth weft-faced compound twills, the threads used in the main warp and binding warp are not twisted. From a slightly later archaeological context (late 10th to early/mid 11th century) at 16–22 Coppergate, York, there is a reliquary pouch, the outer covering of which was woven in a similar compound twill. Although both main and binding warps are Z thrown, as in the Perth compound twills, there is a difference in that the York reliquary pouch has a main warp which is paired (Walton 1989, 369–71).

The fact that the Perth weft-faced compound twills have a single rather than paired main warp ends means that they are slightly unusual in 12th- to 14th-century contexts. Parallels may be noted, however. Two fragments assigned to the 11th to 12th century from the treasury at Beromünster share similar characteristics (Schmedding 1978, Cat Nos 20a and 20b). In these two rectangular shaped silks, the wefts on each face are of a different colour. In No 20a at Beromünster, the weft

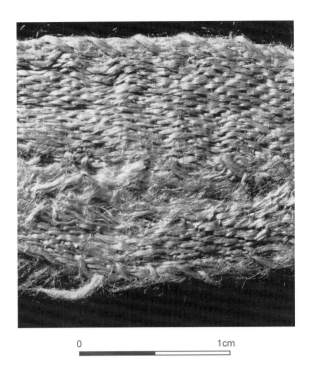

0   1cm

Illus 44 *Twill, silk, weft-faced compound twill with single main warp ends. Cat No 46/A7323.*

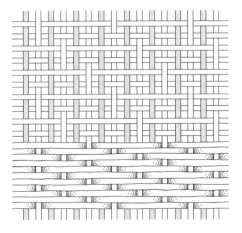

Illus 45 *2/1 weft-faced compound twill.*

on the upper surface is violet, and that on the lower surface is green-blue. The two colours appearing on the upper and lower surfaces of No 20b are light violet and dark violet, respectively. These two fragments share the same structural characteristics displayed by Cat Nos 6/A9500 and 46/A7323, but the warp and weft counts are much higher.

Monochrome samitum is said to be rare (ibid, 37). It has been found as a lining material in St Cuthbert's grave, Durham (Flanagan 1956, 525). It also constitutes the ground of another St Cuthbert fabric, the so-called Rider silk, which has a printed design (Brett 1956). In addition, it was employed in an embroidered chasuble

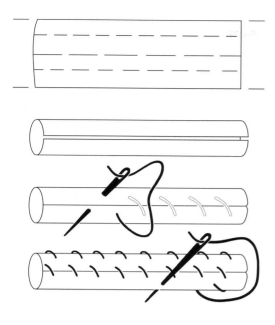

Illus 46 *Detail of construction of Cat No 46/A7323.*

ascribed to St Thomas of Canterbury in the Cathedral of Fermo, Italy; the fabric is blue on the upper surface and white on the lower (Schuette and Müller-Christensen 1963, Plates 57–59). This silk has an inscription which dates it to AD 1116 and which further assigns it to Almería, a noted Spanish weaving centre (May 1957, 10).

Various explanations have been offered to account for the contrast between the choice of single or paired main warp threads in weft-faced compound twills. According to one suggestion, a proportion of one main warp thread to one binding thread is found in earlier fabrics; the development of paired main warp ends permitted the weavers to use finer yarn, thereby affording better weft cover (Flanagan 1956, 507–8, Footnote 3). Further examples of the use of a single main warp are known from fragments, originally dyed red, found in the tomb of ?Henry of Blois (d 1171) in Winchester Cathedral (Crowfoot 1990, 486 No 1039) and in a weft-faced compound twill found during excavations at Lower Brook Street, Winchester. In this second example the warp was probably dyed with weld, and the wefts formed some kind of pattern in yellow and red (ibid, 482 No 1020).

Another proposition is that paired main warp ends have greater design potential in that a smaller design may be enlarged (Flanagan, cited in Walton 1989, 377). It has also been suggested that fabrics with single main ends were suitable for embroidery, as in the embroidered buskins of Archbishop Hubert Walter (d 1205) at Canterbury Cathedral (Muthesius 1982b, 84). The High Street compound twills, however, have survived in a monochrome condition.

Not all weft-faced compound twills have a 1/2 order of interlacing. A single main warp twill, excavated from a late 13th-century level at site Trig Lane, London, is a 1/3 weft-faced compound twill (Crowfoot et al 1992, 107 and Fig 77). In other words, the weft passes under one binding warp and over three. Like the Perth compound weaves, it is monochrome in colour. The Trig Lane silk consists of five small pieces of fabric, sewn together to make what looks like the upper part of a bag or pouch (ibid, 104).

In Scotland, an example of a 1/3 weft-faced compound twill has been analysed from an early or mid 16th-century bishop's tomb at Fortrose (Henshall et al 1956, 26–8). The cloth is patterned in a repeated fleur-de-lys design with two wefts, an untwisted silk yarn and a badly deteriorated pattern weft, which was possibly of vegetable fibre originally twisted with a metal strip. However, this textile is significantly different from the fragments excavated from the High Street and Kirk Close sites in Perth. The ground warp is paired in a proportion of two main warp ends to each binding end. In addition, both warps are fine, lightly S thrown silk. It has been suggested that generally, with few exceptions, silk yarns employed in the west were Z thrown until the 14th century (or the end of the 13th century in Italy), when technological advances in reeling and throwing silk resulted in a change to the production of fine S twisted warp yarns (Crowfoot et al 1992, 124). A silk velvet from Fast Castle in Berwickshire, from a late 15th-century context, has a main warp which is S thrown (Pritchard in Ryder and Gabra-Sanders 1992, 9, and in Gabra-Sanders and Ryder 2001, 129). However, there are some cases of narrow silk ribbons with an S thrown warp which predate the 14th century (see Tabby weaves of silk, above).

Compound weaves may also be woven on the basis of a tabby rather than a twill binding. An extremely high quality textile woven in such a compound weave was exhumed from the presumed tomb of Robert I (the Bruce) in Dunfermline Abbey when it was opened in 1819, although there is a slight possibility that the grave may have contained the body of Alexander III, who died in 1286 (Henshall et al 1956, 22 n1). According to the analysis undertaken by Beckwith and Kerton (ibid, 22–6), the structure of the textile consists of a brocaded tabby, the tabby binding being employed in the ground, the pattern and the brocade. Three pairs of ground warp are used for each binding warp, all Z thrown silk (the binding warp only has a slight twist). There are three wefts; the ground weft is of untwisted silk, the pattern weft consists of a gilt metal strip twisted S on a plied linen core, and the brocade weft is also of untwisted silk. Since the metal is woven throughout the fabric, Beckwith and Kerton identified it as cloth of gold. Probably dating from the early 14th century or late 13th century, the textile is thought to be a product of a loom in northern Italy (ibid, 26).

The fourth silk twill excavated from the High Street is Cat No 233/A09–0122 (Illus 47, 48). This 2/2 twill has reversals in both directions, creating an overall lozenge pattern. With a firm Z thrown warp and untwisted weft, it has a warp count of 35–38 threads and a weft count of 25–27 threads per 10mm. These counts are fairly similar to those of a silk cloth in the treasury at Chur, Switzerland (Schmedding 1978, 88 Cat No 90). The Chur piece is large, and it is crossed with bands of coloured silk wefts and gold threads with a linen core. However, the main weave is a lozenge twill with a firm Z thrown warp and a loose Z twisted weft; both warp and weft are white. Schmedding (ibid, 88) assigned it to 13th-century Spain.

Other lozenge twill silks include a cushion found in the tomb of Queen Berenguela (d 1246) at the convent of the monarchs of Castile and León at Las Huelgas, near Burgos, Spain (Gómez-Moreno 1946, Plate LXVIII no 21), and a rectangular satchel in the treasury of St Servatius, Maastricht (Stauffer 1991, Cat No 84). Both these textiles are crossed by transversal bands of colour; the latter has a Z thrown warp and an untwisted weft like Cat No 233/A09–0122. In the light of these examples, it is significant that the High Street lozenge twill was recovered from deposits dating to the second half of the 13th century

The fragmentary Trig Lane pouch mentioned above also came from a 13th-century context. In spite of the 2/2 and 1/3 interlacings used, respectively, in the compound twills of Cat No 233/A09–0122 and of this pouch, a point of comparison may be made in the loose texture that both display. The use of fine threads in a loosely textured weave is characteristic of another type of 13th-century silk cloth known as cloth of aresta (Desrosiers et al 1989, 223 n10). Of note is a silk recovered from excavations at Kirk Close in Perth belonging to this category (Muthesius 1987, 169–71; Illus 49). The term cloth of aresta is derived from the Latin *pannus de arista*. One of the features of such cloths is the incorporation of a chevron or herringbone twill, hence the Latin term *arista* which, besides meaning an ear of corn, may also be applied to fishbone or herringbone. The reverses in direction across the width of the fabric of the diagonal ridges of the chevron twill correspond to individual repeats of one straight comber unit and one in reverse, in which the direction of the diagonal lines in the twill is changed (Desrosiers et al 1989, 210–11). In the Kirk Close textile the points of the chevrons meet in a vertical band embellished with a large lozenge which separates pairs of confronted birds. A fuller definition has been proposed to account for the technical features of cloth of aresta in the following terms: 'Figured two-sided weft-faced lozenge and diagonal twill weaves, with 2 or 3 lats [wefts], the third lat brocaded or interrupted' (ibid, 213). These textiles always have a warp proportion of one end. In other words, there is only a main warp, since a binding warp is not used. However, Desrosiers et al (ibid, 213) note that the term 'two-sided' does not, strictly speaking, always hold true. Some examples of cloth of aresta are not fully reversible because the third lat creates a 'right' and a 'wrong' surface, or else a tabby may occur on one side as in the Kirk Close textile. In cloth of aresta with a lozenge twill ground, 'the reverse of the cloth always corresponds to the side on which these lozenges are formed by the longer floats'. The Kirk Close textile has such a lozenge ground, but it should be noted that the

0   5cm

Illus 47 *Twill, silk, with lozenge pattern. Cat No 233/A09–0122.*

0   2cm

Illus 48 *Detail of twill, silk, with lozenge pattern. Cat No 233/A09–0122.*

criterion adopted by Desrosiers et al for distinguishing the right surface has been described as side two by Muthesius (1987, 169).

In the dual classification proposed by Desrosiers et al, the Kirk Close textile belongs to Category 1, more precisely, to sub-group 1(L8) because of its ground weave, which is a 'two-sided weft-faced lozenge twill, with a repeat of 8 warp threads and 8 passes' (Desrosiers et al 1989, 215). The birds and vertical bands are executed in two consecutive twill weaves which interlace 5/1 and 3/1/1/1 (Muthesius 1987, Illustration 95). Unlike the 1(L8) textile from the Musée Historique des Tissus, Lyon, illustrated by Desrosiers et al (1989, Figure 2), which has three lats (the third lat interrupted), and is a polychrome textile, the Kirk Close textile has two wefts and the cloth is monochrome, the Z thrown warp and untwisted wefts being golden yellow in colour.

Cloth of aresta is thought to have been woven in Spain in the 13th century (May 1957, 87–8; King 1968, 29). More recently, Desrosiers (1999, 114) has suggested that Category 1 textiles might have been produced in Languedoc, which had links at that time with the Aragonese crown. It is therefore interesting to note the 14th-century archaeological context from which the Kirk Close example was excavated. Such a textile would have been highly prized. It is also possible that sumptuary laws imposed restraints on the wearing or use of such a luxury product. The earliest surviving sumptuary law in Scotland is dated to the 15th century; it gave permission to knights or lords and members of their families to wear silk (see Dress in medieval Perth, below). Hence the Kirk Close silk may have been an heirloom before being finally discarded.

A fascinating point of comparison may be made between this textile and the pewter token (A9279) from the High Street (see PHSAE Fascicule 2, The metalwork). The token came from a context dated to the third quarter of the 13th century, and it shows two addorsed birds, their heads turned backwards towards each other; they are depicted pecking the fruit of a three-branched tree which is centrally placed. Although the birds on the Kirk Close textile are confronted, they too, peck at the leaves or fruit of a three-branched tree. It should be noted that the drawing of the textile in Muthesius (1987, Illus 95) is not accurate in this respect. In both the token and the textile, the birds are stylised, but Bateson suggests that the birds on the token may represent peacocks, in which case the triple branched tree may symbolise the true vine (Christ). The peacocks would then stand for the immortality granted to those who feed from it; in other words, the textile and the token may have been seen as an allegory of the Eucharist (see Fascicule 2, The metalwork, Devotional objects, for further details). Such pewter tokens were actually cast in Scotland, but the textile is perhaps an Aragonese import.

Amongst the cloth of aresta recovered from the royal tombs at Las Huelgas is a textile with pairs of confronted, but backward looking birds (Gómez-

Illus 49 *Detail of silk twill with bird design from Kirk Close, Perth, Cat No 29. (Copyright Perth Museum and Art Gallery)*

Moreno 1946, Plate LXXIa). Manuel Gómez-Moreno placed both lozenge twills, like Cat No 233/A09–0122, and cloth of aresta in a category he designated as the 'Christian Series', noting the influence of the Mudéjar style (that is, art executed by Muslims under Christian rule) in the treatment of the arch portrayed in heraldic shields on the cloth of aresta in the tomb of Alfonso VIII (ibid, 57). Peacock motifs, as in the Kirk Close textile, constitute an artistic theme explored by both Muslims and Christians. A stucco ceiling incorporating peacocks at the convent of Las Huelgas has been attributed to the work of stucco carvers from Andalucía in the 13th century, which at that time was under Muslim control (May 1957, 52–5). Hence the peacock was used as a symbol in both Islamic and Christian iconographic canons.

In addition to the silks represented amongst the High Street textiles, few other types of weave have been found on Scottish sites. A narrow silk strip was recovered from a Phase 1 pit at Queen Street, Aberdeen, dating from the second half of the 13th century. It is 8mm wide with one side selvedge intact. Along this closed edge there is a tabby border of 10 warp threads, but the main weave is a warp-faced satin, interlacing 4/1 and with the ridges forming an S diagonal (Bennett

1982, 199). Technically, satin is a five-end weave which is particularly suited to silk as the weave enhances the glossiness of the fibre. Satin continued to be used in Scotland as demonstrated by a dark reddish brown silk cloth, probably a 1/4 weft-faced twill with a very shallow Z diagonal from the tomb of Gavin Dunbar, Archbishop of Glasgow (d 1547) (Henshall et al 1956, 28–9). The chronological aspects concerning the twist direction of the constituent yarns in these different categories of silk textiles will be reviewed with reference to the Perth tabbies and twills in the General discussion, below.

The presence of imported silks in Scottish burghs, of which Perth has provided most examples, extends the range of imported textiles already known from the work of Henshall et al (1956). In addition, the archaeological contexts demonstrate that silks were used in a wider social sphere than one might suppose from a study of surviving silks in Western treasuries alone. The High Street silks demonstrate the prosperity of at least some of its inhabitants, from the earliest days of the burgh. They also indicate that Perth burgesses were part of the extensive trading networks which were operating in Europe and further afield.

Carpet

The fragment of carpet with its tabby base of jute or sisal, and pile coloured with modern dye, is certainly of recent manufacture. A photograph (Illus 50) has been included as an illustration of how radically the appearance of a textile may be affected even by a relatively short period of burial.

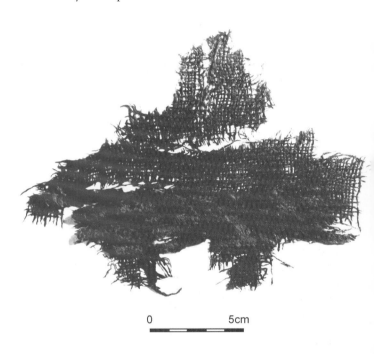

0   5cm

Illus 50 *Carpet (modern). Cat No 403/A11083.*

Carpet.

Cat/Accession	Area	Rig	Feature	Phase
South Sector				
403/A11083	1	VI, VII	Unstratified	u/s

Non loom-woven fabrics

H Bennett, P Z Dransart and the late N Q Bogdan

Felt

Felt may take the form of a flat fabric or a simple three-dimensional article such as a cap or coat. This type of fabric does not have an ordered structure, but is composed of a mass of animal hairs amalgamated by compression in the presence of heat and moisture. As is shown by Mary Burkett's survey (1979, 7–29), felt-making was widespread in the ancient world, where it was used for the production both of mundane goods and such items as fine decorated rugs. It is noted that references to felt are common in Nordic literature from about AD 1000 and it is probable that its use was well established in north-west Europe by that date. Finds of felt have been reported from 13th- and 15th-century contexts in the old town of Oslo (Kjellberg 1982, 137, 147). Virtually nothing is known of the early history of felt in Scotland, but it appears that by the late Middle Ages, if not before, it was being produced on a professional basis in the Scottish burghs. This may be deduced from the existence of hatters – practitioners of a craft in which felt-making was the primary process – in south-east Scotland before 1400 (Craigie 1925, 66). Even so, finds of felt among excavated material from Scotland have been rare. Audrey Henshall (1952, 29) records just one: an undated cap of wool felt from a peat bog in Shetland. Medieval pieces from Scottish sites include a tiny, bright mid-brown fragment excavated from 14th- or 15th-century levels in Kirk Close, Perth (Bennett 1987, 166), a piece from Threave Castle (Bennett nd b) and four fragments from Sillerholes, West Linton (Thea Gabra-Sanders pers comm). Felt has also been recovered from English sites (Crowfoot 1979b, 36; Crowfoot et al 1992, 75).

The finds of felt from the High Street, which came from contexts ranging from the second half of the 12th to the early 14th centuries, are all fragmentary

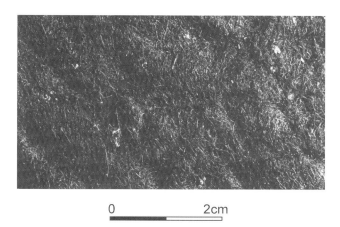

Illus 51 *Felt, wool. Cat No 131/A9126.*

and of undistinguished appearance. Cat No 131/A9126 (Illus 51), which is typical, is thick, irregular and made from coarse fibres; unlike the good quality fragment from Kirk Close, it shows no signs of having been dyed. For Cat No 406/A9821 alone is there any indication of its function: it was found inside a leather boot and appears to have been a lining or inner shoe.

Tablet-woven textiles

Tablet weaving is a method of making narrow bands by the employment of thin perforated plaques or tablets, of wood or some other rigid substance; it can also be used for the production of cordage. To begin, the threads which are to form the warp of the textile are passed through holes in the tablets and held taut; the

Felt.

Cat/Accession	Area	Rig	Feature	Phase
South Sector				
112/A6775	2	V	B5, North Room–Floor/Occupation (1)	IIa–IIff
131/A9126	3	VI	M1.2, Pit 2648	<IIg(IIh)
175/A09–0107	9	VII	B19 (Phase 2a), North Room–Occupation (3c)	IIIb
202/A09–0132a	7	VI	MC119, Pit 7390	<IIIc–IVa
262/A09–0063	9	VII	B18 (Phase 2a), North Room & Hall–Construction (1)	IVb
295/A6696	3	VI	M1.4d	IVb,IVc
387/A09–0070	7	VII	M8a	Va,Vaa
406/A9821	3/4	V, VI	Unstratified	u/s

most common form of tablet is square, with a hole in each corner, accommodating up to four threads. The threading of the warp through the tablets automatically produces a shed (opening) for the weft to pass through (see Illus 52), and the weaving proceeds by the turning of the tablets, forward or back, to create new sheds. In the process, the warp threads held by any given tablet are twisted round each other, locking the weft in place. This gives the work considerable strength, and also its characteristic corded appearance. The products of tablet weaving may be plain, but often they are decorated, as the technique offers exceptional freedom of patterning. Textured patterns may be achieved by threading some tablets from the opposite side to the remainder (thus giving the groups of warp ends contrary twists, as in Illus 52), and by varying the sequence of rotation of individual tablets. Greater possibilities still are offered by the use of warp threads of different colours, and the introduction of one or more brocading wefts. A technical description of tablet weaving, together with indications of its history and geographical distribution, may be found, for example, in Schuette 1956.

During the medieval period silk, sometimes embellished with metal foil, was used extensively in tablet weaving. The products, made for both clergy and well-to-do laity, served as tapes and edgings or applied ornaments on garments and other items, and occasionally took the form of complete objects, such as belts or ecclesiastical stoles (Henshall et al 1956, 29–30). Of the instances of tablet weaving from Scotland, all but one are of silk and fall within the Middle Ages; the exception is the woollen braids on a 1,200-year-old hood, from St Andrew's Parish, Orkney (Henshall 1952, 9–15). The majority exhibit a simple foundation weave, with the patterns executed entirely in brocading in one or more colours. In this group are fragments from the tombs of King Robert I (d 1329), Gavin Dunbar, Archbishop of Glasgow (d 1547) and an unknown bishop of the mid-16th century or earlier, in Fortrose Cathedral (Henshall et al 1956, 29–35); there is also a narrow band brocaded with silver thread, of possible 14th-century date, excavat-ed from Kirk Close, Perth in 1979 (Bennett 1987, 166 Cat No 28). A seal tag

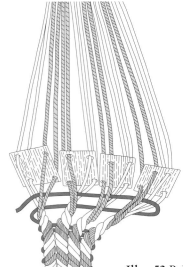

Illus 52 Principle of tablet weaving.

of this structure is appended to a supposed *inspeximus* by King Robert II, dated 1371, but the document proves to have been a later forgery by an English antiquary (Henshall 1964, 159–61). This form of tablet weaving is not, however, represented among the High Street material.

The examples of tablet weaving from the High Street take two shapes: bands and cordage. In all cases the warp and surviving weft are silk, although instances where the weft has decayed entirely may indicate the use of linen thread. This combination of a silk warp with a weft of another fibre would discount such an item from being the product of the Parisian silk guild which, in its statutes, ordered its members (male and female) not to 'warp thread with silk' because the work is 'false and bad' (*fause et mauvèse*) and, if found, 'must be burnt' (Depping 1837, 88; Dixon 1895, 221).

Amongst the finds there are two examples of bands, both from the second half of the 13th century. In Cat No 217/A6694b, the weft has perished and only the accident of the band having been tied in a knot has kept the short lengths of warp together and in sequence. Despite its poor condition and small scale – the band was probably no more than 8mm wide – it is apparent

Tablet-woven textiles.

Cat/Accession	Area	Rig	Feature	Phase
South Sector				
80/A11162b+	3	VI	B4, 'Courtyard'–Occupation	IIc
102/A12651+	4	V	MC081a	IId
117/A9899+	3	V	B23, North Room–Occupation (1a)	IIb–IIff
217/A6694b+	1	VI	B20, Levelling	<IIId–IVaa
234/A09–0124a+	7	VII	MC126, Pit 7402	IVaa,IVb
235/A09–0124b+	7	VII	MC126, Pit 7402	IVaa,IVb
238/A09–0109+	7	VII	B18 (Phase 1/2)	IVaa,IVb
271/A09–0097+	7	VII	B18 (Phase 2b), North Room, Hall & Hall South–Occupation (10)	IVb

+ Silk

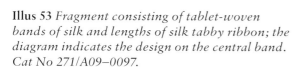

0   3cm

Illus 53 *Fragment consisting of tablet-woven bands of silk and lengths of silk tabby ribbon; the diagram indicates the design on the central band. Cat No 271/A09–0097.*

Illus 54 *Tablet-woven stole, German, 12th–13th century (Victoria and Albert Museum, 142.1894).*

that there was at least a simple form of patterning, for the texture of the centre of the band is distinctly softer than that of the edges. The effect cannot be accounted for either by the yarn or the putative weave; a fine 2 ply yarn has been used for all the warp threads, and close examination suggests that the weave was probably plain throughout, that is, the weft was passed through the work after every quarter turn of the tablets. It appears that the variation in texture has been achieved solely by the simple expedient of threading the six tablets bearing the centre warp ends in the opposite direction to the remainder. In effect, these ends have been twisted in Z direction, against the ply, whereas the border warp threads have been twisted in S direction, reinforcing the ply; this textured weave is without parallel in Scotland. Whether further differentiation was made by using warp threads of different colours is no longer evident. The scale of the band would have made it suitable for a fastening.

The fragments of tablet-woven band which form part of the fabric of Cat No 271/A09–0097 (Illus 53) are a good deal more complex in structure than Cat

No 217/A6694b. The weaving has been so arranged that the warp appearing on the surface forms diagonal lines, giving the effect of a twill; further, two colours have been used, worked into a geometric pattern which is the same on the back of the band as the front, but in counterchange. The style of the geometric ornament is familiar from European textiles of the 12th and 13th centuries, and may be compared in particular with that on a tablet-woven stole, thought to be German work of the period, now in the Victoria and Albert Museum (Illus 54). The double-faced diagonal weave is also known from elsewhere: it was described in detail by Hans Dedekam (1925) in an analysis of woollen bands of the fifth to sixth centuries AD from Norway, and by Grace Crowfoot (1939, 59–63) in relation to the early tenth-century 'girdle' of St Cuthbert; in addition, it was identified by Audrey Henshall (1964, 157–9) as the technique used in the weaving of a silk seal-tag worked with zoomorphic ornament, attached to a charter of William, King of Scots, dated 1189 x 1196. It should be noted, however, that the Perth fragments do not have the plain borders exhibited by these parallels, nor are they embellished with brocading. The work is competent, and slightly finer than the seal-tag, but does not approach the exquisite quality of the Cuthbert piece nor yet the finely controlled craftwork of the Victoria and Albert Museum's stole.

A double-faced tablet-woven band is known from an archaeological context at Baynard's Castle in London, dating from the second quarter of the 14th century (Crowfoot et al 1992, Cat No 143, Fig 100A). It is woven in a lozenge pattern with at least two colours, but the design is simpler than the Perth piece. Since it has a higher weft count (25–26 picks per 10mm) using a plied weft (Z thrown and S plied), rather than a weft with a slight Z twist and a count of approximately 20 picks per 10mm in the Perth piece, it undoubtedly served a different purpose, for instance a girdle or even, as suggested by Crowfoot et al (1992, 132), a spur leather.

The larger group of tablet-woven pieces from the High Street (six items) takes the form not of flat bands but of cords. This shape is achieved by causing the weft to follow a spiral course; instead of being passed to and fro through the fabric it is continually inserted from the same side and drawn tight after each passage, pulling the work into a tube. The cords, which were recovered from layers dating from just after 1150 to the second half of the 13th century, are all unpatterned and apparently in single colours. Three have a diameter of 2mm, while the remaining three have a diameter of 3mm. However, there is some variation in the number of tablets with which the bands were worked, ranging from a possible eight to sixteen tablets. As Audrey Henshall has commented (1964, 162), the results are not unlike shoe laces. She was referring to similar cords used as seal-tags, but the Perth pieces could equally well have served as drawstrings or fastenings, or even for the suspension of personal ornaments; Cat No 102/A12651, which has bound ends, might have been used in this way (Illus 55) A further function has been attested from the late 14th century at Baynard's Castle in London, where two short lengths of silk tablet-weave were found strung with a total of eight amber beads, evidently the remains of a rosary (Crowfoot et al 1992, Fig 106; Egan and Pritchard 1991, 306). The London tubular cords are somewhat later than the High Street examples, since most were dated to the end of the 14th century. As listed by Crowfoot et al (1992, 135), they range in diameter from 1mm to 2.5mm, and were constructed using either 12 or 16 tablets.

A structurally related tubular cord attached to a charter granted by King John (Balliol) at Lindores Abbey, dated 1294, employed eight tablets. Four colours were used in the warp, and one of the tablets was threaded in a different order from the rest. Periodically, the twist was reversed, creating a pattern in the cord (Henshall 1964, 161).

The places of origin of the examples of tablet weaving from medieval Scotland are uncertain. Since they are of silk it is tempting to assume that they were imported ready-made, and Audrey Henshall

Illus 55 *Tablet-woven cord with bound ends, silk. Cat No 102/A12651.*

has tentatively suggested a Spanish origin for one of the Fortrose bands. On the other hand, that the craft of tablet weaving was not totally unknown here is indicated by the find of a fine, four-holed square bone tablet, of possible 9th-century date, from the Brough of Birsay, Orkney (Curle 1982, 60). Since tablet weaving had a specialised use in the Nordic world in the preparation of the warp for a warp-weighted loom, the find is not unexpected. It is not impossible, however, that the craft was also known on the mainland of Scotland, and that some of the Perth finds may have been locally made.

Net

The three examples of net were all deposited during the first decade or so of the 14th century. They may indeed have come from one property for there is reason to believe that Rigs V and VI may have been combined by that date. All three are delicate works, constructed from fine 2 ply silk yarn, and two have embroidered designs carried out in varieties of darning in a form of needlework known, among other names, as *lacis*. Although the third example is plain net, the fragment could well have been part of a similarly ornamented

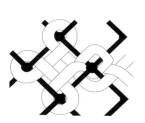

Illus 56 *Interlace stitch.*
Cat No 351/A7577a.

Illus 57 *Embroidered design*
on net. Cat No 351/A7577a.

Illus 58 *Hair-covering*
of embroidered silk net.
Cat No 370/A10112.

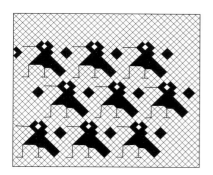

Illus 59 *Embroidered design on net.*
Cat No 370/A10112.

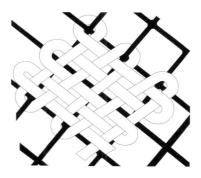

Illus 60 *Surface darning.*
Cat No 370/A10112.

piece. In the embellishment of the net, three different forms of darning have been used. On Cat No 351/ A7577a (Frontispiece) the embroidery has been worked entirely in an open, interlaced stitch, creating a four-lobed form (Illus 56), the repetition of which builds up the cross crosslet design (Illus 57). Cat No 370/A10112 (Illus 58 and Illus 59), by contrast, is worked with solid forms, and the effect of the bird and lozenge design is

altogether less dainty. The lozenges and the bodies of the birds are carried out in a more familiar form of darning; the decorating yarn is run forward and back to lay down a series of parallel threads, and is then woven across them, alternatively under and over, to create a solid fabric (Illus 60). This should properly be called surface darning, for the net serves only to provide a framework for the first set of threads, and is left free behind each motif as is visible on the reverse (Illus 61). A third technique, a cord stitch, has been used to work the beaks and legs of the birds (Illus 62).

Cat Nos 351/A7577a and 370/A10112 are notable among the Perth textiles as being identifiable entities; both are recognisable as decorative hair coverings. The wearing of the hair confined in a net came into vogue among Northern European women by or during the 13th century and, in various forms, continued into the 15th century and beyond (Cunnington and Cunnington 1952, 53; Heinemeyer 1966, 16ff). Parisian guild members who made such nets were called *crespiniers* in their statutes (Depping 1837, 85) and, in England, the contemporary term for this kind of head-dress was *crepin* or *crespine*, direct from the French (*MED*, sv *crepin*; *NED*, sv *crepine*). Among the later manifestations of the fashion is the jewelled caul worn by Margaret of Denmark, wife of James III (1460–1488), on the Trinity Altarpiece of Hugo van der Goes, possibly painted 1478–9, now in the National Gallery of Scotland. The date of deposition of the Perth pieces, however, and the evidence provided by Continental parallels (discussed below) indicate that they belong to the earlier years of the fashion. Too little is known about dress in medieval Scotland for certainty as to how they would have been worn, but if English and Continental modes were followed they may have appeared as on the figure of St Anne, embroidered on a velvet band in c1320 (Illus 63). Here a decorated net covers the hair on the back and sides of the head; it is worn beneath a barbette, the band of linen which passes under the chin, and a fillet, a stiffened linen circlet. Alternatively, the Perth nets may have been worn so as to cover all the hair but a small portion at the front, perhaps with the fillet alone. A further possibility is that both barbette and fillet were omitted, although the Cunningtons (1952, 53) maintained that in England these hair nets 'were never worn alone except by women of the lower class'. A simply dressed woman wearing her hair in a net is depicted in the scene of Iwein and Laudine on the Malterer Hanging, a German couched embroidery of c1310–20, given by the Malterer family to the Convent of St Catherine at Freiburg im Breisgau (Staniland 1991, 42).

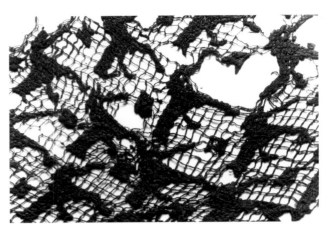

Illus 61 *Detail of reverse of hair-covering of embroidered silk net. Cat No 370/A10112.*

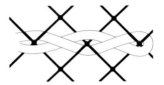

Illus 62 *Cord stitch. Cat No 370/A10112.*

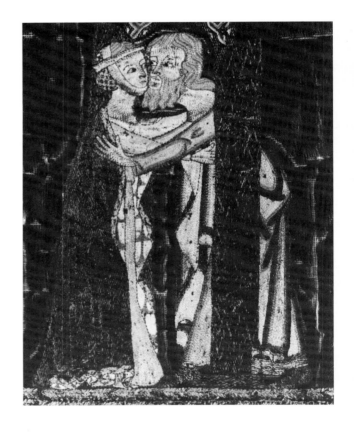

Illus 63 *St Anne, wearing her hair confined in a decorated net or crespine. Detail from embroidered velvet band, England, c1320–40 (Victoria and Albert Museum 8218.1863).*

Net.

Cat/Accession	Area	Rig	Feature	Phase
South Sector				
336/A09–0055+	7	VI	B34–Courtyard	Va
351/A7577a+	3	VI	B1(b), Destruction, Tumble 2775	Va
370/A10112+	3	V, VI	M1.5a	Va,Vaa(VI)

+ Silk

Although the making of net, for use in fishing, hunting, and so on, must have been one of the earliest human textile achievements, this ornamented variety has a much shorter history. In recent times, as may be seen from instruction books of the Victorian era and of the early 20th century (eg, Caulfield and Sawards 1882, sv *Guipure d'Art*; Carita 1908), *lacis* was among the forms of needlework practised by leisured ladies. Pattern books for *lacis* were produced as early as the 16th century (Palliser 1910, 17–18), at which time it was employed by well-to-do women on the Continent in the making of hangings, bed furniture, and so on, and in the embellishment of household linen (Carita 1908, 12); linen, and gold and silver threads, were used, as well as silk. That *lacis* was worked in Scotland at this period, at least at the Court, is indicated by a reference to '*mes ouvrages masches*' in the will made by Mary, Queen of Scots, before the birth of the future James VI in 1566 (Palliser 1910, 22). About *lacis* in the earlier centuries much less is known, but there is sufficient evidence to indicate that during the late Middle Ages it was used for garments and furnishings in both lay and ecclesiastical settings. A distinctive feature of the few early pieces remaining, those from Perth included, is that the embroidery is generally worked diagonally on a ground of lozenges, whereas most post-medieval pieces have been made on a foundation of square meshes.

From England there are references to net-work in inventories of church furnishings from the late 13th century (Roch 1876, cix-cx). There are also four unembroidered mesh hair-nets, all of Z thrown and S plyed silk, from sites in London (Crowfoot et al 1992, 145–9). These are Cat No 399 from Trig Lane, late 13th century; Cat Nos 145 and 153 from Baynard's Castle, second quarter of the 14th century; and Cat No 391, also from Baynard's Castle, late 14th century).

However, the Perth pieces are the first surviving examples of *lacis* from medieval Britain to have come to light. It is, therefore, necessary to look to the Continent for parallels. The graves of the Castilian royal family in the Convent of Las Huelgas, near Burgos in Northern Spain, have yielded three pieces. Two are a pair of cushion covers from the coffin of Sancho (d 1343), illegitimate son of Alfonso XI; they have a heavy geometric design worked in coloured silks and gold thread (Gómez-Moreno 1946, 39, Plate 133). The third, also a cushion cover, from the tomb of Isobel de Molina (d 1292) is embroidered with four-lobed rosettes in the same open interlace stitch employed on Cat No 351/A7577a (ibid, 33, Plate 134); the work is not true *lacis*, however, for the ground is not knotted. As befits their purpose, the fabric of all three cushion covers is considerably more robust than that of the Perth pieces. Closer in both scale and workmanship are several examples from Germany. Among several such in the Boch collection in the Victoria and Albert Museum is a fragment of delicate silk net embroidered in pink, white and green silk yarns (1854.1863); it incorporates the cross motif found in Cat No 351/A7577a, although worked in solid darning rather than interlace stitch. Comparison with German embroideries and silks suggests it was made in the 13th or 14th century. Closer still is another hair net, recovered from a grave of c1300 in the Church of St Elisabeth, Marburg, and now in the Germanisches Nationalmuseum, Nuremberg (Illus 64). The Nuremberg piece has a tablet-woven band attached to the lower edge, whereas the Perth example has a flat braid (see Braids, below), but otherwise the similarity in design and technique is such as to suggest that both were made in the same area, presumably in Germany. In the case of Cat No 370/A10112, although the technique is familiar

Illus 64 *Hair-covering of embroidered silk net, found in Marburg, c1300.*
(© *Germanisches National Museum, Nurnberg*)

from other medieval pieces it is difficult to find parallels for the design. Several examples of *lacis* from Germany are worked with birds or animals, usually of heraldic significance; a fragment of probable 14th-century date in the Victoria and Albert Museum (326.1896) is ornamented with closely-darned escutcheons, some bearing beasts, while another (307.1894) has a diaper design, each alternate lozenge containing a double-headed eagle; a hair net of late 13th- or early 14th-century date in Dusseldorf bears the arms of Middle and Lower Rhenish families, some of which include birds, although in this case the escutcheons have been embroidered separately and then
applied to the net (Heinemeyer 1966, Figs 1–4). None of these examples, however, has a bird motif resembling that on Cat No 370/A10112. The identity of the long beaked, broad tailed bird is dubious and it has been worked so clumsily that it may be doubted whether the embroiderer had a particular species in mind. A possible explanation is that it is a considerably devolved version of a peacock motif (see Twill weaves of silk, above), such as is found, for example, on some Spanish silks of the period, the lozenge being the last remnant of the raised fan of the tail.

Sprang

Sprang may be defined as 'a method of making fabric by manipulating the parallel threads of a warp that is fixed at both ends' (Collingwood 1974, 31). Generally, the threads are stretched over a frame and then plaited or interlaced with the fingers. Because both ends are fixed, the interworking of one half of the warp has a similar, but reversed result in the other half; when the work is complete just one transverse line of fastening is required to lock the contrary twists of the two halves in place and prevent them from untwining. The technique is capable of producing fabrics of widely differing appearance, from an open lace-like mesh to a dense material with a superficial resemblance to closely-worked knitting. This versatility, combined with the elasticity common to all forms of sprang, has suited it to a variety of purposes; the method has been utilised in the making of close-fitting garments such as caps, head-dresses and stockings, as well as bags and military sashes.

As has been shown by both Hald (1950, 249–80) and Collingwood (1974, 35–43), sprang has a long history and wide geographical distribution. The technique is common to, amongst others, Prehispanic Peru, Bronze Age Denmark and Coptic Egypt; in Scandinavia it has continued in use into modern times, as also in parts of south and east Europe and elsewhere. Despite this distribution, no similar tradition can be traced in Britain. Archaeological finds of sprang here have been

Illus 65 *Sprang. Cat No 227/A09–0121.*

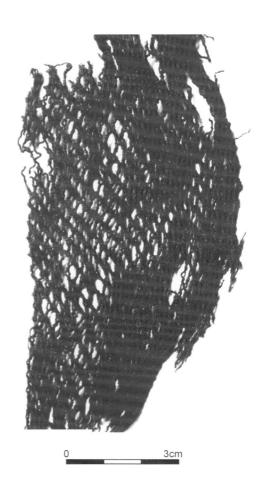

Illus 66 *Sprang worked from very firm worsted yarn. Cat No 227/A09–0121.*

Sprang.

Cat/Accession	Area	Rig	Feature	Phase
South Sector				
227/A09–0121	7	VII	B18 (Phase 1b), North Room–Occupation (5b)	IVa,IVaa

very rare: impressions on a Viking 'tortoise' brooch from Unst, Shetland, may have been left by sprang, but a footless stocking found near Micklegate Bar, York, possibly dating from the period of Roman occupation, may until now have been the only extant example (Henshall 1950; 1952, 16). The find from Perth appears to be the first from a medieval context in Britain. However in Ireland, a piece of openwork sprang constructed from silk thread has been reported from Viking levels at Dublin (Pritchard 1988, 156).

The sprang from Perth is composed of two small fragments made from very firmly spun smooth wool yarn. It was worked into a uniform open mesh in which each interstice is formed by eight intersections of the threads (Illus 65, 66); there are no signs of shaping, or of a meeting line. As has been pointed out by Collingwood (1974, 34), since the thread structures which can be made by sprang can also be attained by other methods, the identification of the technique cannot be regarded as certain where a piece is largely incomplete. Even so, it is difficult to imagine what other technique could have been used in this case. The purpose of the fragments is not clear. The highly elastic open fabric would be very suitable for a hair-covering and, indeed, the same structure is found in the hair net or cap of the early Iron Age from Haraldskar, Denmark (Hald 1950, 52–5, 260) but the fragments are too small for this to be more than conjecture.

Braids

There are five pieces which have been braided from lengths of wool or silk yarn. Three different techniques have been used, all of which have wide currency and are not specific to a particular area or period. Two of the methods produce flat bands, the third, tubular cords. In each case the piece could have been made with the fingers alone, although for the third method bobbins are sometimes employed to help control and order the threads. None of the braids is complete.

The earliest of the group, Cat No 30/A11567a (Illus 67), deposited before 1150, is a flat band about 18mm wide. It is made from thirteen strands of plyed wool yarn worked in a simple plait in which each thread moves diagonally back and forth across the braid, passing alternately under and over the other threads as it goes (Illus 68). Plaits made according to the same principle, but containing fewer threads, have been found in 13th- and 14th-century contexts at Southampton, Oxford, and at least two sites in London (Crowfoot 1975, 336, 338, Fig 275; 1980, 113–114, Fig 52). Elisabeth Crowfoot considered most of these narrow braids are likely to be shoe laces, although the example from Riverside Wall, London, which is divided into two tails at one end, may have served a more decorative purpose. These English medieval finds are all in silk. For a parallel in wool it is necessary to look to Scandinavia in the Viking period, notably a tabby diagonal braid in 24 threads, from a grave dated about AD 1000 at Mammen, Denmark (Hald 1950, 245, Figs 246–247). As Dr Hald commented, though, the technique is an old one and of widespread use, not limited to north-west Europe. She added (ibid, 246–52) that such bands, often patterned, have a prominent place in Scandinavian folk dress, principally as garters. The Perth piece, too, is an appropriate width to have been a garter.

The second flat braid, Cat No 352/A7577b, which is of silk, is sewn to the lower edge of one

Illus 67 *Tabby diagonal braid, wool. Cat No 30/A11567a.*

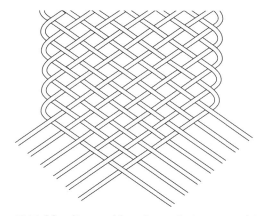

Illus 68 *Tabby diagonal braid, wool. Cat No 30/A11567a.*

Braids.

Cat/Accession	Area	Rig	Feature	Phase
South Sector				
30/A11567a	3	VI	MC037a, Pit 5157	Ia–Ie
166/A9974	3	VI	M1.3	IIi
307/A6637+	3	V, VI	M1.4c	IIIa–IVcc
352/A7577b+	3	VI	B1(b), Destruction, Tumble 2775	Va
391/A09–0021+	7	VII	B53 (Phase 1), North Area–Occupation (3a)	Vb

+ Silk

of the embroidered hair nets, Cat No 351/A7577a
(Frontispiece), which may be dated c1300. The outer
side resembles a diagonal braid, but the inner side is
dissimilar, and from this it is evident that a different
technique has been used from that of the diagonal
braid. The band appears to have been made from seven
double threads (each originally with a loop at each
end) by the method known as finger- or loop-braiding.
The procedure for this form of braiding, which was
formerly used throughout the Nordic world, and is
still current in Norway, is described in detail by both
Dr Gudjónsson (1979, 65–6) and Aagot Noss (1966,
134–136). Again, although well-known in Scandinavia,
the technique was clearly not confined to that area.
Dr Gudjónsson (1979, 67) cited the example of loops
for buttoning made in this manner on a 14th-century
aumonière of possible Rhenish workmanship; Elisabeth
Crowfoot (1975, 336–8) described a complete braid
of five loops from Southampton, deposited in the last
decade of the 13th century; while from a late 13th-
century deposit in London there is a nine-loop braid,
probably part of a silk purse, and a five-loop braid
stitched to a caul of plain netting (Pritchard 1982,
198–9). Twenty-four fingerloop braids made from two
ply thread, using from seven to twenty loops, are also
recorded from London (Crowfoot et al 1992, 138, Table
12). Like the Perth braid, these other medieval pieces
are of silk.

The remaining three braids from Perth are cords.
The two of silk (Cat Nos 307/A6637 (Illus 69) and 391/
A09–0021) are narrow, while the third, Cat No 166/
A9974 (Illus 70) of coarse wool, is massive by contrast.
The first two are composed of 32 and 24 single elements,
respectively; the third is of eight elements, each consisting
of four strands. All three are firm and close-textured
and much less elastic than the flat braids. The technique
is whipcording (Illus 71), the method of working of
which is described in detail by Dr Hald (1950, 243–5,

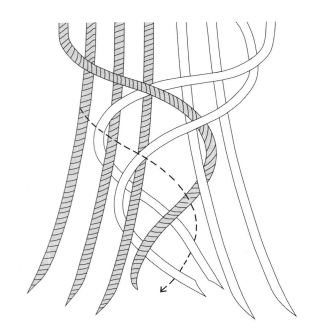

Illus 71 *The principle of whipcording with eight
elements (after Hald 1950).*

Figs 237–245). Plain or patterned, the cords may be of
few or many threads, but always in multiples of four;
short lengths may be made without tools, but bobbins
are employed for longer lengths. Dr Hald notes that
the uses of such braids are very varied, from providing
cords on slings in Palestine to decorative trimmings on
women's skirts in Denmark. The Perth braids appear to
have been designed for strength rather than ornament;
the heavy wool cord would have been suitable for a
handle or perhaps part of a harness, while the silk pieces
may have been drawstrings, or possibly garment ties.

Yarns

Of the 65 finds in this category five, or possibly six, are
of silk, two probably of horsehair, and the rest of wool.
All but four are yarns of a suitable weight for weaving
or needlework, and most are probably scrap from these
activities, or fragments from woven articles.

All the samples of silk are fine 2 ply yarns thrown in
S direction. The yarns in Cat No 330/A7841 resemble
the dark sewing threads used in tabby silk Cat No 346/
A09–0044. With the exception of Cat No 339/A09–
0053, the condition of which is too poor for judgement,
these samples show signs of having been worked. Cat
Nos 17/A11512, 183/A09–0098 and 250/A09–0116
appear to be the remnants of tablet-woven pieces –
bands or cord – the weft from which has perished.
Cat No 223/A7835 may have been a finger braid, but
is unravelled for most of its length. The majority of
the wool yarns are coarse 2 ply, 3–6mm in diameter,
composed of hairy fibres; Z spun and S plyed is the
usual structure. These are identical with the yarns used
in the weaving and, occasionally, the sewing of the

0   2cm

Illus 69 *Braid made by the whipcord method, silk.
Cat No 307/A6637.*

0   2cm

Illus 70 *Braid made by the whipcord method, wool.
Cat No 166/A9974.*

Yarns.

Cat/Accession	Area	Rig	Feature	Phase
South Sector				
3/A9496	1/2	VI	MC006	Ib
7/A11202	1/2	V, VI	M2.1b & B10, South Room–Floor/Occupation (1)	Ic,Icc
10/A11085	4	V, VI	MC017	Ia–Icc>
16/A11080d	3	V	MC025, Pit 5337	(Ia–)Id
17/A11512+	3	V	MC025, Pit 5337	(Ia–)Id
28/A8496	2	VI	P5.1b	Icc,Id
43/A10490	4	VI	B16 (Phase 1), Occupation (1b)	(Id)Ie
44/A7312a?	2	VI	M14b(b)	Ie
45/A7312b?	2	VI	M14b(b)	Ie
49/A7353a	2	VI	M14b(b), Pit 3625	Ie
50/A7353b	2	VI	M14b(b), Pit 3625	Ie
51/A7416a	2	VI	M14b(b), Pit 3625	Ie
52/A7416b	2	VI	M14b(b), Pit 3625	Ie
53/A7429	2	VI	M14b(b), Pit 3625	Ie
54/A7432	2	VI	M14b(b), Pit 3625	Ie
56/A10770	3	V	MC034a	Ie(If)
57/A09–0002	3	V	MC034a	Ie(If)
65/A10414	4	VI	B16 (Phase 2), Destruction	If,IIa
67/A11086	3	VI	P5.3b	If,IIa
71/A10681	3	V	MC049	IIa
†72/A09–0020	3	VI	MC054a, Pit 5267	(IIa)IIb
79/A11162a	3	VI	B4, 'Courtyard'–Occupation	IIc
85/A11090	3	VI	MC066	IIc
86/A10347	4	VI	M1.1f	IIb–IId
88/A10036	4	VI	M1.1c	IId
122/A9520	4	VI	B12, Occupation (1b)	IIe–IIg
124/A9842	4	VI	B12, Pit 2345	IIe–IIg
129/A10071	4	VI	B12, Pit 2345	IIe–IIg
135/A9320Aa	3	VI	M1.2, Pit 2648	<IIg(IIh)
136/A9320Ab	3	VI	M1.2, Pit 2648	<IIg(IIh)
137/A9320Ac	3	VI	M1.2, Pit 2648	<IIg(IIh)
152/A10436	3	VI	M1.2, Pit 2648	<IIg(IIh)
171/A09–0145a	9	VII	B19 (Phase 1), North Room–Occupation (4b)	IIIa
172/A09–0145b	9	VII	B19 (Phase 1), North Room–Occupation (4b)	IIIa
173/A11309	1	VII	MC112b	IIIb
179/A09–0144	9	VII	M13	IIg–IIIb
183/A09–0098+	9	VII	P8.1b & B19 (Phase 2b), South Room–Occupation (1a)	IIIc
194/A09–0082	9	VII	M15	IIId
203/A09–0132b	7	VI	MC119, Pit 7390	<IIIc–IVa
214/A8864	3	V	MC156	IVaa
216/A6694a	1	VI	B20, Levelling	<IIId–IVaa
223/A7835+	3	V	B3 (South), Occupation (1b)	IVa,IVaa
232/A09–0129*	7	VII	MC126, Pit 7402	IVaa,IVb
237/A09–0143	7	VII	MC126, Pit 7402	IVaa,IVb
240/A09–0065	9	VII	B18 (Phase 1/2)	IVaa,IVb
250/A09–0116+	7	VI	M1.4f	IVc
256/A09–0125	7	VI	M1.4f	IVc
265/A09–0112	7	VII	B18 (Phase 2a), External 1, Pit 7314	IVb
266/A09–0118	7	VII	B18 (Phase 2a), External 1, Pit 7314	IVb
268/A09–0128	7	VII	B18 (Phase 2a), External 1, Pit 7314	IVb
285/A09–0095	7	VII	B18 (Phase 2b), Hall & Hall South–Occupation (12a)	IVb

(continued)

Yarns (continued).

Cat/Accession	Area	Rig	Feature	Phase
296/A8099	3	VI	M1.4d	IVb,IVc
300/A8084	3	VI	M1.4d, Pit 2566	IVb,IVc
308/A6642	3	V, VI	M1.4c	IIIa–IVcc
312/A6653d	3	V, VI	M1.4c	IIIa–IVcc
317/A8914	3	V, VI	M1.4c	IIIa–IVcc
327/A8867	2	VI	M1.4e	IVcc(Va)
330/A7841+?	3	VI	P6	IVcc,Va
339/A09–0053+	7	VII	P8.4	Va
341/A09–0087	7	VII	P8.4	Va
345/A09–0047b	7	VII	P8.4	Va
353/A2947	3	V, VI	M1.5a	Va,Vaa(VI)
366/A6628	3	V, VI	M1.5a	Va,Vaa(VI)
383/A09–0073	7	VI, VII	M1.5b	Vaa
401/A6130	4	V	M3c	Vd

All are of wool with the exception of those indicated thus:
+ Silk
+? Possibly silk
* Horsehair ?
† indicates item is not listed in original site Finds Register

heavy tabby fabrics (see Tabby weaves from 2 ply yarns above). There are also a few fine 2 ply yarns. Composed of combed fibres, smooth and firm, they are likely to have been sewing threads. The five samples of single ply thread include a tiny clew of fine Z spun yarn, dyed a bright pink, Cat No 265/A09–0112, and a mass of medium weight strands, Cat No 341/A09–0087, Z spun and in various shades of brown, which appear to be waste perhaps trimmed from the end of a web of cloth.

Cordage

The items in this category are heavier plies than the yarns listed above and may be termed cordage. These have been produced by the simple method of twisting together multiple strands of one or more plies, perhaps with the aid of a cross-bar handle. Cords manufactured by other techniques, namely tablet weaving and braiding, are considered under the appropriate headings above. The most substantial of the four listed here, Cat No 174/A09–0141 (Illus 72), is 10mm in diameter. Made from three strands of 2 ply yarn twisted together firmly and evenly, and of thoroughly professional appearance,

it must originally have been of considerable strength. The fibres have the visual characteristics of horsehair, but this has not been confirmed by analysis. A second example which also appears to be of horsehair, Cat No 15/A11080c, but exists only in a short length, is simply a heavy yarn plied back on itself, leaving a loop at one end. The remaining samples, Cat Nos 26/A09–0026a and 261/A09–0061, are fragments in poor condition, of bulky, rather soft cordage. These are composed of from 18 to 34 smooth Z spun strands of wool yarn twisted together in S direction. Similar cordage has been found on habitation sites elsewhere, for example one of seventh- to eighth-century date from Hessen, north Germany (Tidow and Schmid 1979, 125, Plate 2), but its purpose is not known.

Illus 72 *Cordage, ?horsehair. Cat No 174/A09–0141.*

Cordage.

Cat/Accession	Area	Rig	Feature	Phase
South Sector				
15/A11080c*	3	V	MC025, Pit 5337	(Ia–)Id
26/A09–0026a	3	V	MC025, Pit 5337	(Ia–)Id
174/A09–0141*	9	VII	B19 (Phase 2a), North Room–Floor (1)	IIIb
261/A09–0061	9	VII	B18 (Phase 2a), North Room & Hall–Construction (1)	IVb

All are of wool with the exception of those indicated thus:

* Horsehair ?

General discussion

P Z Dransart, H Bennett and the late N Q Bogdan

Apart from their interest as the first large body of medieval textiles from Scotland, the finds of cloth and related material from the High Street are a potential source of information for a momentous period in the history of Perth (as of Scotland as a whole). Over 75% of the deposits pre-date the 14th century and are exactly contemporary with the two hundred years of relative peace and prosperity which saw the emergence of towns in Scotland. It was the time, indeed, of the rapid development of Perth to a position second only to Berwick as a port and centre of commerce when, it has been argued (Duncan 1974, 42–9), the manufacture of cloth played an important role in the economy of the burgh. Most of the remaining material dates from the early and mid-14th century and therefore relates to the years of the Wars of Independence and the occupation and re-occupation of the burgh by invading forces, which resulted in the demise of Perth as one of the chief towns of Scotland. What then may be learnt from the finds concerning the production of and trade in textiles in the burgh during this period?

Silk

At 7.54% of the finds, silk, both loom-woven and in other forms, is well represented among the High Street textiles; these silks do not come from one level alone, but are drawn from all periods of the excavation. As there is no evidence for silk throwing (spinning) or the weaving of silk yardage in medieval Scotland, all such finds must be regarded as potential imports. Even so, it is not impossible that some of the non-loom-woven items were made locally from imported yarn. The Exchequer Roll for 1331, for instance, mentions the purchase for the royal wardrobe of Parisian silk, *cerici Parisiensis* (*ERS*, i, 380), which since it was bought by weight, not by the piece or length, may be deduced to have been yarn rather than a textile. While such a purchase may have been intended principally for use as sewing thread, it could also have provided the material for making braids or for tablet weaving. In theory the examples of *lacis*, the embroidered silk hair nets, could also have been made locally from yarn bought in, but the similarities of technique and design to probable German work of the period strongly support a foreign origin for these items (see Net, above). Netting needles with an open eye at each end are known at some European sites, for instance from eighth- to 11th-century Mikulžice in the Czech Republic (Kostelníková 1990, 117), a tentatively identified example in wood (yew) from a 13th-century house at Winchester (Biddle and Elmhirst 1990, 817), from 14th- and early 15th-

century deposits in London (Crowfoot et al 1992, 146–7) and from late 15th- to early 16th-century Amsterdam (Baart et al 1977, 126, Cat No 123). A documentary reference to an *agora de rete* (a 'needle to make a net') also appears in an inventory of items sold at public auction at Pisa in 1176 (Robbert 1983, 401; see also below). However, such needles have not been recognised amongst the High Street finds.

In at least some cases, silk yarns were used for decorative stitching. There are instances of two leather uppers of shoes/boots with such stitching (this Fascicule, Leather Cat Nos 229/A7588c and 172/A7580a). In the latter, two rows of white thread enclose a row of pink thread. A colour contrast was also used in repairing or reusing silk fabrics. One of the compound weave silk twills, which had been stitched into a tube, has a pink yarn clinging to its edge (Cat No 46/A7323). Pink silk yarn was also used to repair Cat No 271/A09–0097, an item composed of lengths of tablet weaving and narrow ribbon. In both these cases, a yarn plyed from two strands of pink silk was used to stitch what appears to have been a recycled silk textile of a contrasting colour; the colours may, of course, have faded over time.

That loom-woven silks of this period are imports is beyond doubt and, as suggested above (see Tabby weaves of silk and Twill weaves of silk, above), some of the 11 fragments of woven silk from the High Street might have come from as far afield as Central Asia. They are, perhaps, more likely to have come from the Byzantine or the Islamic world, which at that time reached as far as Spain. The 2/2 lozenge twill (Cat No 233/A09–0122) is likely to have been woven in 13th-century Spain, whether in a Christian or Islamic workshop. The near-by site of Kirk Close also produced a patterned silk either from 13th-century Spain or Aragonese Languedoc (Muthesius 1987; see also above). Another possibility is that the tabbies were woven in Italy or France (Amt 1993, 194).

There are precedents for the discovery of such exotic material in Scotland. Fragments of textiles recovered from the probable grave of Robert I (d 1329) included the remains of silk presumed to have come from Northern Italy (Henshall et al 1956, 22–6). Entries for the same period in the Exchequer Rolls, that is, from 1326 on, indicate that those at Court, at least, had access to clothing and furnishing fabrics from the textile manufacturing centres of Europe and sometimes beyond. There is mention, for instance, of the purchase of large quantities of fabrics in Flanders and of silks and velvet bought in London (*ERS*, i, 119, 385), and in addition to the Parisian silk there are specific references to silk cloth of Antioch and Tripoli and coloured cloth

Table 2 *Direction of twist in woven silks.*

cat/accession no		warp	weft	phase	date of deposition
tabby					
4/A9976*		Z	loose Z	Ib	early 12th century
267/A09–0127*		loose Z	I	IVb	second half of 13th century
271/A09–0097		loose S	loose Z	IVb	second half of 13th century
323/A09–0059*		Z	I	IVc,IVcc	late 13th century
343/A09–0046		loose Z	I	Va	early 14th century
344/A09–0047a		loose Z	I	Va	early 14th century
346/A09–0044*		loose Z	I	Va	early 14th century
362/A6149*		Z	Z	Va,Vaa(VI)	early 14th century
twill (compound)					
6/A9500	main warp	loose Z	I	Ic,Icc	first half of 12th century
	binding warp	loose Z	I		
46/A7323	main warp	loose Z	I	Ie	slightly before 1150
	binding warp	loose Z	I		
342/A09–0088	main warp	Z	I	Va	early 14th century
	binding warp	Z	I		
twill (2/2 lozenge twill)					
233/A09–0122*		Z	I	IVaa,IVb	second half of 13th century
tablet–weave					
80/A11162b		loose Z x 2	†	IIc	mid to later 12th century
102/A12651		2S	†	IId	later 12th century
117/A9899		2S	†	IIb–IIff	second half of 12th century
217/A6694b		2S	†	<IIId–IVaa	mid 13th century or slightly earlier
234/A09–0124a		2S	I x 2	IVaa,IVb	second half of 13th century
235/A09–0124b		2S	†	IVaa,IVb	second half of 13th century
238/A09–0109		Z(?)	†	IVaa,IVb	second half of 13th century
271/A09–0097		2S	loose Z	IVb	second half of 13th century

Notes
Z yarn twisted in clockwise direction
S yarn twisted in anti–clockwise direction
I untwisted yarn
† disintegrated yarn
* denotes textile without a selvedge; warp and weft inferred

(of wool, it seems) of Tarsus (*ERS*, i, 150, 380). The significance of the fragments excavated from Perth, a few of which come from some of the earliest levels of the site (Period I: pre 1150), is the demonstration that these foreign luxury fabrics were being imported for at least two centuries before those recorded in the Exchequer Rolls, and that their use was not confined to a small circle at the Royal Court. The implication is that from the beginning the burgh of Perth had inhabitants of wealth and substance.

Some of the silks, loom-woven and otherwise, were heavily worn when buried; they may have been heirloom goods not discarded until some time after their manufacture. The cloth of aresta from Kirk Close may represent such an inherited item. Nonetheless, there is sufficient variation in date to indicate a continuing degree of prosperity for the inhabitants of the High Street site. Four of the loom-woven silks and a yarn identified as being probably of silk were recovered from the make-up of a path (P8.4). Since these four textiles are offcuts, they could be the product of an Islamic centre or of a Parisian or other European craft guild. Hence they may have been woven close to the date of deposition in the first decades of the 14th century. Whatever the exact date of manufacture of the High Street loom-woven silks, it is noteworthy that over a third of the silk samples recovered came from layers that dated from the period when Perth frequently served as a forward supply base for the English armies. The presence of the embroidered silk hair nets also confirms that there were those in early 14th-century Perth with access to the latest in European fashion. There is, of course, no means of knowing whether these head-dresses belonged to members of local families or came, say, from the households attached to the English garrison.

If the silk textiles are treated as a group consisting of tabby, twill and tablet weaves, it is possible to review the chronological changes in the throwing of yarns employed in such weaves in the light of comparable finds from Scottish sites and further afield. An examination of the literature on changes in the direction of throwing silk yarns indicates that the warp elements in silks of the 12th to 14th centuries are usually either Z thrown or untwisted. Following technological changes in Northern Italy, which took place from the end of the 13th century, fine S thrown warp yarns became gradually available (Crowfoot et al 1992, 124). The direction of twist in the Perth woven silks is presented in Table 2. Dating from the early 12th to the early 14th centuries, the tabbies and twills in the group do indeed have Z thrown yarn in the warp elements (or in system 1 where the warp is inferred). The one exception is the narrow tabby ribbon stitched to the tablet weave in Cat No 271/A09–0097.

Amongst the silk textiles found in Scottish graves (see Twill weaves of silk, above), this chronological distinction holds true; the late 13th- or early 14th-century compound tabby from the probable tomb of Robert I has Z thrown warp elements, while the

more recent compound twill from the 16th-century bishop's tomb at Fortrose has a fine S thrown warp. The distinction holds firm for the 13th-century cloth of aresta from Kirk Close, with its Z thrown warp, while a 15th-century velvet from Fast Castle has an S thrown warp. An exception to the chronological trend is provided by the 13th-century (or possibly later) satin from Aberdeen (Bennett 1982, 199). This satin might be an early example of a silk made from yarns produced from the technological developments in throwing silk occurring originally in Northern Italy.

It has been noted, however, that the warp in narrow silk ribbons did not fit into this chronological pattern. Ribbons excavated from pre-12th-century layers at 16–22 Coppergate, York, have S thrown yarn in both warp and weft and, additionally, a reliquary pouch from the site has an inner lining with S thrown warp and untwisted weft (Walton 1989, 367–70). Therefore the seeming anomaly amongst the Perth tabbies in Cat No 271/A09–0097, in which the warp has a loose S twist angle, would be attributable to the lack of standardisation in throwing silk for weaving into ribbons. A late medieval silk ribbon of tabby weave, which was compounded by the addition of a set of supplementary metal-wrapped warp threads to form a narrow central stripe, from Dairsie, Fife, was woven with an S thrown warp and an untwisted weft (Dransart 2012). The ribbon in Cat No 271/A09–0097 differs from the Dairsie and Coppergate examples because it has a slightly Z twisted weft. Yet the tablet-woven sections to which this ribbon is sewn conform to the general chronological pattern for silk yardage from medieval contexts, since the warp elements consist of Z thrown strands plied with an S twist (note that in plied yarns, the ply direction is generally opposite to that of the original spin). The other tablet-woven bands and cords from the High Street also share these directions in the throwing
and plying of the yarns.

The evidence considered here demonstrates that silks found in Perth and other Scottish burghs were being traded as high status imports before surviving documentary sources record the consumption of silk in royal circles. Besides royalty, the clergy wore sometimes costly vestments and relics were often wrapped in silk. It may therefore be no coincidence that the Kirk Close cloth of aresta came from the vicinity of St John's Kirk. Many of the Perth silks acquire particular significance in that they present particular information about the use of a luxury fabric from a period predating the early 14th-century. The narrow tubular tablet-woven silk cords with a spiral weft from the High Street, for instance, predate similar examples excavated from sites in London. At Perth, they belong to the century between c1160 and c1260, while the earliest of the surviving London examples date from the first half of the 14th century. A structurally related tubular cord survives attached to a charter of King John (Balliol) to Nicholas de Hay, dated 1 August 1294 (Henshall 1964, 161). Since the charter was granted at Lindores, the cord or the component silk yarns could well have been supplied from Perth. In addition six silk items described as 'cords' were detected among the finds excavated from 80–86 High Street, Perth, but the textile report in the final publication of that site offers no analysis of them, making it difficult to incorporate them into a comparative study (Harrison and Janaway 1997, 757).

Animal hair (including wool)

Compared with the finds of silk, the origins of the wool cloths which make up the bulk of the textiles from Perth are much more problematic. The source of the difficulty is that whereas there is sufficient evidence from the documents of the period to indicate the availability of varieties of imported as well as Scottish-made cloths, our actual knowledge of any of them is small and highly imperfect. Thus, although some of the groups of cloths have a distinctive appearance, and were presumably recognisable types, identified by name, it is difficult to connect them with fabrics mentioned in written sources. Also, there are obvious limitations (and dangers) to the possibility of relating material evidence from one site in one burgh to general references to textiles in documents not directly related to that site. There are a few pieces for which foreign manufacture is a reasonable assumption. The best candidate for being regarded as an import is Cat No 82/A12553b, a 2/2 twill which has characteristics unusual among the High Street finds; it has sufficient affinities with material from the Norse sphere to be identified as *vaðmál* imported from there. Other possible imports are Cat Nos 19/A12340b, a 2/1 twill coloured with a rare and expensive dye (see Dyes, above), 97/A09–0001, a 2/1 twill and, perhaps, 84/A12553d, a 2/2 twill. Cat No 35/A11567f, a tabby, may also be guessed to be a stranger. Yet it has to be admitted that no fibre analysis has been done on the yarns used in these proposed imports. Cat No 84/A12553d was probably woven on a vertical loom, and there is evidence for the continued use of this type of loom in medieval Scotland at Aberdeen and at Perth itself. Even *vaðmál* was produced until the 18th century in Orkney and Shetland. Hence the basis for recognising imports and identifying the provenance remain very insecure with our present state of knowledge. The suggestions put forward here, therefore, are at best highly tentative and in need of testing against future discoveries.

Foreign cloth of various kinds was undoubtedly used in medieval Scotland. For much of the period covered by the finds, mentions of specific fabrics are rare but, for the 14th century, the Exchequer Rolls provide repeated reference to two distinct types –striped cloth, *panni de radiato* or *panni radiati*, and coloured cloth, *panni coloris*. Interestingly, some of them are recorded as being supplied to the Royal Household via Perth (*ERS*, i, 65–6). Often the market is not mentioned, but one entry notes the purchase of 23 pieces of each type, together costing the substantial sum of £173 9s 2d,

in Flanders in 1328 (*ERS*, i, 119). There is no further description of the cloth, but the purpose for which it was intended – to provide robes for the knights at the marriage celebrations of the future David II and his Queen Johanna – is suggestive of good quality; further, since highly-finished cloth was the fashion at this period, it was presumably fulled and napped. In other entries the colour of the *panni coloris* is specified, russet, green and red all being mentioned (*ERS*, i, 69, 117, 150), and, as its name suggests, it was clearly a dyed cloth. The red cloth is the cloth of Tarsus mentioned above, but there is no need to suppose that all *panni coloris* came from one place; it may well have been a general term for well-made dyed, fulled and napped cloth. If so, the vigorous cloth industries of Flanders, Artois and northern Italy are all possible 12th- and 13th-century sources, while England had developed its own reputation for luxury cloth making by the 15th century (see below). As has been shown by Professor Whiting (see Dyes, above), dyed cloths are poorly represented at Perth and only among one category group – the 2/1 Twills with nap, ZS – are there indications of a substantial proportion of pieces being dyed to a good standard. Perhaps significantly, this is also the group that contains the best of the fulled, napped and sheared cloths. If *panni coloris* is to be equated with any of the Perth finds it can only be with some of these. Less information still is available for the striped cloth mentioned in the Exchequer Rolls, but it is possible that the description refers to the weft-striped cloths, found in 13th- to 15th-century levels on a number of European sites, of which Cat No 283/A09–0077b may be one (see 2/1 Twill with nap, ZS above).

As indicated above, less than one third of the wool textiles in the High Street sample have the appearance of being fulled. Ellen Schjølberg examined the cover factor of the warp and weft in 2/2 and 2/1 twills excavated from a fire layer dated to 1170 at Bergen, Norway. The cover factor takes into account both the yarn count and the diameter of the yarn (Schjølberg 1998, 210). Among the 2/1 twills are a large number with apparently impossibly high cover factors. The fabrics, therefore must have been subjected to a shrinking process after removal from the loom. She suggested that a specialized setting process must have been used and that these textiles were imported, perhaps from eastern England (Schjølberg 1998, 212–13).

Dyed, fulled and sheared cloths were also being produced in Scotland as indicated by regulations dated to the 13th century or earlier, which limited the making of such to professional craftsmen in the towns (*Ancient Burgh Laws*, 11, 97–8). More specifically, the charter granted by William I (the Lion) to Perth early in the 13th century (probably 1209) implies that the manufacture of this dyed or sheared cloth, *pannus tinctus vel tonsus*, was of considerable importance to the burgesses (*RRS*, ii, no 467). Another prerogative of the Perth burgesses, within Perthshire, was the making of 'mixed' cloth, *pannus mixtus*, but it is not clear what is meant by this term. Perhaps it referred to cloth made from naturally-coloured wools, or a combination of undyed and dyed wools? This uncertainty illustrates the problems of linking the information in the charter to the surviving material from Perth; because the document is essentially concerned with the promotion and protection of the industry, not the quality of the product, there are no technical details. This difficulty in applying documentary evidence to excavated materials is equally valid for cloth production in medieval Scotland as a whole, for which, unlike some other European countries (especially for the late medieval period), there is a dearth of regulations concerning the width of webs, the density of the threads, the quality and preparation of the yarn and so on, which would give a clearer picture of the goods being made.

Among the terms of the Perth charter granted by William I (ibid) is a clause allowing the burgesses of the burgh their own merchant guild 'save for the fullers and weavers' (exceptis fullonibus et telariis). It has been noted that in documents dating from the first half of the 13th century relating to the burgesses of Perth and their property, trade names listed include furbar, taillur, tenteman and tinctor, but exclude webster (weaver) and walker (fuller) (Duncan 1975, 489–90). Therefore Duncan concluded that websters and waulkers belonged to a different social and economic group than the tenteman and dyer, who might aspire to the status of burgess in the burgh. The high standing of the burgesses who were responsible for the dyeing industry has been attributed to the fact that dyers had to trade for expensive dyed stuffs and mordants from abroad, in addition to coping with the complexities of the craft itself (ibid, 490). They would have hired servants to undertake the actual work. Duncan (ibid, 490) found the names of two dyers in the charters relating to Perth which he examined. Hence there is a distinct possibility that red dyed textiles from the High Street, such as Cat No 19/A12340b, were finished locally and were not always imported from abroad, as suggested above.

Waulking, or the fulling of cloth, was extremely hard work until the introduction of mechanised waulkmills or fulling mills. In the Highlands, it was traditionally the women who pounded the wet cloth with their feet, singing waulking songs to assist them in the arduous task (Ross 1895, 20–26). A 17th-century engraving entitled 'The Prospect of ye Town of Dundee from ye East' by John Slezer shows women, with their skirts tucked up, in large wooden vats treading cloth (Cavers 1993, 55), but Slezer might have observed them beating or washing previously fulled cloth. As mentioned previously, the earliest known mill seems to have been set up by Coupar Angus Abbey, Perthshire in c1260 (see Finishing, above). Because of the considerable financial outlay involved in such a project, fulling mills were often funded by major land-owners, whether lay or monastic (Higham 1989, 49). In addition to the mills, potash pits and tenter banks were essential components. Potash was obtained from burned wood or bracken for use as soap in the fulling process. After the cloth was fulled, it was stretched on

frames placed on tenter banks to dry. Such activities would have been conducted outwith the burgh, close to an appropriate water supply, such as the Lade at Perth or even further afield. A study of place names, historical records and the surviving remains in north-west England by Mary Higham (1989) has revealed evidence for the development of a cloth finishing industry by wealthy landowners probably during the 12th and 13th centuries. This aspect of cloth production has yet to be fully studied in Perthshire.

Despite the difficulties of interpreting the Perth charter granted by William I, since the fulled cloths from the High Street, including those which have been additionally finished by napping and shearing, are almost entirely confined to the 2/1 twills, it is a reasonable supposition that it is among examples of this weave that locally-made cloth is to be found. As has been noted above, some of the 2/1 twills with nap are of good quality, but equally, there are others of unimpressive or even poor appearance, this lack of quality being more marked among the fulled 2/1 twills without nap. It cannot necessarily be supposed that all the well-made pieces are imports and the inferior ones the local products, for despite the almost universal reputation of Scottish cloth at the end of the Middle Ages for coarseness and bad workmanship (for example Halyburton's Ledger, xl–xli) it is possible that cloth production in Scotland was in a healthier state in earlier years, that is, before the troubles of the 14th century.

The 2/1 twills from the High Street have much in common with contemporary fabrics woven in a 2/1 binding from other northern European sites, such as those from 10th- to 15th-century Novgorod (Thompson 1967, 96–7); late 10th- to 13th-century Poland (Kamínska and Nahlik 1960, 116); various sites in Holland (Vons-Comis 1982a, 162); 14th-century London (Crowfoot et al 1992, 31); and 12th- to 14th-century York (Walton 1989, 383). By far the largest category represented in the High Street assemblage is that of 2/1 twill without nap, ZS. It was noted above that fabrics in this category tend to have a firmer spun, more regular Z twisted element (identified as the warp) interwoven with a fuzzier, more woolly and looser S spun element (identified as the weft). This contrast in character between the yarns of the two systems imparts a certain quality to the cloth which may, to the modern observer, appear unfavourable when compared with earlier European textiles. Some cloths dating from the ninth to eleventh centuries found, for example at Birka, Sweden (Geijer 1938, 22–9), and York (Hedges 1982, 102–4) belong to the same category, but they have an even, tightly twisted combed warp and a combed weft. They are closely woven, with a high thread count and are often diamond twills. There is evidence for this tradition in Scotland, but from a later date, from Coldingham Priory, Berwickshire, and from the High Street itself (see above). Yet textile Cat No 97/A09–0001 also displays frequent weaving errors, probably due to problems occurring in the lifting of the heddles. This cloth represents a paradox apart from its 'foreign' appearance. It has a high thread count, which one would associate with a quality product, but faults, possibly caused by broken heddles, mar the appearance in a textile woven from evenly spun worsted yarn. One might expect to find errors associated with a weave executed in a low thread count, as in a third- to fourth-century AD diamond twill textile with a mistake in the knitting of the heddles and an error in the lifting of the shafts from Thorsberg, Germany, discussed by Möller-Wiering (2011, 62–3).

If the general run of fulled cloth from the High Street is typical of the artisanal fabrics produced in the burgh at the time, the mixed quality suggests that attempts to foster the industry had been partially successful. The reasons can only be guessed at; one might venture to suggest that if weavers were held in such low esteem then much of their handiwork may have been produced quickly, with little attention to detail. It may be that there had been a failure to develop the appropriate technology, although with so few indications concerning the introduction to Scotland of the equipment associated with the growth of professional cloth production in Europe – that is, the spinning wheel, cards, the horizontal loom and the fulling mill (see Spinning, Selvedges, Finishing, above) – this surmise is hard to determine. What is clear from the High Street textiles is that some cloths with a heavily napped surface are present from the 12th century onward, that is before evidence for the introduction of the new technologies. The same argument applies to the felt, present in low frequencies in all but Period I (pre-1150). Less clear is whether the textiles recovered from the excavation were made by specialist artisan weavers (usually presumed to be male) or whether domestic production took place in rural communities, in which case craftswomen may well have been active (Duncan 1975, 471).

In contrast with the excavations at Novgorod, where six working parts of horizontal looms were identified by Kolchin among the wood remains, but no firm evidence for the vertical loom was detected (Thompson 1968, 146), the High Street has yielded evidence for the warp-weighted loom, but not one part of a horizontal loom has been detected. If weavers did not have their own guild in the 13th century, then women may well have contributed to the production of cloth within the burgh, if it is acceptable to equate the vertical loom with women weavers, as is usually assumed (Hoffman 1964, 258–65).

Another factor may have been a shortage of raw material. Scotland, of course, was a wool-producing country, but much of the product was exported; throughout the Middle Ages wool was responsible for three quarters of the country's export earnings, reaching a peak in the 13th century (A Stevenson pers comm). Perhaps, therefore, despite attempts to protect local sources by controlling the sale of wool – as in William I's charter – the best of it continued to feed the looms of Europe, and those of Flanders in particular. If so, insufficient wool of the appropriate quality,

notably the prime white wool, may have been available for the home industry. Whatever the accuracy of this suggestion, there is nothing among the Perth finds to contradict the view that at this period Scotland was essentially an exporter of raw wool. The presence of considerable numbers of what are believed to be bale pins from the High Street site probably provides additional evidence for the trade of wool (see Textile tools, below). Wooden bale pins have been used until recently in the West Riding of Yorkshire to fasten bales of wool in a covering of sacking for transport (Morris 2000, 2329).

The implication of the regulations outlined above is that cloth woven in Scottish burghs was a product of relatively small craft industries while that produced in rural areas would have been mainly undyed and subject to little or no finishing. It would have been made on a domestic basis, the yarn both prepared and woven up in the household. An alternative is that, as in later centuries, the yarn was taken to a customary weaver – although it is not known how far specialist or semi-specialist weavers were available outside the burghs at this period. Again, with so few indications concerning this mode of production, the cloth cannot be identified with certainty among the material from Perth. It is a reasonable supposition that country or domestic cloths are represented among the predominant twill weaves, the larger number of which appear to have been left in the natural colour of the wool and bear either scant signs of finishing or none at all. A tentative suggestion may be made that 2/2 Twills without nap, ZZ were produced outwith the burgh since they maintain a constant presence in all periods represented by the High Street finds. This is not true of other categories of textiles and fabrics, which are either greatly reduced or absent in Period III (the first half of the 13th century). This pattern of decline occurs generally in the archaeological material recovered from the High Street; it has been attributed variously to a disastrous fire in Phase IIff and the notable flood of 1209 (see Fascicule 1, The excavation, 52; 119–20).

Later the twills were to become the coarse twills – plaidings, fingrums and the like – which were exported from eastern Scotland in such quantity in the 17th century (Gulvin 1973, 19–21). But it must be noted that far from being homogeneous, the 2/2 and 2/1 twills without nap include cloths of varying types and widely differing quality, and there is no means of knowing how large a proportion were locally, or even Scottish made.

For another main group of fragments from the High Street – the 53 coarse tabby fabrics made from 2 ply yarn concentrated particularly in the 12th century – local manufacture may be suggested with more confidence, unless of course this category of textile served as packaging. In view of the state of development of the native sheep especially in Periods I and II (see The wool and hair, below), it must be supposed that there was a considerable quantity of coarse, hairy wool available, not suitable for the production of normal cloth, which could have been utilised in this way. Further, it is difficult to imagine that it would have been economic to transport such a low-quality product over any distance.

Yet the presence of fine-generalised medium, medium and semi-fine fleece types should be noted in the sample of analysed fleeces at the High Street. From 15th-century Fast Castle, Berwickshire, semi-fine fleece was found to occur in a higher than expected proportion (25% of analysed samples) in both textiles and raw wool (Ryder and Gabra-Sanders 1992, 15–17; Gabra-Sanders and Ryder 2001, 131–5). This fleece has been understood to represent the 'white, fine and excellent wool' described by Hector Boece in the early 16th century, later known as the Old Scottish Short-woolled Sheep (Ryder and Gabra-Sanders 1992, 17; Gabra-Sanders and Ryder 2001, 135). This early occurrence was followed by the later appearance of similar types in England (ibid). It has been pointed out that during medieval times, generalised medium fleece would have been regarded as fine (ibid). In the examples analysed from the High Street, the fine-generalised medium, medium and semi-fine types tend to occur in Periods IV and V (1250–1350>). Given that a far higher number of samples were tested from Period II (the second half of the twelfth century) than any other period, and only two from Period I (the first half of the twelfth century), it is unsafe to draw firm conclusions. However, it may be implied that there was an improvement in fleece types through time at Perth. Further research on the Perth material would probably produce more evidence concerning the development of fleece types in the area.

Bast fibres

For the reasons explained (see Fibres above), the absence from the site of the third major textile material available during the period under discussion – namely linen – is not remarkable; the presence of empty needle holes in both the cloths and the leatherwork, and the finding of glass linen-smoothers (see Fascicule 4, The glass, 119), provide useful confirmation that linen and related vegetable fibres, such as hemp, were used but have not survived. A 12th-century manuscript illumination (Illus 3), albeit probably of northern English provenance, shows Eve spinning a bast fibre from a distaff that she holds between her knees; the manner in which the distaff is dressed is characteristic of prepared flax.

The extent of the use of vegetable fibre is another matter. Flax (*Linum usitatissimum* L.) was undoubtedly available in a number of forms. There is mention in the customs lists of both linen thread and thread to make nets (*Ancient Burgh Laws*, 105–06). The Exchequer Rolls for the 14th century record the importation of four different grades of yardage: canvas, linen cloth, napery and towelling (eg *ERS*, i, 119). For the Scottish production of linen, though, little evidence is

available. Linen occurs in Viking graves in Scandinavia and Scotland; for instance, two fragments of tabby contained in oval brooches accompanying the burial of a woman at Kneep, Lewis, are probably linen (Bender Jørgensen 1987, 166). During excavations south of Bernard Street, Leith, a decayed piece of linen in a tabby weave was found at the top of a pot containing a coin hoard, which was deposited 1470–5 (Bennett and Habib 1985, 423). Despite the conditions of preservation which permitted the survival of almost complete woollen garments on some Norse farm sites in Greenland, linen has only been recovered in a fragile state, usually when carbonisation occurred. Just one fragment of a narrow braid stitched to *vaðmál* survived in an uncarbonised condition on the site of a farm at Hvalsey Church (Østergård 2009, 78). At the High Street, such accidental burning leading to the survival of linen was not reported.

In the case of the Greenland sites, it is possible that linen was an import rather than being produced locally. In order to explore whether or not bast fibres were being grown in Perth, it is necessary to look for indirect types of evidence. Excavations at Pool on the Isle of Sanday, Orkney, indicate that flax was grown there in Norse times, although the earliest occurring *Linum* plant remains in Scotland date back to the Bronze Age and Neolithic (Bond and Hunter 1987, 175). The plant may be used to produce both linseed oil from the seeds, and flax fibres, for spinning into linen yarn, from the stems (ibid, 175–6). It is preferable, however, to harvest the stems before the seeds are mature if they are to be processed into yarn (Barber 1992, 12), an activity which would have the effect of reducing the number of seeds in archaeological deposits.

In medieval Aberdeen, flax remains including seeds were recovered from Queen Street (Fraser and Dickson 1982, 241–2) and 45–75 Upperkirkgate (Kenward and Hall 2001, 287). Fragments of textiles which may be of linen have occasionally been excavated from 13th- and 14th-century contexts in the north of England. A partially mineralised tabby from 33–35 Eastgate, Beverley, was identified as being of vegetable bast fibre (either flax or hemp) by Walton (1992b, 610). Further examples, possibly of vegetable fibre, are known from 16–22 Coppergate, York, where a tabby was more positively identified as flax (Walton 1989, 441 Cat No 1445). The difficulty in identifying the species in processed plant fibres is paralleled by the documentary use of the term 'linen' in English, which can refer to fabric types, such as bed linen, made from plant fibres or to fabric made specifically from flax (Cruikshank 2011, 240).

One of the midden layers on the 45–75 Upperkirkgate site also yielded one piece from a hemp plant (a *Cannabis* achene) but, as Kenward and Hall (2001, 287) commented, although hemp was useful as a fibre for spinning and a source of oil-seed, it is difficult to envisage how it might have been used on the basis of one fragment. Flax and hemp flourish under different geographical and climatic regimes, the former requiring more moisture and displaying a greater sensitivity to weather conditions than the more varied conditions under which hemp can be grown (Eckhel 1988, 59). Remains of both hemp and flax were recovered from layers dated to the 12th to 14th century at Park Street, Birmingham; of interest is that hemp was detected in deposits filling a ditch (Ciaraldi 2009, 246–9). Large amounts of stems provisionally identified as hemp were found lying horizontally in an organic layer in another section of moat at The Row, Digbeth where slowly flowing water would have been suitable for the retting of bast fibres (ibid, 256–7). Retting is a means of partially rotting the stems to break down the woody parts and separate the fibre.

The common stinging nettle (*Urtica dioica* L.) is another useful source of vegetable fibre, and its abundant presence is attested among the High Street plant remains (see Fascicule 4, The botanical remains, 72). Unfortunately, there is no indication whether its economic potential was exploited in medieval Perth. In order to extract the fibre, it may be processed in a similar fashion to flax. However, ethnographic accounts demonstrate that fibres may be obtained from nettle stems by beating, scraping and rubbing without the need for retting (Hald 1980, 125–6). Since nettle fibre is thought to be even more perishable than flax (ibid, 126), the chances of identifying it in archaeological deposits are extremely rare. A carbonised sample of a textile woven in a 2/2 chevron twill from a 10th-century deposit at 16–22 Coppergate, York (Walton 1989, 312 Catalogue No 1334) was found to differ from other vegetable fibres and was thought to be nettle.

Given the comparative material discussed above, the discovery at the High Street site of flax seeds in ten different contexts (see Fascicule 4, The botanical remains, 69) and what had probably been a flax-breaking mallet (see Fascicule 2, Wood Cat No 8/A11104) suggests some local processing of flax or other bast fibres. Four linen smoothers found in deposits laid down during the second half of the 13th century provide evidence that linen was used if not produced (see Fascicule 4, The glass, 119; see also below). That some of the shoes were sewn with wool or hair (see

The Leather, this fascicule), neither of which is well suited to the purpose, may point to periodic shortages of linen. Such a shortage would not be altogether surprising given the military history of Perth in the late 13th and 14th centuries.

The preparation of flax involves the extraction of the stem fibres in the process of retting, after which the stems are beaten with a wooden tool such as the High Street mallet, which dates from the second quarter of the 12th century, or a tool known as a flax break, which is thought to have come into use during the 14th century (Leadbeater 1976, 14). Retting may be done with different sources of water – under dew, in stagnant water or in running water (Leadbeater 1976, 59). Dew-retted fibres produce grey or darker brown fibres, while retting in stagnant or running water gives a honey-cream colour (Leadbeater 1976, 61). Hence the latter methods may have been preferred if the linen was later to be bleached white. The development of a linen industry would have required the construction of ponds from which the water could periodically be discharged if retting was to be done in stagnant conditions, or crates constructed and filled with the flax stems and left in the river for ten to twenty days, if running water was to be used (ibid, 59). Alternatively the flax might simply have been spread out in a suitable position under trees (which retain morning dew) for six to eight weeks (ibid, 61).These activities would have been easily disrupted by the attacks to which Perth was subject during the Wars of Independence. Photographs of peasant families processing flax in the former Yugoslavia may be seen in Radauš Ribarić and Rihtman Aguštin (1988, 74–5); they present a vivid impression of the extent of the land and water necessary to process in quantity flax fibres from harvested stems.

Hence the coarse tabby fabrics in the Perth textile assemblage might have been regarded as alternatives to lower grades of vegetable fabrics, whether because wool was cheaper or linen not so readily available. In either case, it seems likely that the large scale production and bleaching of linen in Perth lay in the future. The post-medieval development of the textile industry in the burgh is briefly discussed in Fascicule 1, 23.

The wool and hair

M L Ryder

Introduction

In seeking evidence of the type of sheep kept in Britain during the Middle Ages it is necessary to go back to prehistoric times when the main breed of sheep seems to have been the small brown Soay sheep that now survives in a feral state on St Kilda off north-west Scotland. Evidence for this comes from the similarity of Neolithic bone remains with those of the Soay, and the similarity of wool in Bronze Age cloth with the fleece of the Soay (Ryder 1968).

The primitive features shared by the Soay with the wild ancestor are a short tail (all modern breeds have a long tail); a coloured fleece in which the belly is white (most modern breeds are completely white); and an annual moult (the wool of virtually all modern breeds grows continuously). To these major and obvious differences between wild sheep and modern domestic breeds can be added the change from a hairy coat to a woolly fleece; the wool of the Soay is already much less hairy than the coat of the wild sheep, but there are hairy and woolly types.

Colour changed next with the appearance of white sheep in the Iron Age, but there was in fact a range of colour: black, white, and grey, in addition to the brown of the Soay (Ryder 1987).

This vari-coloured sheep still had hairy as well as woolly fleece types and a spring moult. It appears to have been common until after the Middle Ages, and widespread throughout Europe, since small pockets of relic breeds survive in isolated areas (Ryder 1983a). Many of the surviving breeds have a short tail, but only the rams are horned: the skeleton is, however, otherwise similar to the Soay (see below). But the wild-pattern white belly has gone (or at least is

extremely rare), and so this marks the Soay as truly unique among domestic sheep. Grey animals are, however, a notable feature and the type could be described as 'European grey or vari-coloured'.

The surviving breeds of this type in Britain are the Orkney and Shetland. During the 19th century these two breeds formed a single population, but the Shetland has since been selectively bred for white woolly fleeces, and so only the Orkney retains the full range of colour and fleece type (Ryder 1968). The tendency to shed meant that in the past the wool had to be obtained by plucking (Ryder 1992), but this has mostly been bred out today, so that most sheep are shorn.

Roman textiles from Britain and the Continent show that more changes in fibre diameter were taking place at that time. The predominant wool type during the Roman period, in addition to being white, is fine to the naked eye, but microscopic examination reveals that the wool contains medium fibres, and so is of generalised medium type. Hairy medium wools were still common, however, and these predominated at Vindolanda on Hadrian's Wall for instance (Ryder 1983a). A comparison of Roman and Saxon wools is shown in Table 3.

Ryder (1968) summarised previous textile remains from Scotland and Viking wools from the north were on the whole more hairy than either the Roman or medieval examples examined up to that date. Twelve of 14 Viking yarns were hairy medium, one was generalised medium, and one true medium. The six medieval yarns comprised one hairy medium, four generalised medium, and one fine type. All the Viking and medieval wools had natural pigmentation.

Table 3 *Comparison of Roman and Saxon wools.*

	Vindolanda (Roman)		all other Roman (including Europe)		Saxon (England only)	
H		(1)		–		–
HM	34%	(19)	14%	(12)	23%	(10)
GM	34%	(19)	15%	(13)	23%	(10)
FGM	18%	(10)	39%	(34)	30%	(13)
M	2%	(1)	3.5%	(3)	5%	(2)
S	4%	(2)	1.5%	(1)		–
F	9%	(5)	27%	(23)	19%	(8)

H = hairy
HM = hairy medium
GM = generalised medium
FGM = fine, generalised medium
M = true medium
S = short
F = fine

Table 4 *Wool fibre diameter measurements and incidence of hairy pigmented fibres.*

fleece type		n	overall diameter	modal diameter		mean diameter		medium hairy fibres		pigmented fibres	
			range	range	mean	range	overall mean	range	mean	range	mean
H	Perth	17	12–124	20–30	24.5	33.4–46.8	39.8	1–57%	22%	0–100%	35%
	Aberdeen	2	12–128	54&66	60.0	52.6&54.9	53.8	19&31%	25%	7&13%	10%
HM	Perth	39	12–100	20–40	26.3	26.4–43.3	34.5	0–51%	17%	0–100%	57%
	Aberdeen	3	14–90	24–30	26.6	26.8–32.8	29.6	5–9%	7%	2–10%	5%
GM	Perth	16	10–60	20–31	24.9	24.4–33.3	29.5	0–10%	4%	1–100%	25%
	Aberdeen	7	10–58	20–24	22.6	21.6–30.8	26.7	0–11%	3%	0–21%	6%
FGM	Perth	6	12–52	23–24	23.8	24.2–28.8	26.7	2–20%	4%	0–100%	7%
	Aberdeen	1	12–56	–	16	–	23.6–9.6	–	–	–	8%
M	Perth	7	10–66	26–40	32.3	31.0–38.6	33.7	0–65%	15%	0–100%	14%
	Aberdeen	2	14–60	30&32	31.0	28.2&32.5	30.4	1&4%	2.5%	0&4%	2%
S	Perth	4	10–50	24–30	27.0	26.0–28.9	27.6	0–46%	22%	0	0
	Aberdeen	–									
F	Perth	–									
	Aberdeen	1	12–36	–	18	–	21.0–4.3	–	0	–	0

Measurements expressed in microns, that is, thousandths of a mm

H = hairy
HM = hairy medium
GM = generalised medium
FGM = fine, generalised medium
M = true medium
S = short
F = fine

Material and methods

From the vast amount of cloth and hair found, a range of apparently different hair and unspun fibre finds was selected for identification only but 93 yarns were chosen from the cloth to give a random sample of the wools for microscopic examination and measurement. Samples from Aberdeen, supplied by Dr Helen Bennett, were included for comparison. Diameter measurements were made of 100 (or close to 100) fibres from each wool sample using a projection microscope. The definition of fleece type and the criteria on which they are determined from the diameter distribution are detailed by Ryder (1983a).

Findings

Hair and unspun fibres

Hair from the following species was identified: horse (A6698), pig (A9140), ox (A6700, A9526), goat (A6629, A6690, A6776, A7342), plus two cloths woven of goat hair (Cat Nos 63/A9993a, 64/A9993b). There were also four unspun sheep's wool samples (A7065, A8082, Cat No 369/A8911, A10483) the measurements of which are included with the yarn measurements summarised

below. Two cloths (Cat Nos 4/A9976, 362/A6149) were made of silk. Some apparent hair finds turned out to be plant material.

Further details

Horse (A6698)
Mostly coarse non-medullated hair with heavy pigmentation. Could be from the tail.

Pig (A9140)
Hairs have characteristic fraying tip of the pig.

Ox (A6700)
Pointed staple seen with naked eye suggested hairy sheep.

Ox (A9526)
Straightness under microscope indicates cow. One was 40mm and the other 80mm long. The diameter distributions were typical of cattle hair.

The goat samples were measured to assist identification; two were 60mm long, one 70mm and one 90mm. These compared with a mean winter length of 148mm in some

Table 5 *Summary of fleece types in British medieval wools.*

		H		HM		GM		FGM		M		S		F	
Winchester	11th century	14%	(1)	57%	(4)	29%	(2)	–		–		–		–	
London, Baynard's Castle	1200	–		25%	(2)	63%	(5)	–		–		–		12%	(1)
York	12th–13th centuries	27%	(3)	37%	(4)	27%	(3)	–		9%	(1)	–		–	
Southampton	13th–14th centuries	–		11%	(2)	58%	(11)	–		5%	(1)	5%	(1)	21%	(4)
London, Baynard's Castle	14th century	13%	(3)	8%	(2)	8%	(2)	38%	(9)	4%	(1)	13%	(3)	16%	(4)
London, Baynard's Castle	15th century	7.5%	(2)	11%	(3)	15%	(4)	18%	(5)	11%	(3)	30%	(8)	7.5%	(2)
Yorkshire	15th century	–		33%	(2)	(66%)	(4)	–		–		–		–	
Perth	12th–14th centuries	19%	(17)	44%	(39)	18%	(16)	6%	(5)	8%	(7)	5%	(4)	–	
Aberdeen	13th–14th centuries	12.5%	(2)	19%	(3)	44%	(7)	6%	(1)	12.5%	(2)	–		6%	(1)
average		10%		27%		36%		8%		6%		6%		7%	

H = hairy
HM = hairy medium
GM = generalised medium
FGM = fine, generalised medium
M = true medium
S = short
F = fine

Scottish feral goats, which are likely to represent past domestic animals (Ryder 1970). Of the five diameter distributions determined (including the hair in the four yarns), two had the mean diameter, modal value and skewed distribution typical of the winter coat, and three had the symmetrical distribution found in the summer coat by Ryder (1970).

Wool

Only 30% of the Perth wools analysed lacked natural pigmentation, but as few as 14% showed evidence of dye (mostly red and yellow, with occasional blue and green) under the microscope, and these included some wools with a few naturally pigmented fibres, which indicates grey or roan wool. Eleven of the 16 Aberdeen yarns had slight natural pigmentation (up to 20% fibres with pigment). It was common for only the coarser fibres to be pigmented, as in grey wool.

The four unspun wool staples comprised three hairy fleece types, two 40mm long and the other 60mm, and one hairy medium wool which was 25mm long.

A summary of the fibre diameter measurements of all the wools is shown in Table 4, along with those of the Aberdeen samples for comparison. The hairy medium-generalised medium type predominates, few of the modern short and medium types emerged.

But there is a high proportion of true hairy and hairy medium wools, compared with for instance the Aberdeen examples, among which the generalised medium fleece predominated. Comparison with other sites is made in Table 5 and covered in the discussion below.

Table 6 gives a classification of fleece types by yarn and catalogue number, and also indicates the extent of pigmentation and the presence of dye. A high proportion of cloths have the same fleece type in each yarn and, indeed may in fact be from the same wool. Because of the difficulty of determining which is the warp and which the weft, the yarns have been designated 1 and 2, but the presumed warp is always designated 1. Where a different wool was used, that in the warp is usually coarser.

Discussion

No attempt was made to study the breed type of any material other than the wool from sheep. More detailed investigation and measurement should, however, yield much more information than the simple identification listed here.

The wool finds form an extremely interesting and valuable collection in being not only the largest group

Table 6 *Tabulation of fleece type and pigment by yarn.*

Cat/accession	phase	weave	system	H	HM	GM	FGM	M	S	pigment	dye
South Sector											
29/A7439	Id,Ie	tabby	(1)	+	−	−	−	−	−	+++	−
			(2)	−	+	−	−	−	−	+++	−
92/A10193b	IId	2/2 twill	(1)	−	−	−	−	+	−	−	+
			(2)	−	−	−	+	−	−	−	+
93/A10193c	IId	2/1 twill	(1)	−	+	−	−	−	−	++	−
			(2)	−	−	−	−	+	−	+	−
98/A10332	IId	2/1 twill	(1)	+	−	−	−	−	−	+++	−
			(2)	−	+	−	−	−	−	+++	−
99/A10787	IId	2/1 twill	(1)	−	+	−	−	−	−	++	−
			(2)	−	+	−	−	−	−	++	−
107/A10784	IId,IIe	tabby	(1)	+	−	−	−	−	−	++	−
			(2)	+	−	−	−	−	−	++	−
108/A6125	IId–IIf	2/1 twill	(1)	−	+	−	−	−	−	+	−
			(2)	−	+	−	−	−	−	+	−
113/A8863a	IIa–IIff	2/1 twill	(1)	−	+	−	−	−	−	+	−
			(2)	−	−	+	−	−	−	+	−
115/A8871	IIa–IIff	2/1 twill	(1)	−	+	−	−	−	−	+	−
			(2)	+	−	−	−	−	−	++	−
116/A6716	IIa–IIff	2/1 twill	(1)	−	+	−	−	−	−	+	−
			(2)	−	+	−	−	−	−	+	−
125/A9478a	IIe–IIg	2/1 twill	(1)	−	−	−	−	+	−	−	−
			(2)	−	−	+	−	−	−	−	−
128/A9481	IIe–IIg	2/1 twill	(1)	+	−	−	−	−	−	−	−
131/A9126	<IIg(IIh)	felt	−		+	−	−	−	−	+	−
139/A9506	<IIg(IIh)	2/1 twill	(1)	−	−	−	−	+	−	+++	−
			(2)	−	−	+	−	−	−	+++	−
143/A9536c	<IIg(IIh)	2/1twill	(1)	−	+	−	−	−	−	+	−
			(2)	−	+	−	−	−	−	+	−
153/A11266	<IIg(IIh)	tabby	(1)	−	+	−	−	−	−	+++	−
			(2)	−	+	−	−	−	−	+++	−
158/A8432	IIi	2/1 twill	(1)	−	−	+	−	−	−	−	−
			(2)	−	−	+	−	−	−	−	−
164/A9108	IIi	2/1 twill	(1)	−	−	+	−	−	−	−	−
			(2)	−	−	+	−	−	−	−	−
166/A9974	IIi	braid	(1)	+	−	−	−	−	−	+++	−
			(2)	+	−	−	−	−	−	+	−
167/A9056	IIi	2/2 twill	(1)	−	+	−	−	−	−	+++	−
			(2)	−	+	−	−	−	−	+++	−
168/A9057a	IIi	2/1 twill	(1)	+	−	−	−	−	−	++	−
			(2)	−	+	−	−	+	−	+++	−
181/A8085	IIIa–IIIc	2/2 twill	(1)	−	+	−	−	−	−	+++	−
			(2)	−	+	−	−	−	−	+++	−
199/A9766a	<IIIc–IVa	2/1 twill	(1)	−	+	−	−	−	−	+++	−
			(2)	−	−	+	−	−	−	−	−
211/A9903a	IVa	2/1 twill	(1)	−	+	−	−	−	−	+	−
			(2)	−	−	+	−	−	−	−	−
212/A9903b	IVa	2/1 twill	(1)	−	−	+	−	−	−	−	−
			(2)	−	−	+	−	−	−	−	−
213/A9905	IVa	2/1 twill	(1)	+	−	−	−	−	−	−	+
			(2)	−	+	−	−	−	−	−	+
221/A6126	IVa,IVaa	tabby	(1)	+	−	−	−	−	−	++	−
			(2)	−	+	−	−	−	−	+++	−
228/A6124a	IVb	2/1 twill	(1)	−	−	−	−	+	−	−	−
			(2)	−	−	−	−	−	−	−	−

Table 6 *(continued)*

Cat/accession	phase	weave	system	H	HM	GM	FGM	M	S	pigment	dye
231/A9906	IVb	2/1 twill	(1)	−	−	−	−	+	−	−	−
			(2)	−	−	+	−	−	−	−	−
297/A8101	IVb,IVc	2/1 twill	(1)	−	−	−	−	+	−	+	+
			(2)	−	−	−	−	−	+	−	+
299/A9904	IVb,IVc	tabby	(1)	−	+	−	−	−	−	+	−
			(2)	+	−	−	−	−	−	+	−
302/A8097b	IVb,IVc	2/1 twill	(1)	−	−	−	−	+	−	−	+
			(2)	−	−	−	+	−	−	−	+
348/A6710a	IVcc,Va	2/1 twill	(1)	−	+	−	−	−	−	+++	−
			(2)	−	−	+	−	−	−	+++	−
349/A6710b	IVcc,Va	2/1 twill	(1)	−	−	−	−	−	+	+	+
			(2)	−	+	−	−	−	−	+	+
361/A6148	Va,Vaa(VI)	2/2 twill	(1)	−	+	−	−	−	−	+++	−
			(2)	−	+	−	−	−	−	+++	−
364/A6626	Va,Vaa(VI)	2/1 twill	(1)	−	−	−	+	−	−	+++	−
			(2)	−	+	−	−	−	−	+++	−
368/A8861	Va,Vaa(VI)	2/1 twill	(1)	−	−	+	−	−	−	+++	−
			(2)	−	+	−	−	−	−	+++	−
371/A6146	Va,Vaa	2/1 twill	(1)	−	−	−	+	−	−	−	−
			(2)	−	−	−	+	−	−	−	−
397/A6709	Vaa–Vc(VI)	2/1 twill	(1)	−	+	−	−	−	−	−	−
			(2)	−	−	−	+	−	−	−	−
398/A8869	Vb–Vc	tabby	(1)	−	+	−	−	−	−	+++	−
			(2)	−	+	−	−	−	−	+++	−
404/A1268	u/s	2/1 twill	(1)	−	+	−	−	−	−	+	−
			(2)	−	+	−	−	−	−	+	−
North Sector											
410/A7336	(1)2	tabby	(1)	−	+	−	−	−	−	+++	−
			(2)	−	+	−	−	−	−	+++	−

H = hairy
HM = hairy medium
GM = generalised medium
FGM = fine, generalised medium
M = true medium
S = short

of medieval wools found in the British Isles, but second only to the Vindolanda Roman collection in size. Such large samples enable a meaningful assessment of the proportion of different fleece types among the sheep to be made for the first time.

The high proportion of coloured wools from Perth and Aberdeen indicate the persistence of sheep with natural pigment into the Middle Ages, survivors of which persist today in the Orkney/Shetland type.

Staple lengths of 40mm and 60mm are the same as reported by Ryder (1983a) in samples from London (Baynard's Castle) and Winchester respectively. The fourth staple, which was only 25mm long, may not represent a full year's growth. Among the survivors of the hairy medium-generalised medium type, even the finer varieties have a fleece longer than 60mm, but in the hairy variety it is commonly over twice this length.

Table 5, which compares the Perth and Aberdeen wools with other British medieval examples, indicates that the range of fleece types in Scotland is typical. On the other hand, the relatively small sample size of all but the Perth collection means that some of the other findings may not give a true representation. The occurrence of true fine wools (notably one from Aberdeen) does not necessarily indicate import from the continent since a fine diameter distribution can be found in such breeds as the primitive Orkney.

Fragment counts of the mammal bones from this excavation (see Fascicule 4, The mammal bone, Table 15) indicate 63.5% from cattle, 22.2% sheep/goat, 4.9% goat, 8.3% pig, and 1% from horse. The high proportion of cattle, sheep and goat horn cores suggests a horner's shop, while the leather together with much hair and some raw wool suggests skin working.

Table 7 *Hair identification.*

Accession	context	species	area	rig	feature	phase
South Sector						
A7342	C3625	goat	2	VI	M14b(b), Pit 3625	Ie
A7065	C3601	sheep	2	V	M14b(c)	Ie–If
63/A9993a	C2386	goat	4	VI	B16 (Phase 2), Destruction	If,IIa
64/A9993b	C2386	goat	4	VI	B16 (Phase 2), Destruction	If,IIa
A6776	C3589	goat	2	VI	MC061	IIb
A6629	C3577	goat	2	V	B5, North Room–Floor/Occupation (2)	IIa–IIff
A9526	C2611	ox	3	VI	M1.2, Pit 2648	<IIg,IIh
A9140	C2267	pig	4	VI	B13, Occupation (1ba)	IIh
A10483	C2462C	sheep	3	VI	M1.3	IIi
A8082	C2516	sheep	3	VI	B2, Floor (2a)	IVa,IVaa
A6698	C2508	horse	3	V	P2.3a	IVaa
A6700	C2480	ox	3	V	MC155	IVb,IVc
369/A8911	C2404	sheep	3	V, VI	M1.5a	Va,Vb(VI)
A6690	C2048	goat	2	-	Unstratified	u/s

Sheep bones predominated in medieval excavations in High Street, Edinburgh (Chaplin and Barnetson 1976, 232–8). The lowest levels of 15th-century deposits had horned sheep skulls of both sexes, while higher levels had hornless skulls from which Armitage (1976, 239) suggested that there were two distinct varieties. Since all the Scottish breeds not of recent origin are either horned in both sexes, or horned in the ram only, it is not clear what these varieties might be. Another possibility is that they represent a single type in which some of the ewes are horned and others polled, the Soay in fact being a breed in which not all the ewes have horns.

Textile tools

P Z Dransart and the late N Q Bogdan

The evidence for textile production and usage presented in this fascicule derives largely from the direct examination of the yarns and fabrics themselves. Certain tool categories used in the preparation of raw materials, their export, and in the production and handling of fabrics are also present amongst the finds from the High Street. While the items listed in the tables below are considered in more detail in Fascicules 2 and 4, here the reader's attention is drawn to these tool categories and how they might have been used in the yarn and cloth making activities represented by the textiles themselves. The focus is on the use of tools in certain technological processes, including the baling of fleece, the spinning of yarn and the weaving and fulling of cloth. This chapter examines evidence for the domestic production of yarn and textiles in the medieval burgh of Perth as well as trade in wool and cloth with the Low Countries, for which some documentary evidence has survived. Therefore this section should be read in conjunction with the discussion of the textiles and fabrics, particularly as related to spinning and the evidence for loom types. This discussion is organised on the basis of the processes used in transforming fibre into yarn, yarn into fabric, and fabric into garments, as in a *chaîne de production* discussed in the work of Alain Ferdière (1984, 210).

Certain categories of tools are scarce or absent amongst the excavated material (for example, loom parts, pins and thimbles). Possible reasons for their absence or for their scarcity are considered below.

Baling fleece

A large number of wooden pins is represented in the list of textile related tools. Many are likely to have served as bale pins, which would have been used to hold in place the outer wrapping of bales in which shorn fleece was transported. They have a tapered shape, lack a head, and were whittled from wood. According to Carole Morris (2000, 2329), fleeces from the West Riding of Yorkshire were until recently wrapped in sacking secured by wooden pins. Coarse tabbies woven from 2 ply yarns were found amongst the High Street textiles, therefore the question arises whether such textiles might have served to secure woollen bales, with the wooden pins holding the tabby cloth in place, either in the course of importation into or export from the medieval burgh of Perth.

Medieval Scots sold considerable quantities of wool to the major cloth producing centres in the Low Countries. During the 12th and 13th centuries, cities in Flanders and Artois gained a predominant position in producing and exporting broadcloth. This dominance was challenged by the success of smaller local communities in manufacturing cloth. Expertise in textile production spread to Brabant and Holland and, by the 15th century, centres in eastern England had gained a reputation for producing broadcloth, too (Sortor 1989, 1475). Certain textile producers in these regions gained a reputation for spinning yarn, weaving and finishing woollen broadcloths of the highest quality. The sale of both fleeces and draperies had to meet stringent edicts, and those of Saint-Omer in Artois contain details of considerable interest concerning Scotland. Perth was specifically mentioned in an edict dating sometime in the second half of the 13th century or the first quarter of the 14th century (Espinas and Pirenne 1920, 234–5):

> *Le laine d'Escoche k'on resake en cheste vile doit*
> *poursuir ausi bone desous con deseure, sor 60 s.*
> *Et ki melleroit laine d'Abardaine, ne laine de*
> *Berewic, ne de Monros, avœc laine de Pert, il*
> *seroit à 60 s. Et chil ki le vent doit dire de quel*
> *vile ele est, sor 60 s.*

In other words, wool sourced in Scotland had to be sold in Saint-Omer, and of a consistent quality that was as good below as above ('ausi bone desous con desueure'). If the fleeces did not meet this standard, a fine of 60 shillings was levied. Equally, the fleeces were not to be mixed. Anyone mixing Aberdeen fleece with that of Berwick, Montrose or Perth would be fined 60 shillings, the levy also charged if any merchant failed to say from which burgh the wool came. The principle of keeping fleece supplied from Aberdeen, Berwick, Montrose and Perth separate was also used as a model for dealing with wool from different countries, which it was also forbidden to mix. Contravention of this edict also carried a fine of 60 shillings (ibid, 240):

> *On a conmandei ke nus ne venge laine, ne melle*
> *laines de Irlande ne de Wales avœc laine d'Escoche,*
> *sor 60 s. Et ke nus ne venge laine de Yrlande por laine*
> *d'Escoche, ne laine de Wales por laine d'Escoche.*
> *Mais le vende de chascune terre à par lui, sor 60 s.*

In this edict, it is forbidden to mix wools from Ireland or Wales with that of Scotland. Merchants are ordered not to sell wool from Ireland as that of Scotland, or wool from Wales as that of Scotland.

A schedule of wool prices dating from c1270 has survived from Douai. It provides a list of abbeys and hospitals (mostly Cistercian) in England, Wales and Scotland selling wool to Douai. The prices of wool in a sack-weight equivalent to 364lb are presented in *livres parisis* and in pounds sterling. From Perth, wool traded through the abbey of 'Cupre' (Coupar Angus) was listed as 35 livres parisis per sack, equivalent to £10.938 sterling (Munro 1978, Table 1). In this listing, the mean per sack for Scottish wool was slightly lower than the mean prices for Wales and England (ibid, 125). The Coupar Angus price was the same as that of Melrose (Roxburgh) and Glenluce (Wigtown), a similarity that was also maintained in the undated price list of Francesco Balducci Pegolotti in *La practica della mercatura* (ibid, Table 1). However English and Scottish wool sacks were both charged the same customs duty in the Saint-Omer edicts (Espinas and Pirenne 1920, 267).

It appears that not all of the wools sold under the name of the local monastic house came from abbey lands. Wool harvests collected from small producers were known as *collecta*. Munro (1978, 127) suggested that Cistercian and other orders were well placed to enter into contractual arrangements with Italian and Flemish firms by taking out substantial loans from these companies and by agreeing to deliver large amounts of wool, which came from the abbey's own flocks as well as from those of lay owners.

There is little documentary evidence for the specific details of trade in Scottish wools. The trading activities of Thomas of Coldingham, burgess and merchant in Berwick-upon-Tweed, have been preserved in early 14th-century records issued by Durham Cathedral Priory (Donelly 1980, 105). Working with partners, Thomas handled the sale of a substantial amount of wool and hides, including at least 90 woolsacks, acquired from the Priory between 1310 and 1315. It appears that his transactions included payments at a rate lower than one might expect through a *pre manibus* arrangement in which the merchant made cash payments for the fleece harvests of future years (ibid, 108). Durham Priory provided wool from the clip of its own flocks, from Norham and from Coldingham, its Scottish cell. It is also likely that *collecta* wools also contributed to the sacks that were delivered to Thomas (ibid).

Monastic houses were presumably regarded as being more credit-worthy than individual wool producers. In contrast, the Saint-Omer edicts make it clear that its guild members were not to enter into credit arrangements with Scots producers of wool (Espinas and Pirenne 1920, 241)

> *On a conmandei ke nus bourgois ne vallet à bourgois soit si hardis k'il croie nules markandises en Escoche, ne laines, sor 60 lb. Et ausitost ke il l'aroit creue, il aroit perdu toutes ses frankises et 60 lb.*

This edict warns a burgher or a burgher's assistant against placing trust in merchandise or wools when in Scotland, under the pain of a £60 forfeit. Moreover, as soon as a merchant entered into a credit agreement he would lose all his franchises as well as a £60 forfeit.

Another edict specifically bans merchants from lending money in Scotland on wools bought in advance (ibid, 246):

> *On a deffendu ke nus presteche deniers en Escoche sour laines achater devant, sour 60 lb. et se bourgeoisies perdue.*

Despite these stringent restrictions on the part of traders in the Low Countries, Thomas of Coldingham's woolsacks were probably made up of clips from a wide geographical area. To conform to the expectations of the Saint-Omer guilds, however, they would have required to have had their source identified. If Thomas's activities in acquiring wool from Durham Priory can be used as an analogy for Perth, then it is likely that wool traded through the burgh or through Coupar Angus came from a wide area in the heart of Scotland. The finding of a cloudberry seed (*Rubus chamaemorus*) in a late 13th-century context (see Fascicule 4, The botanical remains, 77) suggests the pasturing of sheep (or, more probably, goats) at high altitudes. The wool must have been taken to the burgh and packed in heavy, securely identified bales to meet the criteria of cities such as Saint-Omer and Ypres.

When the wool was converted into yarn and cloth, it still retained the identity of its place of origin. The edicts from Ypres state that textiles woven from Scottish wools should have a yellow stripe (*une roie gaune*) woven into the selvedge (Espinas and Pirenne 1920, 462):

> *Chascun drap ke on fait de laine d'Escoche doit avoir une roie gaune au darrain coron dou drap, sour 60 s. et le drap pierdut.*

The fine for infringing this edict followed the standard pattern seen at Saint-Omer: 60 shillings and the cloth confiscated.

From the High Street excavation, a cloth bale seal has been tentatively identified (see Fascicule 2, The metalwork, Cat No 142/A04–0466). It was possibly used to identify a bale of cloth imported from an important textile producing centre. Such seals were made from lead; usually there were two discs, each bearing its own stamp, connected by a strip of metal. By the early 14th century, they were frequently added to cloths woven in Ypres (Endrei and Egan 1982, 47–9), but other centres also had their own seals. It is worth noting the Period Va context (dated to the early 14th century) in which this find was made. However, it seems that cloth was imported into Perth from at least 1209, since the charter of William I permitted foreign traders to sell their goods in the burgh itself, between the festivals of Ascension and Lammas. Indeed, the Laws of the Four Burghs (Edinburgh, Roxburgh, Berwick and Stirling) stated that 'na strangear merchand arrivand with schippis and merchandise sall cut claith or sell in penny worthis bot in grete, and that wythin burgh and to the merchandis of the burgh' (*Ancient Burgh*

Laws 1868, statute XLI). These restrictions have been interpreted as offering some protection to local cloth producers and merchants (Stavert 1993, iv). That 'hukstaris' be forbidden to sell their wares 'befor that undern be rungyn in wynter and mydmorne in somer' (that is, before the third hour of 9am in Winter and the first hour of 6am in summer) indicates an awareness that poor light conditions would make it difficult for buyers to see the quality of their purchases (ibid, statute LXVI).

Fibre preparation

As well as serving as a centre for the export of wool, Perth was also a place where yarns and cloth were produced. Whereas the trading of wool had to comply with the standards set by the guilds of the dominant cloth producing centres in the Low Countries, local practices in fibre preparation (whether woollen or bast) and cloth production seem to have been perfomed in a socio-technological domain that had much in common with Scandinavian practices.

Amongst the excavated finds from the High Street are artefacts indicating that the preparation of both wool and bast fibres took place. The identification of at least one item that might have served as a flax-breaking mallet amongst the tools made from wood (see Fascicule 2, The wood, Cat No 8/A11104) suggests that bast fibres were prepared locally. Other more fragmentary club-like artefacts might also have served to beat flax in order to extract fibres prior to spinning, or as laundry beaters. Mallets or pounders with a cylindrical head were used to beat the stem fibres of flax which had previously been prepared by rippling, to remove the seed heads, and retting, to loosen the fibres from the outer covering of the flax stems (see Bast fibres in the General Discussion above). It is thought that their use was superseded by a tool called a flaxbreak from the 14th century in some areas of Europe (Leadbeater 1976, 14). Part of a wooden flax- (or hemp-) break, with a notched edge, has been tentatively identified from a Greenland farm at Narsaq (Østergård 2009, 76).

A number of pounding tools were recovered from excavations at Bryggen (the wharf) in Bergen, Norway. Ingvild Øye (1988, 27–9) remarked that these tools were found in layers dating from before 1170 to c1413 and she reported that one bore a runic inscription interpreted as 'Unhappy is the man who has a wife like you'. The activity of pounding the retted stems (an activity which is referred to as 'beetling' in a description of cloth production at 16–22 Coppergate site in York) was a vigorous one and Walton Rogers (1997, 1725) commented that surviving tools often display much damage. This pounding was followed by scutching, using a paddle- or blade-shaped wooden tool to remove unwanted remnants of plant waste clinging to the fibres. A photographic record of flax fibre pre-paration, including the use of a mallet, in the former Yugoslavia is presented in Radauš Ribarić and Rihtman Aguštin (1988, 76–7).

After these operations, bundles of flax fibres were separated by drawing them through a series of iron teeth set into wooden blocks, the first set having coarser and the second and subsequent sets having finer teeth. Some iron spikes in the High Street material have been identified as single heckle or wool comb teeth (see Fascicule 2, The metalwork, Iron Cat Nos 109–134). Walton Rogers (1997, 1727–31) observed that it is difficult to distinguish the teeth of wool combs from those of heckles. Therefore she preferred to call them 'fibre-processing spikes', a category which also includes ripple spikes. She noted that through time iron spikes with a rounded or rounded-rectangular cross section became longer in the period about AD1200 (ibid, Figs 802 and 803).

The absence of evidence for hand cards in Scotland prior to 1349 has been mentioned above. Carding is a means of preparing fleece before spinning it into yarn with a woollen finish, as illustrated by the seated woman in Illus 5. Until late in the 14th century, carding was prohibited in the guild rules of the cloth producing centres of the Low Countries (van Uytven 1983, 175). It is likely that at least some of the iron spikes would have been used in the combing of fleece at the High Street, especially for spinning into yarn with a worsted finish.

Another means of preparing wool is performed by the hands alone; no tools are required. The spinner takes a lock of fleece and teases it out to open the matted tip. She then turns the lock round to hold the shorn end between her thumb and forefinger, with her other hand pulling out the fibres more or less parallel with each other to produce a continuous roving. This form of preparation produces a semi-worsted yarn (Leadbeater 1976, 35).

Spinning

That spinning, whether of wool or of bast fibres, was done with the aid of a drop spindle in the medieval burgh of Perth is attested by the appearance not only of whorls made of wood, stone and bone, but also of wooden spindles, which would have been inserted into the whorl. Of the 41 whorls listed, 33 are of stone, seven of bone and one of wood. The preferential survival of the stone whorls is probably due to their being made from a non-organic material. These whorls were fashioned from sandstones, siltstone, schist, clay and mudstones, all presumably of local manufacture (see Fascicule 4, The stone objects, 127–8). By the 18th century, stone spindles in Scotland were called 'rocks'. Paradoxically, however, the wooden whorl from the High Street excavation is from an early layer on the site, dated to the first half of the 12th century.

It is posible that another type of whorl was present amongst the finds excavated from the High Street. Objects made from perforated pig metapodia are identified as toggles in the worked bone catalogue, although Arthur MacGregor (see Fascicule 4, The worked bone, 104) suggested an alternative use as a toy mounted on a doubled cord, which might have been pulled to cause the bone to spin. Such perforated bones have also been reported as a component of a single cross-arm spindle in the provinces of Shansi and Shantung in Mongolia and in rural China (Hochberg 1980, 26). A foot bone of a sheep, goat or zebu is used for the cross-arm and the shaft is formed from an iron hook or a piece of bamboo provided with a hooked barb at the top (ibid, 27). In northern China, people use these spindles to produce short lengths of yarn such as wicks for candles, sewing thread for shoes and in domestic sewing and repairing tasks. Such a usage is a possibility for the Perth perforated metapodia. Given the conditions of preservation on the High Street site, however, one might expect to find evidence for a shaft and, in the section on Dress in medieval Perth (below), these bones are discussed as serving as toggles.

To use a spindle, the spinner rotated it by giving it a sharp twist with one hand while drafting out the prepared fibre in the other hand. The spun yarn was then transferred to the spindle by winding it round the shaft above the whorl, if it was placed lower down the spindle shaft (Illus 3), or under the whorl if it was placed high up the spindle shaft (Illus 4). According to Bette Hochberg (1980, 30), high whorl spindles have a fast rotation, which is suited to the spinning of a yarn with a hard twist. Heavier whorls are used in the spinning of flax, the fibres of which are required to be spun with a stronger twist than wool (Grierson 1985, 8).

Evidence for the spindle or muckle wheel has not been detected among the finds, although it is possible that it was introduced to the High Street during Period V (the first half of the 14th century). There are several reasons why drop spindles continued in use. One of their most important characteristics is their portability, which means that spinners can engage in multiple tasks. A spinner does not have to remain in one place, as is the case with the muckle wheel (Illus 5). Therefore spinning and plying are tasks that can be done while herding animals or on the way to market. An illumination accompanying Psalm 91 in the Luttrell Psalter (BL, Add MS 42130, f. 166b) depicts a woman feeding chickens while holding a long distaff under her left arm. A drop spindle hangs from the fibre wound round the distaff. On the High Street site, spindle whorls made their way into middens, were dropped in a well or on paths, and were abandoned inside buildings. Six whorls came from occupation layers in the rooms of Building 18, dated to the second half of the 13th century, and a further six were recovered from occupation layers associated with Building 53, interpreted as a workshop area with evidence for metalworking (see Fascicule 1, 75–6; 191), dated to the first half of the 14th century. This distribution suggests that spinning was done in and around the houses of Perth's medieval burgh as the spinners engaged with their daily round of chores.

Observations made by one of the authors during ethnographic fieldwork in a highland community of llama, alpaca and sheep herders in northern Chile confirm the portability and versatility of spinning with drop spindles, even when spinning wheels are present. In this community spinning is done by women, men and children (Dransart 2002). Although most households have metal spinning wheels, they are rarely used. Drop spindles are preferred, the spinning wheels occasionally being used by the men to ply yarn.

In the spinning traditions of medieval Scotland, the yarns required for weaving were singles; they consisted in the main of unplyed yarns. The available evidence (iconographic and documentary) indicates that spinners in European countries were most likely to be women. Women had to produce large quantities of yarn, which meant that a spinner had to make the most of the time available to her. In a discussion of spinning as a poorly paid occupation for women and as a cultural activity with ideological overtones, Jones and Stallybrass (2000, 125) commented that, when introduced, the spinning wheel came to indicate 'attachment to home rather than to wandering the countryside'. They cite estimations for the early modern period that it would take the yarn spun by at least six to eight spinners to provide a weaver with a sufficient quantity for one day's work (ibid, 299). According to another estimate for 15th- to 16th-century Germany, more than 20 carders and spinners would have been needed to provide a weaver with yarn for producing between 60 and 100 bolts of cloth per annum (Wiesner 1986, 194).

In a manual called *Livre des Mestiers* by a Bruges schoolmaster, produced in several versions from 1369 for teaching French and Flemish terms, the spinning wheel is criticised for producing yarn with knots (van Uytven 1983, 175). There is some evidence that 15th-century merchants still preferred hand spun yarn, especially for the warp (Kerridge 1985, 6). Long after the spindle wheel had come into use in some areas of Western Europe, weavers favoured yarn spun on a drop spindle because the spinner was able to impart a greater amount of twist to the yarn in a controlled manner. This preference indicates the potential quality of the yarns that medieval spinners produced. Hence it is no surprise that the Perth whorls were made in a range of materials, and in different weights, as appropriate for the production of different qualities of yarn.

The spindle is also a versatile implement in that it is easy to produce yarn with a twist in either the Z or the S direction. To spin yarn with a Z twist, the spinner rotates the spindle in a clockwise motion and, for an S twist, in an anti-clockwise motion. Spinning wheels can also be turned in either direction. However, with a spindle or muckle wheel, the belt has to be crossed and the wheel turned in a clockwise motion in order to rotate the spindle in an anticlockwise direction in the production of S spun or S ply yarn (Leadbeater 1976, 95). The spinner in Illus 5 has crossed the band driving the spindle, and she turns the wheel in a clockwise direction using a stick held in her right hand. She holds the unspun fibre in her left hand, controlling the amount of fibre that is drawn down into the yarn. The motion of the large wheel caused the small whorl on the spindle to rotate for many turns, allowing the spinner to walk backwards, drawing out the thread before the momentum of the wheel ceased. As a result, this wheel was sometimes called the 'walking wheel' (Grierson 1985, 11). It is possible that the Luttrell illumination shows the carding of wool and the spinning of woollen yarn for use as weft in cloth that could have belonged to one of the 2/1 ZS twill categories discussed above.

No distaffs were identified amongst the wooden tools excavated on the High Street. A distaff is a short, hand-held device or a long pole round which the fibre was dressed. A long distaff was tucked under the left arm, enabling the spinner to walk while drafting the fleece with the left hand and twisting the spindle with the right (Hochberg 1980, 54). Alternatively, the spinner sat and held the distaff between her knees (Illus 3). The long distaffs that were depicted in manuscript illuminations dressed with fibre held in place by a spirally wound ribbon would probably have been used in the spinning of long fibres, such as flax.

However, wool might also be spun with the aid of a distaff. Another form of distaff consists of a length of plaited cord tied into a loop and worn over the spinner's left wrist. The combed or carded fleece then would be wound round the 'bracelet', resting on the tassel formed by the knotted cord. This method is suitable for spinning a fibre with short or medium staple (Hochberg 1980, 54). This type of distaff would be difficult to recognise in the archaeological record.

When the spindle was full the spinner converted the yarn into a hank by winding it round a yarn-winder, a wooden example of which was found inside a room in Building 5 (see PHSAE Fascicule 2, The wood, Cat No 421). The hank thus produced could then be washed to remove any traces of oiling used in spinning wool fibre into yarn. Prior to spinning it was normal practice to extract the natural lanolin in the shorn fleece and also any smearing with butter or tar of the sheep that had occurred before shearing (to ameliorate the effect of parasites). The scoured fleece would then be oiled. This procedure of scouring and greasing was part of the production process of woollen rather than worsted yarns. In France and the Low Countries a distinction was made between the greased or 'wet' production of cloth – *draperies ointes* (French) or *gesmoutte draperie* (Flemish) – and 'dry' – *draperies sèches* (French) or *droge draperie* (Flemish) (Munro 2009, 5). Grierson (1985, 5) listed the following ingredients recorded as having being put to use in early modern Scotland for such greasing purposes: 'unsalted butter, fish liver oil, whale oil, whale oil and tar melted together, tallow made from sheep's fat, lard, butter from ewe's milk, rape oil. Clarified goose grease, swine's grease, olive oil, fulmar oil, the worst sort of butter and the juice expressed from the root of the common fern'. After spinning the fleece, the yarn would be wound into a hank on the yarn-winder; it was then washed. Yarn wound into a hank by this means is also suitable for dyeing, because it enables the dye to penetrate the yarn evenly while preventing tangling from occurring. After dyeing, weavers usually wound the yarn into a tightly formed ball because it is easier to warp a loom in such a form.

Warping and weaving

When warping a loom, a weaver might make use of a device known as a paddle to keep several threads under control during the procedure. One has very tentatively been identified from Rig V (see Fascicule 2, The wood, Cat No 219/A4854), but the function of this enigmatic item is not clear. Nine possible warping paddles were identified from the Bryggen excavation; those from stratified contexts were dated from 1170 to c1413 (Øye 1988, 77). Made from one piece of wood, they consist of a flat handle and a wider part pierced with holes. The Perth example has a row of seven holes. This number and arrangement of holes differs from the three illustrated Bryggen examples (ibid, Fig III.13).

Looms were substantial pieces of equipment but very little evidence for them has survived amongst the Perth finds. It is possible that the substantial beams used to make a loom were reused when the loom itself fell into disuse. Typically a loom has the shape of a frame which holds one or two beams round which the the warp is wound to hold it taut. Generally speaking, two main types were used in medieval Europe. The older type was warp-weighted and it was upright. The warp was hung under tension from the upper beam (from a starting edge as discussed above), weighted by a series of free-hanging weights made of clay or stone (Hoffman 1964, 5). Groups of warp ends were tied to each loom weight. The loom was also provided with heddles, which were made from a continuous yarn supported on a rod (ibid, 133–5), for lifting and lowering selected threads. The selection of threads enabled the weavers to open a shed, the space into which they inserted the weft. They stood in front of the loom to enter the weft, working from the top down.

While no recognisable loom parts have been noted amongst finds from the High Street, some of the tools which accompanied the use of the warp-weighted loom are present. These take the form of pin-beaters which, along with the sword-beater which came to light in 1898 in the Watergate, Perth, provide positive evidence for the use of warp-weighted looms in the burgh during medieval times. Pin-beaters were small curved and pointed tools made of wood or bone. Both weaving swords and pin-beaters were used for beating in the weft as weaving progressed. According to Hoffman (1964, 320–1), the pin-beater was used to beat the weft upwards in a textile of a fairly high warp density. She reported an experiment of the 1950s in which weavers produced a 20 ell length of wadmal, using pin-beaters to beat up the weft first with the shed open and a second time after closing it (ibid, 135–6). The sword-beater was used after the weavers closed the shed by lowering the heddle.

In a reconstruction drawing of a warp-weighted loom based on a study by Walton Rogers (1997, 1751) of the textile related finds from Coppergate, York, pins are shown as having been inserted through the side selvedges to bind the edges of the cloth to the upright frame of the loom. Such pins could have been made from wood and would have helped to prevent the warp from bunching as the weaving progressed. It is possible that some of the wooden pins listed from the High Street might have served such a purpose.

The presence of tools associated with the warp-weighted loom strenghtens the suggestion that a domestic weaving industry took place in family homes in the burgh. If the use of pin-beaters was associated with cloth of a fairly high warp density, this textile production was potentially of a good standard. The women of the household would have been in control of these spinning and weaving activities. Evidently a craftsman-based guild organisation of weaving was already present by the 13th century in Scottish medieval burghs, including Perth (Stavert 1993, iv, but see the section above on animal fibres in The textiles: General discussion). Therefore the horizontal loom, which was eventually to replace the warp-weighted loom, is likely to have been present during the period covered by this fascicule. Both types of loom were probably used in the medieval burgh of Perth to produce textiles on the basis of different social arrangements.

Working parts from horizontal looms were found amongst the finds of wood dating from about 1220 at Novgorod (Thompson 1968). Such looms were provided with two beams to tension the warp: a beam at the far end of the loom and another called the breast beam, next to which the weaver sat. The weaver worked in a direction from the front of the loom to the back, entering the weft from either the left or right, and beating the weft towards himself. On completing a woven length, he cut the cloth from the loom. Scissors found on the High Street are considered in the next section.

Fulling and tailoring

The tenter hook from Rig V (see Fascicule 2, The metalwork, Iron Cat No 135/A7837b) might have been used with a series of such hooks to attach a length of wet, fulled cloth to a frame for drying (see General discussion, above). Fulling is a process of scouring and trampling a textile woven from woollen yarns in a large tub of warm water mixed with fuller's earth and perhaps urine as well. This process felted the fibres and obscured the weave. In the best cloths, it took from three to five days to reduce the cloth by up to fifty percent of its original size (Munro 2009, 5).

The greatest shrinkage occurred in the direction of the weft than in the warp, due to the looser spin in the former (ibid, 55 n25). By drying the textile on a frame, a controlled shrinking occurred, making the textile wrinkle free and thicker than it was when it

was removed from the loom. In calculating the warp density, the weavers would have taken into account whether or not the finished cloth was to be fulled or not.

Following this treatment, the cloth was napped to raise a surface of loose ends in the wool fibres. This task was performed by using a hand-held wooden tool mounted with teasels (Carus-Wilson 1957, 110). Such a tool would most likely not survive easily in archaeological deposits and none have been reported from the High Street. In the Assize of Petty Customs, however, teasels are listed (along with woad) as being liable to the payment depending on quantity: 'thai sal hafe for ilk ton at the entre four peniis, and for ilk thousand tassallis [teasels] a peny, and ilk barell of tasill twa peniis' (*Ancient Burgh Laws* 1868, 107). These rates for every ton, for every thousand teasels and every barrel suggest that they were imported in high numbers.

The raised surface on the cloth then underwent a shearing; the shears for this task were large and flat-ended (Carus-Wilson 1957, 106). A cloth might undergo several teasellings and shearings, the first at the fuller's premises and the last before being cut by a tailor. According to Carus-Wilson (ibid, 107) the task of grinding to maintain the cutting edge of the shears was a highly skilled one.

The presence of shears, scissors and metal and bone needles listed among the textile tools and the evidence derived from a study of the offcuts of cloth that are represented amongst the High Street finds provide a material trace for the activities of tailors and seamstresses who worked in the medieval burgh. Both shears and scissors have two blades, which provide cutting edges that strike against each other. In shears the blades are connected by arms to a sprung bow and in scissors they are riveted together, the arms ending in a bow. However there is not always a clearcut distinction in the use of the two terms (Beaudry 2006, 117). In modern parlance the scissors depicted in the Taymouth Hours (Illus 73) might be referred to as the shears of a tailor. Their large size suggests that they would have been employed to cut the cloth for making the dark mourning habit, which is shown in the tailor's hands in its finished state. Despite the finished appearance of the garment, the caption at the foot of the page identified the tailor as St Francis cutting a monk's habit.

A large number of metal needles were recovered from parts of the site that favoured the preservation of such small items (see Fascicule 2, The metalwork). Made of iron or copper alloy, they are represented frequently in different phases. Twenty-two copper alloy needles were found in a 12th-century pit (Pit 3040). Overall, the needles measure from 0.5mm to 4mm in width and are round in section. They would have been suitable for stitching the range of fabrics reported in this fascicule, from the fine silks to the coarse tabbies. The finest fabrics would have required sharp needles; the evidence from Norse Greenland indicates that sewers

Illus 73 *St Francis cutting cloth, from the Taymouth Hours, f. 180v (British Library, Yates Thompson 13).* (© *The British Library Board*).

sharpened the points on small whetstones, which had a perforation at one end for hanging from a belt (Østergård 2009, 112). At Perth there were also needles made from bone, although some of them may have served as dress pins (see Fascicule 4, The worked bone, 103).

This evidence demonstrates the ubiquity of stitching, in the making, remaking and repair of clothing. When not in use, the needles might have been stored in small needlecases made from bone or wood. Objects tentatively categorised as bone bobbins are described in Fascicule 4; and there are two carefully lathe-turned wooden examples (see Fascicule 2, The wood, Cat Nos 98/A11403 and 101/A10570), which are comparable with two of the bone ones (see Fascicule 4, The worked bone, Cat Nos 24/A05−0202 and 33/A5369). The wooden bobbins, however, date from Period II and the bone one from Periods IV and V. One of the bone bobbins (65/A2498) displays a considerable amount of handling in the polish on its outer surface as befits an object that would have been in daily use. As suggested by Arthur MacGregor in Fascicule 4, these artefacts were probably multi-functional and, in addition to storing needles, they may also have served as reels to carry thread (see also Walton Rogers 1997, 1786).

Very few pins were detected in the Perth deposits. Most are decorative and they would have been used as much for ornamentation as for holding layers of clothing together. Amongst the pins made of wood, pin A05−0139 differs from the others in being smaller in size and having a rounded head. It was excavated from a midden dated to the first half of the 14th century. Bone, antler and metal were more common materials for making pins to fasten garments and to dress hair, or for use in weaving and tailoring

activities. Following the suggestion made by Morris (2000, 2309) for a small number of pins with shaped heads excavated from the site of 16–22 Coppergate, York, this pin might have served as an alternative to counterparts made from more durable materials. She argued that wooden pins would not have been as strong but they would have been readily and quickly made.

A tryptich painted by Stefan Lochner in c1440, housed in Cologne Cathedral, includes a group of richly dressed young women, some of whom have shiny metal pins in their hair or dress (Egan and Pritchard 1991, 298). Such pins were used to hold the elements of the wearer's headdress together rather than being put to use as a dress-making aid. Of the few metal pins recovered from the High Street, most are decorated (see Fascicule 2, The metalwork). Five of the undecorated pins were of bronze, one having traces of plating, and a further example was of gilded iron. This last item and two of the bronze ones have survived as shanks and may have been needles rather than pins. It seems, therefore, that pins were not used in any numbers in medieval Perth. Although Mary Beaudry's cultural history of what she called 'the lowly pin' cited evidence for extremely large quantities on some medieval European sites from the 14th century onwards, she observed that professional tailors and seamstresses did not usually use pins as an aid in sewing (2006, 10).

Female sewers and male tailors in Perth evidently did not have much use for metal thimbles, either, as only one was found in an unstratified context. Thimbles found on other sites in Scotland include two from the Meal Vennel, Perth (one cast in copper alloy from Phase 6 and the other in sheet copper alloy from Phase 7) (Cox 1996, 770), two from Fast Castle (one in copper alloy with a maker's mark dated to 1520–1620 in Period III and the other in cast copper alloy from Period III–IV) (Gabra-Sanders 2001b, 92) and one from Uttershill Castle, Penicuik, which was found in a fill of rubble in the undercroft (Alexander et al 1998, 1033). These few thimbles are likely to date from contexts that are considerably more recent in date than the stratified textiles and tools discussed here and it is possible that the thimble from the High Street is of a relatively recent date too.

In following the cultural history of thimbles, Beaudry (2006, 90) saw a tool called a needle pusher as a precursor, being used to push a needle through hide or heavy canvas. Metal needle rings were used in China from the second century AD. In contrast, few European literary references to such devices predate Hildegard von Bingen's writing in the mid-12th century. Because Hildegard used the term *zieriskranz* ('ornamental wreath'), it is assumed that she used a ring instead of the domed thimble, which became the usual type associated with the large-scale production of brass thimbles in Nuremberg by at least 1373 (ibid, 93). In Alexander Neckham's 12th-century listing of a Parisian chambermaid's tool kit, he mentioned 'a leather case protecting the finger from needle pricks, vulgarly called a "thimble"' (translated in Holmes 1952, 83). Presumably people continued, until at least the 13th century, to use ring-shaped devices of bronze or leather when sewing. There is a possibility that thimble rings made of leather have not survived at Perth, or have not been recognised amongst the finds.

The paucity of evidence for thimbles in Perth contrasts with their availability in other parts of Europe. An Italian inventory dated 1176 provides an insight into the thimbles made from different metals that were carried by a wealthy Venetian, Gratianus Gradenigo. He died, perhaps murdered, while travelling at sea. An inventory in a notarial document drawn up in Pisa listed his personal effects, which must have been more numerous because the evidence suggests that some of his possessions were stolen before or following his death (Robbert 1983, 387). Notwithstanding the suspicious absence of some of them, it appears that he was transporting lengths of cloth and supplies for tailors and seamstresses. Amongst these supplies are the following items:

Anulos duos 1 de ferro et alterum de rame pro cusire 6d.
[two thimbles, for sewing, one iron, another copper 6d.]
ii anulos 1 de ferro et alterum de rame de cusire 6d.
[two sewing thimbles, one iron, another copper 6d.]
annulos iiii de rame de cusire 12d.
[four thimbles of copper for sewing 12d.]
anulos duos 1 de ferro et alterum de ramo pro cusire 6d.
[two sewing thimbles, one iron, another copper 6d.]
1 anulum argentum 5s.
[one silver thimble 5s.]
accuraiolum de osso 6d.
[one needle case of bone 6d.]
bucigones de osso 1 et alium de ligno cum agoro 16d.
[needle covers of bone and another of wood, with

needle 16d.]
agora de rete 5d.
[needle to make a net 5d.]
filum 6d.
[thread 6d.]
aspam 1 2d.
[1 asp 2d.]

Therefore this single inventory listed more thimbles than have been published from excavations of Scottish late medieval/early modern sites, throwing into relief the extreme scarcity of thimbles recorded from medieval Scotland. Of interest in the list of articles carried by the Italian is the 'needle to make a net', given the discussion of the knotted net, above.

Laundry

The final category of tool discussed here consists of linen smoothers, indicating that either the finishing or the laundry of linen counted amongst the activities conducted in the medieval burgh of Perth. Smoothing implements made from glass or stone were used to impart a surface sheen as a finishing treatment or, as Frances Pritchard (1984, 67) suggested, to reduce the wrinkling of laundered items of linen, which crumples easily.

Like cloth woven from wool yarns, linen fabrics might be coarse in quality or fine. Coarse linens were probably beaten to make them soft (a process known as beetling) or were glazed by placing the cloth on a firm surface and rubbing the linen smoother across it (Bond and Hunter 1987, 179). Linen smoothers, formed from a large, flattened ball of dark glass, are known from Viking sites, dating from the tenth century (Hunter 1985, 65) but they also begin to occur frequently on rural and urban sites of the Carolingian Period in the territories of central France (Ferdière 1984, 227–8, Moireau 1993, 184), which leads one to suspect that they were used domestically after washing linen garments. On the High Street site, linen smoothers were identified in contexts in Rigs V and VII, the latter from a destruction phase of Building 18 (see Fascicule 4, The glass, 119).

Conclusion

The tool categories considered here have been discussed in the light of the processes involved in the baling of wool for export, spinning yarn, weaving, fulling, tailoring and washing cloth. Combined with the analysis of the textiles themselves, comparison with finds from sites such as Bryggen, Bergen, and in the light of the surviving guild edicts from St-Omer and Ypres, the activities that took place in the medieval burgh of Perth have emerged in more detail than is possible for other Scottish sites. The evidence considered here suggests that although the inhabitants of Perth must have been aware of the changing conditions and rules under which guilds were controlling the production of cloth in the Low Countries, Italy and England, there was still a domestic sphere of production that perhaps was more closely paralleled by Scandinavian practices. The baling of wool and the production of textiles and garments were important activities in Perth. Garment making, however, would also have included the remaking of items from reused cloth. This aspect of utilising the products of the crafts considered here will be examined in more detail in the next section, on the evidence for dress from the High Street excavation.

Textile tools.

Accession	Artefact	Area	Rig	Feature	Phase
South Sector					
A11409	whorl (wood)	4	V, VI	MC017	Ia–Icc>
A8104	pin-beater (bone)	1/2	VI	B8, Occupation (2)	(Icc)Id
A11104	flax-breaking mallet (wood)	3	V	MC031, Pit 5096	Ia–Id
A10492a	pin (wood)	4	VI	B16 (Phase 1), Occupation (1b)	(Id)Ie
A7582b	pin (wood)	2	VI	M14b(b), Pit 3625	Ie
A10873	comb tooth (metal)	2	V	M14b(a), Pit 3830	Id
A05–0011	pin (wood)	3	V	MC034a	Ie(If)
A7073a	pin (wood)	2	VI	MC044b	If
A7073b	pin (wood)	2	VI	MC044b	If
A10362	pin (wood)	4	VI	B16 (Phase 2), Destruction	If,IIa
A6581	comb tooth (metal)	2	VI	MC061	IIb
A1630a	needle (metal	1	V	M14a, Pit 3040	Id–IIc
A1630b	needle (metal)	1	V	M14a, Pit 3040	Id–IIc
A1630c	needle (metal)	1	V	M14a, Pit 3040	Id–IIc
A1630d	needle (metal)	1	V	M14a, Pit 3040	Id–IIc
A1630e	needle (metal)	1	V	M14a, Pit 3040	Id–IIc
A1630f	needle (metal)	1	V	M14a, Pit 3040	Id–IIc
A1630g	needle (metal)	1	V	M14a, Pit 3040	Id–IIc
A1630h	needle (metal)	1	V	M14a, Pit 3040	Id–IIc
A1630i	needle (metal)	1	V	M14a, Pit 3040	Id–IIc
A1630j	needle (metal)	1	V	M14a, Pit 3040	Id–IIc
A1630k	needle (metal)	1	V	M14a, Pit 3040	Id–IIc
A1630l	needle (metal	1	V	M14a, Pit 3040	Id–IIc
A1630m	needle (metal)	1	V	M14a, Pit 3040	Id–IIc
A1630n	needle (metal)	1	V	M14a, Pit 3040	Id–IIc
A1630o	needle (metal)	1	V	M14a, Pit 3040	Id–IIc
A1630p	needle (metal)	1	V	M14a, Pit 3040	Id–IIc
A1630q	needle (metal)	1	V	M14a, Pit 3040	Id–IIc
A1630r	needle (metal)	1	V	M14a, Pit 3040	Id–IIc
A1630s	needle (metal)	1	V	M14a, Pit 3040	Id–IIc
A1630t	needle (metal)	1	V	M14a, Pit 3040	Id–IIc
A1630u	needle (metal)	1	V	M14a, Pit 3040	Id–IIc
A1630v	needle (metal)	1	V	M14a, Pit 3040	Id–IIc
A10763	comb tooth (metal)	3	VI	MC066	IIc
A11100	pin (wood)	3	VI	MC066	IIc
A9925	needle (metal)	1	VI	M1.1c	IId
A11403	bobbin (wood)	3	VI	M1.1c, Pit 5005	IId
A11097b	pin (wood)	3	VI	MC080	IId,IIe
A11097a	pin (wood)	3	VI	MC080	IId,IIe
A10570	bobbin (wood)	3	VI	MC080	IId,IIe
A12278	needle (metal)	1	VI	MC071	IIb–IIff
A12326	needle (metal)	1	VI	MC071	IIb–IIff
A12281	whorl (stone)	1	VI	MC071	IIb–IIf
A12517	whorl (stone)	1	VI	MC071	IIb–IIf
A6697	comb tooth (metal)	2	V	B5, North Room–Floor/Occupation (1)	IIa–IIff
A9280	shears (metal)	4	VI	B12, Occupation (1b)	IIe–IIg
A9510	whorl (bone)	4	VI	B12, Occupation (2a)	IIe–IIg
A9486	comb tooth (metal)	4	VI	B12, Pit 2340	IIe–IIg
A9489	pin (wood)	4	VI	B12, Pit 2345	IIe–IIg
A8489	needle (metal)	4	V, VI	M11	IIh

(continued)

Accession	Artefact	Area	Rig	Feature	Phase
A9513	comb tooth (metal)	4	V, VI	M11	IIh
A9895	pin-beater (bone)	3	VI	M1.3	IIi
A8640a	pin (wood)	3	VI	M1.3	IIi
A8640b	pin (wood)	3	VI	M1.3	IIi
A04–0637	needle (metal)	9	VII	P8.0	IIIa,IIIb
A9096	needle (metal)	4	V	MC116	IIe–IIIc
A06–0072	whorl (stone)	9	VII	P8.1c	IIIc
A9299	spindle (wood)	3	VI	M6a	IIg–IIId
A9727b	pin (wood)	3	VI	M6a	IIg–IIId
A112238	club (wood)	3	V	M6b	IIg–IVa
A8512	whorl (stone)	3	V	M6b	IIg–IIId
A7837b	tenter hook (metal)	3	V	P2.2b	IVa
A8484	whorl (stone)	3	V	P2.2b	IVa
A7872	linen smoother (glass)	4	V	MC143	IVaa
A6354	comb tooth (metal)	4	V	MC143	IVaa
A8095	needle(metal)	3	V	P2.2a & P2.3a	IVa,IVaa
A8112	pin (wood)	4	V	MC158a, Pit 2228	IVaa
A4854	comb board? (wood)	2	V	B26, Floor/Occupation (8b)	IIg–IVaa
A5455	whorl (bone)	1	VI	B20, Occupation (1a)	<IIId–IVa
A6736	club (wood)	1	VI	B20, Occupation (2b)	<IIId–IVa
A9541	whorl (stone)	3	VI	B2, T2846	IVa,IVaa
‡A8357a	shears (metal)	3	VI	B2, Floor (2a)	IVa,IVaa
A9281	shears (metal)	3	V	B3 (South), T2570	IVa,IVaa
A7831c	comb tooth (metal)	3	V	B3 (South), Occupation (1b)	IVa,IVaa
A04–0687	shears (metal)	7	VII	P3..3	IVa–IVb
A04–0475	shears (metal)	9	VII	B18 (Phase 1b), North Room & South Room–Occupation (6)	IVa,IVaa
A06–0078	whorl (stone)	7	VII	B18 (Phase 1b), North Room & South Room–Occupation (6)	IVa,IVaa
A10–0017	linen smoother (glass)	9	VII	B18 (Phase 1b), Destruction	IVa,IVaa
A5220	needle (metal)	4	VI	B11, T2206, WW2206	IVaa
A6459	comb tooth (metal)	3	V	MC158b, Pit 2526A	IVaa
A04–0632b	needle (metal)	7	VII	MC126, Pit 7402	IVaa,IVb
A04–0642a	needle (metal)	7	VII	MC126, Pit 7402	IVaa,IVb
‡A04–0653a	needle (metal)	7	VII	MC126, Pit 7402	IVaa,IVb
A04–0653b	needle (metal)	7	VII	MC126, Pit 7402	IVaa,IVb
A10–0029	linen smoother (glass)	7	VII	MC126, Pit 7402	IVaa,IVb
A04–0593b	needle (metal)	7	VII	B18 (Phase 1/2)	IVaa,IVb
A04–0598b	needle (metal)	7	VII	B18 (Phase 1/2)	IVaa,IVb
A04–0644	needle (metal)	7	VII	B18 (Phase 1/2	IVaa,IVb
†A04–0688	shears (metal)	7	VII	B18 (Phase 1)	IVaa,IVb
A05–0202	bobbin (bone)	7	VII	B18 (Phase 1), MF7307	IVaa,IVb
A05–0157	pin (wood)	9	VII	B18 (Phase 1/2)	IVaa,IVb
A06–0054	whorl (stone)	9	VII	B18 (Phase 2a), Pit 9301	IVb
A05–0214	pin (wood)	7	VII	B18 (Phase 2a), External 1, Pit 7314	IVb
A04–0578	comb tooth (metal)	7	VII	B18 (Phase 2a), North Room & Hall–Construction (1)	IVb
A04–0569	needle (metal)	7	VII	B18 (Phase 2a), North Room & Hall–Construction (1)	IVb
A05–0090	pin (wood)	9	VII	B18 (Phase 2b), North Room, Hall & Hall South–Occupation (10)	IVb
A11–0022	whorl (bone)	7	VII	B18 (Phase 2b), North Room, Hall & Hall South–Occupation (10)	IVb
A06–0067	whorl (stone)	7	VII	B18 (Phase 2b), North Room, Hall & Hall	IVb

(continued)

Accession	Artefact	Area	Rig	Feature	Phase
				South–Occupation (10)	
A06–0066	whorl (stone)	7	VII	B18 (Phase 2b), North Room, Hall & Hall South–Occupation (10)	IVb
A06–0034	whorl (stone)	9	VII	B18 (Phase 2b), Hall–Occupation (11b)	IVb
A11–0021	needle (bone)	7	VII	B18 (Phase 2b), Hall & Hall South–Occupation (12a)	IVb
A04–0319	comb tooth (metal)	9	VII	B18 (Phase 2b), Hall & Hall South–Occupation (12a)	IVb
A06–0076	whorl (stone)	10	VIII	MC153	IVb
A05–0219	pin (wood)	7	VI	M1.4f	IVc
A04–0645	comb tooth (metal)	7	VI	M1.4f	IVc
A11–0023	whorl (bone)	10	VIII	M9b(a)	IVc
A10363a	pin (wood)	3	V	MC155, Pit 2691	IVb,IVc
A10363b	pin (wood)	3	V	MC155, Pit 2691	IVb,IVc
A10870a	scissors (metal)	3	V	MC155, Pit 2691	IVb,IVc
A5444	pin (wood)	3	VI	M1.4d	IVb,IVc
A5369	bobbin (bone)	3	VI	M1.4d	IVb,IVc
A8078f	needle (metal)	3	VI	M1.4d, Pit 2566	IVb,IVc
A6363c	needle (metal)	3	V, VI	M1.4c	IIIa–IVcc
A5182	whorl (stone)	3	V, VI	M1.4c	IIIa–IVcc
A7355	pin (wood)	3	V, VI	M1.4c	IIIa–IVcc
A10727e	comb tooth (metal)	3	V, VI	M1.4c	IIIa–IVcc
A5432a	pin (wood)	3	V, VI	M1.4c	IIIa–IVcc
A5432b	pin (wood)	3	V, VI	M1.4c	IIIa–IVcc
A5432c	pin (wood)	3	V, VI	M1.4c	IIIa–IVcc
A5514	comb tooth (metal)	3	V, VI	M1.4c	IIIa–IVcc
A04–0511	needle (metal)	7	VII	P8.3	IVc,IVcc
A04–0483	needle (metal)	7	VII	M9a	IVc,IVcc
A04–0179	needle (metal)	9	VII	M9a	IVc,IVcc
A04–0184	needle (metal)	9	VII	M9a	IVc,IVcc
A04–0191	needle (metal)	9	VII	M9a	IVc,IVcc
A04–0315	needle (metal)	9	VII	M9a	IVc,IVcc
A06–0055	whorl (stone)	7	VII	M9a	IVc,IVcc
A06–0013	whorl (stone)	9	VII	M9a	IVc,IVcc
A05–0032	pin (wood)	9	VII	M9a	IVc,IVcc
A05–0019a	pin (wood)	9	VII	M9a	IVc,IVcc
A05–0019b	pin (wood)	9	VII	M9a	IVc,IVcc
A05–0119a,b	spindle (wood) & whorl (bone)	9	VII	M9a	IVc,IVcc
A10–0023	linen smoother (glass)	10	VIII	M9b(b)	IVc,IVcc
A06–0062	whorl (stone)	10	VIII	M9b(b)	IVc,IVcc
A05–0160	pin (wood)	10	VIII	M9b(b)	IVc,IVcc
A05–0089a	pin (wood)	10	VIII	M9b(b), MF6027	IVc,IVcc
A05–0183	club (wood)	10	VIII	M9b(b), MW6086	IVc,IVcc
A05–0170	pin (wood)	7	VI	M1.4i	IVcc
A05–0172a	pin (wood)	7	VI	M1.4i	IVcc
A05–0172b	pin (wood)	7	VI	M1.4i	IVcc
A5448b	pin (wood)	3	VI	P6	IVcc,Va
A10000	pin/needle (bone)	3	VI	P6	IVcc,Va
A6758b	pin (wood)	3	VI	M1.4e	IVcc(Va)
A4500	whorl (stone)	2	VI	B34, MF2759	Va
A05–0143a	pin (wood)	7	VI	B34–Courtyard	Va
A05–0143b	pin (wood)	7	VI	B34–Courtyard	Va
A05–0143c	pin (wood)	7	VI	B34–Courtyard	Va
A05–0143d	pin (wood)	7	VI	B34–Courtyard	Va

(continued)

Accession	Artefact	Area	Rig	Feature	Phase
A04–0465	needle (metal)	7	VII	P8.4	Va
A04–0466	cloth bale seal? (metal)	7	VII	P8.4	Va
A05–0141	pin (wood)	7	VII	P8.4	Va
A05–0142a	pin (wood)	7	VII	P8.4	Va
A05–0142b	pin (wood)	7	VII	P8.4	Va
A05–0142c	pin (wood)	7	VII	P8.4	Va
A05–0144a	pin (wood)	7	VII	P8.4	Va
A05–0144b	pin (wood)	7	VII	P8.4	Va
A05–0145	pin (wood)	7	VII	P8.4	Va
A05–0152a	pin (wood)	7	VII	P8.4	Va
A05–0152b	pin (wood)	7	VII	P8.4	Va
A05–0153a	pin (wood)	7	VII	P8.4	Va
A05–0153b	pin (wood)	7	VII	P8.4	Va
A05–0171	pin (wood)	7	VII	P8.4	Va
A05–0056a	pin (wood)	9	VII	P8.4	Va
A05–0056b	pin (wood)	9	VII	P8.4	Va
A5757A	needle/pin (bone)	1	V, VI	M5c	(IVc–)Va
A5749	yarn-winder (wood)	2	V	B1(a), South Room–Floor (2b)	IVcc,Va
A6719a	pin (wood)	3	VI	P6 & B1(b)–Demolition, Tumble 2775	IVcc,Va
A6719b	pin (wood)	3	VI	P6 & B1(b)–Demolition, Tumble 2775	IVcc,Va
A5407	pin (wood)	2	VI	B1(b), Tumble 2775	IVcc,Va
A1169a	comb tooth (metal)	3	V, VI	M1.5a	Va,Vaa(VI)
A6569	needle (metal)	3	V, VI	M1.5a	Va,Vaa(VI)
A1177	pin (wood)	3	V, VI	M1.5a	Va,Vaa(VI)
A2121	pin (wood)	3	V, VI	M1.5a	Va,Vaa(VI)
A2124	pin (wood)	3	V, VI	M1.5a	Va,Vaa(VI)
A5450a	pin (wood)	3	V, VI	M1.5a	Va,Vaa(VI)
A5450b	pin (wood)	3	V, VI	M1.5a	Va,Vaa(VI)
A5450c	pin (wood)	3	V, VI	M1.5a	Va,Vaa(VI)
A5752a	pin (wood)	3	V, VI	M1.5a	Va,Vaa(VI)
A5752b	pin (wood)	3	V, VI	M1.5a	Va,Vaa(VI)
A5758Ba	pin (wood)	3	V, VI	M1.5a	Va,Vaa(VI)
A5758Bb	pin (wood)	3	V, VI	M1.5a	Va,Vaa(VI)
A5758Bc	pin (wood)	3	V, VI	M1.5a	Va,Vaa(VI)
A5758Bd	pin (wood)	3	V, VI	M1.5a	Va,Vaa(VI)
A5766a	pin (wood)	3	V, VI	M1.5a	Va,Vaa(VI)
A5766b	pin (wood)	3	V, VI	M1.5a	Va,Vaa(VI)
A5766c	pin (wood)	3	V, VI	M1.5a	Va,Vaa(VI)
A5766d	pin (wood)	3	V, VI	M1.5a	Va,Vaa(VI)
A5780	pin (wood)	3	V, VI	M1.5a	Va,Vaa(VI)
A5783	pin (wood)	3	V, VI	M1.5a	Va,Vaa(VI)
A3815	whorl (stone)	3	VI, VII	M1.5a	Va,Vaa(VI)
A04–0113	needle (metal)	7	VI, VII	M1.5b	Vaa
A04–0125	needle (metal)	7	VI, VII	M1.5b	Vaa
A04–0327	needle (metal)	7	VI, VII	M1.5b	Vaa
A04–0385	needle (metal)	7	VI, VII	M1.5b	Vaa
A04–0369	comb tooth (metal)	7	VI, VII	M1.5b	Vaa
A04–0119	comb (metal)	7	VI, VII	M1.5b	Vaa
A05–0040a	pin (wood)	7	VI, VII	M1.5b	Vaa
A05–0040b	pin (wood)	7	VI, VII	M1.5b	Vaa
A05–0040c	pin (wood)	7	VI, VII	M1.5b	Vaa
A05–0045	pin (wood)	7	VI, VII	M1.5b	Vaa
A05–0061	pin (wood)	7	VI, VII	M1.5b	Vaa
A05–0106a	pin (wood)	7	VI, VII	M1.5b	Vaa

(continued)

Accession	Artefact	Area	Rig	Feature	Phase
A05–0106b	pin (wood)	7	VI, VII	M1.5b	Vaa
A05–0106c	pin (wood)	7	VI, VII	M1.5b	Vaa
A05–0106d	pin (wood)	7	VI, VII	M1.5b	Vaa
A05–0108a	pin (wood)	7	VI, VII	M1.5b	Vaa
A05–0108b	pin (wood)	7	VI, VII	M1.5b	Vaa
A05–0108c	pin (wood)	7	VI, VII	M1.5b	Vaa
A05–0108d	pin (wood)	7	VI, VII	M1.5b	Vaa
A05–0108e	pin (wood)	7	VI, VII	M1.5b	Vaa
A05–0109a	pin (wood)	7	VI, VII	M1.5b	Vaa
A05–0109b	pin (wood)	7	VI, VII	M1.5b	Vaa
A05–0109c	pin (wood)	7	VI, VII	M1.5b	Vaa
A05–0109d	pin (wood)	7	VI, VII	M1.5b	Vaa
A05–0109e	pin (wood)	7	VI, VII	M1.5b	Vaa
A05–0109f	pin (wood)	7	VI, VII	M1.5b	Vaa
A05–0116a	pin (wood)	7	VI, VII	M1.5b	Vaa
A05–0116b	pin (wood)	7	VI, VII	M1.5b	Vaa
A05–0116c	pin (wood)	7	VI, VII	M1.5b	Vaa
A05–0122	pin (wood)	7	VI, VII	M1.5b	Vaa
A05–0123	pin (wood)	7	VI, VII	M1.5b	Vaa
A05–0124a	pin (wood)	7	VI, VII	M1.5b	Vaa
A05–0124b	pin (wood)	7	VI, VII	M1.5b	Vaa
A05–0124c	pin (wood)	7	VI, VII	M1.5b	Vaa
A05–0124d	pin (wood)	7	VI, VII	M1.5b	Vaa
A05–0124e	pin (wood)	7	VI, VII	M1.5b	Vaa
A05–0124f	pin (wood)	7	VI, VII	M1.5b	Vaa
A05–0124g	pin (wood)	7	VI, VII	M1.5b	Vaa
A05–0124h	pin (wood)	7	VI, VII	M1.5b	Vaa
A05–0124i	pin (wood)	7	VI, VII	M1.5b	Vaa
A05–0124j	pin (wood)	7	VI, VII	M1.5b	Vaa
A05–0126	pin (wood)	7	VI, VII	M1.5b	Vaa
A05–0127a	pin (wood)	7	VI, VII	M1.5b	Vaa
A05–0127b	pin (wood)	7	VI, VII	M1.5b	Vaa
A05–0127c	pin (wood)	7	VI, VII	M1.5b	Vaa
A05–0127d	pin (wood)	7	VI, VII	M1.5b	Vaa
A05–0139	pin (wood)	7	VI, VII	M1.5b	Vaa
A11–0018	needle (bone)	7	VI, VII	M1.5b	Vaa
A04–0243	needle (metal)	7	VII	M8a	Va,Vaa
A04–0244	needle (metal)	7	VII	M8a	Va,Vaa
A04–0279	needle (metal)	7	VII	M8a	Va,Vaa
A04–0442	comb tooth (metal)	7	VII	M8a	Va,Vaa
A05–0099a	pin (wood)	7	VII	M8a	Va,Vaa
A05–0099b	pin (wood)	7	VII	M8a	Va,Vaa
A05–0101	pin (wood)	7	VII	M8a	Va,Vaa
A05–0102	pin (wood)	7	VII	M8a	Va,Vaa
A05–0103	pin (wood)	7	VII	M8a	Va,Vaa
A05–0104a	pin (wood)	7	VII	M8a	Va,Vaa
A05–0104b	pin (wood)	7	VII	M8a	Va,Vaa
A05–0104c	pin (wood)	7	VII	M8a	Va,Vaa
A05–0110	pin (wood)	7	VII	M8a	Va,Vaa
A06–0022	whorl (stone)	9	VII	M8a	Va,Vaa
A06–0026	whorl (stone)	9	VII	M8a	Va,Vaa
A11–0015	pin-beater (bone)	7	VII	M8a	Va,Vaa
A05–0115a	pin (wood)	7	VII	M8a, Pit 7183	Va,Vaa
A05–0115b	pin (wood)	7	VII	M8a, Pit 7183	Va,Vaa

(continued)

Accession	Artefact	Area	Rig	Feature	Phase
A05–0115c	pin (wood)	7	VII	M8a, Pit 7183	Va,Vaa
A05–0088a	pin (wood)	7	VII	B53 (Phase 1), Central Area–T7152	Vb
A05–0088b	pin (wood)	7	VII	B53 (Phase 1), Central Area–T7152	Vb
A05–0097a	pin (wood)	7	VII	B53 (Phase 1), Central Area–T7152	Vb
A04–0261	comb tooth (metal)	7	VII	B53 (Phase 1), Central Area–Occupation (2a)	Vb
A06–0032	whorl (stone)	7	VII	B53 (Phase 1), Central Area–Occupation (2a)	Vb
A06–0033	whorl (stone)	7	VII	B53 (Phase 1), Central Area–Occupation (2a)	Vb
A04–0246	needle (metal)	7	VII	B53 (Phase 1), Central Area–Occupation (3c)	Vb
A05–0084a	pin (wood)	7	VII	B53 (Phase 1), Central Area–Occupation (3c)	Vb
A05–0084b	pin (wood)	7	VII	B53 (Phase 1), Central Area–Occupation (3c)	Vb
A05–0084c	pin (wood)	7	VII	B53 (Phase 1), Central Area–Occupation (3c)	Vb
A05–0084d	pin (wood)	7	VII	B53 (Phase 1), Central Area–Occupation (3c)	Vb
A05–0086a	pin (wood)	7	VII	B53 (Phase 1), Central Area–Occupation (3c)	Vb
A05–0086b	pin (wood)	7	VII	B53 (Phase 1), Central Area–Occupation (3c)	Vb
A05–0081a	pin (wood)	7	VII	B53 (Phase 1), North Area–D7080	Vb
A05–0081b	pin (wood)	7	VII	B53 (Phase 1), North Area–D7080	Vb
A05–0081c	pin (wood)	7	VII	B53 (Phase 1), North Area–D7080	Vb
A04–0198	scissors (metal)	7	VII	B53 (Phase 1), North Area–Occupation (1b)	Vb
A05–0080	pin (wood)	7	VII	B53 (Phase 1), North Area–Occupation (1b)	Vb
A05–0020	pin (wood)	7	VII	P8.5	Vb,Vbb
A05–0051	pin (wood)	7	VII	B53 (Phase 2), North Area–T7072	Vbb
A04–0159	comb tooth (metal)	7	VII	B53 (Phase 2), South Area–Occupation (7a)	Vbb
A05–0031a	pin (wood)	7	VII	B53 (Phase 2), South Area–Occupation (7a)	Vbb
A05–0031b	pin (wood)	7	VII	B53 (Phase 2), South Area–Occupation (7a)	Vbb
A05–0055a	pin (wood)	7	VII	B53 (Phase 2), South Area–Occupation (7a)	Vbb
A05–0055b	pin (wood)	7	VII	B53 (Phase 2), South Area–Occupation (7a)	Vbb
A05–0059a	pin (wood)	7	VII	B53 (Phase 2), South Area–Occupation (7a)	Vbb
A05–0059b	pin (wood)	7	VII	B53 (Phase 2), South Area–Occupation (7a)	Vbb
A06–0021	whorl (stone)	7	VII	B53 (Phase 2), North Area–Occupation (7a)	Vbb
A06–0028	whorl (stone)	7	VII	B53 (Phase 2), North Area–Occupation (7a)	Vbb
A11–0010	pin/needle (bone)	7	VII	B53 (Phase 2), South Area–Occupation (7a)	Vbb
A04–0188	needle (metal)	7	VII	B53 (Phase 2), North Area–Occupation (7b)	Vbb
A05–0046a	pin (wood)	7	VII	B53 (Phase 2), North Area–Occupation (7b)	Vbb
A05–0046b	pin (wood)	7	VII	B53 (Phase 2), North Area–Occupation (7b)	Vbb
A05–0049a	pin (wood)	7	VII	B53 (Phase 2), North Area–Occupation (7b)	Vbb
A05–0049b	pin (wood)	7	VII	B53 (Phase 2), North Area–Occupation (7b)	Vbb
A05–0049c	pin (wood)	7	VII	B53 (Phase 2), North Area–Occupation (7b)	Vbb
A05–0076a	pin (wood)	7	VII	B53 (Phase 2), North Area–Occupation (7b)	Vbb
A05–0047	pin (wood)	7	VII	B53 (Phase 2), North Area–Occupation (8)	Vbb
A04–0170	comb tooth (metal)	7	VII	B53 (Phase 2), South Area–Occupation (9b)	Vbb
A11–0011	whorl (bone)	7	VII	B53 (Phase 2), North Area–Occupation (9b)	Vbb
A05–0052	pin (wood)	7	VII	B53 (Phase 2), North Area–Occupation (12)	Vbb
A06–0025	whorl (stone)	7	VII	B53 (Phase 2), North Area–Occupation (12)	Vbb
A04–0126	comb tooth (metal)	7	VII	B53 (Phase 2), North Area–Occupation (14)	Vbb
A05–0057	pin (wood)	7	VII	B53 (Phase 2), North Area–Occupation (14)	Vbb
A11–0007	needle (bone)	7	VII	B53 (Phase 2), North Area–Occupation (14)	Vbb
A05–0035	pin (wood)	7	VII	B53 (Phase 2), North Area–Occupation (15), H7075, T7076	Vbb
A06–0027	whorl (stone)	10	VIII	M8b	Va,Vaa(–Vc)
A2498	bobbin (bone)	2	V, VI	M4a	Vaa–Vc(VI)
A3108	whorl (stone)	2	V, VI	M4a	Vaa–Vc
A4501	whorl (stone)	2	V, VI	M4a	Vaa–Vc
A4502	whorl (stone)	2	V, VI	M4a	Vaa–Vc
A3932a	comb tooth (metal)	4	V, VI	M3a	Vb–Vc

(continued)

Accession	Artefact	Area	Rig	Feature	Phase
A3932b	comb tooth (metal)	4	V, VI	M3a	Vb–Vc
A5513	comb tooth (metal)	4	V, VI	M3a	Vb–Vc
A6463	comb tooth (metal)	4	V, VI	M3a	Vb–Vc
A5460	pin (wood)	4	V, VI	M3a	Vb–Vc
A5754	pin (wood)	4	V, VI	M3a	Vb–Vc
A5757B	pin (wood)	4	V, VI	M3a	Vb–Vc
A5765a	pin (wood)	4	V, VI	M3a	Vb–Vc
A5765a	pin (wood)	4	V, VI	M3a	Vb–Vc
A5765b	pin (wood)	4	V, VI	M3a	Vb–Vc
A5765c	pin (wood)	4	V, VI	M3a	Vb–Vc
A4478	shears (metal)	4	V, VI	M3a, T2180	Vb–Vc
A5449	pin (wood)	4	V, VI	M3a, T2187	Vb–Vc
A05–0008a	pin (wood)	4	VII	M7	Vc
A05–0008b	pin (wood)	4	VII	M7	Vc
A05–0006a	pin (wood)	4	VII	M7	Vc
A10733	needle (metal)	4	VI	M3b	Vd
A1111a	pin (wood)	4	VI	M3b	Vd
A1111b	pin (wood)	4	VI	M3b	Vd
A1133b	pin (wood)	4	VI	M3b	Vd
A5775a	pin (wood)	4	VI	M3b	Vd
A5775b	pin (wood)	4	VI	M3b	Vd
A1353a	bobbin (bone)	4	VI	M3b	Vd
A1353b	bobbin (bone)	4	VI	M3b	Vd
A5440a	pin (wood)	4	VI	P1a	Vd
A5440b	pin (wood)	4	VI	P1a	Vd
A2424b	pin (wood)	4	V	M3c	Vd
A5437a	pin (wood)	4	V	M3c	Vd
A5437b	pin (wood)	4	V	M3c	Vd
A5438a	pin (wood)	4	V	M3c	Vd
A5438b	pin (wood)	4	V	M3c	Vd
A5753a	pin (wood)	4	V	M3c	Vd
A5753b	pin (wood)	4	V	M3c	Vd
A6161	pin (wood)	4	V	M3c	Vd
A04–0524	needle (metal)	10	VIII	B50(a), Construction–T6149	IVc–Vc(–Vdd)
A1899	club (wood)	4	VI	M3e, Pit 2111	Vdd>
A11052	whorl (bone)	2	VI	Building T, Well 3819	VIa–VIf
A6035	whorl (stone)	2	VI	Building T, Well 3819	VIa–VIf
A10345	pin (wood)	3	V	Unstratified	u/s
A12566a	pin (wood)	3	V, VI	Unstratified	u/s
A12566b	pin (wood)	3	V, VI	Unstratified	u/s
A12566c	pin (wood)	3	V, VI	Unstratified	u/s
A1077	whorl (stone)	3	V, VI	Unstratified	u/s
A05–0053a	pin (wood)	7	VII	Unstratified	u/s
A05–0053b	pin (wood)	7	VII	Unstratified	u/s
A05–0114a	pin (wood)	7	VI/VII	Unstratified	u/s
A05–0114b	pin (wood)	7	VI/VII	Unstratified	u/s
A05–0114c	pin (wood)	7	VI/VII	Unstratified	u/s
A05–0004a	pin (wood)	7–10	VI–VIII	Unstratified	u/s
A05–0004b	pin (wood)	7–10	VI–VIII	Unstratified	u/s
A05–0004c	pin (wood)	7–10	VI–VIII	Unstratified	u/s
A05–0005	pin (wood)	7–10	VI–VIII	Unstratified	u/s
A06–0014	whorl (stone)	7–10	VI–VIII	Unstratified	u/s
A04–0082	thimble (metal)	9	VII	Unstratified	u/s
A06–0015	whorl (stone)	9	VII	Unstratified	u/s

(continued)

Accession	Artefact	Area	Rig	Feature	Phase
North Sector (Area 5)					
A0511	pin (wood)	5, A	–	Lade (4)	6–12(b–e)
A0919	pin (wood)	5, A	–	Lade (4)	6–12(b–e)
A0339	pin-beater (bone)	5, A	–	Lade (4)	6–12(b–e)
A0021	pin-beater (bone)	5, A	–	Unstratified	19
North Sector (Area 6)					
A3922a	comb tooth (metal)	6	–	Drain, T1066	H
A3922b	comb tooth (metal)	6	–	Drain, T1066	H
South/North Sectors					
†L1483/ A04-0630c	needle (metal)	–	–	–	–
Cat No 703/ A?	pin (wood)	–	–	–	–
†A05–0085/ L2054	pin (wood)	–	–	–	–
Cat No 670/ L2660	pin (wood)	–	–	–	–
Cat No 427/ L3303	pin (wood)	–	–	–	–

† indicates accession number may be suspect/wrongly copied
‡ indicates not found at time of writing

Whorls.

Accession	Artefact	Area	Rig	Feature	Phase
South Sector					
A11409	whorl (wood)	4	V/VI	MC017	Ia–Ic>
A12281	whorl (stone)	1	VI	MC071	IIb–IIf
A12517	whorl (stone)	1	VI	MC071	IIb–IIf
A9510	whorl (bone)	4	VI	B12, Occupation (2a)	IIe–IIg
A06–0072	whorl (stone)	9	VII	P8.1c	IIIc
A8512	whorl (stone)	3	V	M6b	IIg–IIId
A8484	whorl (stone)	3	V	P2.2b	IVa
A5455	whorl (bone)	1	VI	B20, Occupation (1a)	<IIId–IVaa
A9541	whorl (stone)	3	VI	B2, T2846	IVa,IVaa
A06–0078	whorl (stone)	7	VII	B18 (Phase 1b), North Room & South Room–Occupation (6)	IVa,IVaa
A06–0054	whorl (stone)	9	VII	B18 (Phase 2a), Pit 9301	IVaa,IVb
A11–0022	whorl (bone)	7	VII	B18 (Phase 2b), North Room, Hall & Hall South–Occupation (10)	IVb
A06–0067	whorl (stone)	7	VII	B18 (Phase 2b), North Room, Hall & Hall South–Occupation (10)	IVb
A06–0066	whorl (stone)	7	VII	B18 (Phase 2b), North Room, Hall & Hall South–Occupation (10)	IVb
A06–0034	whorl (stone)	9	VII	B18 (Phase 2b), Hall–Occupation (11b)	IVb
A06–0076	whorl (stone)	10	VIII	MC153	IVb
A11–0023	whorl (bone)	10	VIII	M9b(a)	IVc
A5182	whorl (stone)	3	V, VI	M1.4c	IIIa–IVcc
A06–0055	whorl (stone)	7	VII	M9a	IVc,IVcc
A06–0013	whorl (stone)	9	VII	M9a	IVc,IVcc
A05–0119b	whorl (bone)	9	VII	M9a	IVc,IVcc
A06–0062	whorl (stone)	10	VIII	M9b(b)	IVc,IVcc
A4500	whorl (stone)	2	VI	B34, MF2759	Va
A3815	whorl (stone)	3	V, VI	M1.5a	Va,Vaa(VI)
A06–0022	whorl (stone)	9	VII	M8a	Va,Vaa
A06–0026	whorl (stone)	9	VII	M8a	Va,Vaa
A06–0032	whorl (stone)	7	VII	B53 (Phase 1), Central Area–Occupation (2a)	Vb
A06–0033	whorl (stone)	7	VII	B53 (Phase 1), Central Area–Occupation (2a)	Vb
A06–0028	whorl (stone)	7	VII	B53 (Phase 2), North Area–Occupation (7a)	Vbb
A06–0021	whorl (stone)	7	VII	B53 (Phase 2), North Area–Occupation (7a)	Vbb
A11–0011	whorl (bone)	7	VII	B53 (Phase 2), North Area–Occupation (9b)	Vbb
A06–0025	whorl (stone)	7	VII	B53 (Phase 2), North Area–Occupation (12)	Vbb
A06–0027	whorl (stone)	10	VIII	M8b	Va,Vaa(–Vc)
A3108	whorl (stone)	2	V, VI	M4a	Vaa–Vc
A4501	whorl (stone)	2	V, VI	M4a	Vaa–Vc
A4502	whorl (stone)	2	V, VI	M4a	Vaa–Vc
A11052	whorl (bone)	2	VI	Building T, Well 3819	VIa–VIf
A6035	whorl (stone)	2	VI	Building T, Well 3819	VIa–VIf
A1077	whorl (stone)	3	V, VI	Unstratified	u/s
A06–0014	whorl (stone)	7–10	VI–VIII	Unstratified	u/s
A06–0015	whorl (stone)	9	VII	Unstratified	u/s

Dress in medieval Perth: the evidence from the site

P Z Dransart

Of the 411 fabrics excavated from the High Street, a large number seem to have served in garments to clothe the inhabitants of the burgh. They exist as small offcuts of new cloth or as larger pieces that were worn, reused in the recycling of garments and finally discarded. The different processes used to make the fabrics and textiles, which have been studied in the sections above, indicate that the labour involved was considerable. The purpose of this section is to consider the High Street fabrics in the light of how people might have worn them. A comparative approach is adopted to examine other finds from the site that actually depict clothed persons, and to make further comparisons with other materials from countries with which Perth was in contact in the Middle Ages.

Despite the large number of samples of textiles and other fabrics recovered from the site, many difficulties hinder an adequate study of the clothing worn by the inhabitants of the medieval burgh. Detailed evidence for clothing in Scotland from the 12th to mid-14th centuries is rare due to the dearth of sculpture, painting and the like resulting from the campaigns of iconoclasm wrought by Reformers and Covenanters. Therefore visual representations produced by medieval Scots of themselves are often lacking and there is little with which to compare the fragmentary evidence from Perth. Where a greater abundance of iconographic evidence has survived, dress historians still encounter problems. In a study of European medieval clothing, Françoise Piponnier and Perrine Mane (1995, 117–18) noted that there appears to be a relative lack of change through time in the dress of peasants, while the more abundant iconographic and documentary references available regarding the clothing of the wealthy reveal greater variation in style amongst the rich.

The Perth textiles, however, provide a special insight into a particular aspect of dress because they provide information on the qualities of the fabrics with which the inhabitants of Perth clothed themselves across different social categories. Therefore this section is proposed as a preliminary study for research should more finds become available in the future. The procedure adopted here is to examine the properties of the different categories of cloth used in medieval Perth and to consider their suitability as changes took place in the cut of the garments, which may be observed in surviving iconographic and documentary evidence from western European countries. The first step will be to address the relative cost of clothing in medieval times. Establishing that this cost would have been far higher for most of the inhabitants of the medieval burgh of Perth than for its 21st-century inhabitants provides a context for examining dress as an expression of social

distinctions as well as helping to understand how dress contributed to an articulation of those differences. The following discussion considers the weaves and draping qualities of cloth as well as the evidence from the site for pins, buttons and badges that formed part of the means by which those social identities were articulated.

Relative economic values in cloth and clothing

Economic historians have examined the monetary values of textiles relative to the purchasing power of individuals in different income groups. Louise Buenger Robbert's (1983) study of an inventory of the personal effects of a murdered Venetian, Gratiano Gradenigo, provided a basis for analysing prices for food and clothing in 12th-century Pisa and Venice. A set of clothing owned by Gradenigo would have represented 15 days' work for the Pisan notary who inscribed the inventory and 25 days' work for the cashier. Robbert (ibid, 390) asked her readers to reflect whether contemporary readers would spend a month's wages on a suit of clothing, including shoes. For the couriers, guards and porters who were appointed to oversee the sale of Gradenigo's possessions, his high quality garments would have been unattainable. She calculated that a guard who was paid 2d a day would have had to have worked 24 weeks to pay for an inexpensive set of garments (ibid, 390).

Since the publication of Robbert's article in the early 1980s, the relative cost of mass produced clothing to consumers declined, especially in the 1990s. Therefore it is of interest to examine John Munro's (2009) study of the changing values of cloth produced in the Low Countries. One of the main products of looms in Flanders and Artois were the Hondschoote *says* or serges. Some of these cloths might well be counted amongst the category 2/1 Twill without nap, ZS, which was particularly well represented in the High Street textiles in Periods IV and V (that is, in the second half of the 13th and first half of the 14th centuries; see Illus 74). The peak in this category, coinciding with Period IV, occurred when serges were predominant in 13th-century textile production in the Low Countries (ibid, 8). There was competition in this trade from other countries, including Italy and England, because these textiles were relatively cheap and they did not undergo complex finishing processes. The political and economic situation changed in the Low Countries from the 1290s, with the outbreak of warfare, combined with a demographic fall in the 14th century brought about by the Black Death. These changes resulted in a restructuring of Flemish textile

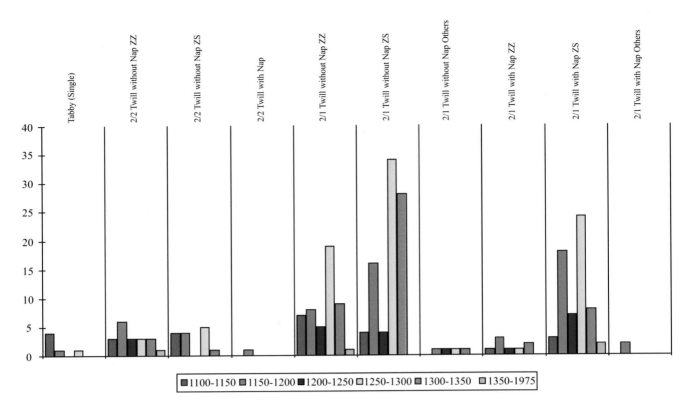

Illus 74 *Textiles suitable for clothing.*

production that increasingly focused on the weaving of 'heavy-weight luxury woollens', which were marketed in northern Europe, including the Baltic (ibid, 2). In the light of fluctuations in the cost of different qualities of cloth, Munro examined the monetary values of textiles relative to the purchasing power of a master mason in Antwerp during the first half of the 16th century. He concluded (ibid, 52) that 'For the 13.725 days' wages required for that master mason's purchase of the supposedly 'cheap' Hondschoote single say (1538–44), the same Toronto [Canada] carpenter today would also earn a very considerable sum: $3,631 (or about €2,269). Instead, today's Toronto carpenter would need to spend only a very few days' wage income to purchase a very fine wool-based suit.'

Both Robbert (1983) and Munro (2009) recognise the difficulties in studying the relative values of cloth and differences in the purchasing power between people in the past and present. However, these examples from 12th-century northern Italy and 16th-century Antwerp demonstrate the high cost of garments before the 21st century. If they can be used analogically for the situation in Perth, they help to provide a context for understanding the implications of a clause in the medieval Forest Laws of Scotland, in which the penalty included the confiscation of the cloak or outermost garment from a person found trespassing in a royal forest (Gilbert 1979, 305):

> If any stranger be found in the forest on any forbidden route [and] if he swears on the cross that he did not know that the road was forbidden nor that he knew

the right road, the forester shall lead him to [continue to] traverse [the forest] without harm. But if the man is not ignorant he ought to be taken and led to the king's castle and there, outside the gate, when witnesses have been brought, the forester shall take his outermost garment and whatever is in his purse which he needed and let him hand over his person to the porter of the castle to be kept during the king's pleasure.

Therefore infringement of the Forest Laws incurred a very steep penalty which included the confiscation of the offender's outer garment. This penalty would have fallen more harshly on the poorer offenders than the rich.

Cutting one's cloak according to one's cloth

Suitability of the High Street textiles for clothing

If the decorative hair-coverings (see Net, above) are the only pieces recognisable as more-or-less complete garments amongst the High Street textiles, and the pieces of felt in Cat No 406/A9821 (see Felt, above) formed the lining of a boot, how suitable were the other fabrics for clothing? The very coarse plain weave tabbies can be discounted as they might have been used as packaging, unless shrouds are counted as garments (see Tabby weaves from two ply yarns, above). It seems reasonable, however, to assume that many of the textiles considered in this report were originally destined for clothing. A similar conclusion was reached by Bennett (1987, 166) concerning the textiles from the nearby excavations at Kirk Close, Perth, where most of the 29 fabrics were considered to be 'of suitable weights for clothing or blankets or other light furnishings'. One of the textiles excavated from 80–86 High Street, Perth was a sleeve assembled from three panels of 2/1 twill, ZZ, probably dyed with madder (Harrison and Janaway 1997, 758 No 137). Another indicator to support the notion that many of the textiles in this report once served to clothe people is that napped surfaces have been considered a characteristic of garments (Möller-Wiering 2011, 127).

The evidence found for tailoring activities on the High Street site, including shears, scissors and needles (see Textile tools, above), also lends support to this idea. Indeed, some of the textiles themselves have the appearance of being discarded offcuts. While the finished garments were removed from the site, small and apparently unwanted scraps remained and eventually formed part of the archaeological record. Cat Nos 277/A09–0049a and 138/A9326 fall into this category. Both are 2/1 Twills with nap, ZS, and both have cut edges. The latter is an example of an extremely high quality dyed cloth and, unsurprisingly, only a small fragment was allowed to go to waste. Other textiles take the form of long strips, such as Cat Nos 309/A6653a and 114/A8863b, which latter is cut in a slight curve. At least some of the silks were used as bindings or tapes, including Cat Nos 6/A9500 and 46/A7323, which are narrow lengths of samitum. The worn piece of tabby, cut on the bias, Cat No 362/A6149, might also have bound the edge of a garment. One would expect to find such shapes on the site as by-products of the fitting of garments made from new or reworked cloth. Yet other textiles are irregular in outline, with rectangular pieces removed (for example Cat Nos 82/A12553b, Illus 31 and 290/A09–0093, Illus 41; these bear witness to the cutting of fabric which undoubtedly took place in the High Street in medieval times. It is significant that the trade name of *taillur* occurs in a document dating from the first half of the 13th century relating to the burgesses of Perth and their property (Duncan 1975, 489). In addition, a tailor was listed among about 80 burgesses and artisans named in submissions made to Edward I of England in 1291 (ibid, 487). The relationship between the tailoring or cut of a garment and the type of weave in which the cloth is woven will be discussed further below, after a description of the garment types that are likely to have been worn in medieval Perth.

Clothing as a vestimentary code

The high relative cost of garments for many of the inhabitants of Perth suggests that if dress served to mark statuses, such as gender, age and ethnicity, those identities were not easily changed. Some groups of people probably wore the livery of their employer; their dress would have denoted their occupation and rank. Although some of these distinctions would

have been pronounced, others may have been more subtle, especially as most of the Perth textiles have a monochrome appearance. This study rests on the premise that dress constituted a vestimentary system, to borrow a phrase adopted by Piponnier and Mane (1995, 6), which contributed to the articulation of social life in medieval Perth. Attending to the modes of dress in a social system in this manner draws on a semiotic analysis of the clothing worn by different groups of people constituting the society being studied; see also Adorno 1981. The identities considered here do not convey the sense of uniqueness and individuality that make one person different from others; rather they refer to membership of group categories, emphasising statuses related to ethnicity, gender, occupation and rank. Therefore different cate-gories of people adopted or were compelled to wear certain garments, or specific combinations of garments, thereby contributing to the maintenance of the identity of those categories as social groups.

During the centuries represented by finds from the High Street, Normans and Flemings settled in Scotland whether from England or directly from Normandy and other parts of France, Artois and the Low Countries (Barrow 1973, 316–17). The process of Normanisation of Scotland is popularly associated with Margaret, second wife of Malcolm III. The daughter of a Hungarian mother and Edward Atheling of England, she acquired a reputation for piety. Nevertheless, her confessor Thurgot wrote a hagiography in which he described her fondness for rich clothing alongside Norman tastes and preferences (cited in Barrow 1973, 315):

She caused merchants to come by land and sea from various regions and to bring very many precious wares that were still unknown in Scotland. The Scots were compelled by the queen to buy clothing of different colours and various ornaments of dress.

Members of the Royal Court evidently distinguished themselves by wearing rich dress because *The Anglo–Saxon Chronicle* reported for the year 1075 that King Malcolm and Queen Margaret received Edgar Atheling, presenting him with 'skins covered with purple cloth and robes of marten's skin and of grey fur and ermine and costly robes and golden vessels of silver'. As Edgar lost nearly all these gifts in a shipwreck, the Scottish monarchs gave him more 'immense treasure' as he set off to King William's court in Normandy (ibid, 316). This presentation of sumptuous clothing as part of a careful cultivation and propagation of Norman tastes, which Margaret allegedly fostered among the ruling classes, formed part of the background to changing attitudes towards dress as the burgh of Perth gained in importance from the 11th century.

The priest and chronicler, John of Fordun (*Chron Fordun*, ii, 237), said of David I (reigned 1124–1153) that he brought to his kingdom the luxuries of foreign nations, changing its coarse stuffs for precious vestments, and covering its ancient nakedness with purple and fine

Illus 75 *Seal of John I (Balliol), portrayed dressed as a knight.*

Illus 76 *Seal of John I (Balliol), portrayed seated on his throne and dressed as a civilian.*

linen. While the High Street has provided evidence for the importing of luxury goods in the form of silk, the equation of non-Norman dress with 'nakedness' is a perception examined more fully below.

If dress served as a metaphor to denote status and ethnic belonging, the derisory title by which King John Balliol is known to scholars and school children alike is significant. Following his surrender to the English in 1296 and the stripping of the red and gold emblems of the kings of Scotland from his clothing, he became known as Toom Tabard; he was found wanting at a time when military leadership was required. Humiliated by Edward I of England, John Balliol failed to match up to the image of the warrior presented on his own seal, where he is depicted wearing a hauberk and hose of mail, a helm and a sleeveless tabard (Illus 75; cf Illus 76). At the time of his surrender, English invading forces occupied Perth. The loyalties of the inhabitants of Perth must have been severely tested during the War of Independence (see Fascicule 1, Historical background). The adoption or rejection of Norman standards of dress throughout this period was not merely a question of fashion since complex political issues and concerns regarding ethnic identity were involved in addition to the relative costs of replacing one's clothing.

The piety embodied in the perceived Norman identity of Saint Margaret was complemented by a strong military ethos. A 'mail-clad, cone-helmeted *chiualer* or knight' (Barrow 1973, 316) is a particularly persuasive image of Norman identity. Dress historians have noted the influence that military clothing exerted over civilian dress (Evans 1952, 14). A tunic known as the *cotte*, worn by women and men, is said to have evolved from a men's garment worn over the *haubert* (hauberk), a tunic of chain mail, during the early 13th century in France. Throughout that century, military garb continued to have an effect on civilian clothing. Before proceeding to examine how the Perth textiles might have been used in garments, it is proposed to present a brief survey of what people wore in countries with which medieval Perth was in contact.

Clothing in 12th- to 14th-century Europe

Manuscript illustrations, sculpture and seals provide the basis for this description of dress. The depiction of high status individuals on seal matrices is one of the few sources of figurative imagery for high status Scots, especially women. What follows is a summary based on a study by Joan Evans (1952) of French medieval dress, a description of English medieval dress (Cunnington and Cunnington 1952) and on an inspection of Romanesque sculpture, ivories and manuscript illuminations published in Zarnecki (1971). It should be mentioned that the Cunningtons' book relies fairly heavily on French pictorial sources in constructing a history of English medieval dress.

Twelfth century

Women wore a long kirtle or gown over a smock or chemise. After the first quarter of the 12th century, the bodice of this gown became close fitting, expanding to a series of soft folds to the ground below the level of the hips. The neck might be cut into a V shape, to reveal the top of the smock. Sleeves were close fitting at the wrists but later in the century they widened from the elbow to form long hanging cuffs. Characteristic of high status women, this new cut is attested in the dress of a Scot by the seal of Margaret, Duchess of Brittany (died 1171), sister of William the Lion. The seal shows her narrow-waisted gown, pleated at the hem, while extravagant cuffs trailed to the ground (Laing 1866, 24) (Illus 77).

A thick cord of wool, linen or silk formed a girdle tied round the waist or hips. Evans (1952, 6) reported that in France married women wore a belt over the uppermost *bliaut*, or super-tunic, pulling up the fabric in folds to hide it; only girls went without a belt. A female column figure on the West front of Chartres Cathedral, c1140–50 (Zarnecki 1971, Plate 95), wears a girdle in one of the methods described by the Cunningtons (1952, 38): 'passed round the front of the waist and knotted or crossed over

Illus 77 *Margaret, Duchess of Brittany (after Laing 1866).*

the small of the back, then brought forward and down-ward and tied in front, the ends hanging in middle almost to the ankles'. A long, loose super-tunic was worn over the gown. It also became closer fitting round the upper part of the body and developed exaggerated sleeve cuffs. Particularly elaborate trimmings at the hem and the wide cuffs of a super-tunic are shown in an ivory of the Virgin by Zarnecki (1971, Plate 158). This kind of super-tunic was not suited to a gown with pendant cuffs. Women wore a ground length cloak, tied at the front, usually with loose cords.

Underneath the main garments women wore cloth stockings or hose, held in place by woollen garters above or below the knees. Shoes were pointed in shape and were without raised heels.

Often the hair was covered by a veil and noble women wore gold bands or diadems to keep the veil in place. From c1130 to 1170, when pendant cuffs were fashionable, a long narrow band with streaming ends might be tied over the veil and knotted on one side. A wimple or neck covering of fine white linen or silk became common from the middle of the century until c1340. Tucked into the neck of the gown, its ends were drawn up to frame the face, and a veil was usually worn over the top of the head. Alternatively, from the late 12th to the 14th centuries, women wore a barbette, a linen band passing from under the chin to the temples, and a fillet, also of linen, encircling the head.

Hair is sometimes shown plaited in two very long braids with a veil on top of the head (ibid, Plate 95). According to the Cunningtons (1952, 40), these tresses were bulked out with false hair or tow and were either tipped with ornaments or encased in silk *fouriaux* (see Tabby weaves of silk, above).

The main garments for men corresponded to those of women: tunic, super-tunic, cloak, legwear and shoes. However, the length of men's tunics varied, reaching to the knee, mid- calf or ankle. As with women's tunics and super-tunics, sleeves became wider (Zarnecki 1971, Plate 158). In contrast with women's clothing,

the tunic skirt was sometimes slit up the front to thigh level. A bronze tomb plate dated shortly after 1080 in Merseburg Cathedral shows Anti-King Rudolf of Swabia in a mid-calf length tunic with close fitting bodice, tight cuffs at the wrists and full skirt. His cloak is fastened at the right shoulder (ibid, Plate 104). This form of cloak is also featured in a psalter from St Albans Abbey, dated c1120–30, depicting the return of the Magi (ibid, Plate 195).

According to the Cunningtons (1952, 11), the 12th-century cloak or mantle was cut 'on the square and not on a circle'. It was clasped on the right shoulder, leaving the right arm free, or on the left shoulder. Alternatively, it was fastened in front beneath the chin. The Cunningtons (ibid, 31) also note that noble men had mantles lined with fur, while peasants had hooded skin cloaks with the hair surface outside.

Although not always depicted in illuminations, men of all classes wore breeches tied at the waist, reaching above or below the knee. During the course of the 12th century, these breeches became shorter, assuming the form of undergarments. Apparently, linen was the preferred material (ibid, 31). Men's hose were either short or long, in which case they overlapped the breeches. A variety of shoes or boots were worn, for instance the granite relief carving of King David as a musician at Santiago de Compostela, dated c1120, has high shoes tied at the ankle (Zarnecki 1971, Plate 124).

A variety of hoods, closed capes and caps were worn by men, one of the most distinctive being the pointed Phrygian cap, worn in England from the 10th to the end of the 12th centuries, but lingering into the 13th century (Cunnington and Cunnington 1952, 33). The coif was to continue into the next century and beyond. It was a plain linen bonnet which covered the ears and was tied under the chin (ibid, 34). Another type of cap which lasted into the 13th century was round in shape with a stalk on top (Zarnecki 1971, Plate 197). Men wore their hair short or shoulder length; beards and moustaches were common, although young men were often clean shaven.

Thirteenth to early fourteenth centuries

Women and men continued to wear the same basic garments throughout the 13th century and into the first part of the 14th century. However, the streamers and pendant cuffs characteristic of the 12th century were no longer fashionable. The characteristic crimped folds and sometimes fluttering garments of the Romanesque were replaced by heavier draped fabrics of the Gothic style (Evans 1952, 10). This change is a significant one and, as discussed below, it is related to changes in cloth production. The drapery was to become even more voluminous in the 15th and 16th centuries. Necklines became lower or were cut into a V opening, which was fastened with a brooch. Round and ring brooches were excavated from the High Street (see Fascicule 2, The metalwork), and a carved boss from Elgin, dated to the late 13th or early 14th century, demonstrates how such brooches were used (Illus 78; NMAS 1982, C2). Sleeves could be close fitting or loose. This more robust style of dress is shown in a Scottish context on the seal of Dervorgilla, daughter of Alan, Lord of Galloway and Margaret, daughter of David, Earl of Huntingdon. She was the mother of King John Balliol (Illus 79) Laing 1866, 14).

In France, both women and men wore a *cotte* (tunic) and an over-coat, the *surcot*, which was sometimes sleeved and split at the sides, or was sleeveless with deep armholes (Evans 1952, 14). Characteristic of this period was the width of the armholes in sleeved garments, sloping up from the waist (ibid, 15).

In 13th-century England, women wore a large garment known as the surcote on top of the gown. It had wide sleeves or was sleeveless (Cunnington and Cunnington 1952, 48). Men wore a variety of super-tunics or surcotes, including a sleeveless tabard of mid-calf length or longer. It was worn without a belt and was sometimes slit up the front to the level of the waist (ibid, 42). Cloaks, mantles and legwear tended to resemble those of the preceding century. However, c1200, noble men wore criss-crossed bindings on the legs. Boots or buskins were loose with coloured tops (ibid, 44–7).

During the second quarter of the 14th century changes occurred in both female and male garments (ibid, 55). Clothes were cut more closely, and men's tunics were shorter, revealing long tight-fitting hose worn on the legs. While some types of headgear for both women and men continued from the 13th century, hoods developed 'an extension of the point of the cowl into a hanging tail' known as the liripipe (ibid 62–5). Buttons, which were previously decorative, became more functional as fastenings, and cloaks were cut on a circle. Since most of the High Street textiles predate c1350, these changes will not be considered here. The adoption of the shaped *pourpoint* (doublet) by young French warriors in the mid-14th century and contemporary reactions to it has been discussed by Piponnier (1989), while the response by the authors of moralising tracts to the new garment styles, which emphasised sexual difference (tightly hosed legs in men's dress and narrow bodices in women's), has been discussed by Blanc (1989). What the ensuing discussion attempts to do is to consider these changes in relation to the types of weaves used in the different categories of cloth known from the Perth excavations.

The qualities of surface finish

Given that garments similar to those described in the preceding section were worn across wide parts of Europe, including Scandinavia (Østergård 1982), it is likely that such forms were donned by Perth's burgesses, too. There would have been variations, however, in qualities such as the weaves, dyestuffs and finishing techniques used in producing the cloth. The

Illus 78 *Boss from Elgin Cathedral.*

Illus 79 *Dervorgilla de Balliol (after Laing 1866).*

analysis of a 2/1 twill dating from the 13th century (Cat No 283/A09–0077b, Illus 42 indicates that weft-striped textiles were present in clothing worn in Perth. However, most of the garments were probably more subtly distinctive. A reference to striped garments in the 13th-century Statutes of the Church of Aberdeen disapproved of the wearing by ecclesiastics of 'brightly coloured and striped clothing' (Scarlett 1987, 67). The striped cloth, *panni de radiato*, and coloured cloth, *panni coloris*, mentioned in the Exchequer Rolls for the fourteenth century (see The textiles: General discussion) may have been beyond the reach of many people in Perth.

The dye analysis reported above indicates that red was the most frequently used dye colour, but blue and yellow were also detected, and there is a possibility that red and blue were combined to produce either purple or black. An unusual tabby fabric from medieval excavations in Scotland is striped in one system with brown and pink yarns. It was found, unstratified, in a workman's trench in the old Council Chambers, High Street, Perth (Bennett 1987, 171 Catalogue No 32). However, it may well date from the late 14th century and it might not be contemporary with the High Street textiles. It is likely that most people wore plain clothing in the period considered here and that brightly coloured and striped garments were still rare.

Although plain, self-coloured fabrics were probably the norm in medieval Perth, it should not be understood that the textiles used to make items of dress were uniform. Illus 74 is a bar diagram displaying the frequencies of the different cloth categories, excluding the coarse two ply tabby weaves. The inference to be drawn from Illus 74 is that few garments would have been made from tabby weave. Many were made from 2/2 twills, or 2/1 twills with or without nap. Some of these cloths were fulled, obscuring the weave in the finished garment.

Anni Albers (1965, 59) pointed out that the character of the raw material and that of the weave employed in the construction of a textile are interrelated. The main advantage of wool is its capacity to insulate, and this characteristic is diminished in a tabby weave, which is somewhat open and rigid unless it is subjected to some form of finishing treatment. Albers observed that twill textiles form a more pliable cloth than tabby weaves, thereby accentuating the softness of the wool. In addition, warp and weft yarns may be set more closely in twill, providing more warmth in a heavier fabric (ibid, 60). The insulating properties of wool were presumably of utmost importance to the inhabitants of medieval Perth. However, the potential for twill woven fabrics to drape well was perhaps also appreciated.

During the 11th and 12th centuries, the draped human figure provided European artists working in various media (stone, paint, metal and ivory) with one of their most important sources of visual inspiration. The folds in garments were usually depicted with great clarity, and often in a highly exaggerated fashion. One of the stylistic devices employed by European artists was Byzantine 'damp-fold' drapery which showed clothing moulded to the human body as though it were wet, in order to emphasise the human form (Zarnecki 1971, 117). Evidence for this curvilinear damp-fold tradition in Scotland is provided by a fragmentary sculpture from Jedburgh (Thurlby 1981). In France, high status women and men wore a long tunic (*chainse*) of goffered or pleated linen under a shorter over-tunic (*bliaut*); the king was reported as having a natural silk *bliaut* laced at the side with gold (Evans 1952, 5). However, it is perhaps more likely that the woollen twills worn by the inhabitants of Perth were used in garments comparable with those of Scandinavians, for which there is some iconographic evidence.

The chess pieces found on the south shore of Uig Bay on the west of the Isle of Lewis in the Outer Hebrides provide evidence for the dress of queens, kings, bishops, knights and foot soldiers or warders (or rooks). Stylistically they have been dated to c1135–1170, with the mitres worn by the bishops suggesting a time frame after c1150 (Taylor 1978, 14–15). They are considered to be the product of a Scandinavian workshop. Of special interest are the soft folds in the long garments worn by the seated queens and standing warriors (Illus 80–4).

A large fold is represented at the hem of the tunic worn by queens and warders alike. This fullness may have been achieved by inserting gores (triangular inserts) into a central seam cut into the front and back of the garment.

Illus 80 *Lewis chess piece: King (front and rear). (© Trustees National Museums Scotland)*

Illus 81 *Lewis chess piece: King (after NMAS 1892).*

Illus 82 Lewis chess piece: Queen (front and rear). (© Trustees National Museums Scotland)

Illus 83 *Lewis chess piece: Bishop (front and rear).* (© *Trustees National Museums Scotland*)

Illus 84 *Lewis chess piece: warder or footsoldier (front and rear).* (© *Trustees National Museums Scotland*)

This practice was both widespread and long-lived since it appears in a linen tunic from the Treasury of Notre Dame Cathedral, Paris, said to have belonged to St Louis (Louis IX), who died in 1270. The long sleeves of the garment were cut from trapezoidal shapes of fabric, the wider end being sewn to the armhole and narrower end forming the cuff. If two such shapes are cut from a length of cloth, fully occupying the width, four long triangles are left along the side selvedges. In the St Louis tunic, such offcuts were inserted as gores into slits cut into the front and back of the tunic (Burnham 1980; Crowfoot et al 1992, 176–7). This shaping is also clearly visible in a tunic depicted on a stained glass window in Bourges Cathedral (Illus 85). Presumably there were differences in the quality of the cloth represented in the tunics on Lewis chess pieces; the central fold of the queen's tunic in Illus 82) is draped in a sequence of five subsidiary U-shaped undulations, while that of the warder hangs rigidly, falling from the chest level of the wearer (Illus 84). The tunics of some of the other chess queens were depicted with equally fine robes falling in folds in different formations (Robinson 2004, 16–18).

Kings from the Lewis chess sets are shown wearing a semicircular cloak which is open at the right and pinned at the right shoulder (Illus 80, 81). Another such cloak is worn by Malcolm IV (the Maiden) in the large initial M on the charter granted to Kelso Abbey (NMAS 1892, 18). Dated to 1159 or shortly thereafter, it is of a similar period as the Lewis figures.

The garments of a man found buried in peat from Bocksten, in the southern Swedish province of Halland, provide actual examples of tunic and cloak with these characteristics, albeit from a later estimated date, c1350–1360. He wore a cloak, tunic, hose, footwraps and leather shoes; all the garments were woven in 2/1 twill using wool yarns (Nockert 1982, 278). His tunic had a round neck opening in the middle of the cloth, and four gores were inserted in the front, back, and side seams. Although damaged, the cloak was thought to be semicircular with a circle cut out for the head and an opening at the right (ibid, 278).

Illus 85 *The Mother of the Prodigal Son holding a tunic. Stained glass window at Bourges Cathedral.* (*After Kraus 1967*)

How common was the wearing of garments with a napped surface in Perth?

During the 13th and early 14th centuries on the High Street, 2/1 twill without nap outstripped other weaves at a period when 2/1 twill with nap was more unevenly represented. Textile specialists have noted that, elsewhere in Europe, 2/1 twill rose in proportion to other weaves from the late tenth century onwards (Kamínska and Nahlik 1960, Fig 20; Crowfoot 1979b, 38). It virtually replaced 2/2 twills at the 16–22 Copper-gate site in York (Walton 1989, 383). The choice of Z spun warp and S spun weft in such textiles seems to have been linked with the process of fulling and the subsequent mechanisation of the process, introduced on the Continent by the late 11th century and by the end of the 12th century in England (Carus-Wilson 1954, 189–90, 210). In Scotland, the earliest record of a fulling mill dates from c1260 (see Finishing, above).

In twill cloths with an even, Z spun warp and a softer, less even, S spun weft, the weft face lends itself to being raised into a napped surface. Such textiles might have been worn with the raised surface on the outside, to provide protection against wind and rain, as suggested by Kamínska and Nahlik (1960) in Polish textiles from Gdansk. Alternatively, the fluffy weft face might have been turned to the inside, with the smooth warp yarn providing the outer surface of the garment as suggested by coarse 2/2 twills from Bergen studied by Ellen Schjølberg (1998, 209) or, on the basis of the seams, by fragments from Baynard's Castle, London examined by Crowfoot (1979b, 38).

At Perth, good quality cloths with a raised nap on both surfaces, cloths with a nap on one surface only, and cloths with a lower thread count and slight nap on both surfaces are all present in the archaeological deposits (see 2/1 Twill with nap, ZS above). Therefore people must have worn garments variously with napped and unnapped surfaces outermost. However, the category 2/1 twill without nap, ZS contains a larger sample (87 textiles) than the corresponding category with nap. These cloths were evidently left without nap on purpose, since the category of 2/1 twills without nap, ZZ is also fairly well represented, with 19 samples from the second half of the 13th century alone, and 49 samples overall. A twill cloth woven from Z spun warp and Z spun weft throws the diagonal ridges of the weave into greater relief (ibid, 38). These twill weaves must have been valued for their visual characteristics in medieval Perth, in addition to the draping qualities of the cloth. It is likely that most of the burgh's inhabitants wore garments made from such twill weaves without nap.

While such weaves were frequently worn in Perth, notable changes in women's and men's clothing were occurring in France and the Low Countries. Flanders had pioneered technological developments in the weaving of luxury woollens from the early or mid-11th century, and was exporting broadcloth of uniform width (Duncan 1975, 464). Broadcloth

was a tabby weave with mixed spinning (ZS); it was dyed, fulled, teasled and sheared (Munro 2009). This finishing treatment was important since the relatively open binding of the tabby meant that the warp and weft yarns would have been less densely set compared with twill weaves. If it were not for the fulling and the raising of the nap in the finishing process, the resulting cloth would have had fewer insulating properties than a twill fabric.

Textiles excavated from Baynard's Castle in London (dating from the second quarter to late 14th century) provide direct evidence for an increase in the use of broadcloth. The main London sequence only has a significant degree of overlap with the High Street textile assemblage in the first half of the 14th century. It is interesting to note that most of the published London textiles are tabby weaves, the shift from twill to tabby being very marked in this period (Crowfoot et al 1992, 26–7, 43). Evidence for this shift has also been noted in the Netherlands and at the north German towns of Lübeck and Hameln (ibid, 44).

The contrast between the Perth and London textiles may be exemplified by Perth Cat No 19/A12340b, a 2/1 twill with nap, ZS, dyed with kermes, dating from the first half of the 12th century, and Cat No 50 from Baynard's Castle in London, a wool tabby, ZS, dyed with kermes and dating from the second quarter of the 14th century. Unfortunately, Crowfoot et al (ibid, 45) do not provide full technical details for this textile, but they do mention that there are a few pieces of tabby cloth which are designated as 'medium to fine grade' and that six such samples from the late 14th-century deposits 'are finer than those from the earlier part of the century'.

Broadcloth was so called because of its standard width. As woven, it measured about 100 inches wide before fulling. According to Kenneth Ponting (1987, 78), in Scotland a loom width of 50 inches was more normal, fulled to a width of 40 inches. The extra width which imported broadcloth afforded may have helped to provoke changes in the way garments were cut. Fulled tabby woven cloth did not have the same draping qualities as twill weaves and these factors seem to have given scope for tailors to develop garment styles using more gores combined with more complicated cutting and stitching. The tailoring of the garment compensated for the loss in the draping qualities characteristic of twills.

Such garments fitted the body more closely than the clothes with long loose folds of the 12th and 13th centuries, which meant that openings became necessary to enable the wearer to put on the garment. Tightly fitted sleeves were buttoned at the cuff, using more buttons than were necessary to achieve a decorative effect. Fragments from sleeves and edges of garments with small cloth buttons are known from Baynard's Castle in London, dating from the 14th century. One of the pieces had at least 42 cloth buttons in a length measuring 315mm (Crowfoot et al 1992, 168–72, No 216).

Complete garments are extremely rare in the archaeological record, although a considerable number are known from Herjolfsnæs, a Norse site in Greenland. Excavation of 110–120 relatively intact burials yielded evidence for interment of the dead in wooden coffins or, presumably when wood was in scarce supply, wrapped in shrouds consisting of garments (Østergård 1982, 271; 2009, 23–4). Under the direction of Poul Nørlund in 1921, about 23 tunics or robes, 16 hoods, four hats/caps and four single stockings were recovered in a more or less complete condition (Østergård 2009, 26). One main garment type was worn by both women and men; it had shoulder seams and was slipped over the head. A long slit was cut into the back and front of the tunic, into which one or two gores were inserted. One, two or four gores were also set into the side seams. These lateral gores extended from the hem right up to the armhole, but the front and back gores reached only to the level of the waist (Hald 1980, 340 and Figure 408). At the level of the waist, the gores were narrow but they increased in width at the level of the hips down to the hem. The overall effect was of a wide, flaring skirt flowing from a narrower bodice, without the need for seaming at the waist. One tunic measured more than four metres at the hem (Østergård 1982, 272; 2009, 168). A comparable use of gores occurred in a tunic from Moselund, Denmark, but the central slit cut to accommodate the gores in the front and back seams was left open up to waist level (Hald 1980, Fig 409).

The cut of these garments had something in common with the new styles found in other European countries, but the Greenland and Moselund tunics were made from twill fabrics, not broadcloth. Another distinctive characteristic is that the same basic garment type was worn by women and men. The Norse inhabitants of Herjolfsnæs wore hoods with liripipes, as did the French in the 14th century (Wahlgren 1986, Figs 93–101; Østergård 2009, 203–18), but iconographic evidence demonstrates that a high degree of gender differentiation in clothing was taking place in France and England, especially among young people. Nothing could be further removed from the mid-calf length, wide skirted tunics worn by Norse men than the short and tightly fitted *pourpoint* of Charles de Blois (d 1364), with padded bust, seamed waistline and buttoned front (Piponnier 1989, Fig 1).

Although the High Street textiles are fragmentary, they demonstrate the importance of twill weaves for clothing people. Luxury broadcloth was beyond the reach of many, but the continued use of twill weaves would not have prevented tailors and seamstresses from adapting the cut of the garments to the cloth available to their clients. The colouring of the clothing would have been fairly homogeneous and largely restricted to the natural browns of undyed wool. Variations between different garments would have been largely based on the choice of twill employed (2/2 or 2/1), or whether the surface was napped or not. Hence characteristics such as the 2/2 diamond twill of Cat No 18/A12340a, woven in smooth and lustrous yarn, would have contrasted greatly with Cat No 22/A12340e, a 2/1 twill with a napped and mottled surface achieved by interspersing three natural brown colours in what was probably the weft.

The dress of the elite

The double effigy of Walter Stewart, Earl of Menteith and his countess, Mary, at Inchmahome Priory on an island in the Lake of Menteith (Illus 86) provides a glimpse of the dress standards probably adopted by the wealthier inhabitants of 13th-century Perth. Walter is said to have died in c1295 (Fawcett 1986, 22), although the effigy may have been prepared before that date. Mary wears a long tunic and super-tunic which trail along the ground. The upper garment is slit at the sides and has deep, dolman-like sleeves, which were popular in the 13th century. Round her waist she wears a narrow belt or girdle. A long cloak is attached by a cord across her chest, and she holds the lowermost corner in her right hand.

Illus 86 *Effigies of Walter Stewart, Earl of Menteith and his countess, Mary.*

Her veil is held in place by a fillet or band, which passes round the head. An alternative form of headgear dating from the late 12th to 14th centuries involved the use of a barbette and fillet, as depicted on an otherwise weathered effigy in the parish church of Bourtie, Aberdeenshire (Brydall 1895, Figure 4). Possible evidence for a similar arrangement is visible on a fragmentary wooden carving from the High Street (see Fascicule 2, The wood, Cat No 650/A11092), although it is not clear whether the lower item is a barbette partially obscured by a veil, or whether it is the corner of a wimple, covering the ear of the wearer (Illus 87–9).

The Earl of Menteith is attired in a super-tunic, which presumably covers a tunic of chain mail. Like that of the countess, it is split at the sides, but it is much shorter, reaching only to the knee. The details of the sleeves are not clear, because his left arm is covered by a long shield, and his right arm lies underneath the countess. In addition to a belt at his waist, he wears another belt diagonally across the hips. This would presumably have held his sword in place, but it is now missing. In symmetry with the countess, he wears a cloak, the lower left hand corner of which is brought across his left hip; although longer than his super-tunic, it is shorter than that of his wife. Evidently Scottish nobles kept abreast of Continental fashions. During the 13th century in France the *surcot* (the super-tunic), as worn over the *haubert* or hauberk, became shorter with the introduction of hose and shoes of mail. At the end of the first quarter of the 13th century, the *surcot* was approximately mid-calf length, and it had shortened to just below the knee by the middle of the century (Evans 1952, 12 and Plate 9).

Effigies of Scottish knights dating from the 13th and early 14th centuries, like the Earl of Menteith, display belts worn around the waist or hips. According to Brydall (1895, 336), the belt was an integral part of knightly attire, it was 'worn upon all occasions, in the hall, at the banquet-table, and on the field of battle' and was 'often exceedingly rich'.

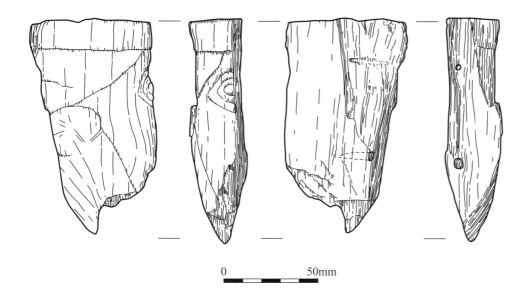

0   50mm

Illus 87 *Carved wooden head from Perth High Street. Wood Cat No 650/A11092 (Scale 1:2).*

Illus 88 *Adapted from MS 2397 Biblioteca Marciana, Venice.*

Illus 89 *After Strutt BM (now British Library), Ms Sloane 3983(in Cunnington and Cunnington 1952).*

Military garb

Late in the 12th century, a pilgrim seems to have
returned to Perth from Canterbury with an ampulla,
possibly wearing it, as described by Brian Spencer
(1975, 245), suspended from a cord round the neck
and prominently displayed on the wearer's chest. It
was eventually discarded in a midden in the first half
of the 13th century (see Fascicule 2, The metalwork,
Devotional objects, Cat No 1/A9264). The reverse
depicts the martyrdom of Thomas Becket with one
of the assassins wearing a knee-length hauberk and
scabbard at his right side (Illus 90). Cross-hatched
lines are used to represent the texture of the chain
mail and, from the absence of these lines on his legs,
it would seem that he wore cloth hose. He also lacks
the super-tunic seen on 13th-century depictions of
knights, including the Menteith effigy. His head is
protected by a helmet.

As an idealised depiction of a Norman knight
dressed for combat, it probably represented an earlier
standard of garb. In France, high status men wore
the hauberk until the mid-12th century, after which it
became more widespread (Evans 1952, 3–4). Hooded,
to protect the neck, its sleeves sometimes also had
pocket-like ends to cover the hands. The 11th-century
form of conical helmet with nose-flap continued in
use, with the addition of an added flap of fringed
leather over the nape of the neck and two or four
bands of metal to strengthen the crown. Early in
the 13th century, the closed helm was adopted, with
rounded top and an angular front provided with eye
slits and breathing holes (Illus 75). By the 14th
century, it had become flattened, slightly conical in
shape, and it was lengthened by overlapping bands of
metal at the neck (ibid, 12). With the adoption of the
closed helm, the identity of the wearer was obscured
and heraldic devices were applied to the super-tunic
(ibid, 12). Following the Eighth Crusade, towards the
end of the 13th century, rectangular metal plates were
introduced to shield the shoulders, and this protective
coating was made progressively more elaborate with
the addition of leather or plates of steel (ibid, 13).
However, surviving effigies of knights in Scotland
indicate that certain standard fittings were either rare
(such as mamelières, placed over the pectorals on
a 15th century effigy) or absent, for instance thigh-
pieces termed tuilles (Brydall 1895, 336).

Copper alloy and pewter links from chain mail
occur on archaeological sites (for example at Threave
Castle, Kirkcudbrightshire; Caldwell 1981, 107–11).
From the High Street, chain mail (see Fascicule 2, The
metalwork, Iron Cat No 708/A04–0555a) and spurs,
including a gilded example (Cat No 703/A04–0551),
were recovered from deposits associated with the
second phase of Building 18, an impressively sized
hall (see Fascicule 1, 172–8). These finds come from
deposits dated to the second half of the 13th century,
from a level prior to the English occupation of Perth
at the end of the century. Gilded spurs were only used

Illus 90 *The assassination of St Thomas Becket.*
Ampulla from Perth High Street.
Devotional Cat No 1/A9264.

by knights during this period, confirming the high
status of some of the finds from this archaeological
context (see Fascicule 2, The metalwork). One might
wonder why military gear was encountered in a
burgess's house. From a documentary source dated
1296, however, it is known that the Earl of Warenne
remitted a charge in which 'master Thomas the doctor'
accused Thomas Brun of stealing 'a coat of mail, value
20s., [and] a tabard, value half a mark' from his house in
Perth. In this case 'a little sack with boxes of ointment'
had a far greater monetary value than the coat of mail
and tabard (the sack and its contents were stated to be
worth 100s.) and, in the absence of the plaintiff, the
case was dismissed (*CDS*, ii, 191). In the light of the
present discussion, one should note the combination
of the hauberk and the tabard, or super tunic.

It is likely, however, that not all men drafted
into military service owned complete military garb.
The chronicler Jean Froissart, who was born at
Valenciennes c1337, described knights and squires
wearing armour and being mounted on rounseys and
coursers during a Scottish invasion of Northumberland
in 1327. He explained that the greater number of Scots
'commoners', whom he seems to have admired for their
military prowess, were 'armed each in his own fashion'
and riding small ponies (Froissart 1979, 47).

Even if the chain mail found at Perth was worn by a
knight, its use was not the prerogative of the Normans
alone. There was a long tradition for its use in Celtic
regions, dating back to the Iron Age. Effigy slabs in the
West Highlands frequently depict warriors in a quilted
or padded tunic, known as the aketon, and a cape of
chain mail with a bascinet on the head (Brydall 1895,

Fig 2; Dunbar 1989, 169). In 1521, the historian John Major mentioned that Scots covered 'the whole body with a coat of mail, made of iron rings' (cited in Dunbar 1989, 23). However, he added that 'common folk among the Wild Scots' donned a patched linen garment daubed with pitch, over which they wore an overcoat of deerskin. There was a long tradition for distinguishing Highland Scots because, from a Norman perspective, their battle-dress differed radically from Norman ideals. Major used the epithet 'Wild Scots' in reference to Gaelic speakers and the next section examines what evidence there is for the expression of ethnic diversity in dress in Perth.

Clothing and ethnic identity in Perth

The identities of Gaelic speakers

The discussion thus far has considered the Perth finds in the light of the Normanisation of Scotland and in reference to trading contacts with areas such as the Baltic, the Low Countries and Artois. Despite the complimentary terms with which Froissart regarded Scottish military achievements, foreign authors of literary sources from at least the 12th century tended to make a strong distinction between themselves and the Scots, about whom they wrote in pejorative terms on the basis of different standards of dress. A disparaging speech (cited in Anderson 1908, 197) was attributed to the Norman Walter Espec by Abbot Ailred of Rievaulx (d 1166):

> Who then would not laugh, rather than fear, when to fight against such men runs the worthless Scot with half-bare buttocks? . . . now (the Scots) challenge to war their conquerors, their masters; they oppose their naked hide to our lances, our swords and our arrows, using calf-skin for a shield, inspired by irrational contempt of death rather than by strength.

In a similar vein, Henry of Huntingdon (d c1155) put the following words into the mouth of Ralph Nowel, Bishop of Orkney: 'Why do we hesitate then to advance against unarmed and naked men?' (ibid, 197–8 n 6). A more specific reference was made by Ralph de Diceto to the army which William I (the Lion) raised in 1173, when he characterised the men as 'an endless host of Galwegians ... men agile, unclothed, remarkable for much baldness' (ibid, 247). Difference in dress standards focusing on the perceived 'nakedness' of the Scots soldiers is highlighted by these Norman chroniclers in connection with military activities. For the Normans, military prowess was given visual expression in the chain mail, helm, tabard, belts and other accoutrements necessary for making war; their masculinity was marked by their military dress. These material items provided them with the necessary means for social domination and for assuming the rights and privileges of overlordship. Geoffrey Barrow (1973, Chapter 10) demonstrated how Scottish monarchs

granted lands to individual subjects in a system of military feudal tenure with knight service. This process became more sustained during the second half of the 12th century in Gaelic-speaking areas beyond the Forth and Tay (ibid, 284–5). The brothers who were kings in succession, Malcolm IV (the Maiden) and William I (the Lion), received the military service of companies of trained knights in a social climate paralleled in other countries, such as France, Flanders, Brittany and England. According to Barrow (ibid, 286), it was more practicable to grant enfeoffments of land to people than to pay wages to professional soldiers.

Participation in the Crusades brought Scots soldiers to the attention of writers abroad. The authors of contemporary 12th-century accounts recognised a *'Scotorum more'* or a particularly Scottish custom in dress style in the bare-legged soldiers who passed through their countries. In a history of the first crusade written before 1112, Guibert de Nogent provided sketches of the groups of men who travelled through France on their way to the Holy Land. He characterised the Scots as being 'bare-legged, with their shaggy cloaks' (Duncan 1950, 211). A pilgrim to Compostela in Spain compared the Navarrese to the Scots, saying that the former 'wear dark clothes, short, to the knees only, in the manner of the Scots' (Galbreath 1949, 198). The pilgrim token from Rig VII at High Street might have held special significance for the Gaelic-speaking community (see Fascicule 2, The metalwork, Devotional objects, Cat No 6/A04–0505) because it shows the crucified figure of St Andrew wearing a short tunic, belted and with a fringe or band at the hem (Illus 91). It had a ring at each corner, although only one now survives, for stitching to the wearer's hat, which Spencer (1975, 244–5) says was the normal place for displaying the evidence of having gone on a pilgrimage after the 13th century. However, the dress of the saint is different from that

Illus 91 *Pilgrim token of St Andrew. Devotional Cat 6/A04–0505.*

delineated on a stone mould found in North Berwick, where he wears a long tunic (Richardson 1907, 431).

It is not clear whether outsiders were able to distinguish the Scots from the Irish (Duncan 1950, 211). Irish men also went abroad without leggings. The small, stylised figures attached to the 12th-century Lemanaghan shrine, illustrated by Henry (1970, Plates 44 and 45), wear knee-length garments and are bare-footed. Although produced in the same century as the Lewis chess pieces, it depicts different garment types. There is, however, a curious point of correspondence shared by the Lewis kings and the Lemanaghan figures in the elaborate styling of the hair and beards. In addition, the long tunic sleeves of the shrine figures fall in corrugated folds round the wrists and arms, like the cuffs of the Lewis queens. These characteristic folds also appear at the wrists of a man and woman, probably representing Christ and Ecclesia, on a stone baptismal font in Tryde church, Sweden (Zarnecki 1971, Plate 130). The stylisation at work here did not prevent artists from expressing regional differences in dress that provoked commentators to draw ethnic distinctions.

The shaggy mantle (presumably worn above a short undergarment by the Scots travellers whom Guibert de Nogent saw) had a long history. Fragments of textiles with a pile imitating sheepskin are known from several archaeological sites of the Migration, Viking and medieval periods in north-west Europe (Hedges 1982, 114). An example of a fragment of a tabby with a pile made by inserting sections of yarn is known from Kildonan, Isle of Eigg (Henshall 1952, 15). Elsewhere other examples with a ground weave of tabby, 2/2 diamond twill or 2/1 twill and a pile that was either spun or left unspun have been reported from Cronk Moar, Isle of Man (Bersu and Wilson 1966, 80–3), from sites in York (Hedges 1982, 122; Walton 1989, 434 and 442), from Heynes, Iceland (Guðjónsson 1962) and from Lund, Sweden (Lindström 1982, 182).

An untailored garment, the shaggy mantle was wrapped round the body of the wearer. On an eighth-century Pictish stone at Hilton of Cadboll, a high status horsewoman riding side saddle is depicted wearing a capacious mantle gathered in folds round her body, pinned at the chest by a pennanular brooch (Allen 1903, Figure 59). This form of dress is in contrast with the high status tunics and flowing garments of men on Pictish stones with their iconographic references to classical garments and Sassanian imagery, inspired by textiles and metalwork (Henderson 1998, 134–40). In Ireland, a shaggy cloak was associated with the miracles of St Brigit. A large part of what is called the 'mantle of St Brigit', mentioned in an inventory dated 1347, survives in the treasury of St Salvator's Cathedral, Bruges (McClintock 1936; Dransart 2007, 176–7).

Amongst the surviving Perth textiles, Cat No 84/A12553d is unusual for its light shaggy surface. It has an unusual selvedge, which is likely to have been a starting edge for weaving on a vertical loom (Illus 15). Deposited in the mid-12th century in a backland courtyard, this textile possibly indicates a dress standard associated with a rural inhabitant, who might have been a Gaelic-speaker, the language being current in the area of Perth during the 12th and 13th centuries. A distortion in the threads of the weave suggests that it was once pinned, perhaps by a brooch or a bone pin to keep the cloth in place on the wearer.

On the basis of literary and iconographic evidence, it is evident that shaggy mantles were worn by people in different stations of life and that, increasingly, outsiders saw them as indicating a Gaelic-speaking ethnic identity. It has been suggested that a drawing made by Albrecht Dürer in 1521 of soldiers (one of whom wears a shaggy mantle), often understood to be Irish, were perhaps galloglasses, or Hebridean mercenaries participating in an Irish war party (Dunbar 1989, 26). Fragments, with a spun pile and dyed with kermes, have been excavated from a 16th-century context at Drogheda, Ireland (Heckett 1992, 158–9), the dyesource indicating that the owner would have been a person of rank. It may also be suggested that 'Ane hieland mantill of black freis pasmentit with gold and lynit with blak taffetie' recorded in an inventory dated 1578 of items in Edinburgh Castle belonging to James VI and Mary Queen of Scots was a high status garment (Dunbar 1989, 24–5).

Yet the poet Spenser vilified the 'Irish' mantle as 'a fitt house for an outlaw, a meete bedd for a rebell, and an apt cloke for a theif' (cited in Carus-Wilson 1954, 26). Paradoxically, such mantles proved to be a popular export item to England, via the port of Bristol, in the 15th century. As Carus-Wilson (ibid, 26) comments, these 'capacious' mantles 'could serve as garment, bed, or even tent when necessary'.

Drawings of a man and a woman wearing shaggy mantles were included in a compendium entitled *Recueil de la Diversité des Habits* and published in Paris in 1562. However there are differences in the manner in which they are treated – the portrayal of the woman is far more pejorative in its associations than that of the captain, who wears a stylised rendition of a fringed shaggy cloak (Illus 92). In contrast, the woman is wrapped in a large skin cloak, with the hair or fleece inside, and wears skin shoes (Dunbar 1989, 27). The captions to these illustrations, 'the wild woman of Scotland' and 'the wild captain', demonstrate that such dress was no longer seen as civilised, a point stressed by Heckett (1992, 162). Although these drawings appear to be fanciful, the personages they depicted reappeared in the margin of Speed's 1610 map of Ireland (ibid, 165). The woman and man are shown as one of the three types of couples representing different social classes within Irish society. It is important to note that on Speed's map, the women and men are depicted clearly wearing typically European clothing, according to their respective ranks, but the shaggy mantle, as an ethnic marker, is the outermost garment (Dransart 2007, 162).

References to the shaggy mantle continued late into the 17th century (ibid, 178). New standards of dress, however, were already emerging from the 16th century onwards that distinguished Scottish and Irish speakers

La fauuage d'Efcoffe.

Si tu mets l'œil deffus cefte figure
A celle fin que certain tu en foys,
C'eft la fauuage au pays Efcoffoys,
De peaux veftue encontre la froidure.

Le capitaine Sauuage.

Vous pourrez voir entre les Efcoffoys,
Tel Capitaine faifant là leur feiours,
Qui fouuent font nuyfance aux Angloys,
Peu de profit leur fait faire maints tours.

Illus 92 *'La sauvage d'Écosse' ('wild woman of Scotland') and 'Le capitaine sauvage' ('wild captain'). Fanciful depictions of a Scots woman and man from* Recueil de la diversité des habits *(1562). (By courtesy of the Bibliothèque Municipale de Tours, Rés 3540, Fonds Marcel)*

of Gaelic. In Ireland, the increasing availability of linen was used by women in headgear consisting of great rolls of cloth. Men donned thickly folded shirts with 30 or more yards of material in a saffron colour (Carus-Wilson 1954, 25). During the reign of Henry VIII, the English attempted to suppress this expression of ethnic identity by forbidding the use of saffron dye and by setting an upper limit of seven yards per shirt (Heckett 1992, 163). Their attempts met with little success. Meanwhile, in Scotland men were already beginning to adopt the belted plaid which, in time, became the kilt (Dunbar 1989, 29–30).

Sumptuary laws

In addition to the dress codes instituted by the authorities of different religions, sumptuary laws were enacted in various European states in relation to dress standards and feasting. Such legislation was aimed at regulating extravagant clothing and jewellery, and over-indulgence in the consumption of food (Marcus 1975, 193; Shaw 1979, 81). It has been interpreted as ostensibly serving to protect poor people from unnecessary expenditure, but it also maintained social distinctions (Amt 1993, 74).

The earliest surviving sumptuary law in Scotland is dated March 1430 (Shaw 1979, 81). It outlines the standards of dress allowed to members of broad social classes. No restrictions were specified for men classified as knight or lord with an annual income of at least 200 merks and their heirs. Persons of lesser rank were not allowed to wear clothes of silk or certain furs, nor were embroidery of pearls or precious metal permissible. Other items, such as belts, brooches and chains were allowed. From the High Street, there is ample evidence for such items, including decorated buckles, round brooches and copper pins, as well as plain ring-brooches (see Fascicule 2, The metalwork). Moulds used in casting indicate that brooches were made in the burgh (see Fascicule 4, The stone objects, 135–7). The richer furs were denied to burgesses, apart from aldermen (that is, provosts), bailies and members of the town council. Among rural dwellers, yeomen and commoners were not to wear 'hewyt' (coloured) clothing below knee length, not were 'ragyt' garments allowed (probably referring to slashed items of dress). According to the terms of the act, wives were to wear clothing appropriate to the status of their husbands. The restrictions on the wives and servants of commoners were treated in greatest detail; they were not to wear long trains, long-necked hoods, full sleeves or expensive kerchiefs. This legislation sought to control the colour, trimming and yardage used in the clothing of commoners (Shaw 1979, 82; online Records of the Parliaments of Scotland [RPS] at www.rps.ac.uk, legislation 1430/12–14).

Subsequent sumptuary laws passed in Scotland were more explicitly worded and they also maintained differential standards on the basis of social standing (Shaw 1979, 83). Implied rather than explicitly stated in this legislation is that, in a marriage between two persons of different status, the wife had to adopt the dress worn by women in her husband's social category. In other words, there was no social encouragement for a woman to marry below her status (hypogamy) or above it (hypergamy). It is not known whether the circumstances which prompted these 15th-century laws were similar to those of previous centuries, although it may be noted that double effigies present spouses dressed as social equals (Illus 86).

It is unclear when the practice began of wealthy patrons giving their worn clothes to their servants for recycling. It presumably predated the act of 1581, which permitted servants to receive used garments from their employers. The same act also allowed women of all classes to wear previously restricted headdresses (Shaw 1979, 84; *RPS*, legislation 1581/10/37). The 16th-century context of this act may well not apply to Perth of the 12th to 14th centuries, but the presence of the neatly cut silk tabbies (Cat Nos 343/A09–0046 and 344/A09–0047a) does suggest that high status fabric was recycled in the burgh, perhaps from headdresses, as suggested above (see Tabby weaves of silk, above).

Because sumptuary legislation was frequently re-enacted in different countries, people must repeatedly have flouted the law. Shaw (1979, 81) pointed out that Scottish parliamentary records are fragmentary up to 1466 and it is possible that earlier legislation existed. A particularly detailed law from Venice, dated 1299, has survived (Amt 1993, 74). It stipulated the numbers of women who might accompany a bride at her wedding and restricted the number of new dresses to four in her trousseau. There was a strict prohibition on the use of pearls (ibid, 75):

6. Item, that henceforth no man or woman or lady may wear borders of pearls, under penalty of 20 *soldi di grossi*, except that brides, if they wish, may have borders of pearls on their wedding dress a single time, and similarly one headpiece of pearls; and they may not place the aforesaid borders on any gown other than the wedding gown. And the aforesaid borders, which are placed on the wedding dress and cloak, may not be worth more than 20 *soldi di grossi* altogether, under the aforesaid penalty.

7. And that no person may wear an embroidered border beyond the value of five *lire de piccoli*; and no person may place any embroidered border on a cloak or on fur. Strings of pearls for the hair are totally forbidden and prohibited, so that no woman or lady may wear them henceforth, under penalty of 100 *soldi* for each time she is found contravening this law. And also she may not have more than one row of gold or amber buttons worth more than 10 *soldi di grossi*, under the aforesaid penalty of 100 *soldi*, nor any hair ornament of pearls worth more than 100 *soldi*, under the aforesaid penalty.

This stringent legislation made exemption only for ladies visiting the court, when travelling to or returning from the palace itself. Seed pearls were used in the medieval period in embroideries to embellish both religious and secular dress. They were combined with larger pearls or other costly items, as in an embroidered cuff on a deep purple silk dalmatic with the insignia of the Holy Roman Empire, dated 1130–1140, from the royal workshops of Roger II, King of Sicily, in Palermo (Staniland 1991, Fig 53). Scotland was a source for large pearls, which were exported to England and probably further afield. Commercial pearl fishing survived into the 20th century in the vicinity of Perth (Woodward 1994, 82–6). No pearls were recovered during the excavation, but bivalves of the pearl mussel were recovered (see Fascicule 4, The mollusca, 61). It would not be surprising if pearls were employed in the costliest of garments worn during the 12th and 13th centuries in Perth, perhaps in the form of a border like the hem of one of the Lewis kings (Illus 80). It should be remembered that in the sumptuary law of 1430, pearls were not permitted for people below the class of knights or lords (*RPS*, legislation 1430/12).

Although the use of buttons goes back to at least the Bronze Age in Europe, cloth buttons are normally dated from the 14th century onwards. During the 13th century, metal buttons or brooches served instead (Crowfoot et al 1992, 168). One gold- and three copper alloy-covered buttons from High Street are circular in shape (see Fascicule 2, The metalwork, non-ferrous Cat Nos 67–70). In Cat No 68/A8070, with a diameter of 28mm, gold covers a lead base pierced to hold a now missing wire loop. It and two of the other buttons have rouletted or repoussé decoration (Cat Nos 69/A9286a and 67/A10757). Of interest is the design of the gold button, an eight-petalled flower, which resembles the seven-petalled motif on the brooch worn at the right shoulder of King David as depicted in stained glass at Augsburg Cathedral, c1135 (Illus 93). It is possible that this button was used on the type of cloak described above as worn by the Lewis chess kings and Malcolm IV on the Kelso charter.

The occurrence of gold and alloy buttons, silk hair-coverings and silk tablet woven braids bears witness to the wealth of some of the inhabitants of Perth. In particular, the hair-coverings (see Net, above) and the gold button have stylistic links with Germany, and the presence of these luxury items may reflect the trading activities undertaken by the burgesses of Perth and their north European counterparts. The success of these merchants in obtaining such goods may well have prompted the enactment of sumptuary legislation.

At the other end of the social hierarchy, people fastened their clothes with other sorts of devices. A thistle-headed bone pin (see Fascicule 4, The worked bone, 103 and 108 Cat No 9/A7079) provides a decorative example, despite the irregular cut of the head. Perforated pins made from simply worked pig fibulae were also perhaps used as dress pins, with a

Illus 93 *The Prophet Daniel and King David. Stained glass window at Augsburg Cathedral, c1135. (After Zarnecki 1971)*

Saints and prelates

Many of the material remains from the High Street seem to have been left as remnants of artisanal and mercantile activities. The establishment of Canons Regular of St Augustine at Scone by Alexander I, during the second decade of the 12th century (Duncan 1975, 131), would have resulted in a demand for dark cloth suitable for habits. According to Duncan (ibid, 470), the canons were given permission by Malcolm IV, who raised the status of the priory to that of an abbey, to retain 'a smith, skinner and tailor' under the same conditions granted to the burgesses of Perth. Malcolm's charter listed three '*ministros*', namely '*vnum fabrum* [smith] *vnum pelliparium* [skinner] *et vnum sutorem* [souter]' [*RRS*, i, no 243]. Duncan took the sewer [from the Latin *suere*, 'to sew'] to be a tailor rather than a cobbler. Hence it is likely that cloth for the monks' habits was acquired in Perth. Although Augustinians and Benedictines, an order which also flourished in 12th-century Scotland, are usually thought of as wearing black habits, the cloth probably was not dyed but was simply the darkest natural colour available. It is therefore possible that some of the cloth excavated from the High Street site might have been destined for a religious order. Some of the textiles in the lists of 2/2 and 2/1 twills discussed above in the section on loom-woven fabrics would have provided non-ostentatious material for habits, especially those without a nap woven using yarn spun from heavily pigmented fleece.

Another order associated with black habits is that of the Dominicans, who founded a friary in Perth in 1231. They were granted land where the castle had been situated and, after the 1240s, the Dominican Friary became the residence of the Scottish monarchs when they visited Perth (see Fascicule 1, Historical background, 7). Later, the Whitefriars (the Carmelites) and the Grey-friars (the Franciscans) established foundations in the environs of Perth during the period considered here, and a Carthusian monastery or Charterhouse was founded.

The habits of the medieval orders differed in detail, but they shared in common the principle of simplicity and an avoidance of luxury. Based on medieval dress norms, monastic vestments were subject to a far slower rate of change than lay dress (Evans 1952, 67–8). In the differing standards as to what constituted monastic life, the Augustinian Canons had a less strict monastic discipline than the Benedictines. Writing at the end of the 11th or beginning of the 12th century, Simeon of Durham looked back to the time, in the days of St Cuthbert, when the monastery of Coldingham, Berwickshire, housed nuns and monks. According to Simeon, the nuns had 'devoted themselves to the sewing of robes of the finest workmanship, in which they either adorned themselves like brides, thereby endangering their own estate of life and profession, or they gave them to men who were strangers, for the purpose thereby securing their friendship' (cited in Amt 1993,

yarn threaded through the perforation to secure the pin to the garment. These potentially multi-functional items had been in use down the centuries in north-western Europe (Walton Rogers 1997, 1783). The perforated pig metapodials (see Fascicule 4, The worked bone,104) provide another instance of a necessary dress accessory made with great simplicity. Apart from the perforation, the bone is all but unmodified and, if they were toggles, apparently they were of a highly successful design since they were found in contexts dating from the earliest to the latest periods of the High Street site. Other toggles were fashioned from strips of rolled up leather (The leather, this fascicule).

232). This statement equates fine clothing with what was, to Simeon, inappropriate behaviour on the part of the nuns.

Yet it has to be admitted that priests robed in their vestments were clad in the fine linens and silks denied to other members of the various monastic communities in Christendom; the body of St Cuthbert himself was laid to rest in the most luxurious of silks (Crowfoot 1939; Battiscombe 1956). Simeon alleged that the nuns, who lived long before his time, despised 'the sanctity of their profession' in directing their handiwork to what he considered to be the wrong ends. The reporting of alleged moral misdeeds, rather than acknowledging the good practices of monastic houses, has been noted by Amt (1993, 246). This tendency may explain why the history of Elcho Priory, founded close to Perth sometime before 1247, has been described as 'obscure' (Cowan and Easson 1976, 146). It was a house of Cistercian nuns. An extremely fragmentary grave slab from the Priory, now in Perth Museum, shows the hem of the robes of a nun, presumably a prioress, with a dog at her feet. Dated to the 14th century, it perhaps had a similar format to the more complete slab from Dundrennan Abbey (Illus 94). The Dundrennan slab is thought to represent a noble benefactress, a kinswoman of the Lords of Galloway (Brydall 1895, 367). The monks of Dundrennan belonged to the Cistercian order, but Lincluden Priory, founded by Uchtred, Lord of Galloway before 1174, housed a community of black nuns of the Benedictine Order (Cowan and Easson 1976, 143).

In Scotland, precious silk cloths have been found interred with Archbishop Gavin Dunbar and in an unidentified bishop's tomb at Fortrose, as discussed above (see Twill weaves of silk, above). These remains are fragmentary, and unfortunately the 13th-century mural painting in the choir of Inchcolm Abbey of seven clerics is damaged at the level of the heads and shoulders (Paterson 1950, Plate 7). However, the fine folds of the drapery, outlined in black, red and yellow, are clearly visible. At the hem of each robe, there are panels bearing a lozenge design. The fineness of the drapery is akin to the more schematic depiction of the garments worn by the figures on the admittedly worn High Street ampulla, which presents the Virgin and Child on one side and the Coronation of the Virgin on the other (see Fascicule 2, The metalwork, Devotional objects, Cat No 3/A04–0214). Like the Thomas Becket ampulla, it would have been worn on the chest of the wearer as evidenced by the rings for suspending the cord round the neck, one of which has survived.

The bishops among the Lewis chess pieces (Illus 82) and the depiction (Illus 95) of St Thomas Becket on the ampulla from the High Street (see Fascicule 2, The metalwork, Devotional objects, Cat No 1/A9264) provide a clear idea of how clerics were robed in northern European countries. Priestly garments for celebrating mass derive from antecedents in classical Rome; they achieved a degree of formality still recognisable today from the sixth to ninth centuries AD (Hogarth 1987, 8). When robing, priests first donned an amice,

Illus 94 *Effigy slab of a noblewoman at Dundrennan Abbey (after Brydall 1895).*

Illus 95 *Thomas Becket ampulla. Devotional Cat No 1/A9264.*

a rectangular neck-piece with cords crossed over the chest, which were wrapped behind (Evans 1952, 68). They then put on an alb, the basic garment for clerics, a loose tunic usually made of fine linen (Schmedding 1978, no 289). Next they donned a tunicle or dalmatic. Both these garments were similar in shape, but the tunicle was of a plain fabric, while the dalmatic was often of richly woven or embroidered silk. These two garments were shorter than the alb and were often fringed and slit at the sides. Deacons wore a dalmatic as the outer garment (Evans 1952, Plates 75 and 76) and subdeacons a tunicle (Hogarth 1987, 9). A stole was arranged next; bishops placed it round the neck with each end hanging straight down, priests crossed it over the chest and deacons wore it on the diagonal (Evans 1952, 71). A maniple was placed round the left wrist; originally a *sudarium* (a cloth for wiping the hands), it had now become a decorative feature which usually matched the stole (ibid, 71). Priests, bishops and archbishops wore a chasuble over the dalmatic. It was a large garment derived from the Roman circular outer robe with a hole for the head, one of the names for it being *casula*, meaning 'little house' (Hogarth 1987, 8). The chasuble was often beautifully embroidered with bands known as orphreys, as visible in the rear view on Illus 83. Bishops and archbishops wore a mitre on the head, and archbishops might be further distinguished by the pallium, a circular band worn over the chasuble with long bands hanging down front and back. The nuns of Sant' Agnese in Rome wove these bands using the white wool of dedicated lambs and they were presented to arch-bishops and some abbots of the large monasteries within three months of their consecration (Evans 1952, 74).

The 12th-century St Thomas Beckett ampulla from Perth (Illus 90) depicts the saint wearing a finely pleated alb. It does not have an apparel, that is a panel of embroidery at the front at the level of the hem, nor do the Lewis bishops display such a panel. The apparel is considered to be a 13th-century feature (ibid, 69), and an example is present on the alb in Sens Cathedral, traditionally said to have been worn by St Thomas (Illus 96). Apparels are also depicted on the albs worn by the Inchcolm Abbey clerics.

On the other side of the ampulla, Saint Thomas is robed in mass vestments, in which he was buried (Vogt 2010, 125). He is depicted wearing a mitre, amice and chasuble. In the first half of the 12th century mitres were worn with the peaks above each ear, but mid-century they were turned so that the points were placed front and back, as is the custom today. An early example in France of the new style of mitre is dated 1144 (Evans 1952, 76). Both the Lewis bishops and Saint Thomas have mitres with the points at front and behind. The

low sides and the shallow angle of the point also indicate a late 12th century date (Vogt 2010, 123). Afterwards, mitres became higher and more pointed. In the Lewis bishops, the amice is a relatively modest affair, but that of St Thomas is quite elaborate and the lozenges probably represent embroidery. According to Evans (1952, 69), collars of stiff embroidery date from 1144 in France.

The image of St Thomas depicts the chasuble in a series of concertina like pleats, an arrangement which has the effect of creating a point at front and back. At Sens, a dark violet silk chasuble in the cathedral treasury traditionally ascribed to Saint Thomas is embellished with gold embroidery (Illus 97, 98). The form of this

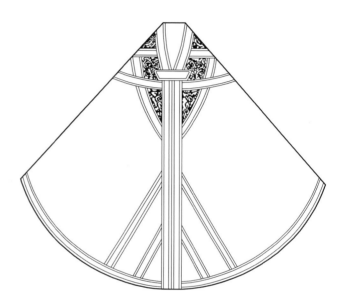

Illus 97 *Front view of a chasuble from Sens Cathedral ascribed to St Thomas Becket. (After Evans 1952)*

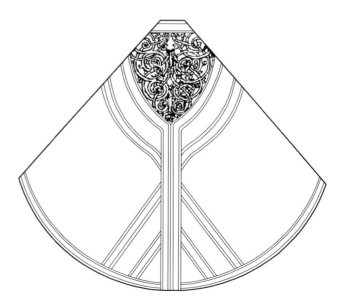

Illus 98 *Rear view of a chasuble from Sens Cathedral ascribed to St Thomas Becket. (After Evans 1952)*

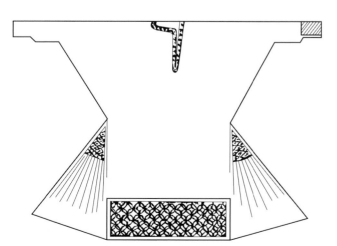

Illus 96 *Alb from Sens Cathedral ascribed to St Thomas Becket. (After Evans 1952)*

vestment changed considerably over the years from its original circular shape. In its large form, the fabric at the sides was gathered up over the shoulders to free the arms. One of the Lewis bishops (Illus 83; NMAS 1892, 375, Number NS 24) has simple, heavy folds over the arms, and the lifted chasuble reveals the dalmatic and alb beneath. An example of a voluminous chasuble arranged in a series of narrow pleats is worn by the figure of St Nicholas on the seal of the medieval burgh of Aberdeen (Laing 1866, Plate XIV.6). Although appended to a document dated 1357, the matrix from which it was impressed dates from the first half of the 12th century on stylistic grounds. More recently, chasubles were cut into a point and now they are shield shaped, front and back, making the garment lighter and less cumbersome.

The robing of priests and their acolytes for mass would have provided the inhabitants of Perth with the sight of costly linen and silk garments that were of a delicacy and vivid colour to which they were not accustomed in their daily lives. From the discussion above of the evidence for the working of silk and linen on the High Street, it is probable that fabrics supplied through Perth were used to make vestments that were in keeping with ecclesiastical standards observed elsewhere in Christendom. The everyday garb of nuns, monks and lay persons differed greatly from that of priests when robed for mass.

Conclusions

In the previous parts of this section, attention focused on the skills and processes involved in transforming raw fibres, whether of animal protein or plant origin, into finished cloth. Here the material presence of cloth has been examined, especially its draping qualities as worn by people of different ranks, statuses, genders and ethnicities. The chain of procedures studied in this volume demonstrates how medieval people valued different qualities in cloth, depending on the fibres and dyes used to make it and the labour required to bring out the desired characteristics, even though much of it, to modern eyes, seems to be homogeneous in colour. From the beautiful drape of the finest woollen twill weaves, the lustre of silks and the crisp handle of laundered linen, to the luxury of fluffy, napped broadcloths, Perth's inhabitants would have had an eye for such characterful fabrics even though their own garments may have been of a humbler sort. The draping qualities of the twills that enhanced the dignity of the wearer and, in the later phases of the medieval burgh, the broadcloths that provided tailors and seamstresses with scope to cut and shape garments, thereby enhancing the gender characteristics of the human form, give a tangible insight into the dress worn by the people. This study of the European-wide interconnectedness of cloth production and trade from the herding of local sheep on the hills surrounding Perth, the tending of silk worms in Mediterranean countries and the cultivation of bast fibres in various places, the processing of all these fibres, to the making of finished garments and their subsequent recycling, demonstrates the time-consuming skills that contributed to the value with which cloth was held.

The socio-technological thread explored here was one that was sometimes frayed as communities sought to maintain their trading privileges and, on a wider political level, when they were caught up in processes of Normanisation. In seeking to understand how people clothed themselves in medieval Perth, this study has emphasised the diversity of dress and group identities. However, our conceptual views should allow for a certain degree of contrariness as far as dress is concerned. Paradoxically, some members of the 13th- and 14th-century church were among the staunchest supporters of Scotland's independence, although in office they donned the standardised vestments of western Christendom. A telling expression of the desire of the clergy for both an independent Scotland and an independent Scottish Church can be seen in the actions of Robert Wishart, Bishop of Glasgow in 1306. Instead of excommunicating Robert I (the Bruce) for his part in the assassination of John Comyn, he produced from his episcopal store rich robes for a new king, and a banner with the arms of the previous king, 'which the indefatigable old man had been carefully hiding in his treasury for precisely this purpose and moment' (Barrow 1988, 149). In this case ceremonial garment forms were deployed in strategies that enhanced the activities of church and state.

Amongst the finds from the High Street a striking image of a cloaked figure prefigured a type of decoration that was to characterise 14th- and 15th-century dress throughout Europe. An anthropomorphic carved ivory handle (see Fascicule 4, Hall, 102–3 and 113 Illus 52, Cat No 45/A11–0013; Illus 99) wears a hooded garment with leaves resembling ornamental shapes known as dagges. These ornamental cut-outs, first used in the 13th century, were of cloth and they were used in the edging of garments such as capes and hoods. The fulled tabby cloth that was becoming increasingly available during the 14th century was suitable for cutting into such complex shapes. Edges were left unhemmed, since they would not fray easily (indeed one might note that fashion designers reintroduced such cut edges at the edges of garments in the first decade of the 21st century). Examples of an oak leaf dagge and long pendant leaf are known from Baynard's Castle in London (Crowfoot et al 1992, 194 and 198, Cat Nos 70 and 253). That the Perth knife handle looks to the future in Scotland is attested by 15th- and 16th-century carvings such as the angels bearing a monstrance on the Sacrament House at Deskford, Banffshire (Illus 100), and the sartorial extravagance which was to become typical of those centuries.

Illus 99 *Detail of anthropomorphic walrus ivory handle. Worked bone Cat No 45/A11–0013.*

Illus 100 *Elegantly clothed angels bearing a monstrance. Deskford Sacrament House, Banffshire, 15th–16th-century carving. (Courtesy Robert Gordon University)*

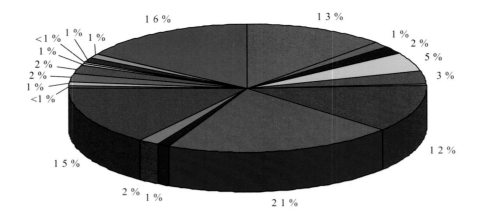

■ Tabby (2 Ply)	■ Tabby (single)	■ Silk Tabby
■ 2/1 Twill without Nap, ZZ	■ 2/1 Twill without Nap, ZS	■ 2/1 Twill without Nap, others
☐ Silk Twills	■ Carpet	■ Felt
■ Braids	■ Cordage	■ Yarns
☐ 2/2 Twill without Nap, ZZ	■ 2/2 Twill without Nap, ZS	■ 2/2 Twill with Nap
■ 2/1 Twill with Nap, ZZ	■ 2/1 Twill without Nap, ZS	■ 2/1 Twill with Nap, Others
■ Tablet-Woven Textiles	☐ Net	☐ Sprang

1100-1150

1150-1200

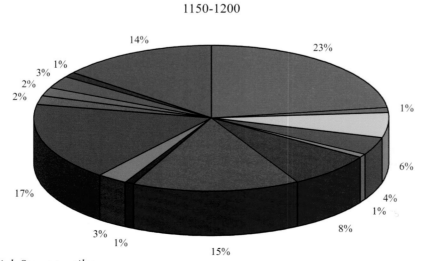

Illus 101 *Perth High Street textiles.*

The textiles catalogue
H Bennett, the late N Q Bogdan and P Z Dransart

*Notes on dyes, natural pigmentation of wools
and wool types are based on comments by Professor
M C Whiting (MW) and Dr Michael Ryder (MR).*

*Flavonols kaempferol, quercitin and rhamnetin are
abbreviated as K, Q and R.*

*Wools are designated: H hairy, HM hairy medium,
GM generalised medium, FGM fine, generalised
medium, M true medium, and S short.*

*† indicates item is not listed in original site Finds
Register, numbered 31a1 in RCAHMS archive.*

1 2/2 Twill without nap ZS Wool
Nine fragments of dark brown, light weight, unfelted 2/2 twill,
firm to the touch; the threads are unevenly packed. Dimensions:
c250mm by 50mm in all. System 1: smooth Z spun yarn, 10–12
threads per 10mm. System 2: similar S spun yarn, 15 threads
per 10mm.
A09–0003; C4797–4; MC004; Phase Ia; Rigs V and VI
Not illustrated

2 2/1 Twill without nap ZS Wool
Two small pieces (and a number of fragments), in poor
condition, of mid-brown, light weight 2/1 twill, unfelted but
slightly soft to the touch. Dimensions: a) 35mm by 75mm; b)
30mm by 30mm. System 1: smooth Z spun yarn, 11 threads per
10mm. System 2: similar S spun yarn, 9 threads per 10mm.
A9992; C3822–1; MC006, T3852; Phase Ib; Rig VI
Not illustrated

3 Yarn Wool
Coarse, mid-brown, 2S ply yarn, about 3mm in diameter. Length
230mm.
A9496; C3759–1/2; MC006; Phase Ib; Rig VI
Not illustrated

4 Tabby Silk
One larger and two small fragments of yellowish mid-brown
tabby with a fine warp and very thick weft; detailed examination
has suggested that glittering particles on the surface are mica
or quartz and not a metallic substance as originally supposed.
All three fragments are irregular in shape. Dimensions: a) 90mm
by 84mm; b) 54mm by 35mm; c) 35mm by 34mm. System 1:
very fine, Z twisted yarn, 32 threads per 10mm. System 2:
thick (about 1mm) slightly Z twisted yarn, which is of a matte
appearance, 16–17 threads per 10mm.
A9976; C3822–1; MC006, T3852; Phase Ib; Rig VI
Illus 26, 27

5 Tabby (2 ply yarn) Wool
Two unconserved, folded fragments of tabby. Tabby woven
from 2 ply yarns, dark brown in colour and with relatively coarse
fibres. Dimensions; a) 60mm by 50mm, b) 55mm by 50mm by
10mm. System 1: Z spun and 2S plied, 3 threads per 10mm.
System 2: the same.
A10072; C3829–1; MC010a, SA3829; Phase Ib; Rig VI
Not illustrated

6 Twill Silk
Two fragments, very worn, each consisting of two strips of pale
yellowish brown, 1/2 weft-faced compound twill. The ridges of
the twill form an S-diagonal. Both pieces consist of two strips
of fabric which are oversewn together along a long margin. The
other long margin retains traces of overstitching, but it is worn
and the details are unclear. In addition, there is overstitching
down the middle of each piece. One of the strips has a third
fragment of cloth of the same weave attached to only one side
of the piece, where it is attached by overstitching. These two
pieces are very similar to, and perhaps part of, the same fabric
as 46/A7323 below. Main warp and binding warp: fine, slightly
Z twisted yarn. There is a proportion of one main end to each
binding end; there are 16 binding warp ends per 10mm, and
about 16 main warp ends per 10mm. The main warp ends are
largely obscured and difficult to count. There are two wefts, of
untwisted yarn, which is coarser in diameter than the warp. The
weft count is 24 threads per 10mm on each face of the fabric.
The sewing thread is slightly S twisted silk yarn in a similar
shade to the fabric. Dimensions: a) 13mm by 185mm, b) 18mm
by 105mm.
A9500; C3792–1; B15 (West/East), PH3792; Phase Ic,Icc; Rigs
V and VI
Not illustrated

7 Yarn Wool
Very dark brown, coarse, hairy 2S ply yarn, 4–5mm in diameter.
Length 165mm.
A11202; C3737–1/2; M2.1b and B10, South Room–Floor/
Occupation (1); Phase Ic,Icc; Rigs V and VI
Not illustrated

8 2/1 Twill without nap ZZ Wool
Two fragments of dark brown, medium weight, closely woven
2/1 twill, unfelted and slightly harsh to the touch. Dimensions:
a) 90mm by 20mm, b) 70mm by 15mm. System 1: Z spun yarn,
8 threads per 10mm. System 2: similar yarn, 10 threads per
10mm.
A12612B; C3797–1/2; B10, South Room–Occupation (2b);
Phase Icc; Rig V
Not illustrated

9 2/2 Twill without nap ZS Wool
Two pieces of very dark brown, medium weight 2/2 twill, unfelted and firm to the touch; the yarns are unevenly packed and slightly variable in thickness. Dimensions: a) 70mm by 65mm, b) 65mm by 50mm. System 1: smooth Z spun yarn, about 9 threads per 10mm. System 2: the same.
A8086; C3690–1/2; B10, South Room–Floor (3); Phase Icc; Rig V
Not illustrated

10 Yarn Wool
Very dark brown, coarse 2S ply yarn, about 4mm in diameter. Length 122mm.
A11085; C4533–4; MC017; Phase Ia–Icc>; Rigs V and VI
Not illustrated

11 Tabby (2 ply yarn) Hair–?goat
Unconserved fragment, folded and in a fragile condition. The fabric is a very dark brown, coarse tabby. Dimensions: c140mm by 80mm by 40mm. System 1: S spun and 2Z plied, 2 threads per 10mm. System 2: S spun and 2Z plied with a loose ply angle, 2.5 threads per 10mm.
A11506; C4592–4; MC017; Phase Ia–Icc>; Rigs V and VI
Not illustrated

12 Tabby (2 ply yarn) Wool
One piece of dark brown, very heavy tabby, open-textured and harsh to the touch, with about 100mm of closed edge, of simple structure, remaining on one margin. Dimensions: 200mm by 120mm. System 1: warp, firm 2 ply yarn, Z spun and S plyed, 3–3.5 threads per 10mm. System 2: weft, similar yarn, 2–3 threads per 10mm.
A11155; C5079–3; MC031, Pit 5096; Phase Ia–Id; Rig V
Not illustrated

13 2/1 Twill without nap ZS Wool
One piece of reddish dark brown, light weight, unfelted 2/1 twill. Dimensions: 40mm by 105mm. System 1: smooth Z spun yarn, 16 threads per 10mm. System 2: similar S spun yarn, 16 threads per 10mm.
A11080a; C5097–3; MC025, Pit 5337; Phase (Ia–)Id; Rig V
Not illustrated

14 2/1 Twill without nap ZS Wool
Two pieces of coarse, heavy weight 2/1 twill, the smaller with the remains of closed edge, of simple structure, on one long margin; the yarns appear to have been spun from unsorted wool, as they are mottled in various shades of brown, and are of variable thickness. Dimensions: a) 140mm by 245mm; b) 90mm by 15mm. System 1: smooth Z spun yarn, 6 threads per 10mm. System 2: thicker S spun yarn 5 threads per 10mm.
A11080b; C5097–3; MC025, Pit 5337; Phase (Ia–)Id; Rig V
Not illustrated

15 Cordage ?Horse hair
Coarse hairs in various shades of brown, Z spun into a very thick thread which has been twisted back onto itself to create a firm 2 ply yarn about 10mm in diameter; only one end is complete. Length 200mm.
A11080c; C5097–3; MC025, Pit 5337; Phase (Ia–)Id; Rig V
Not illustrated

16 Yarn Wool
Fragments of mottled mid-brown, 2S ply yarn, 3mm in diameter.
A11080d; C5097–3; MC025, Pit 5337; Phase (Ia–)Id; Rig V
Not illustrated

17 Yarn Silk
Sixteen (?) pieces of fine, golden brown, loosely twisted 2S ply silk yarn; the threads are matted together, apparently arranged in groups of four, and are kinked as if they were originally woven; probably the remains of a piece of tablet weaving, the weft of which has disintegrated. Length up to 295mm.
A11512; C5097–3; MC025, Pit 5337; Phase (Ia–)Id; Rig V
Not illustrated

18 2/2 Twill without nap ZS Wool
One piece of dark brown, medium weight, unfelted and slightly loose-woven 2/2 diamond twill with inaccurate meetings, the threads unevenly packed. As far as can be judged from the fragment remaining, the pattern was intended to be symmetrical in the Z spun System, with 12 threads in each half of the diamond, but is asymmetrical in the second. In one area the pattern breaks down. This, if the Z spun yarn is regarded as the warp, is attributable to irregularities in the lifting of the heddles. Dimensions: 270mm by 100mm. System 1: smooth Z spun yarn, 6–7 threads per 10mm. System 2: similar S spun yarn, 6–7 threads per 10mm.
A12340a; C5097–3; MC025, Pit 5337; Phase (Ia–)Id; Rig V
Illus 11

19 2/1 Twill with nap ZS Wool
One piece of bright bluish-red, light weight, felted 2/1 twill; there is a light nap on one surface; there are fragments of the same fabric matted to one long margin, probably the location of a seam, but no sewing thread is visible. Dimensions: 155mm by 54mm. System 1: fine Z spun yarn, 13 threads per 10mm. System 2: similar S spun yarn, 13 threads per 10mm. Dye: kermes (MW).
A12340b; C5097–3; MC025, Pit 5337; Phase (Ia–)Id; Rig V
Illus 43

20 Tabby Wool
One narrow strip of soft, light-medium weight striped tabby, the threads in System 1 closely spaced and entirely covering those in System 2. The piece may possibly be the remains of some narrow textile such as a garter, but as there are no closed edges surviving this is uncertain. Dimensions: 90mm by 17mm. System 1 (warp?): smooth S spun threads, about 24 threads per 10mm; 32 threads remain, 24 of them bright yellowish brown, with 7 dark brown threads on one side and 1 on the other. System 2 (weft?): fine, smooth Z spun threads, in poor condition, widely spaced, 6 threads per 10mm.
A12340c; C5097–3; MC025, Pit 5337; Phase (Ia–)Id; Rig V
Illus 22

21 Tabby (2 ply yarn) Wool
One piece of dark brown, very heavy weight tabby, comparatively close-woven. Dimensions: 110mm by 180mm. System 1: firm 2 ply yarn, Z spun and S plyed, 2.5–3 threads per 10mm. System 2: the same.
A12340d; C5097–3; MC025, Pit 5337; Phase (Ia–)Id; Rig V
Not illustrated

22 2/1 Twill with nap ZS Wool

Two pieces of medium weight 2/1 twill, now worn, with the remains of a raised nap on one surface; the threads in System 2 are variable in thickness, and those in both systems are unevenly packed. Dimensions: a) 220mm by 58mm, b) 88mm by 15mm. System 1: fine, mainly light yellow brown, Z spun yarn, about 11 threads per 10mm. System 2: heavier S spun yarn, light yellow brown picks alternate with mid-brown or dark brown picks, about 12 threads per 10mm. The irregular striped effect created by the alternating colours is most visible on the face of the fabric in which the heavier S spun yarns predominate, but the effect is rendered less clear by the raising of the nap.
A12340e; C5097–3; MC025, Pit 5337; Phase (Ia–)Id; Rig V
Not illustrated

23 Tabby Wool

One piece of mid-brown, heavy medium weight unfelted tabby of uneven appearance; the yarn is variable in thickness and there are a number of shedding mistakes; there are traces of a possible seam line about 10mm from one long margin but there is no sewing thread. Dimensions: 135mm by 185mm. System 1: smooth Z spun yarn, 8 per 10mm. System 2: similar yarn, 8–9 per 10mm. No dye (MW).
A11551a; C5116–3; MC025, Pit 5337; Phase (Ia–)Id; Rig V
Not illustrated

24 2/2 Twill without nap ZS Wool

One piece, very worn, of even mid-brown, medium weight, unfelted 2/2 twill, slightly soft to the touch. Dimensions: 105mm by 150mm. System 1: plump, glossy Z spun yarn, 6–7 threads per 10mm. System 2: thicker and softer S spun yarn, 6 threads per 10mm. No dye: MW.
A11551b; C5116–3; MC025, Pit 5337; Phase (Ia–)Id; Rig V
Not illustrated

25 Tabby (2 ply yarn) Wool

Two pieces of worn, dark brown, heavy, open-textured tabby. Dimensions: a) 160mm by 80mm; b) 60mm by 50mm. System 1: very firm 2 ply yarn, Z spun and S plied, about 3 threads per 10mm. System 2: similar.
A09–0006; C5336–3; MC025, Pit 5337; Phase (Ia–)Id; Rig V
Not illustrated

26 Cordage Wool

Poor condition; 34 smooth, fine Z spun strands have been twisted together in S direction to create a soft cord about 6mm in diameter; two lengths of the cordage have been twisted with some unspun wool fibres. Length c90mm.
A09–0026a; C5336–3; MC025, Pit 5337; Phase (Ia–)Id; Rig V
Not illustrated

27 2/1 Twill without nap ZZ Wool

One fragment of dark brown, light weight, unfelted 2/1 twill, close-woven and firm to the touch. Dimensions: 53mm by 12mm. System 1: fine hard Z spun yarn, 17 threads per 10mm. System 2: similar yarn, 13–14 threads per 10mm.
A09–0026b; C5336–3; MC025, Pit 5337; Phase (Ia–)Id; Rig V
Not illustrated

28 Yarn Wool

Two pieces of very dark brown, coarse, hairy, firm 2S ply yarn, about 4mm in diameter. Length: a) 75mm, b) 165mm.
A8496; C3702–2; P5.1b; Phase Icc,Id; Rig VI
Not illustrated

29 Tabby (2 ply yarn) Wool

One piece (and two fragments) of mottled dark brown, very heavy tabby, coarse to the touch, but comparatively even and close-woven of its kind, with one long edge closed; the closed edge is of simple structure. Dimensions: 680mm by 210mm. System 1: warp, firm 2 ply yarn, Z spun and S plied, 3.5 threads per 10mm. System 2: weft, similar yarn, 2 threads per 10mm. Wool type: warp H, pigment +++, no dye; weft HM, pigment +++ no dye (MR).
A7439; C3652–2; MC030b; Phase Id,Ie; Rig VI
Illus 17

30 Braid Wool

Three fragments of braid, one with a knot joining two parts, plaited from thirteen elements; each element is a length of firm 2S ply, mid-brown yarn, slightly variable in thickness and tension. Length c280mm in all; width c18mm.
A11567a; C5158–3; MC037a, Pit 5157; Phase Ia–Ie; Rig VI
Illus 67, 68

31 2/2 Twill without nap ZZ Wool

One piece of sandy brown, medium weight, unfelted 2/2 twill, harsh to the touch. Dimensions: 60mm x 45mm. System 1: Z spun yarn, about 8 threads per 10mm. System 2: the same. No dye (MW).
A11567b; C5158–3; MC037a, Pit 5157; Phase Ia–Ie; Rig VI
Not illustrated

32 2/1 Twill without nap ZZ Wool

Seven fragments of light brown, light weight, unfelted 2/1 twill, harsh to the touch; one piece has 30mm of closed edge - a tubular selvedge of five threads, woven in tabby on one margin. Dimensions: c85mm by 70mm in all. System 1: warp, fine hard Z spun yarn, 11–12 threads per 10mm. System 2: weft, similar yarn, about 10 threads per 10mm.
A11567c; C5158–3; MC037a, Pit 5157; Phase Ia–Ie; Rig VI
Not illustrated

33 2/2 Twill without nap ZZ Wool

Two pieces (and three fragments), very worn, of bright mid-brown, light weight, unfelted 2/2 twill. Dimensions: a) 160mm by 40mm; b) 115mm by 40mm. System 1: smooth Z spun yarn, 12 threads per 10mm. System 2: similar yarn, about 10 threads per 10mm.
A11567d; C5158–3; MC037a, Pit 5157; Phase Ia–Ie; Rig VI
Not illustrated

34 Tabby Wool

Eight fragments of mid-brown, very heavy tabby, now matted and in poor condition. Dimensions: c120mm by 120mm. System 1: Z spun yarn, about 9 threads per 10mm. System 2: thicker (?) Z spun yarn, about 3 threads per 10mm (largely obscured by System 1).
A11567e; C5158–3; MC037a, Pit 5157; Phase Ia–Ie; Rig VI
Not illustrated

35 Tabby Wool
Numerous fragments of mid-brown, very light weight, open-textured tabby, very firm to the touch, the threads in both systems widely spaced; both spinning and weaving are generally even. Dimensions: c180mm by 180mm. System 1: very fine hard Z spun yarn, 15 threads per 10mm. System 2: similar yarn, 14 threads per 10mm. No dye (MW).
cf Crowfoot et al 1992, 43 Cat No 397 for worsted tabby, from Trig Lane, London, c1270.
A11567f; C5158–3; MC037a, Pit 5157; Phase Ia–Ie; Rig VI
Illus 20

36 Tabby (2 ply yarn) Wool
One piece of mottled mid-brown, very heavy tabby, slightly soft to the touch and constructed from yarn variable in thickness. Dimensions: 400mm by 230mm. System 1: 2 ply yarn, Z spun and S plyed, about 2.5 threads per 10mm. System 2: similar yarn, about 2 threads per 10mm.
A11567g; C5158–3; MC037a, Pit 5157; Phase Ia–Ie; Rig VI
Not illustrated

37 2/1 Twill with nap ZZ Wool
One piece of golden mid-brown, medium weight 2/1 twill, compact, and with comparatively even texture. Dimensions: 145mm by 60mm. System 1: smooth, firm Z spun yarn, 11 threads per 10mm. System 2: similar yarn, 12 threads per 10mm.
A11567h; C5158–3; MC037a, Pit 5157; Phase Ia–Ie; Rig VI
Not illustrated

38 2/1 Twill without Nap ZZ Wool
One piece, worn, of pinkish mid-brown, light weight, unfelted 2/1 twill, slightly soft to the touch; the spinning is regular, but the cloth has an uneven appearance. Dimensions: 235mm by 150 mm. System 1: fine Z spun yarn, 24 threads per 10mm. System 2: similar yarn, 18–19 threads per 10 mm. Dye: madder (MW).
A11567i; C5158–3; MC037a, Pit 5157; Phase Ia–Ie; Rig VI
Not illustrated

39 2/1 Twill without nap ZZ Wool
Three pieces of mid brown, light weight unfelted 2/1 twill, firm to the touch. Dimensions: a) 135mm by 55mm; b) 115mm by 40mm; c) 55mm by 30mm. System 1: smooth Z spun yarn, 12 threads per 10mm. System 2: similar yarn, 14–15 threads per 10mm.
A11567j; C5158–3; MC037a, Pit 5157; Phase Ia–Ie; Rig VI
Not illustrated

40 2/2 Twill without nap ZZ Wool
Two pieces of medium weight, closely woven 2/2 twill; the general appearance of the fabric is bright mid-brown, although the yarn varies in shade; the pieces are slightly felted in parts but this appears to be the result of wear. Dimensions: a) 90mm by 95mm; b) 100mm by 22mm. System 1: smooth Z spun yarn, 10 threads per 10mm. System 2: less firm Z spun yarn, 10 threads per 10mm.
A12342; C5158–3; MC037a, Pit 5157; Phase Ia–Ie; Rig VI
Not illustrated

41 2/1 Twill without nap ZZ Wool
Three pieces of bright mid-brown, light weight, unfelted, 2/1 twill, evenly spun and woven; piece a) has traces of a seam line, but no thread survives; a similar fabric to Cat No 59/A11142. Dimensions: a) 105mm by 50mm; b) 95mm by 35mm; c) 85mm by 35mm. System 1: fine Z spun yarn, 20 threads per 10mm. System 2: the same.
A11524; C5121–3; MC037b, WW5121; Phase Ib–If; Rig VI
Not illustrated

42 Tabby (2 ply yarn) Wool
One piece of mottled mid/dark brown, very heavy tabby, comparatively even and close-woven of its type. Dimensions: 310mm by 165mm. System 1: 2 ply yarn, S spun and Z plyed, 2.5 threads per 10mm. System 2: the same.
cf Bennett 1982, 199 Cat No 157 for eight fragments of woollen tabby with 2 ply yarn which is S spun and Z plied from Broad Street, Aberdeen, probably dating from the 14th century.
A12614; C4743–4; B16 (Phase 1), Pit 4742; Phase (Id)Ie; Rig VI
Not illustrated

43 Yarn Wool
Coarse, hairy, 2S ply yarn, about 4mm in diameter. Length 50mm.
A10490; C4505–4; B16 (Phase 1), Occupation (1b); Phase (Id) Ie; Rig VI
Not illustrated

44 Yarn Wool
Very dark brown, coarse, firm 2 S ply yarn, 3mm in diameter. Length 150mm.
A7312a; C3622–2; M14b(b); Phase Ie; Rig VI
Not illustrated

45 Yarn Wool
Dark brown, coarse, firm 2Z ply yarn, 2–3mm in diameter. Length 140mm.
A7312b; C3622–2; M14b(b); Phase Ie; Rig VI
Not illustrated

46 Twill Silk
A long strip of pale yellowish brown 1/2 weft-faced compound twill, folded along the weft axis, with the edges oversewn together in the form of a tube. The ridges of the twill form an S diagonal. There are three rows of overstitching; the first joins the edges of the fabric together in a tubular shape, and two more rows are executed along the folds at each side, to make a flat strip. Main warp and binding warp: fine, slightly Z twisted yarn. There is a proportion of one main end to each binding end. There are 14–15 binding warp ends per 10mm and 14–15 main warp ends per 10mm. The two wefts are of untwisted yarn, which is coarser in diameter than the warp. The weft count is 18 threads per 10mm on each face of the fabric. Some long exposed warp floats are visible on one face. The sewing thread is slightly S twisted silk yarn in a similar shade to the fabric. In addition, there is a short length of Z2S silk yarn, dyed pink, clinging to one of the stitched edges of the tube. This piece is very similar to Cat No 6/A9500. Dimensions: 16mm by 440mm.
A7323; C3622–2; M14b(b); Phase Ie; Rig VI
Illus 44

47 Tabby (2 ply yarn) Wool
One piece of mottled mid-brown, very heavy tabby, open-textured and slightly soft to the touch. System 1: 2 ply yarn, Z spun and S plyed, 2 threads per 10mm. System 2: similar yarn, 2–3 threads per 10mm.
A7339; C3622–2; M14b(b); Phase Ie; Rig VI
Not illustrated

48 Tabby (2 ply Yarn) Wool
One piece of mottled mid/dark brown, very heavy tabby, coarse to the touch and comparatively close-woven, with the remains of a simple closed edge on one margin. Dimensions: 670mm by 220mm. System 1: warp, firm 2 ply yarn, Z spun and S plyed, 2.5–3 threads per 10mm. System 2: weft, the same.
A7568; C3622–2; M14b(b); Phase Ie; Rig VI
Not illustrated

49 Yarn Wool
Two pieces, knotted together, of coarse, firm 2S ply dark brown yarn, 2–4mm in diameter. Length 150mm.
A7353a; C3625–2; M14b(b), Pit 3625; Phase Ie; Rig VI
Not illustrated

50 Yarn Wool
Coarse, hairy, very dark brown, 2S ply yarn, about 5mm in diameter. Length 215mm.
A7353b; C3625–2; M14b(b), Pit 3625; Phase Ie; Rig VI
Not illustrated

51 Yarn Wool
Dark brown, coarse, hairy, firm 2Z ply yarn, about 3mm in diameter. Length 155mm.
A7416a; C3625–2; M14b(b), Pit 3625; Phase Ie; Rig VI
Not illustrated

52 Yarn Wool
Very dark brown, coarse, hairy, 2S ply yarn, 3–4mm in diameter. Length 530mm.
A7416b; C3625–2; M14b(b), Pit 3625; Phase Ie; Rig VI
Not illustrated

53 Yarn Wool
Four pieces of very dark brown, coarse, hairy 2S ply yarn, 4–5mm in diameter. Length a) 120mm; b) 115mm; c) 80mm; d) 55mm.
A7429; C3625–2; M14b(b), Pit 3625 Phase Ie; Rig VI
Not illustrated

54 Yarn Wool
Two pieces of coarse, hairy, loosely 2S plyed, mid-brown yarn. Length a) 205mm; b) 165mm.
A7432; C3625–2; M14b(b), Pit 3625; Phase Ie; Rig VI
Not illustrated

55 Tabby (2 Ply yarn) Wool
One piece (and a number of fragments) of mottled mid-brown, very heavy tabby, of irregular appearance; the yarn is variable in thickness and tension and the threads are unevenly spaced; on one margin parts of a simple closed edge are intact. Dimensions: 380mm by 295mm. System 1: warp, 2 ply yarn, Z spun and S plyed, about 3 threads per 10mm. System 2: weft, similar, 2–3 threads per 10mm.
A09–0035; C5319–3; P5.3a; Phase If; Rig VI
Not illustrated

56 Yarn Wool
Coarse, hairy 2S ply, dark brown yarn, about 3mm in diameter. Length 170mm.
A10770; C5067–3; MC034a; Phase Ie(If); Rig V
Not illustrated

57 Yarn Wool
Two pieces of mottled mid/dark brown, coarse, hairy, 2S ply yarn, 3–4mm in diameter. Length a) 360mm; b) 90mm.
A09–0002; C5314–3; MC034a; Phase Ie(If); Rig V
Not illustrated

58 2/1 Twill with nap ZS Wool
Three pieces of even mid-brown, medium weight, lightly felted 2/1 twill, with a slight nap, now worn, on both surfaces; piece a) has one long edge turned 5mm under with a double fragment of the same fabric attached presumably the remains of a seam; the sewing thread has not survived; a) 80mm by 60mm, b) 40mm by 50mm, c) 60mm by 70mm. System 1: Z spun yarn, 12–14 threads per 10mm. System 2: thicker S spun yarn, 8 threads per 10mm.
A09–0011; C5324–3; MC034a; Phase Ie(If); Rig V
Not illustrated

59 2/1 Twill without nap ZZ Wool
One piece of bright mid-brown, light weight 2/1 twill, unfelted, close-woven and firm to the touch; the spinning is fine and even and the threads are regularly packed. This fabric is similar to Cat No 41/A11524. Dimensions: 185mm by 35mm. System 1: firm Z spun yarn, 23 threads per 10mm. System 2: similar yarn, 18 threads per 10mm.
A11142; C5089–3; MC053c; Phase If; Rig VI
Not illustrated

60 2/1 Twill without nap ZS Wool
One piece of dark brown, medium weight, lightly felted, uneven 2/1 twill. Dimensions: 120mm by 70mm. System 1: Z spun yarn, about 10 threads per 10mm. System 2: softer S spun yarn, about 5 threads per 10mm.
A11143; C5089–3; MC053c; Phase If; Rig VI
Not illustrated

61 Tabby (2 ply yarn) Wool
One piece of very dark brown, heavy tabby, comparatively close-textured and even. Dimensions: 310 mm by 130mm. System 1: firm 2 ply yarn, Z spun and S plyed, about 3 threads per 10mm. System 2: firm 2 ply yarn, Z spun and S plyed, about 3 threads per 10mm.
A12381; C5105–3; MC053c; Phase If; Rig VI
Not illustrated

62 Tabby (2 ply yarn) Wool
Seventeen fragments (about 7000 sq mm) of mottled mid/dark brown, very heavy tabby, open textured and comparatively soft to the touch, now very worn. System 1: 2 ply yarn, S spun and Z plyed, 2–3 per mm. System 2: similar.
A2828; C3604–2; MC044b; Phase If; Rig VI
Not illustrated

63 Tabby (2 ply yarn) Goathair
One piece of mottled light/dark brown, exceptionally heavy, coarse, uneven tabby, with 130mm of simple closed edge remaining on one margin; the spinning of the yarn varies from moderately firm to very weak. Dimensions: 250mm by 190mm. System 1: warp, 2 ply yarn, Z spun and S plyed, 1.5 threads per 10mm (but more closely packed towards the selvedge) System 2: weft, similar yarn, about 1.5 threads per 10mm. Goat +++ in both systems (MR).
cf a goat hair tabby woven from 2 ply yarns, which are Z spun and S plied, dating from 1380–1400 from site Baynard's Castle, London (Crowfoot et al 1992, Cat No 319). Other goat hair tabbies from medieval sites in London were spun and plied in the opposite directions (ibid, Table 8).
A9993a; C2386–4; B16 (Phase 2), Destruction; Phase If,IIa; Rig VI
Illus 18

64 Tabby (2 ply yarn) Goathair
One piece (and a number of fragments) of mottled mid/dark brown, very heavy tabby, slightly open-textured and coarse to the touch. On one edge there are the remains of a selvedge composed of five warp threads, the outermost two threads being treated as one element, and the remaining three as another element; it is not known whether this structure is the remains of a starting edge, or simply a strengthened side selvedge. Dimensions: 110mm by 210mm. System 1: warp (? runs parallel to closed edge), 2 ply yarn, Z spun and S plyed, 2 threads per 10mm. System 2: the same. Goathair, pigment +++ in warp and + in weft (MR).
A9993b; C2386–4; B16 (Phase 2), Destruction; Phase If,IIa; Rig VI
Illus 14

65 Yarn Wool
Unconserved very dark brown yarn with coarse fibres; Z spun and 2S plied, with a loose ply angle. Length 122mm.
A10414; C2386–4; B16 (Phase 2), Destruction; Phase If,IIa; Rig VI
Not illustrated

66 Tabby (2 ply yarn) Wool
Four fragments of mottled mid/dark brown, heavy tabby, of slightly open texture; the tension of the yarn and the spacing of the threads are uneven. Dimensions: a) 110mm by 75mm; b) 50mm by 70mm; c)110mm by 40mm; d) 70mm by 100mm. System 1: 2 ply yarn, Z spun and S plyed, about 2 threads per 10mm. System 2: similar yarn, 2–2.5 threads per 10mm.
A12534; C2386–4; B16 (Phase 2), Destruction; Phase If,IIa; Rig VI
Not illustrated

67 Yarn Wool
Three pieces of mottled mid/dark brown, coarse 2S ply yarn, about 4mm in diameter. Length a) 170mm; b) 55mm; c) 60mm.
A11086; C5052–3; P5.3b; Phase If,IIa; Rig VI
Not illustrated

68 Tabby (2 ply yarn) Wool
Two pieces (and a number of fragments) of mottled mid/dark brown, very heavy tabby, coarse to the touch, but evenly spun and woven; there is 30mm of closed edge, of simple structure, on one margin of one piece. Dimensions: a) 150mm by 180mm; b) 240mm by 150mm. System 1: warp, firm 2 ply yarn, Z spun and S plyed, 3 threads per 10mm. System 2: weft, similar yarn, 2 threads per 10mm.
A11510a; C5137–3; P5.3b; Phase If,IIa; Rig VI
Not illustrated

69 2/1 Twill without nap ZZ Wool
One small piece (and four smaller fragments) of bright mid-brown, light weight 2/1 twill of uneven appearance, unfelted and firm to the touch. Dimensions: 65mm by 42mm. System 1: firm Z spun yarn, 14 threads per 10mm. System 2: similar yarn, 12 threads per 10mm. Dye: Q, R, unknown? (MW).
A11510b; C5137–3; P5.3b; Phase If,IIa; Rig VI
Not illustrated

70 2/1 Twill with nap ZS Wool
One fragment of reddish mid-brown, light weight, slightly felted 2/1 twill with a light nap on both surfaces. System 1: Z spun yarn, 13–14 threads per 10mm. System 2: similar S spun yarn, 10–11 threads per 10mm.
A11510c; C5137–3; P5.3b; Phase If,IIa; Rig VI
Not illustrated

71 Yarn Wool
Two fragments of very dark brown, even 2S ply coarse yarn, about 3mm in diameter. Length a) 50mm; b) 160mm.
A10681; L3741; C5034–3; MC049; Phase IIa; Rig V
Not illustrated

72 Yarn Wool
Coarse, dark brown, 2S ply yarn. Length 92mm.
A09–0020; C5266–3; MC054a, Pit 5267; Phase (IIa)IIb; Rig VI
Not illustrated

73 Tabby (2 ply yarn) Wool
One piece of very dark brown, heavy tabby, comparatively close-textured. Dimensions: 100mm by 65mm. System 1: 2 ply yarn, Z spun and S plyed, 3.5 threads per 10mm. System 2: similar yarn, 2 threads per 10mm.
A6625; C3589–2; MC061; Phase IIb; Rig VI
Not illustrated

74 2/1 Twill with nap ZS Wool
One piece of bright mid-brown, light-medium weight, closely woven 2/1 twill, with a slight nap, now worn, on both surfaces; there is 50mm of closed edge – probably a side selvedge – on one margin; the warp threads are paired for 7mm to strengthen the edge. Dimensions: 130mm by 105mm. System 1: warp, fine Z spun yarn, 14 threads per 10mm. System 2: weft, similar S spun yarn, 12–13 threads per 10mm.
A11154; C5023–3; MC048; Phase (Ia–)IIa–IIc; Rig VI
Not illustrated

75 Tabby (2 ply yarn) Wool
Two pieces of very dark brown, heavy tabby, comparatively even and close-woven. Dimensions: a) 310mm by 280mm; b) 105mm by 200mm. System 1: firm 2 ply yarn, Z spun and S plyed, 2–2.5 threads per 10mm. System 2: similar yarn, 3 threads per 10mm.
A11673a; C5156–3; MC056, Pit 5155; Phase Ia–IIc; Rig VI
Not illustrated

76 Tabby (2 ply yarn) Wool
One piece of very dark brown, very heavy tabby, comparatively close-textured, with about 550mm of closed edge, of simple structure, on one margin. Dimensions: 620mm by 210mm. System 1: warp, 2 ply yarn, Z spun and S plyed, 2–2.5 threads per 10mm. System 2: weft, similar, 2 threads per 10mm.
A11673b; C5156–3; MC056, Pit 5155; Phase Ia–IIc; Rig VI
Not illustrated

77 2/2 Twill without nap ZS Wool
Unconserved, crumpled fragment of very dark brown, light weight, unfelted 2/2 twill. Dimensions: c85mm by 63mm by 8mm. System 1: Z spun, 8 threads per 10mm. System 2: S spun, 8 threads per 10mm.
A10417; C4489–3; B4, Floor; Phase IIc Rig VI
Not illustrated

78 Tabby (2 ply yarn) Wool
One piece (and four fragments) of mottled mid/dark brown, very heavy tabby, coarse to the touch, with 290mm of closed edge, of simple structure, on one long margin; the yarn is variable in both tension and thickness resulting in an uneven fabric; a length of thick, coarse 2 ply yarn, similar to that used in the weaving has been sewn (?) through the fabric at the closed edge for 60mm. Dimensions: 355mm by 270mm. System 1: warp, 2 ply yarn, Z spun and S plyed, about 2 threads per 10mm. System 2: weft, 2 ply yarn, Z spun and S plyed, about 2 threads per 10mm.
A10724; C5028–3; B4, 'Courtyard' Occupation; Phase IIc; Rig VI
Not illustrated

79 Yarn Wool
Two pieces of very dark brown, coarse, hairy 2S ply yarn, probably from Cat No 78/A10724. Length a) 215mm; b) 305mm.
A11162a; C5028–3; B4, 'Courtyard' Occupation; Phase IIc; Rig VI
Not illustrated

80 Tablet weaving Silk
Three fragments of cord, now bright mid-brown, originally about 2mm or 3mm in diameter. The cord has been woven with eight (?) four-hole tablets, from soft silk yarn, with a spiral weft which has all but disintegrated (there are possible traces of a frayed weft at one end). The warp has a slight Z twist, and it was used in pairs. Two fragments are knotted together, and measure 320mm overall. The third fragment is 185mm long; it has an overhand knot approximately at mid point.
A11162b; C5028–3; B4, 'Courtyard' Occupation; Phase IIc; Rig VI
Not illustrated

81 2/1 Twill without nap ZS Wool
One piece of dark brown, light-medium weight, lightly felted 2/1 twill; the yarn in both systems is very variable in thickness and tension, and there are a number of shedding mistakes. Dimensions: 190mm by 490mm. System 1: Z spun yarn, 10–13 threads per 10mm. System 2: heavier less firmly spun, S spun yarn, about 9 threads per 10mm.
A12553a; C5028–3; B4, 'Courtyard' Occupation; Phase IIc; Rig VI
Not illustrated

82 2/2 Twill without nap ZS Wool
Probably *vaðmal*. One piece of medium weight, unfelted, slightly loose-woven 2/2 twill, in two shades of brown. Dimensions: 270mm by 280mm. System 1: smooth Z spun, dark brown yarn, 11–12 threads per 10mm. System 2: softer S spun, mid-brown yarn, 8 threads per 10mm.
A12553b; C5028–3; B4, 'Courtyard' Occupation; Phase IIc; Rig VI
Illus 31

83 2/1 Twill (?) with nap ZS Wool
Two strips of reddish mid-brown, heavily felted fabric; the structure is obscured by the dense nap on both surfaces, but is probably 2/1 twill. Dimensions: a) 125mm by 20mm; b) 120mm by 10mm. System 1: Z spun, no count possible. System 2: S spun, no count possible.
A12553c; C5028–3; B4, 'Courtyard' Occupation; Phase IIc; Rig VI
Not illustrated

84 2/2 Twill with nap ZZ Wool
One piece of dark brown, light weight 2/2 twill, loosely woven. The fabric shows no sign of milling and the weave is clearly visible, but there is a light, shaggy 'nap', which has not been sheared, on both surfaces; this results, perhaps, from the use of yarn spun from fleece prepared by combing but without the short staple removed. There is a closed edge on one long margin with the transverse threads looped and twisted before being returned to the fabric. This is almost certainly a starting edge. There is a knot in the warp, and at one point there is a gap in the fabric where the threads have been pushed apart, perhaps by a pin. Dimensions: 50mm by 245mm. System 1: warp, firm Z spun yarn, 10 threads per 10mm. System 2: weft (parallel to closed edge), similar yarn, 15 threads per 10mm.
A12553d; C5028–3; B4, 'Courtyard' Occupation; Phase IIc; Rig VI
Illus 15, 32

85 Yarn Wool
Two fragments of mottled dark brown, coarse hairy 2S ply yarn, about 4mm in diameter. Length a) 90mm; b) 125mm.
A11090; C5055–3; MC066; Phase IIc; Rig VI
Not illustrated

86 Yarn Wool
Two unconserved fragments of dark brown yarn, with coarse fibres; Z spun and 2S plied with a maximum width of 5mm. Length a) 55mm; b) 30mm.
A10347; C2382–4; M1.1f; Phase IIb–IId; Rig VI
Not illustrated

87 Tabby (2 ply yarn) Wool
One fragment of dark brown, very heavy tabby, close textured and soft to the touch; the yarn is irregular in tension and thickness. Dimensions: 130mm by 100mm. System 1: 2 ply yarn, Z spun and S plyed, 2 threads per 10mm. System 2: 2 ply yarn, Z spun and S plyed, 2 threads per 10mm.
A8857; C3584–2; MC069, Pit 3584; Phase (IIc)IId; Rig VI
Not illustrated

88 Yarn Wool
Unconserved very dark brown yarn, with coarse fibres; Z spun and 2S plied, 3mm diameter. Length at least 200mm.
A10036; C2365–4; M1.1c; Phase IId; Rig VI
Not illustrated

89 2/2 Twill without nap ZZ Wool
One piece of mottled brown, coarse, heavy, unfelted 2/2 twill; the yarn varies in thickness and also in colour - the result of spinning from unsorted wool. Dimensions: 290mm by 240mm. System 1: smooth Z spun yarn, 4–5 threads per 10mm. System 2: smooth Z spun yarn, 4–5 threads per 10mm.
A10075; C2365–4; M1.1c; Phase IId; Rig VI
Not illustrated

90 2/1 Twill without nap ZS Wool
One fragment of mid-brown, light weight, unfelted 2/1 twill. Dimensions: 55mm by 15mm. System 1: smooth Z spun yarn, 13 threads per 10mm. System 2: thicker S spun yarn, 11 threads per 10mm.
A10076; C2365–4; M1.1c; Phase IId; Rig VI
Not illustrated

91 2/1 Twill without nap ZZ Wool
One piece, worn, of mid-brown, light weight, unfelted 2/1 twill; 70mm by 60mm. System 1: fine Z spun yarn, 15 threads per 10mm. System 2: the same.
A10193a; C2365–4; M1.1c; Phase IId; Rig VI
Not illustrated

92 2/2 Twill without nap ZZ Wool
One piece of reddish dark brown light medium weight, closely woven 2/2 twill, with a closed edge on one long margin; the edge has been strengthened by the outmost three warp threads being treated as one; both surfaces are slightly matted but this appears to be the result of wear. Dimensions: 155mm by 10mm. System 1: warp, fine hard Z spun yarn, 15 threads per 10mm (estimate). System 2: weft, softer Z spun yarn, 11 threads per

10mm. Wool type: warp M, no pigment, green-brown dye; weft FGM, no pigment, trace of blue dye (MR).
A10193b; C2365–4; M1.1c; Phase IId; Rig VI
Not illustrated

93 2/1 Twill without nap, Others Wool
One fragment, worn, of coarse, heavy 2/1 twill. The fabric appears to have had a coloured pattern. Dimensions: 50mm by 70mm. System 1: warp, fine, dark, S spun threads and lighter Z spun threads, softer and more variable in thickness; about 4 threads per 10mm. System 2: two pairs of fine, light brown, S spun threads (each pair acting as one element), alternate with two thicker, S spun dark brown threads; one dark thread is approximately as wide as each pair of light threads; 3 threads per 10mm. Wool type: System 1 HM, pigment ++, no dye; System 2 M, pigment +, no dye (MR).
A10193c; C2365–4; M1.1c; Phase IId; Rig VI
Illus 9

94 2/1 Twill (?) without nap ZZ Wool
One fragment, in poor condition, of coarse, heavy, slightly open fabric, probably 2/1 twill. Dimensions: 80mm by 60mm. System 1: Z spun yarn, variable in thickness and tension, about 4 threads per 10mm. System 2: heavier Z spun yarn, about 4 threads per 10mm.
A10193d; C2365–4; M1.1c; Phase IId; Rig VI
Not illustrated

95 2/2 Twill without nap ZS Wool
Two pieces (and two fragments) of mid-brown, medium weight 2/2 twill, closely woven and slightly felted; on both pieces one margin has been turned under to a depth of about 15mm and caught down with a firm 2S ply sewing thread of similar colour. Dimensions: a) 115mm by 130mm; b) 130mm by 105mm. System 1: smooth, firm Z spun yarn, 8 threads per 10mm. System 2: similar S spun yarn 8 threads per 10mm. Dye: Q, K, R, unknown (MW).
A10624a; C2365–4; M1.1c; Phase IId; Rig VI
Not illustrated

96 2/2 Twill without nap ZZ Wool
Three pieces of coarse, heavy medium weight, mid-brown, slightly felted 2/2 twill, the threads variable in thickness and unevenly packed. Dimensions: a) 100mm by 55mm; b) 160mm by 85mm; c) 175mm by 100mm. System 1: smooth but uneven Z spun yarn, about 10 threads per 10mm. System 2: similar yarn, 6–7 threads per 10mm.
A10624b; C2365–4; M1.1c; Phase IId; Rig VI
Not illustrated

97 2/1 Twill without nap ZS Wool
Two pieces of dark brown/faded grey-brown, closely woven 2/1 twill. The warp is smooth and even; it is closely spaced and on one face it entirely covers the weft. Both fragments have one closed edge of simple structure, with the warp running parallel to the selvedge. In both pieces there are frequent weaving errors probably caused by shedding problems. Dimensions: a) 347mm by 67mm; b) 316mm by 45mm. System 1: warp, Z spun, in a) 20 threads per 10mm and in b) 24–26 threads per 10mm. System 2: weft, S spun, in a) 14 threads per 10mm and in b) 12

threads per 10mm.
A09–0001; C4706–4; M1.1c; Phase IId; Rig VI
Not illustrated

98 2/1 Twill without nap ZZ Wool
One piece, in a poor state of preservation, of heavy weight, black 2/1 twill, unfelted, soft and open-textured, uneven in both spinning and weaving; there is a tear, about 120mm long, at one end, which has been mended by oversewing with fine, very firmly Z spun yarn used double; 430mm by 280mm. System 1: smooth but irregular Z spun yarn, 4–7 threads per 10 mm. System 2: similar yarn, 5–6 threads per 10mm. Wool type: System 1 H, pigment +++; System 2 HM, pigment +++ (MR). No dye (MW).
A10332; C4470–3; M1.1c, Pit 5005; Phase IId; Rig VI
Not illustrated

99 2/1 Twill with nap ZS Wool
Two strips of dark brown, medium weight, compact and felted 2/1 twill; the nap is pronounced on one side but less so on the other; the long edges of piece a) are curled in, as if they had been seamed. Dimensions: a) 220mm by 35mm; b) 205mm by 35mm. System 1: Z spun yarn, about 16 threads per 10mm. System 2: thicker S spun yarn, about 11 threads per 10mm. Wool type: HM, pigment ++, no dye in both systems (MR).
A10787; C4470–3; M1.1c, Pit 5005; Phase IId; Rig VI
Not illustrated

100 2/1 Twill without nap ZS Wool
Three pieces of sandy brown, light medium weight 2/1 twill, unfelted but comparatively close-woven and soft to the touch. Dimensions: a) 345mm by 365mm; b) 90mm by 155mm; c) 195mm by 180mm. System 1: Z spun yarn, 13 threads per 10mm. System 2: similar S spun yarn, 12 threads per 10mm.
A11550; C4470–3; M1.1c, Pit 5005; Phase IId; Rig VI
Illus 36

101 Tabby (2 ply yarn) Wool
Two pieces of mottled mid/dark brown, very heavy tabby, comparatively close-textured. Dimensions: a) 205mm by 170mm; b) 130mm by 100mm. System 1: 2 ply yarn, Z spun and S plyed, 2 threads per 10mm. System 2: the same.
A12343; C4470–3; M1.1c, Pit 5005; Phase IId; Rig VI
Not illustrated

102 Tablet weaving Silk
Three fragments of a length of cord, about 2mm in diameter, now mid-brown, constructed from 16 strands of 2S ply silk yarn; the cord appears to have been tablet-woven with a spiral weft, but the weft has disintegrated and the cord become partially unravelled. Two pieces of the cord have been knotted together and 20mm below the knot the ends are bound for 18mm with single ply silk yarn of a similar colour and an upper layer of a darker 2 ply yarn; below the binding the component threads of the cord fall loose but may originally have been woven. Length two pieces together 340mm; remaining fragment 410mm.
A12651; C4687–4; MC081a; Phase IId; Rig V
Illus 55

103 Tabby (2 ply yarn) Wool
One piece of mottled mid/dark brown very heavy tabby, slightly open-textured. Dimensions: 370mm by 210mm. System 1: hairy 2 ply yarn, Z spun and S plyed, 1.5–2 threads per 10mm. System 2: similar yarn, about 2 threads per 10mm. No dye (MW).
A12650; C4705–4; MC084; Phase IId, IIe; Rig VI
Not illustrated

104 2/2 Twill without nap ZZ Wool
Two pieces (and one fragment) of dark brown, light weight, unfelted 2/2 twill, with the weave changing direction part way across the larger piece; probably the same fabric as Cat No 105/A10057. Dimensions: a) 60mm by 70mm; b) 55mm by 65mm. System 1: smooth Z spun, 13 threads per 10mm. System 2: the same.
A9975; C4459–3; M1.1d; Phase IId, IIe; Rig VI
Illus 10, 29

105 2/2 Twill without nap ZZ Wool
One piece (and one fragment) of even dark brown, light weight, unfelted 2/2 twill; part way across the piece the twill reverses (see Illus 18, 19 and textile Cat No 104/A9975). Dimensions: 115mm by 100mm. System 1: smooth Z spun yarn, 13 threads per 10mm. System 2: the same. No dye (MW).
A10057; C4468–3; M1.1d; Phase IId, IIe; Rig VI
Not illustrated

106/Tabby (2 ply yarn) Wool?
One piece of mottled mid/dark brown, exceptionally heavy, coarse and uneven tabby, with 315mm of simple closed edge on one margin; the yarn, which is spun from coarse, springy fibres, is irregular in thickness and tension. Dimensions: 420mm by 430mm. System 1: warp, slack 2 ply yarn, Z spun and S plyed, about 1.5 threads per 10mm. System 2: weft, similar yarn, 1–2 threads per 10mm.
A10668; C4492–3; M1.1a; Phase IId, IIe; Rig VI
Not illustrated

107 Tabby (2 ply yarn) Wool
One piece of dark brown, very heavy tabby, coarse and open-textured. Dimensions: 150mm by 200mm. System 1: 2 ply yarn, S spun and Z plyed, about 2.5 threads per 10mm. System 2: similar yarn, about 2 threads per 10mm. Wool type: H, pigment ++, no dye in both systems (MR).
A10784; C4492–3; M1.1a; Phase IId, IIe; Rig VI
Not illustrated

108 2/1 Twill without nap ZZ Wool
One piece of even mid brown, medium weight, unfelted 2/1 twill, closely woven and firm to the touch, with 50mm of closed edge of simple structure remaining on one margin; the warp threads are closely packed, and on one surface the fabric is strongly warp-faced. Dimensions: 180mm by 140mm. System 1: warp, fine smooth Z spun yarn, 18 threads per 10mm. System 2: weft, thicker Z spun yarn, 9 threads per 10mm. Wool type: HM, pigment +, no dye in both systems (MR).
A6125; C3582–2; M1.1d and M1.1e; Phase IId–IIf; Rig VI
Illus 33

109 Tabby (2 ply yarn) Wool
One piece of very dark brown, heavy tabby, harsh to the touch
and comparatively close-woven. Dimensions: 90mm by 130mm.
System 1: very firm 2 ply yarn, S spun and Z plyed, about 3
threads per 10mm. System 2: the same. No dye (MW).
A9907; C3582–2; M1.1d and M1.1e; Phase IId–IIf; Rig VI
Not illustrated

110 2/1 Twill with nap ZS Wool
One strip of even mid-brown, medium weight 2/1 twill, felted
and with the nap raised on both surfaces. Dimensions: 35mm
by 160mm. System 1: soft Z spun yarn, 10 threads per 10mm.
System 2: similar S spun yarn, 10 threads per 10mm.
A9901; C4451–3; M1.1e; Phase IIf; Rig VI
Not illustrated

111 2/1 Twill without nap ZZ Wool
One piece of bright mid-brown, light-medium weight 2/1 twill,
unfelted but closely woven, even in spinning and weaving.
Dimensions: 115mm by 95mm. System 1: firm Z spun yarn,
12 threads per 10mm. System 2: similar yarn, 11 threads per
10mm.
A6649; C3590–2; B5, North Room–Floor/Occupation (1); Phase
IIa–IIff; Rig V
Not illustrated

112 Felt Wool
Fragments of mid-brown, heavy weight felt, in poor condition.
Dimensions: c200mm by 60mm in all.
A6775; C3590–2; B5, North Room–Floor/Occupation (1); Phase
IIa–IIff; Rig V
Not illustrated

113 2/1 Twill without nap ZZ Wool
Four pieces of mid-brown, light medium weight unfelted 2/1
twill. Dimensions: a) 80mm by 65mm; b) 70mm by 50mm; c)
45mm by 35mm; d) 40mm by 35mm. System 1: smooth Z spun
yarn, 11 threads per 10mm. System 2: heavier (?) Z spun, 10–11
threads per 10mm. Wool type: System 1 HM, pigment + (little
and few), no dye; System 2 GM, pigment + (few), no dye (MR).
A8863a; C3577–2; B5, North Room–Floor/Occupation (2);
Phase IIa–IIff; Rig V
Not illustrated

114 2/1 Twill (?) with nap ZS Wool
One long strip of heavy, mid-brown cloth with a nap on both
surfaces; the weave appears to be 2/1 twill but is largely
obscured by heavy dressing; both colour and texture are
uneven. Dimensions: 400mm by 10–20mm. System 1: Z spun,
no count possible. System 2: thicker, S spun, no count possible.
No dye (MW).
A8863b; C3577–2; B5, North Room–Floor/Occupation (2);
Phase IIa–IIff; Rig V
Not illustrated

115 2/1 Twill (?) with nap ZS Wool
One strip of heavy, very felted, mid-brown cloth with nap on
both surfaces, similar to Cat No 114/A8863b. Dimensions:
270mm by 30mm. System 1: Z spun, no count possible System
2: spun, no count possible. Wool type: System 1 HM, pigment +,

no dye; System 2 H, pigment ++, no dye (MR).
A8871; C3577–2; B5, North Room–Floor/Occupation (2); Phase
IIa–IIff; Rig V
Not illustrated

116 2/1 Twill with nap ZS Wool
One piece of very heavily felted, mid-brown, medium weight
2/1 twill with the nap raised on both surfaces. Dimensions:
110mm by 40mm. System 1: fine Z spun yarn, about 10 threads
per 10mm. System 2: S spun yarn, about 12 threads per 10mm
(estimated). Wool type: HM, pigment +, no dye in both systems
(MR).
A6716; C3587–2; B5, North Room–MW3587; Phase IIa–IIff; Rig
V
Not illustrated

117 Tablet weaving(?) Silk
Fragment of cord in poor condition, about 3mm in diameter,
composed of light brown, fine 2S ply silk yarn; probably
originally tablet-woven with a spiral weft. Length 115mm.
A9899; C2607–3; B23, North Room–Occupation (1a); Phase
IIb–IIff; Rig V
Not illustrated

118 Tabby (2 ply yarn) Wool
Two pieces of very dark brown, heavy tabby, coarse to the
touch. Dimensions: a) 80mm by 40mm; b) 40mm by 60mm.
System 1: very firm 2 ply yarn, S spun and Z plyed, about 3
threads per 10mm. System 2: similar.
A09–0007; C2607–3; B23, North Room–Occupation (1a);
Phase IIb–IIff; Rig V
Not illustrated

119 Tabby (2 ply yarn) Wool
Three pieces of very dark brown, heavy tabby, coarse to the
touch and comparatively close-textured. Dimensions: a) 102mm
by 68mm; b) 130mm by 140mm; c) 55mm by 47mm. System
1: very firm 2 ply yarn, Z spun and S plyed, 3.5–4 threads per
10mm. System 2: the same. Dye: minute trace of unknown blue
dye? (MW).
A09–0136; C9556–9; B27, North Room and South Room–
Occupation (1a); Phase <IIc–IIff; Rig VII
Not illustrated

120 Tabby (2 ply yarn) Wool
One piece of very dark brown, heavy tabby, like Cat No 119/
A09–0136 and probably part of the same fabric. Dimensions:
290mm by 260mm. System 1: very firm 2 ply yarn, Z spun and S
plyed, 3.5–4 threads per 10mm. System 2: the same.
A09–0137; C9556–9; B27, North Room and South Room–
Occupation (1a); Phase <IIc–IIff; Rig VII
Not illustrated

121 2/2 Twill without nap ZS Wool
One piece, very worn, of mid-brown, light medium weight,
unfelted 2/2 twill. Dimensions: 115mm by 70mm. System 1:
fine smooth Z spun yarn, 11–13 threads per 10mm. System 2:
heavier S spun yarn, 8 threads per 10mm.
A10496; C2385–4; M10; Phase IId–IIg; Rig V
Not illustrated

122 Yarn Wool
Unconserved bundle of yarn, very fragile and in a brittle
condition. Dark brown, with coarse fibres; Z spun and 2S plied,
5–7mm wide.
A9520; C2342–4; B12, Occupation (1b); Phase IIe–IIg; Rig VI
Not illustrated

123 Tabby (?) (2 ply yarn) Wool?
Unconserved, matted fragment in a fragile condition. The weave
is probably tabby, and the yarns are coarse, some 5–6mm in
diameter, very dark brown in colour. Dimensions: c60mm by
55mm by 15mm. System 1: Z spun and 2S plied, 1.5 threads
per 10mm. The yarns in System 2 are of a similar colour, but the
details are unclear.
A9891; C2342–4; B12, Occupation (1b); Phase IIe–IIg; Rig VI
Not illustrated

124 Yarn Wool
One fragment, in poor condition, of coarse 2S ply yarn. Length
150mm.
A9842; C2346–4; B12, Pit 2345; Phase IIe–IIg; Rig VI
Not illustrated

125 2/1 Twill with nap ZS Wool
One piece of mid-brown, medium weight, felted 2/1 twill, with
the nap, now worn, raised on both surfaces. Dimensions:
120mm by 50mm. System 1: Z spun yarn, 14 threads per 10mm.
System 2: slightly heavier S spun yarn, 12 threads per 10mm.
Wool type: System 1 M, no pigment, no dye; System 2 GM, no
pigment, no dye (MR).
A9478a; C2346–4; B12, Pit 2345; Phase IIe–IIg; Rig VI
Not illustrated

126 2/1 Twill with nap ZZ Wool
Two pieces, very worn, of rich mid-brown, light weight 2/1 twill
with a slight nap on one surface. Dimensions: a) 110mm by
30mm; b) 120mm by 30mm. System 1: fine Z spun yarn, 13–14
threads per 10mm. System 2: similar yarn, about 11 threads per
10mm.
A9478b; C2346–4; B12, Pit 2345; Phase IIe–IIg; Rig VI
Not illustrated

127 2/1 Twill without nap ZS Wool
One piece of dark brown, light weight, close-woven, unfelted 2/1
twill. Dimensions: 70mm by 45mm. System 1: Z spun yarn, 18
threads per 10mm. System 2: similar S spun yarn, 12 threads
per 10mm. No dye (MW).
A9478c; C2346–4; B12, Pit 2345; Phase IIe–IIg; Rig VI
Not illustrated

128 2/1 Twill with nap ZS Wool
Three pieces of moderately heavy 2/1 twill with slight nap on
both surfaces, of very irregular appearance; the yarns are
mottled, in shades from light to dark brown, suggesting the
use of unsorted wool; the threads in both warp and weft are
irregularly spaced. Dimensions: a) 180mm by 80mm; b) 120 by
75mm; c) 80 by 40mm. System 1: Z spun yarn, comparatively
firm but variable in tension, 7–8 threads per 10mm. System 2:
thicker and less firm S spun yarn, about 4 threads per 10mm.
Wool type: warp H, no pigment, no dye (MR).
A9481; C2346–4; B12, Pit 2345; Phase IIe–IIg; Rig VI
Not illustrated

129 Yarn Wool
Two fragments of coarse, dark brown, 2S ply yarn, 2mm in
diameter. Dimensions: a) 80mm; b) 105mm.
A10071; C2346–4; B12, Pit 2345; Phase IIe–IIg; Rig VI
Not illustrated

130 2/1 Twill without nap ZS Wool
One piece of dark reddish brown, light medium weight 2/1 twill,
lightly felted and soft to the touch; the threads are irregularly
packed and the fabric has an uneven appearance. Dimensions:
160mm by 80mm. System 1: Z spun yarn, 12 threads per 10mm.
System 2: S spun yarn, variable in thickness, about 12 threads
per 10mm.
A8833; C2285–4; B12, Occupation (1/2); Phase IIe–IIg; Rig VI
Not illustrated

131 Felt Wool
One piece of mid-brown, heavy weight felt, now of variable
thickness. Dimensions: 200mm by 200mm. Wool type: H,
pigment +, no dye (MR).
A9126; C2611–3; M1.2, Pit 2648; Phase <IIg(IIh); Rig VI
Illus 51

132 2/1 Twill without nap ZS Wool
One piece of dark brown, light weight, unfelted close-woven 2/1
twill; the spinning is firm and even and the threads are evenly
packed but there are weaving faults visible in both systems.
Dimensions: 175mm by 57mm. System 1: fine, hard Z spun yarn,
20 threads per 10mm. System 2: the same.
A9129; C2611–3; M1.2, Pit 2648; Phase <IIg(IIh); Rig VI
Not illustrated

133 Tabby Wool
One fragment of very dark brown, medium weight, unfelted
tabby. Dimensions: 35mm by 40mm. System 1: plump, glossy
Z spun yarn, 6 threads per 10mm. System 2: similar yarn, 5–6
threads per 10mm.
A9130; C2611–3; M1.2, Pit 2648; Phase <IIg(IIh); Rig VI
Not illustrated

134 2/1 Twill without nap ZS Wool
One piece of dark brown, light weight, unfelted 2/1 twill; the
threads are irregularly packed and variable in thickness; 300mm
by 180mm. System 1: smooth Z spun yarn, 18 threads per
10mm. System 2: softer S spun yarn, 12 threads per 10mm. No
dye (MW).
A9271; C2611–3; M1.2, Pit 2648; Phase <IIg(IIh); Rig VI
Not illustrated

135 Yarn Wool
Fragment of dark brown yarn, S spun and 2Z plied, 4mm
diameter. Length 125mm.
A9320Aa; C2611–3; M1.2, Pit 2648; Phase <IIg(IIh);Rig VI
Not illustrated

136 Yarn Wool?
Fragment of mottled dark brown yarn with coarse fibres, Z spun,
3–4mm diameter. Length 105mm.
A9320Ab; C2611–3; M1.2, Pit 2648; Phase <IIg(IIh); Rig VI
Not illustrated

137 Yarn Wool?

At least two fragments of dark brown yarn with coarse fibres, Z spun, 3.5mm diameter. There are two knots present, one of which is a larkshead knot. Length 145mm.

A9320Ac; C2611–3; M1.2, Pit 2648; Phase <IIg(IIh); Rig VI

Not illustrated

138 2/1 Twill with nap ZS Wool

Small offcut of bright bluish-red, felted 2/1 twill with a raised nap on both surfaces. The raised nap obscures the weave. Dimensions: 60mm by 6mm. System 1: Z spun, estimated 12 threads per 10mm. System 2: S spun, approximately 14 threads per 10mm.

A9326; C2611–3; M1.2, Pit 2648; Phase <IIg(IIh); Rig VI

Not illustrated

139 2/1 Twill without nap ZS Wool

One piece of very dark brown, medium weight, unfelted 2/1 twill, woven from smooth, glossy yarns. Dimensions: 160mm by 130mm. System 1: Z spun yarn, about 15 threads per 10mm. System 2: similar S spun yarn, 11 threads per 10mm. Wool type: System 1 M, pigment +++; System 2 GM, pigment +++ (MR). No dye (MW).

A9506; C2611–3; M1.2, Pit 2648; Phase <IIg(IIh); Rig VI

Not illustrated

140 2/2 Twill without nap ZZ Wool

One piece of dark brown, medium weight, unfelted 2/2 twill, closely woven and firm to the touch. Dimensions: 120mm by 120mm. System 1: firm Z spun yarn 10 threads per 10mm. System 2: the same.

A9522; C2611–3; M1.2, Pit 2648; Phase <IIg(IIh); Rig VI

Not illustrated

141 2/1 Twill with nap ZS Wool

One piece of distinct reddish brown, medium weight 2/1 twill, heavily felted and compact, with the nap raised on both surfaces. Dimensions: 30mm by 30mm. System 1: fine Z spun yarn, about 10 threads per 10mm. System 2: thicker S spun yarn, about 10 threads per 10mm (estimated).

A9536a; C2611–3; M1.2, Pit 2648; Phase <IIg(IIh); Rig VI

Not illustrated

142 2/1 Twill with nap, Others (SS) Wool

One fragment of mid-brown, medium weight 2/1 twill, felted and soft to the touch. Dimensions: 10mm by 85mm. System 1: S spun yarn, about 8 threads per 10mm. System 2: similar yarn, about 8 threads per 10mm. cf a 2/1 twill without nap, SS, probably 14th-century, from Kirk Close, Perth (Bennett 1987, 164). Another 2/1 twill, felted on both sides, with S warp and S weft is from 30–46 Upperkirkgate, Aberdeen (Phase 2b) (Gabra-Sanders 2001a, 232).

A9536b; C2611–3; M1.2, Pit 2648; Phase <IIg(IIh); Rig VI

Not illustrated

143 2/1 Twill (?) with nap ZS Wool

Three pieces of mid-brown, heavy medium weight, heavily felted fabric, with nap on both surfaces; the weave is almost totally obscured, but may be 2/1 twill. Dimensions: a) 160mm by 20mm; b) 72mm by 11mm; c) 65mm by 10mm. System 1: Z spun, no count possible. System 2: S spun, no count possible. Wool type: HM, no pigment, no dye in both systems (MR).

A9536c; C2611–3; M1.2, Pit 2648; Phase <IIg(IIh); Rig VI

Not illustrated

144 2/1 Twill without nap ZZ Wool

Unconserved fragment of mid brown, light weight, closely woven, unfelted 2/1 twill; 47mm by 76mm. The piece is trapezoidal in shape, with four cut edges. System 1: Z spun, 16 threads per 10mm. System 2: S spun, 16 threads per 10mm.

A10409a; C2611–3; M1.2, Pit 2648; Phase <IIg(IIh); Rig VI

Not illustrated

145 2/1 Twill with nap ZS Wool

Unconserved fragment, folded back on itself. The fabric is a light weight 2/1 twill, rich mid-brown in colour, with a raised nap on the surface in which the S spun elements predominate. There is a closed edge 130mm long, consisting of a selvedge, 10mm wide, of tabby weave in which the Z elements are used double and the S elements single. Dimensions: c100mm by 50mm. System 1: Z spun, 14 threads per 10mm. System 2: S spun, 13 threads per 10mm.

A10409b; C2611–3; M1.2, Pit 2648; Phase <IIg(IIh); Rig VI

Not illustrated

146 2/1 Twill (?) with nap ZS Wool

Unconserved fragment, folded, plus one even smaller fragment of a felted, deep red 2/1(?) twill with a raised nap on both surfaces. The nap renders identification insecure. Dimensions c20mm by 14mm by 6mm. System 1: Z spun, no count possible. System 2: S, no count possible.

A10409c; C2611–3; M1.2, Pit 2648; Phase <IIg(IIh); Rig VI

Not illustrated

147 2/1 Twill without nap ZS Wool

Unconserved crumpled fragment of irregular shape. The fabric is a light weight, unfelted 2/1 twill, dark brown in colour. Dimensions: c110mm by 65mm by 15mm. System 1: Z spun, smooth and regular, 14 threads per 10mm. System 2: S spun, slightly coarser, 12 threads per 10mm.

A10409d; C2611–3; M1.2, Pit 2648; Phase <IIg(IIh); Rig VI

Not illustrated

148 2/1 (?) Twill with nap ZZ Wool

Unconserved fragment, folded, plus a small piece of the same textile which adheres to Cat No 149/A10409f. The fabric is a light weight, felted 2/1 twill, very dark brown in colour, with a raised nap on both surfaces which tends to obscure the weave. Dimensions: c70mm by 18mm by 10mm. System 1: Z spun, 10 threads per 10mm. System 2: the same.

A10409e; C2611–3; M1.2, Pit 2648; Phase <IIg(IIh); Rig VI

Not illustrated

149 2/1 Twill without nap ZS Wool

Unconserved fragment, crumpled, in fragile condition and covered in mud. Light weight, unfelted (?) 2/1 twill, light yellow-brown in colour. Dimensions: c95mm by 90mm by 15mm. System 1: Z spun, count not possible. System 2: S spun, count not possible. A piece of Cat No 148/A10409e adheres to this textile.

A10409f; C2611–3; M1.2, Pit 2648; <IIg(IIh); Rig VI

Not illustrated

150 Tabby (2 ply yarn) Wool
One fragment, in very poor condition, of mid-brown, very heavy tabby; the yarn in System 2 has largely disintegrated. Dimensions: 95mm by 30mm. System 1: very firm 2 ply yarn, Z spun and S plyed, about 3 threads per 10mm. System 2: loosely plyed 2 ply yarn, Z spun and S plyed, about 2.5 threads per 10mm.
A10412; C2611–3; M1.2, Pit 2648; Phase <IIg(IIh); Rig VI
Not illustrated

151 Tabby (2 ply yarn) Wool
One piece of dark brown, exceptionally heavy tabby, constructed from very coarse yarn of irregular thickness. Dimensions: 750mm by 440mm. System 1: 2 ply yarn, Z spun and S plyed, about 2 threads per 10mm. System 2: similar yarn, about 1.5 threads per 10mm.
A10427; C2611–3; M1.2, Pit 2648; Phase <IIg(IIh); Rig VI
Not illustrated

152/ Yarn Wool
One length of very heavy 2S ply yarn in poor condition. Length 200mm.
A10436; C2611–3; M1.2, Pit 2648; Phase <IIg(IIh); Rig VI
Not illustrated

153 Tabby (2 ply yarn) Wool
Two pieces of very dark brown, exceptionally heavy tabby, open-textured and coarse to the touch; the thickness of the yarn and the spacing of the threads are variable. Dimensions: a) 240mm by 200mm; b) 120mm by 60mm. System 1: very firm 2 ply yarn, Z spun and S plyed, about 3 threads per 10mm. System 2: similar yarn, 3–4 threads per 10mm. Wool type: HM, pigment +++, no dye in both systems (MR).
A11266; C2611–3; M1.2, Pit 2648; Phase <IIg(IIh); Rig VI
Not illustrated

154 2/1 Twill without nap ZS Wool
One fragment of dark brown, light weight, unfelted 2/1 twill, harsh to the touch. Dimensions: 40mm by 50mm. System 1: fine Z spun yarn, 16 threads per 10mm. System 2: similar yarn, 12 threads per 10mm.
A9121; C2611–3; M1.2, Pit 2648; Phase <IIg(IIh); Rig VI
Not illustrated

155 2/1 Twill (?) with nap ZS Wool
One fragment of dark red, light weight but heavily felted fabric; the heavy nap on both surfaces obscures the structure which is probably 2/1 twill. Dimensions: 65mm by 6mm. System 1: fine Z spun yarn, no count possible System 2: similar S spun yarn, no count possible.
A11288; C2611–3; M1.2, Pit 2648; Phase <IIg(IIh); Rig VI
Not illustrated

156 Tabby (?) (2 ply yarn (?)) Wool
Unconserved textile in an extremely poor, compacted and brittle condition. The yarns are dark brown in colour, with coarse fibres, but identification is insecure.
A8497; C2264–4; M11; Phase IIh; Rigs V and VI
Not illustrated

157 2/1 Twill (?) with nap, Others Wool
One strip, with a selvedge on one long edge, of very heavy mid-brown cloth; the weave appears to be 2/1 twill but the structure is obscured by heavy felting and the close packing of the threads. Dimensions: 500mm by 10–25mm. System 1: warp, loosely twisted 2 ply threads, some constructed from fine Z spun yarn and others from softer S spun yarn, no count possible. System 2: weft, S spun yarn, probably used in pairs, about 4 pairs per 10mm.
A8366; C2250–4; M1.3; Phase III; Rig VI
Not illustrated

158 2/1 Twill without nap ZS Wool
One piece of light weight, even mid-brown 2/1 twill, lightly felted, close-woven and slightly soft to the touch. Dimensions: 55mm by 50mm. System 1: Z spun yarn, 12 threads per 10mm. System 2: S spun yarn, 11 threads per 10mm. Wool type: GM, no pigment, no dye (yellow discolour) in both systems (MR).
A8432; C2462C–3; M1.3; Phase IIi; Rig VI
Not illustrated

159 Tabby (2 ply yarn) Wool
One fragment of dark brown, very heavy tabby. Dimensions: 80mm by 55mm. System 1: firm 2 ply yarn, Z spun and S plyed, 3 threads per 10mm. System 2: similar yarn, 2.5 threads per 10mm.
A8505a; C2462C–3; M1.3; Phase IIi; Rig VI
Not illustrated

160 2/1 Twill without nap ZS Wool
One piece of dark brown, light-medium weight 2/1 twill, unfelted, coarse to the touch and of uneven appearance. Dimensions: 30mm by 90mm. System 1: Z spun yarn, 10 threads per 10mm. System 2: similar S spun yarn, 9 threads per 10mm.
A8505b; C2462C–3; M1.3; Phase IIi; Rig VI
Not illustrated

161 2/1 Twill without nap ZS Wool
One piece of mid-brown, light weight 2/1 twill, lightly felted and slightly soft to the touch; the threads are irregularly packed and, in one System, very variable in thickness, resulting in an uneven fabric. Dimensions: 103mm by 95mm. System 1: fine, smooth Z spun yarn, about 12 threads per 10mm. System 2: S spun yarn, variable in thickness, about 12 threads per 10mm.
A8725; C2462C–3; M1.3; Phase IIi; Rig VI
Not illustrated

162 2/1 Twill with nap ZZ Wool
One fragment of reddish dark brown, light weight 2/1 twill, with a light nap on both surfaces. Dimensions: 13mm by 16mm. System 1: fine, but soft, Z spun yarn, about 15 threads per 10mm. System 2: similar yarn, about 12 threads per 10mm.
A10070; C2462C–3; M1.3; Phase IIi; Rig VI
Not illustrated

163 2/1 Twill with (?) nap ZS Wool
One fragment, in poor condition, of reddish dark brown, light weight 2/1 twill, lightly felted and with the possible remnants of a raised nap on both surfaces. Dimensions: 25mm by 35mm. System 1: Z spun yarn, about 12 threads per 10mm. System 2: S spun yarn, about 10 threads per 10 mm.
A8832; C2597–3; M1.3; Phase IIi; Rig VI
Not illustrated

164 2/1 Twill with nap ZS Wool
One piece of even mid-brown, heavy medium weight 2/1 twill, heavily felted and with nap, now partially worn away, on both surfaces. Dimensions: 70mm by 55mm. System 1: Z spun yarn, about 14 threads per 10mm. System 2: S spun yarn, about 12 threads per 10mm. Wool type: GM, no pigment, no dye in both systems (MR).
A9108; C2597–3; M1.3; Phase IIi; Rig VI
Not illustrated

165 2/1 Twill without nap ZS Wool
One piece of reddish dark brown, light weight 2/1 twill, of uneven texture, unfelted but slightly soft to the touch. Dimensions: 205mm by 100mm. System 1: fine Z spun yarn, 15 threads per 10mm. System 2: similar S spun yarn, 14 threads per 10mm.
A9138; C2597–3; M1.3; Phase IIi; Rig VI
Not illustrated

166 Braid Wool
Braided cord, 13–15mm in diameter, made on the whipcord principle (see Illus 71) from mottled mid/dark brown Z spun yarn – 32 strands arranged in eight groups of four. Length 295mm. Wool type: sample 1 H, pigment +++, no dye; sample 2 H, pigment +, no dye (MR).
A9974; C2597–3; M1.3; Phase IIi; Rig VI
Illus 70

167 2/2 Twill without nap ZZ Wool
Three pieces of dark brown, light weight, unfelted 2/2 twill, close woven and firm to the touch. Dimensions: a) 110mm by 140mm; b) 90mm by 75mm; c) 60mm by 90mm. System 1: firm Z spun yarn, 15 threads per 10mm. System 2: similar yarn, 13–15 threads per 10mm. Wool type: HM, pigment +++ in both systems (MR). No dye (MW).
A9056; C2603–3; M1.3; Phase IIi; Rig VI
Not illustrated

168 2/1 Twill without nap, Others Wool
Three pieces of dark brown, very heavy weight, unfelted 2/1 twill, moderately firm to the touch. Dimensions: a) 250mm by 235mm; b) 115mm by 180mm; c) 50mm by 95mm. System 1: glossy, firmly Z spun yarn, variable in thickness, 8 threads per 10mm. System 2: each element composed of a pair of threads, one Z spun and one S spun, 4–5 pairs per 10mm. Wool type: System 1 H, pigment ++, no dye; System 2 HM, pigment +++, no dye (MR).
A9057a; C2603–3; M1.3; Phase IIi; Rig VI
Illus 39

169 2/1 Twill without nap ZS Wool
One piece of light weight, dark brown, 2/1 twill, evenly spun and woven, unfelted but soft to the touch. Dimensions: 70mm by 150mm. System 1: fine Z spun yarn, 14 threads per 10mm. System 2: similar S spun yarn, 12–13 threads per 10mm.
A9057b; C2603–3; M1.3; Phase IIi; Rig VI
Not illustrated

170 2/1 Twill without nap ZZ Wool
Two pieces of very dark brown, heavy weight, unfelted 2/1 twill. Dimensions: a) 132mm by 45mm; b) 72mm by 35mm. System 1: plump, glossy Z spun yarn, about 7 threads per 10mm. System 2: the same.
A09–0142; C9520–9; B19 (Phase 1), North Room–Occupation (4b); Phase IIIa; Rig VII
Not illustrated

171 Yarn Wool
Very coarse, hairy, mottled mid-brown 2S ply yarn. 5–6mm in diameter. Dimensions: 252 mm.
A09–0145a; C9520–9; B19 (Phase 1), North Room–Occupation (4b); Phase IIIa; Rig VII
Not illustrated

172 Yarn Wool
Very coarse, hairy, mottled 3S ply yarn, 5–7mm in diameter. Length 168mm.
A09–0145b; C9520–9; B19 (Phase 1), North Room–Occupation (4b); Phase IIIa; Rig VII
Not illustrated

173 Yarn Wool
Fragment of dark brown, firm, smooth 2S ply yarn, about 2mm in diameter. Length 95mm.
A11309; C3874–1; MC112b; Phase IIIb; Rig VII
Not illustrated

174 Cordage ? Horse hair
Two pieces, knotted together at both ends, of firm, even dark brown cordage, about 10mm in diameter. The cord is composed of three elements, each a firm 2Z ply yarn, twisted together in S direction. Length 1040mm. There is a further fragment, knotted, of the same cord about 80mm long.
A09–0141; C9479–9; B19 (Phase 2a), North Room–Floor (1); Phase IIIb; Rig VII
Illus 72

175 Felt Wool
Fragments, in poor condition, of mid-brown felt. Dimensions: c65mm by 80mm in all.
A09–0107; C9473–9; B19 (Phase 2a), North Room–Occupation (3c); Phase IIIb; Rig VII
Not illustrated

176 2/1 Twill with nap ZS Wool
One piece of heavy medium weight, dark brown, felted 2/1 twill, with the nap raised on one side; both spinning and weaving are uneven. Dimensions: 75mm by 130mm. System 1: Z spun yarn, about 8 threads per 10mm. System 2: S spun yarn, softer and thicker, about 8 threads per 10mm.
A09–0110; C9473–9; B19 (Phase 2a), North Room–Occupation (3c); Phase IIIb; Rig VII
Not illustrated

177 2/1 Twill without nap ZS Wool
One piece of mid-brown, light medium weight, 2/1 twill, unfelted but soft to the touch, and of uneven texture. Dimensions: 140mm by 190mm. System 1: smooth Z spun yarn, 10–11 threads per 10mm. System 2: S spun yarn, variable in thickness, 9–10 threads per 10mm. Dye: indigotin (MW).
A09–0108; C9476–9; B19 (Phase 2a), North Room–Occupation (3c); Phase IIIb; Rig VII
Not illustrated

178 2/1 Twill with nap ZS Wool
One piece of even mid-brown, medium weight, compact 2/1 twill, with a slight nap on both surfaces; there is an indentation running parallel to and about 5mm away from one edge which may indicate a seam line. Dimensions: 100mm by 80mm. System 1: Z spun yarn, 11–12 threads per 10mm. System 2: slightly thicker S spun yarn, 13 threads per 10mm.
A09–0111; C9476–9; B19 (Phase 2a), North Room–Occupation (3c); Phase IIIb; Rig VII
Not illustrated

179 Yarn Wool
Very dark brown, coarse 2S ply yarn, probably from Cat No 180/A09–0138 (tabby; 2 ply yarn). Length 90mm.
A09–0144; C9502–9; M13; Phase IIg–IIIb; Rig VII
Not illustrated

180 Tabby (2 ply yarn) Wool
One fragment of dark brown, very heavy tabby. Dimensions: 103mm by 92mm. System 1: 2 ply yarn, Z spun and S plyed, 2.5–3 threads per 10mm. System 2: the same. No dye (MW).
A09–0138; C9509–9; M13; Phase IIg–IIIb; Rig VII
Not illustrated

181 2/2 Twill without nap ZZ Wool
One piece of very dark brown, light medium weight, unfelted 2/2 twill, close woven and comparatively even in spinning and weaving. There is a closed edge on one short margin – a tubular selvedge of seven threads of a similar yarn to that used in the main body of the fabric, but the weave of the selvedge is tabby. Dimensions: 45mm by 40mm. System 1: warp, smooth, firm Z spun yarn, 12 threads per 10mm. System 2: weft, similar yarn, 10 threads per 10mm. Wool type: HM, pigment +++, no dye in both systems (MR).
cf a Norwegian Migration Period textile, identified as a blanket, from a chieftain's grave at Evebø/Eide, a 2/2 twill, fulled, ZZ, with tubular selvedges. However the selvedges only have three or five warp ends, and the main fabric has a lower warp and weft count than the Perth textile (Raknes Pederson 1982, 75–6, Figures 1 and 2).
A8085; C2242–4; M1.4a(a); Phase IIIa–IIIc; Rig VI
Illus 13

182 2/1 Twill with nap ZS Wool
One piece of bright mid-brown, medium weight 2/1 twill, felted and with the nap raised on both surfaces. Dimensions: 30mm by 70mm. System 1: Z spun yarn, 8–9 threads per 10mm. System 2: softer and thicker S spun yarn, 8 threads per 10mm.
A09–0094; C9443–9; P8.1b and B19 (Phase 2b), South Room–Occupation (1a); Phase IIIc; Rig VII
Not illustrated

183 Yarn Silk
Fragments of yellowish mid-brown, fine 2S ply silk; the yarn is kinked as if it was originally woven, perhaps with tablets. Length up to 120mm.
A09–0098; C9443–9; P8.1b and B19 (Phase 2b), South Room–Occupation (1a); Phase IIIc; Rig VII
Not illustrated

184 2/1 Twill without nap ZS Wool
One narrow strip, with one long edge closed, of very dark brown, light medium weight, unfelted 2/1 twill, closely woven and firm to the touch; there are no special arrangements for the closed edge and it is not clear whether the weave is that of a main fabric or whether the entire strip is itself the selvedge of a fabric, the remainder of which has not survived. Dimensions: 317mm by 7mm. System 1: warp, smooth firm Z spun yarn, 14 threads per 10mm. System 2: weft, thicker S spun yarn, 12 threads per 10mm.
A09–0106; C9462–9; B19 (Phase 2b), North Room–Floor (1); Phase IIIc; Rig VII
Not illustrated

185 2/1 Twill with nap ZZ Wool
One fragment of reddish mid-brown, light weight, closely woven 2/1 twill, soft, and with the remains of a light nap on both surfaces. Dimensions: 22mm by 13mm. System 1: fine even Z spun yarn, about 16 threads per 10mm. System 2: softer Z spun yarn, 12 threads per 10mm.
A09–0096; C9439–9; B19 (Phase 2b), North Room–Floor (2b); Phase IIIc; Rig VII
Not illustrated

186 2/1 Twill with nap ZS Wool
One piece of light brown, heavy weight 2/1 twill, with a slight nap on both surfaces and a closely woven but uneven texture. Dimensions: 55mm by 32mm. System 1: Z spun yarn, about 10 threads per 10mm. System 2: considerably thicker and softer S spun yarn, variable in diameter, about 5 threads per 10mm.
A09–0086; C9413–9; B19 (Phase 2b), North Room–Occupation (3); Phase IIIc; Rig VII
Not illustrated

187 2/1 Twill with nap ZS Wool
One piece of heavy medium weight, olive brown 2/1 twill, with slight nap on both surfaces; the fibres are now brittle. Dimensions: 200mm by 25mm. System 1: Z spun yarn of irregular thickness, about 10 threads per 10mm. System 2: similar S spun yarn, about 8 threads per 10mm. No dye (MW).
A09–0091; C9438–9; B19 (Phase 2b), South Room–Occupation (2a); Phase IIIc; Rig VII
Not illustrated

188 2/2 Twill without nap ZZ Wool
One piece of dark brown, light weight, unfelted 2/2 twill, close-woven and firm to the touch. Dimensions: 120mm by 50mm. System 1: smooth firm Z spun yarn, 10 threads per 10mm. System 2: similar yarn, 8–10 threads per 10mm.
A09–0084; C9414–9; P8.1c; Phase IIIc; Rig VII
Not illustrated

189 2/1 Twill with nap ZS Wool
Three pieces of even mid-brown, medium weight 2/1 twill, heavily felted and with nap on both surfaces, but now worn. Dimensions: a) 125mm by 45mm; b) 25mm by 70mm; c) 35mm by 15mm. System 1: fine soft Z spun yarn, 9–10 threads per 10mm. System 2: thicker S spun yarn, 9–10 threads per 10mm.
A09–0089; C9414–9; P8.1c; Phase IIIc; Rig VII
Not illustrated

190 2/1 Twill without nap ZZ Wool
One piece of worn, dark brown, light medium weight 2/1 twill, unfelted but slightly soft to the touch, with about 105mm of closed edge of simple structure, on one margin. Dimensions: 225mm by 186mm. System 1: fine Z spun yarn, 13 threads per 10mm. System 2: similar yarn, 10–11 threads per 10mm.
A09–0130; C7383–7; M6a; Phase IIg–IIId; Rig VI
Not illustrated

191 2/1 Twill without nap ZZ Wool
One piece of dark brown, light weight, unfelted, close woven and firm 2/1 twill, even in spinning and weaving. Dimensions: 147mm by 110mm. System 1: fine hard Z spun yarn, 18 threads per 10mm. System 2: similar yarn, 16 threads per 10mm.
A09–0058; C9401–9; M15; Phase IIId; Rig VII
Not illustrated

192 2/1 Twill without nap ZS Wool
One piece of worn, mid-brown, medium weight, unfelted 2/1 twill; the yarns in both systems are variable in thickness and tension and the threads are unevenly packed. Dimensions: 320mm by 250mm. System 1: Z spun yarn, 8–10 threads per 10mm. System 2: S spun yarn, 7–10 threads per 10 mm.
A09–0078; C9404–9; M15; Phase IIId; Rig VII
Not illustrated

193 2/1 Twill without nap ZZ Wool
One piece of very dark brown, light medium weight 2/1 twill, unfelted and firm to the touch. Dimensions: 65mm by 75mm. System 1: smooth, firm Z spun yarn, 10–11 threads per 10mm. System 2: similar yarn, 9 threads per 10mm.
A09–0081; C9404–9; M15; Phase IIId; Rig VII
Not illustrated

194 Yarn Wool
Three fragments of coarse, dark brown 2S ply yarn, plus three further unplyed fragments. Maximum length is 113mm, and the diameter of the plied yarns is 3mm.
A09–0082; C9404–9; M15; Phase IIId; Rig VII
Not illustrated

195 2/1 Twill with nap ZS Wool
Fragment of distinct red brown, medium weight 2/1 twill, very compact and with the nap raised on both surfaces. Dimensions: 33mm by 38mm. System 1: Z spun yarn, 14 threads per 10mm. System 2: thicker S spun yarn, about 8–9 threads per 10mm.
A09–0083; C9404–9; M15; Phase IIId; Rig VII
Not illustrated

196 2/1 Twill without nap ZZ Wool
One worn fragment of dark brown, light weight, unfelted 2/1 twill. Dimensions: 25mm by 40mm. System 1: Z spun yarn, 13 threads per 10mm. System 2: similar yarn, 10 threads per 10mm. No dye (MW).
A09–0123; C7340–7; M15; Pit 9415; Phase IIId; Rig VII
Not illustrated

197 2/2 Twill without nap ZZ Wool
Two pieces of dark brown, light medium weight 2/2 twill, unfelted and very firm to the touch; the threads are very unevenly packed and there are a number of weaving mistakes. Dimensions: a) 160mm by 245mm; b) 360mm by 420mm. System 1: fine hard Z spun yarn, 11–18 threads per 10mm. System 2: similar yarn, 11–15 threads per 10mm. No dye (MW).
A8520; C2581–3; M6b; Phase IIg–IIId; Rig V
Not illustrated

198 2/1 Twill without nap ZS Wool
Two pieces of dark brown, light weight 2/1 twill, lightly felted, comparatively close woven and soft to the touch; the threads are unevenly packed and variable in thickness. Dimensions: a) 68mm by 105mm; b) 38mm by 110mm. System 1: fine smooth Z spun yarn, about 17 threads per 10mm. System 2: heavier S spun yarn, about 9 threads per 10mm.
A9497; C2644–3; MC119, Pit 7390; Phase <IIIc–IVa; Rig VI
Not illustrated

199 2/1 Twill without nap ZS Wool
One fragment of heavy weight, unfelted 2/1 twill; the colour is generally sandy brown, but with a few dark threads in System 1; but the piece is too small to judge whether this represents deliberate striping or is simply the result of using unsorted wool. Dimensions: 30mm by 50mm. System 1: plump Z spun yarn, 7 threads per 10mm. System 2: similar S spun yarn, 7 threads per 10 mm. Wool type: System 1 HM, pigment +++ (black), no dye; System 2 GM, no pigment, no dye (MR).
A9766a; C2644–3; MC119, Pit 7390; Phase <IIIc–IVa; Rig VI
Not illustrated

200 2/1 Twill without nap ZS Wool
One piece of reddish mid-brown light weight, unfelted 2/1 twill. Dimensions: 45mm by 40mm. System 1: fine Z spun yarn, 12 threads per 10mm. System 2: slightly heavier S spun yarn, 12 threads per 10mm.
A9766b; C2644–3; MC119, Pit 7390; Phase <IIIc–IVa; Rig VI
Not illustrated

201 2/1 Twill without Nap ZS Wool
Three small pieces (and two fragments) of bright mid-brown, light medium weight 2/1 twill, lightly felted and comparatively close woven. Dimensions: a) 50mm by 33mm; b) 45mm by 38mm; c) 42mm by 35mm. System 1: fine Z spun yarn, 12 threads per 10mm. System 2: heavier S spun yarn, 8 threads per 10mm.
A9766c; C2644–3; MC119, Pit 7390; Phase <IIIc–IVa; Rig VI
Not illustrated

202 Felt? Wool
Fragments of reddish dark brown matted wool; it is not clear whether these are the remains of felt or simply matted unsorted fibres. Dimensions: c65mm by 30mm in all.
A09-0132a; C7386-7; MC119, Pit 7390; Phase <IIIc-IVa; Rig VI
Not illustrated

203 Yarn Wool
Two lengths, knotted together, of firm 2S ply, bright mid-brown yarn, 2-3mm in diameter, constructed from smooth Z spun yarn. Length 400mm in all.
A09-0132b; C7386-7; MC119, Pit 7390; Phase <IIIc-IVa; Rig VI
Not illustrated

204 Tabby Wool
Two strips of heavy weight tabby, each with a closed edge on one long margin, perhaps selvedges rather than part of the main fabric; the first System which runs parallel to the closed edge, probably the warp, is closely packed and largely covers the second System which is composed of finer yarn used double; at the edge of the fabric the double threads pass round the outermost two warp threads before returning into the fabric. Dimensions: a) 135mm by 35mm; b) 100mm by 25mm. System 1: warp, plump, smooth, S spun mid-brown yarn, 9 threads per 10mm; 22 threads remain on the larger piece. System 2: weft, lighter weight S spun yarn, used double, 3 pairs threads per 10mm; in most, but not all sheds, one thread is a similar shade to the warp and the second is dark brown. Minute trace of unknown blue dye (?) (MW).
A09-0133a; C7386-7; MC119, Pit 7390; Phase <IIIc-IVa; Rig VI
Illus 21

205 2/2 Twill without nap ZS Wool
One piece, very worn, of coarse, heavy, unfelted 2/2 twill, the yarn varying in colour from light to mid-brown. Dimensions: 263mm by 35mm. System 1: smooth Z spun yarn, 6-7 threads per 10mm. System 2: heavier S spun yarn, 4-5 threads per 10mm.
A09-0133b; C7386-7; MC119, Pit 7390; Phase <IIIc-IVa; Rig VI
Not illustrated

206 2/1 Twill without nap ZZ Wool
Four pieces, very worn, of even light brown, light medium weight 2/1 twill, unfelted and with an open texture. Dimensions: a) 180mm by 35mm; b) 153mm by 28mm; c) 75mm by 14mm; d) 59mm by 29mm. System 1: smooth Z spun yarn, 9 threads per 10mm. System 2: the same.
A09-0134a; C7386-7; MC119, Pit 7390; Phase <IIIc-IVa; Rig VI
Not illustrated

207 2/1 Twill without nap ZZ Wool
One fragment of dark red-brown, light weight 2/1 twill, unfelted but close woven and firm to the touch, unusually well executed in both spinning and weaving. Dimensions: 95mm by 12mm. System 1: fine, smooth, Z spun yarn, 18 threads per 10mm. System 2: similar yarn, 16 threads per 10mm.
A09-0134b; C7386-7; MC119, Pit 7390; Phase <IIIc-IVa; Rig VI
Not illustrated

208 2/1 Twill without nap ZS Wool
One piece of reddish mid-brown, light weight, unfelted 2/1 twill; the threads are variable in tension and unevenly packed. Dimensions: 131mm by 90mm. System 1: Z spun yarn, about 13 threads per 10mm. System 2: S spun yarn, more variable in thickness, 11-13 threads per 10mm.
A09-0135a; C7386-7; MC119, Pit 7390; Phase <IIIc-IVa; Rig VI
Not illustrated

209 2/1 Twill with nap ZS Wool
One piece of sandy brown, light medium weight 2/1 twill, of uneven appearance, with a light nap on both surfaces. Dimensions: 122mm by 119mm. System 1: Z spun yarn, 15 threads per 10mm. System 2: slightly heavier S spun yarn, 10 threads per 10mm.
A09-0135b; C7386-7; MC119, Pit 7390; Phase <IIIc-IVa; Rig VI
Not illustrated

210 2/1 Twill without nap ZS Wool
One piece of light medium weight, unfelted 2/1 twill, dark brown but lighter in patches, moderately even in spinning and weaving. Dimensions: 112mm by 116mm. System 1: fine smooth Z spun yarn, 10 threads per 10mm. System 2: heavier S spun yarn, 9 threads per 10mm.
A09-0135c; C7386-7; MC119, Pit 7390; Phase <IIIc-IVa; Rig VI
Not illustrated

211 2/1 Twill without nap ZZ Wool
One piece of even mid-brown, light medium weight 2/1 twill, unfelted but close woven and slightly firm to the touch. Dimensions: 125mm by 15mm. System 1: smooth Z spun yarn, about 16 threads per 10mm. System 2: similar yarn, 10-12 threads per 10mm. Wool type: System 1 HM, pigment +, no dye; System 2 GM, no pigment, no dye (MR).
A9903a; C2536-3; P2.2b; Phase IVa; Rig V
Not illustrated

212 2/1 Twill without nap ZS Wool
One fragment of even mid-brown, medium weight 2/1 twill, without nap, felted, compact and slightly soft to the touch. Dimensions: 20mm by 50mm. System 1: fine Z spun yarn, about 15 threads per 10mm. System 2: heavier S spun yarn, about 12 threads per 10mm. Wool type: GM, no pigment, no dye in both systems (MR).
A9903b; C2536-3; P2.2b; Phase IVa; Rig V
Not illustrated

213 2/1 Twill with nap ZS Wool
Two pieces of distinct red-brown, medium weight, heavily felted and compact 2/1 twill, with a pronounced nap on both sides. Dimensions: a) 50mm by 30mm; b) 80mm by 25mm. System 1: firm Z spun yarn, no count possible. System 2: spun yarn, no count possible. Wool type: System 1 H, no pigment; System 2 HM, no pigment; red dye in both (MR). Madder present in quantity (MW).
A9905; C2536-3; P2.2b; Phase IVa; Rig V
Not illustrated

214 Yarn Wool
Fragment of heavy, 2Z ply mottled mid/dark brown yarn; 45mm.
A8864; C2512–3; MC156; Phase IVaa; Rig V
Not illustrated

215 2/1 Twill with nap ZS Wool
One triangular piece of heavy medium weight, even mid-brown,
felted 2/1 twill, with pronounced nap (now partially worn) on both
sides. Dimensions: 60mm by 85mm. System 1: Z spun yarn,
about 10 threads per 10mm. System 2: S spun, 12 threads per
10mm.
A09–0057; C9358–9; B18 (Phase 1a), Middle Room/Hall–
Occupation (1b); Phase IVa,IVaa; Rig VII
Not illustrated

216 Yarn Wool
Very dark brown, coarse, hairy 2S ply yarn, about 4mm in
diameter. Length 59mm.
A6694a; C3564–1; B20, Levelling; Phase <IIId–IVaa; Rig VI
Not illustrated

217 Tablet weaving Silk
Fragment, in poor condition, of a tablet-woven band, the weft
of which has disintegrated. The band, originally perhaps 8mm
wide, is composed of 56 warp threads–very fine 2S ply silk
yarn–now a yellowish beige with patches of a brighter orange
colour, arranged in 14 groups of four. The four border groups on
each side are twisted in S direction, the remaining central six in
Z direction. Length 75mm.
A6694b; C3564–1; B20, Levelling; Phase <IIId–IVaa; Rig VI
Not illustrated

218 2/1 Twill without nap ZS Wool
Two pieces of dark brown, light weight, unfelted 2/1 twill, close
woven and firm to the touch, with a closed edge of simple
structure on one long margin of one piece; the two long margins
of piece (b) and one long margin of piece (a) are turned in by
5–8mm, as if they have been seamed, but there is no trace of
sewing thread. Dimensions: a) 105mm by 50mm; b) 105mm by
75mm. System 1: fine hard Z spun yarn, 16 threads per 10mm.
System 2: S spun yarn, more variable in thickness, 13–14
threads per 10mm.
A6634; C3553–1; B20, Occupation (1a); Phase <IIId–IVaa; Rig
VI
Not illustrated

219 2/1 Twill without nap ZS Wool
One piece (and a fragment) of dark brown, light medium weight
2/1 twill, unfelted but close woven and slightly soft to the touch;
both spinning and weaving are uneven; 240mm by 165mm.
System 1: smooth Z spun yarn, 12 threads per 10mm. System 2:
softer S spun yarn, 12 per 10mm.
A11662; C3552–1; B20, Occupation (2b); Phase <IIId–IVaa; Rig
VI
Not illustrated

220 2/1 Twill without nap ZS Wool
One piece of mid-brown, light weight 2/1 twill, unfelted and
open textured but soft to the touch, of uneven appearance; the
thickness of the yarn in both systems is variable. Dimensions:
45mm by 43mm. System 1: Z spun yarn, 10–11 threads per
10mm. System 2: similar S spun yarn, 7 threads per 10mm.
A09–0139; C7363–7; MC130; Phase <IIIc–IVaa; Rig VII
Not illustrated

221 Tabby (2 ply yarn) Wool
One piece of mottled mid/dark brown, very heavy tabby, coarse
to the touch, and slightly open in texture. Dimensions: 480mm
by 400mm. System 1: 2 ply yarn, Z spun and S plyed, 2.5
threads per 10mm. System 2: similar yarn, 2 threads per 10mm.
Wool type: System 1 H, pigment ++, no dye; System 2 HM,
pigment +++, no dye (MR).
A6126; C2498–3; B2, WW2498; Phase IVa,IVaa; Rig VI
Not illustrated

222 2/2 Twill without nap ZS Wool
Three fragments, very worn, of bright mid-brown, medium
weight 2/2 twill. Dimensions: c90mm by 40mm in all. System 1:
smooth Z spun yarn, 6 threads per 10mm. System 2: similar S
spun yarn, about 6 threads per 10mm.
A9902; C2796–2; B2, Late Occupation/Abandonment (2) and
M1.4d; Phase IVa–IVc; Rig VI
Not illustrated

223 Yarn ? Silk
Group of at least 16 lengths of dark brown, fine, firm, 2S ply
yarn. The width of the unit is 5mm. It is not clear whether the
group was originally worked together, eg to form a cord, as
the component yarns seem to lie in groups of four. The yarn
resembles that used in the stitching of silk tabby 346A09–0044.
Length up to 205mm.
A7835; C2546–3; B3 (South), Occupation (1b); Phase IVa,IVaa;
Rig V
Not illustrated

224 2/1 Twill without nap ZZ Wool
One piece of dark brown, light weight, unfelted, firm 2/1 twill
with 55mm of closed edge of simple structure remaining on one
margin; the warp threads are more closely packed for 4mm at
the selvedge. Dimensions: 35mm by 67mm. System 1: warp,
fine hard Z spun yarn, 17 threads per 10mm. System 2: weft,
similar yarn, 15 threads per 10mm.
A09–0075a; C9331–9; B18 (Phase 1b), North Room–Floor;
Phase IVa,IVaa; Rig VII
Not illustrated

225 2/1 Twill without nap ZZ Wool
One piece of very dark brown, medium weight, very closely
woven 2/1 twill, hard to the touch. Dimensions: 120mm by
17mm. System 1: smooth, plump Z spun yarn, 10–11 threads
per 10mm. System 2: similar yarn, 9–10 threads per 10mm.
A09–0075b; C9331–9; B18 (Phase 1b), North Room–Floor;
Phase IVa,IVaa; Rig VII
Not illustrated

226 2/1 Twill without nap ZZ Wool
Three pieces of dark brown, light weight, unfelted, close
woven and firm 2/1 twill, evenly spun and woven; piece (c) has
260mm of closed edge, of simple structure, on one long margin.
Dimensions: a) 385mm by 150mm; b) 115mm by 60mm; c)
285mm by 25mm. System 1: fine hard Z spun yarn, 18 threads
per 10mm. System 2: similar yarn, 15 threads per 10mm.
A09–0120; C7334–7; B18 (Phase 1b), North Room–Occupation
(5b); Phase IVa,IVaa; Rig VII
Not illustrated

227 Sprang Wool
Two fragments of sprang, worked in very fine, hard, dark
brown, S spun yarn. The yarn has been worked into an elastic,
octagonal mesh, the octagons being approximately 3mm across
when expanded. Dimensions: a) 90mm by 25mm; b) 50mm by
15mm (not expanded).
A09–0121; C7334–7; B18 (Phase 1b), North Room–Occupation
(5b); Phase IVa,IVaa; Rig VII
Illus 65, 66

228 2/1 Twill with nap ZS Wool
Seven fragments of bright sandy brown, light medium weight
2/1 twill, lightly felted and with the remains of a slight nap on
both surfaces; the nap has a distinct red tinge. Dimensions: a)
110mm by 55mm; b) 45mm by 35mm; c) 40mm by 55mm; d)
50mm by 20mm; e) 40mm by 30mm; f) 35mm by 25mm. System
1: Z spun yarn, 10 threads per 10mm. System 2: thicker and
more irregular S spun yarn, 8–9 threads per 10mm. Wool type:
System 1 M; no pigment, no dye in both systems (MR).
A6124a; C2211–4; MC160, Pit 2232; Phase IVb; Rig VI
Not illustrated

229 2/1 Twill without nap ZS Wool
Two pieces of dark brown, light weight, lightly felted 2/1 twill,
slightly soft to the touch. Dimensions: a) 130mm by 70mm; b)
65mm by 100mm. System 1: smooth Z spun yarn, 13 threads
per 10mm. System 2: heavier S spun yarn, 13 threads per
10mm.
A6124b; C2211–4; MC160, Pit 2232; Phase IVb; Rig VI
Not illustrated

230 2/1 Twill with nap ZS Wool
Two fragments of dark reddish brown, medium weight, very
heavily felted and compact fabric; the structure is obscured but
is probably 2/1 twill. System 1: Z spun yarn, no count possible
System 2: S spun yarn, no count possible. Dye: madder (MW).
A6124c; C2211–4; MC160, Pit 2232; Phase IVb; Rig VI
Not illustrated

231 2/1 Twill with nap ZS Wool
One piece of dark, red brown, medium weight, felted 2/1 twill,
with the nap (now partially worn away) raised on both surfaces.
Dimensions: 20mm by 175mm. System 1: fine, smooth Z spun
yarn, 10 threads per 10mm. System 2: thicker S spun yarn, 10
threads per 10mm. Wool type: System 1 M, no pigment, no dye;
System 2 GM, no pigment, no dye (MR).
A9906; C2211–4; MC160, Pit 2232; Phase IVb; Rig VI
Not illustrated

232 Yarn Horse hair?
Very firm 2S ply dark brown yarn, about 3mm in diameter.
Length 190mm.
A09–0129; C7336–7; MC126, Pit 7402; Phase IVaa,IVb; Rig VII
Not illustrated

233 2/2 Twill Silk
One piece, worn and with an irregular outline, of golden
yellow, fine 2/2 lozenge twill with point repeat. A short length
of dark brown silk yarn with a tight Z twist clings to this textile.
Dimensions: 134mm by 145mm. System 1: firm Z spun yarn,
35–38 threads per 10mm. System 2: untwisted yarn, 25–27
threads per 10mm. 13th century.
A09–0122; C7342–7; MC126, Pit 7402; Phase IVaa,IVb; Rig VII
Illus 47, 48

234 Tablet weaving (?) Silk
Firm cord, 2mm in diameter, composed of about 44 lengths
of very fine 2S ply light yellowish-brown yarn, twisted in Z
direction. The surface of the cord is very close textured and
the structure is not clear, but it has possibly been tablet-woven
with a spiral weft. Where visible, the weft yarns are of silk, used
double, but they are in a worn condition. Length 320mm.
A09–0124a; C7342–7; MC126, Pit 7402; Phase IVaa,IVb; Rig VII
Not illustrated

235 Tablet weaving Silk
Two pieces, in poor condition, of tablet-woven, light yellowish-
brown brown cord, about 3mm in diameter. The cord has been
woven from loosely spun 2S ply yarn, possibly on 10 four-hole
tablets, with a spiral weft which has since disintegrated. Length
a) 180mm; b) 130mm.
A09–0124b; C7342–7; MC126, Pit 7402; Phase IVaa,IVb; Rig VII
Not illustrated

236 2/1 Twill with nap ZS Wool
Fragment, very worn, of mid-brown, light weight 2/1 twill, soft
to the touch and with a light nap on one surface; both spinning
and weaving are relatively even. Dimensions: 80mm by 30mm.
System 1: fine Z spun yard, 12 threads per 10mm. System 2:
similar S spun yarn, 10 threads per 10mm.
A09–0124c; C7342–7; MC126, Pit 7402; Phase IVaa,IVb; Rig VII
Not illustrated

237/Yarn Wool
Fragment of course, hairy, very dark brown 2S ply yarn, about
3mm in diameter. Length 75mm.
A09–0143; C7342–7; MC126, Pit 7402; Phase IVaa,IVb; Rig VII
Not illustrated

238 Tablet weaving Silk
Two lengths, in poor condition, of tablet-woven cord, 2mm in
diameter. The cord has been woven from Z (?) twisted silk yarn,
now bright yellowish brown, on eight (?) four-hole tablets, with
a spiral weft which has since disintegrated. Dimensions: a)
120mm; b) 225mm.
A09–0109; C7310–7; B18 (Phase 1/2); Phase IVaa,IVb; Rig VII
Not illustrated

239 2/2 Twill without nap ZZ Wool
One piece of dark brown, light weight, unfelted 2/2 twill, closely and evenly woven. Dimensions: 80mm by 105mm. System 1: smooth Z spun yarn, 16 threads per 10mm. System 2: similar yarn but more variable in thickness, 15–17 threads per 10mm.
A09–0069; C9216–9; B18 (Phase 1/2); Phase IVaa,IVb; Rig VII
Not illustrated

240 Yarn Wool
Fragment of coarse, firm, Z spun and 2S ply dark brown yarn, diameter 3mm. Length 38mm.
A09–0065; C9153–9; B18 (Phase 1/2); Phase IVaa,IVb; Rig VII
Not illustrated

241 2/1 Twill (?) with nap ZS Wool
One small strip of even mid-brown, heavy medium weight fabric with the nap raised on both surfaces; heavy finishing has almost totally obscured the weave, which is probably 2/1 twill. System 1: Z spun yarn, about 10 threads per 10mm. System 2: S spun yarn, about 10 threads per 10mm.
A09–0067; C9153–9; B18 (Phase 1/2); Phase IVaa,IVb; Rig VII
Not illustrated

242 2/1 Twill without nap ZS Wool
One fragment, very worn, of mid-golden brown, medium weight, unfelted 2/1 twill, open textured but soft to the touch. Dimensions: 75mm by 30mm. System 1: plump, glossy Z spun yarn, 6 threads per 10mm. System 2: similar S spun yarn, 4–5 threads per 10mm.
A09–0033; C9159–9; B18 (Phase 1/2), MF9194; Phase IVaa,IVb; Rig VII
Not illustrated

243 2/2 Twill without nap ZZ Wool
One fragment of very dark brown, medium weight, unfelted and closely woven 2/2 twill. Dimensions: 25mm by 50mm. System 1: smooth, firm Z spun yarn, 9 threads per 10mm. System 2: the same.
A09–0034; C9159–9; B18 (Phase 1/2), MF9194; Phase IVaa,IVb; Rig VII
Not illustrated

244 2/1 Twill without nap ZS Wool
One fragment, very worn, of light medium weight, lightly felted 2/1 twill. Dimensions: 35mm by 28mm. System 1: fine, smooth Z spun yarn about 8 threads per 10mm. System 2: softer and thicker S spun yarn, about 6 threads per 10mm.
A09–0062; C9159–9; B18 (Phase 1/2), MF9194; Phase IVaa,IVb; Rig VII
Not illustrated

245 2/1 Twill without nap ZS Wool
One piece of very dark brown, light weight 2/1 twill, unfelted but close woven. Dimensions: 65mm by 83mm. System 1: smooth, firm Z spun yarn, 15–16 threads per 10mm. System 2: similar S spun yarn, 13–14 threads per 10mm.
A09–0100; C7294–7; M1.4f; Phase IVc; Rig VI
Not illustrated

246 Tabby (2 ply yarn) Wool
One fragment, in poor condition, of dark brown, exceptionally coarse and heavy tabby with 25mm of closed edge, of simple structure, on one margin. Dimensions: 140mm by 80mm. System 1: warp, 2 ply yarn, Z spun and S plyed, about 2 threads per 10mm. System 2: weft, similar yarn, about 1.5 threads per 10mm.
A09–0101; C7294–7; M1.4f; Phase IVc; Rig VI
Not illustrated

247 2/1 Twill without nap ZS Wool
One piece of bright mid-brown, light weight 2/1 twill, unfelted but close woven and firm to the touch. Dimensions: 75mm by 45mm. System 1: smooth Z spun yarn, 13 threads per 10mm. System 2: slightly thicker S spun yarn, 11 threads per 10mm.
A09–0113; C7326–7; M1.4f; Phase IVc; Rig VI
Not illustrated

248 2/1 Twill without nap ZS Wool
One piece of very dark brown, light weight 2/1 twill, unfelted but close woven and firm to the touch; both spinning and weaving are even. Dimensions: 187mm by 42mm. System 1: smooth firm Z spun yarn, 18 threads per 10mm. System 2: similar S spun yarn, 15 threads per 10mm.
A09–0114; C7326–7; M1.4f; Phase IVc; Rig VI
Not illustrated

249 2/1 Twill without nap ZS Wool
One piece, now worn, of dark brown, light weight 2/1 twill, unfelted but close woven and firm to the touch; there is a ridge parallel to and about 7mm away from one margin which probably represents a seam line, but no sewing thread survives. Dimensions: 155mm by 120mm. System 1: smooth firm Z spun yarn, 16 threads per 10mm. System 2: similar S spun yarn, 15 threads per 10mm.
A09–0115; C7326–7; M1.4f; Phase IVc; Rig VI
Not illustrated

250 Yarn Silk
Two groups of lengths of fine, firm 2S ply silk yarn in at least two shades of mid-brown; in group (a) the threads are knotted together; the yarn is kinked as if it was originally woven; probably the remains of a tablet-woven band, the weft of which has disintegrated. Length a) 195mm; b) 300mm.
A09–0116; C7326–7; M1.4f; Phase IVc; Rig VI
Not illustrated

251 2/1 Twill without nap ZS Wool
One piece of very dark brown, medium weight, unfelted 2/1 twill, close woven and firm to the touch. Dimensions: 69mm by 75mm. System 1: smooth Z spun yarn, 9–10 threads per 10mm. System 2: similar S spun yarn, 9–10 threads per 10mm.
A09–0117a; C7326–7; M1.4f; Phase IVc; Rig VI
Not illustrated

252 2/2 Twill without nap ZS Wool
One piece of uneven mid-brown, light medium weight 2/2 twill, unfelted and slightly loose woven; 102mm by 119mm. System 1: fine Z spun yarn, 16 threads per 10mm. System 2: similar S spun yarn, 10 threads per 10mm.
A09–0117b; C7326–7; M1.4f; Phase IVc; Rig VI
Not illustrated

253 2/1 Twill without nap ZZ Wool
Two fragments of dark brown, light weight, unfelted, hard 2/1 twill, evenly spun and woven. Dimensions: a) 45mm by 24mm; b) 48mm by 50mm. System 1: smooth, firm Z spun yarn, 20 threads per 10 mm. System 2: similar yarn, 16–18 threads per 10mm.
A09–0126; C7326–7; M1.4f; Phase IVc; Rig VI
Not illustrated

254 2/1 Twill without nap ZZ Wool
One piece of dark brown, light weight, unfelted firm 2/1 twill, with about 15mm of closed edge – of simple structure – on one margin. Dimensions: 78mm by 32mm. System 1: smooth even Z spun yarn, 16–18 threads per 10mm. System 2: similar yarn, 12 threads per 10mm.
A09–0119a; C7335–7; M1.4f; Phase IVc; Rig VI
Not illustrated

255 2/1 Twill without nap ZS Wool
Three fragments of mottled mid/dark brown, light medium weight, unfelted 2/1 twill of uneven appearance. Dimensions: a) 90mm by 50mm; b) 37mm by 42mm; c) 42mm by 50mm. System 1: Z spun yarn, 12 threads per 10mm. System 2: S spun yarn, about 10 threads per 10mm.
A09–0119b; C7335–7; M1.4f; Phase IVc; Rig VI
Not illustrated

256 Yarn ? Wool
One piece (and three fragments) of very dark brown, coarse, hairy, loosely 2S plyed yarn, about 6mm in diameter. Length 330mm.
A09–0125; C7335–7; M1.4f; Phase IVc; Rig VI
Not illustrated

257 2/1 Twill with nap ZS Wool
One strip of bright mid-brown, medium weight 2/1 twill, lightly felted and soft to the touch. The nap is pronounced on one surface and slight on the other. A closed edge remains on one long margin, but although the warp threads are more closely packed towards the edge, there appear to be no special arrangements. Dimensions: 340mm by 24mm. System 1: warp, fine smooth Z spun yarn, 14 threads per 10mm. System 2: weft, softer and thicker S spun yarn, 9–10 threads per 10mm.
A09–0131; C7384–7; B18 (Phase 2a and 2b), T7385; Phase IVb; Rig VII
Not illustrated

258 2/1 Twill with nap ZS Wool
Two pieces of bright mid-brown, medium weight, heavily felted 2/1 twill; the nap is pronounced on one side and slight on the other. Dimensions: a) 100mm by 40mm; b) 215mm by 32mm. System 1: firm Z spun yarn, 12 threads per 10mm. System 2: similar S spun yarn, 10–12 threads per 10mm.
A09–0103; C7306–7; B18 (Phase 2a), North Room and Hall–Construction (1); Phase IVb; Rig VII
Not illustrated

259 2/1 Twill without nap, Others Wool
One piece of dark brown, light weight, unfelted, closely woven 2/1 twill, constructed from very smooth, even, firmly spun yarns. Dimensions: 170mm by 105mm. System 1: Z spun yarn, 15–18 threads per 10mm. System 2: similar S spun yarn, 15–16 threads per 10mm for a width of 120mm, then similar Z spun yarn, 17–18 threads per 10mm for the remaining 50mm.
A09–0104; C7306–7; B18 (Phase 2a), North Room and Hall–Construction (1); Phase IVb; Rig VII
Illus 38

260 2/1 Twill with nap ZS Wool
One piece (and a number of fragments) of mid-reddish brown, light weight 2/1 twill, with the remains of a light nap on both surfaces. Dimensions: 85mm by 75mm. System 1: fine Z spun yarn, about 10 threads per 10mm. System 2: slightly softer and thicker S spun yarn, about 10 threads per 10mm.
A09–0030; C9165–9; B18 (Phase 2a), North Room and Hall–Construction (1); Phase IVb; Rig VII
Not illustrated

261 Cordage Wool
Two fragments of cordage, each about 4mm in diameter, knotted together, consisting of fine, smooth Z ply yarns twisted together in the S direction; there are 18 elements in one piece and 25 in the other. Length 130mm.
A09–0061; C9165–9; B18 (Phase 2a), North Room and Hall–Construction (1); Phase IVb; Rig VII
Not illustrated

262 Felt (?) Wool
Fragments, very worn, of a dense, heavy medium weight sandy brown fabric, possibly genuine felt rather than the remains of a felted woven fabric. Dimensions: c45 by 20mm in all.
A09–0063; C9165–9; B18 (Phase 2a), North Room and Hall–Construction (1); Phase IVb; Rig VII
Not illustrated

263 2/1 Twill with nap ZS Wool
Two fragments of sandy brown, light weight, lightly felted 2/1 twill, with a slight nap on one surface. Dimensions: a) 55mm by 80mm; b) 34mm by 20mm. System 1: fine Z spun yarn, 13 threads per 10mm. System 2: thicker and softer S spun yarn, 11 threads per 10mm.
A09–0102; C7304–7; B18 (Phase 2a), North Room and Hall–Construction (2); Phase IVb; Rig VII
Not illustrated

264 2/1 Twill without nap ZZ Wool
Three pieces of dark brown, light weight, unfelted 2/1 twill, with both spinning and weaving even; piece (c) has a ridge running parallel to and about 7mm away from one margin, which probably represents a seam line, but no sewing thread survives. Dimensions: a) 220mm by 160mm; b) 55mm by 60mm; c) 65mm by 45mm. System 1: fine hard Z spun yarn, 18 threads per 10mm. System 2: similar Z spun yarn, 15 threads per 10mm.
A09–0105; C7311–7; B18 (Phase 2a), External 1, Pit 7314; Phase IVb; Rig VII
Illus 34

265 Yarn Wool

Small clew or knot of bright pink, single ply, fine smooth Z spun yarn. The yarn is less than 1mm in diameter. Dimensions: 32mm by 9mm.

A09–0112; C7323–7; B18 (Phase 2a), External 1, Pit 7314; Phase IVb; Rig VII

Not illustrated

266 Yarn Wool

Fragment of mid-reddish brown, fine smooth 2S ply yarn, about 1mm in diameter. Length 70mm.

A09–0118; C7323–7; B18 (Phase 2a), External 1, Pit 7314; Phase IVb; Rig VII

Not illustrated

267 Tabby Silk

One piece of fine, dull crimson red tabby, with fragments of a light brown 2S silk thread, very loosely plied, sewn through the fabric towards one edge. The textile is trapezoidal in shape, and has four cut edges. The yarn of System 2 is slightly coarser and more variable in diameter than the Z twisted yarn of System 1. In one area of coarser yarn, there are two threads in the same shed. A series of fine crease marks are visible on the textile, the trend of the creases is in the direction of system 1. Dimensions: 118mm by 64mm. System 1: fine, slightly Z twisted yarn, about 42mm threads per 10mm. System 2: untwisted yarn, 38 threads per 10mm.

A09–0127; C7323–7; B18 (Phase 2a), External 1, Pit 7314; Phase IVb; Rig VII

Not illustrated

268 Yarn Wool

Fragment of very coarse, hairy, Z spun, loose 2S ply mid-brown yarn about 10mm in diameter. Length 166mm.

A09–0128; C7343–7; B18 (Phase 2a), External 1, Pit 7314; Phase IVb; Rig VII

Not illustrated

269 2/2 Twill without nap ZZ Wool

One fragment of mid-brown, light weight, unfelted 2/2 twill, evenly spun and woven. Dimensions: 33mm by 37mm. System 1: fine, hard Z spun yarn, 17 threads per 10mm. System 2: similar yarn, 13 threads per 10mm.

A09–0099a; C7298–7; B18 (Phase 2b), North Room, Hall and Hall South–Occupation (10); Phase IVb; Rig VII

Not illustrated

270 Tabby (2 ply yarn) Wool

One fragment of very dark brown, heavy tabby, comparatively close woven. Dimensions: 80mm by 60mm. System 1: firm 2 ply yarn, Z spun and S plyed, 3.5 threads per 10mm. System 2: similar yarn, 2.5–3 threads per 10mm.

A09–0099b; C7298–7; B18 (Phase 2b), North Room, Hall and Hall South–Occupation (10); Phase IVb; Rig VII

Not illustrated

271 Tablet weaving Silk

Two fragments. The larger fragment (a) very worn, composed of three incomplete, patterned, tablet-woven bands and two lengths of tabby ribbon, joined width-wise to form a flat fabric, each length of ribbon separating two lengths of tablet weaving. The bands and the ribbon are silk throughout. Also detached fragment (b) of tablet-woven band. The bands, which are 16mm wide (except for one which has lost one selvedge but was presumably originally uniform with the others) appear to have been cut from one length. The weft, now golden brown but possibly originally white, is slightly Z twisted and entirely covered by the warp threads; there are about 20 weft picks threads per 10mm. There are 176 (?) warp threads, all 2S ply yarn, worked on 44(?) four-hole tablets in double-faced diagonal weave. The overall appearance of the warp is light brown, but some have a distinct greenish-yellow tinge (occupying a third of the width at one side of the tablet-woven bands) while others appear to have been white (or possibly pink). The bands are woven with a geometric design, light on dark on one side and reversed on the other, but the faded state of the yarns makes it uncertain whether one repeating motif has been used throughout the length of the bands. The ribbon, now also yellowish brown, is slightly under 5mm wide, with 22 warp ends of loosely S twisted yarn, and a loosely Z twisted weft; there are about 30 picks of weft threads per 10mm. The bands and the ribbons are joined by oversewing the edges with fine, slightly S twisted, yellowish brown yarn. There are also traces of a bright pink 2S ply yarn which seems to have been used for repair; at one point, where the ribbon has apparently worn away, the edges of the two adjacent tablet-woven bands have been drawn together and secured with the pink thread. Dimensions: a) 110mm by 55mm; b) 15mm by 60mm.

A09–0097; C7299–7; B18 (Phase 2b), North Room, Hall and Hall South–Occupation (10); Phase IVb; Rig VII

Illus 53

272 Tabby (2 ply yarn) Wool

One piece of mottled mid-brown, heavy tabby, comparatively close textured. Dimensions: 162mm by 125mm. System 1: firm 2 ply yarn, Z spun and S plyed, 3.5 threads per 10mm. System 2: similar yarn, 3.5–5 threads per 10mm. Dye: trace of madder (MW).

A09–0147; C7299–7; B18 (Phase 2b), North Room, Hall and Hall South–Occupation (10); Phase IVb; Rig VII

Illus 16

273 2/1 Twill with nap ZZ Wool

One piece (and three fragments), very worn, of mid-brown, medium weight, heavily felted 2/1 twill, with the nap raised on both surfaces. Dimensions: 73mm by 45mm. System 1: Z spun yarn, 8–9 threads per 10mm. System 2: slightly heavier Z spun yarn, 7 threads per 10mm.

A09–0024; C9132–9; B18 (Phase 2b), North Room, Hall and Hall South–Occupation (10); Phase IVb; Rig VII

Not illustrated

274 Tabby (2 ply yarn) Wool
One piece of very dark brown, very heavy tabby, coarse to the touch and comparatively compact, with 95mm of closed edge of simple structure, remaining on one margin. Dimensions: 240mm by 130mm. System 1: warp, firm 2 ply yarn, Z spun and S plyed, 3–3.5 threads per 10mm. System 2: weft, similar yarn, 2 threads per 10mm.
A09–0032a; C9132–9; B18 (Phase 2b), North Room, Hall and Hall South–Occupation (10); Phase IVb; Rig VII
Not illustrated

275 2/1 Twill without nap ZS Wool
One fragment of very dark brown, light weight 2/1 twill, compact and smooth to the touch. Dimensions: 40mm by 35mm. System 1: fine, even Z spun yarn, 12 threads per 10mm. System 2: thicker S spun yarn, 10 threads per 10mm.
A09–0032b; C9132–9; B18 (Phase 2b), North Room, Hall and Hall South–Occupation (10); Phase IVb; Rig VII
Not illustrated

276 2/1 Twill without nap ZZ Wool
Two pieces of dark brown, light weight, unfelted 2/1 twill, evenly spun and woven; both pieces have signs of a seam line on one margin, but without traces of sewing thread. Dimensions: a) 143mm by 100mm; b) 110mm by 65mm. System 1: fine hard Z spun yarn, 14 threads per 10mm. System 2: the same.
A09–0045; C9132–9; B18 (Phase 2b); North Room, Hall and Hall South–Occupation (10); Phase IVb; Rig VII
Not illustrated

277 2/1 Twill with nap ZS Wool
One fragment of distinct red-brown, light medium weight 2/1 twill, heavily felted and with the nap raised on both surfaces to give a smooth, even finish. Dimensions: 45mm by 27mm. System 1: fine even Z spun yarn, 10 threads per 10mm. System 2: similar S spun yarn, 8 threads per 10mm.
A09–0049a; C9132–9; B18 (Phase 2b), North Room, Hall and Hall South–Occupation (10); Phase IVb; Rig VII
Not illustrated

278 2/1 Twill without nap ZS Wool
One small piece (and a number of fragments) of light brown, light weight 2/1 twill, unfelted but slightly soft to the touch. The largest piece measures 30mm by 53mm. System 1: fine Z spun yarn, slightly variable in thickness, about 13–14 threads per 10mm. System 2: S spun yarn, 13–14 threads per 10mm.
A09–0049b; C9132–9; B18 (Phase 2b), North Room, Hall and Hall South–Occupation (10); Phase IVb; Rig VII
Not illustrated

279 2/1 Twill without nap ZZ Wool
Three fragments of dark brown, light weight, unfelted 2/1 twill, comparatively even in both spinning and weaving. Dimensions: a) 40mm by 50mm; b) 45mm by 45mm; c) 25mm by 15mm. System 1: smooth firm Z spun yarn, 12 threads per 10mm. System 2: the same. Dye: Q, unknown (MW).
A09–0056a; C9132–9; B18 (Phase 2b), North Room, Hall and Hall South–Occupation (10); Phase IVb; Rig VII
Not illustrated

280 2/1 Twill without (?)nap ZS Wool
Eight fragments, very worn, of light brown, light weight 2/1 twill, lightly felted, close woven and soft to the touch. The weave is indistinct in places but this appears to be the result of wear rather than deliberate raising of the nap. Dimensions: a) 21mm by 17mm; b) 15mm by 20mm; c) 21mm by 25mm; d) 26mm by 21mm; e) 39mm by 14mm; f) 16mm by 27mm; g) 22mm by 18mm; h) 11mm by 25mm. System 1: Z spun yarn, 12 threads per 10mm. System 2: thicker S spun yarn, tightly twisted, about 12 threads per 10mm.
A09–0056b; C9132–9; B18 (Phase 2b), North Room, Hall and Hall South–Occupation (10); Phase IVb; Rig VII
Not illustrated

281 2/1 Twill with nap ZS Wool
One fragment, very worn, (and two smaller scraps) of dark red-brown, light weight 2/1 twill, with a slight nap on one surface. Dimensions: 30mm by 32mm. System 1: fine, soft Z spun yarn, 14 threads per 10mm. System 2: similar S spun yarn, 12 threads per 10mm.
A09–0071; C9132–9; B18 (Phase 2b), North Room, Hall and Hall South–Occupation (10); Phase IVb; Rig VII
Not illustrated

282 2/1 Twill without nap ZS Wool
One fragment of reddish mid-brown, light medium weight 2/1 twill, soft and lightly felted. The yarns are brittle and in poor condition. There are the remains of a closed edge with two pairs of heavy, Z spun, dark brown threads, each pair acting as one element, in the outermost two places. This may be a starting edge (cf Hoffmann 1964, Figs 70–76). Dimensions: 25mm by 70mm. System 1: fine Z spun yarn, 8–9 threads per 10mm. System 2 (parallel to closed edge), slightly softer and thicker S spun yarn, about 10 threads per 10mm.
A09–0077a; C9132–9; B18 (Phase 2b), North Room, Hall and Hall South–Occupation (10); Phase IVb; Rig VII
Illus 35

283 2/1 Twill with nap ZS Wool
Seven fragments, in very poor condition, of mid-brown, medium weight 2/1 twill, closely woven and soft to the touch, with traces of a slight nap. On three of the pieces, the thick S spun yarn on one of the margins is replaced by fine S spun yarn similar in weight to that in System 1; the threads are closely packed (about 12 in 5mm). These may represent a weft stripe, but the fragments are too damaged for certainty. Dimensions: c150mm by 70mm in all. System 1: fine, even Z spun yarn, 10 threads per 10mm. System 2: considerably heavier S spun yarn, variable in thickness and tension, 7–9 threads per 10mm.
A09–0077b; C9132–9; B18 (Phase 2b), North Room, Hall and Hall South–Occupation (10); Phase IVb; Rig VII
Illus 42

284 2/1 Twill without nap ZZ Wool
Two pieces (and a fragment) of dark brown, light weight, closely woven, unfelted 2/1 will, firm to the touch. Dimensions: a) 145mm by 115mm; b) 43mm by 35mm. System 1: firm Z spun yarn, about 18 threads per 10mm. System 2: similar yarn, 14–15 threads per 10mm.
A09–0027; C9179–9; B18 (Phase 2b), North Room, Hall and Hall South–Occupation (10); Phase IVb; Rig VII
Not illustrated

285 Yarn Wool
Fragment of very heavy dark brown 2S ply yarn about 5mm in diameter. Length 115mm.
A09–0095; C7289–7; B18 (Phase 2b), Hall and Hall South–Occupation (12a); Phase IVb; Rig VII
Not illustrated

286 2/1 Twill without nap ZZ Wool
One fragment of dark brown, light weight, unfelted 2/1 twill, closely woven and firm to the touch. Dimensions: 85mm by 9mm. System 1: fine Z spun yarn, 15 threads per 10mm (estimated) System 2: similar yarn 12 threads per 10mm.
A09–0022; C9095–9; B18 (Phase 2b), Hall and Hall South–Occupation (12a); Phase IVb; Rig VII
Not illustrated

287 2/1 Twill without nap ZZ Wool
One piece of dark brown, light weight, unfelted 2/1 twill, evenly spun and woven. Dimensions: 203mm by 170mm. System 1: smooth, firm Z spun yarn, 13 threads per 10mm. System 2: the same.
A09–0039; C9095–9; B18 (Phase 2b), Hall and Hall South–Occupation (12a); Phase IVb; Rig VII
Not illustrated

288 2/1 Twill without nap ZZ Wool
One piece, worn, of dark brown, light weight, unfelted 2/1 twill, comparatively even in spinning and weaving. Dimensions: 65mm by 70mm. System 1: Z spun yarn, 14 threads per 10mm. System 2: similar yarn, 16 threads per 10mm.
A09–0092a; C7235–7; B18 (Phase 2b), North Room and Hall–Floor (2); Phase IVb; Rig VII
Not illustrated

289 2/1 Twill without nap ZS Wool
Two pieces of light medium weight, mid-brown 2/1 twill, firm to the touch and unfelted, apart from one margin on each piece which may have been seamed. The thickness of the yarn in both systems is variable. Dimensions: a) 185mm by 205mm; b) 120mm by 75mm. System 1: Z spun yarn, 10–12 threads per 10mm. System 2: slightly heavier S spun yarn, about 11 threads per 10mm.
A09–0092b; C7235–7; B18 (Phase 2b), North Room and Hall–Floor (2); Phase IVb; Rig VII
Not illustrated

290 2/1 Twill with nap ZS Wool
One piece of distinct red-brown, medium weight 2/1 twill, with the nap raised on both surfaces; both the nap and the red tint are more pronounced on the surface in which the S spun yarns predominate. Both spinning and weaving are uneven. Dimensions: 215mm by 242mm. System 1: Z spun yarn, about 12 threads per 10mm. System 2: thicker and softer S spun yarn, about 10 threads per 10mm.
A09–0093; C7235–7; B18 (Phase 2b), North Room and Hall–Floor (2); Phase IVb; Rig VII
Illus 41

291 2/1 Twill without nap ZS Wool
Three pieces (and some fragments) of dark brown, light weight, unfelted 2/1 twill. Dimensions: a) 127mm by 80mm; b) 140mm by 60mm; c) 98mm by 75mm. System 1: smooth, fine Z spun yarn, 11 threads per 10mm. System 2: similar but less regular S spun yarn, 10 threads per 10mm.
A09–0038; C9103–9; B18 (Phase 2b), Hall South–Occupation (13a); Phase IVb; Rig VII
Not illustrated

292 Tabby (2 ply yarn) Wool
One piece (and two fragments) of dark brown, heavy tabby, coarse to the touch and slightly open textured. Dimensions: 205mm by 180mm. System 1: very firm 2 ply yarn, Z spun and S plyed, 3–4 threads per 10mm. System 2: similar yarn, 3 threads per 10mm.
A09–0029; C9156–9; B18 (Phase 2b), Hall South–Occupation (13b); Phase IVb; Rig VII
Not illustrated

293 2/1 Twill without nap ZS Wool
One piece of dark reddish brown, light weight, unfelted 2/1 twill. Dimensions: 45mm by 50mm. System 1: Z spun yarn, 10 threads per 10mm. System 2: similar S spun yarn, 14 threads per 10mm.
A9127; C2530–3; MC155, Pit 2691; Phase IVb,IVc; Rig V
Not illustrated

294 2/1 Twill without nap ZS Wool
Two pieces (and five fragments) of dark brown, light weight 2/1 twill, unfelted, close woven and firm to the touch. Both spinning and weaving are comparatively even. Dimensions: a) 190mm by 100mm; b) 65mm by 95mm. System 1: smooth firm Z spun yarn, 20 threads per 10mm. System 2: similar S spun yarn, 17–18 threads per 10mm.
A6128; C2476–3; M1.4d; Phase IVb,IVc; Rig VI
Not illustrated

295 Felt Wool
Two pieces of dark brown heavy felt, uneven in colour and texture. Dimensions: a) 105mm by 65mm; b) 100mm by 50mm.
A6696; C2476–3; M1.4d; Phase IVb,IVc; Rig VI
Not illustrated

296 Yarn Wool
Very dark brown, coarse, hairy 2S ply yarn, 3–4mm in diameter. Length 170mm.
A8099; C2476–3; M1.4d; Phase IVb,IVc; Rig VI
Not illustrated

297 2/1 Twill with nap ZS Wool
One piece of distinct red-brown, medium weight 2/1 twill, felted and with a pronounced nap (now partially worn) on both sides. Dimensions: 110mm by 30mm. System 1: fine Z spun yarn, about 12 threads per 10mm. System 2: thicker, softer S spun yarn, about 7 threads per 10mm. Wool type: System 1 M, pigment +; System 2 S, no pigment; both with traces of red dye (MR). Dye: madder (MW).
A8101; C2476–3; M1.4d; Phase IVb,IVc; Rig VI
Illus 40

298 2/1 Twill (?) with nap ZS Wool
One fragment of bright, even mid-brown, light weight but heavily felted fabric, with the nap raised on both sides: the finish is exceptionally smooth and even and suggests a high quality product; the structure is largely obscured but is probably 2/1 twill. Dimensions: 35mm by 20mm. System 1: fine even Z spun yarn, no count possible. System 2: similar S spun yarn.
A8515; C2476–3; M1.4d; Phase IVb,IVc; Rig VI
Not illustrated

299 Tabby (2 ply yarn) Wool
Two pieces of dark brown, heavy tabby, coarse to the touch; the threads are irregularly packed giving a close texture in some parts and an open texture in others. Dimensions: a) 45mm by 120mm; b) 60mm by 120mm. System 1: firm 2 ply yarn, S spun and Z plyed, 3–5 threads per 10mm. System 2: similar yarn, 2–3 threads per 10mm. Wool type: System 1 HM, pigment +, no dye; System 2 H, pigment +, no dye (MR).
A9904; C2476–3; M1.4d; Phase IVb,IVc; Rig VI
Not illustrated

300 Yarn Wool?
Dark brown, coarse fibre, Z spun yarn with a diameter which varies from 2mm to 8mm. Length 810mm.
A8084; C2577–3; M1.4d, Pit 2566; Phase IVb,IVc; Rig VI
Not illustrated

301 2/1 Twill with nap ZS Wool
One piece of reddish mid-brown, light medium weight 2/1 twill, lightly felted and with a slight nap, now worn, on both surfaces; neither spinning nor weaving is particularly even. Dimensions: 200mm by 35mm. System 1: fine Z spun yarn, 14–15 threads per 10mm. System 2: thicker S spun yarn, about 10 threads per 10mm. Dye: both indigotin and madder present (MW).
A8097a; C2577–3; M1.4d, Pit 2566; Phase IVb,IVc; Rig VI
Not illustrated

302 2/1 Twill with nap ZS Wool
Four fragments of sandy brown, light medium weight 2/1 twill, lightly felted and with a slight nap on both surfaces. Dimensions: a) 50mm by 20mm; b) 60mm by 12mm; c) 30 by 10mm; d) 50mm by 5mm. System 1: fine Z spun yarn, 12 threads per 10mm. System 2: thicker S spun yarn, 8 threads per 10mm. Wool type: System 1 M, no pigment; System 2 FGM, no pigment; indications of a pale yellow dye in both systems (MR).
A8097b; C2577–3; M1.4d, Pit 2566; Phase IVb,IVc; Rig VI
Not illustrated

303 2/1 Twill (?) with nap ZS Wool
One piece of dark brown, medium weight, very heavily felted and compact fabric; the weave is obscured, but may be 2/1 twill. Dimensions: 43mm by 60mm. System 1: fine Z spun yarn, no count possible. System 2: S spun (?), no count possible.
A12372a; C2577–3; M1.4d, Pit 2566; Phase IVb,IVc; Rig VI
Not illustrated

304 2/1 Twill without nap ZS Wool
Two fragments of light weight, mid-brown 2/1 twill, lightly felted, close woven and soft to the touch. Dimensions: a) 15mm by 20mm; b) 15mm by 25mm. System 1: fine Z spun yarn, 15 threads per 10mm. System 2: similar S spun yarn, 12 threads per 10mm.
A12372b; C2577–3; M1.4d, Pit 2566; Phase IVb,IVc; Rig VI
Not illustrated

305 2/1 Twill without nap ZS Wool
One piece of very dark brown, light medium weight 2/1 twill, unfelted but comparatively soft to the touch; 80mm by 70mm. System 1: smooth but uneven Z spun yarn, 10–12 threads per 10mm. System 2: more even S spun yarn, 12 threads per 10mm.
A03–0253; L1344B; C7258–7; M1.4h; Phase IVc; Rig VI
Not illustrated

306 Tabby (2 ply yarn) Wool
One piece (and four fragments) of mottled dark brown, very heavy tabby, coarse to the touch and comparatively even in both spinning and weaving. Dimensions: 260mm by 180mm. System 1: very firm 2 ply yarn, Z spun and S plyed, 3 threads per 10mm. System 2: the same. See yarn Cat No 312/A6653d.
A6144; C2462A-3; M1.4c; Phase IIIa–IVcc; Rigs V and VI
Not illustrated

307 Braid Silk
Length of flattened whipcording, 3mm wide, constructed from bright mid-brown, soft 2S ply yarn; there are thirty two elements. Length 196mm.
A6637; C2462A-3; M1.4c; Phase IIIa–IVcc; Rigs V and VI
Illus 69

308 Yarn Wool
Very coarse, hairy, very dark brown 2S ply yarn, about 5mm in diameter. Length 115mm.
A6642; C2462A-3; M1.4c; Phase IIIa–IVcc; Rigs V and VI
Not illustrated

309 2/1 Twill without nap ZS Wool
One piece of uneven dark brown, light weight, unfelted 2/1 twill, evenly spun and woven. Dimensions: c40mm by 160mm. System 1: Z spun yarn, 14 threads per 10mm. System 2: S spun yarn, 13 threads per 10mm.
A6653a; C2462A-3; M1.4c; Phase IIIa–IVcc; Rigs V and VI
Not illustrated

310 2/1 Twill without nap ZS Wool
One fragment of mid-brown, light weight, unfelted 2/1 twill, evenly spun and woven. Dimensions: 37mm by 16mm. System 1: fine Z spun yarn, 19 threads per 10mm. System 2: similar S spun yarn, 15 threads per 10mm.
A6653b; C2462A-3; M1.4c; Phase IIIa–IVcc; Rigs V and VI
Not illustrated

311 2/1 Twill without nap ZS Wool
One fragment of very dark brown, light weight, unfelted 2/1 twill, the yarns slightly variable in thickness. Dimensions: 32mm by 27mm. System 1: firm Z spun yarn, 18 threads per 10mm. System 2: similar S spun yarn, 13–14 threads per 10mm.
A6653c; C2462A-3; M1.4c; Phase IIIa–IVcc; Rigs V and VI
Not illustrated

312 Yarn Wool

Dark brown, firm, thick 2S ply yarn, possibly from Cat No 306/A6144 above; from 2–3mm diameter. Length 130mm.
A6653d; C2462A–3; M1.4c; Phase IIIa–IVcc; Rigs V and VI
Not illustrated

313 Tabby (2 ply yarn) Wool

Five pieces, very brittle and worn, of very dark brown, very heavy tabby; the threads are widely and unevenly spaced and the tension and thickness of the yarn are variable. One piece has 40mm of closed edge, of simple structure, on one margin. Diameter: a) 200mm by 140mm; b) 225mm by 120mm; c) 165mm by 85mm; d) 125mm by 135mm; e) 55mm by 30mm. System 1: warp, 2ply yarn, S spun and Z plyed, 1.5–3 threads per 10mm. System 2: weft, the same.
A6701; C2462A–3; M1.4c; Phase IIIa–IVcc; Rigs V and VI
Not illustrated

314 2/1 Twill without nap ZZ Wool

Two pieces of dark brown, light weight, unfelted 2/1 twill, firm to the touch. Dimensions: a) 85mm by 75mm; b) 43mm by 55mm. System 1: fine Z spun yarn, 16 threads per 10mm. System 2: less even Z spun yarn, 13–15 threads per 10mm.
A6708; C2462A–3; M1.4c; Phase IIIa–IVcc; Rigs V and VI
Not illustrated

315 2/1 Twill with nap ZS Wool

Two fragments of sandy brown, light weight, lightly felted 2/1 twill, with the remains of a light nap on both surfaces. Dimensions: a) 45mm by 50mm; b) 60mm by 25mm. System 1: Z spun yarn, 10 threads per 10mm. System 2: similar S spun yarn, about 11 threads per 10mm.
A7352a; C2462A–3; M1.4c; Phase IIIa–IVcc; Rigs V and VI
Not illustrated

316 2/1 Twill with nap ZS Wool

One fragment of reddish mid-brown, light weight 2/1 twill, slightly felted and with the remains of a light nap on both surfaces. Dimensions: 47mm by 47mm. System 1: smooth Z spun yarn, about 12 threads per 10mm. System 2: slightly heavier, and less even, S spun yarn, 11–13 threads per 10 mm.
A7352b; C2462A–3; M1.4c; Phase IIIa–IVcc; Rigs V and VI
Not illustrated

317 Yarn Wool

Unconserved bundle of yarns in poor condition, measuring approximately 90mm by 35mm. The yarn is dark brown, with coarse fibres; S spun and 2Z plied with a loose ply angle, 2–3mm in diameter.
A8914; C2462A–3; M1.4c; Phase IIIa–IVcc; Rigs V and VI
Not illustrated

318 2/1 Twill with nap ZS Wool

Two pieces, very worn, of bright sandy brown, light weight 2/1 twill, soft to the touch; there is a light nap on one surface, although this is possibly the result of wear. Dimensions: a) 75mm by 60mm; b) 75mm by 55mm. System 1: Z spun yarn, 9–10 threads per 10mm. System 2: softer S spun yarn, 8 threads per 10mm.
A7424; C2537–3; M1.4c; Phase IIIa–IVcc; Rigs V and VI
Not illustrated

319 2/1 Twill without nap ZS Wool

Four small pieces (and a number of fragments) of dark brown, light weight 2/1 twill, unfelted but close woven and comparatively soft to the touch. Dimensions: a) 60mm by 80mm; b) 90mm by 75mm; c) 85mm by 60mm; d) 100mm by 60mm. System 1: Z spun yarn, 12 threads per 10mm. System 2: softer S spun yarn, about 10 threads per 10mm.
A09–0010; C9021–9; P8.3; Phase IVc,IVcc; Rig VII
Not illustrated

320 2/1 Twill without nap ZS Wool

One fragment of bright mid-brown, medium weight 2/1 twill. Dimensions: 20mm by 70mm. System 1: smooth Z spun yarn, 10 threads per 10mm. System 2: thicker and softer S spun yarn, 8–10 threads per 10mm.
A09–0085; C7218–7; M9a; Phase IVc,IVcc; Rig VII
Not illustrated

321 2/1 Twill without nap ZZ Wool

One piece of dark brown, light medium weight 2/1 twill, unfelted but closely woven and compact; both spinning and weaving are even. Dimensions: 635mm by 308mm. System 1: smooth Z spun yarn, 12 threads per 10mm. System 2: similar yarn, 10 threads per 10mm.
A09–0051; C7226–7; M9a; Phase IVc,IVcc; Rig VII
Not illustrated

322 2/1 Twill without nap ZZ Wool

One small piece (and five fragments) of mid-brown, light weight, unfelted hard 2/1 twill, even in spinning and weaving. Dimensions: 55mm by 60mm. System 1: fine Z spun yarn, 16 threads per 10mm. System 2: similar yarn, 14 threads per 10mm.
A09–0076; C7231–7; M9a; Phase IVc,IVcc; Rig VII
Not illustrated

323 Tabby Silk

One fragment of fine, closely woven bright brown tabby. It should be noted that the long dimension does not follow system 1, since the piece is cut on the bias. All edges are cut, and the fragment has the shape of an attenuated triangle with a notch protruding from one of the long edges. Dimensions: 115mm by 25mm. System 1: fine, slightly Z twisted yarn, 41–45 threads per 10mm. System 2: contains two yarns, an untwisted yarn, of which there are 48–50 threads per 10mm, and a coarser yarn with a slight Z twist, of which there are 19 threads per 5mm. This coarser yarn is visible in bands at upper and lower angles of the fragment, but these surviving bands are at most 8mm deep.
A09–0059; C7238–7; M9a; Phase IVc,IVcc; Rig VII
Not illustrated

324 2/2 Twill without nap ZS Wool

Four pieces of medium weight, dark brown, unfelted but close woven 2/2 twill, firm to the touch. Dimensions: a) 80mm by 75mm; b) 60mm by 42mm; c) 35mm by 30mm; d) 25mm by 20mm. System 1: smooth Z spun yarn, 8 threads per 10mm. System 2: similar S spun yarn, 8 threads per 10mm.
A09–0014; C9013–9; M9a; Phase IVc,IVcc; Rig VII
Illus 30

325 2/1 Twill without nap ZZ Wool
One piece of dark brown, light weight, evenly spun and woven, unfelted 2/1 twill. Dimensions: 60mm by 65mm. System 1: smooth Z spun yarn, 15 threads per 10mm. System 2: similar yarn, 14–16 per 10mm.
A09–0080; C6108–10; M9b(b); Phase IVc,IVcc; Rig VIII
Not illustrated

326 2/1 Twill with nap ZS Wool
One fragment of reddish mid-brown, medium weight felted 2/1 twill with traces of nap on both surfaces. Dimensions: 77mm by 60mm. System 1: Z spun yarn, about 14 threads per 10mm. System 2: similar S spun yarn, 10 threads per 10mm.
A7616; C2543–3; M1.4e; Phase IVcc(Va); Rig VI
Not illustrated

327 Yarn Wool
Unconserved loose bundle of yarn, rich dark brown in colour, but with coarse fibres, S spun and 2Z plied. The diameter is 3mm.
A8867; C2782–2; M1.4e; Phase IVcc(Va); Rig VI
Not illustrated

328 2/1 Twill without nap ZS Wool
One piece of dark brown, light weight, unfelted 2/1 twill. Dimensions: 110mm by 120mm. System 1: smooth Z spun yarn, 10 threads per 10mm. System 2: slightly heavier S spun yarn, 8 threads per 10mm.
A6631; C2452–3; M1.4e, Pit 2446; Phase IVcc(Va); Rig VI
Not illustrated

329 2/1 Twill with nap ZS Wool
One piece of black, heavy medium weight 2/1 twill, felted and compact, with a distinct nap on both surfaces. Probably the same fabric as Cat No 347/A8859. Dimensions: 280mm by 50mm. System 1: Z spun yarn, about 10 threads per 10mm. System 2: softer S spun yarn, 6 threads per 10mm.
A6644; C2427–3; P6; Phase IVcc,Va; Rig VI
Not illustrated

330 Yarn Silk ?
Nine lengths (up to 217mm long) of very fine, very dark brown 2S ply yarn; possibly sewing thread. Each yarn is less than 0.5mm diameter, and the total width of the group is 3mm. cf the dark brown yarn used to stitch silk tabby Cat No 346/A09–0044.
A7841; C2544–3; P6; Phase IVcc,Va; Rig VI
Not illustrated

331 2/1 Twill without nap ZS Wool
One piece of mid to dark brown, light medium weight 2/1 twill, unfelted but compact and slightly soft to the touch. Dimensions: 80mm by 50mm. System 1: smooth Z spun yarn, of irregular thickness, 10 threads per 10mm. System 2: similar S spun yarn, 7–8 threads per 10mm.
A6152; C2759–2; B34, MF2759; Phase Va; Rig VI
Not illustrated

332 2/1 Twill without nap ZS Wool
Two pieces of light weight, dark brown unfelted 2/1 twill, close woven and slightly soft to the touch; probably the same fabric as Cat No 333/A6652a. Dimensions: a) 75mm by 88mm; b) 65mm by 35mm. System 1: fine smooth Z spun yarn, 18 threads per 10mm. System 2: similar S spun yarn, 18 threads per 10mm.
A6151; C2421–3; B34, Floor; Phase Va; Rig VI
Not illustrated

333 2/1 Twill without nap ZS Wool
Three pieces of dark brown, light weight, unfelted but closely woven 2/1 twill. Dimensions: a) 110mm by 170mm; b) 113mm by 149mm; c) 65mm by 45mm. System 1: fine, even Z spun yarn, 18 threads per 10mm. System 2: similar S spun yarn, 18 threads per 10mm. No dye (MW).
A6652a; C2421–3; B34, Floor; Phase Va; Rig VI
Not illustrated

334 2/1 Twill without nap ZZ Wool
One piece, very worn, of light weight, bright mid-brown, unfelted 2/1 twill. Dimensions: 95mm by 80mm. System 1: Z spun yarn, 13–15 threads per 10mm. System 2: similar yarn, 11 threads per 10mm. No dye (MW).
A6652b; C2421–3; B34, Floor; Phase Va; Rig VI
Not illustrated

335 2/1 Twill without nap ZS Wool
One piece of mid-brown, light weight 2/1 twill, unfelted but slightly soft to the touch; both spinning and weaving are even. Dimensions: 75mm by 80mm. System 1: smooth Z spun yarn, 13 threads per 10mm. System 2: similar S spun yarn, 11 threads per 10mm.
A09–0052; C7191–7; B34–Courtyard; Phase Va; Rig VI
Not illustrated

336 Net Silk
Fragments (about 220mm by 130mm in all) of fine net, now a yellowish brown shade, constructed from firm 2S silk yarn. The yarn is knotted every 3–4mm to form a simple lozenge mesh. The net is similar to but slightly heavier than the ground of the two examples of lacis (Cat Nos 351/A7577a, 352/A7577b and 370/A10112).
cf four knotted mesh hairnets are known from sites in London, constructed from 2S silk yarn, dating from the late 13th to late 14th centuries (Crowfoot et al 1992, 145–9).
A09–0055; C7191–7; B34–Courtyard; Phase Va; Rig VI
Not illustrated

337 2/1 Twill without nap, Others Wool
One piece of light medium weight, dark brown, unfelted 2/1 twill; there are a number of shedding (?) mistakes and the cloth has a careless appearance. Dimensions: 195mm by 205mm. System 1: smooth but irregular Z spun yarn interspersed at intervals of 12 to 14 threads by two S spun elements in regular succession across the width of the textile, about 13 threads per 10mm. System 2: heavier S spun yarn, about 9 threads per 10mm.
A09–0041; C7200–7; B34–Courtyard; Phase Va; Rig VI
Illus 37

338 2/1 Twill without nap ZZ Wool
One piece of dark brown, light weight, unfelted and slightly open-textured 2/1 twill, relatively even in both spinning and weaving. Dimensions: 270mm by 115mm. System 1: smooth Z spun yarn, 14 threads per 10mm. System 2: similar yarn, 13 threads per 10mm.
A09–0050; C7200–7; B34–Courtyard; Phase Va; Rig VI
Not illustrated

339 Yarn Silk ?
Six fragments, very worn, of Z spun, 2S ply yellow-brown yarn, now partially unplied. The greatest length is 240mm, and the yarns have a diameter of 1mm or less. One length is Z plied with a rich mid-brown yarn which is coarser than the S plied yarns.
A09–0053; C7185–7; P8.4; Phase Va; Rig VII
Not illustrated

340 2/1 Twill without nap ZZ Wool
One piece of light medium weight, unfelted, dark brown 2/1 twill, moderately firm to the touch. Dimensions: 60mm by 105mm. System 1: smooth Z spun yarn, variable in thickness, 10 threads per 10mm. System 2: similar yarn, 10–11 threads per 10mm.
A09–0054; C7185–7; P8.4; Phase Va; Rig VII
Not illustrated

341 Yarn Wool
A mass of smooth Z yarn in various shades of brown, all about 1mm in diameter and mostly 100–150mm long, possibly waste cut from the end of a web of cloth.
A09–0087; C7185–7; P8.4; Phase Va; Rig VII
Not illustrated

342 Twill Silk
Two fragments, very worn, of dark golden yellow 1/2 weft-faced compound twill. The ridges of the twill form Z-diagonals. Both pieces are roughly triangular in shape. In (b) one of the margins consists of a side selvedge with no special treatment other than the closer spacing of approximately 18 warp ends; the other two edges are cut. In (a) the edges are cut, but the outline is worn. The main warp and binding warp are of fine, firmly Z twisted yarn. There is a proportion of one main end to each binding end, with 17 binding warp ends threads per 10mm and 17 main warp ends threads per 10mm. There are two wefts, of untwisted yarn which is coarser in diameter then the warp. The weft count is of 24 threads per 10mm on each face of the fabric. Dimensions: a) 120mm by 33mm; b) 62mm by 55mm.
A09–0088; C7185–7; P8.4; Phase Va; Rig VII
Not illustrated

343 Tabby Silk
One piece of bright mid-brown, fine tabby. There is a selvedge intact on one long edge; the warp threads are more closely packed towards the closed edge and the weft passes round a bundle of threads serving as the outermost warp end. The other three edges are cut and the piece is rectangular in shape. At a distance of about 45mm from the selvedge, two warp ends are paired. All the other warp ends are used singly. The weft is coarser in diameter than the warp, and it is more densely packed in some areas than in others. The fragment is in a deteriorated condition at one end, and there are wear mark in

the direction of the weft. Dimensions: 300mm by 152mm. System 1: warp, fine slightly Z twisted yarn, 35–37 threads per 10mm. System 2: weft, untwisted yarn, about 32–35 threads per 10mm.
A09–0046; C7208–7; P8.4; Phase Va; Rig VII
Not illustrated

344 Tabby Silk
One piece of bright mid-brown, fine tabby with a selvedge intact on one long edge. Similar in every respect to and probably part of the same fabric as Cat No 343/A09–0046, apart from the one paired warp which is not a feature of this piece. This fragment also has three cut edges and is rectangular in shape, but it is in a more deteriorated condition. A series of fine crease marks trend in the direction of the weft. System 1: warp, fine lightly Z twisted yarn, 33–35 threads per 10mm. System 2: weft, untwisted yarn, about 31–35 threads per 10mm.
A09–0047a; C7208–7; P8.4; Phase Va; Rig VII
Not illustrated

345 Yarn Wool?
Mottled dark brown, coarse, hairy, 2S ply yarn, 5–6mm in diameter. Length 225mm.
A09–0047b; C7208–7; P8.4; Phase Va; Rig VII
Not illustrated

346 Tabby Silk
Two fragments, sewn together, of bright but fairly dark brown fine tabby. One edge on each piece has been turned in to a depth of 4–5mm. The two folded edges are linked with a rich dark brown 2S ply yarn. The hems are held down with a row of running stitch along the edge of the hem. On the larger fragment, there is another row of running stitches parallel to, and at a distance of 25mm from, the folded edge of the hem. All the stitching is executed in a similar silk 2S yarn. The two sides of the fragment measure, respectively, a) 45mm by 50mm, b) 20mm by 45mm. The piece as a whole has four cut edges, but it is somewhat irregular in shape. Dimensions: 72mm by 55mm overall. System 1: fine, slightly Z twisted yarn, 35–38 threads per 10mm. System 2: untwisted yarn, about 32–34 threads per 10mm. The threads of system 2 are coarser in diameter than those of system 1.
A09–0044; C7209–7; P8.4; Phase Va; Rig VII
Illus 23

347 2/1 Twill with nap ZS Wool
One fragment of black, heavy medium weight, heavily fulled 2/1 twill with the nap raised on both surfaces. Probably the same fabric as Cat No 329/A6644. Dimensions: 55mm by 29mm. System 1: Z spun yarn, about 10 threads per 10mm. System 2: softer S spun yarn, about 6 threads per 10mm.
A8859; C2403–3; P6 & B1(b), Destruction; Phase IVcc,Va; Rig VI
Not illustrated

348 2/1 Twill without nap ZS Wool
One piece of very dark brown, light weight, unfelted 2/1 twill, the threads unevenly packed. Dimensions: 115mm by 100mm. System 1: fine, hard Z spun yarn, 15 threads per 10mm. System 2: softer S spun yarn, 11 threads per 10mm. Wool type: System 1 HM, pigment +++, no dye; System 2 GM, pigment +++, no dye (MR).
A6710a; C2477–3; B1(a), T2477; Phase IVcc,Va; Rig V
Not illustrated

349 2/1 Twill without nap ZZ Wool
One piece of even dark brown, light weight 2/1 twill, unfelted but soft to the touch; uneven spinning and shedding mistakes give the cloth a careless appearance. Dimensions: 85mm by 130mm. System 1: Z spun yarn, 14 threads per 10mm. System 2: similar yarn, 12–16 threads per 10mm. Wool type: System 1 S, pigment +, dark dye; System 2 HM, pigment +, red dye (MR).
A6710b; C2477–3; B1(a), T2477; Phase IVcc,Va; Rig V
Not illustrated

350 2/1 Twill without nap ZZ Wool
One piece of dark brown, light weight, unfelted 2/1 twill, close woven and firm to the touch, with 45mm of closed edge, of simple structure, remaining on one margin. Dimensions: 130mm by 85mm. System 1: warp, smooth Z spun yarn, 18 threads per 10mm. System 2: weft, similar yarn, 18–20 threads per 10mm.
A6695; C2464–3; B1(a), Levelling; Phase IVcc,Va; Rig V
Not illustrated

351 Net (darned) (and braid) Silk
352 Braid (and net (darned)) Silk
One strip (Cat No 351/A7577a), incomplete and heavily worn, of lacis (embroidered net) – the remains of a decorative hair-covering. An incomplete length of narrow braid (Cat No 352/A7577b) is attached to the lower edge. The ground is of fine, firm 2S ply silk yarn, now mid-brown. At the upper edge the threads are twisted together in pairs and were presumably gathered onto a foundation loop (cf Illus 64, example in Germanisches National Museum, Nurnberg). Below this the threads are knotted to form a mesh of lozenges with 3mm sides, to a depth of 15mm. Thereafter, further threads are knotted in, to double the number, and the work continues for a further 110mm. This last section is ornamented with a cross crosslet design (Illus 57) darned in with 2S ply silk yarn, softer than, but now a similar shade to, the ground. The braid at the lower edge is composed of seven loops of very dark brown 2S ply silk yarn. The width of the braid varies from 2mm to 4mm, the result of variations in tension during the working. The lower edge of the net appears to have been attached to the braid by sewing with a length of dark brown yarn, similar to that used in the manufacture of the braid. Dimensions: net 150mm by 360mm; braid length 300mm. About 1300.
A7577a,b; C2542–3; B1(b), Destruction, Tumble 2775; Phase Va; Rig VI
Illus 56, 57 and Frontispiece

353 Yarn Wool
Six fragments of thick but slightly soft S spun, 2Z ply yarn in various shades of mid to dark brown, 3mm diameter. This is possibly from Cat No 358/A6127e (Tabby, 2 ply yarn). Dimensions: 25–40mm overall.
A2947; C2404–3; M1.5a; Phase Va,Vaa(VI); Rigs V and VI
Not illustrated

354 2/1 Twill without nap ZS Wool
Two pieces of very dark brown, light medium weight 2/1 twill, unfelted and of uneven texture. Dimensions: a) 95mm by 115mm; b) 75mm by 47mm. System 1: smooth Z spun yarn of irregular thickness, 12 threads per 10mm. System 2: similar S spun yarn, 10 threads per 10mm.
A6127a; C2404–3; M1.5a; Phase Va,Vaa(VI); Rigs V and VI
Not illustrated

355 2/1 Twill with nap ZZ Wool
One piece of even mid-brown, light medium weight, compact 2/1 twill, with nap on both surfaces. Dimensions: 95mm by 35mm. System 1: fine Z spun yarn, 13–14 threads per 10mm. System 2: the same.
A6127b; C2404–3; M1.5a; Phase Va,Vaa(VI); Rigs V and VI
Not illustrated

356 2/2 Twill without nap ZZ Wool
One fragment of light medium weight, mid-brown, unfelted 2/2 twill, even in colour and texture. Dimensions: 30mm by 25mm. System 1: smooth Z spun yarn, 12 threads per 10mm. System 2: similar yarn, 9 threads per 10mm.
A6127c; C2404–3; M1.5a; Phase Va,Vaa(VI); Rigs V and VI
Not illustrated

357 2/1 Twill without nap ZS Wool
One fragment of light medium weight, mid-brown, 2/1 twill, unfelted but comparatively compact and soft to the touch. Dimensions: 55mm by 30mm. System 1: Z spun yarn, 11–12 threads per 10mm. System 2: similar S spun yarn, 9–10 threads per 10mm. No dye (MW).
A6127d; C2404–3; M1.5a; Phase Va,Vaa(VI); Rigs V and VI
Not illustrated

358 Tabby (2 ply yarn) Wool
Fragment of mottled mid/dark brown, very heavy tabby, comparatively close woven and soft to the touch. Dimensions: 45mm by 55mm. System 1: 2 ply yarn, S spun and Z plyed, 2.5 threads per 10mm. System 2: similar yarn, 2 threads per 10mm. See yarn Cat No 353/A2947.
A6127e; C2404–3; M1.5a; Phase Va,Vaa(VI); Rigs V and VI
Not illustrated

359 2/1 Twill without nap ZS Wool
One piece of light medium weight, dark brown, 2/1 twill, lightly felted and comparatively compact and soft to the touch. Dimensions: 60mm by 43mm. System 1: Z spun, about 11 threads per 10mm. System 2: similar S spun yarn, about 10 threads per 10mm.
A6145a; C2404–3; M1.5a; Phase Va,Vaa(VI); Rigs V and VI
Not illustrated

360 2/1 Twill without nap ZS Wool
Two pieces of mid-brown, medium weight, lightly felted 2/1 twill, uneven in spinning and weaving. Dimensions: a) 95mm by 90mm; b) 75mm by 40mm. System 1: Z spun yarn, 9–11 threads per 10mm. System 2: S spun yarn, 7 threads per 10mm.
A6145b; C2404–3; M1.5a; Phase Va,Vaa(VI); Rigs V and VI
Not illustrated

361 2/2 Twill without nap ZS Wool
One piece, very worn, of dark brown, heavy weight, unfelted, loosely woven 2/2 twill' Dimensions: 120mm by 80mm. System 1: smooth Z spun yarn, 7 threads per 10mm. System 2: similar S spun yarn, 6–7 threads per 10mm. Wool type: HM, pigment +++, no dye in both systems (MR).
A6148; C2404–3; M1.5a; Phase Va,Vaa(VI); Rigs V and VI
Not illustrated

362 Tabby Silk

One worn fragment of very fine open tabby, donkey brown in colour. The fragment has the shape of an irregular parallelogram. In both systems the threads are widely spaced. The fabric is crumpled, with creases trending in the direction of system 1. Dimensions: 93mm by 111mm. System 1: very fine Z twisted yarn, 51–54 threads per 10mm. System 2: very fine Z twisted yarn, 33 threads per 10mm.

A6149; C2404–3; M1.5a; Phase Va,Vaa(VI); Rigs V and VI

Illus 24, 25

363 2/1 Twill without nap ZS Wool

Three fragments of dark brown, light weight 2/1 twill, unfelted but close woven and slightly soft to the touch; both spinning and weaving are comparatively even. Dimensions: a) 42mm by 30mm; b) 35mm by 20mm; c) 15mm by 25mm. System 1: fine Z spun yarn, 10 threads per 10mm. System 2: similar S spun yarn, 10 threads per 10mm.

A6150; C2404–3; M1.5a; Phase Va,Vaa(VI); Rigs V and VI

Not illustrated

364 2/1 Twill without nap ZS Wool

One piece of very dark brown, light medium weight, unfelted 2/1 twill, the threads unevenly packed. Dimensions: 70mm by 70mm. System 1: Z spun yarn, about 12 threads per 10mm. System 2: S spun yarn, about 9 threads per 10mm. Wool type: System 1 FGM, pigment +++; System 2 HM, pigment +++ (MR). No dye (MW).

A6626; C2404–3; M1.5a; Phase Va,Vaa(VI); Rigs V and VI

Not illustrated

365 2/1 Twill (?) with nap ZZ Wool

Six fragments of dark brown, light weight, felted 2/1 twill(?), with the nap raised on both surfaces. Dimensions: c120mm by 60mm in all. System 1: fine Z spun yarn, 18 threads per 10mm. System 2: similar yarn, 17 threads per 10mm. No dye (MW).

A6627; C2404–3; M1.5a; Phase Va,Vaa(VI); Rigs V and VI

Not illustrated

366 Yarn Wool

Three pieces of thick, soft, loosely Z spun, mid-brown yarn, about 4mm in diameter. Length a)195mm; b) 165mm; c) 70mm.

A6628; C2404–3; M1.5a; Phase Va,Vaa(VI); Rigs V and VI

Not illustrated

367 2/1 Twill without nap ZZ Wool

Three pieces of dark brown, light weight, unfelted 2/1 twill, comparatively evenly spun and woven. Dimensions: a) 80mm by 90mm; b) 70mm by 70mm; c) 90mm by 30mm. System 1: smooth Z spun yarn, 12 threads per 10mm. System 2: the same.

A6648; C2404–3; M1.5a; Phase Va,Vaa(VI); Rigs V and VI

Not illustrated

368 2/1 Twill without nap ZS Wool

One piece of dark brown, light weight, unfelted 2/1 twill, slightly soft to the touch. Dimensions: 85mm by 65mm. System 1: Z spun yarn, 15 threads per 10mm. System 2: S spun yarn, 10–11 threads per 10mm. Wool type: System 1 GM, pigment +++, no dye; System 2 HM, pigment +++, no dye (MR).

A8861; C2404–3; M1.5a; Phase Va,Vaa(VI); Rigs V and VI

Not illustrated

369 2/1 Twill with nap ZS Wool

Two small pieces (and three fragments) of dark brown, light weight 2/1 twill, with the remains of a nap on both surfaces. Dimensions: a) 70mm by 50mm; b) 39mm by 40mm. System 1: fine Z spun yarn, 11–12 threads per 10mm. System 2: similar S spun yarn, 11–12 threads per 10mm.

A8911; C2404–3; M1.5a; Phase Va,Vaa(VI); Rigs V and VI

Not illustrated

370 Net (darned) Silk

Two fragments, now an even mid-brown shade, and heavily worn, of lacis (embroidered net). The ground is fine, firm S spun silk thread knotted into lozenges with sides 3–4mm long. On this a pattern has been darned – with a soft 2S ply silk yarn used double – consisting of a repeating bird motif, arranged in diagonal rows, the rows alternating with rows of small lozenges. The lozenges are generally single but on piece (b), there is one row of double lozenges. Also on piece (b), which is in very poor condition, there are the remains of a ring of joined lozenges within which the threads of the ground cease to be knotted and are held by a central foundation ring of yarn about 5mm in diameter. This structure indicates the fragments are the remains of a hair-covering similar to Cat Nos 351/A7577a and 352/A7577b. Dimensions: a) 100mm by 180mm; b) 265mm by 165mm.

A10112; C2404–3; M1.5a; Phase Va,Vaa(VI); Rigs V and VI

Illus 58–62

371 2/1 Twill without nap ZZ Wool

Two pieces of dark brown, light weight, unfelted 2/1 twill. a) 80mm by 40mm; b) 110mm by 30mm. System 1: fine Z spun yarn, 14 threads per 10mm. System 2: the same. Wool type: FGM, no pigment, no dye in both systems (MR).

A6146; C2405–3; M1.5a; Phase Va,Vaa; Rigs V and VI

Not illustrated

372 2/1 Twill without nap ZS Wool

Two fragments of dark brown, light weight 2/1 twill, lightly felted and soft to the touch. Dimensions: a) 13mm by 21mm; b) 14mm by 18mm. System 1: fine Z spun yarn, 15 threads per 10mm. System 2: similar S spun yarn, 9–10 threads per 10mm. Dye: Q, K, R? (MW).

A8880; C2405–3; M1.5a; Phase Va,Vaa; Rigs V and VI

Not illustrated

373 2/1 Twill without nap ZS Wool

Three pieces (and a number of fragments) of dark brown, light weight 2/1 twill, unfelted but soft to the touch. Dimensions: a) 50mm by 25mm; b) 35mm by 40mm; c) 45mm by 40mm. System 1: Z spun yarn, 15 threads per 10mm. System 2: S spun yarn, more variable in thickness, 9–10 threads per 10mm.

A09–0017; C7079–7; M1.5b; Phase Vaa; Rigs VI and VII

Not illustrated

374 2/1 Twill without nap ZS Wool

Four pieces (and some fragments) of mottled mid/dark brown, light medium weight, unfelted but slightly soft 2/1 twill. Dimensions: a) 110mm by 185mm; b) 75mm by 80mm; c) 60mm by 100mm; d) 50mm by 35mm. System 1: Z spun yarn of irregular thickness, about 11 threads per 10mm. System 2: finer

S spun yarn, about 8 threads per 10mm. No dye (MW).
A09–0019; C7079–7; M1.5b; Phase Vaa; Rigs VI and VII
Not illustrated

375 2/2 Twill without nap ZZ Wool
One piece (and a fragment) of dark brown, medium weight, unfelted 2/2 twill. Dimensions: 75mm by 53mm. System 1: plump, smooth Z spun yarn, 10 threads per 10mm. System 2: similar yarn, 8 threads per 10mm.
A09–0023a; C7079–7; M1.5b; Phase Vaa; Rigs VI and VII
Not illustrated

376 2/1 Twill without nap ZZ Wool
One piece (and two fragments) of dark brown, light weight, unfelted 2/1 twill; the threads in system 1 are closely packed and almost cover those in system 2. Dimensions: 110mm by 20mm. System 1: fine hard Z spun yarn, about 18 threads per 10mm. System 2: similar yarn, 8 threads per 10 mm.
cf Cat No 537 from 45–75 Gallowgate, Aberdeen (Gabra-Sanders 2001a, 225 and 232) and Cat No 159 from 42 St Paul Street, Aberdeen (Bennett 1982, 199).
A09–0023b; C7079–7; M1.5b; Phase Vaa; Rigs VI and VII
Not illustrated

377 2/1 Twill with nap ZS Wool
One piece of very dark brown, light medium weight, lightly felted 2/1 twill, with a slight nap on both surfaces. Dimensions: 50mm by 32mm. System 1: Z spun yarn, 12–13 threads per 10mm. System 2: thicker S spun yarn, 8–9 threads per 10mm.
A09–0060; C7082–7; M1.5b; Phase Vaa; Rigs VI and VII
Not illustrated

378 2/1 Twill without nap ZS Wool
One piece of dark brown, light medium weight, 2/1 twill, unfelted but soft to the touch; the yarn in both systems is variable in thickness. Dimensions: 185mm by 45mm. System 1: Z spun yarn, 10–12 threads per 10mm. System 2: S spun yarn, 8–9 threads per 10mm.
A09–0072a; C7082–7; M1.5b; Phase Vaa; Rigs VI and VII
Not illustrated

379 2/1 Twill without nap ZS Wool
One fragment, very worn, of dark brown, medium weight 2/1 twill, open textured but soft to the touch; the yarn in both systems is variable in tension and thickness. Dimensions: 45mm by 40mm. System 1: Z spun yarn, about 8 threads per 10mm. System 2: S spun yarn, about 6 threads per 10mm.
A09–0072b; C7082–7; M1.5b; Phase Vaa; Rigs VI and VII
Not illustrated

380 2/1 Twill without nap ZZ Wool
One piece of dark brown, light weight unfelted 2/1 twill, firm to the touch. Dimensions: 210mm by 100mm. System 1: smooth, firm Z spun yarn, 13 threads per 10mm. System 2: similar yarn, 12 threads per 10mm.
A09–0037; C7169–7; M1.5b; Phase Vaa; Rigs VI and VII
Not illustrated

381 2/2 Twill without nap ZZ Wool
One piece of very dark brown, medium weight unfelted 2/2 twill with a number of shedding mistakes. Dimensions: 175mm by 180mm. System 1: smooth firm Z spun yarn, 13 threads per 10mm. System 2: Z spun yarn, thicker and more variable in tension, 7 threads per 10mm.
A09–0042; C7169–7; M1.5b; Phase Vaa; Rigs VI and VII
Not illustrated

382 2/1 Twill without nap ZS Wool
One piece of dark brown, light medium weight unfelted 2/1 twill, slightly open textured and firm to the touch. Dimensions: 90mm by 140mm. System 1: smooth Z spun yarn, 12 threads per 10mm. System 2: similar S spun yarn, 10 threads per 10mm.
A09–0064; C7169–7; M1.5b; Phase Vaa; Rigs VI and VII
Not illustrated

383 Yarn Wool
About twenty strands, up to 70mm long, of reddish mid-brown soft S spun yarn; the yarn is kinked as if it was once woven. The yarns are variable in diameter, approximately 1mm.
A09–0073; C7169–7; M1.5b; Phase Vaa; Rigs VI and VII
Not illustrated

384 Tabby (2 ply yarn) Wool
One piece of dark brown, heavy tabby, of comparatively close and even texture. Dimensions: 170mm by 135mm. System 1: firm 2 ply yarn, Z spun and S plyed, 3 threads per 10mm. System 2: similar yarn, 4 threads per 10mm.
A09–0043; C7162–7; M8a; Phase Va,Vaa; Rig VII
Not illustrated

385 2/1 Twill with nap ZS Wool
Two pieces of mottled mid-brown, light medium weight 2/1 twill, soft to the touch and with the remains of a light nap on both surfaces; both spinning and weaving are uneven. Dimensions: a) 163mm by 165mm; b) 43mm by 50mm. System 1: soft Z spun yarn, 13 threads per 10mm. System 2: thicker S spun yarn, about 8 threads per 10mm.
A09–0040; C7163–7; M8a; Phase Va,Vaa; Rig VII
Not illustrated

386 2/1 Twill without nap ZS Wool
One piece of very dark brown, medium weight, unfelted and open textured 2/1 twill, firm to the touch; the threads are irregularly spaced. Dimensions: 170mm by 105mm. System 1: smooth Z spun yarn, about 11 threads per 10mm. System 2: thicker S spun yarn, 6–9 threads per 10mm. No dye (MW).
A09–0036; C7182–7; M8a; Phase Va,Vaa; Rig VII
Not illustrated

387 Felt Wool
Fragments, in poor condition, of rich mid-brown heavy weight felt, uneven in texture. Dimensions: c70mm by 80mm in all.
A09–0070; C7201–7; M8a; Phase Va,Vaa; Rig VII
Not illustrated

388 2/1 Twill without nap ZS Wool
One piece of dark brown 2/1 twill, similar to Cat No 389/A09–0074 and probably part of the same fabric. Dimensions: 90mm by 155mm. System 1: even Z spun yarn, 13 threads per 10mm. System 2: similar S spun yarn, 10 threads per 10mm.
A09–0015; C9012–9; M8a; Phase Va,Vaa; Rig VII
Not illustrated

389 2/1 Twill without nap ZS Wool
Two pieces, one with 55mm of simple closed edge on one margin, of dark brown, light medium weight 2/1 twill, unfelted but compact and slightly soft to the touch. Dimensions: a) 155mm by 183mm; b) 90mm by 100mm. Probably part of fabric Cat No 388/A09–0015. System 1: even Z spun yarn, 13 threads per 10mm. System 2: similar S spun yarn, 10 threads per 10mm.
A09–0074; C7205–7; M8a; T7206; Phase Va,Vaa; Rig VII
Not illustrated

390 2/1 Twill without nap ZS Wool
Two pieces of very dark brown, light medium weight, unfelted 2/1 twill, both with a closed edge, of simple structure, remaining on one margin. The weaving is close but uneven. Dimensions: a) 232mm by 95mm; b) 150mm by 104mm. System 1: warp, smooth, glossy, Z spun yarn, about 12 threads per 10mm. System 2: weft, similar S spun yarn, about 12 threads per 10mm.
A09–0146; C7113–7; B53 (Phase 1), Central Area–Occupation (2a); Phase Vb; Rig VII
Not illustrated

391 Braid Silk
Length of very firm whipcording, now mid-brown; 2mm in diameter. The braid is constructed from (?) 24 lengths of soft 2S ply silk yarn. Length 75mm.
A09–0021; C7110–7; B53 (Phase 1), North Area–Occupation (3a); Phase Vb; Rig VII
Not illustrated

392 2/1 Twill without nap ZS Wool
Two fragments of dark brown, light weight, closely woven 2/1 twill, lightly felted and slightly soft to the touch; both spinning and weaving are even. Dimensions: a) 55mm by 50mm; b) 40mm by 50mm. System 1: very fine Z spun yarn, 15 threads per 10mm. System 2: similar S spun yarn, 15 threads per 10mm.
A09–0013; C7107–7; B53 (Phase 1), North Area–Occupation (4); Phase Vb; Rig VII
Not illustrated

393 Tabby (2 ply yarn) Wool
Four pieces of mottled mid/dark brown, heavy tabby, open-textured and harsh to the touch; two of the pieces have lengths of selvedge, of simple structure, intact on one edge. Dimensions: a) 570mm by 135mm; b) 250mm by 105mm; c) 190mm by 105mm; d) 150mm by 90mm. System 1: warp, very firm 2 ply yarn, Z spun and S plyed, 5–6 threads per 10mm. System 2: weft, similar yarn, about 3 threads per 10mm.
A09–0008; C7064–7; P8.5; Phase Vb,Vbb; Rig VII
Not illustrated

394 2/1 Twill without nap ZS Wool
One piece of dark brown, light medium weight, unfelted 2/1 twill, the threads irregularly spaced, giving an uneven appearance. Dimensions: 90mm by 115mm. System 1: fine Z spun yarn, about 12 threads per 10mm. System 2: similar but more irregular S spun yarn, 8–9 threads per 10mm.
A09–0016; C7072–7; B53 (Phase 2), North Area–T7072; Phase Vbb; Rig VII
Not illustrated

395 2/1 Twill without nap ZS Wool
Three pieces of dark brown, light weight 2/1 twill, unfelted but soft to the touch; both spinning and weaving are slightly uneven. Dimensions: a) 110mm by 125mm; b) 35mm by 25mm; c) 45mm by 25mm. System 1: smooth Z spun yarn, 15 threads per 10mm. System 2: S spun yarn, 15–16 threads per 10mm.
A09–0025; C7099–7; B53 (Phase 2), South Area–Occupation (6); Phase Vbb; Rig VII
Not illustrated

396 2/1 Twill without Nap ZS Wool
One piece (and a number of fragments), very worn, of dark reddish brown, light weight 2/1 twill, lightly felted and soft to the touch. Dimensions: 90mm by 115mm. System 1: Z spun yarn, 15 threads per 10mm. System 2: S spun yarn, 12 threads per 10mm.
A09–0012; C7034–7; B53 (Phase 2), North Area–Occupation (15); Phase Vbb; Rig VII
Not illustrated

397 2/1 Twill with nap ZS Wool
One piece of sandy brown, medium weight 2/1 twill, lightly felted with a slight nap on one surface; the piece ran red when washed. Dimensions: 65mm by 45mm. System 1: fine Z spun yarn, about 12 threads per 10mm. System 2: thicker, more irregular, S spun yarn, about 8 threads per 10mm. Wool type: System 1 HM, no pigment, no dye; System 2 FGM, no pigment, no dye (MR).
A6709; C2737–2; M4a; Phase Vaa–Vc(VI); Rigs V and VI
Not illustrated

398 Tabby (2 ply yarn) Wool
One piece of mottled mid-brown, very heavy tabby, soft to the touch; the yarn in both systems is very variable in thickness and tension. Dimensions: 90mm by 60mm. System 1: 2 ply yarn, S spun and Z plyed, about 3 threads per 10mm. System 2: 2 ply yarn, Z spun and S plyed, about 3 threads per 10mm. Wool type: HM, pigment +++, no dye in both systems (MR).
A8869; C2176–4; M3a; Phase Vb–Vc; Rigs V and VI
Not illustrated

399 2/1 Twill without nap ZS Wool
One piece of rich mid-brown, medium weight, lightly felted 2/1 twill; both spinning and weaving are uneven. Dimensions: 150mm by 60mm. System 1: Z spun yarn, about 8 threads per 10mm. System 2: heavier S spun yarn, 6–7 threads per 10mm.
A8910; C2715–2; P1b; Phase Vd; Rig VI
Not illustrated

400 Tabby (2 ply yarn) Wool
Two worn fragments of very dark brown, heavy tabby, open textured but comparatively even in both spinning and weaving. Dimensions: a) 45mm by 40mm; b) 40mm by 35mm. System 1: 2 ply yarn, Z spun and S plyed, 4 threads per 10mm. System 2: similar yarn, 3 threads per 10mm.
A8858; C2123–4; M3b; Phase Vd; Rig VI
Not illustrated

401 Yarn Wool
Five fragments, each about 20mm long, of smooth, soft, reddish mid-brown, Z spun yarn.
A6130; C2174–4; M3c; Phase Vd; Rig V
Not illustrated

402 2/1 Twill with Nap ZS Wool
Three roughly triangular pieces and one strip of dark brown, medium weight, felted 2/1 twill, with a slight nap on both surfaces; two of the pieces are ridged a short distance from and parallel to one edge suggesting a seam line; a) 190mm by 120mm, b) 215mm by 120mm, c) 150mm by 105mm, d) 265mm by 15mm. System 1: Z spun yarn, 10–11 threads per 10mm. System 2: S spun yarn, about 8 threads per 10mm.
A09–0028; C7008–10; B51, T7008; Phase Vd,Vdd; Rig VIII
Not illustrated

403 Carpet Jute or sisal base, man-made(?) pile
Two pieces of carpeting consisting of a tabby base constructed from stiff ribbon-like yarn, the threads widely spaced, 5–6 threads per 10mm, with a pile of greenish-blue felted threads arranged in rows about 7mm wide and now about 2mm deep; the method by which the pile is attached to the base is not clear, but probably an adhesive has been used. The pieces appear to be of very recent origin. Dimensions: a) 250mm by 165mm; b) 250mm by 40mm. Professor Whiting (MW) commented that a sample of the pile sent for dye analysis 'contained an acidic blue/green dyestuff, not indigo sulphonic acid, and I cannot find any reference to a chemical candidate for this dye earlier than 1879'. Modern.
A11083; C3870–1; Unstratified; Rigs VI and VII
Illus 50

404 2/1 Twill without nap ZZ Wool
One piece of mottled mid/dark brown, very heavy 2/1 twill, open-textured and firm to the touch, with 85mm of closed edge remaining on one margin. The warp threads are more closely packed at the closed edge but the structure is simple; at one point, two weft threads have been passed through the same shed. Dimensions: 160mm by 120mm. System 1: warp, glossy, plump Z spun yarn, of irregular thickness, about 6 threads per 10mm. System 2: weft, similar yarn, 4 threads per 10mm. Wool type: HM, pigment +, no dye in both systems (MR).
A1268; C2716–2; Unstratified; Rigs V and VI
Not illustrated

405 2/1 Twill with nap ZS Wool
One piece of even mid-brown, heavy 2/1 twill, heavily felted and with a light nap on one surface and a heavier nap on the other. Dimensions: 235mm by 55mm. System 1: fine Z spun yarn, variable in tension and thickness, 12 threads per 10mm. System 2: S spun yarn, 9–10 threads per 10mm.
A2827; C2001–3/4; Unstratified; Rigs V and VI
Not illustrated

406 Felt Wool
Numerous fragments in poor condition, of mid-brown, medium weight felt taken from inside a leather boot; there are no visible needle holes or signs of seams or other constructional features. Dimensions: c200mm by 70mm in all.
A9821; C2001–3/4; Unstratified; Rigs V and VI
Not illustrated

407 Tabby (2 ply yarn) Wool
Six pieces of dark brown, very heavy tabby, coarse to the touch and uneven in both spinning and weaving; two of the pieces have a length of closed edge, 110mm and 170mm respectively, intact on one margin. Dimensions: a) 220mm by 200mm; b) 60mm by 50mm; c) 140mm by 140mm; d) 155mm by 220mm; e) 185mm by 100mm; f) 140mm by 165mm. System 1: warp, 2 ply yarn, S spun and Z plyed, 3–4 threads per 10mm. System 2: weft, similar yarn, 3.5–4 threads per 10mm.
A09–0005; C7000–7–10; Unstratified; Rigs VI–VIII
Not illustrated

408 2/1 Twill with nap ZS Wool
One piece of dark red-brown, medium weight heavily felted 2/1 twill, compact and with nap on both surfaces. Dimensions: 85mm by 35mm. System 1: fine Z spun yarn, about 14 threads per 10mm. System 2: similar S spun yarn, about 10 threads per 10mm.
A09–0066; C7000–7–10; Unstratified; Rigs VI–VIII
Not illustrated

409 2/2 Twill without nap ZZ Wool
One piece of mottled mid/dark brown, heavy medium weight, unfelted, closely woven 2/2 twill. Dimensions: 100mm by 110mm. System 1: smooth Z spun yarn, 12 threads per 10mm. System 2: similar yarn, 8 threads per 10mm.
A09–0009; C7001–7/9; Modern, T7014; Phase VI; Rig VII
Not illustrated

North Sector (Area 5)

410 Tabby (2 ply yarn) Wool
One piece of dark brown, very heavy tabby, open textured and comparatively soft to the touch; now very worn. Dimensions: 60mm by 100mm. System 1: 2 ply yarn, loose Z spun and S plyed, about 2 threads per 10mm. System 2: the same. Wool type: HM, pigment +++ in both systems (MR). No dye (MW).
A7336; C0489–5; Ditch; Phase (1)2
Not illustrated

North Sector (Area 6)

411 2/1 Twill without nap ZS Wool
One piece of light medium weight, dark brown 2/1 twill, unfelted
and firm to the touch, the threads unevenly spaced' Dimensions:
70mm by 100mm. System 1: Z spun yarn, 12–13 threads per
10mm. System 2: S spun yarn, 10–11 threads per 10mm. No
dye (MW).
A6147; C1028–6; 'Garden'; Phase G
Not illustrated

THE LEATHER

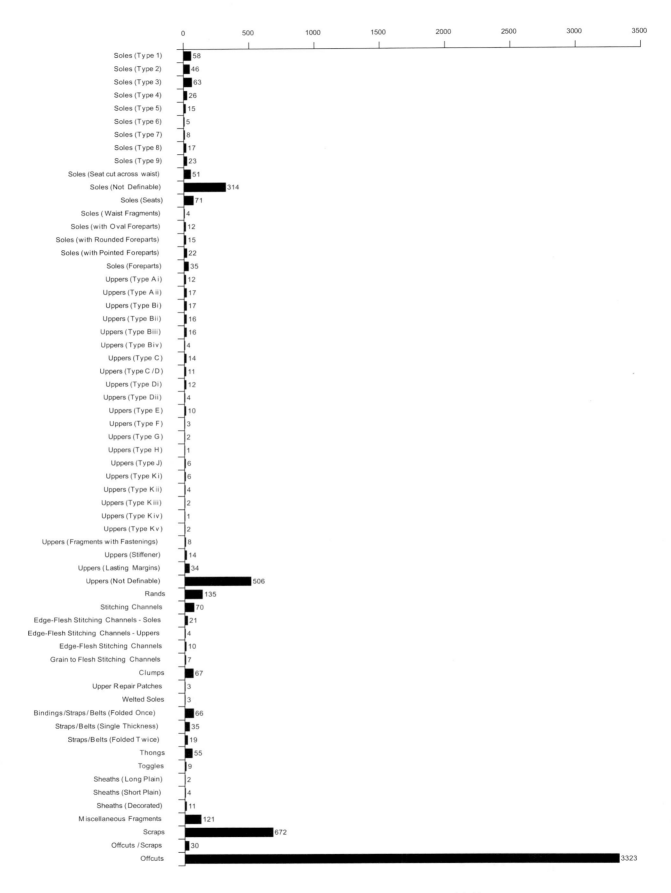

Illus 102 *Bar diagram showing the frequencies of different categories*
of leatherwork recovered from Perth High Street Archaeological Excavation.

Introduction

Clare Thomas with the late N Q Bogdan

Over 6000 fragments of leather were found, including shoes, straps, sheaths, offcuts, scraps and miscellaneous articles. Most of the shoes were very worn, and many had been cut, probably for the reuse of a less worn part. The presence also of large quantities of offcuts and scraps suggests that the assemblage is largely composed of waste material from cobbling, ie the repair of old shoes and the manufacture of new ones from old leather.

The leather was distributed over the whole site, with large concentrations in pits and middens, especially in the later layers. Leather items as a whole appear to increase throughout the occupation of the site, in common with other finds categories, although the numbers of sole and upper fragments fell considerably during Period III (first half of the 13th century). However, it should be borne in mind that these apparent differences may be at least in part due to the physical extent of the deposits themselves: for example evidence for Period I was only recovered from Areas 1–4, while that for the later Periods II and III also included Area 9. Evidence for Periods IV and V was even more extensive and included Areas 7 and 10.

Shoes form the largest single category of objects, with many matching soles and uppers, a few of which are still joined together. Evidence survives for methods of construction and repair. Soles can be divided into nine types and uppers into ten, respectively, some of which belong predominantly to particular phases, for example, Sole Type 3 to Period IV (second half of the 13th century), and Upper Type A to Periods I and II (first and second halves of the 12th century respectively).

Straps form a much smaller but still significant group. Some, folded once, were probably bindings for shoes and clothing, and therefore strictly speaking are not straps. The others, however, would almost certainly have been used as fastenings. These included toggles, thongs, straps of single thickness and more substantial belts, formed of strips of leather, folded twice and stitched up the centre of the reverse.

The sheaths, though few in number, are important, as 11 were intricately decorated. All were most probably civilian in character, made to hold the wearers'everyday knives. Most of the sheaths can be assigned to particular phases, the dates of which compare well with those suggested by external parallels.

At the time of the excavation, the study of Scottish medieval leather was in its infancy. In 1963, Dunbar published a welted shoe of mid-16th century date, from Skirling Castle, Peebles-shire (1963, 244–5). This was apparently followed by an 18-year interlude, until the publication in 1981 of Threave Castle, Galloway, where a small but distinct group of soles and uppers dating from the late 14th to early 15th centuries was found (Thomas 1981, 123–6).

Since then, reports have been published or prepared on leather from Aberdeen (Stones 1982; Thomas 2001a), Kirkwall (Thomas 1982), Perth (Thomas 1987; Thomas and Walsh 1995), Fast Castle (Thomas 2001b), Jedburgh (Thomas 1995), Spynie Palace (Thomas 2002) and Whithorn (Nicholson 1997). A very large assemblage, of over 13,000 fragments, was recovered from the Bon Accord site, Aberdeen. However, approximately 75% of this consists of waste material (Thomas forthcoming d).

Many parallels are available from England. Much of the early work on English mediaeval shoes was done by Miss June Swann, keeper of the shoe collection at Northampton Museum and by John Thornton, formerly of the Northampton College of Technology. June Swann has concentrated on questions of style, John Thornton on methods of construction and repair. Thornton has published reports on shoes from many sites, including Worcester (1969a, 56–62); Shrewsbury (1961, 187, 199, 200, 205–6); Clare Castle, Suffolk (1959, 146–52); York (Goodfellow and Thornton 1972, 97–105) and Durham (Carver 1979, 26–35). The only caveat about his otherwise excellent reports is that his dating is usually based only on style, with little or no apparent reference to the archaeological context.

More securely dated reports include Southampton (Platt and Coleman Smith 1975, 296–302); Clarendon Hotel, Oxford (Sturdy 1958, 75–7); King's Lynn (Clarke and Carter 1977, 349–66); Dover (Mynard 1969, 101–4); London Custom House site (Tatton-Brown 1975, 154–67; Grew and de Neergaard 1988; Cowgill et al 1987; Egan and Pritchard 1991; Pritchard 1991, 211–41); York (MacGregor 1982, 242–53; Tweddle 1986, 237–56; Mould et al 2003), Exeter (Friendship-Taylor 1984, 323–33); Newcastle (Dixon 1988, 93–103); Leicester (Allin 1981a and b); Winchester (Thornton 1990a, b, c, d); Sandwell Priory (Thomas 1991); and Plymouth (Gaskell-Brown 1986, 53–8). A large and interesting group of leather from the Barbican ditch and Castle Moat, Oxford has also been published, but it is not very closely dated (Hassall 1976, 276–96).

Very good parallels are also available from some of mediaeval Scotland's trading partners in Scandinavia, Germany and the Netherlands. Shoes and other leather artefacts similar in style and construction to those from the High Street have been found in Lund (Sweden) (Blomqvist 1938, 189; 1945, 138); Bergen (Norway) (Larsen 1992); Amsterdam (Groenman-van Waateringe 1975); Haithabu (Groenman-van Waateringe 1984); Lübeck (Groenman-van Waateringe and Guiran 1978, 161–73; 169–74; Vons-Comis 1982b,

239–50; Groenman-van Waateringe and Krauwer 1987, 75–84); Konstanz (Schnack 1992a and 1994); Bremen (Schnack 1993); and Schleswig (Schnack 1992b). Other parallels are also available from Dublin (Ard Mhúseam na H-Eireann 1973) and Novgorod (Thompson 1967, 80–4; Brisbane 1992).

The surviving threads or yarns have been examined by Dr Helen Bennett and P Dtransart of National Museums Scotland (NMS); the latter's report appears in Appendix 1.

Approximately one third of the leather has been conserved, initially by the excavation's own conservator, subsequently by the laboratory of NMS. A report by Tom Bryce on the conservation of the leather appears in Appendix 2. Appendix 3 contains a discussion of the shrinkage of the leather during conservation.

A report on the identification of the animal species appears in Appendix 4. Only the conserved leather was examined. Much of it was too worn to enable the follicle pattern to be recognised. Where the follicle patterns were clear, these were nearly all identified as cattle hide. A few examples, however, are sheepskin or goatskin.

The conserved leather has been deposited in Perth Museum and Art Gallery.

In the ensuing discussion, the leather has been considered first by category, then by type, with due reference to its chronological distribution over the site, and to external parallel. A glossary of technical terms relevant to leather has been included, as well as explanations of methods of construction. A selective catalogue follows the discussion; a full catalogue is preserved in Perth Museum and Art Gallery and in the site archive in the Royal Commission on the Ancient and Historical Monuments of Scotland, Edinburgh. All measurements quoted are post-conservation.

Shoes

Close to 2000 fragments of turnshoes were found, including soles, uppers, clump soles, rands and other stitching channels. Many of these were small fragments, but a substantial number of soles and uppers were nearly complete. Of the nine surviving examples of soles and uppers still joined together, some have rands and/or clump soles. In 43 other cases, matching soles and uppers were recognised. Unfortunately, the sole and upper types are not always identifiable, as so little survives, but correlation of the recognisable sole and upper types is still very useful. The soles can be divided, by shape, into nine types, while differences in design and method of fastening produce 10 upper types, some with sub-divisions. Most of the types belong predominantly to one phase or another, although earlier and/or later examples usually occur as well. Tunnel stitch holes indicate that many soles were repaired with clumps, often on both seat and forepart. Sole/upper seams have also been re-stitched; in some cases the original stitching channels have been replaced with thongs. In one rare instance, an upper has been patched. Several shoes have been distorted by bunions, with damage done to both sole and upper. Three welted soles were also found; these were unstratified.

Methods of construction

All the evidence, apart from three welted soles mentioned above, points to turnshoe construction, where as Thornton (1973b, 47) says 'the shoe is made inside out (normally with the flesh side outwards) by sewing the lasting margin of the upper to the edge of a single sole which also acts as an insole. The shoe is then turned the right way round so that the grain side of the leather is on the outside of the shoe and the upper/sole seam is now inside'.

The soles have all the characteristics of turnshoe soles; the stitching channels have edge–flesh holes, with stitch length c4–7mm; the flesh sides are uppermost, while the grain sides show typical signs of wear derived from contact with the ground, particularly on the outside of the seat and on the centre forepart, as, for instance Cat No 2333/A03–0291a (Illus 147). They are distinct from insoles of welted shoes, which have a longer stitch length, c6–10mm, and which bear the impression of feet, but which do not show wear marks caused by direct contact with the ground. Moreover, such insoles usually have the grain side uppermost (Thornton 1973a, 8–12).

Many fragments of rand have been found, seven still attached to the sole and four of these still joined to the upper as well: rand and sole Cat Nos 783/A9372a and 788/A9546; sole, rand and upper Cat Nos 5241/A03–0216 (Illus 146), 813/A11220b, 3427/A03–0051a–d and 343/A6772c (Illus 145). Thornton (1973b, 46) defines a rand as 'a long narrow strip of leather of roughly triangular cross-section included in an upper/bottom seam to make it more waterproof or decorative'.

It fills the space between sole and upper and also strengthens the seam, as it lengthens the stitch, allowing it to stretch more. Some of the Perth rands are triangular in cross-section, for instance Cat No 5781/A0800c,d, but many are flat, for example Cat No 5241/A03–0216. The latter is an example of a wide rand apparently used to protect the upper; it extends for c9mm beyond the edge of the sole both at inner waist and at the front of the forepart, with two fragments overlapping at the front, thus protecting it from being scuffed. In his report on the leather from Roushill, Shrewsbury, Thornton (1961, 206) describes what appears to be the nearest parallel, a rand which widens at the back of the seat; in this case, however, the rand appears to project outwards, instead of curving against the upper. Thornton suggested that this may have been a protective measure. There is no evidence for wide rands used to attach extra soles (Thornton 1973a, 9, 11).

Uppers were attached to soles by lasting margins with grain to flesh stitching channels, with oval holes c1.5mm by 3mm, and with stitch lengths of 4–7mm, as on the corresponding channels on the soles. Fragments of uppers were joined together with butted edge–flesh seams, invisible on the grain side, as on Cat No 931/A12305. The stitching is usually very neat, with small rectangular/round holes, diameter c0.5–1mm and with stitch lengths of 2.5–4mm, as on the upper Cat No 931/Al2305. Stiffeners were often used to strengthen quarters. The grain side of the stiffener was usually placed against the flesh side of the quarters. One example, however, Cat No 313/A12310, has the flesh side of the stiffener facing the quarters. The lasting margin of the stiffener was sewn into the sole–upper seams and thus pierced with oval grain to flesh stitch holes. The top edge was attached by hem stitching to the flesh side of the quarters, where small tunnel stitches are often visible. The hem stitch leaves a scalloped pattern on the stiffener itself as on Cat No 478/Al2309b; an impression of this is sometimes apparent on the quarters (Illus 126).

A hem stitch was also used for the attachment to uppers of top bands and facings. Top bands were straps of leather, folded once and added to the top edge of the upper, as a decorative binding. These straps are discussed farther under the heading 'Straps folded once', as not all straps of this construction are necessarily parts of shoes– some may be bindings for clothes. Facings were apparently used to reinforce the tie-holes of upper Types C and D. No facings actually survive from this site, but the stitch holes used to attach them do, in the form of small tunnel stitches on the flesh side of the leather, on either side of the tie-holes.

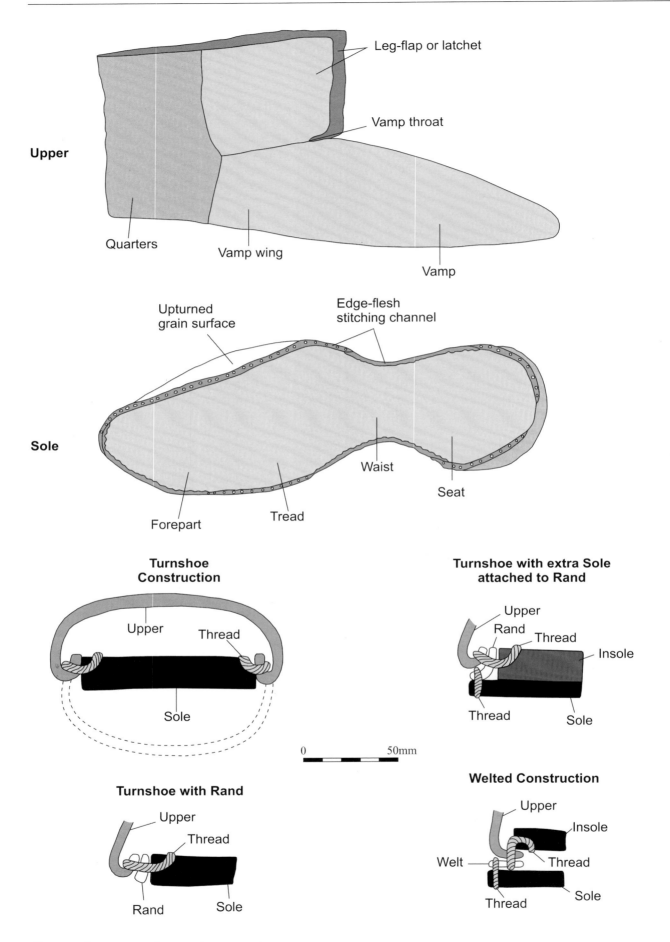

Illus 103 *Shoe terminology and construction.*

Examples of V- and Y-shaped facings have been found at Oxford (Hassall 1976, 251) and London (Tatton-Brown 1975, 159–60).

Tunnel stitching on the flesh side of uppers may also have been used to secure a lining: two uppers have diagonal or vertical rows of such stitching (Cat Nos 3670/A7791, Illus 140 and 1287/A6451c,d, Illus 136), while another has a horizontal row, parallel with the lasting margin (Cat No 163/A7787j, Illus 141). A fourth upper contains a scrap of felt, as well as other traces of felt, despite having no stitching which might have held it in place (Cat No 5769/A9821b). Two other uppers had partial liners, consisting of extensions to the quarters that had been turned inwards (Cat Nos 255/A12287a, Illus 130 and 296/A12632b, Illus 130).

Parallels for the latter feature are known from Aberdeen (Thomas 2001a, 243, illus 186 nos 578–579,) and Durham (Carver 1979, 26–35), but other evidence for the medieval use of linings in the British Isles appears to be non-existent, although they are mentioned in Wardrobe accounts (Grew and de Neergaard 1988, 48). The only available parallels are from Continental Europe, but even here they are scarce. The best evidence comes from Schleswig, where 80 examples survive. All, apart from one exception, were associated with high boots, equivalent to PHSAE Type H, and dated from the 14th century onwards. The lower part of the lining was secured by inclusion in the sole–upper seam; on some examples, vertical rows of tunnel stitching were used to hold the leg portion in place. The exception probably belonged to a Halbschuh or ankle-boot. The linings were all made of goatskin. Schnack comments on the paucity of evidence for linings; she could only find parallels from Lubeck, Pleskau and Frankfurt-am-Oder. The last included 15th-century examples of felt linings (Schnack 1992b, 118).

The thread used to stitch these shoes was apparently nearly all wool, as shown by woollen thread which survived in situ on at least 53 examples (see Illus 120, 121, 146). As discussed at greater length by Dr Dransart in Appendix 1, the use of wool is most unusual.

The closest contemporary parallel is from Kirk Close, Perth (Thomas 1987, 176). Examples from London (Pritchard 1991, 219, 221) and Winchester (Thornton 1990c, 708) belong to the 10th and 11th centuries. Eight examples of wool were noted at York; five of these dated to the late 9th to mid 11th centuries, three to the 12th to 13th centuries (MacGregor 1982, 138, 140; Mould et al 2003, 3259–61). Later examples of woollen thread from Dungiven date to the late 16th or early 17th centuries (Henshall and Seaby 1962, 119, 129, 135). The normal thread was linen, but no linen at all has survived from this site.

However, the use of linen for textiles is indicated by glass-smoothers and a possible flax-breaking mallet (see Fascicule 4, The glass; Fascicule 2, The worked wood). A single thread of linen was recovered from South Methven Street, Perth and flax seeds, probably waste from oil production, were found at both Kirk Close and South Methven Street (Robinson 1987, 206). The almost complete lack of linen from medieval Perth is almost certainly explained by the fact that bast fibres do not survive well buried in damp conditions (Bennett 1987, 159; Thomas 1987, 176).

A study of the dating of the examples of wool shows that it occurred in all phases and thus was not just used at one particular period, which might have suggested a temporary shortage of linen. Thongs were sometimes used to attach clump soles and to repair sole–upper seams but were not employed in the original construction, as they had been in earlier periods, as, for instance, in Anglo-Saxon Winchester (Thornton 1973a, 7). Silk was found on two boots, both of 12th-century date. On Cat No 229/A7588c (Illus 140) silk was used as a decorative binding for the top edge, while the top band of Cat No 172/A7580 (Illus 148) was stitched with a row of pink silk between two rows of white. Silk, though a luxury, was relatively common in 12th-century Europe (The textiles, this volume). Other examples of uppers stitched with silk have been found in London (Pritchard 1988, 77) and Bergen (Pedersen 1992, 143–50).

These shoes were probably made on wooden lasts, although none were found at the High Street site. An example from York was shaped for the left foot, and still had a few scraps of leather nailed to it (MacGregor 1982, 144–5, Fig 74). Similar finds are also known from Haithabu (Groenman-vanWaateringe 1984, 18, Abb. 5), Schleswig (Schnack 1992b, 34), Oslo (Schia 1977, 321) and Novgorod (Brisbane 1992, 183). Even when lasts do not survive, their use is indicated by the presence of lasting marks, such as a small hole on an upper (Type Bi), Cat No 461/A10511; this upper also had a small tunnel-like depression, possibly caused by bracing the boot to the last. Small nail holes have also been found on soles from Newcastle (Dixon 1988, 94; 1989, no 83) and Schleswig (Schnack 1992b, 34–5).

As mentioned above, three unstratified welted soles were found. These almost certainly date from the 16th century or later, as welted shoe construction was only developed in Britain after cAD1500. In this method, a wide rand or welt was used to link upper and insole to a separate outer sole. Firstly, the upper was lasted, or shaped on to the last, and secured by nails or bracing thread. Next, upper and insole were sewn to the welt. Thirdly, the outer sole was stitched to the last. This method simplified construction, as the finished shoe

Table 8 *The chronological distribution of the use of wool as a yarn.*

period	I	II	III	IV	V	unstratified
instances of wool	1	23	4	7	14	4

no longer required turning, thus enabling it to be much more substantial. Repairs to the outer sole–welt seam were also easy (Thornton 1973a, 11; 1973b, 48). The welt is distinguished from the earlier rand by having two grain to flesh stitching channels, not one. The upper still has a grain to flesh stitching channel on its lasting margin, but with a longer stitch length of 6–10mm. Early insoles are very similar to a turnshoe sole, with an edge–flesh stitching channel, but again with a longer stitch length and usually with the grain side up. Later insoles are stitched through a rib on the flesh side. Outer soles have a grain to flesh stitching channel (Thornton 1973a, 11; 1973b, 48).

Repairs (Illus 104)

Evidence for repair survives on many fragments; soles were frequently patched, sole/upper seams were occasionally re-stitched or replaced with thongs and in a very few cases the upper was patched.

Worn soles were repaired with clumps, which were approximately of seat or forepart shape and which were attached to the relevant area by tunnel stitching, whose holes are visible on both clumps and original soles. For example, sole Cat No 222/A7436a has part of a seat clump still attached; tunnel stitch holes indicate that the forepart has also been repaired (Illus 104). The clumps on this sole, and on another, Cat No 286/A03–0017a, were attached by thongs, which survive (Illus 104). Clump soles also occur separately, as eg, a right forepart clump with pointed toe, Cat No 3865/A03–0068 (Illus 104), and a seat clump Cat No 3511/A03–0251 (Illus 104). Another seat clump Cat No 5855/A03–0133f, has been formed out of two fragments, most probably scraps from soles, joined together with a butted edge–flesh seam: a most unusual and very economical repair (Illus 104). Some soles were repaired more than once, as, for instance Cat No 625/A9885a (Illus 104), where both seat and forepart have been repaired at least twice; one crack along a line of tunnel-holes may have been caused by strain from the repair stitching itself. Similarly, the centre forepart of Cat No 452/A10048a has cracked and worn along the line of stitching for a clump that covered an earlier tear across the front of the sole (Illus 147).

Clump soles surviving in situ or tunnel stitch holes for them show that 85 soles had been patched. Type 1 soles were the most patched, with 28 examples, which represent 33% of the repaired soles, or 50% of their type. Substantial proportions of the two-part soles had been repaired: 28.5% of Type 7, 6% of Type 8, and 24% of Type 9.

Repairs to sole–upper seams are suggested by close concentrations of stitch holes in both sole and upper stitching channels, as on Cat Nos 4123/A03–0214a, 5608/A03–0065, 783/A9372a, 332/A6774b and 5821/A0801b. However, it is possible that these soles and uppers have been reused, in conjunction with new or other reused components, rather than repaired.

Thongs were used to replace worn sole/upper seams, as on sole and upper Cat No 222/A7436a (Illus 104) and probably also vamps Cat Nos 3072/A8668g (Illus 144) and 2777/A03–0124c (Illus 146). On another example, left sole Cat No 3594/A6220b, five thong holes have replaced the very worn edge–flesh stitching channel. The thong holes are c24mm, 12mm, 27mm and 19mm apart; the new seam would have been far from waterproof (Illus 122). The use of a thong to repair a sole–upper seam was also noted at Schleswig (Schnack 1992b, 124–8).

Upper Cat No 626/A9885b has had part of its lasting margin replaced by a patch; the new stitch holes are very irregular. The quarters of this upper had also been patched (Illus 104). However, this was an unusual method of repair, with only four other examples from this site (Cat Nos 267/A7044Bg, Illus 130; 2807/A03–0274b, not illustrated; 2337/A03–0291e and 456/A10048e, Illus 147). This suggests that uppers requiring patching were discarded or cut for reuse. Patches on uppers would have been much more obtrusive than clumps on soles or repairs to seams. Furthermore, uppers would not have worn as badly as a single sole. Some uppers may have been repaired more subtly, by the substitution of new or reused parts; this is especially possible for side-pieces. This method of repair may explain some of the two-part uppers of Types J and D, for example, Cat No 1105/A03–0287c, which has a sidepiece on either side of the foot (Illus 137; J Swann pers comm).

There are few examples of repairs to uppers. Uppers which had splits stitched together were found at Kirk Close, Perth (Thomas 1987, 177, nos 17 and 19) and at Redcliffe Street, Bristol (Thomas forthcoming b), while one of the Schleswig uppers had been patched (Schnack 1992b, 124–8). A child's ankle-shoe from Coppergate, York also has a repaired slit in the vamp (Mould et al 2003). Repaired soles and uppers, and separate clump soles, were most numerous in Period IV, followed by Periods II and V.

Reuse

Some of the leather was reused rather than repaired, probably in the manufacture of new shoes from old (translation) and also in cobbling, the repair of shoes and other items. Evidence for this takes the form of cut-up uppers, and soles with shapes cut from them. Cut-up uppers appear in all periods, but particularly in Periods II (1150–1200) and IV (1250–1300). Cut-out soles (apart from Soles (seats cut across the waist)) only occur in Period V (14th century) deposits. It is also noticeable that the more complete uppers date from the earlier phases. The more fragmentary uppers from the later phases may be a further reflection of a recycling industry.

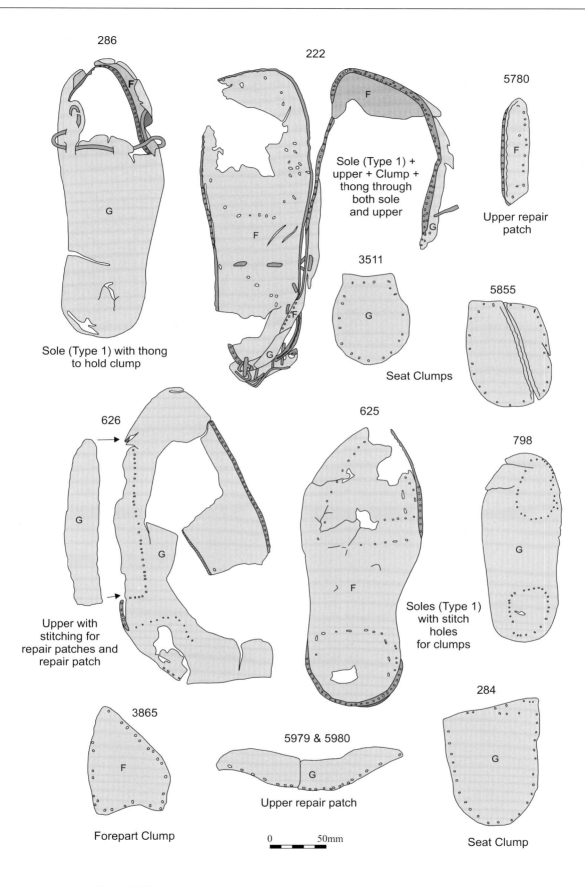

286

Sole (Type 1) with thong
to hold clump

222

Sole (Type 1) +
upper + Clump +
thong through
both sole
and upper

5780

Upper repair
patch

3511

Seat Clumps

5855

626

Upper with
stitching for
repair patches and
repair patch

625

Soles (Type 1)
with stitch
holes
for clumps

798

3865

Forepart Clump

5979 & 5980

Upper repair patch

0   50mm

284

Seat Clump

Illus 104 *Repairs.*

Repairs (Illus 104).

Cat/Accession	Leather type	Area	Rig	Feature	Phase
South Sector					
28/A10800b	Sole (Type 6)	1	V	MC008, T3774	Ib
68/A8809c	Sole (Type 1)	1/2	V, VI	M2.1b & B10, South Room–Floor/Occupation (1)	Ic,Icc
121/A03–0006	Sole (Type 1)	4	V	MC023, Well 4774	Icc,Id
127/A12306	Upper (Type Aii)	3	V	MC025, Pit 5337	(Ia–)Id
128/A12308a	Sole (Type 1)	3	V	MC025, Pit 5337	(Ia–)Id
163/A7787j	Upper (Type H)	1/2	VI	B6(Phase 1) South Room–Floor (1)	Ie
218/A7648b	Upper (Type Aii)	2	VI	M14b(b), Pit 3625	Ie
222/A7436a	Clump, Sole (Type 1), Upper & Thong	2	VI	P5.2b	Ie
255/A12287a	Upper (Type Bi)	3	V	MC034a	Ie(If)
262/A7044Bb	Sole (Type 1)	2	VI	MC044b	If
267/A7044Bg	Upper (Type Bi)	2	VI	MC044b	If
286/A03–0017a	Sole (Type 1)	3	V	MC053a	If
334/A03–0011	Sole (Type 1)	3	VI	MC054a, Pit 5267	(IIa)IIb
344/A6772d	Upper	2	VI	MC061	IIb
352/A6773a	Sole (Type 2)	2	VI	MC061	IIb
375/A12282a	Sole (Type 7)	1	VI	MC065, Pit 3908	IIa–IIc
400/A12293b	Sole (Type 1)	3	VI	MC056, Pit 5155	Ia–IIc
401/A12293c	Sole (seat)	3	VI	MC056, Pit 5155	Ia–IIc
449/A6771	Upper (Type E)	2	VI	B4, Byre – Occupation	IIc
452/A10048a	Sole (Type 1)	4	VI	M1.1f, Pit 2383	IIb,IIc
453/A10048b	Sole (Type 2)	4	VI	M1.1f, Pit 2383	IIb,IIc
456/A10048e	Upper (Type J)	4	VI	M1.1f, Pit 2383	IIb,IIc
462/A10599a	Sole (Type 1)	3	VI	M1.1c, Pit 5005	IId
471/A12285c	Sole (Type 1)	3	VI	M1.1c, Pit 5005	IId
473/A12285e	Upper (Type Biv)	3	VI	M1.1c, Pit 5005	IId
478/A12309b	Upper (Type Aii)	3	VI	M1.1c, Pit 5005	IId
625/A9885a	Sole (Type 1)	4	V	M10	IId–IIg
626/A9885b	Upper	4	V	M10	IId–IIg
635/A10778b	Sole	3	V	M10	IId–IIg
777/A9371c	Sole	3	VI	M1.2, Pit 2648	<IIg(IIh)
778/A9371d	Upper (Type Biii)	3	VI	M1.2, Pit 2648	<IIg(IIh)
779/A9371e	Upper (Type E)	3	VI	M1.2, Pit 2648	<IIg(IIh)
821/A11221a	Sole (Type 4)	3	VI	M1.2, Pit 2648	<IIg(IIh)
919/A12536a	Sole (Type 2)	4	VI	M1.3	IIi
922/A11639a	Sole (Type 1)	1	VI	MC111	IIb–IIIb
923/A11639b	Sole (Type 1)	1	VI	MC111	IIb–IIIb
970/A11261a	Sole (Type 8)	4	V	MC116	IIe–IIIc
1003/A8011a	Sole (rounded forepart)	4	VI	M1.4a(a)	IIIa–IIIc
1026/A03–0317a	Sole (Type 1)	9	VII	P8.1b	IIIc
1028/A03–0317c	Grain to flesh stitching channel	9	VII	P8.1b	IIIc
1076/A12535b	Sole	4	V, VI	MC128	IIIb,IIIc
1103/A03–0287a	Sole (Type 2)	9	VII	P8.1c	IIIc
1130/A03–0263a	Sole (Type 2)	9	VII	M15	IIId
1148/A5893c	Upper	1	V	M12	IIg–IIIc(–IVa)
1287/A6415c	Upper (Type Di)	3	V	P2.2b	IVa
1314/A7989a	Sole (Type 3)	4	V	MC143	IVaa

(continued)

Cat/Accession	Leather type	Area	Rig	Feature	Phase
1553/A03–0422a	Sole (Type 4)	7	VII	MC130	<IIIc–IVaa
1555/A03–0422c	Upper (Type Bi)	7	VII	MC130	<IIIc–IVaa
1743/A03–0347a	Sole (Type 2)	7	VII	MC126, Pit 7402	IVaa,IVb
1744/A03–0347b	Sole	7	VII	MC126, Pit 7402	IVaa,IVb
1752/A03–0350a	Sole (Type 2)	7	VII	MC126, Pit 7402	IVaa,IVb
1754/A03–0350c	Sole (Type 3)	7	VII	MC126, Pit 7402	IVaa,IVb
1761/A03–0360a	Sole/Upper repair patch	7	VII	MC126, Pit 7402	IVaa,IVb
1763/A03–0360c	Clump	7	VII	MC126, Pit 7402	IVaa,IVb
1804/A03–0367a	Sole (Type 4), upper (Type Di) & thong	7	VII	MC126, Pit 7402	IVaa,IVb
2181/A03–0385a	Sole (Type 7)	7	VII	MC126, Pit 7402	IVaa,IVb
2333/A03–0291a	Sole (Type 3)	7	VI	M1.4f	IVc
2339/A03–0308b	Sole (Type 3)	7	VI	M1.4f	IVc
2371/A03–0332h	Upper	7	VI	M1.4f	IVc
2569/A03–0329a	Sole (Type 1)	7	VII	B18 (Phase 1/2)	IVaa,IVb
2651/A03–0316a	Sole (Type 1)	7	VII	B18 (Phase 1/2), Pit 7324	IVaa,IVb
2682/A03–0202c	Upper	9	VII	B18 (Phase 1/2), Pit 9301	IVaa,IVb
2714/A03–0311a	Sole (Type 2)	7	VII	B18 (Phase 2a), External (1), Pit 7314	IVb
2719/A03–0314c	Rand	7	VII	B18 (Phase 2a), External (1), Pit 7314	IVb
2777/A03–0124c	Upper	9	VII	B18 (Phase 2b), North Room, Hall & Hall South–Occupation (10)	IVb
2779/A03–0232	Sole (Type 4)	9	VII	B18 (Phase 2b), North Room, Hall & Hall South–Occupation (10)	IVb
2807/A03–0274b	Upper (Type Ai)	7	VII	B18 (Phase 2b), Hall, Pit 7290	IVb
2841/A03–0313	Sole (oval forepart)	10	VIII	M9b(a)	IVc
2842/A03–0319a	Sole (seat)	10	VIII	M9b(a)	IVc
3066/A8668a	Sole (Type 1)	3	VI	M1.4d	IVb,IVc
3072/A8668g	Upper	3	VI	M1.4d	IVb,IVc
3102/A6240	Upper (Type C)	2	VI	M1.4d	IVb,IVc
3240/A9888b	Sole (Type 3)	3	V, VI	M1.4c	IIIa–IVcc
3242/A4940a	Upper (Type Biv)	4	V, VI	M1.4b	IVb–IVcc
3384/A03–0233a	Sole	7	VII	M9a	IVc,IVcc
3427/A03–0051a	Upper, sole, rand	9	VII	M9a, Pit 9026	IVc,IVcc
3598/A4329a	Sole (Type 2)	3	VI	M1.4e	IVcc(Va)
3858/A03–0047	Sole (Type 4)	7	VI, VII	M1.5b	Vaa
3859/A03–0048a	Sole (Type 8)	7	VI, VII	M1.5b	Vaa
3861/A03–0048c	Sole	7	VI, VII	M1.5b	Vaa
3863/A03–0067a	Sole (Type 4)	7	VI, VII	M1.5b	Vaa
3886/A03–0125a	Sole	7	VI, VII	M1.5b	Vaa
3927/A03–0136c	Miscellaneous fragment	7	VI, VII	M1.5b	Vaa
4124/A03–0214b	Sole (Type 4)	7	VII	P8.4	Va
4284/A4901b	Sole (Type 3)	1	V, VI	M5a	IVb–Vc
4816/A6237b	Sole (Type 9)	3	V, VI	M1.5a	Va,Vaa
4972/A03–0174l	Sole (oval forepart)	7	VII	M8a	Va,Vaa
5016/A03–0174ddd	Sole (Type 9)	7	VII	M8a	Va,Vaa

(continued)

Cat/Accession	Leather type	Area	Rig	Feature	Phase
5221/A03–0138a	Sole (Type 7)	7	VII	M8a, T7193	Va,Vaa
5241/A03–0216	Upper, sole (Type 2) & rand	7	VII	B53(Phase 1), Central Area–T7152	Vb
5251/A03–0029b	Sole (Type 8)	7	VII	P8.5	Vb,Vbb
5318/A4390f	Upper (Type Ki)	4	V,VI	M3a	Vb–Vc
5336/A03–0018b	Sole (Type 9)	7	VII	M7	Vc
5337/A03–0018c	(Type 9)	7	VII	M7	Vc
5608/A03–0065	Sole (Type 4)	10	VIII	MC174, Pit 7013	(Va–)Vd(Vdd)
5772/A12574b	Sole (Type 3)	3/4	V, VI	Unstratified	u/s
5779/A0800a	Sole (Type 2)	3/4	V, VI	Unstratified	u/s
5780/A0800b	Clump/Upper repair patch	3/4	V, VI	Unstratified	u/s
North Sector					
5889/A7805c	Upper (Type Biv)	5		CG005	4(5)
South/North Sectors					
5979/L1694f,g	Uppers			Unstratified	u/s

Evidence for similar reuse has been found on
many sites, especially at Kirk Close, Perth (13th–14th
centuries) (Thomas 1987, 185); Norwich (Ayers and
Murphy 1983); Redcliffe Street, Bristol (Thomas
forthcoming b); Newcastle (mid-13th–mid-14th
centuries) (Dixon 1988, 94); Leicester (Allin 1981a,
150–1) and Schleswig (especially 13th century)
(Schnack 1992b, 126–8).

Measurements

As stated in the introduction, all measurements quoted are post-conservation and are expressed in millimetres.

Shoe sizes

An attempt has been made to translate sole lengths into modern United Kingdom shoe sizes. As the figures for shrinkage during conservation show considerable variation, between 0% and 29%, it was decided to use only the sole lengths that can be measured on the pre-conservation drawings for this purpose. These drawings have two drawbacks: firstly, they only represent part of the leather recovered from the site;

secondly, they were made by an unskilled workforce. Hence, not all the leather is represented, and the measurements must be regarded as approximate. For this reason, no attempt has been made to try to calculate lengths of uppers. However, despite these problems, lengths were obtained for 86 complete or nearly complete soles.

No allowance has been made for shrinkage during burial, as this is much disputed. On the one hand, Thornton believed in a reduction of c10%. Carol van Driel-Murray, however, suggests that shoes in water-logged conditions may actually have expanded. In her experience, it is immediately after excavation that leather shrinks, unless it is at once kept in water (Grew and de Neergaard 1988, 103; van Driel-Murray 1987).

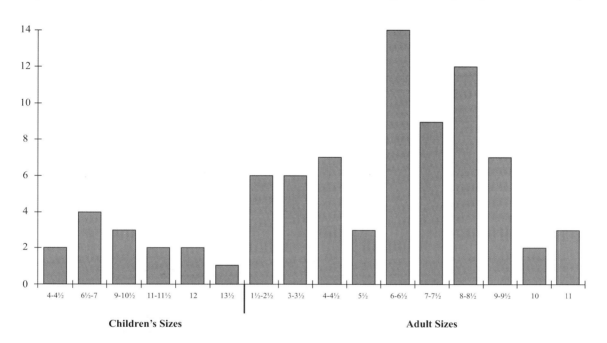

Illus 105 *Number of shoe sizes (overall).*

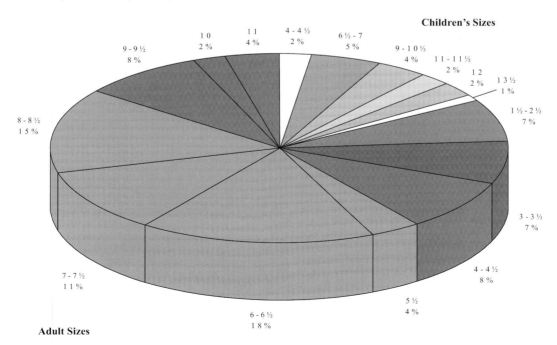

Illus 106 *Percentage of shoe sizes (overall).*

Table 9 *Shoe sizes.*

Cat/ccession	pre-conservation length	post-conservation length	UK shoe size	continental shoe size	shrinkage	phase
Sole (Type 1)						
54/A9886a	282	255	8	42	10%	Ic
58/A8635a	228	212.5	2	34	7%	Ic,Icc
62/A8704a	194–198	167.5	Childs 11	29	14%	Ic,Icc
68/A8809c	310–315	287	11	45	7%	Ic,Icc
103/A03–0001	292	263	9	43	10%	Ia–Icc>
104/A10798a	205	193	Childs 12	30½	6%	Ib–Id
120/A03–0005	267+	250+	6½+	40+	6%	Icc,Id
121/A03–0006	291+	266+	9+	43+	9%	Icc,Id
125/A12297a	205	186	Childs 12	30½	9%	(Ia–)Id
185/A7600a	278	257	8	42	7.5%	Ie
208/A7434	243	207	3½	36	15%	Ie
286/A03–0017a	284	263	8½	42½	7%	If
323/A10600	281+	255+	8+	42+	9%	IIa
331/A6774a	307–315	271	11?	45?	12%	IIb
334/A03–0011	313	274	11?	45?	12%	(IIa)IIb
389/A12296a	160	142	Childs 7	27½	11%	IIa–IIc
406/A12493a	300	277	10	44	8%	Ia–IIc
475/A12302a	268	244	6½	40	9%	IId
491/A12290a	261	231	6	39½	11.5%	IIb–IIf
625/A9885a	294	264	9	43	10%	IId–IIg
798/A10366	198	179	Childs 11½	29½	10%	<IIg(IIh)
846/A8544	280	240	8	42	14%	IIIa–IIIc
923/A11639b	242	219	3½	36	9.5%	IIb–IIIb
2652/A03–0316b	190	165.5	Childs 10½	28½	13%	IVaa,IVb
Sole (Type 2)						
173/A7580b	245	221.5	4	37	10%	Ie
175/A7589a	280	275	8	42	2%	Ie
611/A9879a	231	212	2	34	8%	IId–IIg
1103/A03–0287a	278	256.5	7½–8	41½–42	8%	IIIc
1144/A4817a	266	233	6½	40	11%	IIg–IIIc(–IVa)
1659/A03–0417a	250+	235+	4½+	37½+	6%	IVa–IVb
1743/A03–0347a	285+	247+	8½+	42½+	13%	IVaa,IVb
1809/A03–0374a	283+	267.5+	8–8½+	42–42½+	5.5%	IVaa,IVb
2361/A03–0331a	268	240	6½	42½	10%	IVc
2714/A03–0311a	161	144	Childs 7	24	10.5%	IVb
2872/A4894	183	168	Childs 9½	27½	8%	IVb,IVc
3335/A03–0261a	159	138	Childs 6½	23½	13%	IVc,IVcc
3877/A03–0120b	275	253	7½	41½	8%	Vaa
4493/A4289a	137	127	Childs 4	20½	7%	Va,Vaa(VI)
4815/A6237a	226	206	1½	33½	9%	Va,Vaa
5241/A03–0216	288	262.5	8½–9	42½–43	9%	Vb
5768/A9821a	260	229	5½	39	12%	u/s
5779/A0800a	268	239	6½	40	11%	u/s
Sole (Type 3)						
740/A9144	270	243	7	41	10%	<IIg(IIh)
783/A9372a	258	242	5½	39	6%	<IIg(IIh)
788/A9546a	285	259.5	8½	42½	9%	<IIg(IIh)

(continued)

Cat/ccession	pre-conservation length	post-conservation length	UK shoe size	continental shoe size	shrinkage	phase
831/A8518a	268	251.5	6½	40	6%	IIh
1095/A03–0270a	265	252	6	39½	5%	IIIc
1106/A03–0304a	300	267	10	44	11%	IIIc
1195/A9883	287	271	9	43	6%	IIg–IIId
1426/A6187a	244	228.5	3½	36	6%	IVaa
1991/A03–0362a	267	248	6½	40	7%	IVaa,IVb
2333/A03–0291a	286	257	8½	42½	10%	IVc
2750/A03–0293	280	259	8	42	7.5%	IVb
2985/A10521	251	227.5	4½	37½	9%	IVb,IVc
3033/A3459	225	200	1½	33½	11%	IVb,IVc
3246/A6195	270	253	7	41	6%	IVb–IVcc
3321/A03–0066a	242+	226.5+	3½+	36+	6%	IVc,IVcc
3405/A03–0052a	249+	233+	4½	37½	6%	IVc,IVcc
3707/A03–0134a	278	260	7½	41½	7%	Va
4229/A6373	271+	236+	7+	41+	13%	IVcc,Va
5871/A03–0008	258	242	5½	39	6%	u/s
Sole (Type 4)						
821/A11221a	247	237.5	4	37	4%	<IIg(IIh)
1042/A8546	266	240	6½	40	10%	IIe–IIIc
1206/A8680a	272	253	7	41	7%	IIg–IIId
1553/A03–0422a	238+	215+	3+	35½+	10%	<IIIc–IVaa
1804/A03–0367a	234	230	2½	35	2%	IVaa,IVb
2728/A03–0295a	275	254	7½–8	41½	9%	IVb
2779/A03–0232	287	254.5	8½–9	42½–43	11%	IVb
3863/A03–0067a	266+	238.5	6½+	40+	10%	Vaa
4811/A6189	265	241	6½	40	9%	Va,Vaa
4827/A03–0106	242	222.5	3½	36	8%	Va,Vaa
5240/A03–0090	291	273.5	9	43	5%	Vb
5608/A03–0065	177+	165+	Childs 9+	27+	7%	(Va–)Vd(Vdd)
Sole (Type 5)						
403/A12295	281	240	8	42	15%	Ia–IIc
1504/A03–0405	261+	255+	6+	39½+	2%	<IIIc–IVaa
3117/A8681a	246	226	4	37	8%	IVb,IVc
3857/A03–0044	225+	215+	1½+	33½+	4%	Vaa
3985/A03–0170b	262	240	6	39½	8%	Vaa
5329/A6399a	270	238	7	41	12%	Vb–Vc
Sole (Type 6)						
28/A10800b	249	240	4½	37½	3.6%	Ib
43/A8525	238	208	3	35½	13%	Ic
314/A10365a	296	256	9½	43½	14%	IIa
Sole (Type 7)						
3624/A6077c	218+	202+	Childs 13½+	32+	7%	IVcc(Va)

Average shrinkage of above soles 8.7%

The sizes recorded vary between a child's 4 and an adult 11. A study of their frequencies (Illus 105) shows that adult 6 to 9½ were the most common, followed by adult 1½ to 4½. There was also a small group of children's sizes, 4 to 12, and a very few large examples, adult 10 to 11. Another ten soles, which were not included in the original drawings, have been identified as children's, on the basis of their overall length; no attempt, however, has been made to define a specific modern size. The three main groups possibly represent men's, youths' and women's, and children's, with allowance being made between the groups. As noted under the study of Soles (Children's), the children's sizes were mainly restricted to Soles Types 1 and 2, with one each of Types 3, 4 and 7.

Soles

Of the 785 fragments of soles found, 261 (33%) were reasonably complete and could be divided into nine types, distinguished by variations in shape. Types 1–6 are whole soles; Type 7 consists of soles sewn across the tread, or middle of the forepart; Types 8 and 9 are seats and foreparts, respectively, sewn across the waist and probably originally joined together; several pairs match. Soles that are obviously children's have been compared with adult types, but have been considered separately, to see if dating trends differed. It was not possible to define the types of the rest of the sole fragments, though variations, such as toe shapes, were noted as far as possible. One group has been listed separately, as they are mostly of 14th-century date; these are seats that have been cut across the waist, possibly for reuse.

The types have been defined by shape, especially that of the toe, but also taking into account overall alignment and proportions of the sole, width of waist and curvature of forepart. Schnack (1992b, 38–46) used similar but stricter criteria in her work on the Schleswig soles, ending up with 13 types and three sub-types. These she then placed into four groups, based on the width and shape of the waists. Thus her Group 1 consisted of Types 1–4, with broad, virtually symmetrical soles and no waists. Groups 2 (Types 5–7), 3 (Types 8–10) and 4 (Types 11–13) had progressively more marked waists. Group 1 proved to be the earliest, being predominantly of 11th-century date, followed by Group 2, mainly from the 13th century, and Groups 3 and 4, chiefly of 13th- and 14th-century date. However, these datings were by no means absolute, as Group 1, 2 and 4 soles were also found in 12th-century layers.

In his division of the Bergen soles, Larsen relied on strict mathematical statistics. He came to the conclusion that the most important measurements were the length of the sole and the width of the waist, which he expressed as a ratio. However, he also recognised the relevance of seat and forepart widths, and of overall alignments. As a result, he produced four types, I, II, III and IV, and four variants, A1–A4 (Larsen 1992, 27–30). Larsen also found that his sole types fell into broad dating trends. Thus Types 1 and A3 and A4 were the commonest forms from before 1170 to 1198, while Type IV was of much later date, chiefly 1332 to 1476. Type II, on the other hand, appeared in substantial numbers throughout the site's time-span (Larsen 1992, 38).

Carter's report on the King's Lynn leather also used the length:waist ratio as an expression of sole shape. Thus, if the length of a sole is 120mm, the width of the waist 30mm, then A:C=3.00. In this case, however, no allowance was made for variations in forepart or toe shape that were not represented by the ratio. Carter claimed that this method could be used for dating purposes, and quoted the evidence from King's Lynn.

Table 10 *A:C values of soles by type, where A=length, C=width of waist.*

sole type	A:C	average
1	2.43–4.25	3.43
2	3.3–5.62	4.17
3	3.89–7.76	5.66
4	4.66–6.36	5.64
5	4.21–10.68	6.02
6	3.05–4.45	3.7

Types 7, 8 and 9 not applicable

Table 11 *A:C values of soles by period, where A=length, C=width of waist.*

period	date	A:C	average
I	(1100–1150)	2.87–5.08	3.52
II	(1150–1200)	2.43–7.36	5.17
III	(1200–1250)	3.6–7.76	5.17
IV	(1250–1300)	3.45–10.68	5.18
V	(1300–1350>)	3.79–7.06	5.47

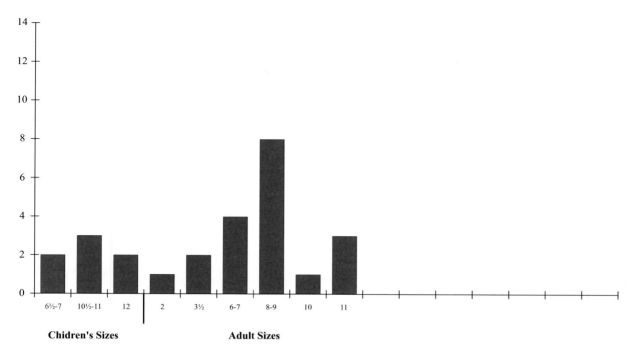

Illus 107 *Soles, Type 1.*

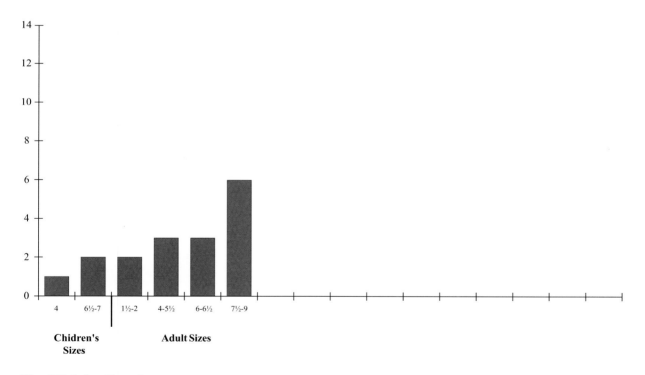

Illus 108 *Soles, Type 2.*

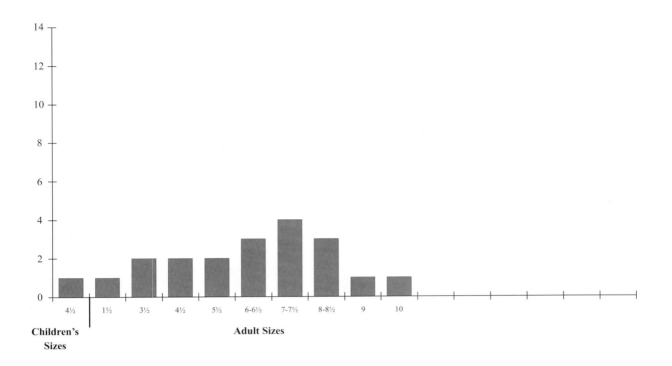

Illus 109 *Soles, Type 3.*

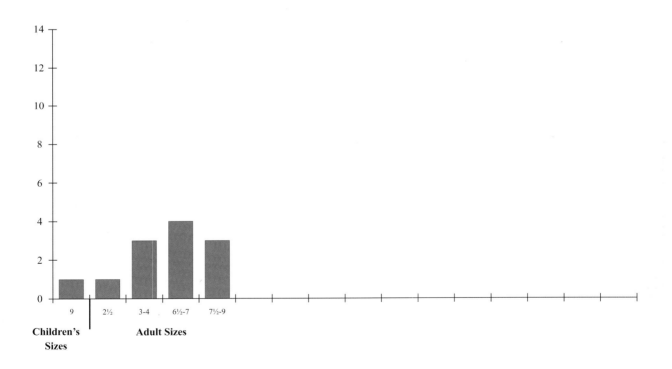

Illus 110 *Soles, Type 4.*

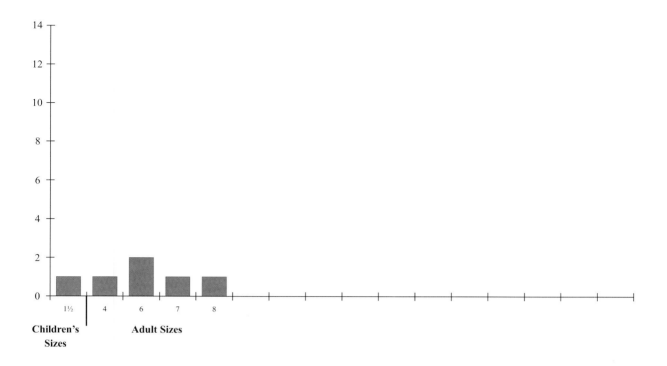

Illus 111 *Soles, Type 5.*

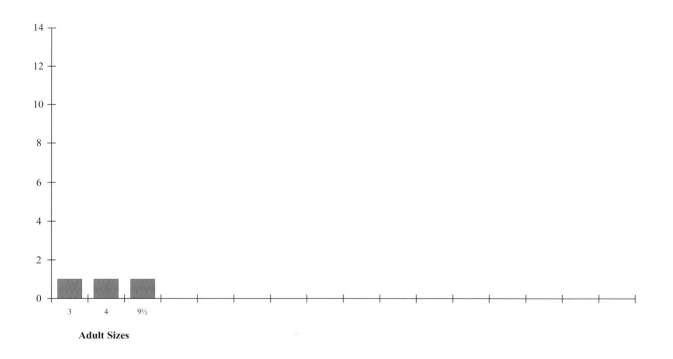

Illus 112 *Soles, Type 6.*

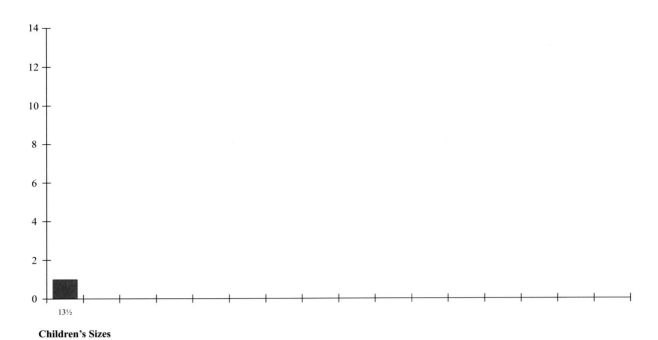

Children's Sizes

Illus 113 *Soles, Type 7.*

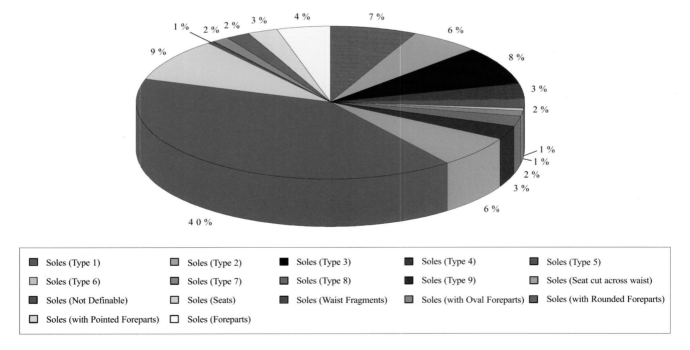

Illus 114 *Sole categories (percentage).*

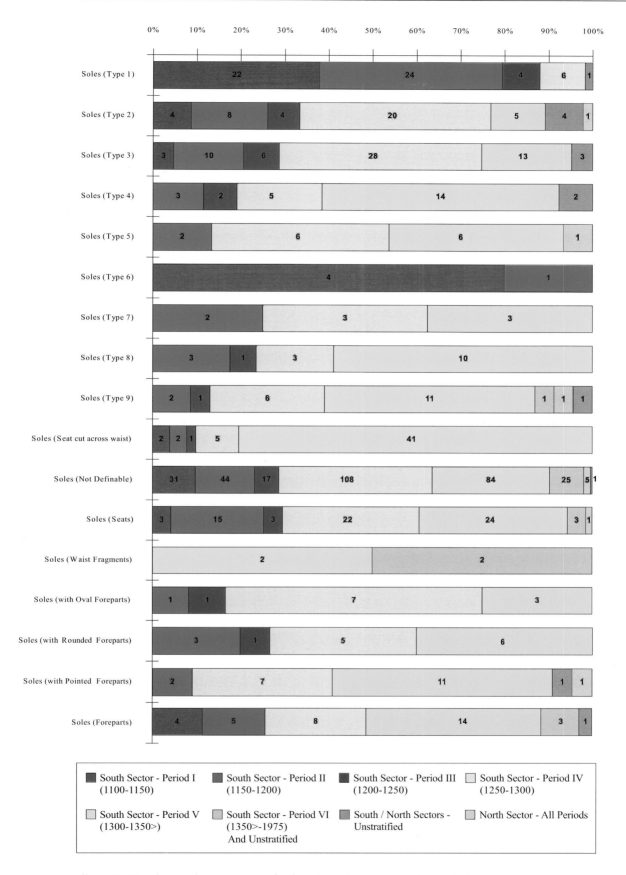

Illus 115 *Number and percentage of sole categories arranged by period.*

None of the 21 Period I (c1050–1250) soles had an A:C greater than 4.4. His 45 soles from Period II (c1250–1350) ranged between 3.9 and 8.0 but were normally between 5.0 and 7.0. The seven Period III (c1350–1500) soles have an A:C up to 12.00 (Clarke and Carter 1977, 355–61).

At Perth High Street, general dating trends can be observed. Type 1 soles, which are broad and straight, are mostly of 12th-century date; the more shapely Types 2 and 3 soles belong principally to the 13th century, while the pointed soles of Types 4 and 5 are mainly of 14th-century date. However, there are exceptions; Type 1 soles also occur in late 13th century contexts; Types 2 and 3 cover a 200–year span from the early 12th century; Type 4 soles date from the 12th century. Pointed soles also include straighter, broader examples of 12th-century date (Type 6). The dating of each type will be discussed in greater detail below. Here it is sufficient to note that sole shapes obviously varied in popularity; several different types were in use at the same time; choice of a particular shape would have depended not just on fashion but also on the needs and preferences of the wearer. Hence, it would be unwise to attempt a definitive dating of sole types.

This argument is supported by Allin (1981b, 9–10), who, in her discussion of the leather from Leicester, challenged the close dating of soles purely on stylistic grounds, emphasising the tendency for styles to be repeated. The above point is important, in view of Carter's use of length:waist ratios as a dating tool, as mentioned above.

This ratio has been applied to the Perth soles, taking into account both types and Periods (see Tables 10 and 11). Types 1 and 6 have virtually identical A:C values, as do Types 3, 4 and 5 (apart from one anomaly), while Type 2 values are slightly higher than those of Types 1 and 6, but lower than those of Types 3, 4 and 5. So far, Carter's theory appears to work, as Types 1 and 6 are earlier than the rest. On the other hand, the ratios do not seem to distinguish between Type 3 and the later Types 4 and 5. This is because the method is over simplified and is not sufficiently sensitive to variations in the shape and width of the forepart, and in the shape of the toe. Carter's theory also appears to work on a chronological basis, but only just. Thus the average ratio rises from 3.52 in Period I to 5.17 in Period II. However, at this point the average levels out, rising only to 5.18 in Period IV and peaking to 5.47 in Period V. Accordingly, Carter's theory only proves that, between the 12th and 14th centuries, waists became proportionately narrower. It can be used as a general guide to possible date of a sole, as it differentiates be-tween wide and narrow waists, but it cannot be used for closer dating, as it does not distinguish between the different foreparts of similarly waisted soles.

Soles, Type 1
(Illus 104, 107, 116, 117, 124, 139, 145, 146 and 147)

Type 1 consists of 58 broad and straight soles, with either no waist or only a very slight narrowing and with a straight-sided forepart, ending in a broad rounded or oval toe. Rather shapeless, they would have been easily cut out. At the High Street, they belonged predominantly to the 12th century (Periods I and II), with at least 38% (22) from Period I and 44% (26) from Period II. The distribution shows only a few concentrations, with four from Pit 5337, five from Midden 14b(b) and five from Pit 5005 in Midden 1.1c. Otherwise, these soles were found singly or in twos (Illus 104, 116, 117, 124, 139, 145, 146, 147).

Dated parallels from other sites range between the 12th and 13th centuries and include 42 St Paul Street and Gallowgate Middle School, Aberdeen (predominantly mid 12th–early 13th centuries) (Stones 1982, 191–7; Thomas 2001a, 243); the Clarendon Hotel, Oxford (c1120–1220) (Sturdy 1958, 75–7); King's Lynn (Period I: c1050–1250) (Clarke and Carter 1977, 355–7); Durham (11th century?) (Carver 1979, 31–3, Figs 19–20); Exeter (13th century) (Friendship-Taylor 1984, 324–7, Fig 184, nos 4 and 6); Winchester (13th century) (Thornton 1990b, 612–15, Fig 163, no 1938, Fig 164, no 1948); Coppergate, York, (9th–13th centuries) (Mould et al 2003); Waterford (late 11th–13th centuries) (O'Rourke 1997, 720, Fig 18.5, 18.6); Bergen (12th–14th centuries) (Larsen 1992, 27–8) and Schleswig (12th–14th centuries) (Schnack 1992b, 38–46, Abb. II, nos 1a, 5, 2a, 6, 8).

Soles, Type 2 (Illus 118, 124, 137, 140, 146 and 147)

The 46 Type 2 soles are also straight, but have a more pronounced shape, with definite waists and with curved foreparts, ending in oval or rounded toes. They mainly belong to the second half of the 13th century, with 42% (20) from Period IV. They are scattered over the site in ones and twos, with only three larger groups: three from Midden 14b(b), four from Pit 7402 (MC126) and three from Midden 1.4f (Illus 118, 124, 137, 140, 146, 147). Parallels mainly from the 12th to 14th centuries are known from Kirk Close, Perth (13th–14th centuries) (Thomas 1987, 176–177); 42 St Paul Street (mid-12th–early 14th century), Aberdeen (Stones 1982, 191–7); 45–75 Gallowgate (1250–1400) and Gallowgate Middle School (12th–13th centuries), Aberdeen (Thomas 2001a, 243); King's Lynn (Period I, c1050–1250) (Clarke and Carter 1977, 355–7); London (early–late 14th century) (Tatton-Brown 1975, 157, Fig 27, nos 9, 22, 43, 51, 52; Grew and de Neergaard 1988, 62, Fig 96, 65, Fig 99); Barbican Ditch, Oxford (13th–15th centuries) (Hassall 1976, 277, Fig 18, nos 6, 9, 10); Durham (11th century?) (Carver 1979, 31–3, Fig 19, 20); Leicester (15th century) (Allin 1981a, 150–1, Fig 57.13,14, Fig 58.18, Fig 59.28); Bristol (13th–14th centuries) (Thomas forthcoming a); Nantwich (14th

Soles, Type 1 (Illus 104, 116, 124, 139 and 145–7).

Cat/Accession	Area	Rig	Feature	Phase
South Sector				
5/A12300a	1	V, VI	MC002	Ia
54/A9886a	1/2	V, VI	M2.1b	Ic
58/A8635a	1/2	V, VI	M2.1b & B10, South Room–Floor/Occupation (1)	Ic,Icc
62/A8704a	1/2	V, VI	M2.1b & B10, South Room–Floor/Occupation (1)	Ic,Icc
68/A8809c	1/2	V, VI	M2.1b & B10, South Room–Floor/Occupation (1)	Ic,Icc
103/A03–0001	4	V/VI	MC017	Ia–Icc>
104/A10798a	4	VI	MC018, Pit 2398	Ib–Id
120/A03–0005	4	V	MC023, Well 4774	Icc,Id
121/A03–0006	4	V	MC023, Well 4774	Icc,Id
125/A12297a	3	V	MC025, Pit 5337	(Ia–)Id
128/A12308a	3	V	MC025, Pit 5337	(Ia–)Id
129/A12308b	3	V	MC025, Pit 5337	(Ia–)Id
136/A12291	3	V	MC025, Pit 5337	(Ia–)Id
143/A7789b	2	VI	P5.2a	Ie
165/A7256a	2	VI	M14b(b)	Ie
170/A7573	2	VI	M14b(b)	Ie
185/A7600a	2	VI	M14b(b)	Ie
208/A7434	2	VI	M14b(b), Pit 3625	Ie
217/A7648a	2	VI	M14b(b), Pit 3625	Ie
222/A7436a	2	VI	P5.2b	Ie
262/A7044Bb	2	VI	MC044b	If
286/A03–0017a	3	V	MC053a	If
313/A12310	3	V	MC039, Pit 2609	If,IIa
323/A10600	3	V	MC049, Pit 5259	IIa
331/A6774a	1/2	VI	P5.4a	IIb
334/A03–0011	3	VI	MC054a, Pit 5267	(IIa)IIb
343/A6772c	2	VI	MC061	IIb
353/A6773b	2	VI	MC061	IIb
363/A2296a	1	V	M14a, Pit 3040	Id–IIc
385/A12304	1	VI	MC065, Pit 3908	IIa–IIc
389/A12296a	1	VI	MC065	IIa–IIc
400/A12293b	3	VI	MC056, Pit 5155	Ia–IIc
406/A12493a	3	VI	MC056, Pit 5155	Ia–IIc
452/A10048a	4	VI	M1.1f, Pit 2383	IIb,IIc
462/A10599a	3	VI	M1.1c, Pit 5005	IId
469/A12285a	3	VI	M1.1c, Pit 5005	IId
470/A12285b	3	VI	M1.1c, Pit 5005	IId
471/A12285c	3	VI	M1.1c, Pit 5005	IId
475/A12302a	3	VI	M1.1c, Pit 5005	IId
491/A12290a	1	VI	MC071	IIb–IIf
504/A3447a	2	VI	M1.1d & M1.1e	IId–IIf
505/A3447b	2	VI	M1.1d & M1.1e	IId–IIf
541/A6371	2	V	B5, North Room–Floor/Occupation (2)	IIa–IIff
625/A9885a	4	V	M10	IId–IIg
634/A10778a	3	V	M10	IId–IIg
797/A10043	3	VI	M1.2, Pit 2648	<IIg(IIh)
798/A10366	3	VI	M1.2, Pit 2648	<IIg(IIh)
846/A8544	4	V, VI	M11	IIIa–IIIc
922/A11639a	1	VI	MC111	IIb–IIIb>
923/A11639b	1	VI	MC111	IIb–IIIb>
1026/A03–0317a	9	VII	P8.1b	IIIc
1878/A03–0353a	7	VII	MC126, Pit 7402	IVaa,IVb
2569/A03–0329a	7	VII	B18 (Phase 1/2)	IVaa,IVb
2651/A03–0316a	7	VII	B18 (Phase 2a), Pit 7324	IVaa,IVb
2652/A03–0316b	7	VII	B18 (Phase 2a), Pit 7324	IVaa,IVb
3066/A8668a	3	VI	M1.4d	IVb,IVc
3599/A4329b	3	VI	M1.4e	IVcc(Va)
5737/A12307a	1	VI, VII	Unstratified	u/s

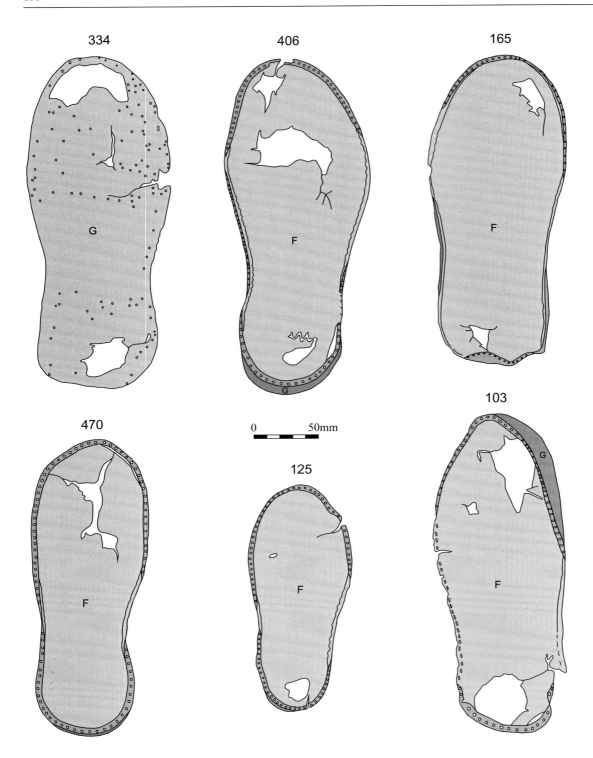

Illus 116 *Soles, Type 1.*

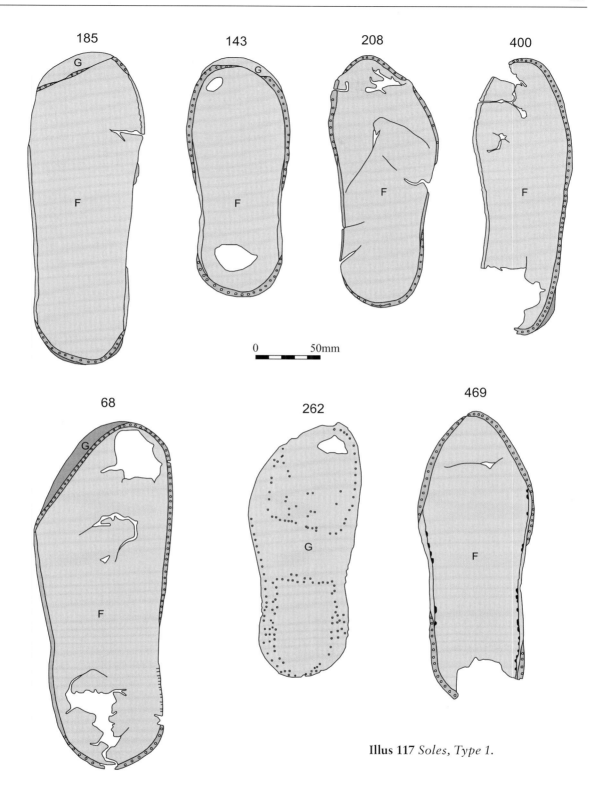

Illus 117 *Soles, Type 1.*

Soles, Type 2 (Illus 118, 124, 137, 140 and 146–7).

Cat/Accession	Area	Rig	Feature	Phase
South Sector				
147/A11595a	3	VI	MC037a, Pit 5157	Ia–Ie
173/A7580b	2	VI	M14b(b)	Ie
175/A7589a	2	VI	M14b(b)	Ie
176/A7589b	2	VI	M14b(b)	Ie
306/A12635b	4	V	B16b, Pit 4726	Id–IIa
352/A6773a	2	VI	MC061	IIb
453/A10048b	4	VI	M1.1f, Pit 2383	IIb,IIc
472/A12285d	3	VI	M1.1c, Pit 5005	IId
611/A9879a	4	V	M10	IId–IIg
776/A9371b	3	VI	M1.2, Pit 2648	<IIg(IIh)
897/A11260a	3	VI	M1.3	IIi
919/A12536a	4	VI	M1.3	IIi
933/A03–0327a	9	VII	P8.0	IIIa,IIIb
1103/A03–0287a	9	VII	P8.1c	IIIc
1130/A03–0263a	9	VII	M15	IIId
1144/A4817a	1	V	M12	IIg–IIIc(–IVa)
1309/A11215	3	V	P2.2b	IVa
1659/A03–0417a	7	VI	P3.3	IVa–IVb
1743/A03–0347a	7	VII	MC126, Pit 7402	IVaa,IVb
1752/A03–0350a	7	VII	MC126, Pit 7402	IVaa,IVb
1809/A03–0374a	7	VII	MC126, Pit 7402	IVaa,IVb
1879/A03–0353b	7	VII	MC126, Pit 7402	IVaa,IVb
2361/A03–0331a	7	VI	M1.4f	IVc
2364/A03–0332a	7	VI	M1.4f	IVc
2481/A03–0392c	7	VI	M1.4f	IVc
2714/A03–0311a	7	VII	B18 (Phase 2a), External (1), Pit 7314	IVb
2747/A03–0297a	7	VII	B18 (Phase 2a), North Room & Hall–Construction (1)	IVb
2754/A03–0288a	7	VII	B18 (Phase 2b), North Room, Hall & Hall South–Occupation (10)	IVb
2760/A03–0092	9	VII	B18 (Phase 2b), North Room, Hall & Hall SouthOccupation (10)	IVb
2775/A03–0124a	9	VII	B18 (Phase 2b), North Room, Hall & Hall SouthOccupation (10)	IVb
2776/A03–0124b	9	VII	B18 (Phase 2b), North Room, Hall & Hall SouthOccupation (10)	IVb
2872/A4894	3	V	MC155	IVb,IVc
3067/A8668b	3	VI	M1.4d	IVb,IVc
3335/A03–0261a	7	VII	P8.3 & M9a, PW7267	IVc,IVcc
3419/A03–0217a	7	VII	B18 (Phases 2a & 2b) & M9a, PH7237	(IVb)IVc,IVcc
3598/A4329a	3	VI	M1.4e	IVcc(Va)
3877/A03–0120b	7	VI, VII	M1.5b	Vaa
4493/A4289a	3	V, VI	M1.5a	Va,Vaa(VI)
4815/A6237a	3	V, VI	M1.5a	Va,Vaa
5241/A03–0216	7	VII	B53 (Phase 1), Central Area– T7152	Vb
5256/A03–0079	7	VII	B53 (Phase 2), North Area–Occupation (7b)	Vbb
5738/A12307b	1	VI, VII	Unstratified	u/s
5768/A9821a	3/4	V, VI	Unstratified	u/s
5779/A0800a	3/4	V, VI	Unstratified	u/s
5792/A0817a	3/4	V, VI	Unstratified	u/s
North sector				
5942/A0807a	5, A		Lade (4)	6–12(b–e)

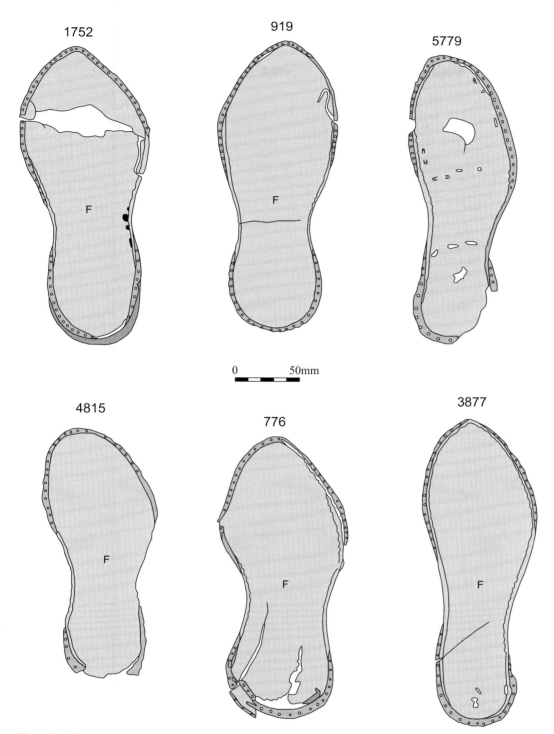

Illus 118 *Soles, Type 2.*

century?) (Hutchings 1983, 81–2, Fig 16, L 16); Chapel Lane Staith, Hull (late 13th–early 14th century) (Jackson 1979, 47–57, Fig 22, 7, 10); Coppergate, York (12th–14th centuries) (Mould et al 2003); Waterford (12th–13th centuries) (O'Rourke 1997, 720, Fig 7); Bergen (late 12th–late 15th centuries) (Larsen 1992, 27–28, Type II) and Schleswig (12th century) (Schnack 1992b, 38–46, Abb. II, Form II, Fig 3 no 14).

Soles, Type 3 (Illus 119, 120, 145 and 147)

Type 3 soles, of which there are 63, are mostly of a natural foot shape with pronounced waists and curved foreparts, inclined inwards slightly, and ending in oval toes. Two unusual soles have had pieces cut out. Cat No 1314/A7989a (Illus 120) has a long narrow hole, pointed at each end, with an edge–flesh stitching channel up each edge, suggesting that a worn sole had been patched in an extraordinary way. Cat No 4533/A6400 (Illus 120) is a very worn sole that has had triangles cut out of the thinnest part of seat and forepart. It is possible that an apprentice made these cuts; on the other hand, the triangles may have been deliberately cut by someone requiring thin and supple pieces of leather. A piper informs me that he requires very thin pieces of leather for his bagpipes; he cuts these from old shoes (Information from Mr Duncan McDiarmid, Castle Menzies Farm, Weem, Aberfeldy, Perthshire; Illus119, 120, 141, 145, 147).

Type 3 soles range in date from the 12th to the 14th centuries, but belong predominantly to the second half of the 13th century, with 46% (28) from Period IV. Again, they are mainly distributed singly or in twos, but have a few concentrated groups, with five from Midden 1.2, Pit 2648, three from Midden 1.3, three from Pit 7402 (MC126), four from Midden 1.4f, five from Building 18 (Phase 2), three from Building 1 and three from Midden 8a. This was a very common medieval shape of sole, with dated parallels mainly from the 13th and 14th centuries, from Kirk Close, Perth (13th–14th centuries) (Thomas 1987, 176–7); Gallowgate Middle School (12th–13th centuries) and 45–75 Gallowgate (1250–1375), Aberdeen (Thomas 2001a, 243); Weoley Castle, Birmingham (13th century) (Oswald 1963, 132); Low Petergate, York (12th–14th centuries) (Goodfellow and Thornton 1972, 97–104); London (early 13th century; early–mid 14th century) (Tatton-Brown 1975, 154–8; Grew and de Neergaard 1988, 56, Fig 84); King's Lynn (c1250–1350) (Clarke and Carter 1977, 357–60); Barbican Ditch, Oxford (13th–15th century) (Hassall 1976, 275–8); Queen Street, Newcastle (mid-13th–mid-14th century) (Dixon 1988, Fig 35, nos 203–205); Leicester (early–mid-14th century) (Allin 1981a, 147, Fig 55.1); Exeter (14th century?) (Friendship-Taylor 1984, 326, 329, Fig 185, 28, 40); Winchester (late 11th–mid-13th centuries) (Ottaway 1982, 128–30); Sandwell Priory (13th–15th centuries) (Thomas 1991, 104); Bristol Bridge (13th–14th centuries) (Thomas forthcoming a); Plymouth (13th–15th centuries) (Gaskell-Brown 1986, Fig 17.1);

Nantwich (mid 14th-century?) (Hutchings 1983, 80–2, Fig 16, L12, L14); Chapel Lane Staith, Hull (late 13th century–1350) (Jackson 1979, Fig 22, 11, 12); Hull (late 13th–early 14th centuries) (Armstrong 1977, 51–60, Fig 20, 3–5, 13); Beverley (12th–13th centuries) (Armstrong 1987, Fig 23, nos 27–28); Coppergate, York (13th–14th centuries) (Mould et al 2003); Waterford (13th century) (O'Rourke, 1997, 720 Fig 18.5, 18.7); Bergen (late 12th and mid-13th–early 15th centuries) (Larsen 1992, 28) and Schleswig (Form 9: 13th–14th centuries; Form 12: 12th century) (Schnack 1992b, 38–46, Abb. II, Form 9 and 12, Fig 3, nos 9–11, 15–16).

Less well dated examples come from Minster Pool, Lichfield (Gould and Thornton 1973, 53–7); Clare Castle, Suffolk (Thornton 1959, 136–52); Oakham Castle, Rutland (Gathercole 1958, 31–3); Parliament Street, York (Tweddle 1986, 242–53); Whithorn (Nicholson 1997); Redcliffe Street, Bristol (Thomas forthcoming b) and Jedburgh (Thomas 1995).

Soles, Type 4 (Illus 121, 124 and 145)

The 26 soles of Type 4 are slender and elegant, with narrow waists and gently curved pointed foreparts. They fall into two groups, 8 symmetrical with a central point, and 17 asymmetrical, but not as markedly as those of Type 5. They date from the mid-12th to the mid-14th centuries, with 53% (14) belonging to the 14th century (Period V). The majority (10) of the asymmetrical variants came from 14th century contexts (Period V). Otherwise, the date ranges are very similar. As with the other types, they were mostly found singly, with four small groups: two from Midden 1.2, Pit 2648; two from Building 18 (Phase 2); three from Midden 1.5b; two each from Middens 1.5a and 8a; and two from Building 53 (Phase 1 (Illus 121, 124, 139, 145).

Very similar soles, of late 14th- to early 15th-century date were found at Threave Castle, Galloway (Thomas 1981, 123–124). Other published parallels, chiefly of 13th- to 14th-century date, include Gallowgate Middle School, Aberdeen (12th–13th centuries); King's Lynn (c1350–1500); Barbican Ditch, Oxford (13th–15th centuries); Dover (early 14th century); Southampton (late 13th century); Leicester (early 14th–15th centuries); London (late 14th century); Coppergate, York (12th–14th centuries); Waterford (13th century) and Bristol Bridge (13th–14th centuries) (Thomas 2001a, 243; Clarke and Carter 1977, 360–1; Hassall 1976, 277–8, Fig 18.8; Mynard 1969, 101–4, Fig 20; Platt and Coleman-Smith 1975, 296–8, Fig 261, nos 250–254; Allin 1981a, 147–148; Grew and de Neergaard 1988, 67, Fig 101; Mould et al 2003; O'Rourke 1997, 720, Fig 18.5, 18.6; Thomas forthcoming a).

Soles, Type 5 (Illus 122)

Thirteen of the 15 Type 5 soles recovered also have pointed toes and are similar to those of Type 4 but are less slender, with broader, more curved foreparts.

Soles, Type 3 (Illus 119, 120, 124, 145 and 147).

Cat/Accession	Area	Rig	Feature	Phase
South Sector				
116/A03–0002a	4	V, VI	MC023	Icc,Id
156/A7787c	1/2	VI	B6 (Phase 1), South Room–Floor (1)	Ie
177/A7589c	2	VI	M14b(b)	Ie
502/A03–0003a	3	V	P2.1a	IIb–IIf
740/A9144	3	VI	M1.2, Pit 2648	<IIg(IIh)
774/A9365	3	VI	M1.2, Pit 2648	<IIg(IIh)
783/A9372a	3	VI	M1.2, Pit 2648	<IIg(IIh)
788/A9546a	3	VI	M1.2, Pit 2648	<IIg(IIh)
795/A9884a	3	VI	M1.2, Pit 2648	<IIg(IIh)
831/A8518a	4	V, VI	M11	IIh
857/A8527a	4	VI	M1.3	IIi
866/A8634a	3	VI	M1.3	IIi
908/A11235b	3	VI	M1.3	IIi
937/A11644	1	VII	MC112b	IIIb
1035/A8009a	3	V	MC117, Pit 4695	IIe–IIIc
1095/A03–0270a	9	VII	P8.1c	IIIc
1106/A03–0304a	9	VII	P8.1c	IIIc
1195/A9883	3	V	M6b	IIg–IIId
1215/A9373a	3	V	M6b	IIg–IIId
1300/A8810a	3	V	P2.2b	IVa
1314/A7989a	4	V	MC143	IVaa
1387/A8021a	3	V/VI	MC144, WW2221	<IIId–IVaa
1426/A6187a	4	V	MC156	IVaa
1753/A03–0350b	7	VII	MC126, Pit 7402	IVaa,IVb
1754/A03–0350c	7	VII	MC126, Pit 7402	IVaa,IVb
1991/A03–0362a	7	VII	MC126, Pit 7402	IVaa,IVb
2333/A03–0291a	7	VI	M1.4f	IVc
2338/A03–0308a	7	VI	M1.4f	IVc
2339/A03–0308b	7	VI	M1.4f	IVc
2340/A03–0308c	7	VI	M1.4f	IVc
2713/A03–0299	7	VII	B18 (Phase 2a), External (1), Pit 7314	IVb
2722/A03–0307a	7	VII	B18 (Phase 2a), External (1), Pit 7314	IVb
2725/A03–0413a	7	VII	B18 (Phases 2a & 2b), T7385	IVb
2750/A03–0293	7	VII	B18 (Phase 2a), North Room & Hall Construction (2)	IVb
2761/A03–0104a	9	VII	B18 (Phase 2b), North Room, Hall & Hall South–Occupation (10)	IVb
2985/A10521	3	V	MC155, Pit 2691	IVb,IVc
3033/A3459	3	VI	M1.4d	IVb,IVc
3048/A8335	3	VI	M1.4d	IVb,IVc
3125/A03–0253a	7	VI	M1.4h	IVc
3239/A9888a	3	V, VI	M1.4c	IIIa–IVcc
3240/A9888b	3	V, VI	M1.4c	IIIa–IVcc
3246/A6195	4	V, VI	M1.4b	IVb–IVcc
3321/A03–0066a	9	VII	P8.3	IVc,IVcc
3382/A03–0249a	7	VII	M9a	IVc,IVcc
3405/A03–0052a	9	VII	M9a	IVc,IVcc
3501/A03–0186a	10	VIII	M9b(b)	IVc,IVcc
3593/A6220a	3	VI	M1.4e	IVcc(Va)
3707/A03–0134a	7	VI	B34, Occupation	Va
3719/A03–0160c	7	VI	B34, Courtyard	Va
3873/A03–0116b	7	VI, VII	M1.5b	Vaa

(continued)

Soles, Type 3 (Illus 119, 120, 124, 145 and 147) (continued).

Cat/Accession	Area	Rig	Feature	Phase
4123/A03–0214a	7	VII	P8.4	Va
4228/A6419	3	V	B1(a), T2789	IVcc,Va
4229/A6373	3	V	B1(a), South Room, Pit 2460	IVcc,Va
4248/A4943c	2	V	B1(b), Demolition	Va
4284/A4901b	1	V, VI	M5a	IVb–Vc
4528/A6198a	3	V, VI	M1.5a	Va,Vaa(VI)
4533/A6400	3	V, VI	M1.5a	Va,Vaa(VI)
4886/A03–0128a	7	VII	M8a	Va,Vaa
4887/A03–0128b	7	VII	M8a	Va,Vaa
5020/A03–0212a	7	VII	M8a	Va,Vaa
5772/A12574b	3/4	V, VI	Unstratified	u/s
5807/A0811a	3/4	V, VI	Unstratified	u/s
5871/A03–0008	7–10	VI–VIII	Unstratified	u/s

Another two (Cat Nos 5335/A03–0018a, 5908/A0113) have lost their toes but their overall shape is similar. They are almost all of mid-13th- to mid-14th-century date, with two examples from Midden 1.4i and Path 8.4, one from Midden 1.4e and one each from Middens 5a, 3a and 7 (Illus 122).

Published parallels, ranging in date from the 13th to the 15th centuries, include London (early 13th century, mid–late 14th century); Leicester (14th–15th centuries); Exeter (mid 14th–15th centuries); Sandwell Priory (15th century); Bayham Abbey (late 15th century–1525); Plymouth (13th–15th centuries); Scale Lane/Lowgate, Hull (late 14th century); Barbican Ditch (13th–15th centuries), Castle Moat (13th/14th–17th/18th centuries), Oxford; Coppergate, York (13th–14th centuries); Waterford (13th century); Amsterdam (1275–1350); Bergen (Type III?: 14th–15th centuries) and Schleswig (Form 13: 12th century) (Grew and de Neergaard 1988, 57–66, Fig 90, 98, 100; Allin 1981a, 148–9, Fig 56, 9, Fig 57, 11, 12, Fig 60, 33; Friendship-Taylor 1984, 324–7, Fig 184, nos 12 and 19, Fig 185, 27; Thomas 1991, 104, nos 14–15; Jones and Thornton 1983, Fig 53, nos 4 and 5; Gaskell-Brown 1986, Fig 17, nos 8 and 9; Armstrong 1980, 68, nos 68–69; Hassall 1976, 276–7, Fig 18, 2, 288–289, Fig 22, 24; Mould et al 2003; O'Rourke 1997, 720, Fig 18.5; Baart et al 1977, 74, 78; Larsen 1992, 28; Schnack 1992b, 38–46, Abb. II, Fig 4, nos 1–3).

Soles, Type 6 (Illus 122)

The five Type 6 soles are broad and straight, with a central point. Cat Nos 1/A12303a, 28/A10800b and 43/A8525 are almost symmetrical, with only a very slight narrowing at the waist. Despite their points, these soles bear more resemblance to those of Type 1 than to other pointed soles. Cat Nos 6/A12300b and 314/A10365 are asymmetrical, and have more marked waists, although these are still fairly wide. The point of Cat No 314/A10365 has been turned outwards slightly. It may have

been stuffed, possibly with moss, although strands of hemp were found in a pointed toe from Plymouth (Gaskell-Brown 1986, Fig 17, 13). Cat No 6/A12300b ends in a pointed extension, which may also have been stuffed. All examples of this category were recovered from 12th century deposits. Cat No 314/A10365a was discovered within a context group that had been laid down shortly after 1150, the other four examples all dated from the first half of the 12th century. They include some of the earliest leatherwork from the High Street (Illus 122).

There are few published parallels for either variant. Those for Type 6a include York (Coppergate and Swinegate, 10th–14th centuries; Low Petergate, 12th–14th centuries; and Schleswig Forms 3a, 4: 11th–12th centuries; Form 7: 12th–13th centuries (Mould et al 2003; Carlisle 1998, unpublished archive report; Goodfellow and Thornton 1972, 100, Fig 23, no 6; Schnack 1992b, 38–46, Abb. II, Fig 2, nos 10–15, Fig 3, nos 5 and 6).

A sole very similar to Cat No 314/A10365a was found at Whithorn, dating to the second half of the 12th century (Nicholson 1997, 504, Fig 10.141.LR 19.6). Other close parallels from Brooks Wharf, Upper Thames Street, London, were accompanied by uppers with vamps cut with V-notches exactly matching the points on the soles (12th–14th centuries) (Thomas forthcoming c). Parallels for Cat No 6/A12300b include Durham (11th century) and London (early–mid-12th century) (Carver 1979, 31–3, Fig 19.1655/750216(a); Grew and de Neergaard 1988, 52, Fig 83; Pritchard 1991, 230, 234, Fig 3.118). According to Pritchard, these shoes with exaggerated points resemble those described by the chronicler Orderic Vitalis; these, he claimed, were imitations by the lower classes of 'shoes with pointed toes curled like scorpions' tails and rams' horns' which were popular at the court of William Rufus in the last decade of the 11th century (Pritchard 1991, 230).

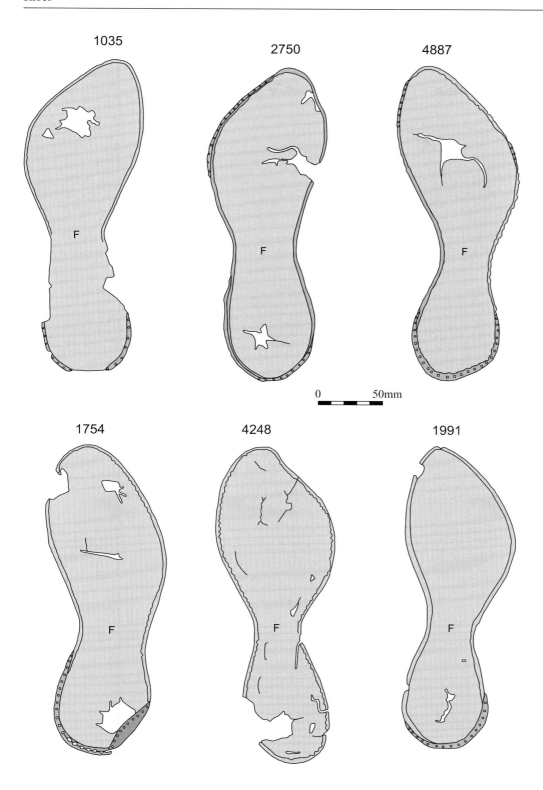

Illus 119 *Soles, Type 3.*

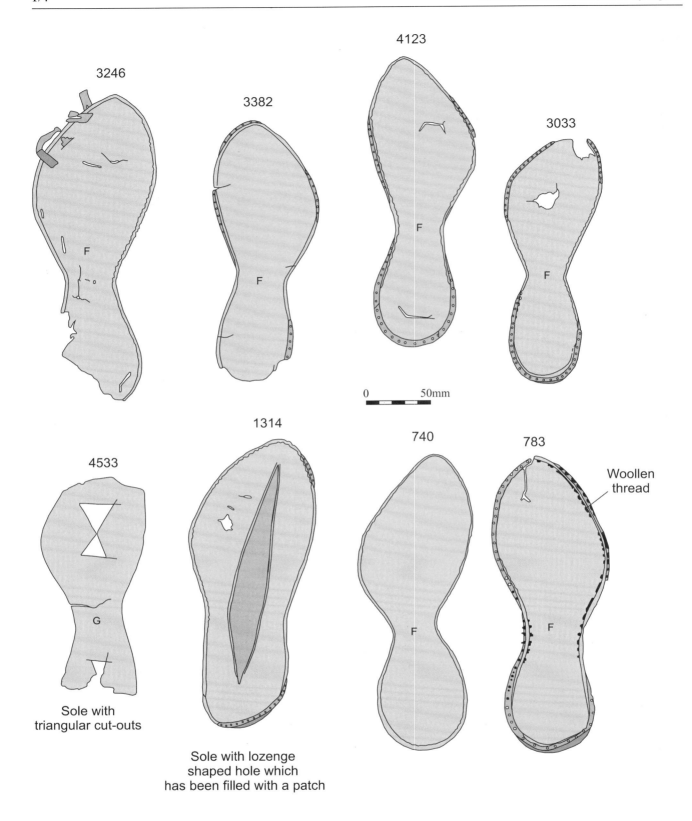

Illus 120 *Soles, Type 3.*

Soles, Type 4 (Illus 117, 121, 124 and 145).

S=symmetrical; As=asymmetrical

Cat/Accession	S/As	Area	Rig	Feature	Phase
South Sector					
325/A03–0009b	S	3	V	MC049, Pit 5259	IIa
811/A11219b	As	3	VI	M1.2, Pit 2648	<IIg(IIh)
821/A11221a	S	3	VI	M1.2, Pit 2648	<IIg(IIh)
1042/A8546	As	3	V	MC117, Pit 4695	IIe–IIIc
1206/A8680a	S	3	V	M6b	IIg–IIId
1553/A03–0422a	S	7	VII	MC130	<IIIc–IVaa
1804/A03–0367a	As	7	VII	MC126, Pit 7402	IVaa,IVb
2365/A03–0332b	As	7	VI	M1.4f	IVc
2728/A03–0295a	As	7	VII	B18 (Phases 2a & 2b), WW7308	IVb
2779/A03–0232	As	9	VII	B18 (Phase 2b), North Room, Hall & Hall South–Occupation (10)	IVb
3704/A9273b	S?	3	VI	B34, Floor	Va
3858/A03–0047	As	7	VI, VII	M1.5b	Vaa
3863/A03–0067a	As	7	VI, VII	M1.5b	Vaa
3896/A03–0132a	As	7	VI, VII	M1.5b	Vaa
4124/A03–0214b	As	7	VII	P8.4	Va
4530/A6245a	As	3	V, VI	M1.5a	Va,Vaa(VI)
4811/A6189	S?	3	V, VI	M1.5a	Va,Vaa
4827/A03–0106	As	7	VII	M8a	Va,Vaa
5113/A03–0151a	S	7	VII	M8a, Pit 7183	Va,Vaa
5238/A03–0097	As	7	VII	B53 (Phase 1), Central Area–Occupation (2a)	Vb
5240/A03–0090	As	7	VII	B53 (Phase 1), Central Area–Occupation (3c)	Vb
5250/A03–0029a	As	7	VII	P8.5	Vb,Vbb
5301/A4917a	n–c	4	V, VI	M3a	Vb–Vc
5608/A03–0065	As	10	VIII	MC174, Pit 7013	(Va–)Vd(Vdd)
5739/A12307c	S	1	VI, VII	Unstratified	u/s
5810/A12487a	As	2	V, VI	Unstratified	u/s

Soles, Type 7 (Illus 123)

The eight Type 7 soles are of a natural shape, similar to those of Types 3 and 5, but with an edge–flesh stitching channel across the tread, or middle of the forepart, for the attachment of a separate toe-piece. These seams are most probably not part of the original construction but repair measures taken when the toes had worn. This argument is further supported by the fact that sole Cat No 5599/A4352a also has an edge–flesh stitching channel across the middle of the seat. No separate toe-pieces have survived. It is also possible that these soles are examples of the manufacture of new shoes from old. 75% (6) of these soles are of mid-13th to mid-14th-century date (Periods IV and V); the others came from a pit that dated from the third quarter of the 12th century (Illus 123).

The only published parallels are from Low Petergate, Coppergate and Swinegate, York (12th–14th centuries), King Edward Street, Perth and Sewer Lane, Hull (late 13th–early 14th centuries). The last example consists of a three-part sole, mid and rear forepart and toe of forepart (Goodfellow and Thornton 1972, 102, Fig 25 no 28; Mould et al 2003; Carlisle 1998, unpublished archive report; Thomas and Walsh 1995, 971; Armstrong 1977, 51–60).

Soles, Types 8 and 9 (Illus 123 and 145)

Types 8 and 9 consist of 17 seats and 23 foreparts, respectively, each sewn across the waist with an edge–flesh stitching channel, thus forming composite soles. Five matching pairs survive: Cat Nos 447/A6722–Type 4?; 970/A11261a, 971/A11261b–Type 2; 916/A12490a, 917/A12490b–Type 2; 3859/A03–0048a, 3860/A03–0048b–Type 3?; and 2300/A03–0276a, 2301/A03–0276b–Type not definable (Illus 123, 145).

The majority of both seats and foreparts date from the later 13th to mid-14th centuries. Indeed 52% (21) of these associated categories were recovered from deposits that had been laid down during the first half of the 14th century (Period V), and another 22% (9) came from context groups that dated from the second half of the 13th century (Period IV). While they were mainly of later date, at least five (13%) were also discovered in 12th century deposits. These included the earliest, 447/A6722, which was recovered from an occupation layer within a byre attached to the south gable of a small backland house (Building 4) which, on dendrochronological evidence, had been erected shortly after 1150. A study of the distribution shows that 12 were found singly, the rest in nine groups: Building 4, Midden 1.3, Midden 1.4f, Building 18 (Phase 2),

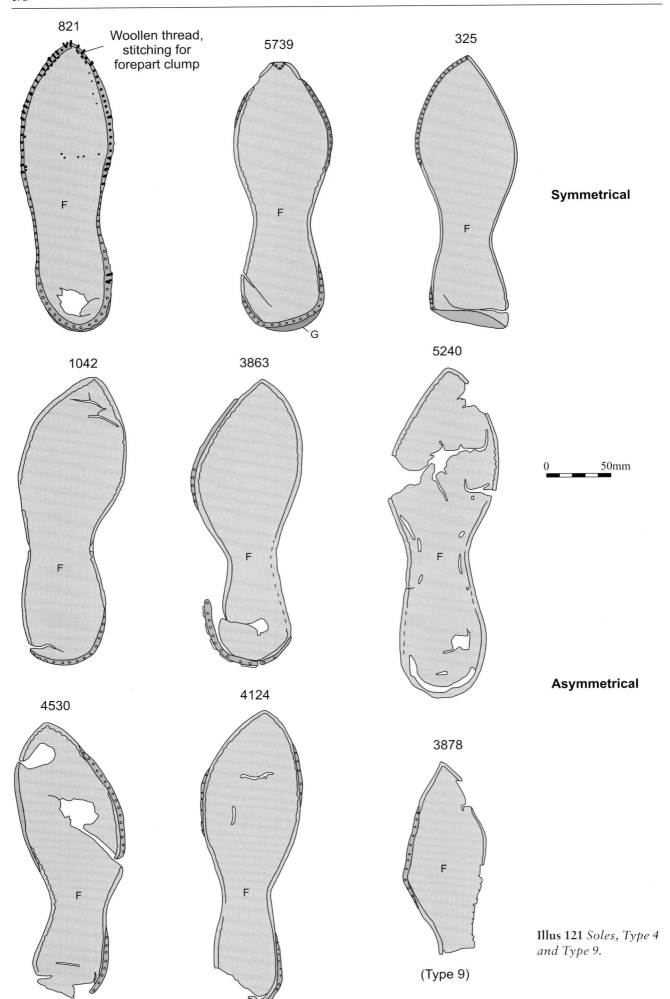

Illus 121 *Soles, Type 4 and Type 9.*

Soles, Type 5 (Illus 122).

Cat/Accession	Area	Rig	Feature	Phase
South Sector				
403/A12295	3	VI	MC056, Pit 5155	Ia–IIc
654/A9558	4	V	M10, Pit 2330	IId–IIg
1361/A8007a	4	V	MC143	IVaa
1504/A03–0405	7	VII	MC130	<IIIc–IVaa
3117/A8681a	3	VI	M1.4d, Pit 2566	IVb,IVc
3517/A03–0224a	7	VI	M1.4i	IVcc
3562/A03–0244a	7	VI	M1.4i	IVcc
3594/A6220b	3	VI	M1.4e	IVcc(Va)
3857/A03–0044	7	VI, VII	M1.5b	Vaa
3985/A03–0170b	7	VI, VII	M1.5b	Vaa
4283/A4901a	1	V, VI	M5a	IVb–Vc
5329/A6399a	3	V, VI	M3a	Vb–Vc
5335/A03–0018a	7	VII	M7	Vc
5611/A4290	1	V	M5d	Vc–Vdd
North Sector				
5908/A0113	5, A		CG017	4–11

Soles, Type 6 (Illus 122).

Cat/Accession	Sole type	Area	Rig	Feature	Phase
South Sector					
1/A12303a	Type 6a	1	VI	MC002	Ia
6/A12300b	Type 6b	1	V, VI	MC002	Ia
28/A10800b	Type 6a	1	V	MC008, T3774	Ib
43/A8525	Type 6a	1/2	V, VI	M2.1b	Ic
314/A10365a	Type 6b	3	V	MC049	IIa

Middens 8a, 7 and 3c each with two; and Middens 1.5a and Midden 1.5b each with six.

This use of separate seats and foreparts is not very common at Perth; it was economical, utilising small pieces of leather, possibly reusing the better part of an old sole; on the other hand, it was not very strong, as the seam joining seat and forepart would have been subjected to great strain. It could represent either original construction or translation or cobbling (the making of new shoes from worn ones). It is unlikely to be part of a repair; a clump sole, attached by tunnel stitching, would have been more usual.

Similar separate seats and foreparts, predominantly of 13th–14th century date, have also been found at King's Lynn (1250–1350); Dover (late 14th century); London (early–late 14th century); Coventry; Low Petergate and Parliament Street, (12th–14th centuries) Coppergate and Swinegate, (13th–14th centuries) York; Town Wall, Roushill, Shrewsbury; Lich Street, Worcester; Newcastle (mid 13th–mid 14th century); Austin Friars (late 14th century) and Market Place, Leicester; Kirk Close, Perth (13th–14th centuries); Bristol Bridge (13th–14th centuries) and Redcliffe Street, Bristol; Chapel Lane Staith, Hull (late 13th–early 14th century); Sewer Lane, Hull (late 13th–early 14th centuries); Hartlepool and Schleswig (11th–14th centuries, especially 13th

century) (Clarke and Carter 1977, 360, Fig 168, nos 68–70; Mynard 1969, 103–4, Fig 20, L6, L7; Grew and de Neergaard 1988, 60, Fig 94, 68, Fig 102, 69, Fig 103, 70, Fig 104; Tatton-Brown 1975, 156–8, Fig 27, nos 47, 74; Thomas 1980, 11, 44–78/51/17, 78/51/20, 64–65–49/194/1, 49/194/2, 72–73–49/226/4, 49/226/10; Goodfellow and Thornton 1972, 104, Fig 26, no 28; Tweddle 1986, 242–53, Fig 110, 786; Mould et al 2003; Carlisle 1998, unpublished archive report; Thornton 1961, 200, 206, Fig 53.2; Thornton 1969a, 58–9, no 5; Dixon 1988, 94, Fig 35, no 206; Allin 1991a, 148, Fig 55, 6, 1991b, 12, 27, Fig 3, 24; Thomas 1987, 176–7; Thomas forthcoming a and b; Jackson 1979, Fig 22, 6 and 7; Armstrong 1977, 51–60; Jackson 1987, 47–8, Fig 23, 1 and 3; Schnack 1992b, 51–2, Abb. 19, Fig 6).

Soles, children's (Illus 124)

Twenty-six soles that are obviously children's have been listed separately to ascertain whether there were any variations in the popularity and dating of children's soles.

Eight (31%) soles were of Type 1; seven of these dated to the 12th century and one to the second half of the 13th century. Half of the ten (38%) Type 2 soles belonged to the second half of the 13th century, while two were of 12th-century date. One (Cat No 4493/

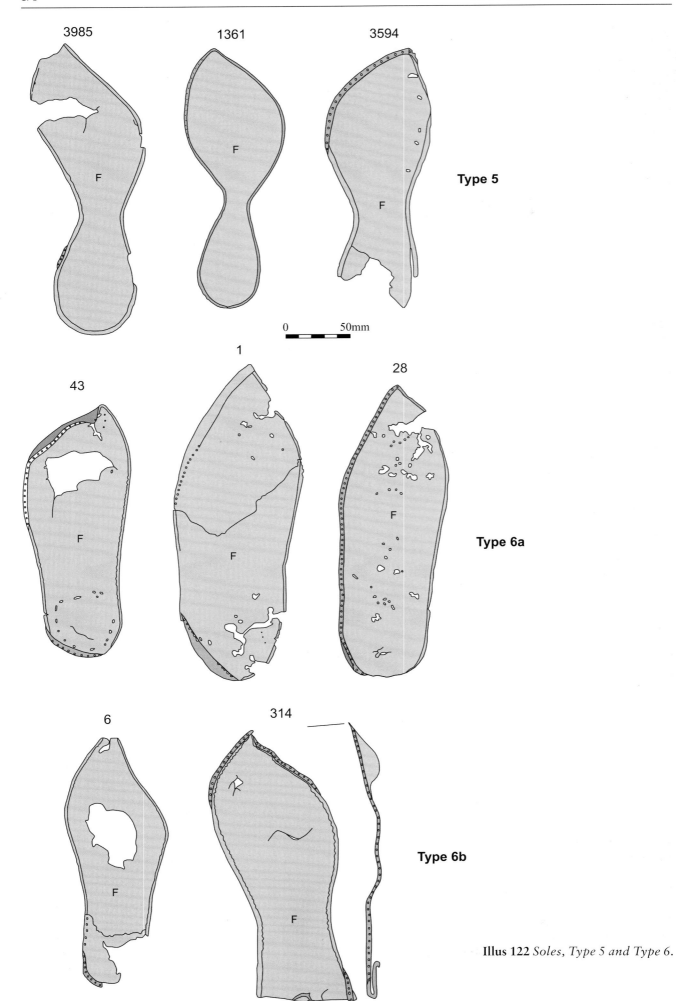

Illus 122 *Soles, Type 5 and Type 6.*

Soles, Type 7 (Illus 123).

Cat/Accession	Area	Rig	Feature	Phase
South Sector				
375/A12282a	1	VI	MC065, Pit 3908	IIa–IIc
376/A12282b	1	VI	MC065, Pit 3908	IIa–IIc
2181/A03–0385a	7	VII	MC126, Pit 7402	IVaa,IVb
3068/A8668c	3	VI	M1.4d	IVb,IVc
3624/A6077c	3	VI	M1.4e	IVcc(Va)
5021/A03–0212b	7	VII	M8a	Va,Vaa
5221/A03–0138a	7	VII	M8a, T7193	Va,Vaa
5599/A4352a	4	V	M3c	Vd

Soles, Type 8 (Illus 123 and 145).

Cat/Accession	Area	Rig	Feature	Phase
South Sector				
447/A6722	2	VI	B4 'Byre' Occupation	IIc
450/A10773a	3	VI	MC066	IIc
916/A12490a	4	VI	M1.3	IIi
970/A11261a	4	V	MC116	IIe–IIIc
1506/A03–0410a	7	VII	MC130	<IIIc–IVaa
2300/A03–0276a	7	VI	M1.4f	IVc
3539/A03–0234a	7	VI	M1.4i	IVcc
3720/A03–0160d	7	VI	B34, Courtyard	Va
3859/A03–0048a	7	VI, VII	M1.5b	Vaa
3882/A03–0121a	7	VI, VII	M1.5b	Vaa
3925/A03–0136a	7	VI, VII	M1.5b	Vaa
4308/A1251a	3	V, VI	M1.5a	Va,Vaa(VI)
4501/A6188a	3	V, VI	M1.5a	Va,Vaa(VI)
4550/A1253a	3	V, VI	M1.5a	Va,Vaa
4812/A6221a	3	V, VI	M1.5a	Va,Vaa
5251/A03–0029b	7	VII	P8.5	Vb,Vbb
5598/A6475	4	V	M3c	Vd

A4289a), and quite possibly two (Cat No 5942/A0807a) were of 14th-century date. Types 3 and 4 were each represented by one example, dating to the early and mid 14th century, respectively. A single child's Type 5 sole was recovered from Trench A, from a layer dating to the 12th–13th centuries. A Type 7 sole was of late 13th-century date (Illus 124).

Thus, Type 2 emerges as the most popular, with Type 1 second. The more elegant and shapely types, such as 3, 4 and 5 were hardly used. The dating trends reflect those of the adult types. This evidence for children's soles is in agreement with that from London, especially from Baynard's Castle, where children's soles were modestly shaped, keeping to the shape of the foot; the more elaborate and exaggerated styles were not used for children (de Neergaard 1985, 14–20).

Soles, pointed fragments (Illus 159)

Three pointed triangular objects, each with two edge–flesh stitching channels, may be parts of shoes. The third edge on each is very thin, as if worn; tunnel stitches, similar to those found on clump soles, run parallel to this third edge on two of them. They are unlikely to be the fronts of foreparts, as they are exceedingly narrow and pointed. It has been suggested that they are the pointed extensions of seats found on early (10th–11th century) soles. The tunnel stitch holes suggest that they might have been used as clump soles, for repair. They were originally assigned to Miscellanea, and are illustrated with them (Illus 159). All three came from Phase Vaa and are thus of early 14th-century date, which makes the seat extension theory unlikely.

Soles, seat cut across waist

The 51 seats that had been cut across the waist have been listed separately, as the majority (82%) of them come from Period V (14th century) deposits. These 14th-century seats include several large groups, eg three from M1.5b, eight from P8.4, three from M1.5a, ten from M8a, seven from M3a, three from M7 and two from M3b and M3c. Indeed it is noteworthy that nearly half (48%) of this category came from one property, Rig VII.

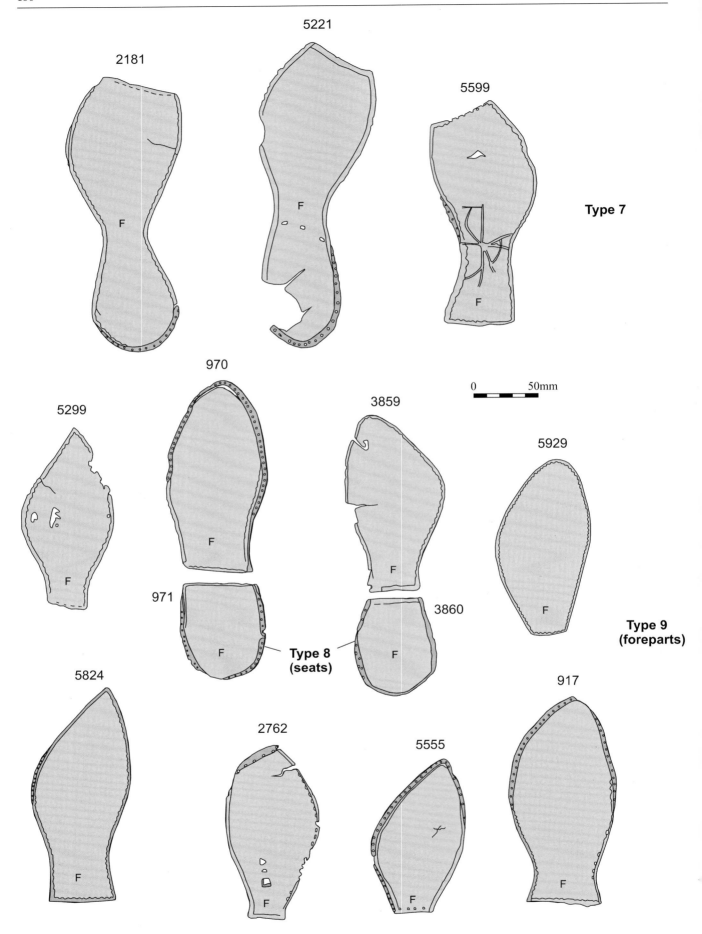

Illus 123 *Soles, Type 7, Type 8 seats and Type 9 foreparts.*

Soles, Type 9 (Illus 123 and 145).

Cat/Accession	Area	Rig	Feature	Phase
South Sector				
447/A6722	2	VI	B4, 'Byre'–Occupation	IIc
917/A12490b	4	VI	M1.3	IIi
971/A11261b	4	V	MC116	IIe–IIIc
1275/A3448a	2	V	P2.2a	IVa
1434/A6474a	4	V	MC156	IVaa
1691/A7792	3	V	B3(South)–Occupation (1b)	IVa,IVaa
2301/A03–0276b	7	VI	M1.4f	IVc
2704/A03–0296a	7	VII	B18 (Phase 1/2), MF 7307	IVaa,IVb
2762/A03–0104b	9	VII	B18 (Phase 2b), North Room, Hall & Hall South–Occupation (10)	IVb
3860/A03–0048b	7	VI, VII	M1.5b	Vaa
3878/A03–0120c	7	VI, VII	M1.5b	Vaa
3947/A03–0140a	7	VI, VII	M1.5b	Vaa
4479/A2284a	3	V, VI	M1.5a	Va,Vaa(VI)
4816/A6237b	3	V, VI	M1.5a	Va,Vaa
4828/A03–0175a	7	VII	M8a	Va,Vaa
5016/A03–0174ddd	7	VII	M8a	Va,Vaa
5299/A6247	2	V, VI	M4a	Va–Vc
5336/A03–0018b	7	VII	M7	Vc
5337/A03–0018c	7	VII	M7	Vc
5555/A6242a	4	V	M3c	Vd
5824/A03–0127a	7	VI, VII	Unstratified	u/s
North Sector				
5929/A0110a	5, A		Lade (4)	6–12(b–e)
South/North Sectors				
5982/L2766a			Unstratified	u/s

These seats show varying degrees of wear, suggesting that they have been cut off worn soles, either to be reused, as separate seats or as clump soles, or else to allow reuse of a better preserved forepart.

Soles, indeterminate forms

It was not possible to ascribe 473 sole fragments to particular types, as they were too worn or incomplete. Where possible, these have been listed as seats, waists or foreparts. Seven (1%) soles of indeterminate form were recovered from the excavations within the North Sector of the site, and 464 from its South Sector. The majority (65%) of these South Sector fragments come from Periods IV and V (1250–1350>): Period I: 37 (8%); Period II: 69 (15%); Period III: 22 (5%); Period IV: 160 (34%); Period V: 144 (31%); unstratified: 32 (7%).

The fragments were distributed all over the site, with particular concentrations in B10 (5), M14b(b) (11), MC044b (5), MC061 (5), B4 (9), B5 (6), M10 (13), M1.2 (9), M1.3 (7), MC128 (6), P2.2b (5), MC126 (8), M1.4f (20), B18 (21), M9b(a) (6), M1.4d (19), M1.4c (10), M1.4b (7), P8.3 (6), M9a (17), M1.4e (10), P8.4 (10), B1 (9), M5a (7), M1.5a (19), M1.5b (13), M8a (35), M4a (5), M3a (11), P1a (11) and M3c (8). (B=Building; M=Midden, P=Path, MC=Miscellaneous Context; see also Appendix 7).

Soles, children's (Illus 124).

Cat/Accession	Sole type	Area	Rig	Feature	Phase
South Sector					
62/A8704a	Sole (Type 1)	1/2	V, VI	M2.1b & B10, South Room–Floor/Occupation (1)	Ic,Icc
104/A10798a	Sole (Type 1)	4	VI	MC018, Pit 2398	Ib–Id
125/A12297a	Sole (Type 1)	3	V	MC025, Pit 5337	(Ia–)Id
182/A7597a	Sole	2	VI	M14b(b)	Ie
187/A7797a	Sole	2	VI	M14b(b)	Ie
306/A12635b	Sole (Type 2)	4	V	B16b, Pit 4726	Id–IIa
353/A6773b	Sole (Type 1)	2	VI	MC061	IIb
389/A12296a	Sole (Type 1)	1	VI	MC065	IIa–IIc
505/A3447b	Sole (Type 1)	2	VI	M1.1d & M1.1e	IId–IIf
798/A10366	Sole (Type 1)	3	VI	M1.2, Pit 2648	<IIg(IIh)
897/A11260a	Sole (Type 2)	3	VI	M1.3	IIi
1678/A4895a	Sole	2	V	B3(South), Construction–Levelling	IVa,IVaa
1831/A03–0378a	Sole	7	VII	MC126, Pit 7402	IVaa,IVb
2652/A03–0316b	Sole (Type 1)	7	VII	B18 (Phase 1/2), Pit 7324	IVaa,IVb
2714/A03–0311a	Sole (Type 2)	7	VII	B18 (Phase 2a), External (1), Pit 7314	IVb
2747/A03–0297a	Sole (Type 2)	7	VII	B18 (Phase 2a), North Room & Hall–Construction(1)	IVb
2760/A03–0092	Sole (Type 2)	9	VII	B18 (Phase 2b), North Room, Hall & Hall South–Occupation (10)	IVb
2872/A4894	Sole (Type 2)	3	V	MC155	IVb,IVc
3335/A03–0261a	Sole (Type 2)	7	VII	P8.3 & M9a, PW7267	IVc,IVcc
3624/A6077c	Sole (Type 7)	3	VI	M1.4e	IVcc(Va)
3873/A03–0116b	Sole (Type 3)	7	VI, VII	M1.5b	Vaa
4493/A4289a	Sole (Type 2)	3	V, VI	M1.5a	Va,Vaa(VI)
5608/A03–0065	Sole (Type 4)	10	VIII	MC174, Pit 7013	(Va–)Vd (Vdd)
5792/A0817a	Sole (Type 2)	3/4	V, VI	Unstratified	Unstratified
North Sector					
5908/A0113	Sole (Type 5)	5, A		CG017	4–11
5942/A0807a	Sole (Type 2)	5, A		Lade (4)	6–12(b–e)

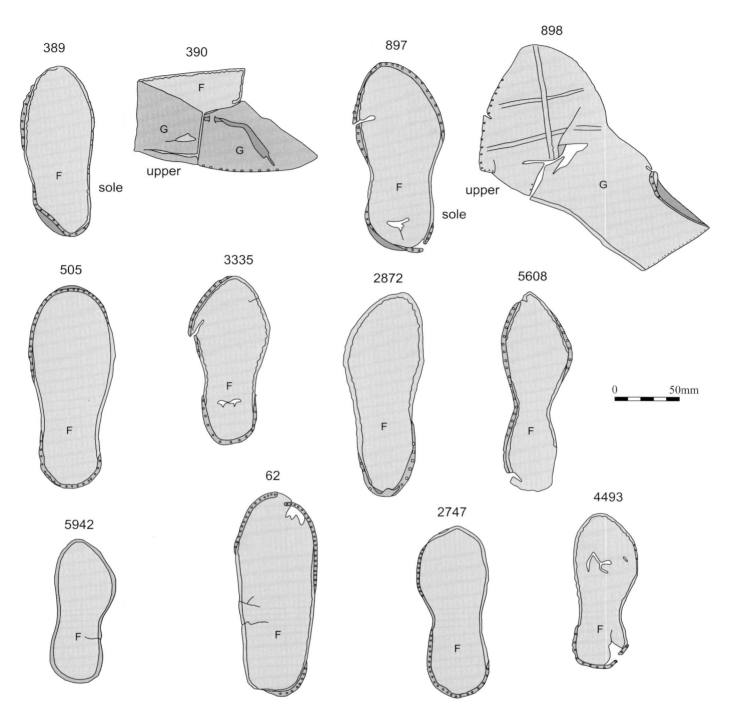

Illus 124 *Children's soles and matching uppers.*

Soles, pointed fragments (Illus 159).

Cat/Accession	Area	Rig	Feature	Phase
South Sector				
3927/A03–0136c	7	VI, VII	M1.5b	Vaa
3928/A03–0136d	7	VI, VII	M1.5b	Vaa
3929/A03–0136e	7	VI, VII	M1.5b	Vaa

Soles, seat cut across waist.

Cat/Accession	Area	Rig	Feature	Phase
South Sector				
2/A12303b	1	V, VI	MC002	Ia
178/A7589d	2	VI	M14b(b)	Ie
366/A7694b	1	V	M14a	Id–IIc
484/A10498	3	VI	M1.1a	IId,IIe
1075/A12535a	4	V/VI	MC128	IIIb,IIIc
2764/A03–0105	9	VII	B18 (Phase 2b), North Room, Hall & Hall South–Occupation (10)	IVb
3231/A6395a	3	V, VI	M1.4c	IIIa–IVcc
3340/A03–0205a	7	VII	M9a	IVc,IVcc
3376/A03–0240a	7	VII	M9a	IVc,IVcc
3604/A4818a	3	VI	M1.4e	IVcc(Va)
3673/A7807a	3	VI	P6	IVcc,Va
3883/A03–0121b	7	VI, VII	M1.5b	Vaa
3948/A03–0140b	7	VI, VII	M1.5b	Vaa
3986/A03–0170c	7	VI, VII	M1.5b	Vaa
4029/A03–0156b	7	VII	P8.4	Va
4035/A03–0158b	7	VII	P8.4	Va
4041/A03–0159a	7	VII	P8.4	Va
4079/A03–0161	7	VII	P8.4	Va
4087/A03–0210a	7	VII	P8.4	Va
4106/A03–0211a	7	VII	P8.4	Va
4125/A03–0214c	7	VII	P8.4	Va
4152/A03–0198a	7	VII	P8.4, Pit 7216	Va
4503/A6188c	3	V, VI	M1.5a	Va,Vaa(VI)
4531/A6245b	3	V, VI	M1.5a	Va,Vaa(VI)
4551/A1253b	3	V, VI	M1.5a	Va,Vaa
4903/A03–0162b	7	VII	M8a	Va,Vaa
4964/A03–0174d	7	VII	M8a	Va,Vaa
4965/A03–0174e	7	VII	M8a	Va,Vaa
5102/A03–0147a	7	VII	M8a, Pit 7183	Va,Vaa
5103/A03–0147b	7	VII	M8a, Pit 7183	Va,Vaa
5114/A03–0151b	7	VII	M8a, Pit 7183	Va,Vaa
5134/A03–0137a	7	VII	M8a, Pit 7183	Va,Vaa
5185/A03–0144a	7	VII	M8a, Pit 7183	Va,Vaa
5199/A03–0129b	7	VII	M8a, T7193	Va,Vaa
5222/A03–0138b	7	VII	M8a, T7193	Va,Vaa
5261/A03–0089b	10	VIII	M8b	Va,Vaa(–Vc)
5300/A6413	2	V, VI	M4a	Va–Vc
5303/A4917c	4	V, VI	M3a	Vb–Vc
5304/A4917d	4	V, VI	M3a	Vb–Vc
5305/A4917e	4	V, VI	M3a	Vb–Vc
5313/A4390a	7	V, VI	M3a	Vb–Vc
5314/A4390b	7	V, VI	M3a	Vb–Vc
5327/A6210	4	V, VI	M3a	Vb–Vc
5331/A4907a	4	V, VI	M3a	Vb–Vc
5338/A03–0018d	7	VII	M7	Vc
5339/A03–0022	7	VII	M7	Vc
5340/A03–0024	7	VII	M7	Vc
5349/A6479a	4	VI	M3b	Vd
5357/A5894a	4	VI	M3b	Vd
5557/A6481	4	V	M3c	Vd
5566/A4602a	4	V	M3c	Vd

Soles, indeterminate forms.

Cat/Accession	Leather type	Area	Rig	Feature	Phase
South Sector					
29/A10800c	Sole	2	V	MC008, T3774	Ib
35/A8652	Sole	2	VI	MC011, Pit 3755	Ib,Ic
83/A7788	Sole (forepart)	1/2	V	B10, South Room–Occupation (2a)	Icc
84/A8662a	Sole	1/2	V	B10, South Room–Floor (2b)	Icc
88/A8682	Sole	1/2	V	B10, South Room–Occupation (2b)	Icc
89/A8688a	Sole	1/2	V	B10, South Room–Occupation (2b)	Icc
90/A8688b	Sole	1/2	V	B10, South Room–Occupation (2b)	Icc
95/A12289a	Sole	4	V/VI	MC017	Ia–Icc>
107/A6403a	Sole	1	V	MC029, Pit 3125	Id
114/A10799a	Sole	4	V, VI	MC023	Icc,Id
130/A12308c	Sole (seat)	3	V	MC025, Pit 5337	(Ia–)Id
135/A12286b	Sole	3	V	MC025, Pit 5337	(Ia–)Id
151/A12311	Sole (forepart)	3	VI	MC037a, Pit 5157	Ia–Ie
157/A7787d	Sole	1/2	VI	B6 (Phase 1), South Room–Floor (1)	Ie
158/A7787e	Sole	1/2	VI	B6 (Phase 1), South Room–Floor (1)	Ie
159/A7787f	Sole	1/2	VI	B6 (Phase 1), South Room–Floor (1)	Ie
160/A7787g	Sole	1/2	VI	B6 (Phase 1), South Room–Floor (1)	Ie
182/A7597a	Sole	2	VI	M14b(b)	Ie
187/A7797a	Sole	2	VI	M14b(b)	Ie
188/A7797b	Sole	2	VI	M14b(b)	Ie
198/A7257c	Sole	2	VI	M14b(b), Pit 3625	Ie
199/A7257d	Sole	2	VI	M14b(b), Pit 3625	Ie
200/A7257e	Sole	2	VI	M14b(b), Pit 3625	Ie
201/A7257f	Sole	2	VI	M14b(b), Pit 3625	Ie
209/A7567a	Sole	2	VI	M14b(b), Pit 3625	Ie
211/A7574a	Sole (forepart)	2	VI	M14b(b), Pit 3625	Ie
213/A7574c	Sole	2	VI	M14b(b), Pit 3625	Ie
214/A7574d	Sole	2	VI	M14b(b), Pit 3625	Ie
219/A7800a	Sole (seat)	2	VI	M14b(b), Pit 3625	Ie
227/A7588a	Sole (forepart)	2	V	M14b(c)	Ie,If
228/A7588b	Sole	2	V	M14b(c)	Ie,If
243/A7310a	Sole (seat)	2	V	M14b(a)	Id
245/A7581a	Sole	2	V	M14b(a)	Id
263/A7044Bc	Sole	2	VI	MC044b	If
264/A7044Bd	Sole	2	VI	MC044b	If
274/A7074a	Sole	2	VI	MC044b	If
275/A7074b	Sole	2	VI	MC044b	If
276/A7074c	Sole	2	VI	MC044b	If
291/A7570a	Sole	2	V	MC046, Pit 3636	If,IIa
292/A7570b	Sole	2	V	MC046, Pit 3636	If,IIa
293/A7570c	Sole	2	V	MC046, Pit 3636	If,IIa
295/A12632a	Sole (oval forepart)	4	V	B16b, Pit 4726	Id–IIa
321/A10505a	Sole	3	V	MC049, Pit 5259	IIa
326/A03–0009c	Sole	3	V	MC049, Pit 5259	IIa
337/A6770a	Sole (seat)	2	VI	MC061	IIb
338/A6770b	Sole (pointed forepart)	2	VI	MC061	IIb
354/A6773c	Sole (forepart)	2	VI	MC061	IIb
355/A6773d	Sole (forepart)	2	VI	MC061	IIb
359/A6946	Sole (seat)	2	VI	MC061	IIb
377/A12282c	Sole (seat)	1	VI	MC065, Pit 3908	IIa–IIc
378/A12282d	Sole	1	VI	MC065, Pit 3908	IIa–IIc
391/A03–0354a	Sole (seat)	1	VI	MC065	IIa–IIc
392/A03–0354b	Sole (seat)	1	VI	MC065	IIa–IIc
401/A12293c	Sole (seat)	3	VI	MC056, Pit 5155	Ib–IIc
426/A6371	Sole (seat)	2	VI	B4, 'Byre'–Occupation	IIc

(continued)

Cat/Accession	Leather type	Area	Rig	Feature	Phase
431/A6483a	Sole (seat)	2	VI	B4, 'Byre'–Occupation	IIc
432/A6483b	Sole	2	VI	B4, 'Byre'–Occupation	IIc
433/A6483c	Sole	2	VI	B4, 'Byre'–Occupation	IIc
434/A6483d	Sole	2	VI	B4, 'Byre'–Occupation	IIc
435/A6483e	Sole	2	VI	B4, 'Byre'–Occupation	IIc
436/A6483f	Sole	2	VI	B4, 'Byre'–Occupation	IIc
437/A6483g	Sole	2	VI	B4, 'Byre'–Occupation	IIc
448/A6747	Sole	2	VI	B4, 'Byre'–Occupation	IIc
497/A10801a	Sole	3	V	P2.1a	IIb–IIf
498/A10801b	Sole	3	V	P2.1a	IIb–IIf
499/A10801c	Sole	3	V	P2.1a	IIb–IIf
500/A10801d	Sole	3	V	P2.1a	IIb–IIf
513/A6391a	Sole (seat)	2	VI	M1.1d & M1.1e	IId–IIf
514/A6391b	Sole	2	VI	M1.1d & M1.1e	IId–IIf
520/A7005b	Sole	1/2	V	B5, T4485	IIa–IIff
525/A6426a	Sole	1/2	V	B5, WW3566	IIa–IIff
532/A6949b	Sole (rounded forepart)	2	V	B5, North Room–Floor/Occupation (1)	IIa–IIff
542/A6376a	Sole (seat)	2	V	B5, North Room–Floor/Occupation (2)	IIa–IIff
543/A6376b	Sole (forepart)	2	V	B5, North Room–Floor/Occupation (2)	IIa–IIff
553/A6948a	Sole	2	V	B5, Destruction	IIa–IIff
616/A11231a	Sole	4	V	M10	IId–IIg
617/A11231b	Sole	4	V	M10	IId–IIg
618/A11231c	Sole	4	V	M10	IId–IIg
619/A11231d	Sole	4	V	M10	IId–IIg
635/A10778b	Sole	3	V	M10	IId–IIg
655/A9553a	Sole (seat)	4	V	M10, Pit 4552	IId–IIg
656/A9553b	Sole (forepart)	4	V	M10, Pit 4552	IId–IIg
657/A9553c	Sole	4	V	M10, Pit 4552	IId–IIg
658/A9553d	Sole	4	V	M10, Pit 4552	IId–IIg
659/A9553e	Sole	4	V	M10, Pit 4552	IId–IIg
660/A9553f	Sole	4	V	M10, Pit 4552	IId–IIg
661/A9553g	Sole	4	V	M10, Pit 4552	IId–IIg
662/A9553h	Sole	4	V	M10, Pit 4552	IId–IIg
733/A9887	Sole	4	VI	B12, Occupation (1b)	IIe–IIg
735/A9367a	Sole (pointed forepart)	4	VI	B12, Occupation (2a)	IIe–IIg
777/A9371c	Sole	3	VI	M1.2, Pit 2648	<IIg(IIh)
784/A9372b	Sole (seat)	3	VI	M1.2, Pit 2648	<IIg(IIh)
789/A9546b	Sole	3	VI	M1.2, Pit 2648	<IIg(IIh)
796/A9884b	Sole	3	VI	M1.2, Pit 2648	<IIg(IIh)
801/A10674	Sole (seat)	3	VI	M1.2, Pit 2648	<IIg(IIh)
802/A10775a	Sole (seat)	3	VI	M1.2, Pit 2648	<IIg(IIh)
804/A11218a	Sole	3	VI	M1.2, Pit 2648	<IIg(IIh)
813/A11220b	Sole, rand, upper	3	VI	M1.2, Pit 2648	<IIg(IIh)
826/A12292	Sole (rounded forepart), upper	3	VI	M1.2, Pit 2648	<IIg(IIh)
847/A8545a	Sole (forepart)	4	V/VI	M11	IIh
874/A8665a	Sole (seat)	3	VI	M1.3	IIi
875/A8665b	Sole (rounded forepart)	3	VI	M1.3	IIi
887/A8821a	Sole	3	VI	M1.3	IIi
909/A11267a	Sole	3	VI	M1.3	IIi
910/A11267b	Sole	3	VI	M1.3	IIi
913/A11268a	Sole	3	VI	M1.3	IIi
914/A11268b	Sole	3	VI	M1.3	IIi
924/A11639c	Sole	1	VI	MC111	IIb–IIIb>
940/A03–0373a	Sole	9	VII	M13	IIg–IIIb

(continued)

Cat/Accession	Leather type	Area	Rig	Feature	Phase
957/A8813a	Sole	4	V	MC116	IIe–IIIc
1001/A8001	Sole	4	V	MC117, Pit 4695	IIe–IIIc
1003/A8011a	Sole (rounded forepart)	4	VI	M1.4a(a)	IIIa–IIIc
1008/A7999	Sole (seat)	4	VI	M1.4a(a)	IIIa–IIIc
1010/A12390a	Sole	4	VI	M1.4a(a)	IIIa–IIIc
1011/A12390b	Sole	4	VI	M1.4a(a)	IIIa–IIIc
1050/A8671h	Sole	3	V	MC117, Pit 4695	IIe–IIIc
1066/A6194a	Sole	4	V/VI	MC128	IIIb,IIIc
1067/A6194b	Sole	4	V/VI	MC128	IIIb,IIIc
1068/A6194c	Sole	4	V/VI	MC128	IIIb,IIIc
1071/A6401a	Sole (seat)	4	V/VI	MC128	IIIb,IIIc
1076/A12535b	Sole	4	V/VI	MC128	IIIb,IIIc
1077/A12535c	Sole	4	V/VI	MC128	IIIb,IIIc
1096/A03–0270b	Sole	9	VII	P8.1c	IIIc
1113/A03–0323b	Sole (seat)	9	VII	P8.1c	IIIc
1114/A03–0323c	Sole (oval forepart)	9	VII	P8.1c	IIIc
1128/A03–0252a	Sole	9	VII	M15	IIId
1146/A5893a	Sole	1	V	M12	IIg–IIIc(–IVa)
1207/A8680b	Sole	3	V	M6b	IIg–IIId
1222/A6070a	Sole	2	V	M6b	IIg–IIId
1259/A03–0421a	Sole (seat)	7	VI	MC124	<IIIc–IVa
1270/A4933a	Sole (pointed forepart)	2	V	P2.2a	IVa
1271/A4933b	Sole (pointed forepart)	2	V	P2.2a	IVa
1280/A8540a	Sole	4	VI	M1.4a(b)	IIIa–IVa
1281/A8540b	Sole	4	VI	M1.4a(b)	IIIa–IVa
1285/A6415a	Sole	3	V	P2.2b	IVa
1286/A6415b	Sole	3	V	P2.2b	IVa
1301/A8810b	Sole (seat)	3	V	P2.2b	IVa
1302/A8810c	Sole (waist fragment)	3	V	P2.2b	IVa
1303/A8810d	Sole (oval forepart)	3	V	P2.2b	IVa
1315/A7989b	Sole	4	V	MC143	IVaa
1374/A8029a	Sole	4	V	MC143	IVaa
1388/A8021b	Sole	3	V/VI	MC144, WW2221	<IIId–IVaa
1389/A8021c	Sole	3	V/VI	MC144, WW2221	<IIId–IVaa
1416/A8020a	Sole	3	V	P2.2a & P2.3a	IVa,IVaa
1442/A7786	Sole	3	V	MC151	IVaa
1479/A6190a	Sole	2	V	B26, Floor/Occupation (8a)	IIg–IVaa
1496/A4827a	Sole (forepart)	1	VI	B20, Levelling	<IIId–IVaa
1603/A03–0424a	Sole (pointed forepart)	7	VII	MC130	<IIIc–IVaa
1635/A11242a	Sole	3	VI	B2, WW2498	IVa,IVaa
1672/A7995a	Sole (seat)	3	V	B3(South), WW2569	IVa,IVaa
1678/A4895a	Sole	2	V	B3(South), Construction–Levelling	IVa,IVaa
1679/A4895b	Sole	2	V	B3(South), Construction–Levelling	IVa,IVaa
1694/A03–0318b	Sole	7	VII	B18 (Phase 1b), Destruction	IVa,IVaa
1701/A4896a	Sole	4	VI	B11, Floor	IVaa
1731/A03–0343a	Sole (pointed forepart)	7	VII	MC126, Pit 7402	IVaa,IVb
1744/A03–0347b	Sole	7	VII	MC126, Pit 7402	IVaa,IVb
1761/A03–0360a	Sole	7	VII	MC126, Pit 7402	IVaa,IVb
1766/A03–0363	Sole	7	VII	MC126, Pit 7402	IVaa,IVb
1831/A03–0378a	Sole	7	VII	MC126, Pit 7402	IVaa,IVb
1886/A03–0357b	Sole (oval forepart)	7	VII	MC126, Pit 7402	IVaa,IVb
1887/A03–0357c	Sole	7	VII	MC126, Pit 7402	IVaa,IVb

(continued)

Cat/Accession	Leather type	Area	Rig	Feature	Phase
1888/A03–0357d	Sole	7	VII	MC126, Pit 7402	IVaa,IVb
2290/A03–0271b	Sole	7	VI	M1.4f	IVc
2291/A03–0271c	Sole	7	VI	M1.4f	IVc
2317/A03–0285a	Sole (seat)	7	VI	M1.4f	IVc
2318/A03–0285b	Sole	7	VI	M1.4f	IVc
2319/A03–0285c	Sole	7	VI	M1.4f	IVc
2320/A03–0285d	Sole	7	VI	M1.4f	IVc
2351/A03–0330a	Sole	7	VI	M1.4f	IVc
2366/A03–0332c	Sole	7	VI	M1.4f	IVc
2367/A03–0332d	Sole	7	VI	M1.4f	IVc
2368/A03–0332e	Sole	7	VI	M1.4f	IVc
2369/A03–0332f	Sole	7	VI	M1.4f	IVc
2374/A03–0333a	Sole (oval forepart)	7	VI	M1.4f	IVc
2375/A03–0333b	Sole	7	VI	M1.4f	IVc
2394/A03–0336	Sole (rounded forepart)	7	VI	M1.4f	IVc
2396/A03–0339a	Sole	7	VI	M1.4f	IVc
2403/A03–0342a	Sole	7	VI	M1.4f	IVc
2448/A03–0387a	Sole (seat)	7	VI	M1.4f	IVc
2449/A03–0387b	Sole	7	VI	M1.4f	IVc
2452/A03–0326a	Sole	7	VI	M1.4f	IVc
2453/A03–0326b	Sole	7	VI	M1.4f	IVc
2555/A03–0289	Sole (seat)	7	VII	B18 (Phase 2a), North Room & Hall–Floor (1)	IVb
2570/A03–0329b	Sole	7	VII	B18 (Phase 1/2)	IVaa,IVb
2571/A03–0329c	Sole	7	VII	B18 (Phase 1/2)	IVaa,IVb
2572/A03–0329d	Sole	7	VII	B18 (Phase 1/2)	IVaa,IVb
2598/A03–0192a	Sole	9	VII	B18 (Phase 1/2)	IVaa,IVb
2600/A03–0184a	Sole (seat)	9	VII	B18 (Phase 1/2)	IVaa,IVb
2639/A03–0231a	Sole (rounded forepart)	9	VII	B18 (Phase 1/2)	IVaa,IVb
2640/A03–0231b	Sole	9	VII	B18 (Phase 1/2)	IVaa,IVb
2672/A03–0180a	Sole (seat)	9	VII	B18 (Phase 1/2), Pit 9276	IVaa,IVb
2680/A03–0202a	Sole (oval forepart)	9	VII	B18 (Phase 1/2), Pit 9301	IVaa,IVb
2705/A03–0296b	Sole	7	VII	B18 (Phase 1/2), MF 7307	IVaa,IVb
2717/A03–0314a	Sole (rounded forepart)	7	VII	B18 (Phase 2a), External (1), Pit 7314	IVb
2718/A03–0314b	Sole	7	VII	B18 (Phase 2a), External (1), Pit 7314	IVb
2723/A03–0307b	Sole (seat)	7	VII	B18 (Phase 2a), External (1), Pit 7314	IVb
2730/A03–0301a	Sole (seat)	7	VII	B18 (Phase 2b), WW7308	IVb
2733/A03–0368a	Sole (seat)	10	VII	B18 (Phases 2a & 2b), MW6155	IVb
2734/A03–0368b	Sole	10	VII	B18 (Phases 2a & 2b), MW6155	IVb
2755/A03–0288b	Sole	7	VII	B18 (Phase 2b), North Room, Hall & Hall South–Occupation (10)	IVb
2780/A03–0245a	Sole (forepart)	9	VII	B18 (Phase 2b), North Room, Hall & Hall South–Occupation (10)	IVb
2781/A03–0245b	Sole	9	VII	B18 (Phase 2b), North Room, Hall & Hall South–Occupation (10)	IVb
2795/A03–0152a	Sole	9	VII	B18 (Phase 2b), North Room, Hall & Hall South–Occupation (10)	IVb
2816/A03–0290	Sole (seat)	10	VIII	M9b(a)	IVc
2839/A03–0312a	Sole	10	VIII	M9b(a)	IVc
2841/A03–0313	Sole (oval forepart)	10	VIII	M9b(a)	IVc
2842/A03–0319a	Sole (seat)	10	VIII	M9b(a)	IVc
2843/A03–0319b	Sole (seat)	10	VIII	M9b(a)	IVc
2857/A03–0302	Sole	10	VIII	M9b(a), T6163	IVc
2860/A4821a	Sole	2	VI	M1.4d & B2, Late Occupation/Abandonment (2)	IVa–IVc

(continued)

Cat/Accession	Leather type	Area	Rig	Feature	Phase
2861/A4821b	Sole	2	VI	M1.4d & B2, Late Occupation/ Abandonment (2)	IVa–IVc
2862/A4821c	Sole	2	VI	M1.4d & B2, Late Occupation/ Abandonment (2)	IVa–IVc
2873/A9142	Sole	3	V	MC155, Pit 2691	IVb,IVc
2878/A9358a	Sole	3	V	MC155, Pit 2691	IVb,IVc
2890/A9363a	Sole (seat)	3	V	MC155, Pit 2691	IVb,IVc
3034/A4941a	Sole	3	VI	M1.4d	IVb,IVc
3056/A8667b	Sole (pointed forepart)	3	VI	M1.4d	IVb,IVc
3057/A8667c	Sole	3	VI	M1.4d	IVb,IVc
3069/A8668d	Sole	3	VI	M1.4d	IVb,IVc
3070/A8668e	Sole	3	VI	M1.4d	IVb,IVc
3084/A3449d	Sole	2	VI	M1.4d	IVb,IVc
3085/A4924a	Sole (seat)	2	VI	M1.4d	IVb,IVc
3086/A4924b	Sole	2	VI	M1.4d	IVb,IVc
3091/A5900b	Sole	2	VI	M1.4d	IVb,IVc
3092/A5900c	Sole	2	VI	M1.4d	IVb,IVc
3093/A5900d	Sole	2	VI	M1.4d	IVb,IVc
3094/A5900e	Sole	2	VI	M1.4d	IVb,IVc
3097/A6226a	Sole	2	VI	M1.4d	IVb,IVc
3103/A6392a	Sole (waist fragment)	2	VI	M1.4d	IVb,IVc
3111/A8028a	Sole (seat)	3	VI	M1.4d, Pit 2566	IVb,IVc
3112/A8028b	Sole (forepart)	3	VI	M1.4d, Pit 2566	IVb,IVc
3113/A8028c	Sole	3	VI	M1.4d, Pit 2566	IVb,IVc
3123/A6205a	Sole (forepart)	2	VI	M1.4d, Pit 2801	IVb,IVc
3124/A6205b	Sole	2	VI	M1.4d, Pit 2801	IVb,IVc
3126/A03–0253b	Sole	7	VI	M1.4h	IVc
3127/A03–0253c	Sole	7	VI	M1.4h	IVc
3145/A6381a	Sole	3	V	M1.4g	IVb,IVc
3172/A3540c	Sole	3	V, VI	M1.4c	IIIa–IVcc
3176/A6072b	Sole	3	V, VI	M1.4c	IIIa–IVcc
3177/A6072c	Sole	3	V, VI	M1.4c	IIIa–IVcc
3178/A6072d	Sole	3	V, VI	M1.4c	IIIa–IVcc
3179/A6072e	Sole	3	V, VI	M1.4c	IIIa–IVcc
3196/A6191a	Sole	3	V, VI	M1.4c	IIIa–IVcc
3197/A6191b	Sole	3	V, VI	M1.4c	IIIa–IVcc
3198/A6191c	Sole	3	V, VI	M1.4c	IIIa–IVcc
3219/A6228a	Sole	3	V, VI	M1.4c	IIIa–IVcc
3225/A6390a	Sole	3	V, VI	M1.4c	IIIa–IVcc
3248/A6233a	Sole (seat)	4	V, VI	M1.4b	IVb–IVcc
3249/A6233b	Sole (seat)	4	V, VI	M1.4b	IVb–IVcc
3250/A6233c	Sole (pointed forepart)	4	V, VI	M1.4b	IVb–IVcc
3251/A6233d	Sole	4	V, VI	M1.4b	IVb–IVcc
3252/A6233e	Sole	4	V, VI	M1.4b	IVb–IVcc
3253/A6233f	Sole	4	V, VI	M1.4b	IVb–IVcc
3254/A4944	Sole (forepart)	4	V, VI	M1.4b	IVb–IVcc
3260/A03–0239a	Sole	7	VII	P8.3	IVc,IVcc
3273/A03–0226a	Sole	7	VII	P8.3	IVc,IVcc
3282/A03–0227b	Sole (seat)	7	VII	P8.3	IVc,IVcc
3307/A03–0250d	Sole (rounded forepart)	7	VII	P8.3	IVc,IVcc
3315/A03–0260d	Sole (forepart)	7	VII	P8.3	IVc,IVcc
3337/A03–0267	Sole	7	VII	P8.3 & M9a, PW7267	IVc,IVcc
3343/A03–0183a	Sole & upper	7	VII	M9a	IVc,IVcc
3352/A03–0246a	Sole	7	VII	M9a	IVc,IVcc
3363/A03–0223a	Sole (seat)	7	VII	M9a	IVc,IVcc
3379/A03–0243a	Sole (forepart)	7	VII	M9a	IVc,IVcc

(continued)

Cat/Accession	Leather type	Area	Rig	Feature	Phase
3380/A03–0243b	Sole (rounded forepart)	7	VII	M9a	IVc,IVcc
3384/A03–0233a	Sole	7	VII	M9a	IVc,IVcc
3391/A03–0255a	Sole	7	VII	M9a	IVc,IVcc
3393/A03–0259a	Sole (oval forepart)	7	VII	M9a	IVc,IVcc
3396/A03–0268a	Sole	7	VII	M9a	IVc,IVcc
3397/A03–0268b	Sole	7	VII	M9a	IVc,IVcc
3417/A03–0275a	Sole	7	VII	B18 (Phases 2a & 2b) & M9a, PH7297	(IVb)IVc,IVcc
3420/A03–0217b	Sole (oval forepart)	7	VII	B18 (Phases 2a & 2b) & M9a, PH7297	(IVb)IVc,IVcc
3427/A03–0051a	Sole, rand, upper	9	VII	M9a, Pit 9026	IVc,IVcc
3428/A03–0051b	Sole, rand, upper	9	VII	M9a, Pit 9026	IVc,IVcc
3429/A03–0051c	Sole, rand, upper	9	VII	M9a, Pit 9026	IVc,IVcc
3430/A03–0051d	Sole, rand, upper	9	VII	M9a, Pit 9026	IVc,IVcc
3432/A03–0049b	Sole	9	VII	M9a, Pit 9026	IVc,IVcc
3546/A03–0238a	Sole	7	VI	M1.4i	IVcc
3563/A03–0244b	Sole	7	VI	M1.4i	IVcc
3565/A7688a	Sole (pointed forepart)	3	VI	M1.4e	IVcc(Va)(VI)
3566/A7688b	Sole	3	VI	M1.4e	IVcc(Va)(VI)
3581/A7778a	Sole	3	VI	M1.4e	IVcc(Va)(VI)
3605/A4818b	Sole	3	VI	M1.4e	IVcc(Va)
3625/A6077d	Sole	3	VI	M1.4e	IVcc(Va)
3642/A6404	Sole	3	VI	M1.4e	IVcc(Va)
3646/A7780a	Sole (forepart)	3	VI	M1.4e	IVcc(Va)
3647/A7780b	Sole	3	VI	M1.4e	IVcc(Va)
3652/A4916	Sole (seat)	2	VI	M1.4e	IVcc(Va)
3653/A4903a	Sole	3	VI	M1.4e, Pit 2446	IVcc(Va)
3660/A5902a	Sole	3	VI	P6	IVcc,Va
3661/A5902b	Sole	3	VI	P6	IVcc,Va
3699/A4299a	Sole (forepart)	3	VI	B34, Floor	Va
3702/A4350	Sole (forepart)	3	VI	B34, Floor	Va
3706/A03–0172b	Sole (forepart)	7	VI	B34, Floor	Va
3721/A03–0160e	Sole (forepart)	7	VI	B34, Courtyard	Va
3760/A03–0190a	Sole (seat)	7	VI	B34, Courtyard	Va
3761/A03–0190b	Sole (forepart)	7	VI	B34, Courtyard	Va
3861/A03–0048c	Sole	7	VI, VII	M1.5b	Vaa
3862/A03–0060	Sole (pointed forepart)	7	VI, VII	M1.5b	Vaa
3879/A03–0120d	Sole (pointed forepart)	7	VI, VII	M1.5b	Vaa
3880/A03–0120e	Sole (pointed forepart)	7	VI, VII	M1.5b	Vaa
3886/A03–0125a	Sole	7	VI, VII	M1.5b	Vaa
3897/A03–0132b	Sole (waist fragment)	7	VI, VII	M1.5b	Vaa
3898/A03–0132c	Sole (oval forepart)	7	VI, VII	M1.5b	Vaa
3926/A03–0136b	Sole	7	VI, VII	M1.5b	Vaa
3943/A03–0139a	Sole (seat)	7	VI, VII	M1.5b	Vaa
3960/A03–0142a	Sole	7	VI, VII	M1.5b	Vaa
3976/A03–0148a	Sole (forepart)	7	VI, VII	M1.5b	Vaa
3977/A03–0148b	Sole (pointed forepart)	7	VI, VII	M1.5b	Vaa
3987/A03–0170d	Sole (rounded forepart)	7	VI, VII	M1.5b	Vaa

(continued)

Cat/Accession	Leather type	Area	Rig	Feature	Phase
4020/A03–0155a	Sole	7	VII	P8.4	Va
4028/A03–0156a	Sole (seat)	7	VII	P8.4	Va
4034/A03–0158a	Sole (rounded forepart)	7	VII	P8.4	Va
4042/A03–0159b	Sole	7	VII	P8.4	Va
4088/A03–0210b	Sole(rounded forepart)	7	VII	P8.4	Va
4089/A03–0210c	Sole (rounded forepart)	7	VII	P8.4	Va
4090/A03–0210d	Sole (rounded forepart)	7	VII	P8.4	Va
4099/A03–0171a	Sole (seat)	7	VII	P8.4	Va
4126/A03–0214d	Sole	7	VII	P8.4	Va
4127/A03–0214e	Sole	7	VII	P8.4	Va
4200/A4906a	Sole	1	V, VI	M5c	(IVc–)Va
4202/A6397a	Sole (forepart)	1	V, VI	M5c	(IVc–)Va
4207/A6232a	Sole (seat)	3	V	B1(a), Construction–Levelling	IVcc,Va
4208/A6232b	Sole (seat)	3	V	B1(a), Construction–Levelling	IVcc,Va
4209/A6232c	Sole	3	V	B1(a), Construction–Levelling	IVcc,Va
4210/A6232d	Sole	3	V	B1(a), Construction–Levelling	IVcc,Va
4217/A4920	Sole	2	V	B1(a), Construction–Levelling	IVcc,Va
4219/A6234a	Sole	2	V	B1(a), Construction–Levelling	IVcc,Va
4232/A4925a	Sole (seat)	3	V	B1(a), North Room–Floor (3a)	IVcc,Va
4241/A1239a	Sole	3	V	B1(b), North Room–Floor (6)	Va
4260/A6374a	Sole (seat)	2	V	B1(b), Demolition, Tumble	Va
4262/A6478a	Sole (seat)	1	V, VI	M5a	IVb–Vc
4263/A6478b	Sole (seat)	1	V, VI	M5a	IVb–Vc
4264/A6478c	Sole	1	V, VI	M5a	IVb–Vc
4265/A6478d	Sole	1	V, VI	M5a	IVb–Vc
4266/A6478e	Sole	1	V, VI	M5a	IVb–Vc
4273/A5892a	Sole (rounded forepart)	1	V, VI	M5a	IVb–Vc
4285/A4923a	Sole	1	V, VI	M5a	IVb–Vc
4289/A0825a	Sole (forepart)	3	V, VI	M1.5a	Va,Vaa(VI)
4290/A0825b	Sole	3	V, VI	M1.5a	Va,Vaa(VI)
4291/A0825c	Sole	3	V, VI	M1.5a	Va,Vaa(VI)
4306/A1223a	Sole	3	V, VI	M1.5a	Va,Vaa(VI)
4309/A1251b	Sole (pointed forepart)	3	V, VI	M1.5a	Va,Vaa(VI)
4395/A2247a	Sole	3	V, VI	M1.5a	Va,Vaa(VI)
4396/A2247b	Sole	3	V, VI	M1.5a	Va,Vaa(VI)
4397/A2247c	Sole	3	V, VI	M1.5a	Va,Vaa(VI)
4480/A2284b	Sole	3	V, VI	M1.5a	Va,Vaa(VI)
4481/A2284c	Sole	3	V, VI	M1.5a	Va,Vaa(VI)
4482/A2284d	Sole	3	V, VI	M1.5a	Va,Vaa(VI)
4483/A2284e	Sole	3	V, VI	M1.5a	Va,Vaa(VI)
4487/A3456a	Sole (forepart)	3	V, VI	M1.5a	Va,Vaa(VI)
4500/A5895	Sole	3	V, VI	M1.5a	Va,Vaa(VI)
4502/A6188b	Sole (seat)	3	V, VI	M1.5a	Va,Vaa(VI)
4504/A6188d	Sole (pointed forepart)	3	V, VI	M1.5a	Va,Vaa(VI)
4529/A6198b	Sole	3	V, VI	M1.5a	Va,Vaa(VI)
4552/A1253c	Sole	3	V, VI	M1.5a	Va,Vaa
4813/A6221b	Sole	3	V, VI	M1.5a	Va,Vaa
4829/A03–0175b	Sole (seat)	7	VII	M8a	Va,Vaa
4830/A03–0175c	Sole (seat), rand	7	VII	M8a	Va,Vaa
4831/A03–0175d	Sole	7	VII	M8a	Va,Vaa
4832/A03–0175e	Sole (pointed forepart)	7	VII	M8a	Va,Vaa
4876/A03–0111c	Sole	7	VII	M8a	Va,Vaa

(continued)

Cat/Accession	Leather type	Area	Rig	Feature	Phase
4880/A03–0179a	Sole	7	VII	M8a	Va,Vaa
4888/A03–0128c	Sole	7	VII	M8a	Va,Vaa
4890/A03–0128e	Sole (pointed forepart)	7	VII	M8a	Va,Vaa
4902/A03–0162a	Sole	7	VII	M8a	Va,Vaa
4904/A03–0162c	Sole	7	VII	M8a	Va,Vaa
4905/A03–0162d	Sole	7	VII	M8a	Va,Vaa
4906/A03–0162e	Sole	7	VII	M8a	Va,Vaa
4907/A03–0162f	Sole	7	VII	M8a	Va,Vaa
4908/A03–0162g	Sole	7	VII	M8a	Va,Vaa
4909/A03–0162h	Sole	7	VII	M8a	Va,Vaa
4910/A03–0162i	Sole	7	VII	M8a	Va,Vaa
4911/A03–0162j	Sole	7	VII	M8a	Va,Vaa
4912/A03–0162k	Sole	7	VII	M8a	Va,Vaa
4913/A03–0162l	Sole	7	VII	M8a	Va,Vaa
4914/A03–0162m	Sole	7	VII	M8a	Va,Vaa
4915/A03–0162n	Sole	7	VII	M8a	Va,Vaa
4916/A03–0162o	Sole	7	VII	M8a	Va,Vaa
4962/A03–0174b	Sole	7	VII	M8a	Va,Vaa
4963/A03–0174c	Sole	7	VII	M8a	Va,Vaa
4966/A03–0174f	Sole	7	VII	M8a	Va,Vaa
4967/A03–0174g	Sole	7	VII	M8a	Va,Vaa
4968/A03–0174h	Sole	7	VII	M8a	Va,Vaa
4969/A03–0174i	Sole	7	VII	M8a	Va,Vaa
4970/A03–0174j	Sole	7	VII	M8a	Va,Vaa
4971/A03–0174k	Sole (oval forepart)	7	VII	M8a	Va,Vaa
4972/A03–0174l	Sole (oval forepart)	7	VII	M8a	Va,Vaa
5022/A03–0212c	Sole (seat)	7	VII	M8a	Va,Vaa
5186/A03–0144b	Sole (seat)	7	VII	M8a, Pit 7183	Va,Vaa
5198/A03–0129a	Sole (seat)	7	VII	M8a, T7193	Va,Vaa
5200/A03–0129c	Sole	7	VII	M8a, T7193	Va,Vaa
5252/A03–0029c	Sole (waist fragment)	7	VII	P8.5	Vb,Vbb
5255/A03–0045	Sole	7	VII	B53 (Phase 2), South Area–Occupation (7a)	Vbb
5291/A4598	Sole (pointed forepart)	2	V, VI	M4a	Va–Vc
5292/A6071a	Sole	2	V, VI	M4a	Va–Vc
5295/A6231	Sole (seat)	2	V, VI	M4a	Va–Vc
5296/A6253	Sole (pointed forepart)	2	V, VI	M4a	Va–Vc
5297/A6212a	Sole (forepart)	2	V, VI	M4a	Va–Vc
5302/A4917b	Sole (seat)	4	V, VI	M3a	Vb–Vc
5306/A4917f	Sole	4	V, VI	M3a	Vb–Vc
5308/A5896a	Sole (seat)	4	V, VI	M3a	Vb–Vc
5315/A4390c	Sole	4	V, VI	M3a	Vb–Vc
5316/A4390d	Sole	4	V, VI	M3a	Vb–Vc
5317/A4390e	Sole	4	V, VI	M3a	Vb–Vc
5322/A4919a	Sole (seat)	4	V, VI	M3a	Vb–Vc
5323/A4919b	Sole (seat)	4	V, VI	M3a	Vb–Vc
5324/A4919c	Sole (forepart)	4	V, VI	M3a	Vb–Vc
5328/A6199	Sole	4	V, VI	M3a	Vb–Vc
5334/A6204	Sole	4	V, VI	M3a	Vb–Vc
5341/A1245	Sole (seat)	4	VI	M3b	Vd
5342/A2283a	Sole (seat)	4	VI	M3b	Vd
5358/A5894b	Sole	4	VI	M3b	Vd
5389/A6223	Sole	4	VI	P1a	Vd
5391/A6248a	Sole (forepart)	4	VI	P1a	Vd
5394/A6197	Sole	4	VI	P1a	Vd

(continued)

Cat/Accession	Leather type	Area	Rig	Feature	Phase
5396/A6394a	Sole (pointed forepart)	4	VI	P1a	Vd
5407/A4247b	Sole	4	VI	P1a	Vd
5408/A4247c	Sole	4	VI	P1a	Vd
5409/A4247d	Sole	4	VI	P1a	Vd
5410/A4247e	Sole	4	VI	P1a	Vd
5460/A1246a	Sole	4	VI	P1a, MF2125	Vd
5461/A1246b	Sole	4	VI	P1a, MF2125	Vd
5462/A1246c	Sole	4	VI	P1a, MF2125	Vd
5486/A0821a	Sole	4	VI	M3b	Vd
5525/A6218a	Sole (seat)	4	VI	M3b	Vd
5552/A6209a	Sole	4	V	M3c	Vd
5569/A4362a	Sole	4	V	M3c	Vd
5592/A6201	Sole (forepart)	4	V	M3c	Vd
5593/A6192a	Sole	4	V	M3c	Vd
5594/A6192b	Sole	4	V	M3c	Vd
5604/A6255a	Sole (forepart)	4	V	M3c	Vd
5616/A0819a	Sole	2	VI	M4c	Vd,Vdd
5708/A0118a	Sole (forepart)	7/10	VII/VIII	Sondage 2003	u/s
5709/A0118b	Sole	7/10	VII/VIII	Sondage 2003	u/s
5710/A0118c	Sole	7/10	VII/VIII	Sondage 2003	u/s
5711/A0118d	Sole	7/10	VII/VIII	Sondage 2003	u/s
5742/A5898b	Sole	2	V, VI	Unstratified	u/s
5743/A5898c	Sole	2	V, VI	Unstratified	u/s
5754/A6383a	Sole	2	V, VI	Unstratified	u/s
5763/A0120a	Sole (seat)	3/4	V, VI	Unstratified	u/s
5776/A2246	Sole (forepart)	7/10	VII/VIII	Sondage 2003	u/s
5794/A0817c	Sole (seat)	3/4	V, VI	Unstratified	u/s
5796/A1234a	Sole	3/4	V, VI	Unstratified	u/s
5797/A1234b	Sole	3/4	V, VI	Unstratified	u/s
5798/A1234c	Sole	3/4	V, VI	Unstratified	u/s
5799/A1234d	Sole	3/4	V, VI	Unstratified	u/s
5800/A1234e	Sole	3/4	V, VI	Unstratified	u/s
5801/A1234f	Sole	3/4	V, VI	Unstratified	u/s
5802/A1234g	Sole	3/4	V, VI	Unstratified	u/s
5803/A1234h	Sole	3/4	V, VI	Unstratified	u/s
5805/A1635a	Sole (seat)	3/4	V, VI	Unstratified	u/s
5811/A12487b	Sole	2	V, VI	Unstratified	u/s
5812/A12487c	Sole	2	V, VI	Unstratified	u/s
5813/A12487d	Sole	2	V, VI	Unstratified	u/s
5814/A12487e	Sole	2	V, VI	Unstratified	u/s
5817/A6222a	Sole	4	V, VI	Unstratified	u/s
5820/A0801a	Sole (forepart)	4	V, VI	Unstratified	u/s
5821/A0801b	Sole	4	V, VI	Unstratified	u/s
5825/A03–0127b	Sole	7	VII, VIII	Unstratified	u/s
5850/A03–0133a	Sole	7	VII, VIII	Unstratified	u/s
5851/A03–0133b	Sole	7	VII, VIII	Unstratified	u/s
5852/A03–0133c	Sole	7	VII, VIII	Unstratified	u/s
5853/A03–0133d	Sole	7	VII, VIII	Unstratified	u/s
5854/A03–0133e	Sole (pointed forepart)	7	VII, VIII	Unstratified	u/s
North Sector					
5887/A7805a	Sole	5	–	CG005	4(5)
5888/A7805b	Sole	5	–	CG005	4(5)
5891/A6236a	Sole	5	–	CG007, Pit 0276	4,5
5892/A6236b	Sole	5	–	CG007, Pit 0276	4,5
5915/A0109a	Sole (pointed forepart)	5,A	–	Lade (4)	6–12 (b–e)
5948/A0804	Sole (seat)	5,A	–	Lade (4)	6–12 (b–e)
5965/A0102	Sole	5,A	–	CG028	15–18
South/North Sectors					
5973/L1694c	Sole (forepart)	–	–	Unstratified	u/s

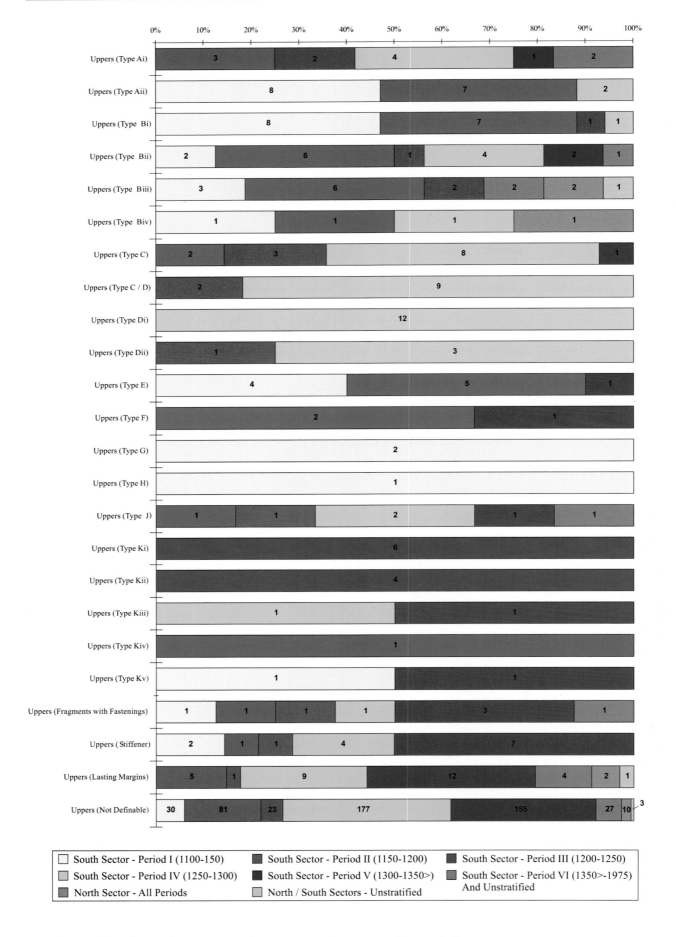

Illus 125 *Number and percentage of upper categories arranged by period.*

Uppers

Of the 722 fragments of upper found, 160 (22%) were complete enough to enable them to be divided into ten Types, A–K (excluding I). The types have been defined by the overall pattern and shape and by the method of fastening. All, except Types H and J, are basically one-piece uppers; in this pattern, an approximately rectangular fragment of leather has been cut and folded round the foot, forming both vamp and quarters, which are joined, usually on the inside of the foot, by a butted edge–flesh seam. Most of these uppers have one or two additional pieces: nearly all have a second leg flap or latchet, as, for example Cat No 218/A7648b, (Type Aii; Illus 127); some have a side-piece linking vamp and quarters, as on Cat No 4288/A4926, (Type Ai), where the side-piece is long and rectangular, reaching from lasting margin to top edge. Some boots, for instance Cat Nos 2486–8/A03–0392h–j, (Type Ai; Illus 128), have two side-pieces, positioned one on top of the other. Another boot, Cat No 358/A6773g, (Type Bii; Illus 131) is made up of five pieces, a large fragment comprising vamp, quarters and part of two leg flaps, two triangular fragments forming the top front corners of both leg flaps and a top band. Such variations from the basic one-piece pattern were probably the result of economy, or occasionally, repair, not style. Types H and J are distinguished by having separate vamps and quarters linked on both the inside and outside of the foot by butted edge–flesh stitching channels. Many uppers, of all types, contain another fragment – a semicircular or triangular heel-stiffener, set on the inside of the quarters.

The following trends emerge from a study of the dating of each type. Types A and B, simple wrap-around boots, the former with no apparent fastening, the latter with varying patterns of thongs, are pre-dominantly of 12th-century date. Also chiefly from 12th-century contexts are Type E, low shoes with small leg flaps or fastenings, Type F, low shoes with no latchets, Type G, high shoes with latchets ending in thongs and Type H, an exceptionally high calf boot with the vamp separate from the quarters. Type J, boots and shoes with separate vamps and quarters, however, belong mainly to the second half of the 13th century, as do Types C and D, boots and shoes respectively, with side lacing. Type K, boots with central fastening, are mainly of late 13th- to mid-14th-century date.

Types A, B, C, G and K consist of ankle-boots, while the Type H upper belongs to a high boot; these were almost certainly worn outdoors. Types D, E and F were low shoes; F in particular, which had no fastenings and no latchets, might have been an indoor slipper.

Thirteen children's uppers were recognised. These belonged to Types Ai (2), Bi (9), Bii (1) and Kiv (1). The Type K upper, although it had a central fastening, was of a much simpler, cruder design than the rest of Type K. The majority of the children's uppers were of mid- to late 12th-century date, with only two from the second half of the 13th century.

Uppers, decorated
(Illus 124, 136, 138, 140, 144 and 148)

Evidence for decoration was found on nine uppers. In three cases, this consisted of a vamp stripe, running from vamp throat to toe. Those on Cat Nos 162/A7787i and 4287/A6398 were made with three and four, respectively, parallel grooves (Illus 138, 144). A child's upper, Cat No 898/A11260b, had a more elaborate pattern, with not only a single groove from throat to toe, but also two grooves at right angles (Illus 124). A fourth upper, Cat No 1089/A03–0278d, had a long vertical rib, formed by two parallel grain to flesh stitching channels (Illus 144).

It is probable that these grooves or ribs would have been stitched with wool or silk; a boot from Coventry, for example, had 'an embroidered stripe of brown wool up the centre front, running from toe to throat' (Thomas 1980, 55–6, 49/185/12). Thornton suggests that a shoe from Lich Street, Worcester, may have been 'stitched horizontally to give the effect of an inserted piping' (Thornton 1969a, 57–8, Fig 13, no 3).

Decorated uppers (Illus 124, 136, 140, 144 and 148)

Cat/Accession	Leather type	Area	Rig	Feature	Phase
South Sector					
162/A7787i	Upper (Type E)	1/2	VI	B6(Phase 1), South Room–Floor (1)	Ie
172/A7580a & 174/A7580c	Top band, upper (Type Aii)	2	VI	M14b(b)	Ie
186/A7600b	Upper (Type G)	2	VI	M14b(b)	Ie
229/A7588c	Upper (Type G)	2	V	M14b(c)	Ie,1f
898/A11260b	Upper (Type Ai)	3	VI	M1.3	IIi
1089/A03–0278d	Upper	9	VII	B19 (Phase 2b), North Room–Floor (2b)	IIIc
1287/A6415c	Upper (Type Di)	3	V	P2.2b	IVa
1288/A6415d	Upper (Type Di)	3	V	P2.2b	IVa
4287/A6398	Upper	1	V, VI	M5a, Pit 3540	IVb–Vc

Coloured silk thread had been used on shoes from London, as, for example, on an upper from Seal House, which had 'three stripes of contrasting red, white and (faded) green' (Grew and de Neergaard 1988, 77–9). Similarly, a 12th-century ankle-shoe from Swinegate, York, has a vamp stripe sewn with pink thread (Mould et al 2003). Vamp stripes were also found at Waterford, Bergen and Schleswig (O'Rourke 1997, 704, 710, Fig 18.3.1, 18.3.2; Larsen 1992, 31–3; Schnack 1992b, Fig 18 no 2, Fig 19, Fig 20 no 2).

Two of the High Street examples (Cat Nos 162/A7787i and 186/A7600b) were recovered from Rig VI deposits that had been laid down shortly before 1150. Three others came from mid-13th-century layers. The earliest of these was detected within a secondary floor-level in the North Room of B19 (Phase 2b), a backland structure in Rig VII. The other two (Cat Nos 1287/A6415c and 1288/A6415d) were found in what should probably be recognised as an occupation layer of a path (P2.2b) that ran along the eastern boundary of Rig V. The sixth example (Cat No 4287/A6398) came from Pit 3540, a pit that dated from some time between the later 13th and the earlier 14th centuries. Parallels from London, York, Schleswig and Bergen are mainly of 12th-century date (Grew and de Neergaard 1988, 77–9; Mould et al 2003; Carlisle 1998, unpublished archive report; Schnack 1992b, 75–8; Larsen 1992, 31–3). This early date fits in with Larsen's suggestion that the decorative vamp stripe owes its origin to 'the functional seam or thonging which held the one-piece shoe together on the top of the foot' (Larsen 1992, 57). A construction seam of this type survives on a 10th century one-piece ankle shoe from Coppergate, York (Mould et al 2003).

Two uppers had been decorated with silk stitching, on the top edge of the quarters (Cat No 229/A7588c, Type G; Illus 140) and on a separate topband or binding (Cat No 172/A7580a, Illus 148; see Straps folded once for further details). Both these uppers came from mid-12th-century contexts.

Another two uppers appear to have had openwork or cutout decoration. A Type G upper, Cat No 186/A7600b, has had a thin strip and three ovals cut out (Illus 140). The closest, though not exact, parallels are found on similarly styled shoes from Schleswig (Schnack 1992b, Figs 45–49, Halbschuh Form G, 93–97). These are, however, later in date (13th to 14th centuries) than the High Street example, which is of mid-12th-century date. Comparable decoration from Bergen is also of 13th- to 14th-century date.

One of the Type Di uppers, Cat Nos 1287/A6415c and 1288/A6415d (Illus 136), has a number of irregular slits. These might have been caused by wear, but, on the other hand, they were possibly intended as decoration, similar to that on several of the Schleswig uppers, which, being of 13th-century date, are broadly contemporary with the High Street example (Schnack 1992b, Halbschuh Form C, 78–84; Fig 22 no 2, Fig 25 no 2, Fig 32 no 2, Fig 33).

Larsen suggests that the effect of openwork decoration may have been enhanced by the use of 'a highly coloured lining', although he admits that the Bergen uppers show no evidence for this (Larsen 1992, 32). Upper Cat Nos 1287/A6415c and 1288/A6415d (Illus 136), however, has a vertical row of tunnel stitching, which could have secured such a lining.

Uppers, Types Ai–ii: ankle boot (Illus 126–8)

Type A consists of 27 ankle boots of one-piece wrap around design with no surviving thongs or tunnel holes for thongs. Ten of these are high ankle-boots (Ai), the rest are low ankle-boots (Aii). As discussed above, these boots are made of one large fragment comprising vamp, quarters and usually a leg flap. Most also have one or more additional fragments—second leg flaps, side-pieces and stiffeners. Nearly all boots had a second leg flap, but it only survives in six examples, as, for instance, Cat Nos 67/A8809b (Illus 128); 174/A7580c (Illus 126); 218/A7648b (Illus 127). Five uppers retain their stiffeners, as, for example, Cat Nos 478/A12309b (Illus 126); 2486–8/A03–0392h–j (Illus 128); 218/A7648b (Illus 127) while a sixth, Cat No 127/A12306 still has the stitch holes for one (Illus 128). Side-pieces survive on eight boots, including Cat Nos 478/A12309b (Illus 126); 277/A7074d (Illus 128); 2486–8/A03–0392h–j (2) (Illus 128); 174/A7580c (Illus 126). Two single slits on Cat No 478/A12309b (Illus 126) might have been for thongs but the complete absence of any other indication for thongs suggest that these slits may represent damage.

5822/A0801c is unusual in that on the inside of the foot it has a very long vamp wing, with vamp and quarters joining in the middle of the stiffener, thus forming a backseam. The quarters of a low boot, Cat No 3327/A03–0066g, has a domed top edge, similar to those found in shoes of Type D.

The vamp of Cat No 898/A11260b has been decorated with an engraved line from throat to toe and with two more at right angles, across the middle of the vamp (Illus 124). Parallels from Worcester, Coventry and London suggest that the lines might have been stitched with wool or silk (Thornton 1969a, 57–8, Fig 13, no 3; Thomas 1980, 55–6, 49/185/12; Grew and de Neergaard 1988, 77–9).

On the High Street site, these ankle boots range in date from the earlier 12th century to possibly as late as the early 14th century. Low ankle boots (Type Aii) seem predominantly to have been of 12th-century date, with 15 (88%) of the 17 coming from Period I and II deposits. The other two (12%) were detected within Rig VII layers that dated from the later 13th century. In the case of the high ankle boots (Type Ai), the dating is not precise. Of the eight stratified examples, (two came from unstratified deposits) at least three, and possibly as many as five, came from Period II (the second half of the 12th century). Equally it is also true that at least three, and possibly as many as five, may have come

Uppers, Type Ai: high ankle boot (Illus 127–8).

Cat/Accession	Area	Rig	Feature	Phase
South Sector				
332/A6774b	1/2	VI	P5.4a	IIb
823/A11221c	3	VI	M1.2, Pit 2648	<IIg(IIh)
898/A11260b	3	VI	M1.3	IIi
1145/A4817b	1	V	M12	IIg–IIIc(–IVa)
1216/A9373b	3	V	M6b	IIg–IIId
2486/A03–0392h, 2487/A03–0392i, & 2488/A03–0392j	7	VI	M1.4f	IVc
2807/A03–0274b	7	VII	B18 (Phase 2b), Hall, Pit 7290	IVb
4288/A4926	1	V, VI	M5a, Pit 3540	IVb–Vc
5822/A0801c	4	V, VI	Unstratified	u/s
5876/A03–0037b	7–10	VI–VIII	Unstratified	u/s

Uppers, Type Aii: low ankle boot (Illus 126–8).

Cat/Accession	Area	Rig	Feature	Phase
South Sector				
67/A8809b	1/2	V, VI	M2.1b & B10, South Room–Floor/Occupation (1)	Ic,Icc
127/A12306	3	V	MC025, Pit 5337	(Ia–)Id
144/A7789c	2	VI	P5.2a	Ie
174/A7580c	2	VI	M14b(b)	Ie
202/A7257g	2	VI	M14b(b), Pit 3625	Ie
218/A7648b	2	VI	M14b(b), Pit 3625	Ie
277/A7074d	2	VI	MC044b	If
362/A7806	2	V	M14b(a)	Id
364/A2296b	1	V	M14a, Pit 3040	Id–IIc
455/A10048d	4	VI	M1.1f, Pit 2383	IIb,IIc
465/A11641	3	VI	M1.1c, Pit 5005	IId
478/A12309b	3	VI	M1.1c, Pit 5005	IId
507/A3447d	2	VI	M1.1d & M1.1e	IId–IIf
918/A12490c	4	VI	M1.3	IIi
921/A12536c	4	VI	M1.3	IIi
2641/A03–0231c	9	VII	B18 (Phase 1/2)	IVaa,IVb
3327/A03–0066g	9	VII	P8.3	IVc,IVcc

from 14th-century deposits (Periods III and IV). These two categories of ankle boot are distributed singly over the site, apart from four concentrations: three from M14b(b), two from M1.1c, three from M1.3 and two from B18.

Parallels include South Methven Street, Perth (15th century?); Gallowgate Middle School (12th–13th centuries), Netherkirkgate, Aberdeen; London (early–mid 12th century; early–mid 14th century); Winchester (late 11th–13th centuries); York; Novgorod; Bremen (11th century?); Bergen (late 12th–early 14th centuries) and Schleswig (11th–12th centuries) (Thomas 1987, 186; Thomas 2001a, 243; Grew and de Neergaard 1988, 11, no 6; Tatton-Brown 1975, 15, Fig 27, no 76; Ottaway 1982, 128–30; Thornton 1990b, 612–13, Fig 163, nos 1937 and 1938; Mould et al 2003; Thompson 1967, 81, Fig 83; Schnack 1993, 62–3, Fig 1a; Larsen 1992, 25–6, Fig 27; Schnack 1992b, 99).

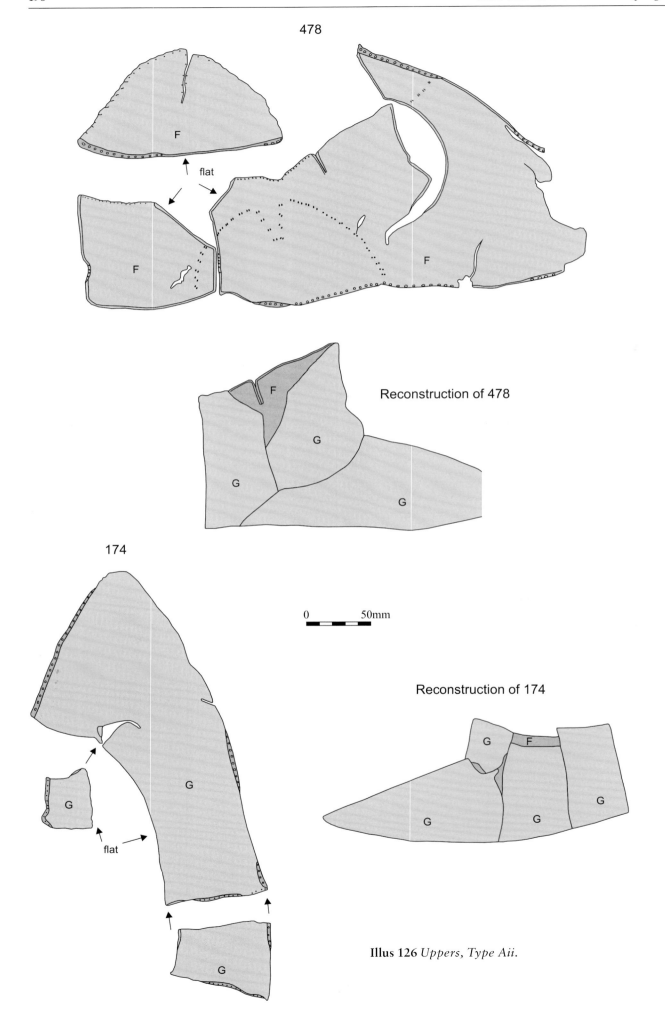

478

Reconstruction of 478

174

0   50mm

Reconstruction of 174

Illus 126 *Uppers, Type Aii.*

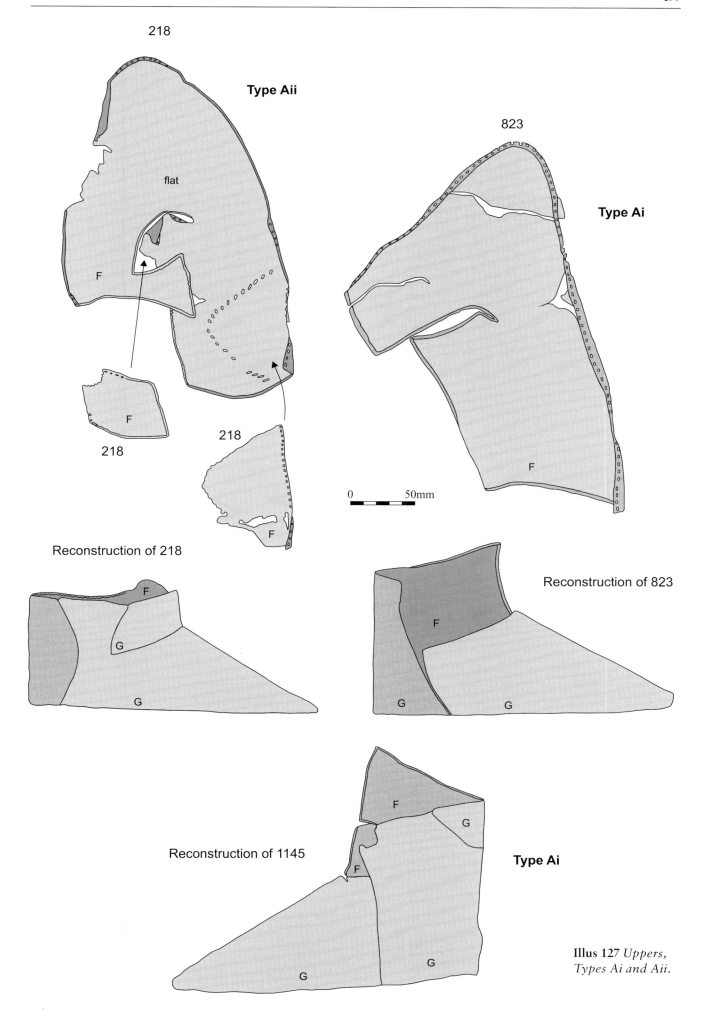

218

Type Aii

823

Type Ai

flat

F

F

218

218

F

0   50mm

F

Reconstruction of 218

F

G

G

Reconstruction of 823

F

G   G

Reconstruction of 1145

F

G

F

Type Ai

G   G

Illus 127 *Uppers,
Types Ai and Aii.*

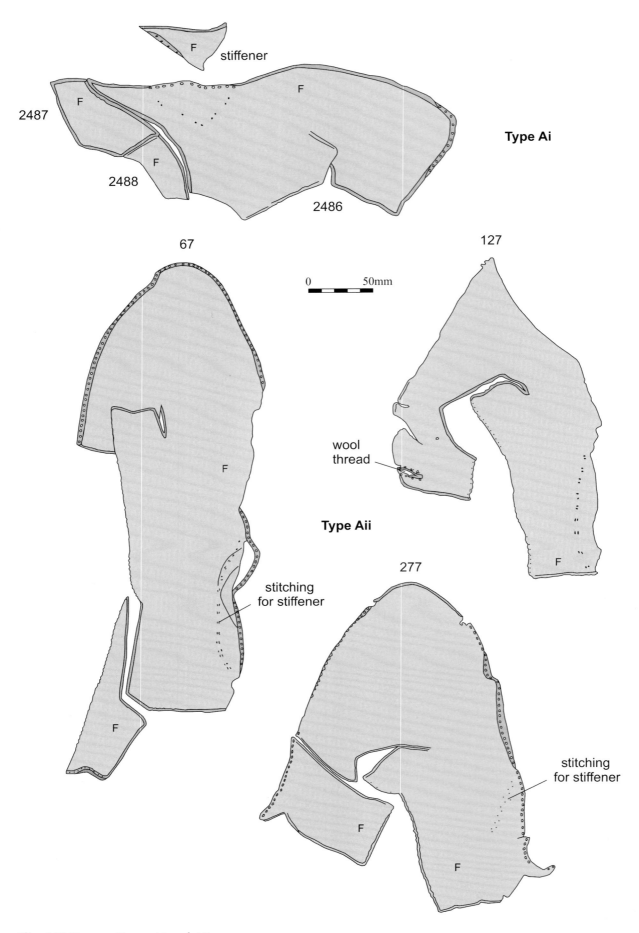

Illus 128 *Uppers, Types Ai and Aii.*

Uppers, Type Bi–iv

Type B consists of 53 boots of one-piece design secured by thongs wrapped round the foot in varying patterns. Type Bi has one horizontal thong, Type Bii two or more horizontal thongs, while Type Biii has two vertical thongs, apparently securing horizontal thongs. Uppers of Type Biv have only a single thong hole surviving.

Uppers, Type Bi: low boot with tunnel hole for thong (Illus 129, 130, 146)

The 17 uppers of Type Bi have tunnel holes for one horizontal thong. The tunnel holes consist of two short parallel vertical slits, about 6mm apart and 4–5mm high; they are usually positioned on each side of the quarters at about the height of the vamp throat, as, for instance, on Cat No 307/A12635c (Illus 146). On some examples, the tunnel hole on the inside of the foot is near the top of the vamp wing as on Cat No 267/A7044Bg (Illus 130).

Cat No 117/A03–0002b, with only one surviving tunnel hole, has clear marks and creases indicating the position of the thong (Illus 129). Cat No 390/Al2296b, with tunnel holes on quarters and vamp wing, has a fragment of thong in situ. On Cat No 508/A3447e, the inner tunnel hole is on a sidepiece.

As with Type A, most uppers of one-piece design include additional fragments. Cat No 183/A7597b has a second leg flap; that of Cat No 30/A10800d (Illus 129) no longer survives. Similarly, Cat No 508/ A3447e still retains its sidepiece, while Cat No 527/ A6803 (Illus 130) does not. Cat No 126/A12297b has a stiffener but its second leg flap is missing (Illus 129). Cat No 357/A6773f has two strips added to the main piece, to increase the height of the leg. On Cat No 117/ A03–0002b, both a leg flap and a sidepiece are missing (Illus 129).

Two boots are unusual in having part of the quarters turned inwards. Cat No 126/A12287a is a low boot with one large fragment comprising vamp, quarters and leg flap. The end of the quarters has been folded inwards and stitched to the flesh side of the quarters. It was not a heel stiffener, as separate stitch holes survive in the correct position. There is also a row of tunnel stitches across the flesh side of the leg flap, possibly for a lining (Illus 129). Similarly, part of the quarters of high boot Cat No 296/A12632b was turned inwards (Illus 130).

Type Bi uppers range in date from early 12th to mid 13th century, but are predominantly (88%) of 12th-century date, with at least eight (47%) examples from Period I (the first half of the 12th century), seven (41%) from Period II. The other two (12%) came from deposits that are unlikely to date from any later than the mid 13th century. The two uppers with quarters turned inwards are both from mid 12th century contexts. These uppers were found singly, apart from two groups of two, M14b(b) and Pit 4726, a cesspit in B16b. All, but one, came from Rigs V or VI.

Dated parallels for this type of boot range from the 11th to the 15th centuries, but are mainly of 12th- to 14th-century date: South Methven Street, Perth (15th century); Gallowgate Middle School, Aberdeen (12th–13th centuries); Low Petergate, York (12th–14th centuries); Coppergate and Swinegate, York; Durham (11th–12th century?); London (first half of the 12th century–mid-13th century); Winchester (late 11th–12th centuries); Whitstable (13th century); Bristol Bridge, Bristol (13th–14th centuries); Waterford (late 11th–12th century); Konstanz (13th century–1500); Bergen (12th–13th centuries); Schleswig (11th–13th centuries) and Lübeck (the end of the 12th century–mid-13th century) (Thomas 1987, 186; Thomas 2001, 243; Goodfellow and Thornton 1972, 97, 102, Fig 25, no 31; Mould et al 2003; Carlisle 1998, unpublished; Carver 1979, 30; Pritchard 1991, 230; Grew and de Neer-gaard 1988, 9–19, Figs 3, 5, 8–9, 12, 22–23; Thornton 1990b, 615–16, Fig 164 no 1947; Thompson 1956, 55–7; Thomas forthcoming a; O'Rourke 1997, 710, Fig 18.3.2; Schnack 1994, 28–9, 3.3, Tafel 21, 22–1949, 4505; Larsen 1992, 19–20, Fig 13; Schnack 1992b, 99–106; Groenman-van Waateringe and Guiran 1978, Typ 5).

The Durham report also refers to an upper which has its lengthy inside quarter folded down to the flesh side by an overseam; this is a hitherto unrecorded feature of an early shoe (Carver 1979, 30). A similar feature was found on one of the uppers from Gallowgate Middle School, Aberdeen. In this case the folded-in portion was rectangular in shape, and had had another rectangular piece stitched above it (Thomas 2001a, 243, [12th–13th centuries]).

Less well dated examples are also known from King Edward Street, 1–5 High Street and Mill Street, Perth; Netherkirkgate, Aberdeen; Coventry; Parliament Street, York; Novgorod; Dublin and Haithabu (Thomas and Walsh 1995, 971; Thomas 1987 186; Thomas 2001a, 243; Thomas 1980, 14, 55–49/185/12 and 1349/195/66; Tweddle 1986, 246–53, Fig 112 nos 815–816; Thompson 1967, 81, Fig 83, 5; Ard Mhusáem na H-Éireann 1973, E 71–16871 and 3981; Groenman-van Waateringe 1975, 24; Groenman-van Waateringe 1984, Typ 6).

Uppers, Type Bii: boot with tunnel holes for two rows of thongs (Illus 131)

Type Bii consists of 16 one-piece boots with tunnel holes for two or more rows of horizontal thongs. Cat No 537/A6416a has a thong wrapped twice around it, passing through two tunnel holes, one above the other, on the closed side of the quarters and through two tunnel holes on the other side, one of which spans the junction of quarters and second leg flap. Cat No 358/A6773g has two tunnel holes, one above the other, on the closed side of the quarters, one tunnel hole on the open side and a single hole at the vamp throat. A length of thong, knotted on the flesh side, passes through the hole at the vamp throat. A second fragment of thong, tied to a third piece, is still threaded through the tunnel hole on the open side (Illus 131).

Uppers, Type Bi–iv.

Cat/Accession	Type	Area	Rig	Feature	Phase
South Sector					
3/A12303c	Bi	1	V, VI	MC002	Ia
30/A10800d	Bi	1	V	MC008, T3774	Ib
117/A03–0002b	Bi	4	V, VI	MC023	Icc,Id
126/A12297b	Bi	3	V	MC025, Pit 5337	(Ia–)Id
161/A7787h	Biii	1/2	VI	B6 (Phase 1), South Room–Floor (1)	Ie
179/A7589e	Bii	2	VI	M14b(b)	Ie
183/A7597b	Bi	2	VI	M14b(b)	Ie
191/A7797e	Bi	2	VI	M14b(b)	Ie
192/A13004a	Bii	2	VI	M14b(b)	Ie
193/A13004b	Biii	2	VI	M14b(b)	Ie
239/A7072b	Biii	2	V	M14b(c)	Ie,If
255/A12287a	Bi	3	V	MC034a	Ie(If)
267/A7044Bg	Bi	2	VI	MC044b	If
285/A9556b	Biv	3	VI	MC053c	If
296/A12632b	Bi	4	V	B16b, Pit 4726	Id–IIa
307/A12635c	Bi	4	V	B16b, Pit 4726	Id–IIa
313/A12310	Biii	3	V	MC039, Pit 2609	If,IIa
357/A6773f	Bi	2	VI	MC061	IIb
358/A6773g	Bii	2	VI	MC061	IIb
360/A6951a	Bii	2	VI	MC061	IIb
390/A12296b	Bi	1	VI	MC065	IIa–IIc
404/A12298a	Biii	3	VI	MC056, Pit 5155	Ia–IIc
411/A12493f	Biii	3	VI	MC056, Pit 5155	Ia–IIc
442/A64831	Biii	2	VI	B4, 'Byre'–Occupation	IIc
461/A10511	Bi	3	VI	M1.1c, Pit 5005	IId
473/A12285e	Biv	3	VI	M1.1c, Pit 5005	IId
508/A3447e	Bi	2	VI	M1.1d & M1.1e	IId–IIf
527/A6803	Bi	1/2	V	B5, South Room–Floor/Occupation (3)	IIa–IIff
537/A6416a	Bii	1/2	V	B5, North Room–Floor/Occupation (1)	IIa–IIff
631/A10047a	Biii	3	V	M10	IId–IIg
730/A9356	Bii	4	VI	B12, Pit 2345	IIe–IIg
778/A9371d	Biii	3	VI	M1.2, Pit 2648	<IIg(IIh)
785/A9372c	Bii	3	VI	M1.2, Pit 2648	<IIg(IIh)
853/A11253	Bii	4	V, VI	M11	IIh
931/A12305	Biii	1	VI	MC111	IIb–IIIb
934/A03–0327b	Biii	9	VII	P8.0	IIIa,IIIb
1088/A03–0278c	Bii	9	VII	B19 (Phase 2b), North Room–Floor (2b)	IIIc
1147/A5893b	Bii	1	V	M12	IIg–IIIc(–IVa)
1208/A8680c	Bi	3	V	M6b	IIg–IIId
1555/A03–0422c	Bi	7	VII	MC130	<IIIc–IVaa
1880/A03–0353c	Bii	7	VII	MC126, Pit 7402	IVaa,IVb
2653/A03–0316c	Bii	7	VII	B18 (Phase 1/2), Pit 7324	IVb
3242/A4940a	Biv	4	V, VI	M1.4b	IVb–IVcc
3320/A03–0262b	Bii	7	VII	P8.3	IVc,IVcc
3621/A4914	Bii	3	VI	M1.4e	IVcc(Va)
5257/A03–0050	Bii	7	VII	B53 (Phase 2), North Area–Occupation (14)	Vbb
5740/A12307d	Biii	1	V, VI	Unstratified	u/s
5755/A6383b	Biii	2	V, VI	Unstratified	u/s
5815/A12487f	Bii	2	V, VI	Unstratified	u/s
North Sector					
5889/A7805c	Biv	5	–	CG005	4(5)
5907/A7585b	Biii	5	–	CG013	(5–)7–9
5943/A0807b	Biii	5, A	–	Lade(4)	6–12(b–e)
South/North Sectors					
5978/L1694e	Biii	–	–	Unstratified	u/s

Uppers, Type Bi: low boot with tunnel hole for thong (Illus 129–30).

Cat/Accession	Area	Rig	Feature	Phase
South Sector				
3/A12303c	1	V, VI	MC002	Ia
30/A10800d	1	V	MC008, T3774	Ib
117/A03–0002b	4	V, VI	MC023	Icc,Id
126/A12297b	3	V	MC025, Pit 5337	(Ia–)Id
183/A7597b	2	VI	M14b(b)	Ie
191/A7797e	2	VI	M14b(b)	Ie
255/A12287a	3	V	MC034a	Ie(If)
267/A7044Bg	2	VI	MC044b	If
296/A12632b	4	V	B16b, Pit 4726	Id–IIa
307/A12635c	4	V	B16b, Pit 4726	Id–IIa
357/A6773f	2	VI	MC061	IIb
390/A12296b	1	VI	MC065	IIa–IIc
461/A10511	3	VI	M1.1c, Pit 5005	IId
508/A3447e	2	VI	M1.1d & M1.1e	IId–IIf
527/A6803	1/2	V	B5, South Room–Floor/Occupation (3)	IIa–IIff
1208/A8680c	3	V	M6b	IIg–IIId
1555/A03–0422c	7	VII	MC130	<IIIc–IVaa

Uppers, Type Bii: boot with tunnel holes for two rows of thongs (Illus 131).

Cat/Accession	Area	Rig	Feature	Phase
South Sector				
179/A7589e	2	VI	M14b(b)	Ie
192/A13004a	2	VI	M14b(b)	Ie
358/A6773g	2	VI	MC061	IIb
360/A6951a	2	VI	MC061	IIb
537/A6416a	1/2	V	B5, North Room–Floor/Occupation (1)	IIa–IIf
730/A9356	4	VI	B12, Pit 2345	IIe–IIg
785/A9372c	3	VI	M1.2, Pit 2648	<IIg(IIh)
853/A11253	4	V, VI	M11	IIh
1088/A03–0278c	9	VII	B19 (Phase 2b), North Room–Floor (2b)	IIIc
1147/A5893b	1	V	M12	IIg–IIIc(–IVa)
1880/A03–0353c	7	VII	MC126, Pit 7402	IVaa,IVb
2653/A03–0316c	7	VII	B18 (Phase 1/2), Pit 7324	IVb
3320/A03–0262b	7	VII	P8.3	IVc,IVcc
3621/A4914	3	VI	M1.4e	IVcc(Va)
5257/A03–0050	7	VII	B53 (Phase 2), North Area–Occupation (14)	Vbb
5815/A12487f	2	V, VI	Unstratified	u/s

Cat Nos 2653/A03–0316c (Illus 146) and 785/A9372c have two and three tunnel holes on either side of the quarters, respectively; the latter upper also has a hole in the vamp wing, with a fragment of thong through it.

Some boots have tunnel holes that were apparently never used. Cat No 3621/A4914 has one obviously used tunnel hole, but above and below it are a pair of short slits, probably unstretched tunnel holes (Illus 131). Similarly, Cat No 192/A13004a (Illus 131) has three tunnel holes, the top one of which consists of a pair of slits and Cat No 358/A6773g, discussed above, has, on the closed side of the quarters, two probably unused tunnel holes above the two already described, suggesting that the boot was originally prepared for four horizontal rows of thonging (Illus 131).

Type Bii uppers, like others of one-piece design, usually contain additional fragments. Cat No 358/A6773g, with five parts, has already been discussed (see Uppers–Introduction above). Cat No 785/A9372c probably originally had a small triangular sidepiece, as well as a second leg flap, both of which Cat No 179/A7589e (Illus 131) also had. Cat No 192/A13004a (Illus 131) still retains its side-piece; the latter example also has a stiffener. The second leg-flap of Cat No 537/A6416a is still in situ, held in place by the thong wrapped round this boot.

Uppers of this type were found in contexts ranging in date from slightly before 1150 until the early 14th century, but were predominantly (50%) of 12th-century date. Two (12.5.%) examples came from Period I, six

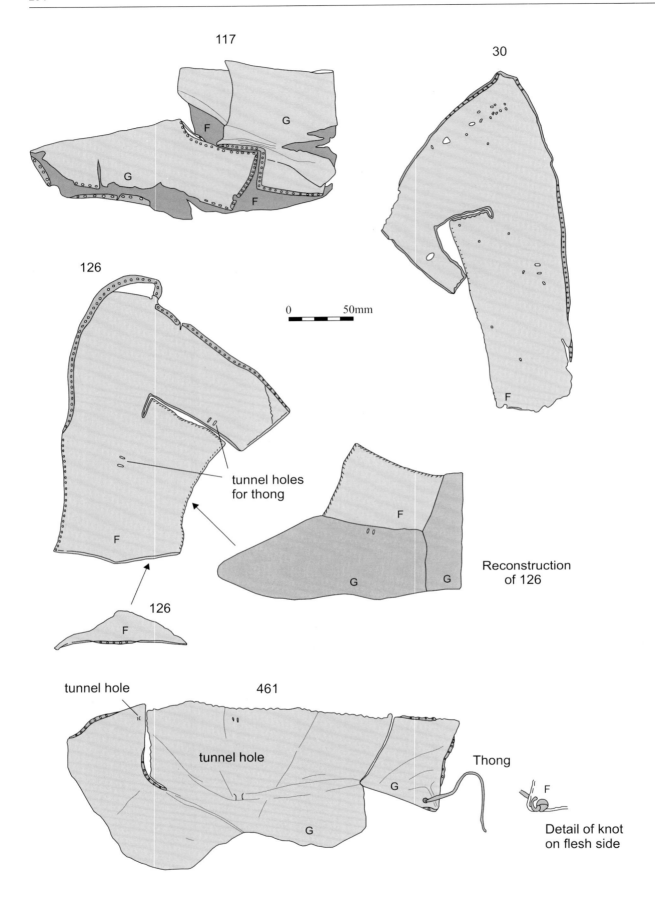

117

30

126

0   50mm

tunnel holes
for thong

Reconstruction
of 126

126

F

tunnel hole

461

tunnel hole

Thong

Detail of knot
on flesh side

Illus 129 *Uppers, Type Bi.*

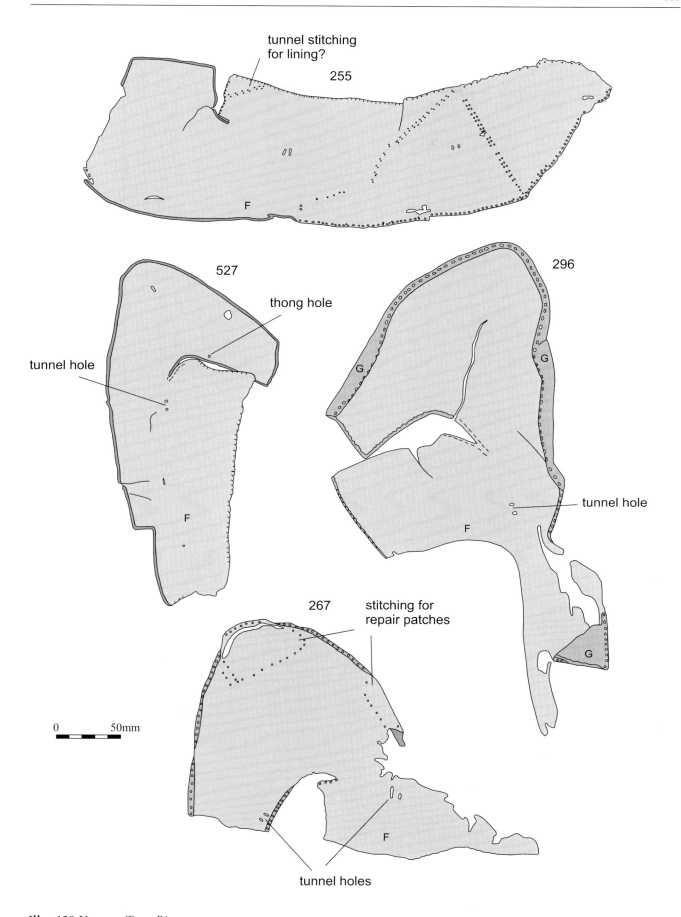

tunnel stitching
for lining?
255

thong hole

tunnel hole

527

296

G

G

F

tunnel hole

F

F

G

267   stitching for
           repair patches

0   50mm

tunnel holes

F

Illus 130 *Uppers, Type Bi.*

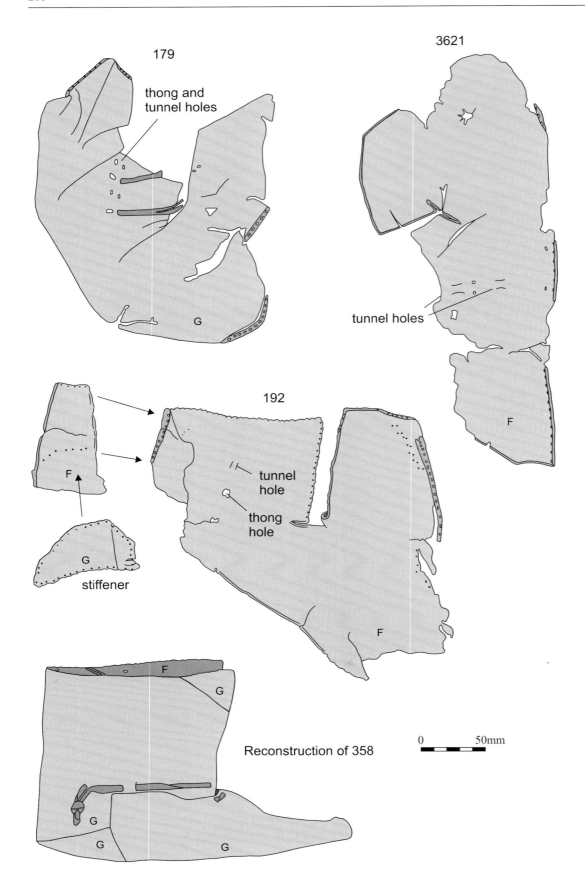

Illus 131 *Uppers, Type Bii.*

(37%) from Period II, two (12.5%) from Period III, four (25%) from Period IV, one (6%) from Period V and one (6%) unstratified. As with those of Type Bi, these uppers occurred singly, except for two groups of two found in M14b(b) and MC061.

Parallels, of mainly 12th- to 14th-century date, include London (early–mid 13th century); Newcastle (mid 13th–mid 14th centuries); Bristol Bridge, Bristol (13th–14th centuries); Coventry; York (12th–13th centuries); Waterford (12th century); Bergen (late 12th–mid 13th centuries); Schleswig (12th–14th centuries); Lübeck (the end of the 12th century–mid 13th century) and Bremen (12th–15th centuries) (Grew and de Neergaard 1988, 14–19, Figs 13–14, 20–21, 24; Dixon 1988, 93–5, Fig 33, nos 192 and 193; Thomas forthcoming a; Thomas 1980, 52–78/51/60 and 162–78/82/56; Mould et al 2003; O'Rourke 1997, 704, Fig 18.4.1; Larsen 1992, 19–20, Fig 14b; Schnack 1992b, 106–14, Figs 64, 66–68, 70–73, 75; Groenman-van Waateringe and Guiran 1978, Typ 6; Schnack 1993, 62–4, Fig 1b).

Uppers, Type Biii: boot with vertical thonging
(Illus 132–4)
Type Biii consists of 16 uppers with vertical thonging, threaded through tunnel holes formed by pairs of short horizontal slits, as on Cat No 5740/Al2307d (Illus 132). These vertical thongs were apparently used to secure wrap-around horizontal thongs, as on Cat No 934/A03–0327b (Illus 134). This upper has, on the closed side of the quarters, a row of vertical thonging with five short stretches of thong on the grain side, through the lowest of which a long horizontal thong has been threaded. This horizontal thong also passes through the second leg flap, which has two vertical rows of thonging; one of these rows spans the junction of the leg flap and vamp wing. Cat No 931/A12305 (Illus 134) also has a vertical thong on each side as

well as a horizontal thong. The vertical thong on the sidepiece ends with a short horizontal stretch on the flesh side at both top and bottom; the top end points towards the quarters, the bottom one towards the vamp throat. It is not clear whether these thongs were turned horizontally in order to secure them, or were originally intended to pass round the foot, with the bottom one perhaps linking up with the surviving horizontal thong which runs from vamp throat to vamp wing. An upper from King's Lynn, which has vertical thongs, suggests the latter possibility; in this case, the bottom ends of the thongs become horizontal, passing forwards, on the flesh side, to single holes on the vamp wings. The vertical thongs on two other uppers, however, are knotted at the base and end there (Clarke and Carter 1977, 352–354, Fig 165, nos 24, 19 and 23). Three uppers from Coventry had clear indentations from horizontal thongs, at the same level as part of the vertical thonging; on 78/82/31, these indentations were 'at a level with the lowest three loops' (of the vertical thonging), while on A830/10, the impression corresponded 'to the position of the lowest loop' (Thomas 1980, 51–78/51/58; 132–49/195/74; 150–A830/10; 155–78/82/31). This evidence strongly supports the suggestion that the vertical thongs were used to secure horizontal wrap-around laces; it is probable that not all the loops of the vertical thongs were used and that often only the lowest loop was used. Vertical thongs were almost certainly also used for their decorative effect.

Six uppers have additional pieces surviving. Cat Nos 161/A7787h (Illus 132) and 239/A7072b (Illus 132) have side-pieces and second leg flaps; Cat No 313/Al2310 (Illus 145) has a sidepiece and a top band. Cat No 934/A03–0327b (Illus 134) has a second leg flap; this upper also has an unusually high vamp wing, reaching to the top edge of the boot.

Uppers, Type Biii: boot with vertical thonging (Illus 132–4).

Cat/Accession	Area	Rig	Feature	Phase
South Sector				
161/A7787h	1/2	VI	B6 (Phase 1), South Room–Floor (1)	Ie
193/A13004b	2	VI	M14b(b)	Ie
239/A7072b	2	V	M14b(c)	Ie,If
313/A12310	3	V	MC039, Pit 2609	If,IIa
404/A12298a	3	VI	MC056, Pit 5155	Ia–IIc
411/A12493f	3	VI	MC056, Pit 5155	Ia–IIc
442/A6483l	2	VI	B4, 'Byre'–Occupation	IIc
631/A10047a	3	V	M10	IId–IIg
778/A9371d	3	VI	M1.2, Pit 2648	<IIg(IIh)
931/A12305	1	VI	MC111	IIb–IIIb
934/A03–0327b	9	VII	P8.0	IIIa,IIIb
5740/A12307d	1	VI, VII	Unstratified	u/s
5755/A6383b	2	V, VI	Unstratified	u/s
North Sector				
5907/A7585b	5	–	CG013	(5–)7–9
5943/A0807b	5, A	–	Lade (4)	6–12(b–e)
South/North Sectors				
5978/L1694e	–	–	Unstratified	u/s

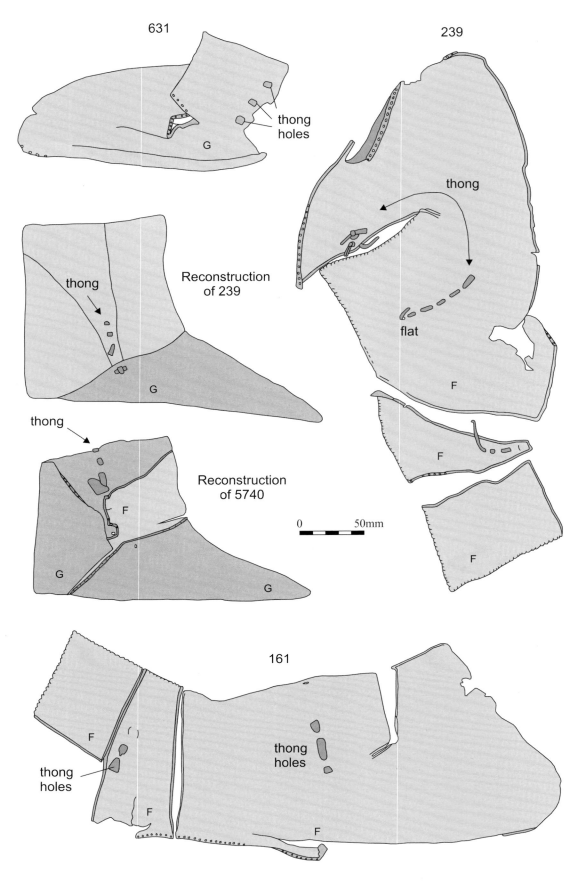

Illus 132 *Uppers, Type Biii.*

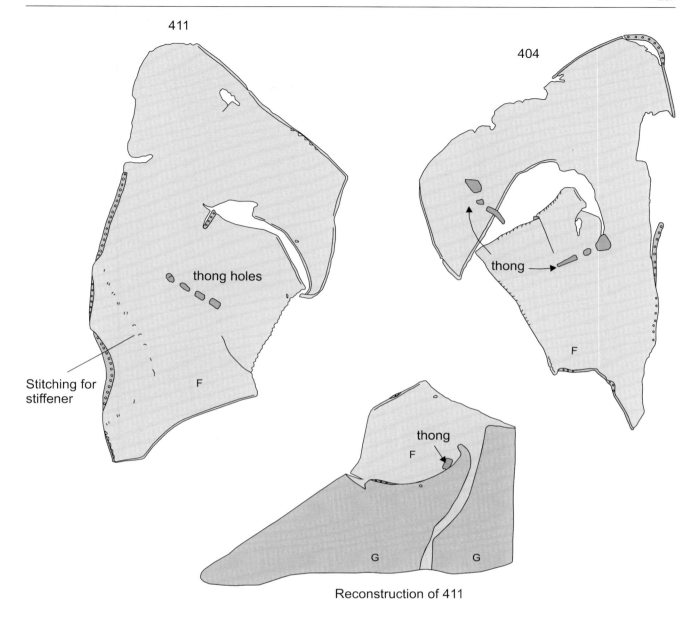

411

404

thong holes

thong

Stitching for
stiffener

F

F

thong

F

G   G

Reconstruction of 411

Illus 133 *Uppers, Type Biii.*

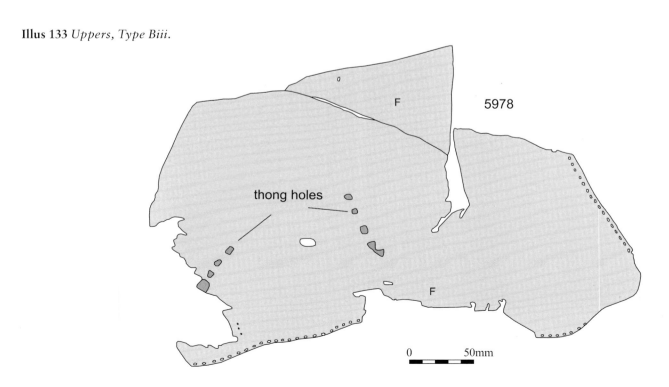

F

5978

thong holes

F

0   50mm

Cat No 931/Al2305 (Illus 134) has a sidepiece, Cat No 5978/L1694e (Illus 133) part of the first leg flap, but both their second leg flaps are missing, as in Cat No 411/Al2493f (Illus 133).

The stratified South Sector Type Biii uppers date from the slightly before 1150 until the early 13th century, belonging mainly to the 12th century, with at least three (18%) examples from Period I, six (37%) from Period II and two (13%) from Period III. Apart from three unstratified examples (Cat Nos 5704/A12307d, 5755/A6383d and 5978/L1694e), two examples of Type Biii boots were also found in Area 5/Trench A. One of these (Cat No 5907/A7585b) came from deposits that dated from the 12th or 13th centuries. The other (Cat No 5943/A0807b), however, came from the infill of Lade (4), the Town Ditch. This infilling was of 14th century and later date. Again, these uppers were found singly, with the exception of two found together in Pit 5155 (MC056). A very well preserved boot of this type was recovered from 1–5 High Street, Perth, but unfortunately it was unstratified (Thomas 1987, 186). Other parallels, predominantly of 12th–13th-century date, include 45–75 Gallowgate (1350–1375) and Gallowgate Middle School (12th–13th centuries), Aberdeen; King's Lynn (1050–1250); London (late 12th–13th centuries); Bristol Bridge, Bristol (13th–14th centuries); Nantwich (12th century?); York (12th–13th centuries); Waterford (12th–13th centuries); Bremen (12th–15th centuries); Bergen (late 12th–early 13th centuries); Schleswig (12th–13th centuries); Lübeck (the end of the 12th century–mid 13th century); Deventer (12th century) and Konstanz (13th–15th centuries) (Thomas 2001a, 243; Clarke and Carter 1977, 352–54, Fig 165, nos 19, 23–24; Grew and de Neergaard 1988, 14–15, Figs 15 and 16; Thomas forthcoming a; Hutchings 1983, 80–1, Fig 16, L 10; Carlisle 1998 unpublished; O'Rourke 1997, 704, Fig 18.1.3; Schnack 1993, 62–4, Fig 1c; Larsen 1992, 19–20, Fig 14b; Schnack 1992b, 107–14, Abb 51 Typ B, Figs 65, 74, 78–79; Groenman-van Waateringe and Guiran 1978, Typ 7; Groenman-van Waateringe 1975, 24–5, Fig 2.6, 34, note 2; Schnack 1994, 29, Taf 22, 23). Undated parallels were found at Coventry, York (Parliament Street), Beverley, S'Hertogen-bosch and Oud Naarden (Thomas 1980, 51, 132, 150, 155; Tweddle 1986, 246–53, Fig 113, no 820; Jackson 1983, 69, Figs 6 and 7 no 3; Goubitz 1983, Type 1; Groenman-van Waateringe 1975, 24–5, Fig 2.6, 34, note 2).

Upper, Type Biv: boot with possible thong hole on vamp wing (Illus 134)

Four boots of one-piece design have only a single thong hole surviving as in Cat No 5889/A7805c (Illus 134), which has a thong, knotted on the flesh side, threaded through a slit in the vamp wing; this boot also has a crease which might have been caused by a wrap-around thong. The other holes on this upper are the result of wear. It is possible that these boots originally had other thong holes and were therefore of Types Bi, Bii or Biii, but none are complete enough to enable further definition.

At least two examples (50%) date from the 12th century, a third to the later 13th century. A fourth is from Area 5; it came, however, from some of the earlier deposits in that area, and could well also be of 12th century date. It is certainly of no later date than the 13th century. The earliest of the Type Biv boots from the South Sector was recovered from a deposit that was laid down shortly before 1150. It is possible that all three of the South Sector Type Biv boots come from one property. The two 12th century examples certainly came from Rig VI, while Cat No 3242/A4940a was found within a midden which had built up after that property had been combined with that to the west of it, Rig V.

Upper, Type C: boot with side lacing (Illus 135)

Type C consists of 14 boots of one-piece design with side lacing linking quarters with vamp wing or side-piece and with the second leg flap. The lacing was threaded through tie-holes, placed parallel to the vertical edges of quarters, vamp wings, side-pieces and leg flaps; these edges have been oversewn. On three examples, including Cat Nos 503/A03–0003b (Illus 135) and 2725/A03–0413a (Illus 135), the edges beneath the lowest tie-hole have been stitched together with an edge–flesh seam. Seven uppers have a row of tunnel stitching on the flesh side, parallel to the tie-holes; this was almost certainly used to attach a strengthener or facing, which would also have been secured by the oversewing on the edge, as in Cat Nos 1043/A8671a, 2745/A03–0294a (Illus 135), 2771/A03–0123a (Illus 135) and 2725/A03–0413a (Illus 135).

No strengtheners or facings have survived from the High Street, but examples were found at The Custom House site, London (early–mid 14th century); the Barbican Ditch, Oxford (13th–15th centuries); King's Lynn (1050–1350); Coppergate, York and at Coventry.

Upper, Type Biv: boot with possible thong hole on vamp wing (Illus 134).

Cat/Accession	Area	Rig	Feature	Phase
South Sector				
285/A9556b	3	VI	MC053c	If
473/A12285e	3	VI	M1.1c, Pit 5005	IId
3242/A4940a	4	V, VI	M1.4b	IVb–IVcc
North Sector				
5889/A7805c	5	–	CG005	4(5)

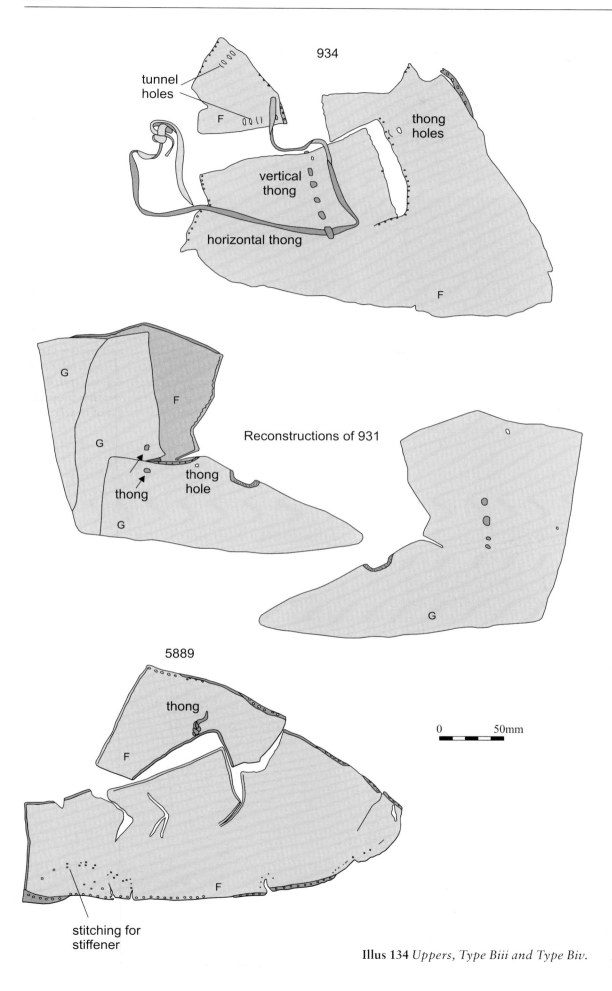

Illus 134 *Uppers, Type Biii and Type Biv.*

These consisted of V-shaped strips of leather, oversewn on all edges, perforated by round holes. At Coventry, three facings were found in situ, while nine other boots had stitching for facings (Tatton-Brown 1975, 159, nos 86, 88, Fig 28, nos 86, 89; Hassall 1976, 281, Fig 20, no 39; Clarke and Carter 1977, 361, Fig 168, no 79, 363, where they were described as binding of a jerkin; Mould et al 2003; Thomas 1980, 13, 14, 23, 40, 48, 56, 59, 71, 74, 92, 95, 105, 128–132, 135, 143, 157).

At the High Street, these Type C boots were found in contexts dating from the second half of the 12th century to the early 14th century, but were mainly (65%) of mid-13th- to early 14th-century date; with two (14%) examples from Period II, three (21%) from Period III, eight (58%) from IV and one (7%) from V. They were distributed singly over the site apart from two, found in P8.1c and M1.4f and four found in B18 (Phase 2).

Parallels, with or without surviving facings, tend to be later, being mainly of 14th- to 15th-century date: 45–75 Gallowgate, Aberdeen (1350–1375); Bristol Bridge, Bristol (13th–14th centuries); London (early– mid 14th century, early–mid 15th century); Sandwell Priory (14th–15th centuries); Exeter (15th century?), Coppergate, York (14th–15th centuries) and Konstanz (14th–15th centuries). Undated parallels were also found at Hull and S'Hertogenbosch (Thomas 2001a; Thomas forthcoming a; Grew and de Neergaard 1988, 27, Fig 39–40, 42–43, Figs 68–70; Thomas 1991, 107, 109, Fig 37, 9; Friendship-Taylor 1984, 324, 327–30; Mould et al 2003; Schnack 1994, 29–30, 3.3.8, Tafel 25–27; Watkin 1987, Fig 130, 423–425; Goubitz 1983, type 3).

Upper, Type C/D: boots and/or shoes with tie holes (not illustrated)

Eleven fragments of uppers have tie holes, most probably for side lacing, but it is not possible to determine whether these are parts of boots or shoes. On five fragments, the edge parallel to the tie holes has been oversewn; three examples also have tunnel stitching for facings, (oversewn) Cat Nos 1136/A03– 0265a, 1137/A03–026 5b, (possibly oversewn) 2796/ A03–0152b, (oversewn) 2706/A03–0296c tunnel stitching, (oversewn) 1704/ A03–0396a, 1705/A03– 0396b, 1706/A03–0396c, 1707/A03–0396d tunnel stitching, 2363/A03–0331c tunnel stitching. All eight fragments are of mid–late 13th-century date. Apart from a single example that was recovered from a Rig VI midden, this category is noteworthy as having come from Rig VII (6) and Rig VIII (4).

Uppers, Types Di and Dii (Illus 136–7)

Type D consists of 16 shoes, not boots, with side lacing. The uppers are of one-piece design, but usually with second leg flaps or latchets and occasionally with side-pieces. The leg flaps or latchets are small and were not apparently used as fastenings. The shoes were laced with thongs threaded through tie-holes; on Type Di, these tie-holes were on adjacent edges of quarters and vamp wing or side-piece, whereas on Type Dii, both rows of tie-holes were on a side-piece, specially split for this purpose. The edges parallel to the tie-holes have been oversewn; several uppers have tunnel stitching for strengtheners or facings. Opposing tie-holes were not usually arranged in pairs, indicating different lacing methods from present ones. Groenman-van Waateringe has considered at length medieval methods of lacing. Of particular interest, with regard to Types C and D, is a method for shoes with an unequal number of tie-holes on either side. This method was observed on a 17th-century shoe. A single lace is looped through the lowest hole of the longer vertical or diagonal row and both ends are then passed through the opposite hole.

Upper, Type C: boot with side lacing (Illus 135).

Cat/Accession	Area	Rig	Feature	Phase
South Sector				
503/A03–0003b	3	V	P2.1a	IIb–IIf
790/A9546c	3	VI	M1.2, Pit 2648	<IIg(IIh)
1043/A8671a	3	V	MC117, Pit 4695	IIe–IIIc
1098/A03–0270d	9	VII	P8.1c	IIIc
1115/A03–0323d	9	VII	P8.1c	IIIc
2292/A03–0271d	7	VI	M1.4f	IVc
2434/A03–0355a	7	VI	M1.4f	IVc
2725/A03–0413a	7	VII	B18 (Phases 2a & 2b), T7385	IVb
2745/A03–0294a	7	VII	B18 (Phase 2a), North Room & Hall– Construction (1)	IVb
2771/A03–0123a	9	VII	B18 (Phase 2b), North Room, Hall & Hall South–Occupation (10)	IVb
2784/A03–0245e	9	VII	B18 (Phase 2b), North Room, Hall & Hall South–Occupation (10)	IVb
2877/A9357c	3	V	MC155, Pit 2691	IVb,IVc
3102/A6240	2	VI	M1.4d	IVb,IVc
4130/A03–0214h	7	VII	P8.4	Va

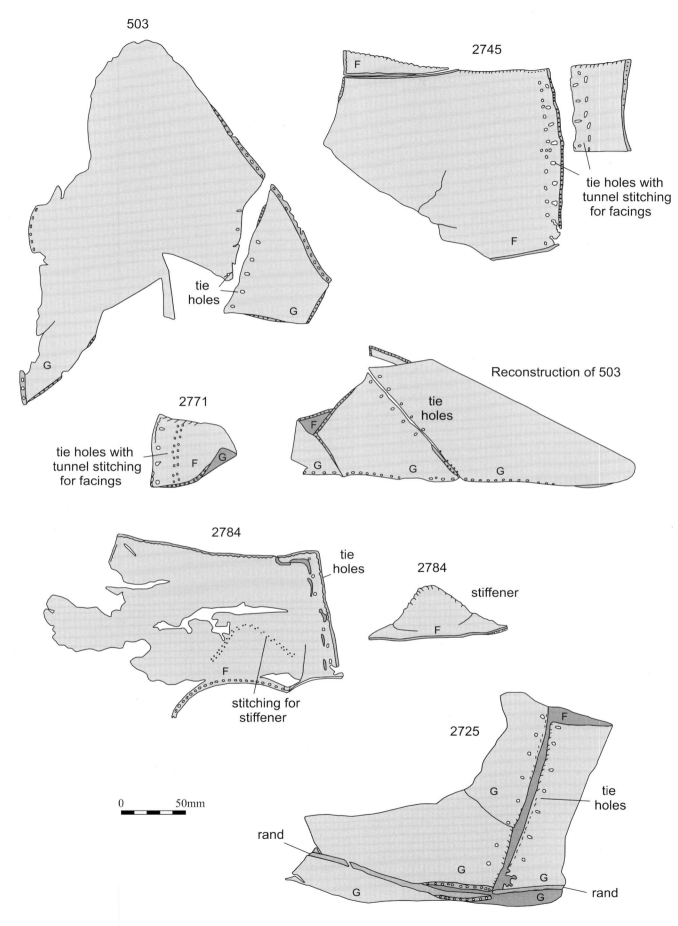

503

2745

tie holes with
tunnel stitching
for facings

tie
holes

G

2771

tie holes with
tunnel stitching
for facings

F   G

Reconstruction of 503

tie
holes

F

G   G   G

2784

tie
holes

2784

stiffener

F

stitching for
stiffener

F

0   50mm

2725

F

G

tie
holes

rand

G

G   G

rand

Illus 135 *Uppers, Type C.*

Upper. Type C/D: boot and/or shoe with tie holes.

Cat/Accession	Area	Rig	Feature	Phase
South Sector				
1136/A03–0265a	9	VII	M15	IIId
1137/A03–0265b	9	VII	M15	IIId
1704/A03–0396a	10	VIII	MC131	<IVa–IVb
1705/A03–0396b	10	VIII	MC131	<IVa–IVb
1706/A03–0396c	10	VIII	MC131	<IVa–IVb
1707/A03–0396d	10	VIII	MC131	<IVa–IVb
2363/A03–0331c	7	VI	M1.4f	IVc
2706/A03–0296c	7	VII	B18 (Phase 1/2), MF 7307	IVaa,IVb
2796/A03–0152b	9	VII	B18 (Phase 2b), North Room, Hall & Hall South–Occupation (10)	IVb
3354/A03–0246c	7	VII	M9a	IVc,IVcc
3418/A03–0275b	7	VII	B18 (Phases 2a & 2b) & M9a, PH7297	(IVb)IVc,IVcc

Upper, Type Di and Dii (Illus 136–7).

Cat/Accession	Type	Area	Rig	Feature	Phase
South Sector					
1105/A03–0287c	Dii	9	VII	P8.1c	IIIc
1287/A6415c	Di	3	V	P2.2b	IVa
1288/A6415d	Di	3	V	P2.2b	IVa
1362/A8007b	Di	4	V	MC143	IVaa
1804/A03–0367a	Di	7	VII	MC126, Pit 7402	IVaa,IVb
2193/A03–0386	Di	7	VII	MC126, Pit 7402	IVaa,IVb
2302/A03–0276c	Di	7	VI	M1.4f	IVc
2303/A03–0276d	Di	7	VI	M1.4f	IVc
2759/A03–0288f	Dii	7	VII	B18 (Phase 2b), North Room, Hall & Hall South–Occupation (10)	IVb
2772/A03–0123b	Di	9	VII	B18 (Phase 2b), North Room, Hall & Hall South–Occupation (10)	IVb
2801/A03–0078	Di	9	VII	B18 (Phase 2b), Hall & Hall South–Occupation (12a)	IVb
3364/A03–0223b	Di	7	VII	M9a	IVc,IVcc
3385/A03–0233b	Dii	7	VII	M9a	IVc,IVcc
3406/A03–0052b	Dii	9	VII	M9a	IVc,IVcc
3434/A03–0073	Di	9	VII	M9a, Pit 9078	IVc,IVcc
3595/A4318a	Di	3	VI	M1.4e	IVcc(Va)

Upper, Type Di: shoe with side lacing (Illus 136–7, 145).

Cat/Accession	Area	Rig	Feature	Phase
South Sector				
1287/A6415c	3	V	P2.2b	IVa
1288/A6415d	3	V	P2.2b	IVa
1362/A8007b	4	V	MC143	IVaa
1804/A03–0367a	7	VII	MC126, Pit 7402	IVaa,IVb
2193/A03–0386	7	VII	MC126, Pit 7402	IVaa,IVb
2302/A03–0276c	7	VI	M1.4f	IVc
2303/A03–0276d	7	VI	M1.4f	IVc
2772/A03–0123b	9	VII	B18 (Phase 2b), North Room, Hall & Hall South–Occupation (10)	IVb
2801/A03–0078	9	VII	B18 (Phase 2b), Hall & Hall South–Occupation (12a)	IVb
3364/A03–0223b	7	VII	M9a	IVc,IVcc
3434/A03–0073	9	VII	M9a, Pit 9078	IVc,IVcc
3595/A4318a	3	VI	M1.4e	IVcc(Va)

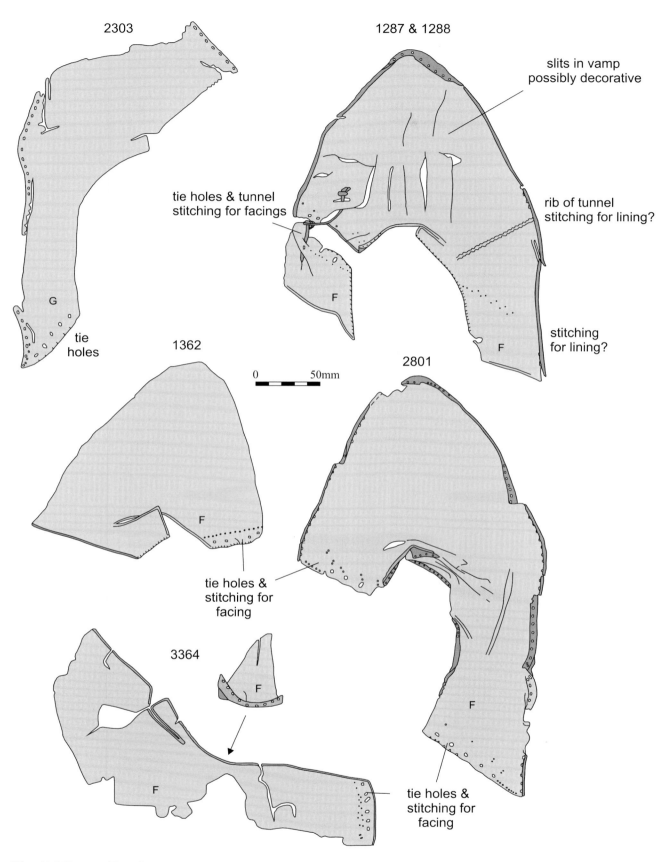

Illus 136 *Uppers, Type Di.*

One end of the lace is passed backwards and forwards, from one side to the other, emerging at the top hole of the longer row. The other end of the lace is threaded up the shorter row, then across to the top hole of the longer row, so that both ends of the lace pass through the same hole, but one from the grain side, the other from the flesh side (Groenman-van Waateringe 1975, 31, Fig 9.2).

In another method of lacing, opposing pairs of holes were linked by single thongs one end of which was sewn to the flesh side of the upper, then threaded through the two holes. Thus, a shoe with three holes on each side would have had three horizontal thongs. A third method used a strip of leather, c15mm wide, split for most of its length; the unsplit end was sewn to the flesh side and the two laces threaded through matching pairs of holes and were then knotted (Groenman-van Waateringe 1975, 30, 31, Fig 9.3, 9.1, 9.5).

Dating from mid to later 13th century, 62% of the Type D shoes came from just one property, Rig VII.

Upper, Type Di: shoe with side lacing
(Illus 136, 137, 145)
Twelve uppers were of Type Di, with the tie-holes on the quarters and on the vamp wing or sidepiece. On one example, Cat No 2801/A03–0078 (Illus 136), the edges beneath the lowest tie-hole have been sewn together with an edge–flesh seam. Tunnel stitching for a facing or strengthener, similar to that found on Type C boots, survives on five uppers: Cat Nos 1287/A6415c and 1288/A6415d (Illus 136), 1362/A8007b (Illus 136), 2801/A03–0078 (Illus 136), 2772/A03–0123b, 3364/A03–0223b (Illus 136).

Two uppers, Cat Nos 1287/A6415c and 1288/A6415d (Illus 136) and 2302/A03–0276c, have side-pieces, with three and six tie-holes respectively. A triangular stiffener survives with upper Cat No 3364/A03–0223b (Illus 136). On Cat No 2193/A03–0386, both a stiffener and a second latchet are missing. Upper Cat Nos 1287/A6415c and 1288/A6415d (Illus 136) has a vertical row of tunnel stitches on the closed side of the vamp wing, possibly to secure a lining, which would have enhanced its openwork decoration. Cat No 1362/A8007b (Illus 136) is included here, although it has separate quarters and vamp; this is possibly the result of repairs.

All 12 Type Di uppers type came from contexts that probably dated from the second half of the 13th century (Period IV). Ten were found in twos, in P2.2b, MC126,

M1.4f, B18 (Phase 2b) and M9a. The majority (50%) came from Rig VII (6), but three were also recovered from both Rig V and Rig VI.

The illustrations of two shoes from King's Lynn (c1250–1350) appear to show tie-holes for side-lacing, but no mention is made of tie-holes in the otherwise detailed descriptions (Clarke and Carter 1977, 350–352, Fig 164, nos 3 and 7). Other parallels are also mainly of 13th- to 14th-century date: London (early–mid 13th century); Newcastle (mid 13th–mid 14th centuries); Bristol Bridge, Bristol (13th–14th centuries); Chapel Lane Staith, Hull (late 13th–mid 14th centuries); Exeter (c1300?); Coppergate, York (13th–14th centuries); Waterford (12th–13th centuries); Bergen (late 12th–mid 14th century); Schleswig (mainly 13th century); Konstanz (especially 13th and 14th centuries); Lübeck (the end of the 12th century–mid-13th century) and Amsterdam (13th–15th centuries) (Grew and de Neergaard 1988, 18–19, Figs 25–26, 56, 89; Dixon 1988, 94, Fig 34, no 199; Thomas forthcoming a; Jackson 1979, Fig 22, nos 20–21, 34; Friendship-Taylor 1984, 324, Fig 184.7; Mould et al 2003; O'Rourke 1997, 706; Larsen 1992, 20–1, Figs 17–18; Schnack 1992b, 78–84, Taf 22–23; Schnack 1994, 24, 3.3.2, Tafel 10–12; Groenman-van Waateringe and Guiran 1978, Typ 1; Groenman-van Waateringe 1975, 25–30, Figs 2.7 and 7.2). Later examples were found at Worcester (mid-15th century; dated by style of toe) and Bremen (14th–the first half of the 15th centuries) (Thornton 1969a, 57–8, no 2; Schnack 1993, 64–5, Fig 2a). Less securely dated or unstratified parallels include Whithorn and Coventry (Nicholson 1997, 502–3; Thomas 1980, 17, 48–78/51/46, 49/214/6 and 78/59/28).

Upper, Type Dii: shoes with side-pieces split for side lacing (Illus 137)
Type Dii consists of four shoes with side lacing. All these uppers have a sidepiece that has been split vertically or diagonally, to form a gusset; parallel to the edges of the gusset are tie-holes. The edges of the gusset have been oversewn; one example, Cat No 1105/A03–0287c, has tunnel stitching for a facing. All the side-pieces extend to the full height of the shoe, from lasting margin to top edge: Cat No 1105/A03–0287c is unusual in having at least four parts, vamp, quarters and inner and outer side-pieces, of which only the side-pieces remain, with a matching Type 2 sole. The outer sidepiece could have been added as a repair measure (Illus 137).

Upper, Type Dii: shoe with side pieces split for side lacing (Illus 137).

Cat/Accession	Area	Rig	Feature	Phase
South Sector				
1105/A03–0287c	9	VII	P8.1c	IIIc
2759/A03–0288f	7	VII	B18 (Phase 2b), North Room, Hall & Hall South–Occupation (10)	IVb
3385/A03–0233b	7	VII	M9a	IVc,IVcc
3406/A03–0052b	9	VII	M9a	IVc,IVcc

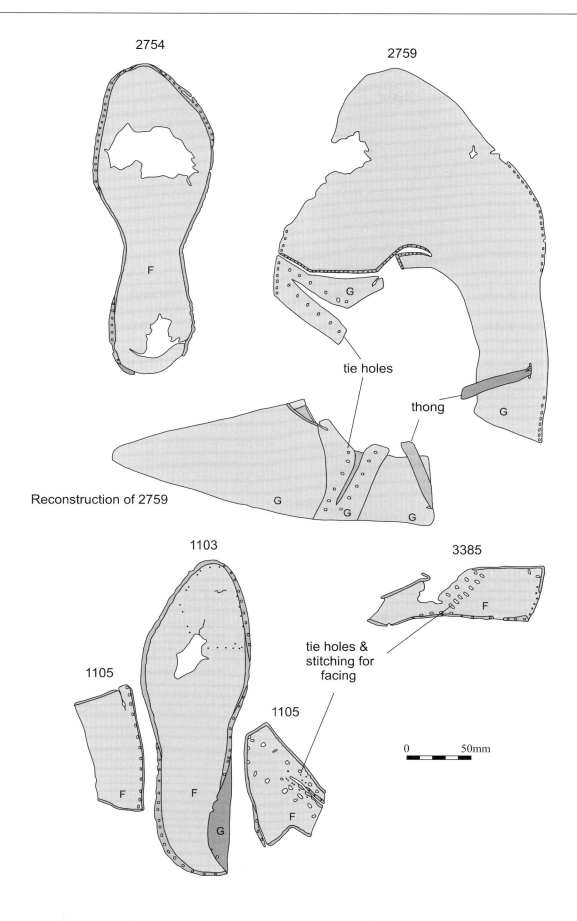

2754

2759

tie holes

thong

Reconstruction of 2759

G

1103

3385

tie holes &
stitching for
facing

1105

1105

0   50mm

Illus 137 *Uppers, Type Dii with matching soles, Type 2.*

All four examples were recovered from Rig VII deposits which are of mid- to late 13th-century date. Two were found in M9a and one each from P8.1c and B18 (Phase 2b).

Parallels for this sub-type are not very common, but are still of 13th–14th century date: London (early–mid-13th century); Bristol Bridge, Bristol (13th–14th centuries); Coppergate, York (13th–14th centuries); Waterford (12th–13th centuries) and Schleswig (chiefly 13th century) (Grew and de Neergaard 1988, 18–19, Fig 27, 57, Fig 90; Thomas forthcoming a; Mould et al 2003; O'Rourke 1997, 706; Schnack 1992b, 78–84, Taf 25, 2, 32, 1).

The only other possible parallel is a fragment from King's Lynn, dating to c1250–1350, described by Carter as an 'instep gusset from front-lacing shoe'. The illustrations show it to be very similar to the sidepiece of Cat No 1105/A03–0287c, except that the King's Lynn example has an edge–flesh stitching channel on its lower edge, not a lasting margin (Clarke and Carter 1977, 350–1, Fig 164, 6).

Upper, Type E: low shoe (Illus 138–9)

Type E consists of ten shoes with uppers of one-piece construction and with neither thongs nor holes for them. In many respects, these shoes were made to a similar pattern as Type A ankle-boots, but were cut lower on the sides of the foot, with the quarters rising to a dome or peak. Cat No 180/A7589f has a separate second latchet, while on Cat No 65/A8808 (Illus 138) both latchets, which do not meet, are made out of the same piece of leather as the vamp and quarters. This upper probably had a sidepiece. Its quarters have a domed or peaked top edge.

Cat No 476/Al2302b (Illus 139) has a stiffener, while stitching for a stiffener survives on four examples, as on Cat Nos 4307/A1233b (Illus 138) and 65/A8808 (Illus 138). The vamp of Cat No 162/A7787i (Illus 138) has been decorated with three approximately parallel lines out from throat to toe. It may have been stitched with coloured wool or silk (see Decorated uppers, above).

All (90%) but one of these uppers are of 12th-century date; the exception was from an early 14th-century

midden (M1.5a) with post-medieval contamination. Apart from two examples which were found in M14b(b) and another two in Pit 5005 (M1.1c), the rest were found singly. Of the nine 12th-century examples of Type E shoes, four of which belonged to Period I and five to Period II, seven came from Rig VI, one from Rig V and one from either Rig V or VI. By the time that Cat No 4307/A1223b was deposited in M1.5a, it is believed that these two properties had been combined.

The closest parallel, from London, is also of 12th-century date (early–mid-12th century; Grew and de Neergaard 1988, 53, Fig 84). A similar example from Worcester has a higher vamp throat, as does an upper from Schleswig (Thornton 1969a, 57–8, Fig 13, no 3, dated 1350–1450 on stylistic grounds; Schnack 1992b, Fig 95, 1, no 7409, 13th–14th centuries). Three of the Whithorn upper fragments have been assigned to this type but as there is no evidence for small latchets, it is possible that they might belong to Type F (Nicholson 1997, 502–503).

Upper, Type F: low shoe without fastenings
(Illus 139, 140)

Type F consists of three uppers of low shoes with no latchets and no apparent fastenings. Cat No 810/A11219a (Illus 139) is most probably a one-piece upper; its quarters have a domed top edge. A similar upper was found at King's Lynn, dated c1250 to 1350 (Clarke and Carter 1977, 350–2, Fig 164, no 12). Cat No 315/A10365b (Illus 139) is possibly a one-piece upper, with quarters and vamp wing joining, but if that were so it would not match the accompanying sole. As the front of the vamp appears to match the sole, it is more probable that the upper had separate quarters. This upper is so worn that it is hard to distinguish between cracked and deliberately cut edges. The toe of this shoe may have been stuffed with moss (see Sole (Type 6) above).

Cat No 3670/A7791 is of one-piece design, with an exceptionally high vamp throat and very low quarters; a separate sidepiece and an insert at the vamp throat no longer survive. The quarters of this shoe were most probably lined, with the lining attached to the flesh side by two rows of tunnel stitching, one parallel to the

Upper, Type E: low shoe (Illus 138–9).

Cat/Accession	Area	Rig	Feature	Phase
South Sector				
65/A8808	1/2	V, VI	M2.1b & B10, South Room–Floor/Occupation (1)	Ic,Icc
162/A7787i	1/2	VI	B6 (Phase 1), South Room–Floor (1)	Ie
180/A7589f	2	VI	M14b(b)	Ie
212/A7574b	2	VI	M14b(b), Pit 3625	Ie
327/A03–0009d	3	V	MC049, Pit 5259	IIa
449/A6771	2	VI	B4 'Byre'–Occupation	IIc
474/A12285f	3	VI	M1.1c, Pit 5005	IId
476/A12302b	3	VI	M1.1c, Pit 5005	IId
779/A9371e	3	VI	M1.2, Pit 2648	<IIg(IIh)
4307/A1223b	3	V, VI	M1.5a	Va,Vaa(VI)

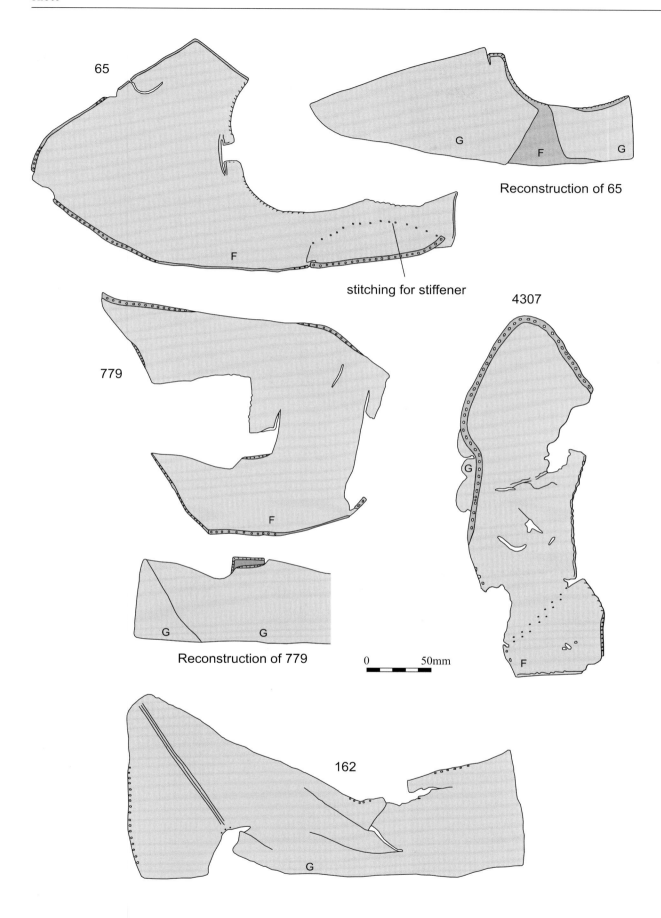

65

Reconstruction of 65

stitching for stiffener

779

4307

Reconstruction of 779

0   50mm

162

Illus 138 *Uppers, Type E.*

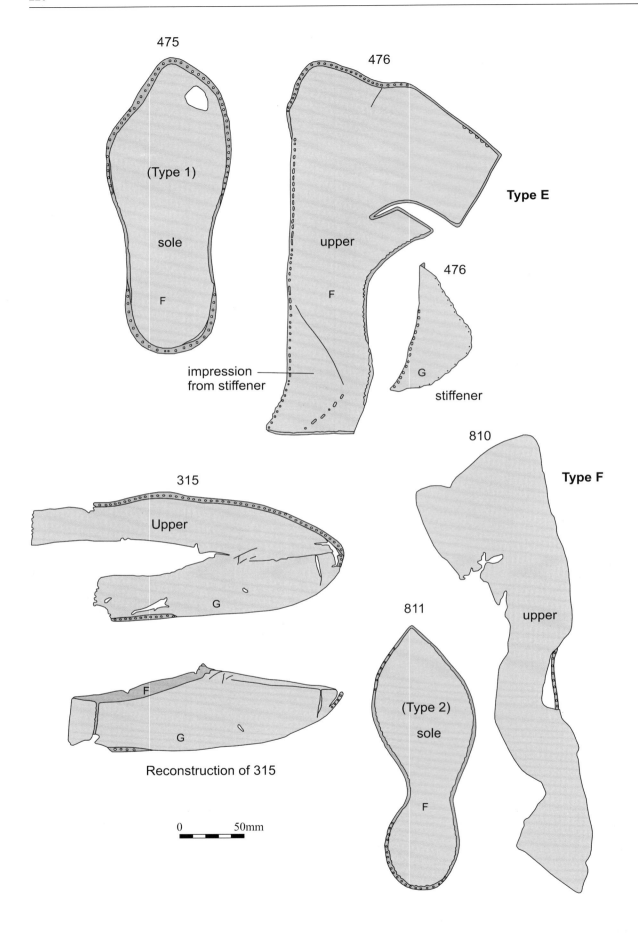

Illus 139 *Uppers, Type E and Type F with two matching soles, Types 1 and 2.*

vertical edge of the quarters, the other on the closed side of the quarters (Illus 140). The nearest parallel is another shoe from King's Lynn, dated c1250–1350 (Clarke and Carter 1977, 350–1, Fig 164, 11).

The two earliest Type F uppers from the High Street were found in Period II deposits that would have dated from the second half of the 12th century, while the third was recovered from a path (P6) which had been laid down in c1300. Two came from Rig VI and one from Rig V. The nearest parallels range in date from the mid-10th to the mid-14th centuries: Winchester (mid–late 10th century, slightly high throat); London (early–mid 12th century and early–mid 13th century); King's Lynn (c1250–1350); Coppergate, York (10th, 11th and 13th centuries); Swinegate, York (late 11th, 12th and 13th centuries); Waterford (12th–13th centuries); Bergen (late 12th–mid 14th centuries) and Schleswig (11th–12th centuries, high vamp throat, with all-over cut-out decoration) (Thornton 1990b, 601–2, Fig 160, no 1878; Grew and de Neergaard 1988, 12, Fig 11, 16, Figs 18–19; Clarke and Carter 1977, 350–1, Fig 164, nos 11 and 12; Mould et al 2003; Carlisle 1998; O'Rourke 1997, 706, Fig 18.2.2; Larsen 1992, 23–4, Figs 23–24; Schnack 1992b, Fig 92.2).

Upper, Type G: shoe with latchet ending in thong (Illus 140)

Type G consists of two high shoes or low boots with latchets ending in thongs for central fastening. Cat No 229/A7588c (Illus 140) is a one-piece upper, comprising vamp, with low vamp throat, vamp wings, quarters and two latchets ending in thongs, tied together. The top edge of the quarters has been oversewn with silk. Upper Cat No 186/A7600b (Illus 140) comprises vamp, vamp wing, low vamp throat with decorative openwork, quarters and one latchet, ending in a thong. The second latchet is missing. Its vamp might have had a coloured

lining, to enhance the decorative effect. Both the High Street examples were recovered from deposits that had been laid down shortly before 1150 from different, but adjoining, properties.

There appears to be only one exact parallel for this type from Coppergate, York (mid-12th century) (Mould et al 2003). A shoe from Southampton, of late 13th century date, has similar latchets, but it is not clear whether they ended in thongs (Platt and Coleman Smith 1975, II, 296–7, Fig 260, no 2141). Two latchets knotted together from Bristol (Bristol Bridge) may also belong to this style (13th–14th centuries; Thomas forthcoming a).

In her report on the shoes from Schleswig, Schnack compares Perth Type G with her Halbschuhform G1 that dates to the 13th and 14th centuries. However, all her shoes appear to be fastened with a strap and buckle; the only example with two thongs is cut exceedingly low at the vamp throat, well below the thongs (Schnack 1992b, 93–7, 137–8, list 7, Tafel 46–49). A similar boot was found at Konstanz, while another three may have been fastened by a latchet ending in two thongs tied through holes in the opposing latchet (late 13th–15th centuries, Schnack 1994, Tafel 18 and 19). The latter feature is also found on ankle-boots from Haithabu, where two thongs were attached to one end of a latchet (Groenman-van Waateringe 1984, Typ 10).

It is possible that the PHSAE Type G is an early form of later latchet and strap and buckle shoes, such as the late 14th century examples from London (Grew and de Neergaard 1988, 32–3, Figs 42–47).

Upper, Type H: high calf boot (Illus 141)

Type H consists of one very high boot (Cat No 163/A7787j), with vamp separate from quarters. Quarters and vamp wing and leg flaps and vamp throat were joined by butted edge–flesh seams; neither thongs nor holes for them survived, suggesting a closed boot,

Upper, Type F: low shoe without fastenings (Illus 139–40).

Cat/Accession	Area	Rig	Feature		Phase
South Sector					
315/A10365b	3	V	MC049		IIa
810/A11219a	3	VI	M1.2, Pit 2648		<IIg(IIh)
3670/A7791	3	VI	P6		IVcc,Va

Upper, Type G: shoe with lachet ending in thong (Illus 140).

Cat/Accession	Area	Rig	Feature	Phase
South Sector				
186/A7600b	2	VI	M14b(b)	Ie
229/A7588c	2	V	M14b(c)	Ie,If

Upper, Type H: high calf boot (Illus 141).

Cat/Accession	Area	Rig	Feature	Phase
South Sector				
163/A7787j	1/2	VI	B6 (Phase 1), South Room–Floor (1)	Ie

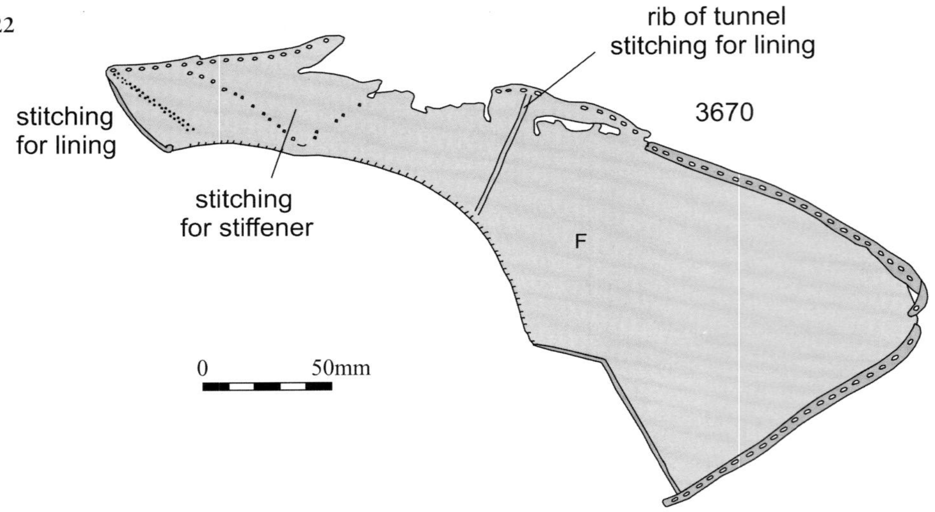

222

stitching
for lining

stitching
for stiffener

rib of tunnel
stitching for lining

3670

F

0   50mm

Type F

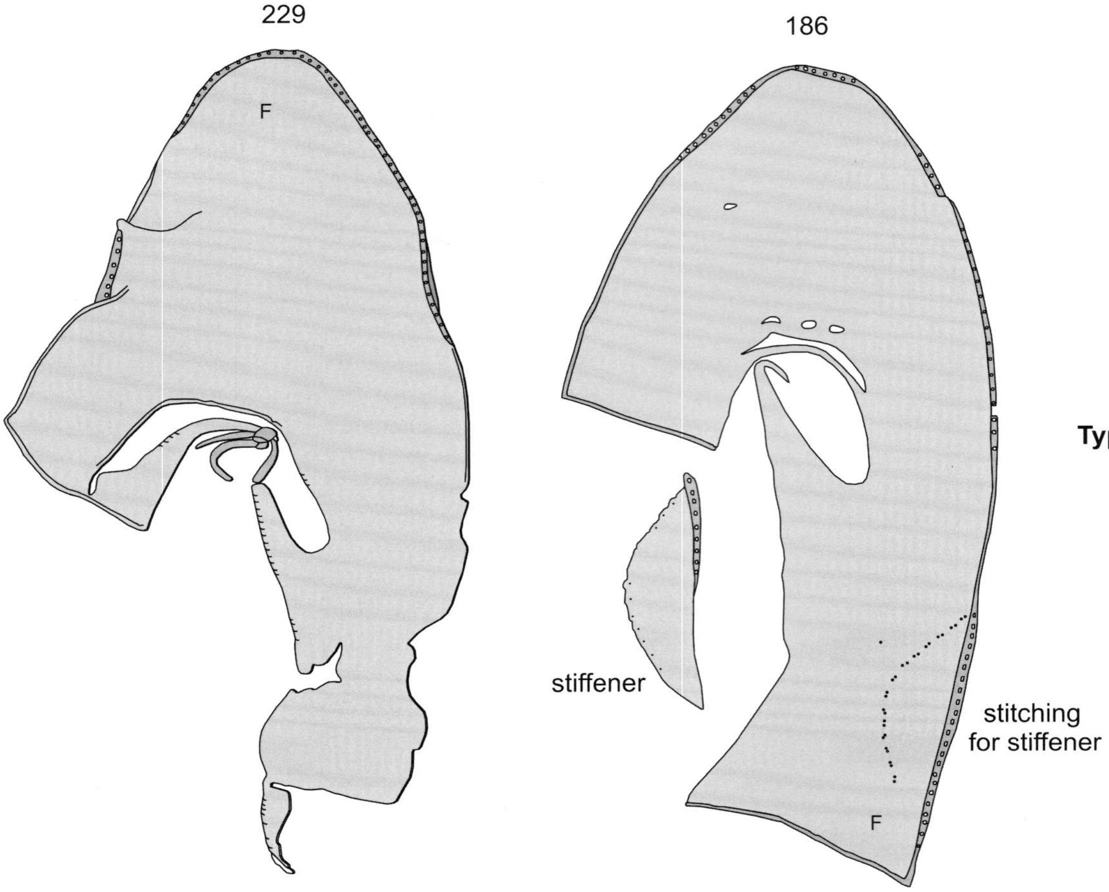

229

F

186

Type G

stiffener

stitching
for stiffener

F

1310

G

F

5769

upper

G

G   F

G   G   G

F

sole
(Type 2)

G

G

wool

F

G

G

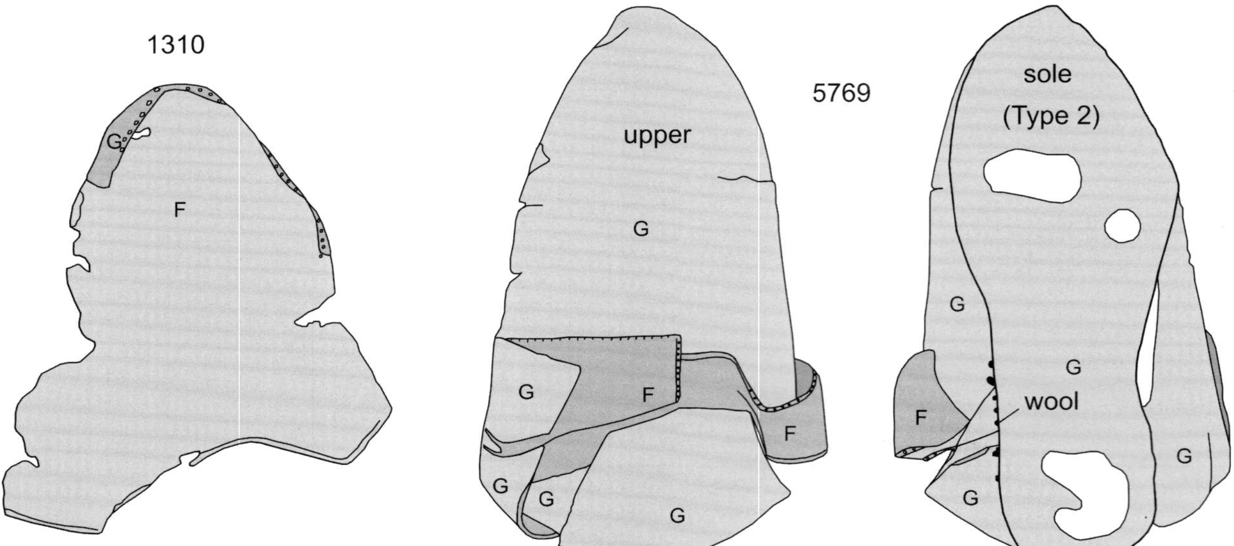

Type J

Left **Illus 140** *Uppers, Type F and Type G; uppers, Type J with attached sole, Type 2.*

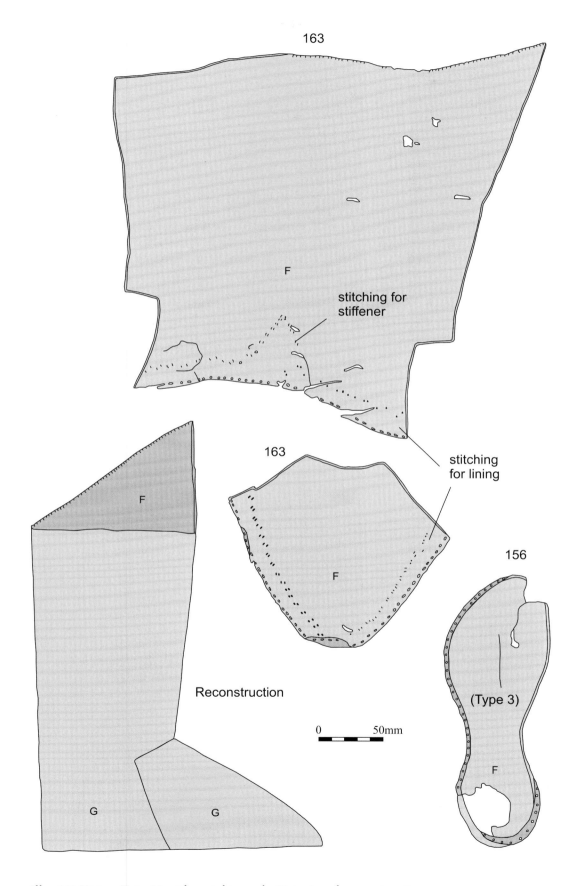

163

F

stitching for
stiffener

163

stitching
for lining

F

156

F

Reconstruction

(Type 3)

0   50mm

F

G   G

Illus 141 *Upper, Type H with matching sole, Type 3 and reconstruction.*

probably similar to a modern wellington boot, with possibly a thong tied round the ankle or leg but not slotted through tunnel holes. The overall style is similar to that of a one-piece design, but, because of the height of the leg, vamp and quarters had to be made of separate pieces. Tunnel stitching for a heel stiffener survives in the quarters, as well as a horizontal row of tunnel stitching, c15mm above the lasting margin of both quarters and vamp, but not crossing the area of the heel stiffener. Its purpose is not clear; possibly it was used to attach the bottom edge of a lining; the top edge might have been secured to the hemstitch on the top edges of the leg. This boot was of mid-12th-century date. It was recovered from a floor layer that had been laid down shortly before 1150.

Cat No 5606/A03–0254 consists of quarters cut to a similar pattern as those of Cat No 163/A7787j, but on a smaller scale, and without a second integral leg flap. As this does not seem big enough to be from a high boot, it has been assigned to Type J. Similarly, Walsh assigned one of the quarters from King Edward Street, Perth to this type. Again, although they are of the same basic shape, they are so much smaller that it is doubtful whether they belong to a high boot (Thomas and Walsh 1995, 971).

The other parallels all come from abroad, and are mostly later in date: Schleswig (13th–14th centuries); Konstanz (c1300–1500); Bergen (second half of the 14th century); Lübeck (the end of the 12th century–mid 13th century) and Novgorod (11th century?). Most of these, however, are not exactly of the same pattern. The nearest are two examples from Schleswig; no 5516 (Tafel 90) and the leather lining of no 4403 (Tafel 86) (Schnack 1992b, 114–21, 141–3, Tafel 83, 84, 86, 90, Stiefelform Typ B; Schnack 1992a, 98–9, Fig 2a; Schnack 1994, Tafel 38; Larsen 1992, 24–5, Fig 26; Groenman-van Waateringe and Guiran 1978, Typ 8; Vons-Comis 1982b, Ab 82, 96e; Thompson 1967, 81, Fig 83, 1).

Schnack also lists parallels from another 12 sites: Pleskau (11th century); Zurich (12th century); Svendborg (12th century); Oslo (13th–14th centuries); Tønsberg (13th–14th centuries); Danzig (13th century); Riga (13th–14th centuries); Stettin (14th century); Warsaw (14th century); Stockholm (14th–15th centuries); Amsterdam (13th–15th centuries); Frankfurt-am-Oder (second quarter of 15th century); Lund (13th–

15th centuries?) and Peiting (?8th–9th centuries, more probably 12th century). Her distribution map shows very clearly that the type is predominantly eastern, ranging from Schleswig to Novgorod, the only western examples coming from Peiting (Germany), Zurich, Amsterdam and Perth (Schnack 1992b, 141–3, 151).

Upper, Type J: boots or shoes with vamp separate from quarters (Illus 140, 143, 147)

It might be more appropriate to call Type J a group rather than a type, as the sole feature uniting these six boots or shoes is the fact that the vamps are separate from the quarters. This may be the result of repair, rather than deliberate two-piece construction.

One boot, Cat No 5769/A9821b (Illus 140), is similar in overall style to Type A, in that it looks like a one-piece wrap-around boot with no tunnel-holes or slits for thongs. However, close inspection demonstrates that it is of composite construction, originally made with four separate pieces. A large and oddly shaped fragment comprises vamp, both vamp wings and one leg flap. Both vamp wings extend far back; one is also very high, reaching to the top edge of the boot, while the second, on the outside of the foot, becomes a leg flap. A small trapezoidal piece forms the quarters; a tiny triangle fills a space between inner vamp wing and quarters. A second leg flap, now missing, would have fitted in above the vamp throat. The interior of the boot was lined with felt, an unexpected luxury in an upper otherwise designed to be as economical as possible (see The Textiles, this volume). It was unstratified.

Only the vamps of Cat Nos 1310/A6377 (Illus 140), 456/A10048e (Illus 147) and 941/A03–0373b survived. Cat No 1310/A6377 had a rounded throat and a vamp wing on either side; it dated to the second half of the 13th century. Cat No 456/A10048e had a continuous edge–flesh stitching channel, forming the edge of vamp throat and both wings; it was of mid-12th-century date. Cat No 941/A03–0373b, of which only a small part was found, belonged to the late 12th or early 13th century. Similar vamps have been found in Coventry (Thomas 1980, 16, 48, 52, 67, 90, 104, 147, 158, Vamp Type 6).

Cat Nos 2753/A03–0281 and 5606/A03–0254 (Illus 143) consist of the quarters and legs of boots with separate vamps (now missing). As mentioned earlier,

Upper Type J: boots or shoes with vamp separate from quarters (Illus 140, 143, 147).

Cat/Accession	Area	Rig	Feature	Phase
South Sector				
456/A10048e	4	VI	M1.1f, Pit 2383	IIb,IIc
941/A03–0373b	9	VII	M13	IIg–IIIb
1310/A6377	3	V	P2.2b	IVa
2753/A03–0281	7	VII	B18 (Phase 2b), North Room, Hall & Hall South–Occupation (10)	IVb
5606/A03–0254	10	VIII	MC174, Pit 7013	(Va–)Vd(Vdd)
5769/A9821b	3/4	V, VI	Unstratified	u/s

Cat No 5606/A03–0254 resembles the quarters of Type H (Cat No 163/A7787j), but on a smaller scale, and is thus unlikely to be part of a very high boot. These boots are of mid–later 14th century date. Thus, two of the stratified examples of these boots belonged to Periods II or III (the second half of the 12th century or earlier 13th century), while three were of late 13th–earlier 14th century date. Examples of Type J uppers were recovered from all four rigs which were excavated.

Other parallels include 45–75 Gallowgate (1350–1375), Gallowgate Middle School (12th–13th centuries), Aberdeen; Newcastle (mid 13th–14th centuries); Winchester (late 11th–mid 13th century) and Schleswig (Thomas 2001a, 249; Dixon 1988, Fig 35, 208B, 212A; Ottaway 1982, 128–30; Schnack 1992b, Fig 98, no 1).

Uppers, Type Ki–v

The 14 uppers (15 fragments) of Type K comprise low boots or high shoes with a central fastening, consisting of a combination of slits and toggles on the latchets and occasionally on the vamp throat. The uppers have been subdivided according to the surviving evidence. Types Ki, Kii and Kiii, with toggles, horizontal thongs and slits, are probably all parts of the same fastening method, while Type Kiv has a similar but much simpler arrangement; Type Kv consists of two very fragmentary boot pieces, with slit or double latchets.

Although this category (Ki–v) included examples which were discovered in 12th and 13th century deposits, it is interesting to note that 11 (73%) of the 15 came from 14th-century layers. Indeed six of these came from the same midden (M1.5b). As many as ten (67%) came from the same area, Area 7.

Uppers, Type Ki (Illus 142)
The five Ki uppers all have toggles and slits. Cat No 3602/A4329e (Illus 142) has two slits on one latchet, three slits and a round hole on the second latchet and a

toggle at vamp throat, threaded through a single hole.

The upper Cat Nos 4030/A03–0156c and 4031/A03–0156d (Illus 142) has a similar arrangement, with two horizontal slits through the latchet, a toggle at the vamp throat and a horizontal slit and a toggle on the second latchet; the toggle at the latchet has been threaded through a tunnel hole and a single hole. Cat No 5638/A1249a (Illus 142) and Cat No 5318/A4390f are probably parts of latchets; the former has two toggles and a trace of a slit, while the latter has four round holes, with a toggle through the bottom one and two thongs, possibly broken toggles, through the two top holes. Cat No 3866/A03–0069a (Illus 142) is also probably a latchet, with a T-shaped slit and two toggles, each threaded through a tunnel hole. The purpose of the tunnel stitching on the flesh side, parallel to the top and outer edges of the latchet, is not clear. It was possibly for attaching the latchet to the rest of the upper. These uppers are all of late 13th- to mid 14th-century date. Two of the six fragments were recovered from P8.4, an early 14th century path which ran along the western boundary of Rig VII.

Uppers, Type Kii (Illus 142)
The four examples of Type Kii uppers have horizontal slits, but no surviving thongs or toggles and are most probably latchets belonging to Type Ki uppers. All four were recovered from early 14th-century features, three from M1.5b.

Uppers Type Kiii (Illus 142, 144)
The two fragments are latchets with three horizontal thongs. The thongs on Cat No 3283/A03–0227d (Illus 144) are each threaded through a tunnel hole, a single hole and a vertical thong. This fragment differs from other examples with vertical thongs (Type Biii), in having the horizontal thongs firmly anchored close to an oversewn edge, suggesting that they were toggles or loops, rather than wrap-around thongs. Cat No 3989/

Uppers, Type Ki–v.

Cat/Accession	Type	Area	Rig	Feature	Phase
South Sector					
230/A7588d	Kv	2	V	M14b(c)	Ie,If
878/A8665e	Kiv	3	VI	M1.3	IIi
3283/A03–0227d	Kiii	7	VII	P8.3	IVc,IVcc
3602/A4329e	Ki	3	VI	M1.4e	IVcc(Va)
3866/A03–0069a	Ki	7	VI, VII	M1.5b	Vaa
3870/A03–0098a	Kii	7	VI, VII	M1.5b	Vaa
3902/A03–0132g	Kii	7	VI, VII	M1.5b	Vaa
3968/A03–0143a	Kv	7	VI, VII	M1.5b	Vaa
3988/A03–0170e	Kii	7	VI, VII	M1.5b	Vaa
3989/A03–0170f	Kiii	7	VI, VII	M1.5b	Vaa
4030/A03–0156c & 4031/A03–0156d	Ki	7	VII	P8.4	Va
4153/A03–0198b	Kii	7	VII	P8.4, Pit 7216	Va
5318/A4390f	Ki	4	V, VI	M3a	Vb–Vc
5638/A1249a	Ki	4	VI	M3e, Pit 2111	Vdd>

3602

toggle

slits

3866

F

Type Ki

4030

F

T shaped slits

4031

toggle

F

5638

F

toggles

G

4153

3870

slits

F

3988

slits

slits now torn

F

Type Kii

F

Type Kiii

3989

loops

G

Type Kv

230

F

0   50mm

Illus 142 *Fragments of uppers, Type K.*

A03–0170f (Illus 142) has three horizontal thongs ending in loops; the thongs have each been passed through a tunnel hole and a single hole. Both these Type Kiii uppers came from contexts that dated from c1300. They came from what were effectively the succeeding phases of the Path 8 sequence between Rigs VI and VII.

Upper, Type Kiv (Illus 143)
Type Kiv consists of one low boot, Cat No 878/A8665e, with a much simpler and cruder fastening, comprising a toggle attached to one latchet and passed through an oval hole in the second latchet. Although the fastening method is basically similar to those of Types Ki–iii, this boot is not strictly comparable, as it is much more roughly finished than the other examples. This boot was discovered in a very late 12th-century backland midden.

Uppers, Type Kv (Illus 142)
Type Kv consists of two fragments. Cat No 230/A7588d (Illus 142) is possibly part of a boot with central fastening; it appears to have a double latchet, one on top of the other. It is not clear if or how this latchet was secured to its partner. This upper came from a deposit that had been laid down very shortly before 1150. As such it was by far the earliest Type K upper detected at the High Street.

Cat No 3968/A03–0143a has a slit latchet, possibly for a central fastening. Like so many of the other variations of Type K upper, it was discovered within M1.5b, an early 14th-century midden in Rigs VI and VII.

The majority of the Type K uppers belong to the late 13th–first half of the 14th century: Period IV, two examples (14%) and Period V, ten examples (71%). The two 12th century examples are atypical.

Uppers, Type Ki (Illus 142).

Cat/Accession	Area	Rig	Feature	Phase
South Sector				
3602/A4329e	3	VI	M1.4e	IVcc(Va)
3866/A03–0069a	7	VI, VII	M1.5b	Vaa
4030/A03–0156c & 4031/A03–0156d	7	VII	P8.4	Va
5318/A4390f	4	V, VI	M3a	Vb–Vc
5638/A1249a	4	VI	M3e, Pit 2111	Vdd>

Uppers, Type Kii (Illus 142).

Cat/Accession	Area	Rig	Feature	Phase
South Sector				
3870/A03–0098a	7	VI, VII	M1.5b	Vaa
3902/A03–0132g	7	VI, VII	M1.5b	Vaa
3988/A03–0170e	7	VI, VII	M1.5b	Vaa
4153/A03–0198b	7	VII	P8.4, Pit 7216	Va

Uppers, Type Kiii (Illus 142, 144).

Cat/Accession	Area	Rig	Feature	Phase
South Sector				
3283/A03–0227d	7	VII	P8.3	IVc,IVcc
3989/A03–0170f	7	VI, VII	M1.5b	Vaa

Uppers, Type Kiv (Illus 143).

Cat/Accession	Area	Rig	Feature	Phase
South Sector				
878/A8665e	3	VI	M1.3	IIi

Uppers, Type Kv (Illus 142).

Cat/Accession	Area	Rig	Feature	Phase
South Sector				
230/A7588d	2	V	M14b(c)	Ie,If
3968/A03–0143a	7	VI, VII	M1.5b	Vaa

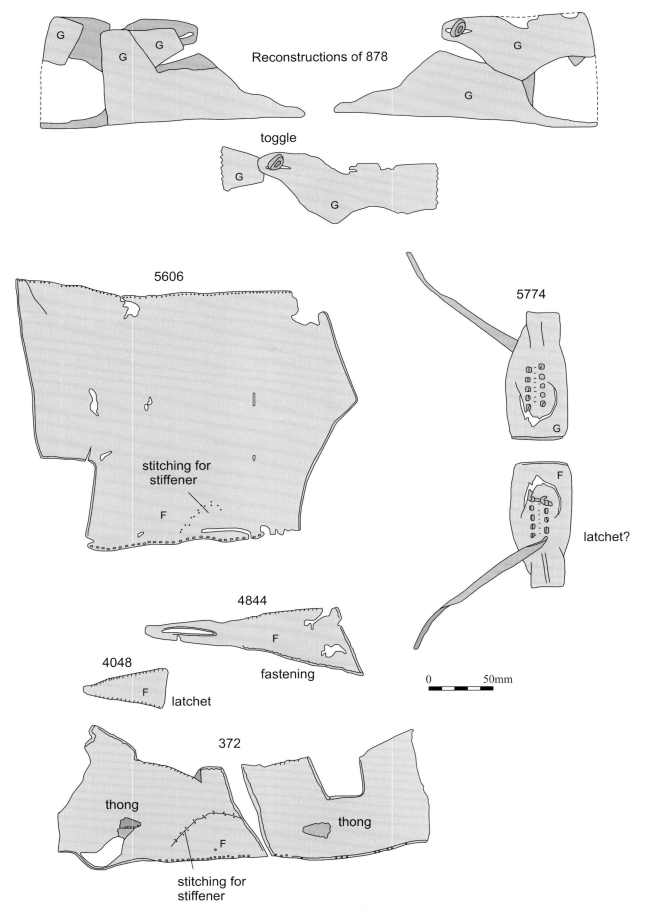

Reconstructions of 878

toggle

5606

5774

stitching for
stiffener

latchet?

4844

fastening

4048

latchet

372

thong

thong

stitching for
stiffener

0   50mm

Illus 143 *Upper Type J, Type Kiv
and fragments of uppers with fastenings.*

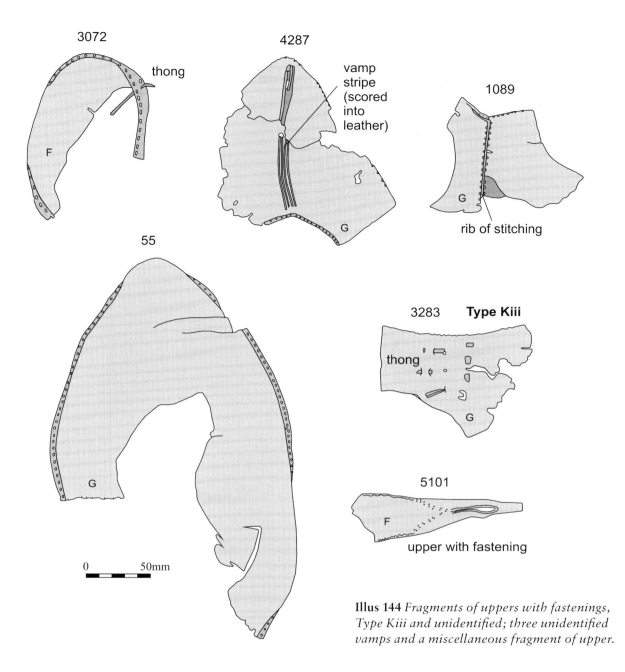

Illus 144 *Fragments of uppers with fastenings, Type Kiii and unidentified; three unidentified vamps and a miscellaneous fragment of upper.*

Substantial fragments of boots of types Ki and Kiii of 13th- to 14th-century date were found at Kirk Close, Perth, while part of a Ki upper was identified at 45–75 Gallowgate, Aberdeen (1350–1375) (Thomas 1987, 179–81, Ki nos 13, 16, 17, Kiii nos 14 and 15; Thomas 2001a, 249).

Other parallels are also of 13th- to 14th-century date: London (mid 13th–mid 14th centuries); Newcastle (mid 13th–mid 14th centuries); Bristol Bridge, Bristol (13th–14th centuries); Barbican Ditch, Oxford (13th–15th centuries); Chapel Lane Staith, Hull (late 13th–early 14th centuries); Coppergate, York (late 13th–14th centuries); Waterford (12th–13th centuries); Amsterdam (with low vamp throat: 1275–1300; ankle-boot: 14th–16th centuries); Bremen (late medieval); Bergen (mid 13th–early 15th centuries); Schleswig (12th–13th centuries); Lübeck (end of 12th century–mid 13th century);

S'Hertogenbosch and Konstanz (14th–15th centuries) (Grew and de Neergaard 1988, 22–3, Figs 32–34; Tatton-Brown 1975, 159–60, Fig 28, nos 77–78, 80; Dixon 1988, 94, Fig 34, no 194; Thomas forthcoming a; Hassall 1976, 279–80, Fig 19, no 24; Jackson 1979, Fig 22, no 19; Mould et al 2003; O'Rourke 1997, 708, Fig 18.2.1; Baart et al 1977; Groenman-van Waateringe 1975, 30–1, Fig 9.4; Schnack 1993, 64–5, Fig 2.c; Larsen 1992, 22–3, Figs 20–22; Schnack 1992b, 121, Fig 93; Groenman-van Waateringe and Guiran 1978, Typ 4; Goubitz 1983; Schnack 1994, 26, 3.3.5, Tafel 16).

Uppers, fragments with fastenings (Illus 143–4)

The eight fragments of leather grouped together here have various forms of fastening (thongs, tie-holes, slits and tunnel holes) but are too fragmentary for further

Uppers, fragments and fastenings (Illus 143, 144).

Cat/Accession	Area	Rig	Feature	Phase
South Sector				
41/A11262	2	VI	MC011, Pit 3755	Ib,Ic
372/A4936	1	V	MC059, Pit 3142	Id–IIc
1111/A03–0310	9	VII	P8.1c	IIIc
2707/A03–0296d	7	VII	B18 (Phase 1/2), MF 7307	IVaa,IVb
4844/A03–0175q	7	VII	M8a	Va,Vaa
5101/A03–0046	9	VII	M8a	Va,Vaa
5362/A5894g	4	VI	M3b	Vd
5774/A12574d	3/4	V, VI	Unstratified	u/s

definition of method of fastening or type of upper. All are probably parts of uppers but it is also possible that some were fastenings of clothing or other objects.

Cat Nos 41/A11262 and 372/A4936 are definitely parts of uppers of high shoes or low boots; Cat No 41/A11262 has two pairs of long slits, possibly elongated tunnel holes, on latchet and quarters. This may originally have been a Type Aii upper, to which thongs were later added rather clumsily. Cat No 372/A4936 (Illus 143) has two thongs, one sewn to the flesh side of the quarters and threaded through a slit, the other through a slit in the vamp. The second thong may have had a buckle attached to it. Cat No 2707/A03–0296d with a thong threaded through three vertical slits, could be part of a Type C or D upper, with thonging similar to that described by Groenman-van Waateringe (1975, 30–1). Cat No 1111/A03–0310 is most unusual in having a double row of five tie-holes. Cat Nos 4844/A03–0175q (Illus 143) and 5101/A03–0046 (Illus 144) are both tapered fragments, with a slit in the pointed end; the edges of the slit of Cat No 5101/A03–0046 have been stitched. Tunnel stitching on the latter suggests that it had been sewn onto an upper. These are possibly latchets or straps.

Cat No 5774/A12574d (Illus 143) is an oblong fragment, with two parallel thongs threaded through four tunnel holes; one thong has a long loose end surviving. Cat No 5362/A5894g has two thongs, plus slits for two more; one thong has been knotted, forming a button. This is possibly a Type K variant, or else part of an article of clothing.

Uppers, stiffeners

The 14 stiffeners listed here have no surviving uppers. Three other stiffeners have been described with their uppers. Three of the above stiffeners were semi-circular, ten triangular. The former came only from 12th-century contexts, while the latter dated from the mid-13th to mid-14th century.

A study of all the evidence for stiffeners, that is, those surviving with their uppers or indicated by stitching, as well as those listed above, shows that triangular forms (33) are almost as common as semi-

circular (35). The semi-circular examples belonged predominantly to the 12th century (71.4%). The majority of the triangular stiffeners were of mid-13th- to mid-14th-century date (60.6%), but a substantial group were of 12th-century date (33.3%).

Analysis of the shape of stiffener used for each type of upper is complicated by lack of evidence from worn or missing quarters. Type A has the lowest percentage of doubt (11%), Type K the highest (93%).

Semi-circular stiffeners were commoner on Types A, B and E (triangular stiffener numbers in brackets): A, 12 (6); B, 13 (6); E, 5 (2). Only triangular stiffeners were associated with Types C (1), D (3), H (1) and J (3).

Uppers, lasting margins (see list)

Uppers, not definable

Where possible, the 506 fragments of upper which were too incomplete or worn for their type to be defined have been described in the catalogue as vamps or quarters. Cat No 4249/A4943d is the quarters of a shoe with a raised or domed top edge, as in some examples of Type D. Cat No 626/A9885b comprises vamp and quarters of a shoe or boot which has been patched twice; one long narrow patch which replaced part of the lasting margin, survives. Cat No 1089/A03–0278d is a small fragment with an unusual vertical rib, formed by two grain to flesh stitching channels, which was probably a decorative feature, similar to a vamp stripe, and was perhaps stitched with coloured wool or thread. Cat No 4287/A6398 is a vamp decorated with a vamp stripe, consisting of four grooves from vamp throat to toe, similar to those on Cat No 162/A7787i (see also Upper [Type E]).

The majority (66%) of these fragmentary uppers recovered from the South Sector of the High Street excavation came from Periods IV and V: 30 (6%) from Period I, 81 (16%) from Period II, 23 (4.5%) from Period III, 177 (35%) from Period IV, 155 (30%) from Period V, 27 (5%) were unstratified, 10 (2%) from all periods in the North Sector and 3 (0.5%) were from either the South or North Sectors.

Uppers, stiffener.

Cat/Accession	Area	Rig	Feature	Phase
South Sector				
106/A10798c	4	VI	MC018, Pit 2398	Ib–Id
289/A03–0017d	3	V	MC053a	If
548/A6412	2	V	B5, North Room–Floor/Occupation (2)	IIa–IIff
1027/A03–0317b	9	VII	P8.1b	IIIc
1399/A8021m	3	V/VI	MC144, WW2221	<IIId–IVaa
1777/A03–0366a	7	VII	MC126, Pit 7402	IVaa,IVb
3603/A4329f	3	VI	M1.4e	IVcc(Va)
3725/A03–0160i	7	VI	B34, Courtyard	Va
3871/A03–0098b	7	VI, VII	M1.5b	Vaa
3978/A03–0148c	7	VI, VII	M1.5b	Vaa
4091/A03–0210e	7	VII	P8.4	Va
4109/A03–0211d	7	VII	P8.4	Va
4826/A03–0218c	7	VII	M8a	Va,Vaa
4925/A03–0162x	7	VII	M8a	Va,Vaa

Uppers, lasting margins.

Cat/Accession	Area	Rig	Feature	Phase
South Sector				
298/A12632d	4	V	B16b, Pit 4726	Id–IIa
299/A12632e	4	V	B16b, Pit 4726	Id–IIa
300/A12632f	4	V	B16b, Pit 4726	Id–IIa
445/A6483o	2	VI	B4, 'Byre'–Occupation	IIc
614/A9879d	4	V	M10	IId–IIg
1029/A03–0317d	9	VII	P8.1b	IIIc
2642/A03–0231d	9	VII	B18 (Phase 1/2)	IVaa,IVb
2643/A03–0231e	9	VII	B18 (Phase 1/2)	IVaa,IVb
2644/A03–0231f	9	VII	B18 (Phase 1/2)	IVaa,IVb
2645/A03–0231g	9	VII	B18 (Phase 1/2)	IVaa,IVb
2683/A03–0202d	9	VII	B18 (Phase 1/2), Pit 9301	IVaa,IVb
2786/A03–0245g	9	VII	B18 (Phase 2b), North Room, Hall & Hall South–Occupation (10)	IVb
3073/A8668h	3	VI	M1.4d	IVb,IVc
3421/A03–0217c	7	VII	B18 (Phases 2a & 2b) & M9a, PH7237	(IVb)IVc,IVcc
3518/A03–0224b	7	VI	M1.4i	IVcc
3819/A03–0164c	7	VI	B34, Courtyard	Va
3958/A03–0140l	7	VI, VII	M1.5b	Vaa
4013/A03–0165a	7	VII	P8.4	Va
4554/A1253e	3	V, VI	M1.5a	Va,Vaa
4555/A1253f	3	V, VI	M1.5a	Va,Vaa
4556/A1253g	3	V, VI	M1.5a	Va,Vaa
4935/A03–0162hh	7	VII	M8a	Va,Vaa
4936/A03–0162ii	7	VII	M8a	Va,Vaa
4937/A03–0162jj	7	VII	M8a	Va,Vaa
5232/A03–0082d	7	VII	B53 (Phase 1), North Area–Occupation (1b)	Vb
5233/A03–0082e	7	VII	B53 (Phase 1), North Area–Occupation (1b)	Vb
5234/A03–0082f	7	VII	B53 (Phase 1), North Area–Occupation (1b)	Vb
5783/A0800e	3/4	V, VI	Unstratified	u/s
5784/A0800f	3/4	V, VI	Unstratified	u/s
5785/A0800g	3/4	V, VI	Unstratified	u/s
5829/A03–0127f	7	VI, VII	Unstratified	u/s
North Sector				
5894/A6236d	5	–	CG007, Pit 0276	4,5
5931/A0110c	5, A	–	Lade (4)	6–12(b–e)
South/North Sectors				
5989/A?	–	–	Unstratified	u/s

Uppers, not definable.

Cat/Accession	Area	Rig	Feature	Phase
South Sector				
13/A9878a	1	V	M0, Pit 3776	Ia(Ib)
14/A9878b	1	V	M0, Pit 3776	Ia(Ib)
19/A10876	1	V	M0, Pit 3776	Ia(Ib)
42/A11232	2	V	MC012, Pit3772	Ic
55/A9886b	1/2	V, VI	M2.1b	Ic
56/A9875	1/2	V, VI	M2.1b	Ic
59/A8635b	1/2	V, VI	M2.1b & B10, South Room–Floor/Occupation (1)	Ic,Icc
96/A12289b	4	V/VI	MC017	Ia–Icc>
105/A10798b	4	VI	MC018, Pit 2398	Ib–Id
148/A11595b	3	VI	MC037a, Pit 5157	Ia–Ie
149/A11595c	3	VI	MC037a, Pit 5157	Ia–Ie
152/A12312a	3	VI	MC037a, Pit 5157	Ia–Ie
166/A7256b	2	VI	M14b(b)	Ie
181/A7589g	2	VI	M14b(b)	Ie
203/A7257h	2	VI	M14b(b), Pit 3625	Ie
210/A7567b	2	VI	M14b(b), Pit 3625	Ie
220/A7800b	2	VI	M14b(b), Pit 3625	Ie
222/A7436a	2	VI	P5.2b	Ie
225/A8494	2	VI	MC042	Ie
244/A7310b	2	V	M14b(a)	Id
246/A7581b	2	V	M14b(a)	Id
253/A7801a	2	V	M14b(a), Pit 3686	Id
260/A6984b	2	VI	MC044b	If
268/A7044Bh	2	VI	MC044b	If
269/A7044Bi	2	VI	MC044b	If
270/A7044Bj	2	VI	MC044b	If
271/A7044Bk	2	VI	MC044b	If
287/A03–0017b	3	V	MC053a	If
288/A03–0017c	3	V	MC053a	If
294/A7121	1/2	VI	P5.3a	If
297/A12632c	4	V	B16b, Pit 4726	Id–IIa
308/A12635d	4	V	B16b, Pit 4726	Id–IIa
309/A12635e	4	V	B16b, Pit 4726	Id–IIa
310/A12635f	4	V	B16b, Pit 4726	Id–IIa
312/A12378b	3	VI	P5.3b	If,IIa
322/A10505b	3	V	MC049, Pit 5259	IIa
333/A7143	1/2	VI	P5.4a	IIb
336/A6749	2	VI	MC061	IIb
339/A6770c	2	VI	MC061	IIb
343/A6772c	2	VI	MC061	IIb
344/A6772d	2	VI	MC061	IIb
345/A6772e	2	VI	MC061	IIb
346/A6772f	2	VI	MC061	IIb
347/A6772g	2	VI	MC061	IIb
367/A7694c	1	V	M14a	Id–IIc
368/A7694d	1	V	M14a	Id–IIc
369/A7694e	1	V	M14a	Id–IIc
370/A7694f	1	V	M14a	Id–IIc
371/A7694g	1	V	M14a	Id–IIc
380/A12282f	1	VI	MC065, Pit 3908	IIa–IIc
393/A03–0370a	1	VI	MC065	IIa–IIc
412/A12493g	3	VI	MC056, Pit 5155	Ia–IIc
414/A6945	2	VI	B4, MW3585	IIc
422/A6408	2	VI	B4, Floor	IIc

(continued)

Cat/Accession	Area	Rig	Feature	Phase
429/A6411a	2	VI	B4, 'Byre'–Occupation	IIc
443/A6483m	2	VI	B4, 'Byre'–Occupation	IIc
444/A6483n	2	VI	B4, 'Byre'–Occupation	IIc
447/A6722	2	VI	B4, 'Byre'–Occupation	IIc
458/A10500	4	VI	M1.1c	IId
464/A10599c	3	VI	M1.1c, Pit 5005	IId
479/A9880	3	VI	MC080	IId,IIe
494/A12290d	1	VI	MC071	IIb–IIf
495/A12290e	1	VI	MC071	IIb–IIf
496/A12290f	1	VI	MC071	IIb–IIf
501/A10801e	3	V	P2.1a	IIb–IIf
521/A7005c	1/2	V	B5, T4485	IIa–IIff
522/A7005d	1/2	V	B5, T4485	IIa–IIff
526/A6426b	1/2	V	B5, WW3566	IIa–IIff
533/A6949c	2	V	B5, North Room–Floor/Occupation (1)	IIa–IIff
534/A6949d	2	V	B5, North Room–Floor/Occupation (1)	IIa–IIff
538/A6416b	2	V	B5, North Room–Floor/Occupation (2)	IIa–IIff
539/A6416c	2	V	B5, North Room–Floor/Occupation (2)	IIa–IIff
546/A6376e	2	V	B5, North Room–Floor/Occupation (2)	IIa–IIff
555/A6948c	1/2	V	B5, Destruction	IIa–IIff
556/A6948d	1/2	V	B5, Destruction	IIa–IIff
558/A6950	1/2	V	B5, Destruction	IIa–IIff
613/A9879c	4	V	M10	IId–IIg
626/A9885b	4	V	M10	IId–IIg
627/A10508a	4	V	M10	IId–IIg
632/A10047b	3	V	M10	IId–IIg
666/A9553l	4	V	M10, Pit 4552	IId–IIg
667/A9553m	4	V	M10, Pit 4552	IId–IIg
668/A9553n	4	V	M10, Pit 4552	IId–IIg
669/A9553o	4	V	M10, Pit 4552	IId–IIg
670/A9553p	4	V	M10, Pit 4552	IId–IIg
671/A9553q	4	V	M10, Pit 4552	IId–IIg
672/A9553r	4	V	M10, Pit 4552	IId–IIg
673/A9553s	4	V	M10, Pit 4552	IId–IIg
674/A9553t	4	V	M10, Pit 4552	IId–IIg
675/A9553u	4	V	M10, Pit 4552	IId–IIg
676/A9553v	4	V	M10, Pit 4552	IId–IIg
677/A9553w	4	V	B4, Pit 4552	IId–IIg
678/A9553x	4	V	M10, Pit 4552	IId–IIg
741/A9364a	3	VI	M1.2, Pit 2648	<IIg(IIh)
780/A9371f	3	VI	M1.2, Pit 2648	<IIg(IIh)
781/A9371g	3	VI	M1.2, Pit 2648	<IIg(IIh)
791/A9546d	3	VI	M1.2, Pit 2648	<IIg(IIh)
800/A10507	3	VI	M1.2, Pit 2648	<IIg(IIh)
813/A11220b	3	VI	M1.2, Pit 2648	<IIg(IIh)
824/A11274a	3	VI	M1.2, Pit 2648	<IIg(IIh)
826/A12292	3	VI	M1.2, Pit 2648	<IIg(IIh)
837/A8638a	4	V, VI	M11	IIh
858/A8527b	4	VI	M1.3	IIi
869/A8649a	3	VI	M1.3	IIi
882/A8666d	3	VI	M1.3	IIi
883/A8666e	3	VI	M1.3	IIi
884/A8666f	3	VI	M1.3	IIi
885/A8666g	3	VI	M1.3	IIi
888/A8821b	3	VI	M1.3	IIi
911/A11267c	3	VI	M1.3	IIi
915/A11268c	3	VI	M1.3	IIi
928/A11639g	1	VI	MC111	IIb–IIIb

(continued)

Cat/Accession	Area	Rig	Feature	Phase
935/A03–0352	9	VII	P8.0	IIIa,IIIb
946/A03–0381a	9	VII	M13, Pit 9493	IIg–IIIb
998/A11273a	4	V	MC116	IIe–IIIc
1012/A12390c	4	VI	M1.4a(a)	IIIa–IIIc
1022/A8691a	4	VI	M1.4a(a)	IIIa–IIIc
1023/A8691b	4	VI	M1.4a(a)	IIIa–IIIc
1032/A8677a	4	V	MC117, Pit 4695	IIe–IIIc
1033/A8677b	4	V	MC117, Pit 4695	IIe–IIIc
1036/A8009b	3	V	MC117, Pit 4695	IIe–IIIc
1078/A12535d	4	V/VI	MC128	IIIb,IIIc
1083/A12492a	4	V/VI	MC128	IIIb,IIIc
1084/A12492b	4	V/VI	MC128	IIIb,IIIc
1089/A03–0278d	9	VII	B19 (Phase 2b), North Room–Floor (2b)	IIIc
1099/A03–0270e	9	VII	P8.1c	IIIc
1100/A03–0270f	9	VII	P8.1c	IIIc
1117/A9881	3	VI	M6a	IIg–IIId
1138/A03–0265c	9	VII	M15	IIId
1139/A03–0265d	9	VII	M15	IIId
1140/A03–0391a	7	VII	M15, Pit 9415	IIId
1142/A03–0266	9	VII	M15, PW9402	IIId
1148/A5893c	1	V	M12	IIg–IIIc(–IVa)
1223/A6070b	2	V	M6b	IIg–IIId
1272/A4933c	2	V	P2.2a	IVa
1274/A4935	2	V	P2.2a	IVa
1291/A7865	3	V	P2.2b	IVa
1305/A8810f	3	V	P2.2b	IVa
1306/A8810g	3	V	P2.2b	IVa
1307/A8810h	3	V	P2.2b	IVa
1319/A7989f	4	V	MC143	IVaa
1320/A7989g	4	V	MC143	IVaa
1322/A8027b	4	V	MC143	IVaa
1323/A8027c	4	V	MC143	IVaa
1324/A8027d	4	V	MC143	IVaa
1325/A8027e	4	V	MC143	IVaa
1396/A8021j	3	V/VI	MC144, WW2221	<IIId–IVaa
1397/A8021k	3	V/VI	MC144, WW2221	<IIId–IVaa
1398/A8021l	3	V/VI	MC144, WW2221	<IIId–IVaa
1419/A6065	3	V	P2.3a	IVaa
1427/A6187b	4	V	MC156	IVaa
1428/A6187c	4	V	MC156	IVaa
1429/A6187d	4	V	MC156	IVaa
1480/A6190b	2	V	B26, Floor/Occupation (8a)	IIg–IVaa
1481/A6190c	2	V	B26, Floor/Occupation (8a)	IIg–IVaa
1482/A6190d	2	V	B26, Floor/Occupation (8a)	IIg–IVaa
1497/A4827b	1	VI	B20, Levelling	<IIId–IVaa
1501/A6635a	1	VI	B20, Occupation (1a)	<IIId–IVaa
1502/A6635b	1	VI	B20, Occupation (1a)	<IIId–IVaa
1547/A03–0418a	7	VII	MC130	<IIIc–IVaa
1636/A11242b	3	VI	B2, WW2498	IVa,IVaa
1637/A11242c	3	VI	B2, WW2498	IVa,IVaa
1638/A11242d	3	VI	B2, WW2498	IVa,IVaa
1662/A03–0420a	7	VI	P3.3	IVa–IVb
1663/A03–0420b	7	VI	P3.3	IVa–IVb
1680/A4895c	2	V	B3 (South), Construction–Levelling	IVa,IVaa
1695/A03–0206	9	VII	B18 (Phase 1b), Destruction	IVa,IVaa
1702/A4896b	4	VI	B11, Floor	IVaa
1745/A03–0347c	7	VII	MC126, Pit 7402	IVaa,IVb
1746/A03–0349a	7	VII	MC126, Pit 7402	IVaa,IVb

(continued)

Cat/Accession	Area	Rig	Feature	Phase
1747/A03–0349b	7	VII	MC126, Pit 7402	IVaa,IVb
1762/A03–0360b	7	VII	MC126, Pit 7402	IVaa,IVb
1811/A03–0374c	7	VII	MC126, Pit 7402	IVaa,IVb
1812/A03–0374d	7	VII	MC126, Pit 7402	IVaa,IVb
1835/A03–0348a	7	VII	MC126, Pit 7402	IVaa,IVb
1881/A03–0353d	7	VII	MC126, Pit 7402	IVaa,IVb
1889/A03–0357e	7	VII	MC126, Pit 7402	IVaa,IVb
1890/A03–0357f	7	VII	MC126, Pit 7402	IVaa,IVb
1891/A03–0357g	7	VII	MC126, Pit 7402	IVaa,IVb
2000/A03–0372a	7	VII	MC126, Pit 7402	IVaa,IVb
2293/A03–0271e	7	VI	M1.4f	IVc
2304/A03–0279a	7	VI	M1.4f	IVc
2305/A03–0279b	7	VI	M1.4f	IVc
2306/A03–0279c	7	VI	M1.4f	IVc
2321/A03–0285e	7	VI	M1.4f	IVc
2322/A03–0285f	7	VI	M1.4f	IVc
2323/A03–0285g	7	VI	M1.4f	IVc
2324/A03–0285h	7	VI	M1.4f	IVc
2325/A03–0285i	7	VI	M1.4f	IVc
2326/A03–0285j	7	VI	M1.4f	IVc
2337/A03–0291e	7	VI	M1.4f	IVc
2342/A03–0308e	7	VI	M1.4f	IVc
2348/A03–0322a	7	VI	M1.4f	IVc
2361/A03–0331a	7	VI	M1.4f	IVc
2370/A03–0332g	7	VI	M1.4f	IVc
2371/A03–0332h	7	VI	M1.4f	IVc
2393/A03–0335	7	VI	M1.4f	IVc
2404/A03–0342b	7	VI	M1.4f	IVc
2433/A03–0345p	7	VI	M1.4f	IVc
2454/A03–0326c	7	VI	M1.4f	IVc
2455/A03–0326d	7	VI	M1.4f	IVc
2489/A03–0392k	7	VI	M1.4f	IVc
2490/A03–0392l	7	VI	M1.4f	IVc
2573/A03–0329e	7	VII	B18 (Phase 1/2)	IVaa,IVb
2574/A03–0329f	7	VII	B18 (Phase 1/2)	IVaa,IVb
2590/A03–0154a	9	VII	B18 (Phase 1/2)	IVaa,IVb
2591/A03–0154b	9	VII	B18 (Phase 1/2)	IVaa,IVb
2638/A03–0203b	9	VII	B18 (Phase 1/2)	IVaa,IVb
2654/A03–0316d	7	VII	B18 (Phase 1/2), Pit 7324	IVaa,IVb
2656/A03–0325a	7	VII	B18 (Phase 1/2), Pit 7324	IVaa,IVb
2657/A03–0325b	7	VII	B18 (Phase 1/2), Pit 7324	IVaa,IVb
2658/A03–0325c	7	VII	B18 (Phase 1/2), Pit 7324	IVaa,IVb
2681/A03–0202b	9	VII	B18 (Phase 1/2), Pit 9301	IVaa,IVb
2682/A03–0202c	9	VII	B18 (Phase 1/2), Pit 9301	IVaa,IVb
2694/A03–0182a	9	VII	B18 (Phase 1/2), Pit 9301	IVaa,IVb
2715/A03–0311b	7	VII	B18 (Phase 2a), External (1), Pit 7314	IVb
2716/A03–0311c	7	VII	B18 (Phase 2a), External (1), Pit 7314	IVb
2735/A03–0368c	10	VII	B18 (Phases 2a & 2b), MW6155	IVb
2736/A03–0368d	10	VII	B18 (Phases 2a & 2b), MW6155	IVb
2737/A03–0368e	10	VII	B18 (Phases 2a & 2b), MW6155	IVb
2748/A03–0297b	7	VII	B18 (Phase 2a), North Room & Hall–Construction (1)	IVb
2765/A03–0113a	9	VII	B18 (Phase 2b), North Room, Hall & Hall South–Occupation (10)	IVb
2766/A03–0113b	9	VII	B18 (Phase 2b), North Room, Hall & Hall South–Occupation (10)	IVb
2767/A03–0113c	9	VII	B18 (Phase 2b), North Room, Hall & Hall South–Occupation (10)	IVb

(continued)

Cat/Accession	Area	Rig	Feature	Phase
2768/A03–0113d	9	VII	B18 (Phase 2b), North Room, Hall & Hall South–Occupation (10)	IVb
2770/A03–0122	9	VII	B18 (Phase 2b), North Room, Hall & Hall South–Occupation (10)	IVb
2777/A03–0124c	9	VII	B18 (Phase 2b), North Room, Hall & Hall South–Occupation (10)	IVb
2785/A03–0245f	9	VII	B18 (Phase 2b), North Room, Hall & Hall South–Occupation (10)	IVb
2833/A03–0306a	10	VIII	M9b(a)	IVc
2840/A03–0312b	10	VIII	M9b(a)	IVc
2844/A03–0319c	10	VIII	M9b(a)	IVc
2858/A7779a	3	VI	M1.4d & B2, Late Occupation/Abandonment (2)	IVa–IVc
2859/A7779b	3	VI	M1.4d & B2, Late Occupation/Abandonment (2)	IVa–IVc
2864/A4821e	2	VI	M1.4d & B2, Late Occupation/Abandonment (2)	IVa–IVc
2865/A4821f	2	VI	M1.4d & B2, Late Occupation/Abandonment (2)	IVa–IVc
2879/A9358b	3	V	MC155, Pit 2691	IVb,IVc
2880/A9358c	3	V	MC155, Pit 2691	IVb,IVc
3035/A4941b	3	VI	M1.4d	IVb,IVc
3058/A8667d	3	VI	M1.4d	IVb,IVc
3072/A8668g	3	VI	M1.4d	IVb,IVc
3077/A8701a	3	VI	M1.4d	IVb,IVc
3081/A3449a	2	VI	M1.4d	IVb,IVc
3082/A3449b	2	VI	M1.4d	IVb,IVc
3083/A3449c	2	VI	M1.4d	IVb,IVc
3087/A4924c	2	VI	M1.4d	IVb,IVc
3088/A4924d	2	VI	M1.4d	IVb,IVc
3106/A6472a	2	VI	M1.4d	IVb,IVc
3107/A6472b	2	VI	M1.4d	IVb,IVc
3108/A8000a	3	VI	M1.4d, Pit 2566	IVb,IVc
3114/A8028d	3	VI	M1.4d, Pit 2566	IVb,IVc
3115/A8028e	3	VI	M1.4d, Pit 2566	IVb,IVc
3116/A8028f	3	VI	M1.4d, Pit 2566	IVb,IVc
3122/A3455	2	VI	M1.4d, Pit 2801	IVb,IVc
3128/A03–0253d	7	VI	M1.4h	IVc
3129/A03–0253e	7	VI	M1.4h	IVc
3130/A03–0253f	7	VI	M1.4h	IVc
3143/A03–0258a	7	VI	M1.4h	IVc
3180/A6072f	3	V, VI	M1.4c	IIIa–IVcc
3200/A6191e	3	V, VI	M1.4c	IIIa–IVcc
3203/A6206a	3	V, VI	M1.4c	IIIa–IVcc
3226/A6390b	3	V, VI	M1.4c	IIIa–IVcc
3233/A6395c	3	V, VI	M1.4c	IIIa–IVcc
3235/A6422a	3	V, VI	M1.4c	IIIa–IVcc
3236/A6422b	3	V, VI	M1.4c	IIIa–IVcc
3255/A03–0228a	7	VII	P8.3	IVc,IVcc
3274/A03–0226b	7	VII	P8.3	IVc,IVcc
3284/A03–0227e	7	VII	P8.3	IVc,IVcc
3285/A03–0227f	7	VII	P8.3	IVc,IVcc
3302/A03–0247a	7	VII	P8.3	IVc,IVcc
3306/A03–0250c	7	VII	P8.3	IVc,IVcc
3316/A03–0260e	7	VII	P8.3	IVc,IVcc
3336/A03–0261b	7	VII	P8.3 & M9a, PW7267	IVc,IVcc
3343/A03–0183a	7	VII	M9a	IVc,IVcc
3344/A03–0183b	7	VII	M9a	IVc,IVcc
3345/A03–0187a	7	VII	M9a	IVc,IVcc
3350/A03–0207c	7	VII	M9a	IVc,IVcc
3355/A03–0246d	7	VII	M9a	IVc,IVcc
3356/A03–0246e	7	VII	M9a	IVc,IVcc

(continued)

Cat/Accession	Area	Rig	Feature	Phase
3377/A03–0240b	7	VII	M9a	IVc,IVcc
3386/A03–0233c	7	VII	M9a	IVc,IVcc
3387/A03–0233d	7	VII	M9a	IVc,IVcc
3407/A03–0083a	9	VII	M9a	IVc,IVcc
3408/A03–0083b	9	VII	M9a	IVc,IVcc
3410/A03–0076a	9	VII	M9a	IVc,IVcc
3427/A03–0051a	9	VII	M9a, Pit 9026	IVc,IVcc
3428/A03–0051b	9	VII	M9a, Pit 9026	IVc,IVcc
3429/A03–0051c	9	VII	M9a, Pit 9026	IVc,IVcc
3430/A03–0051d	9	VII	M9a, Pit 9026	IVc,IVcc
3443/A03–0153a	10	VIII	M9b(b)	IVc,IVcc
3444/A03–0153b	10	VIII	M9b(b)	IVc,IVcc
3452/A03–0168b	10	VIII	M9b(b)	IVc,IVcc
3453/A03–0168c	10	VIII	M9b(b)	IVc,IVcc
3454/A03–0168d	10	VIII	M9b(b)	IVc,IVcc
3455/A03–0168e	10	VIII	M9b(b)	IVc,IVcc
3474/A03–0173a	10	VIII	M9b(b)	IVc,IVcc
3502/A03–0186b	10	VIII	M9b(b)	IVc,IVcc
3512/A03–0264	10	VIII	M9b(b), Pit 6132	IVc,IVcc
3524/A03–0225b	7	VI	M1.4i	IVcc
3525/A03–0225c	7	VI	M1.4i	IVcc
3526/A03–0225d	7	VI	M1.4i	IVcc
3527/A03–0225e	7	VI	M1.4i	IVcc
3547/A03–0238b	7	VI	M1.4i	IVcc
3567/A7688c	3	VI	M1.4e	IVcc(Va)(VI)
3568/A7688d	3	VI	M1.4e	IVcc(Va)(VI)
3584/A7795a	3	VI	M1.4e	IVcc(Va)(VI)
3596/A4318b	3	VI	M1.4e	IVcc(Va)
3626/A6077e	3	VI	M1.4e	IVcc(Va)
3636/A6382a	3	VI	M1.4e	IVcc(Va)
3643/A6406a	3	VI	M1.4e	IVcc(Va)
1025/A6215	3	VI	M1.4e, Pit 2446	IVcc(Va)
3654/A4903b	3	VI	M1.4e, Pit 2446	IVcc(Va)
3655/A6238a	3	VI	P6	IVcc,Va
3662/A5902c	3	VI	P6	IVcc,Va
3663/A5902d	3	VI	P6	IVcc,Va
3664/A5902e	3	VI	P6	IVcc,Va
3671/A7802a	3	VI	P6	IVcc,Va
3687/A1637a	3	VI	B34, MF2407	Va
3708/A03–0134b	7	VI	B34, Occupation	Va
3714/A03–0134h	7	VI	B34, Occupation	Va
3722/A03–0160f	7	VI	B34, Courtyard	Va
3723/A03–0160g	7	VI	B34, Courtyard	Va
3724/A03–0160h	7	VI	B34, Courtyard	Va
3726/A03–0160j	7	VI	B34, Courtyard	Va
3727/A03–0160k	7	VI	B34, Courtyard	Va
3762/A03–0190c	7	VI	B34, Courtyard	Va
3763/A03–0190d	7	VI	B34, Courtyard	Va
3764/A03–0190e	7	VI	B34, Courtyard	Va
3765/A03–0190f	7	VI	B34, Courtyard	Va
3817/A03–0164a	7	VI	B34, Courtyard	Va
3818/A03–0164b	7	VI	B34, Courtyard	Va
3887/A03–0125b	7	VI, VII	M1.5b	Vaa
3903/A03–0132h	7	VI, VII	M1.5b	Vaa
3904/A03–0132i	7	VI, VII	M1.5b	Vaa
3905/A03–0132j	7	VI, VII	M1.5b	Vaa
3906/A03–0132k	7	VI, VII	M1.5b	Vaa
3949/A03–0140c	7	VI, VII	M1.5b	Vaa

(continued)

Cat/Accession	Area	Rig	Feature	Phase
3969/A03–0143b	7	VI, VII	M1.5b	Vaa
3970/A03–0143c	7	VI, VII	M1.5b	Vaa
3979/A03–0148d	7	VI, VII	M1.5b	Vaa
3992/A03–0170i	7	VI, VII	M1.5b	Vaa
4032/A03–0157a	7	VII	P8.4	Va
4033/A03–0157b	7	VII	P8.4	Va
4036/A03–0158c	7	VII	P8.4	Va
4037/A03–0158d	7	VII	P8.4	Va
4048/A03–0159h	7	VII	P8.4	Va
4049/A03–0159i	7	VII	P8.4	Va
4050/A03–0159j	7	VII	P8.4	Va
4051/A03–0159k	7	VII	P8.4	Va
4052/A03–0159l	7	VII	P8.4	Va
4053/A03–0159m	7	VII	P8.4	Va
4054/A03–0159n	7	VII	P8.4	Va
4055/A03–0159o	7	VII	P8.4	Va
4080/A03–0194a	7	VII	P8.4	Va
4086/A03–0204	7	VII	P8.4	Va
4092/A03–0210f	7	VII	P8.4	Va
4108/A03–0211c	7	VII	P8.4	Va
4131/A03–0214i	7	VII	P8.4	Va
4132/A03–0214j	7	VII	P8.4	Va
4154/A03–0198c	7	VII	P8.4, Pit 7216	Va
4155/A03–0198d	7	VII	P8.4, Pit 7216	Va
4176/A03–0199a	7	VII	P8.4, Pit 7216	Va
4177/A03–0199b	7	VII	P8.4, Pit 7216	Va
4178/A03–0199c	7	VII	P8.4, Pit 7216	Va
4179/A03–0199d	7	VII	P8.4, Pit 7216	Va
4180/A03–0199e	7	VII	P8.4, Pit 7216	Va
4181/A03–0199f	7	VII	P8.4, Pit 7216	Va
4182/A03–0199g	7	VII	P8.4, Pit 7216	Va
4201/A4906b	1	V, VI	M5c	(IVc–)Va
4204/A4929a	3	VI	P6 & B1(b), Demolition	IVcc,Va
4206/A6196	3	VI	P6 & B1(b), Demolition	IVcc,Va
4211/A6232e	3	V	B1(a), Construction–Levelling	IVcc,Va
4212/A6232f	3	V	B1(a), Construction–Levelling	IVcc,Va
4222/A6074a	3	V	B1(a), T2477	IVcc,Va
4233/A4925b	3	V	B1(a), North Room–Floor (3a)	IVcc,Va
4242/A1239b	3	V	B1(b), North Room–Floor (6)	Va
4249/A4943d	2	V	B1(b), Demolition	Va
4253/A6410a	2	V	B1(b), Demolition	Va
4267/A6478f	1	V, VI	M5a	IVb–Vc
4268/A6478g	1	V, VI	M5a	IVb–Vc
4269/A6478h	1	V, VI	M5a	IVb–Vc
4286/A4923b	1	V, VI	M5a	IVb–Vc
4287/A6398	1	V, VI	M5a, Pit 3540	IVb–Vc
4311/A1251d	3	V, VI	M1.5a	Va,Vaa(VI)
4312/A1251e	3	V, VI	M1.5a	Va,Vaa(VI)
4399/A2247e	3	V, VI	M1.5a	Va,Vaa(VI)
4400/A2247f	3	V, VI	M1.5a	Va,Vaa(VI)
4401/A2247g	3	V, VI	M1.5a	Va,Vaa(VI)
4402/A2247h	3	V, VI	M1.5a	Va,Vaa(VI)
4403/A2247i	3	V, VI	M1.5a	Va,Vaa(VI)
4494/A4289b	3	V, VI	M1.5a	Va,Vaa(VI)
4526/A6188z	3	V, VI	M1.5a	Va,Vaa(VI)
4527/A6188aa	3	V, VI	M1.5a	Va,Vaa(VI)
4536/A6420	3	V, VI	M1.5a	Va,Vaa(VI)
4553/A1253d	3	V, VI	M1.5a	Va,Vaa

(continued)

Cat/Accession	Area	Rig	Feature	Phase
4818/A6237d	3	V, VI	M1.5a	Va,Vaa
4819/A6237e	3	V, VI	M1.5a	Va,Vaa
4824/A03–0218a	7	VII	M8a	Va,Vaa
4825/A03–0218b	7	VII	M8a	Va,Vaa
4834/A03–0175g	7	VII	M8a	Va,Vaa
4835/A03–0175h	7	VII	M8a	Va,Vaa
4836/A03–0175i	7	VII	M8a	Va,Vaa
4837/A03–0175j	7	VII	M8a	Va,Vaa
4838/A03–0175k	7	VII	M8a	Va,Vaa
4839/A03–0175l	7	VII	M8a	Va,Vaa
4840/A03–0175m	7	VII	M8a	Va,Vaa
4841/A03–0175n	7	VII	M8a	Va,Vaa
4842/A03–0175o	7	VII	M8a	Va,Vaa
4843/A03–0175p	7	VII	M8a	Va,Vaa
4877/A03–0126	7	VII	M8a	Va,Vaa
4878/A03–0131a	7	VII	M8a	Va,Vaa
4889/A03–0128d	7	VII	M8a	Va,Vaa
4920/A03–0162s	7	VII	M8a	Va,Vaa
4921/A03–0162t	7	VII	M8a	Va,Vaa
4922/A03–0162u	7	VII	M8a	Va,Vaa
4923/A03–0162v	7	VII	M8a	Va,Vaa
4924/A03–0162w	7	VII	M8a	Va,Vaa
4926/A03–0162y	7	VII	M8a	Va,Vaa
4927/A03–0162z	7	VII	M8a	Va,Vaa
4974/A03–0174n	7	VII	M8a	Va,Vaa
4975/A03–0174o	7	VII	M8a	Va,Vaa
4976/A03–0174p	7	VII	M8a	Va,Vaa
4977/A03–0174q	7	VII	M8a	Va,Vaa
4978/A03–0174r	7	VII	M8a	Va,Vaa
5023/A03–0212d	7	VII	M8a	Va,Vaa
5024/A03–0212e	7	VII	M8a	Va,Vaa
5025/A03–0212f	7	VII	M8a	Va,Vaa
5026/A03–0212g	7	VII	M8a	Va,Vaa
5027/A03–0212h	7	VII	M8a	Va,Vaa
5028/A03–0212i	7	VII	M8a	Va,Vaa
5029/A03–0212j	7	VII	M8a	Va,Vaa
5030/A03–0212k	7	VII	M8a	Va,Vaa
5031/A03–0212l	7	VII	M8a	Va,Vaa
5032/A03–0212m	7	VII	M8a	Va,Vaa
5105/A03–0147d	7	VII	M8a, Pit 7183	Va,Vaa
5115/A03–0151c	7	VII	M8a, Pit 7183	Va,Vaa
5116/A03–0151d	7	VII	M8a, Pit 7183	Va,Vaa
5136/A03–0137c	7	VII	M8a, Pit 7183	Va,Vaa
5137/A03–0137d	7	VII	M8a, Pit 7183	Va,Vaa
5138/A03–0137e	7	VII	M8a, Pit 7183	Va,Vaa
5139/A03–0137f	7	VII	M8a, Pit 7183	Va,Vaa
5140/A03–0137g	7	VII	M8a, Pit 7183	Va,Vaa
5141/A03–0137h	7	VII	M8a, Pit 7183	Va,Vaa
5201/A03–0129d	7	VII	M8a, T7193	Va,Vaa
5202/A03–0129e	7	VII	M8a, T7193	Va,Vaa
5203/A03–0129f	7	VII	M8a, T7193	Va,Vaa
5204/A03–0129g	7	VII	M8a, T7193	Va,Vaa
5229/A03–0082a	7	VII	B53 (Phase 1), North Area–Occupation (1b)	Vb
5230/A03–0082b	7	VII	B53 (Phase 1), North Area–Occupation (1b)	Vb
5231/A03–0082c	7	VII	B53 (Phase 1), North Area–Occupation (1b)	Vb
5235/A03–0056a	7	VII	B53 (Phase 1), North Area–Occupation (4)	Vb
5241/A03–0216	7	VII	B53 (Phase 1), Central Area–T7152	Vb
5289/A1248a	2	V, VI	M4a	Vaa–Vc

(continued)

Cat/Accession	Area	Rig	Feature	Phase
5309/A5896b	4	V, VI	M3a	Vb–Vc
5319/A4390g	4	V, VI	M3a	Vb–Vc
5330/A6399b	4	V, VI	M3a	Vb–Vc
5355/A6482e	4	VI	M3b	Vd
5356/A6738	4	VI	M3b	Vd
5363/A6200a	4	VI	M3b	Vd
5404/A6414b	4	VI	P1a	Vd
5487/A0821b	4	VI	M3b	Vd
5510/A1227a	4	VI	M3b	Vd
5511/A1227b	4	VI	M3b	Vd
5551/A4607	4	V	M3c	Vd
5558/A6244a	4	V	M3c	Vd
5595/A6192c	4	V	M3c	Vd
5636/A03–0032	10	VIII	B51, Wall 7006	Vd, Vdd
5712/A0118e	7/10	VII/VIII	Sondage 2003	u/s
5713/A0118f	7/10	VII/VIII	Sondage 2003	u/s
5714/A0118g	7/10	VII/VIII	Sondage 2003	u/s
5715/A0118h	7/10	VII/VIII	Sondage 2003	u/s
5716/A0118i	7/10	VII/VIII	Sondage 2003	u/s
5745/A5898e	2	V, VI	Unstratified	u/s
5746/A5898f	2	V, VI	Unstratified	u/s
5747/A5898g	2	V, VI	Unstratified	u/s
5748/A5898h	2	V, VI	Unstratified	u/s
5750/A6207	2	V, VI	Unstratified	u/s
5756/A6402a	2	V, VI	Unstratified	u/s
5757/A6402b	2	V, VI	Unstratified	u/s
5758/A6402c	2	V, VI	Unstratified	u/s
5759/A6402d	2	V, VI	Unstratified	u/s
5760/A6477	2	V, VI	Unstratified	u/s
5764/A0120b	3/4	V, VI	Unstratified	u/s
5773/A12574c	3/4	V, VI	Unstratified	u/s
5774/A12754d	3/4	V, VI	Unstratified	u/s
5816/A12487g	2	V, VI	Unstratified	u/s
5818/A6222b	4	V, VI	Unstratified	u/s
5819/A6222c	4	V, VI	Unstratified	u/s
5826/A03–0127c	7	VI, VII	Unstratified	u/s
5827/A03–0127d	7	VI, VII	Unstratified	u/s
5828/A03–0127e	7	VI, VII	Unstratified	u/s
5832/A03–0127i	7	VI, VII	Unstratified	u/s
5833/A03–0127j	7	VI, VII	Unstratified	u/s
5858/A03–0133i	7	VI, VII	Unstratified	u/s
North Sector				
5890/A7805d	5	–	CG005	4(5)
5893/A6236c	5	–	CG007, Pit 0276	4,5
5917/A0109c	5, A	–	Lade (4)	6–12(b–e)
5918/A0109d	5, A	–	Lade (4)	6–12(b–e)
5919/A0109e	5, A	–	Lade (4)	6–12(b–e)
5920/A0109f	5, A	–	Lade (4)	6–12(b–e)
5921/A0109g	5, A	–	Lade (4)	6–12(b–e)
5922/A0107a	5, A	–	Lade (4)	6–12(b–e)
5930/A0110b	5, A	–	Lade (4)	6–12(b–e)
5960/A0105a	5, A	–	CG024	14–16
South/North Sectors				
5979/L1694f	–	–	Unstratified	u/s
5980/L1694g	–	–	Unstratified	u/s
5992/A?	–	–	Unstratified	u/s

Rands

A total of 135 fragments of rand were found, apart from those still attached to soles or uppers. They ranged in date from the early 12th to the mid-14th century, with particular concentrations in Periods II (25; 18%), IV (50; 37%) and V (30; 22%). The examples of 12th (35; 25%) and 13th century (60; 44%) date are of particular interest in view of Thornton's (1973a, 9) suggestion that they were a 14th-century innovation. However, he himself records their existence in 9th–10th-century Winchester (Thornton 1990b, 593). He also identified rands of a similar date on a thonged shoe from Little Paxton, Cambridgeshire (Thornton 1969b, 91).

Even earlier rands have apparently been recorded on a shoe from the Sutton Hoo ship burial (East 1983, 793, Fig 569, a and b). A different form of rand was found at Swinegate, York; here, a folded strip had been stitched the sole–upper seam of an 11th-century shoe (Carlisle 1998). On the other hand, thin rands that had been noted on some 10th-century shoes from London proved, on closer examination, to be delaminated fragments of the soles' edge–flesh stitching channels (Pritchard 1991, 217–18). Furthermore, Grew and de Neergaard state that rands were not a common feature before the end of the 12th century. It is certainly clear, from the evidence from the High Street and elsewhere, that they were a standard shoe component from the late 12th century, if not earlier.

In 13 instances, fragments of rand were found still attached to soles and/or uppers. Their date range mirrors that of the unattached rands: Periods II, three; IV, five; V, four and unstratified, one.

Rands.

Cat/Accession	Area	Rig	Feature	Phase
South Sector				
97/A12289c	4	V/VI	MC017	Ia–Icc>
98/A12289d	4	V/VI	MC017	Ia–Icc>
99/A12289e	4	V/VI	MC017	Ia–Icc>
100/A12289f	4	V/VI	MC017	Ia–Icc>
145/A7789d	2	VI	P5.2a	Ie
189/A7797c	2	VI	M14b(b)	Ie
190/A7797d	2	VI	M14b(b)	Ie
265/A7044Be	2	VI	MC044b	If
266/A7044Bf	2	VI	MC044b	If
290/A03–0017e	3	V	MC053a	If
313/A12310	3	V	MC039, Pit 2609	If,IIa
343/A6772c	2	VI	MC061	IIb
356/A6773e	2	VI	MC061	IIb
407/A12493b	3	VI	MC056, Pit 5155	Ia–IIc
408/A12493c	3	VI	MC056, Pit 5155	Ia–IIc
409/A12493d	3	VI	MC056, Pit 5155	Ia–IIc
410/A12493e	3	VI	MC056, Pit 5155	Ia–IIc
441/A6483k	2	VI	B4, 'Byre'–Occupation	IIc
451/A10773b	3	VI	MC066	IIc
454/A10048c	4	VI	M1.1f, Pit 2383	IIb,IIc
463/A10599b	3	VI	M1.1c, Pit 5005	IId
492/A12290b	1	VI	MC071	IIb–IIf
493/A12290c	1	VI	MC071	IIb–IIf
506/A3447c	2	VI	M1.1d & M1.1e	IId–IIf
544/A6376c	2	V	B5, North Room–Floor/Occupation (2)	IIa–IIff
545/A6376d	2	V	B5, North Room–Floor/Occupation (2)	IIa–IIff
612/A9879b	4	V	M10	IId–IIg
663/A9553i	4	V	M10, Pit 4552	IId–IIg
664/A9553j	4	V	M10, Pit 4552	IId–IIg
665/A9553k	4	V	M10, Pit 4552	IId–IIg
792/A9546e	3	VI	M1.2, Pit 2648	<IIg(IIh)
813/A11220b	3	VI	M1.2, Pit 2648	<IIg(IIh)
822/A11221b	3	VI	M1.2, Pit 2648	<IIg(IIh)
876/A8665c	3	VI	M1.3	IIi
877/A8665d	3	VI	M1.3	IIi
925/A11639d	1	VI	MC111	IIb–IIIb
926/A11639e	1	VI	MC111	IIb–IIIb
927/A11639f	1	VI	MC111	IIb–IIIb
1097/A03–0270c	9	VII	P8.1c	IIIc
1104/A03–0287b	9	VII	P8.1c	IIIc
1107/A03–0304b	9	VII	P8.1c	IIIc
1129/A03–0252b	9	VII	M15	IIId
1131/A03–0263b	9	VII	M15	IIId
1132/A03–0263c	9	VII	M15	IIId
1133/A03–0263d	9	VII	M15	IIId
1304/A8810e	3	V	P2.2b	IVa
1318/A7989e	4	V	MC143	IVaa
1390/A8021d	3	V/VI	MC144, WW2221	<IIId–IVaa
1391/A8021e	3	V/VI	MC144, WW2221	<IIId–IVaa
1392/A8021f	3	V/VI	MC144, WW2221	<IIId–IVaa
1393/A8021g	3	V/VI	MC144, WW2221	<IIId–IVaa
1394/A8021h	3	V/VI	MC144, WW2221	<IIId–IVaa
1395/A8021i	3	V/VI	MC144, WW2221	<IIId–IVaa
2315/A03–0284c	7	VI	M1.4f	IVc

(continued)

Cat/Accession	Area	Rig	Feature	Phase
2335/A03–0291c	7	VI	M1.4f	IVc
2336/A03–0291d	7	VI	M1.4f	IVc
2341/A03–0308d	7	VI	M1.4f	IVc
2361/A03–0331a	7	VI	M1.4f	IVc
2482/A03–0392d	7	VI	M1.4f	IVc
2483/A03–0392e	7	VI	M1.4f	IVc
2484/A03–0392f	7	VI	M1.4f	IVc
2485/A03–0392g	7	VI	M1.4f	IVc
2719/A03–0314c	7	VII	B18 (Phase 2a), External (1), Pit 7314	IVb
2725/A03–0413a	7	VII	B18 (Phases 2a & 2b), T7385	IVb
2756/A03–0288c	7	VII	B18 (Phase 2b), North Room, Hall & Hall South–Occupation (10)	IVb
2757/A03–0288d	7	VII	B18 (Phase 2b), North Room, Hall & Hall South–Occupation (10)	IVb
2758/A03–0288e	7	VII	B18 (Phase 2b), North Room, Hall & Hall South–Occupation (10)	IVb
2775/A03–0124a	9	VII	B18 (Phase 2b), North Room, Hall & Hall South–Occupation (10)	IVb
2776/A03–0124b	9	VII	B18 (Phase 2b), North Room, Hall & Hall South–Occupation (10)	IVb
2782/A03–0245c	9	VII	B18 (Phase 2b), North Room, Hall & Hall South–Occupation (10)	IVb
2783/A03–0245d	9	VII	B18 (Phase 2b), North Room, Hall & Hall South–Occupation (10)	IVb
2806/A03–0274a	7	VII	B18 (Phase 2b), Hall, Pit 7290	IVb
2863/A4821d	2	VI	M1.4d & B2, Late Occupation/Abandonment (2)	IVa–IVc
3071/A8668f	3	VI	M1.4d	IVb,IVc
3220/A6228b	3	V, VI	M1.4c	IIIa–IVcc
3319/A03–0262a	7	VII	P8.3	IVc,IVcc
3322/A03–0066b	9	VII	P8.3	IVc,IVcc
3323/A03–0066c	9	VII	P8.3	IVc,IVcc
3324/A03–0066d	9	VII	P8.3	IVc,IVcc
3325/A03–0066e	9	VII	P8.3	IVc,IVcc
3326/A03–0066f	9	VII	P8.3	IVc,IVcc
3341/A03–0205b	7	VII	M9a	IVc,IVcc
3353/A03–0246b	7	VII	M9a	IVc,IVcc
3427/A03–0051a	9	VII	M9a, Pit 9026	IVc,IVcc
3428/A03–0051b	9	VII	M9a, Pit 9026	IVc,IVcc
3429/A03–0051c	9	VII	M9a, Pit 9026	IVc,IVcc
3430/A03–0051d	9	VII	M9a, Pit 9026	IVc,IVcc
3435/A03–0086	10	VIII	M9b(b)	IVc,IVcc
3451/A03–0168a	10	VIII	M9b(b)	IVc,IVcc
3520/A03–0224d	7	VI	M1.4i	IVcc
3599/A4329b	3	VI	M1.4e	IVcc(Va)
3600/A4329c	3	VI	M1.4e	IVcc(Va)
3601/A4329d	3	VI	M1.4e	IVcc(Va)
3648/A7780c	3	VI	M1.4e	IVcc(Va)
3649/A7780d	3	VI	M1.4e	IVcc(Va)
3710/A03–0134d	7	VI	B34, Occupation	Va
3711/A03–0134e	7	VI	B34, Occupation	Va
3712/A03–0134f	7	VI	B34, Occupation	Va
3713/A03–0134g	7	VI	B34, Occupation	Va
3864/A03–0067b	7	VI, VII	M1.5b	Vaa
3899/A03–0132d	7	VI, VII	M1.5b	Vaa
3900/A03–0132e	7	VI, VII	M1.5b	Vaa
3901/A03–0132f	7	VI, VII	M1.5b	Vaa
3983/A03–0169	7	VI, VII	M1.5b	Vaa

(continued)

Cat/Accession	Area	Rig	Feature	Phase
4043/A03–0159c	7	VII	P8.4	Va
4044/A03–0159d	7	VII	P8.4	Va
4045/A03–0159e	7	VII	P8.4	Va
4046/A03–0159f	7	VII	P8.4	Va
4047/A03–0159g	7	VII	P8.4	Va
4107/A03–0211b	7	VII	P8.4	Va
4123/A03–0214a	7	VII	P8.4	Va
4128/A03–0214f	7	VII	P8.4	Va
4129/A03–0214g	7	VII	P8.4	Va
4398/A2247d	3	V, VI	M1.5a	Va,Vaa(VI)
4817/A6237c	3	V, VI	M1.5a	Va,Vaa
4830/A03–0175c	7	VII	M8a	Va,Vaa
4833/A03–0175f	7	VII	M8a	Va,Vaa
4917/A03–0162p	7	VII	M8a	Va,Vaa
4918/A03–0162q	7	VII	M8a	Va,Vaa
4919/A03–0162r	7	VII	M8a	Va,Vaa
4973/A03–0174m	7	VII	M8a	Va,Vaa
5104/A03–0147c	7	VII	M8a, Pit 7183	Va,Vaa
5135/A03–0137b	7	VII	M8a, Pit 7183	Va,Vaa
5241/A03–0216	7	VII	B53(Phase 1), Central Area–T7152	Vb
5293/A6071b	2	V, VI	M4a	Vaa–Vc
5768/A9821a	3/4	V, VI	Unstratified	u/s
5769/A9821b	3/4	V, VI	Unstratified	u/s
5781/A0800c	3/4	V, VI	Unstratified	u/s
5782/A0800d	3/4	V, VI	Unstratified	u/s
5857/A03–0133h	–	VI, VII	Unstratified	u/s
North Sector				
5916/A0109b	5, A	–	Lade (4)	6–12(b–e)
South/North Sectors				
5974/L1694a	–	–	Unstratified	u/s
5975/L1694b	–	–	Unstratified	u/s
5976/L1694c	–	–	Unstratified	u/s
5977/L1694d	–	–	Unstratified	u/s

Stitching channels (see list)

Edge–flesh stitching channels: soles (see list)

Edge–flesh stitching channels: uppers (see list)

Edge–flesh stitching channels (see list)

Grain to flesh stitching channels (see list)

There were 146 fragments of stitching channels which survived separately. These included sole and upper edge–flesh stitching channels and lasting margins of uppers. They occurred in all the South Sector periods (Period I: 10, 7%; Period II: 8, 5%; Period III: 6, 4%; Period V: 31, 21%; unstratified: 7, 5%) and with the largest group coming from Period IV (74, 51%), that is the second half of the 13th century. Seven (5%) were also recovered from the North Sector of the High Street excavation and three (2%) had lost their labels in conservation.

Stitching channels.

Cat/Accession	Area	Rig	Feature	Phase
South Sector				
131/A12308d	3	V	MC025, Pit 5337	(Ia–)Id
132/A12308e	3	V	MC025, Pit 5337	(Ia–)Id
133/A12308f	3	V	MC025, Pit 5337	(Ia–)Id
547/A6376f	2	V	B5, North Room–Floor/Occupation (2)	IIa–IIff
932/A03–0380	9	VII	B19 (Phases 1 & 2a), South Room–Floor (2) & Destruction, T9574	IIIa,IIIb
1030/A03–0320a	9	VII	P8.1b	IIIc
1708/A03–0396e	10	VIII	MC131	<IVa–IVb
1709/A03–0396f	10	VIII	MC131	<IVa–IVb
1710/A03–0396g	10	VIII	MC131	<IVa–IVb
1711/A03–0396h	10	VIII	MC131	<IVa–IVb
1712/A03–0396i	10	VIII	MC131	<IVa–IVb
1755/A03–0350d	7	VII	MC126, Pit 7402	IVaa,IVb
1756/A03–0350e	7	VII	MC126, Pit 7402	IVaa,IVb
1757/A03–0350f	7	VII	MC126, Pit 7402	IVaa,IVb
1758/A03–0350g	7	VII	MC126, Pit 7402	IVaa,IVb
1778/A03–0366b	7	VII	MC126, Pit 7402	IVaa,IVb
1779/A03–0366c	7	VII	MC126, Pit 7402	IVaa,IVb
1892/A03–0357h	7	VII	MC126, Pit 7402	IVaa,IVb
1893/A03–0357i	7	VII	MC126, Pit 7402	IVaa,IVb
1894/A03–0357j	7	VII	MC126, Pit 7402	IVaa,IVb
1895/A03–0357k	7	VII	MC126, Pit 7402	IVaa,IVb
1896/A03–0357l	7	VII	MC126, Pit 7402	IVaa,IVb
2182/A03–0385b	7	VII	MC126, Pit 7402	IVaa,IVb
2183/A03–0385c	7	VII	MC126, Pit 7402	IVaa,IVb
2184/A03–0385d	7	VII	MC126, Pit 7402	IVaa,IVb
2185/A03–0385e	7	VII	MC126, Pit 7402	IVaa,IVb
2349/A03–0322b	7	VI	M1.4f	IVc
2405/A03–0342c	7	VI	M1.4f	IVc
2456/A03–0326e	7	VI	M1.4f	IVc
2457/A03–0326f	7	VI	M1.4f	IVc
2458/A03–0326g	7	VI	M1.4f	IVc
2459/A03–0326h	7	VI	M1.4f	IVc
2575/A03–0329g	7	VII	B18 (Phase 1/2)	IVaa,IVb
2576/A03–0329h	7	VII	B18 (Phase 1/2)	IVaa,IVb
2577/A03–0329i	7	VII	B18 (Phase 1/2)	IVaa,IVb
2578/A03–0329j	7	VII	B18 (Phase 1/2)	IVaa,IVb
2601/A03–0184b	9	VII	B18 (Phase 1/2)	IVaa,IVb
2738/A03–0368f	10	VII	B18 (Phases 2a & 2b), MW6155	IVb
2815/A03–0388	10	VIII	MC153	IVb
2845/A03–0319d	10	VIII	M9b(a)	IVc
2846/A03–0319e	10	VIII	M9b(a)	IVc
2847/A03–0319f	10	VIII	M9b(a)	IVc
2850/A03–0328a	10	VIII	M9b(a)	IVc
2851/A03–0328b	10	VIII	M9b(a)	IVc
2852/A03–0328c	10	VIII	M9b(a)	IVc
2853/A03–0328d	10	VIII	M9b(a)	IVc
3286/A03–0227g	7	VII	P8.3	IVc,IVcc
3366/A03–0229a	7	VII	M9a	IVc,IVcc
3423/A03–0077a	9	VII	B18 (Phases 2a & 2b) & M9a, PH7237	(IVb)IVc,IVcc
3424/A03–0077b	9	VII	B18 (Phases 2a & 2b) & M9a, PH7237	(IVb)IVc,IVcc
3475/A03–0173b	10	VIII	M9b(b)	IVc,IVcc
3476/A03–0173c	10	VIII	M9b(b)	IVc,IVcc
3477/A03–0173d	10	VIII	M9b(b)	IVc,IVcc

(continued)

Cat/Accession	Area	Rig	Feature	Phase
3478/A03–0173e	10	VIII	M9b(b)	IVc,IVcc
3479/A03–0173f	10	VIII	M9b(b)	IVc,IVcc
3480/A03–0173g	10	VIII	M9b(b)	IVc,IVcc
3481/A03–0173h	10	VIII	M9b(b)	IVc,IVcc
3504/A03–0208a	10	VIII	M9b(b)	IVc,IVcc
3514/A03–0185a	10	VIII	M9b(b), MF6064	IVc,IVcc
3766/A03–0190g	7	VI	B34, Courtyard	Va
3828/A03–0177c	7	VI	B34, Courtyard	Va
3829/A03–0177d	7	VI	B34, Courtyard	Va
4156/A03–0198e	7	VII	P8.4, Pit 7216	Va
4157/A03–0198f	7	VII	P8.4, Pit 7216	Va
5033/A03–0212n	7	VII	M8a	Va,Vaa
5034/A03–0212o	7	VII	M8a	Va,Vaa
5786/A0800h	3/4	V, VI	Unstratified	u/s
North Sector				
5932/A0110d	5, A	–	Lade (4)	6–12(b–e)
5937/A0119a	5, A	–	Lade (4)	6–12(b–e)
5938/A0119b	5, A	–	Lade (4)	6–12(b–e)

Edge–flesh stiching channels: soles.

Cat/Accession	Area	Rig	Feature	Phase
South Sector				
1134/A03–0263e	9	VII	M15	IIId
1135/A03–0263f	9	VII	M15	IIId
2376/A03–0333c	7	VI	M1.4f	IVc
2532/A03–0401s	7	VII	P8.2b	IVb
2787/A03–0245h	9	VII	B18 (Phase 2b), North Room, Hall & Hall South–Occupation (10)	IVb
3268/A03–0242a	7	VII	P8.3	IVc,IVcc
3388/A03–0233e	7	VII	M9a	IVc,IVcc
3456/A03–0168f	10	VIII	M9b(b)	IVc,IVcc
3820/A03–0164d	7	VI	B34, Courtyard	Va
3826/A03–0177a	7	VI	B34, Courtyard	Va
3827/A03–0177b	7	VI	B34, Courtyard	Va
3959/A03–0140m	7	VI, VII	M1.5b	Vaa
4110/A03–0211e	7	VII	P8.4	Va
4183/A03–0199h	7	VII	P8.4, Pit 7216	Va
5035/A03–0212p	7	VII	M8a	Va,Vaa
5036/A03–0212q	7	VII	M8a	Va,Vaa
5117/A03–0151e	7	VII	M8a, Pit 7183	Va,Vaa
5787/A0800i	3/4	V, VI	Unstratified	u/s
North Sector				
5961/A0105b	5, A	–	CG024	14–16
South/North Sectors				
5972/L1694b	–	–	Unstratified	u/s
5987/A?	–	–	Unstratified	u/s

Edge–flesh stiching channels: uppers.

Cat/Accession	Area	Rig	Feature	Phase
South Sector				
109/A6403c	1	V	MC029, Pit 3125	Id
110/A6403d	1	V	MC029, Pit 3125	Id
4021/A03–0155b	7	VII	P8.4	Va
North Sector				
5883/A0812b	5, A	–	Natural	0

Edge–flesh stiching channels.

Cat/Accession	Area	Rig	Feature	Phase
South Sector				
301/A12632g	4	V	B16b, Pit 4726	Id–IIa
302/A12632h	4	V	B16b, Pit 4726	Id–IIa
303/A12632i	4	V	B16b, Pit 4726	Id–IIa
304/A12632j	4	V	B16b, Pit 4726	Id–IIa
679/A9553y	4	V	M10, Pit 4552	IId–IIg
2491/A03–0392m	7	VI	M1.4f	IVc
2492/A03–0392n	7	VI	M1.4f	IVc
3528/A03–0225f	7	VI	M1.4i	IVcc
4313/A1251f	3	V, VI	M1.5a	Va, Vaa(VI)
4314/A1251g	3	V, VI	M1.5a	Va, Vaa(VI)

Grain–flesh stiching channels.

Cat/Accession	Area	Rig	Feature	Phase
South Sector				
118/A03–0002c	4	V, VI	MC023	Icc, Id
119/A03–0002d	4	V, VI	MC023	Icc, Id
1028/A03–0317c	9	VII	P8.1b	IIIc
3529/A03–0225g	7	VI	M1.4i	IVcc
3530/A03–0225h	7	VI	M1.4i	IVcc
3531/A03–0225i	7	VI	M1.4i	IVcc
5765/A0120c	3/4	V, VI	Unstratified	u/s

Clumps (see list)

Upper repair patches

The 67 clump soles and three upper repair patches listed below do not include those still attached to soles and those indicated by stitch holes on soles. Both seat and forepart clumps survive. One unusual seat clump (Cat No 5855/A03–0133f; Illus 104) has been made out of two separate fragments, joined together with a butted edge–flesh seam. Two items, Cat Nos 1761/A03–0360 and 5780/A0800b (Illus 104), may be upper repair patches.

Another survives with its upper (Cat No 626/A9885b; Illus 104). Clump soles were found in contexts of all periods, but were especially numerous in Period IV (27; 41%). Clump soles surviving in situ or tunnel stitch holes for them show that 85 soles had been patched. Type 1 soles were the most patched, with 28 examples, which represent 33% of the repaired soles, or 50% of their type. Types 2, 3 and 4 accounted for 15%, 9% and 7% of the patched soles, respectively.

Substantial proportions of the two-part soles had been repaired: 28.5% of Type 7, 6% of Type 8, and 24% of Type 9. This reinforces the suggestion that two-part soles represent repairs or cobbling.

Period IV, the second half of the 13th century, produced the most evidence for repairs (40.4%), followed by Periods II (21.3%), V (16.3%) and I (11.3%). (These last figures are based on the combined evidence of surviving separate clumps, those in situ and stitching for them.)

Table 12 *Clump soles and evidence for repair.*

period	date	separate clump soles		clumps in situ and/or stitching		total evidence for repair	
		number	%	number	%	number	%
I	1100–1150	5	9%	11	13%	16	11.3%
II	1150–1200	12	21.4%	18	21%	30	21.3%
III	1200–1250	3	5.3%	6	7%	9	6.4%
IV	1250–1300	24	43%	33	39%	57	40.4%
V	1300–1350>	9	16%	14	16.5%	23	16.3%
unstratified		3	5.3%	3	3.5%	6	4.3%

Clumps.

Cat/Accession	Area	Rig	Feature	Phase
South Sector				
7/A12300c	1	V, VI	MC002	Ia
108/A6403b	1	V	MC029, Pit 3125	Id
115/A10799b	4	V, VI	MC023	Icc,Id
129/A12308b	3	V	MC025, Pit 5337	(Ia–)Id
222/A7436a	2	VI	P5.2b	Ie
223/A7436b	2	VI	P5.2b	Ie
240/A7072c	2	V	M14b(c)	Id–If
259/A6984a	2	VI	MC044b	If
284/A9556a	3	VI	MC053c	If
313/A12310	3	V	MC039, Pit 2609	If,IIa
330/A6769	1/2	VI	P5.4a	IIb
379/A12282e	1	VI	MC065, Pit 3908	IIa–IIc
387/A12374a	1	VI	MC065, T3907	IIa–IIc
438/A6483h	2	VI	B4, 'Byre'–Occupation	IIc
439/A6483i	2	VI	B4, 'Byre'–Occupation	IIc
440/A6483j	2	VI	B4, 'Byre'–Occupation	IIc
528/A6748	2	V	B5, North Room–Floor/Occupation (1)	IIa–IIff
554/A6498b	2	V	B5, Destruction	IIa–IIff
799/A10494	3	VI	M1.2, Pit 2648	<IIg(IIh)
854/A8655	4	VI	B13, Floor (1b)	IIh
920/A12536b	4	VI	M1.3	IIi
936/A03–0358	9	VII	P8.0	IIIa,IIIb
943/A03–0397	9	VII	M13	IIg–IIIb
944/A03–0400a	9	VII	M13	IIg–IIIb
1316/A7989c	4	V	MC143	IVaa
1317/A7989d	4	V	MC143	IVaa
1554/A03–0422b	7	VII	MC130	<IIIc–IVaa
1649/A8522a	3	VI	B2, Floor (2a)	IVa,IVaa
1660/A03–0417b	7	VI	P3.3	IVa–IVb
1661/A03–0417c	7	VI	P3.3	IVa–IVb
1763/A03–0360c	7	VII	MC126, Pit 7402	IVaa,IVb
1810/A03–0374b	7	VII	MC126, Pit 7402	IVaa,IVb
2313/A03–0284a	7	VI	M1.4f	IVc
2314/A03–0284b	7	VI	M1.4f	IVc
2334/A03–0291b	7	VI	M1.4f	IVc
2362/A03–0331b	7	VI	M1.4f	IVc
2542/A03–0375a	7	VII	P8.2b	IVb
2597/A03–0191	9	VII	B18 (Phase 1/2)	IVaa,IVb
2650/A03–0305	7	VII	B18 (Phase 1/2), Pit 7324	IVaa,IVb
2803/A03–0088a	9	VII	B18 (Phase 2b), Hall & Hall South–Occupation (12a)	IVb
3075/A8679	3	VI	M1.4d	IVb,IVc
3118/A8681b	3	VI	M1.4d, Pit 2566	IVb,IVc
3199/A6191d	3	V, VI	M1.4c	IIIa–IVcc
3232/A6395b	3	V, VI	M1.4c	IIIa–IVcc
3237/A6728a	3	V, VI	M1.4c	IIIa–IVcc
3398/A03–0268c	7	VII	M9a	IVc,IVcc
3399/A03–0268d	7	VII	M9a	IVc,IVcc
3508/A03–0221	10	VIII	M9b(b)	IVc,IVcc
3511/A03–0251	10	VIII	M9b(b), Pit 6127	IVc,IVcc
3519/A03–0224c	7	VI	M1.4i	IVcc
3523/A03–0225a	7	VI	M1.4i	IVcc
3865/A03–0068	7	VI, VII	M1.5b	Vaa
3927/AA03–0136c	7	VI, VII	M1.5b	Vaa

(continued)

Cat/Accession	Area	Rig	Feature	Phase
3928/AA03–0136d	7	VI, VII	M1.5b	Vaa
3929/AA03–0136e	7	VI, VII	M1.5b	Vaa
3936/A03–0136l	7	VI, VII	M1.5b	Vaa
3957/A03–0140k	7	VI, VII	M1.5b	Vaa
4310/A1251c	3	V, VI	M1.5a	Va,Vaa(VI)
4532/A6245c	3	V, VI	M1.5a	Va,Vaa(VI)
5242/A03–0119a	7	VII	B53 (Phase 1), Central Area–T7152	Vb
5260/A03–0089a	10	VIII	M8b	Va,Vaa(–Vc)
5403/A6414a	4	VI	P1a	Vd
5556/A6242b	4	V	M3c	Vd
5780/A0800b	3/4	V, VI	Unstratified	u/s
5855/A03–0133f	7	VI, VII	Unstratified	u/s
5856/A03–0133g	7	VI, VII	Unstratified	u/s
North Sector				
5953/A0108a	5, A	–	Lade (3)	6–12(d,e)

Upper repair patches.

Cat/Accession	Area	Rig	Feature	Phase
South Sector				
626/A9885b	4	V	M10	IId–IIg
1761/A03–0360a	7	VII	MC126, Pit 7402	IVaa,IVb
5780/A0800b	3/4	V, VI	Unstratified	u/s

Welted soles.

Cat/Accession	Area	Rig	Feature	Phase
South Sector				
5793/A0817b	3/4	V, VI	Unstratified	u/s
South/North Sectors				
5983/L2766b	–	–	Unstratified	u/s
5984/L2766c	–	–	Unstratified	u/s

Bunions.

Cat/Accession	Leather type	Area	Rig	Feature	Phase
South Sector					
129/A12308b	Sole (Type 1), clump	3	V	MC025, Pit 5337	(Ia–)Id
363/A2296a	Sole (Type 1)	1	V	M14a, Pit 3040	Id–IIc
364/A2296b	Upper (Type Aii)	1	V	M14a, Pit 3040	Id–IIc
406/A12493a	Sole (Type 1)	3	VI	MC056, Pit 5155	Ia–IIc
776/A9371b	Sole (Type 2)	3	VI	M1.2, Pit 2648	<IIg(IIh)
2985/A10521	Sole (Type 3)	3	V	MC155, Pit 2691	IVb,IVc
4153/A03–0198b	Upper (Type Kii)	7	VII	P8.4, Pit 7216	Va

Welted soles (Illus 145)

Three welted outer soles were found at the High Street. All three came from unstratified deposits (Illus 145).

Bunions (Illus 145)

Bulges on five soles and two uppers have almost certainly been caused by *hallux valgus* or bunion joint in the wearer. As the great toe is pushed sideways, the metatarso-phalangeal joint becomes very swollen, creating a bulge on the vamp of the shoe, as on upper Cat No 364/A2296b (Illus 145). As medieval turnshoe soles are slightly dished, the edge of the sole is often pushed out of shape, as on the examples listed above. On sole Cat No 2985/A10521, the strain of the bulge on the sole has also resulted in a hole (Illus 145) (cf Swallow 1973, 29–30).

No indications of any other foot problems, such as hammertoe, were recognised.

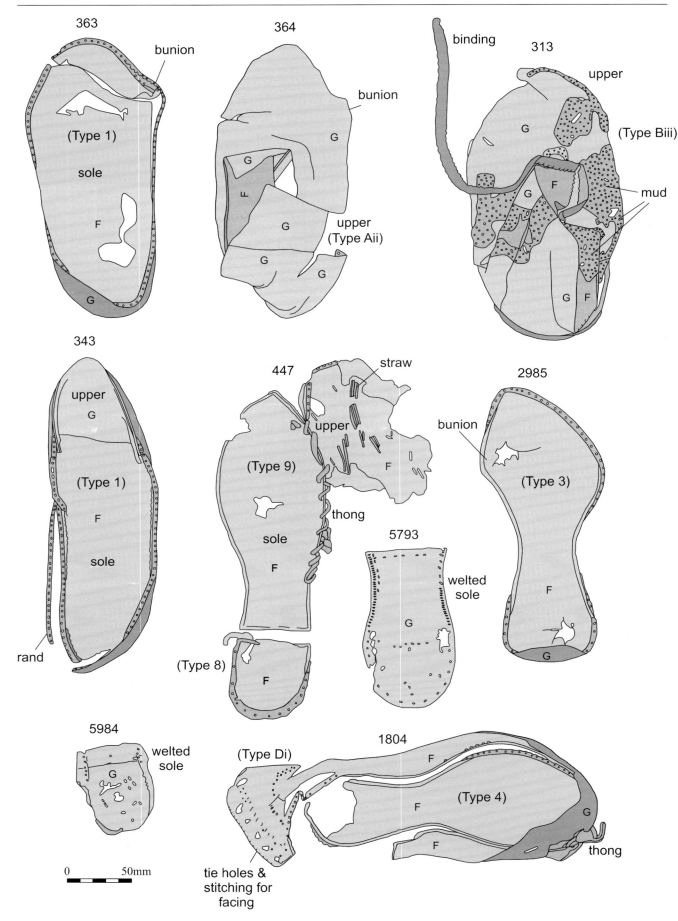

Illus 145 Two soles damaged by bunions, one with matching upper; three soles with uppers attached; two welted soles; one upper with mud (sole not visible).

Soles with attached or matching uppers (Illus 104, 124, 137, 139–41, 145–7).

Cat/Accession	Leather type	Area	Rig	Feature	Phase
South Sector					
28/A10800b	Sole (Type 6)	1	V	MC008, T3774	Ib
30/A10800d	Upper (Type Bi)	1	V	MC008, T3774	Ib
125/A12297a	Sole (Type 1)	3	V	MC025, Pit 5337	(Ia–)Id
126/A12297b	Upper (Type Bi)	3	V	MC025, Pit 5337	(Ia–)Id
156/A7787c	Sole (Type 3)	1/2	VI	B6 (Phase 1), South Room–Floor (1)	Ie
163/A7787j	Upper (Type H)	1/2	VI	B6(Phase 1) 1, South Room–Floor (1)	Ie
173/A7580b	Sole (Type 2)	2	VI	M14b(b)	Ie
174/A7580c	Upper (Type Aii)	2	VI	M14b(b)	Ie
182/A7597a	Sole	2	VI	M14b(b)	Ie
183/A7597b	Upper (Type Bi)	2	VI	M14b(b)	Ie
187/A7797a	Sole	2	VI	M14b(b)	Ie
191/A7797e	Upper (Type Bi)	2	VI	M14b(b)	Ie
222/A7436a	Sole (Type 1), upper, clump, thong	2	VI	P5.2b	Ie
286/A03–0017a	Sole (Type 1)	3	V	MC053a	If
287/A03–0017b	Upper (vamp)	3	V	MC053a	If
306/A12635b	Sole (Type 2)	4	V	B16b, Pit 4726	Id–IIa
307/A12635c	Upper (Type Bi)	4	V	B16b, Pit 4726	Id–IIa
313/A12310	Sole (Type 1), rand, clump, upper (Type Biii)	3	V	MC039, Pit 2609	If,IIa
314/A10365a	Sole (Type 6)	3	V	MC049	IIa
315/A10365b	Upper (Type F)	3	V	MC049	IIa
331/A6774a	Sole (Type 1)	1/2	VI	P5.4a	IIb
332/A6774b	Upper (Type Ai)	1/2	VI	P5.4a	IIb
343/A6772c	Sole (Type 1), rand, upper	2	VI	MC061	IIb
352/A6773a	Sole (Type 2)	2	VI	MC061	IIb
353/A6773b	Sole (Type 1)	2	VI	MC061	IIb
357/A6773f	Upper (Type Bi)	2	VI	MC061	IIb
358/A6773g	Upper (Type Bii)	2	VI	MC061	IIb
363/A2296a	Sole (Type 1), bunion	1	V	M14a, Pit 3040	Id–IIc
364/A2296b	Upper (Type Aii)	1	V	M14a, Pit 3040	Id–IIc
389/A12296a	Sole (Type 1)	1	VI	MC065	IIa–IIc
390/A12296b	Upper (Type Bi)	1	VI	MC065	IIa–IIc
447/A6722	Sole (Types 8 & 9), upper	2	VI	B4, 'Byre'–Occupation	IIc
452/A10048a	Sole (Type 1)	4	VI	M1.1f, Pit 2383	IIb,IIc
453/A10048b	Sole (Type 2)	4	VI	M1.1f, Pit 2383	IIb,IIc
455/A10048d	Upper (Type Aii)	4	VI	M1.1f, Pit 2383	IIb,IIc
456/A10048e	Upper (Type J)	4	VI	M1.1f, Pit 2383	IIb,IIc
462/A10599a	Sole (Type 1)	3	VI	M1.1c, Pit 5005	IId
464/A10599c	Upper	3	VI	M1.1c, Pit 5005	IId
475/A12302a	Sole (Type 1)	3	VI	M1.1c, Pit 5005	IId
476/A12302b	Upper (Type E)	3	VI	M1.1c, Pit 5005	IId
491/A12290a	Sole (Type 1)	1	VI	MC071	IIb–IIf
494/A12290d	Upper	1	VI	MC071	IIb–IIf
504/A3447a	Sole (Type 1)	2	VI	M1.1d & M1.1e	IId–IIf
505/A3447b	Sole (Type 1)	2	VI	M1.1d & M1.1e	IId–IIf
507/A3447d	Upper (Type Aii)	2	VI	M1.1d & M1.1e	IId–IIf
508/A3447e	Upper (Type Bi)	2	VI	M1.1d & M1.1e	IId–IIf
625/A9885a	Sole (Type 1)	4	V	M10	IId–IIg

(continued)

Cat/Accession	Leather type	Area	Rig	Feature	Phase
626/A9885b	Upper	4	V	M10	IId–IIg
810/A11219a	Upper (Type F)	3	VI	M1.2, Pit 2648	<IIg(IIh)
811/A11219b	Sole (Type 4)	3	VI	M1.2, Pit 2648	<IIg(IIh)
813/A11220b	Sole, rand, upper	3	VI	M1.2, Pit 2648	<IIg(IIh)
821/A11221a	Sole (Type 4)	3	VI	M1.2, Pit 2648	<IIg(IIh)
823/A11221c	Upper (Type Ai)	3	VI	M1.2, Pit 2648	<IIg(IIh)
826/A12292	Sole, upper	3	VI	M1.2, Pit 2648	<IIg(IIh)
875/A8665b	Sole (rounded forepart)	3	VI	M1.3	IIi
878/A8665e	Upper (Type Kiv)	3	VI	M1.3	IIi
897/A11260a	Sole (Type 2)	3	VI	M1.3	IIi
898/A11260b	Upper (Type Ai)	3	VI	M1.3	IIi
916/A12490a	Sole (Type 8)	4	VI	M1.3	IIi
917/A12490b	Sole (Type 9)	4	VI	M1.3	IIi
918/A12490c	Upper (Type Aii)	4	VI	M1.3	IIi
933/A03–0327a	Sole (Type 2)	9	VII	P8.0	IIIa,IIIb
934/A03–0327b	Upper (Type Biii)	9	VII	P8.0	IIIa,IIIb
1103/A03–0287a	Sole (Type 2)	9	VII	P8.1c	IIIc
1105/A03–0287c	Upper (Type Dii)	9	VII	P8.1c	IIIc
1144/A4817a	Sole (Type 2)	1	V	M12	IIg–IIIc(–IVa)
1145/A4817b	Upper (Type Ai)	1	V	M12	IIg–IIIc(–IVa)
1215/A9373a	Sole (Type 3)	3	V	M6b	IIg–IIId
1216/A9373b	Upper (Type Ai)	3	V	M6b	IIg–IIId
1300/A8810a	Sole (Type 3)	3	V	P2.2b	IVa
1306/A8810g	Upper	3	V	P2.2b	IVa
1553/A03–0422a	Sole (Type 4)	7	VII	MC130	<IIIc–IVaa
1555/A03–0422c	Upper (Type Bi)	7	VII	MC130	<IIIc–IVaa
1804/A03–0367a	Sole (Type 4), upper (Type Di), thong	7	VII	MC126, Pit 7402	IVaa,IVb
1879/A03–0353b	Sole (Type 2)	7	VII	MC126, Pit 7402	IVaa,IVb
1880/A03–0353c	Upper (Type Bii)	7	VII	MC126, Pit 7402	IVaa,IVb
2333/A03–0291a	Sole (Type 3)	7	VI	M1.4f	IVc
2337/A03–0291e	Upper	7	VI	M1.4f	IVc
2361/A03–0331a	Sole (Type 2), upper, rand	7	VI	M1.4f	IVc
2652/A03–0316b	Sole (Type 1)	7	VII	B18 (Phase 1/2), Pit 7324	IVaa,IVb
2653/A03–0316c	Upper (Type Bii)	7	VII	B18 (Phase 1/2), Pit 7324	IVaa,IVb
2725/A03–0413a	Sole (Type 3), rand, upper (Type C)	7	VII	B18 (Phases 2a & 2b), T7385	IVb
2754/A03–0288a	Sole (Type 2)	7	VII	B18 (Phase 2b), North Room, Hall & Hall South–Occupation (10)	IVb
2759/A03–0288f	Upper (Type Dii)	7	VII	B18 (Phase 2b), North Room, Hall & Hall South–Occupation (10)	IVb
2775/A03–0124a	Sole (Type 2), rand	9	VII	B18 (Phase 2b), North Room, Hall & Hall South–Occupation (10)	IVb
2777/A03–0124c	Upper	9	VII	B18 (Phase 2b), North Room, Hall & Hall South–Occupation (10)	IVb
3321/A03–0066a	Sole (Type 3)	9	VII	P8.3	IVc,IVcc
3327/A03–0066g	Upper (Type Aii)	9	VII	P8.3	IVc,IVcc
3343/A03–0183a	Sole, upper	7	VII	M9a	IVc,IVcc
3419/A03–0217a	Sole (Type 2)	7	VII	B18 (Phases 2a & 2b) & M9a, PH7237	(IVb)IVc,IVcc
3421/A03–0217c	Upper (lasting margin)	7	VII	B18 (Phases 2a & 2b) & M9a, PH7237	(IVb)IVc,IVcc

(continued)

Cat/Accession	Leather type	Area	Rig	Feature	Phase
3427–3430/A03–0051a–d	Sole, rand, upper	9	VII	M9a, Pit 9026	IVc,IVcc
4123/A03–0214a	Sole (Type 3), rand	7	VII	P8.4	Va
4131/A03–0214i	Upper	7	VII	P8.4	Va
5241/A03–0216	Sole (Type 2), upper, rand	7	VII	B53 (Phase 1), Central Area–T7152	Vb
5768/A9821a & 5769/A9821b	Sole (Type 2), rand, upper (Type J)	3/4	V, VI	Unstratified	u/s
5820/A0801a	Sole	4	V, VI	Unstratified	u/s
5821/A0801b	Sole	4	V, VI	Unstratified	u/s
5822/A0801c	Upper (Type Ai)	4	V, VI	Unstratified	u/s
North Sector					
5915/A0109a	Sole (pointed forepart)	5, A	–	Lade (4)	6–12(b–e)
5917/A0109c	Upper	5, A	–	Lade (4)	6–12(b–e)

Soles with attached or matching uppers
(Illus 104, 124, 137, 139–141, 145–7)

Thirteen soles still had uppers attached, while another 40 had matching uppers. Type 1 soles had uppers of Types A (3), B (5), D and J. Type 2 Soles were matched by uppers of Types A (3), B (4), Dii (2) and J. Uppers of Type A (2), C and H were found with Type 3 soles. Type 4 soles had Type A, B and F uppers; two Type 6 soles had matching B and F uppers. Unfortunately none of the matching pairs include Type 5 soles or Type K uppers. Nine soles and 20 uppers were too fragmentary for their type to be defined; this leaves 31 pairs which are hardly representative of the 251 soles of Types 1 and 9 or of the 178 uppers of Types A–K.

Discussion

As described above, the shoes, apart from the three unstratified welted soles, were all of turnshoe construction. Rands were evidently common from the early 12th century onwards. Some shoes were stitched with wool, but it is possible that linen was also used. Silk added a touch of luxury to two boots. The worn out state of many of the fragments and the use of half or three-quarter length soles suggests cobbling, particularly during Periods IV and V (c1250–1350>). The nature of the distribution suggests small concerns, possibly including domestic repairs.

A comparison of the sole types shows that Type 3 (63) and Type 1 (58) were the most common, followed by Type 2 (46), Type 4 (26) and Type 8/9 (17/23). Type B uppers were the most numerous with 53: Bi (17), Bii (16), Biii (16) and Biv (4). Type A (29) came next, followed by Types K (15 fragments of 14 uppers), C (14), D (16) and E (10).

Both sole and upper styles are fairly typical, with many parallels, especially for the soles. The uppers are much more numerous than at most other published sites; hence, it is not surprising that some features are not well represented in the literature. Twelfth-century types included sole Types 1 and 6 and upper Types A, B, E, F, G and H. The more shapely soles of Types 2

and 3 and the side-laced uppers of Types C and D belonged mainly to the second half of the 13th century. Elegant sole Types 4 (asymmetrical variant) and 5, composite sole Types 7, 8 and 9 and the more elaborate uppers of Type K were of late 13th- to mid-14th-century date. Upper Type J covers a much longer time-span, which is not surprising considering it is a broad grouping of footwear with separate vamps and quarters, some of which probably represent repair.

The exceptions serve as a reminder that these dating trends are only a guideline; there are early examples of later styles, for example, Cat No 811/A11221a (Sole, Type 4), or Cat No 156/A7787c (Sole, Type 3). There are also later examples of earlier styles, for instance, Cat No 2652/A03–0316b (Sole, Type 1); its relationship with an upper (Type Dii) in a mid–late 13th-century context shows that it is an instance of a late use of an earlier shape, not a surviving item of rubbish.

The date ranges outlined above, based on contextual data and reinforced by external parallels, are supported further by the absence of certain features of medieval footwear. Thus, there is no evidence at all for soles with pointed seats, and only two possible uppers with raised or notched quarters (Cat Nos 239/A7072b and 785/A9372c), as were found in Winchester (late 9th–10th centuries); Oxford (late Saxon); Durham (Saxo–Norman); York (late 9th–late 11th centuries); London (10th–11th centuries, but also early 12th century from Billingsgate) and Schleswig (11th, also 12th century) (Thornton 1990b, 593; Thornton 1977, 160; Carver 1979, 30; Mould et al 2003; Richardson 1959, 86–90; Goodfellow and Thornton 1972, 97–105; Pritchard 1991, 213–30; Grew and de Neergaard 1988, 10; Schnack 1992b, 39–40). Furthermore, there is no indication of the use of thongs instead of thread for sole–upper seams, nor are there any soles with a raised rib for tunnel stitching, instead of the later edge–flesh stitching channel; these are features found on soles from London (mid-11th century and early 12th cent-ury); Winchester (10th century); Oxford (late Saxon); York (late 9th–11th centuries) and Schleswig (11th–12th centuries) (Pritchard 1991, 218–21; Grew and de Neergaard 1988, 10; Thornton 1990b, 592; Thornton 1977, 160; Mould et al 2003; Schnack 1992b, 35–6).

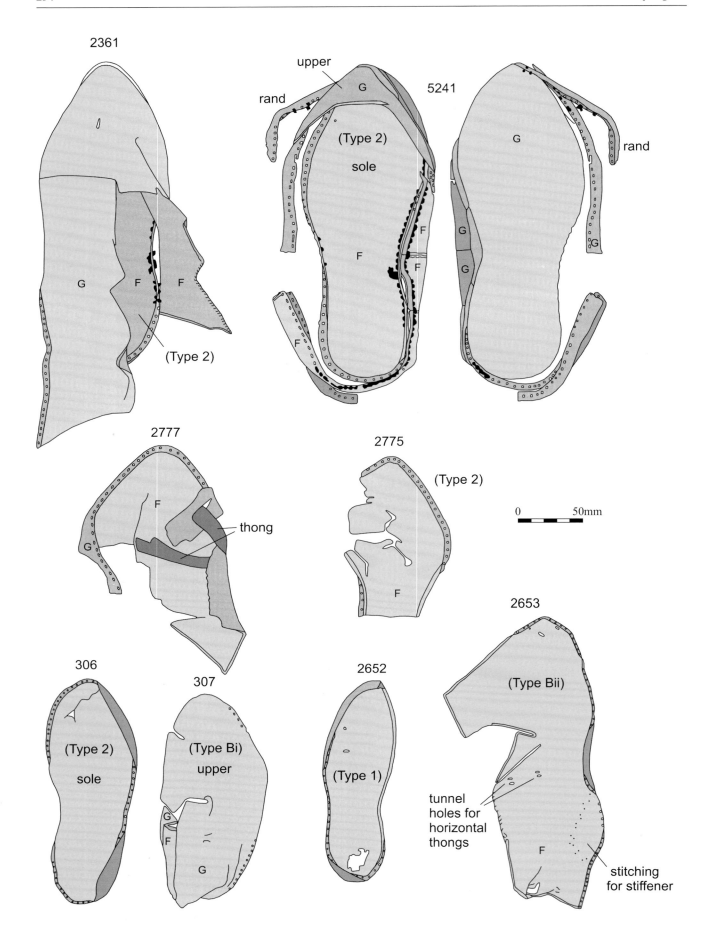

Illus 146 *Two soles with uppers attached; three matching soles and uppers.*

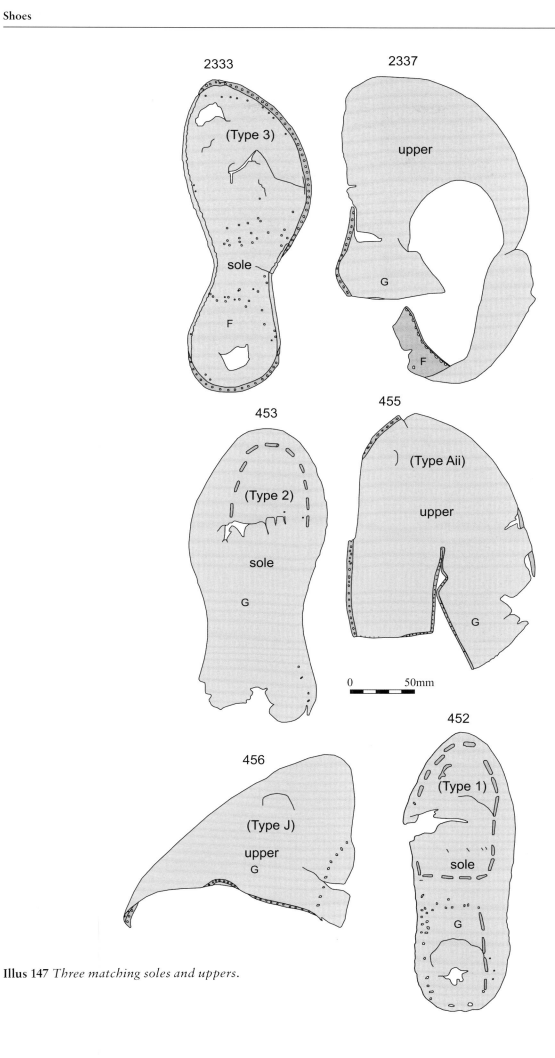

Illus 147 *Three matching soles and uppers.*

Table 13 *Chronological distribtion of upper fragments.*

		period					
		I	II	III	IV	V	unstratified
almost	a	33%	43%	3%	13%	2%	6%
complete	d	22	29	2	9	1	4
	e	29%	26%	5%	4%	2%	12%
large	b	15%	21%	9%	39%	8%	8%
fragments	d	13	18	8	34	7	7
	e	17%	16%	22%	17%	14%	21%
small	c	11.5%	18%	7.5%	45%	12%	6%
fragments	d	41	64	27	161	42	22
	e	54%	58%	73%	79%	84%	67%

a   % of almost complete uppers, by period
b   % of large fragments of uppers, by period
c   % of small fragments of uppers, by period
d   no of pieces, by size
e   % of upper fragments, by size and period

Similarly, although the asymmetrical variants of Type 4 soles resemble those of late 14th–early 15th century date from Threave Castle, the accompanying upper style found there, with its central opening (Type L), is not represented at all in the leather from Perth High Street (Thomas 1981, 123–6). English examples of this type of shoe are also of a comparable date: London (late 14th century); Leicester (14th–15th centuries) and Chapel Lane Staith, Hull (the end of the first quarter of the 14th century–post 1350) (Grew and de Neergaard 1988, 36, 65–7; Allin 1981a, 145–9; Jackson 1979, Fig 22, no 36). The Continental parallels, on the other hand, appear to date from slightly earlier: Amsterdam (1275–1350); Schleswig (13th–14th centuries); Bremen (13th–15th centuries) and Konstanz (13th–15th centuries) (Baart et al 1977, 77, 80; Schnack 1992b, Figs 35–37, Halbschuh D 1; Schnack 1993, 61, 64; Schnack 1992a; Schnack 1994, 25).

Likewise, there are no examples of shoes with a strap and buckle, of the type found in late 14th-century contexts in London and in York, and with a slightly earlier appearance abroad: Amsterdam (1275–1350), Schleswig (13th–14th centuries), Bremen (13th–15th centuries) and Konstanz (13th–15th centuries) (Grew and de Neergaard 1988, 32–3; Mould et al 2003; Baart et al 1977, 74; Schnack 1992b, 93–7, Fig 49, no 1; Schnack 1993, 66, Fig 3b; Schnack 1994, 22).

A study of the phasing shows that more attached or matching soles and uppers survive from the earlier periods than from the later ones: Period I–13%, II–44%, III–7%, IV–26%, V–4%, Unstratified–4%. The reasons for this are not clear. As discussed above, the leather from Periods IV and V (1250–1350>) may represent cobbling, the evidence for which will be examined further in connection with the waste material.

Possibly the leather from the earlier phases represents domestic rubbish, which was dumped and not reused, whereas the later material may have been deposited after it had been cut up for reuse. This might help to explain the smaller numbers of matching or attached soles and uppers from the later phases.

A similar pattern appears from a study of the chronological distribution of upper fragments. The vast majority of large, almost complete uppers belong to 12th-century Periods I and II (33% and 43%) deposits. The more incomplete but still large uppers and the small fragments have a more even distribution, but with the largest concentrations in Period IV (39% and 45% respectively). The increased evidence for translation and cobbling in the later phases onwards probably explains the paucity of virtually whole uppers from Period III.

The shoes also provide some evidence regarding the wealth and status of the medieval population of Perth. First of all, it has been assumed that the shoes were made for sale to the local population, and not for export. This assumption is supported by the worn and patched nature of the shoes, which implies that they were worn, then patched, reused or discarded locally. The worn and patched nature of the shoes indicates that the shoes were well used. However, this is not necessarily an indication of poverty, as turnshoes, with a single sole, would have worn very quickly, almost certainly within a few months, if worn outdoors regularly. Moreover, signs of wear and evidence for repair are a standard feature of shoes from medieval sites. The exceptions are few, such as the shoes from burials at Sandwell Priory, which had been deliberately fitted on the corpses and left on them when they were buried within the Priory. Even these shoes, although in quite good condition, were obviously not new when buried (Thomas 1991, 110).

Furthermore, it is probable that the shoes went through at least two, if not more, stages of ownership, being worn first by one person, then repaired and handed down, for instance to servants, or sold as second-hand, repaired shoes. It used to be common, until the last quarter of the twentieth century, for shoes to be handed down in a family to younger children. This practice only ceased because of concerns that the interior of a shoe, moulded to the shape of one foot, might damage the soft, immature foot of a subsequent wearer. Even today, charity shops quite commonly sell nearly new shoes. Accordingly, the High Street shoes probably represent two different classes of wearer: the original purchaser, and the less well-off recipient or purchaser of a repaired pair.

Two of the High Street shoes also carry a feature that most definitely implies wealth, silk. Although relatively common in 12th-century Europe, it must be regarded as an indication of luxury (The Textiles, this volume). Another possible sign of wealth is the vamp stripes. These have been noted on shoes worn by a king or other important figure in 11th–12th-century manuscripts. However, Grew and de Neergaard (1988, 119) discount the significance of this feature, given the high proportion of shoes with such decoration in the London assemblages.

Nevertheless, vamp stripes imply extra work and, probably, materials and therefore suggest that shoes possessing them were more expensive. Furthermore, although foot-wear with vamp stripes features significantly in the London assemblages, other parallels are not so common, thus suggesting that they are an indicator of wealth. It is therefore of interest that the boot with the most elaborate vamp stripe is a child's.

Another possible indicator of wealth is the linings, represented by a scrap of felt in one boot, and suggested by internal tunnel stitching on three others (Types Di, F and H), and by inturned quarters on two Type Bi uppers.

The shoes also reflect a few signs of bunions. The cause of bunions (hallux valgus) is incompletely understood but may include genetic predisposition, arthritis, gout and other factors all of which may be exacerbated by ill-fitting or tight footwear. Thus this foot condition may have been caused in part by the shoes themselves, although three of the shoes had Type 1 soles, which were least likely to push the big toe inwards. It is possible that these straight, wide soles were deliberately chosen in order to accommodate a swollen joint.

Other leather finds

Straps

One hundred and eighty-four straps were found. The term 'strap' is used loosely to describe fragments of belts, straps, thongs, toggles and strips of leather folded once and most probably used as bindings for shoes and clothing.

Bindings/straps/belts, folded once (Illus 152, 159)

Sixty-six strips of leather were most probably bindings for shoes and clothing. These bindings were formed of long strips folded once; they have an average width of 8.6mm and thickness of 2.3mm. The long cut edges were stitched to the shoe or article of clothing, as demonstrated by the stitch holes and scallop pattern on both the bindings and the uppers. Eight strips were also stitched adjacent to the folded edge. On some strips, the narrow ends of the straps have been stitched. One example, Cat No 172/A7580a (Illus148) (included in these lists but belonging to Cat No 173/A7580b Sole Type 2), had decorative stitching of pink and brown silk. Strap Cat No 5637/A1241 (Illus 152), however, is of a more complex construction and is definitely not a binding. It consists of two strips of leather, one folded once, one of a single thickness, stitched together so that they form a triple thickness of leather, 270mm long, 40mm wide at one end and 17mm at the other. The wider end contains a pointed oval hole, 45mm by 16mm. The narrower end has been perforated by 10 small holes, each c2–3mm in diameter, in two clusters; these were possibly for the attachment of a buckle or for sewing the strap to another object.

These bindings were found in contexts of all periods, but especially during the 12th century: (55%) in Periods I (19; 28%) and II (18; 27%). The binding stitched with silk was of mid-12th-century date, as was the upper stitched with silk (Cat No 229/A7588c, Upper Type G).

Similar bindings were found at Kirk Close (13th–14th centuries) and King Edward Street, Perth; Upper Kirkgate (12th century), Gallowgate Middle School (12th–13th centuries) and 45–75 Gallowgate (c1250–1350), Aberdeen; Jedburgh and Whithorn (Thomas 1987, 183; Thomas and Walsh 1995, 971; Thomas 2001a; Thomas 1995; Nicholson 1997, 507–8). English examples include York (10th century–14th centuries); King's Lynn (11th–13th centuries); Newcastle (mid 13th–mid 14th centuries); Redcliffe Street, Bristol and London (early 13th–late 14th centuries) (Tweddle 1986, 253–6; Mould et al 2003, 3413; Clarke and Carter 1977, 354–5, Fig 164, no 10, Fig 165, nos 20 and 21; Dixon 1988, 94; Thomas forthcoming b; Grew and de Neergaard 1988, 56, 63). Bindings embroidered with silk were also found in York (unstratified), Bergen (late 12th century–1248) and possibly London (mid–late 12th century) (Walton 1989, 410, Fig 170; Larsen 1992, 41–2; Pedersen 1992, 143; Grew and de Neergaard 1988, 76–7, Fig 111).

Straps/belts, single thickness (Illus 151–2, 156, 158)

The 35 straps of single thickness had two long cut edges and two short edges, originally cut but now usually broken. Most examples, for example Cat Nos 3412/A03–0081a (Illus 151) and 3413/A03–0081b (Illus 151), have a row of short diagonal slits parallel to each long edge. These slits were purely decorative; in some cases, they may have been further enhanced by being stitched. Many straps were perforated by round holes, most probably for the pin of a buckle, for example Cat No 1061/A9554a (Illus 151). The area surrounding these holes, usually only one or two, is often worn and cracked, as on Cat No 5958/A0100 (Illus 151). The latter has been dyed a greyish blue; it is the only coloured fragment of leather from the site: the rest are brown or black. Cat Nos 341/A6772a and 342/A6772b (Illus 151) consist of two straps linked together, by being passed through a slit in each other; one strap has a fitting, possibly of copper alloy, at one end. Cat No 4981/A03–0174u has two sets of holes, probably for the attachment of a buckle. This fragment was probably folded between these two sets of holes, over the metal part of the buckle. A grain–flesh stitching channel at one end was probably for attaching the strap to another object. Cat No 5823/A03–0080 is a short strap, with traces of edge–flesh stitching, and with an oval slit or loop at the wider end (Illus 152).

One strap, Cat No 5941/A0802 (Illus 156), has been decorated with rosettes set within spirals or whorls, all within a rectangular frame. The strap is 42mm wide, and is now 181mm long. The frame and innermost ring of spirals have been marked out by small, punched dots, each c1mm in diameter. Dots have also been used for some additional lines and triangular patches. The outer rings of the spirals have been engraved with a blunt tool on wet leather. The rosettes, eight of which survive, were almost certainly all made with the same stamp. Each rosette has seven petals. The rosettes each have a diameter of 11.5mm.

Engraved lines, punched dots and stamped motifs are common features of decorated medieval leather (see Sheaths below). Engraved lines were used to mark out panels, and for some motifs, such as chevrons, hatching, shields and curvilinear designs. Dots punched with a hollow tool were employed to fill in spaces, as, for example, on sheath Cat No 1360/A8002 (Illus 156), where they are enclosed within engraved diamonds. Stamped motifs were either used individually, as with the large fleurs-de-lys set within lozenges on Cat No 3869/A03–0070 (Illus 156), or else repeatedly, to form an all-over pattern, as, for instance, the small fleurs-de-lys on Cat No 5770/A12573 (Illus 156).

Bindings/straps/belts (folded once) (Illus 152, 159).

Cat/Accession	Area	Rig	Feature	Phase
South Sector				
27/A10800a	1	V	MC008, T3774	Ib
33/A11237a	2	VI	MC011	Ib,Ic
57/A9368	1	V, VI	B15 (East/West), PH3792	Ic,Icc
63/A8704b	1/2	V, VI	M2.1b, B10, South Room–Floor/Occupation (1)	Ic,Icc
73/A11222	1/2	V, VI	M2.1b, B10, South Room–Floor/Occupation (1)	Ic,Icc
93/A9551a	4	V, VI	MC017	Ia–Icc>
134/A12286a	3	V	MC025, Pit 5337	(Ia–)Id
142/A7789a	2	VI	P5.2a	Ie
154/A7787a	1/2	VI	B6 (Phase 1), South Room–Floor (1)	Ie
155/A7787b	1/2	VI	B6 (Phase 1), South Room–Floor (1)	Ie
171/A7576	2	VI	M14b(b)	Ie
172/A7580a	2	VI	M14b(b)	Ie
196/A7257a	2	VI	M14b(b), Pit 3625	Ie
197/A7257b	2	VI	M14b(b), Pit 3625	Ie
238/A7072a	2	V	M14b(c)	Ie,If
261/A7044Ba	2	VI	MC044b	If
281/A9555a	3	VI	MC053c	If
282/A9555b	3	VI	MC053c	If
283/A9555c	3	VI	MC053c	If
305/A12635a	4	V	B16b, Pit 4726	Id–IIa
311/A12378a	3	VI	P5.3b	If,IIa
317/A10681a	3	V	MC049	IIa
318/A10681b	3	V	MC049	IIa
324/A03–0009a	3	V	MC049, Pit 5259	IIa
365/A7694a	1	V	M14a	Id–IIc
386/A12377	1	VI	MC065, T3907	IIa–IIc
399/A12293a	3	VI	MC056, Pit 5155	Ia–IIc
477/A12309a	3	VI	M1.1c, Pit 5005	IId
519/A7005a	2	V	B5, T4485	IIa–IIff
531/A6949a	2	V	B5, North Room–Floor/Occupation (1)	IIa–IIff
726/A11643a	4	V	M10, Pit 4554	IId–IIg
775/A9371a	3	VI	M1.2, Pit 2648	<IIg(IIh)
786/A9518a	3	VI	M1.2, Pit 2648	<IIg(IIh)
787/A9518b	3	VI	M1.2, Pit 2648	<IIg(IIh)
853/A11253	4	V, VI	M11	IIh
879/A8666a	3	VI	M1.3	IIi
880/A8666b	3	VI	M1.3	IIi
1087/A03–0278b	9	VII	B19 (Phase 2b), North Room–Floor (2b)	IIIc
1143/A3446	1	V	M12	IIg–IIIc(–IVa)
1239/A8686a	4	V	MC120a	IIh–IVa
1493/A6213	2	V	B26, Floor/Occupation (11b)	IIg–IVaa
1693/A03–0318a	7	VII	B18 (Phase 1b), Destruction	IVa,IVaa
1840/A03–0351a	7	VII	MC126, Pit 7402	IVaa,IVb
1885/A03–0357a	7	VII	MC126, Pit 7402	IVaa,IVb
2271/A03–0426a	7	VII	MC126, Pit 7402	IVaa,IVb
2281/A03–0395a	7	VII	MC146, Pit 7357	<IVb
2289/A03–0271a	7	VI	M1.4f	IVc
2637/A03–0203a	9	VII	B18 (Phase 1/2)	IVaa,IVb
2881/A9358d	3	V	MC155, Pit 2691	IVb,IVc
2882/A9358e	3	V	MC155, Pit 2691	IVb,IVc
3046/A6473d	3	VI	M1.4d	IVb,IVc
3090/A5900a	2	VI	M1.4d	IVb,IVc
3167/A4938a	2	V	M1.4g, Pit 2800	IVb,IVc
3175/A6072a	3	V, VI	M1.4c	IIIa–IVcc

(continued)

Cat/Accession	Area	Rig	Feature	Phase
3622/A6077a	3	VI	M1.4e	IVcc(Va)
3623/A6077b	3	VI	M1.4e	IVcc(Va)
4225/A6393a	3	V	B1(a), T2477	IVcc,Va
4961/A03–0174a	7	VII	M8a	Va,Vaa
5382/A0816a	4	VI	P1a	Vd
5637/A1241	4	VI	M3e, Pit 2111	Vdd>
5741/A5898a	2	V, VI	Unstratified	u/s
5771/A12574a	3/4	V, VI	Unstratified	u/s
5880/A03–0425b	7–10	VI–VIII	Unstratified	u/s
North Sector				
5882/A0812a	5, A	–	Natural	0
5906/A7585a	5	–	CG013	(5–)7–9
South/North Sectors				
5971/L1694a	–	–	Unstratified	u/s

Straps/belts (single thickness) (Illus 151–2, 156, 158).

Cat/Accession	Area	Rig	Feature	Phase
South Sector				
20/A11216a	1/2	VI	MC006	Ib
66/A8809a	1/2	V	M2.1b & B10, South Room–Floor/Occupation (1)	Ic,Icc
341/A6772a	2	VI	MC061	IIb
342/A6772b	2	VI	MC061	IIb
590/A11250a	4	V	M10	IId–IIg
812/A11220a	3	VI	M1.2, Pit 2648	<IIg(IIh)
1061/A9554a	4	V	MC117, Pit 4695	IIe–IIIc
1062/A9554b	4	V	MC117, Pit 4695	IIe–IIIc
1321/A8027a	4	V	MC143	IVaa
2479/A03–0392a	7	VI	M1.4f	IVc
2514/A03–0401a	7	VII	P8.2b	IVb
2554/A04–0430	9	VII	P8.2b	IVb
2636/A03–0176	9	VII	B18 (Phase 1/2)	IVaa,IVb
2817/A03–0273a	10	VIII	M9b(a)	IVc
2875/A9357a	3	V	MC155, Pit 2691	IVb,IVc
2876/A9357b	3	V	MC155, Pit 2691	IVb,IVc
3055/A8667a	3	VI	M1.4d	IVb,IVc
3281/A03–0227a	7	VII	P8.3	IVc,IVcc
3304/A03–0250a	7	VII	P8.3	IVc,IVcc
3305/A03–0250b	7	VII	P8.3	IVc,IVcc
3348/A03–0207a	7	VII	M9a	IVc,IVcc
3349/A03–0207b	7	VII	M9a	IVc,IVcc
3412/A03–0081a	9	VII	M9a	IVc,IVcc
3413/A03–0081b	9	VII	M9a	IVc,IVcc
3414/A03–0081c	9	VII	M9a	IVc,IVcc
3431/A03–0049a	9	VII	M9a, Pit 9026	IVc,IVcc
3703/A9273a	3	VI	B34, Floor	Va
3872/A03–0116a	7	VI, VII	M1.5b	Vaa
3876/A03–0120a	7	VI, VII	M1.5b	Vaa
5406/A4247a	4	VI	P1a	Vd
5607/A03–0054	10	VIII	MC174, Pit 7013	(Va–)Vd(Vdd)
5879/A03–0425a	7–10	VI–VIII	Unstratified	u/s
North Sector				
5924/A0115	5, A	–	Lade (4)	6–12(b–e)
5941/A0802	5, A	–	Lade (4)	6–12(b–e)
5958/A0100	5, A	–	CG024	14–16

A few parallels for stamped rosettes exist, but are not common and are usually much smaller, as on a narrow belt, of late 12th–early 14th-century date, from Chapel Lane Staith Hull; these rosettes have a maximum diameter of 6mm (Jackson 1979, Fig 22, 9). A late 14th-century belt from London has been stamped with small, angular quatrefoils (Egan and Pritchard 1991, 42, Fig 24, no 17, 43). A similar effect is created on another late 14th-century strap from London, which has been decorated with a series of stamped S, each surrounded by a circle of dots (Egan and Pritchard 1991, 40, Fig 22, no 15). A strap from Exeter with stamped S inside roundels was of 14th–15th-century date (Friendship-Taylor 1984, 324, 327, Fig 184, no 11).

Spiral or whorl-like patterns were also used on sheaths to enclose stamped motifs, as, for example, on sheaths nos 444 and 445 from London. On both of these early–mid-14th-century examples, punched dots have been used to help form the shape, as well as to fill in the background. Similar but simpler, cruder whorls occur on a late 14th-century sheath, no 462 (Cowgill et al 1987, 145, 147, 154, 155, Fig 95, nos 444 and 445, Fig 99, no 462).

Engraving, punching and stamping were used throughout the medieval period; however, the use of punched dots to form spirals or roundels does not seem to appear before the early 14th century. The straps from London and Exeter also suggest a 14th-century date for this form of strap decoration. The relative lack of parallels for this strap suggests that it was an unusual item, and should be associated with some form of wealth.

These straps were found in South Sector contexts of all periods (Period I – 2, 6%; Period II – 4, 11%; Period III – 2, 6%; Period V – 5, 14%, but especially in Period IV (18, 51%), the second half of the 13th century. Three (9%) were also recovered from Trench A in the North Sector. Similar straps were found at Kirk Close, Perth (13th–14th centuries); Gallowgate Middle School, Aberdeen (12th–13th centuries); Whithorn; Bristol Bridge, Bristol (13th–14th centuries); York; Newcastle (mid 13th century–mid-14th century); Leicester (c14th–15th centuries); King's Lynn; Custom House site, London (early–mid-14th century); Southampton (late 13th century) and Oxford (13th–14th centuries) (Thomas 1987, 183; Thomas 2001a, 249; Nicholson 1997, 508–9; Thomas forthcoming a; Tweddle 1986, 253–6; Mould et al 2003, 3396–7; Dixon 1988, 94–103; Allin 1981a, 152–3; Clarke and Carter 1977, 361–2, Fig 168, nos 76–82; Tatton-Brown 1975, 163, Fig 30, nos 125 and 126; Platt and Coleman Smith 1975, II, Fig 162, nos 2158–2159, Fig 163, nos 2160–2161; Hassall 1976, 280–2, Fig 19, nos 32–33, Fig 20, no 38, 287, Fig 2, no 15). Some of these straps may have been girdles. Egan and Pritchard (1991, 35) explain how strips of leather were joined together to form floor-length belts.

Straps/belts, folded twice (Illus 149, 150, 153, 158)

Nineteen straps were formed of long strips of leather, folded twice and stitched up the centre of the reverse with a butted edge–grain seam. Four examples (Cat Nos 524/A9369, 459/A10506a, 2312/A03–0280 and 2869/A4939) contained a thin strip of leather,

Straps/belts (folded twice) (Illus 149–50, 153, 158)

Cat/Accession	Area	Rig	Feature	Phase
South Sector				
60/A8636a	1/2	V, VI	M2.1b & B10, South Room–Floor/Occupation (1)	Ic,Icc
94/A9551b	4	V, VI	MC017	Ia–Icc>
113/A8818	2	VI	P5.1a	Icc,Id
153/A12312b	3	VI	MC037a, Pit 5157	Ia–Ie
328/A03–0009e	3	V	MC049, Pit 5259	IIa
459/A10506a	3	VI	M1.1c, Pit 5005	IId
524/A9369	3	V	B5, WW3566	IIa–IIff
731/A9360a	4	VI	B12, Occupation (1b)	IIe–IIg
732/A9360b	4	VI	B12, Occupation (1b)	IIe–IIg
1057/A10623	4	V	MC117, Pit 4695	IIe–IIIc
1112/A03–0323a	9	VII	P8.1c	IIIc
2112/A03–0377a	7	VII	MC126, Pit 7402	IVaa,IVb
2312/A03–0280	7	VI	M1.4f	IVc
2869/A4939	2	VI	M1.4d & B2, Late Occupation/Abandonment (2)	IVa–IVc
3705/A03–0172a	7	VI	B34, Floor	Va
4246/A4943a	2	V	B1(b), Demolition	Va
4247/A4943b	2	V	B1(b), Demolition	Va
5869/A03–0004b	7–10	VI–VIII	Unstratified	u/s
5881/A03–0425c	7–10	VI–VIII	Unstratified	u/s

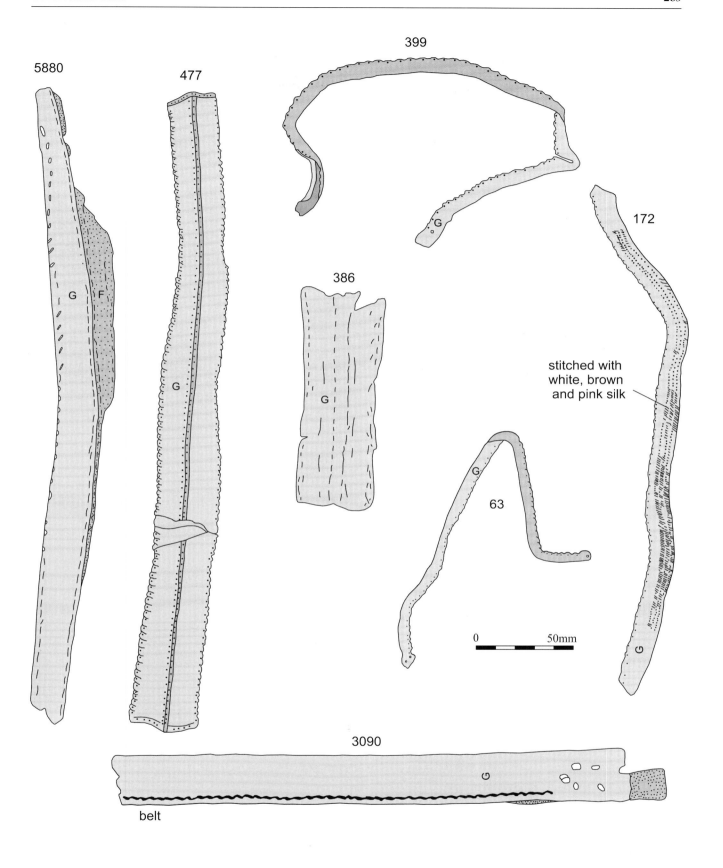

Illus 148 *Straps folded once, bindings and belt.*

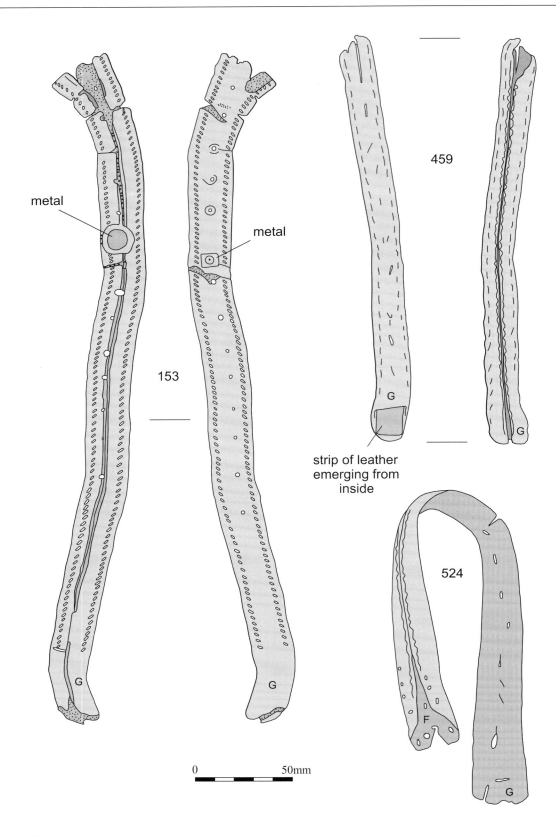

metal

metal

153

459

strip of leather
emerging from
inside

524

0   50mm

Illus 149 *Straps folded twice.*

sandwiched between the front and reverse of the strap; these strips most probably acted as stiffeners. Some straps had a decorative row of short diagonal slits parallel to each folded edge, similar to the slits on the straps of single thickness. The slits have usually been cut through all thicknesses, including the stiffening strips, indicating that they were cut after the leather had been folded. It is possible that some of the rows of slits were stitched for decorative effect, as for example Cat Nos 2312/A03–0280 (Illus 150) and 459/A10506a (Illus 149. Eleven straps, eg Cat Nos 524/A9369 (Illus 149); 3705/A03–0172a (Illus 150); 2312/A03–0280 (Illus 150); 60/A8636a (Illus 150); 153/A12312b (Illus 149), were perforated by round holes; wear and cracks indicate those holes that a buckle pin passed through frequently. Cat No 2312/A03–0280 (Illus 150) has a thong threaded through these holes. One strap with round holes has part of a rivet with a domed head (Cat No 153/A12312b (Illus 149). Cat No 1057/A10623 (Illus 153) is a very large strap, 1075mm long and 58mm wide, with round buckle pin holes and decorative rows of slits, which had most probably been stitched. This strap is possibly part of horse-tack, for instance a girth. However, the edge–flesh seam, linking it probably to another strap, would have been a weak point. It could also be a heavy elaborate belt.

Another fragment, Cat No 328/A03–0009e (Illus 158) (see Miscellaneous fragments), may also be part of one of these straps; one end has been folded over and sewn or nailed in places, presumably to hold a buckle.

This class of straps was found in South Sector contexts of all dates, with four (21%) from Period I, five (25%) from Period II, two (11%) from Period III, three (16%) from Period IV, three (16%) from Period V and two (11%) unstratified examples.

Similar straps with decorative and strengthening stitching were found in London, Winchester (9th century), York, Waterford (12th–13th centuries) and Konstanz (Pritchard 1991, 240; Thornton 1990a, 545–6; Mould et al 2003, 3397–9; O'Rourke 1997, Fig 18.10; Schnack 1994, 42, Tafel 43).

Thongs (Illus 152)

Fifty-five thongs were found. These were of many different lengths, the longest being 470mm long (Cat No 150/A11595d). Widths varied between 1mm and 16mm (Cat Nos 150/A11595d and 3358/A03–0246g). Some, for example Cat Nos 348/A6772h and 349/A6772i, had been knotted together. The possible uses for thongs are innumerable: fasteners for shoes and clothing are the most obvious. They were found in South Sector contexts of all dates: Period I, 11, 20%; Period III, 3, 5%; Period V, 3, 5%, with the largest groups coming from Period II (17, 31%) and Period IV (21, 39%).

Thongs (Illus 152).

Cat/Accession	Area	Rig	Feature	Phase
South Sector				
61/A8636b	1/2	V, VI	M2.1b & B10, South Room–Floor/Occupation (1)	Ic,Icc
150/A11595d	3	VI	MC037a, Pit 5157	Ia–Ie
204/A7257i	2	VI	M14b(b), Pit 3625	Ie
205/A7257j	2	VI	M14b(b), Pit 3625	Ie
206/A7349	2	VI	M14b(b), Pit 3625	Ie
222/A7436a	2	VI	P5.2b	Ie
231/A7588e	2	V	M14b(c)	Ie,If
232/A7588f	2	V	M14b(c)	Ie,If
247/A11444a	3	V	M14b(a)	Id
248/A11444b	3	V	M14b(a)	Id
249/A11444c	3	V	M14b(a)	Id
316/A10604	3	V	MC049	IIa
340/A6770d	2	VI	MC061	IIb
348/A6772h	2	VI	MC061	IIb
349/A6772i	2	VI	MC061	IIb
373/A6636	1	V	MC059, Pit 3142	Id–IIc
402/A12293d	3	VI	MC056, Pit 5155	Ia–IIc
423/A10487a	3	VI	B4, Occupation, MW4476	IIc
427/A6388a	2	VI	B4, 'Byre'–Occupation	IIc
457/A10340	4	VI	M1.1f, Pit 2383	IIb,IIc
460/A10506b	3	VI	M1.1c, Pit 5005	IId
535/A6949e	2	V	B5, North Room–Floor/Occupation (1)	IIa–IIff
536/A6949f	2	V	B5, North Room–Floor/Occupation (1)	IIa–IIff
549/A6729a	2	V	B5, North Room–Floor/Occupation (2)	IIa–IIff
734/A8639	4	VI	B12, Occupation (1/2)	IIe–IIg
814/A11220c	3	VI	M1.2, Pit 2648	<IIg(IIh)
815/A11220d	3	VI	M1.2, Pit 2648	<IIg(IIh)
855/A8654	4	VI	B13, Occupation (1ba)	IIh
929/A11639h	1	VI	MC111	IIb–IIIb
930/A11639i	1	VI	MC111	IIb–IIIb
1085/A03–0283	9	VII	P8.1b & B19 (Phase 2b), South Room–Occupation (1a)	IIIc
1400/A7986a	4	V	B3 (North), Floor (1a)	IVa,IVaa
1401/A7986b	4	V	B3 (North), Floor (1a)	IVa,IVaa
1435/A6474b	4	V	MC156	IVaa
1498/A4827c	1	VI	B20, Levelling	<IIId–IVaa
1499/A4827d	1	VI	B20, Levelling	<IIId–IVaa
1689/A7781a	3	V	B3 (South), Floor (1b)	IVa,IVaa
1804/A03–0367a	7	VII	MC126, Pit 7402	IVaa,IVb
2579/A03–0329k	7	VII	B18 (Phase 1/2)	IVaa,IVb
2580/A03–0329l	7	VII	B18 (Phase 1/2)	IVaa,IVb
2581/A03–0329m	7	VII	B18 (Phase 1/2)	IVaa,IVb
2749/A03–0300	7	VII	B18 (Phase 2a), North Room & Hall–Construction (1)	IVb
2788/A03–0245i	9	VII	B18 (Phase 2b), North Room, Hall & Hall South–Occupation (10)	IVb
2789/A03–0245j	9	VII	B18 (Phase 2b), North Room, Hall & Hall South–Occupation (10)	IVb
2802/A03–0084	9	VII	B18 (Phase 2b), Hall & Hall South–Occupation (12a)	IVb
3036/A6241a	3	VI	M1.4d	IVb,IVc
3037/A6241b	3	VI	M1.4d	IVb,IVc
3078/A8701b	3	VI	M1.4d	IVb,IVc
3079/A8701c	3	VI	M1.4d	IVb,IVc
3351/A03–0207d	7	VII	M9a	IVc,IVcc
3357/A03–0246f	7	VII	M9a	IVc,IVcc
3358/A03–0246g	7	VII	M9a	IVc,IVcc
3867/A03–0069b	7	VI, VII	M1.5b	Vaa
3868/A03–0069c	7	VI, VII	M1.5b	Vaa
3874/A03–0116c	7	VI, VII	M1.5b	Vaa

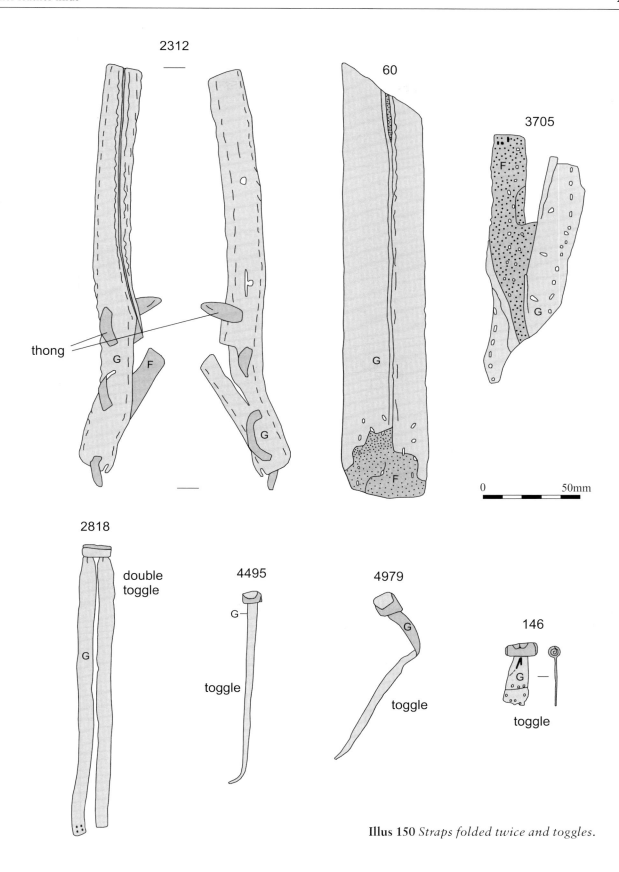

2312

thong

G F

G

60

G

F

3705

F

G

0   50mm

2818

double toggle

G

4495

G

toggle

4979

G

toggle

146

G

toggle

Illus 150 *Straps folded twice and toggles.*

Toggles (Illus 150)

Nine toggles were formed by rolling up very tightly the broad end of a thong then passing the thin end of the thong through a slit in the outer part of the rolled end. The toggle of Cat No 5877/A03–0040a, for example, is 10mm wide and 6mm thick; its emerging thong is 104mm long. Two examples, Cat Nos 28l8/A03–0273b (Illus 150) and 2480/A03–0392b have a wide toggle, with two thongs emerging; in these cases, the broad end of a strip has been rolled up, then split into two thin thongs. These toggles were used as fastenings, particularly on shoes and clothing.

Of the seven toggles that were recovered from stratified deposits, one (Cat No 146/A11658) was recovered from a pit that dated from the first half of the 12th century. The other six came from contexts that belonged to the later 13th or early 14th centuries (Periods IV and V).

Fastenings (Illus 152, 159)

Two fragments are parts of fastenings. Cat No 5873/A03–0028 (Illus 152) is wedge-shaped, with remains of stitching at the wider end, and with two short, straight slits, a semi-circular slit and a small round hole at the narrower end. Cat No 867/A8634b (Illus 159) is a fragment folded into an approximate square, with a thong threaded through it repeatedly, probably for the attachment of another article, such as a sheath.

Keepers (Illus 152)

Two short straps (Cat Nos 2820/A03–0273d and 281/A03–0273e) have been folded and stitched together, forming small loops. These are probably keepers, designed to be stitched around a larger strap, in order to keep the end of the second strap in place, as on a modern watchstrap. Both examples were discovered in a late 13th-century midden in Rig VIII.

Toggles (Illus 150).

Cat/Accession	Area	Rig	Feature	Phase
South Sector				
146/A11658	3	VI	MC037a, Pit 5157	Ia–Ie
2480/A03–0392b	7	VI	M1.4f	IVc
2818/A03–0273b	10	VIII	M9b(a)	IVc
4495/A4289c	3	V, VI	M1.5a	Va,Vaa(VI)
4979/A03–0174s	7	VII	M8a	Va,Vaa
5243/A03–0119b	7	VII	B53 (Phase 1), Central Area–T7152	Vb
5244/A03–0119c	7	VII	B53 (Phase 1), Central Area–T7152	Vb
5749/A5898i	2	V, VI	Unstratified	u/s
5877/A03–0040a	7–10	VI–VII	Unstratified	u/s

Fastenings (Illus 152, 159).

Cat/Accession	Area	Rig	Feature	Phase
South Sector				
867/A8634b	3	VI	M1.3	IIi
5873/A03–0028	7–10	VI–VIII	Unstratified	u/s

Keepers (Illus 152).

Cat/Accession	Area	Rig	Feature	Phase
South Sector				
2820/A03–0273d	10	VIII	M9b(a)	IVc
2821/A03–0273e	10	VIII	M9b(a)	IVc

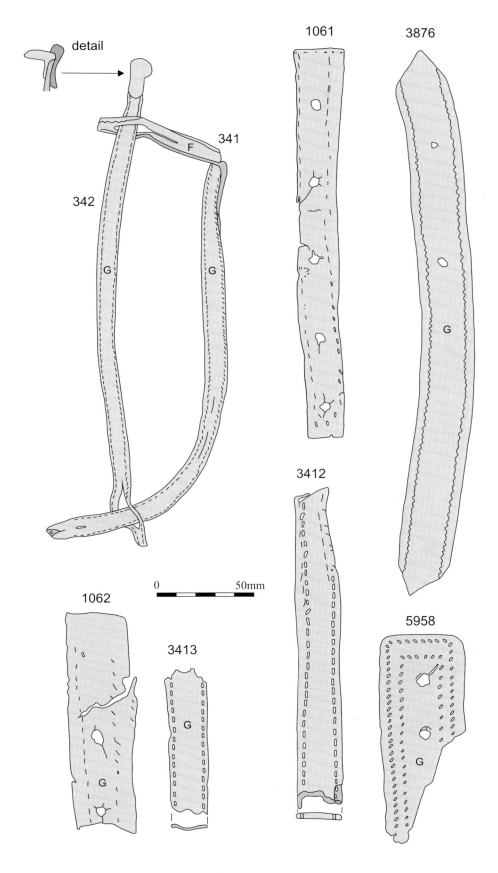

Illus 151 *Straps of single thickness.*

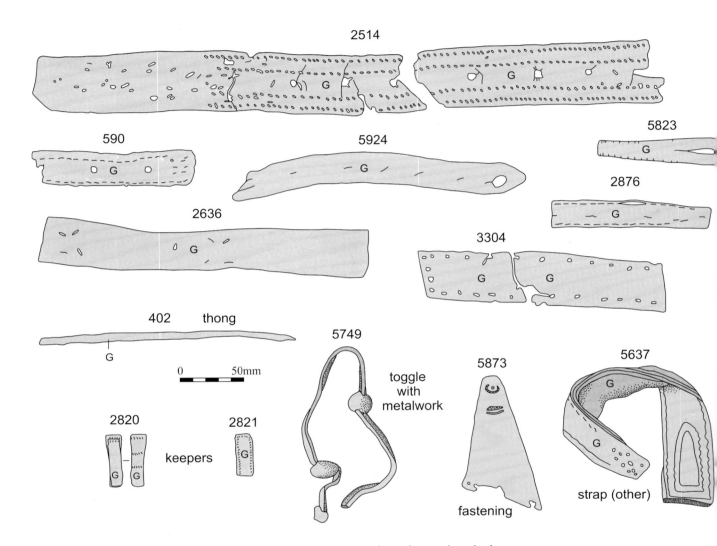

Illus 152 *Straps of single thickness; other strap; keepers; toggle with metalwork; fastening.*

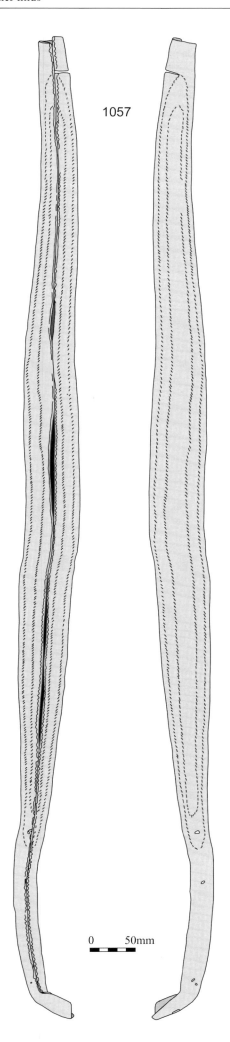

1057

0   50mm

Sheaths (Illus 154–6)

Seventeen sheaths were found; two long examples were probably for daggers, short swords or long knives. The rest were short, intended to hold everyday knives and were almost certainly civilian in character. Eleven of these short sheaths were decorated with a variety of motifs, including hatchings, zigzags, diamonds and fleurs-de-lys. Of the 17 sheaths, two were found in deposits that dated from the late 12th century and four were found in 13th-century deposits Seven, that is just over 50% of the stratified examples, came from contexts that had been laid down during the first half of the 14th century. The majority were recovered from Rig V (3), Rig VI (6) and from Midden 1.5b which was laid down in Rigs VI and VII (3), with another from Rig VII. Mainly recovered singly, it is perhaps noteworthy that two were retrieved from the Courtyard of B34, a small backland building, while another three were recovered from M1.5b which succeeded that building.

Sheaths, long plain (Illus 154)

Cat Nos 739/A9143 (Illus 154) and 5872/A03–0019 (Illus 154) were both made out of a single piece of leather that has been folded twice and stitched together on the reverse with a butted edge–grain seam. Short slits parallel to each folded edge of Cat No 739/A9143 suggest that this sheath may also have been stitched along these edges. This sheath is approximately 630mm long; it is straight, tapering towards its foot. At its upper end, it has a large oval hole with 12 smaller holes above and below, probably for attachment to a belt. It has been suggested that this might be a strap or belt (folded twice) but a long sheath still seems the most likely use.

Cat No 5872/A03–0019 is shorter, only 360mm long and is slightly curved, indicating that it was made for a curved blade, possibly that of a hunting knife; its foot is rounded, not sharply pointed. While Cat No 5872/A03–0019 came from unstratified deposits, Cat No 739/A9143 was detected in a late 12th-century backland pit.

Sheaths, short plain (Illus 154)

Four of the short sheaths were plain, as for example Cat Nos 1116/A9889 (Illus 154) and 5875/A03–0037a (Illus 154). They were constructed from a single piece of leather folded twice and stitched up the centre of the reverse with a butted edge–grain seam, with the exception of Cat No 1116/A9889, which had been sewn with a thong. It was of late 12th- to mid-13th-century date. Cat Nos 3718/A03–0160b and 3984/A03–0170a were of early 14th-century date, while Cat No 5875/A03–0037a was unstratified. Two (50%) of the four sheaths came from Rig VI.

Illus 153 *Long strap folded twice.*

Sheaths, overall (Illus 154–6).

Cat/Accession	Area	Rig	Feature	Phase
South Sector				
570/A9120	4	V	M10	IId–IIg
739/A9143	3	VI	M1.2, Pit 2648	<IIg(IIh)
1116/A9889	3	VI	M6a	IIg–IIId
1224/A8183	4	V	MC120a	IIh–IVa
1360/A8002	4	V	MC143	IVaa
3047/A8334	3	VI	M1.4d	IVb,IVc
3717/A03–0160a	7	VI	B34, Courtyard	Va
3718/A03–0160b	7	VI	B34, Courtyard	Va
3869/A03–0070	7	VI, VII	M1.5b	Vaa
3875/A03–0118	7	VI, VII	M1.5b	Vaa
3984/A03–0170a	7	VI, VII	M1.5b	Vaa
5220/A03–0130	7	VII	M8a, T7193	Va,Vaa
5395/A3192	4	VI	P1a	Vd
5770/A12573	3/4	V, VI	Unstratified	u/s
5868/A03–0004a	7–10	VI–VIII	Unstratified	u/s
5872/A03–0019	7–10	VI–VIII	Unstratified	u/s
5875/A03–0037a	7–10	VI–VII	Unstratified	u/s

Sheaths, long plain (Illus 154).

Cat/Accession	Area	Rig	Feature	Phase
South Sector				
739/A9143	3	VI	M1.2, Pit 2648	<IIg(IIh)
5872/A03–0019	7–10	VI–VIII	Unstratified	u/s

Sheaths, short plain (Illus 154).

Cat/Accession	Area	Rig	Feature	Phase
South Sector				
1116/A9889	3	VI	M6a	IIg–IIId
3718/A03–0160b	7	VI	B34, Courtyard	Va
3984/A03–0170a	7	VI, VII	M1.5b	Vaa
5875/A03–0037a	7–10	VI–VII	Unstratified	u/s

Sheaths, decorated (Illus 155–156)

The 11 decorated sheaths were made out of a single piece of leather. In two examples (Cat Nos 1360/A8002 (Illus 156) and 5220/A03–0130 (Illus 156), the leather had been folded once and the edges sewn together with a grain to flesh seam. The rest had been folded twice and stitched up the centre of the reverse with a butted edge to grain seam. Four sheaths had a projecting upper part, to accommodate a wide haft: Cat Nos 1224/A8183 (Illus 155); 1360/A8002 (Illus 156); 3047/A8334 (Illus 155); and 5868/A03–0004a (Illus 155). The lower part of Cat No 1224/A8183 (Illus 155) had been folded twice, but the upper part only once. Holes for the attachment of the sheath to a belt or clothing or even to a larger sheath were noted on the reverse of six sheaths: Cat Nos 1224/A8183 (Illus 155); 3047/A8334 (Illus 155); 3869/A03–0070 (Illus 156); 5220/A03–0130 (Illus 156); 5770/A12573 (Illus 156); and 5868/A03–0004a (Illus 155). On three examples, these holes had penetrated as far as the decorated front of the sheath: Cat Nos 3047/A8334, 5770/A12573 and 5868/A03–0004a. It has been noted that suspension holes are usually crude and often do not respect the decoration; they were probably made by the owner or user of the sheath (Cowgill et al 1987, 5).

Three methods of decoration were used: engraving, punching and stamping. Lines such as those marking out panels, hatching, chevrons, curvilinear designs, shield motifs and lozenges enclosing stamped patterns, were engraved with a blunt tool, most probably onto wet leather (*LMMC*, 185). One sheath, Cat No 1360/A8002 (Illus 156), had been punched with a hollow tool, to produce dots enclosed within diamonds. Three sheaths, Cat Nos 3869/A03–0070 (Illus 156), 5770/A12573 (Illus 156) and 5395/A3192 (Illus 156), have been stamped, most probably with a metal stamp (ibid). The first two sheaths were stamped with fleurs-de-lys,

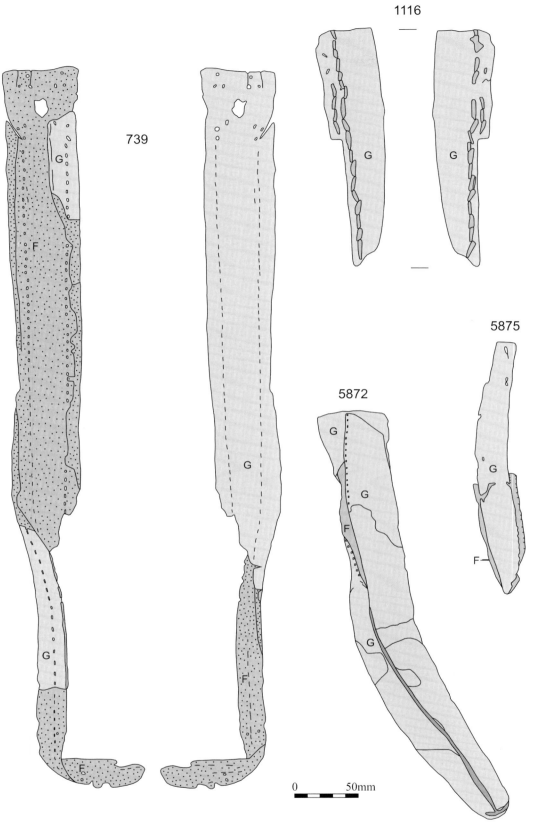

Illus 154 *Plain sheaths.*

the third with a bird, possibly a hawk, sitting on a perch. None of the images are clear; this may be caused by wear to the sheath itself, but it is possible that the stamps were worn when used.

The decoration of the four sheaths with projecting upper parts has been divided into separate panels. The upper part of Cat No 1224/A8183 (Illus 155), for example, has a rectangular panel with three rows of two ovals or shields, while the lower panel has been filled with a simple curvilinear design. The reverse has been scored with irregular hatching. Similarly, the upper panel of Cat No 5868/A03–0004a (Illus 155) has been decorated with bands of diagonal hatching, while a rope pattern fills the lower part of the sheath. Bands of diagonal hatching also occur on the top part of the reverse; the lower part is undecorated. Alternating zones of diagonal lines have been engraved on the front of the projection of Cat No 3047/A8334 (Illus 155); the rest of the upper part of the sheath, including the reverse, has been divided into three panels, each filled with alternating diagonal lines. The panel at the front has small shields engraved between the diagonal lines. The front of the lower part of the sheath has been decorated with a simple curvilinear design, enclosed within a long thin panel bordered by dots. Shallow dots and stylised elongated S on the lower part of the fold of the sheath, as well as the upper panel referred to above, indicate that the sheath was decorated before it was folded. Cat No 1360/A8002 (Illus 156) has the same decoration, top and bottom, but divided into two separate panels. The decoration consists of neatly engraved diamonds, each enclosing a punched hole. The zones on either side of the diamonds contain panels with bands of four diagonal strokes. The fold has been decorated with chevrons, indicating that this sheath was also decorated before it was folded.

The sheaths without a projecting part use the same decorative motifs but are usually not divided into upper and lower panels. Cat No 570/A9120 (Illus 155) is decorated on both front and rear with bands of diagonal hatching, while Cat No 3875/A03–0118 (Illus 155) bears vertical zigzags, two on the front and one on the reverse. The small scrap of Cat No 3717/A03–0160a (Illus 155), which was probably part of a sheath, was engraved with a very rough lattice pattern. The fold and part of the front of Cat No 5220/A03–0130 (Illus 156) has been decorated with a star pattern of two interlocking ovals, possibly representing shields. The remaining area on the front has been filled with rectangles, alternately plain or containing vertical or horizontal strokes. Cat No 3869/A03–0070 (Illus 156) is more elaborately decorated, with a division into upper and lower panels. The upper panel is divided into three horizontal bands. The top one is filled with six spirals, the middle one is plain; the lowest band contains rectangles enclosing shields and debased lozenges that enclose fleurs-de-lys. The lower panel is decorated with opposing zigzags, forming lozenges that enclose worn and sometimes indistinct fleurs-de-lys.

Cat Nos 5770/A12573 (Illus 156) and 5395/A3192 (Illus 156) have been stamped all over, the former with fleurs-de-lys, the latter with a bird, all enclosed within lozenges or diamonds (see above).

These sheaths ranged in date from the late 12th to the mid-14th century (Period II, 1, 9%; Period IV, 3, 27%; Period V, 5, 46%; Unstratified, 2, 18%). The earliest was Cat No 570/A9120, with diagonal hatching, from a late 12th-century context. Cat No 1224/A8183, with shields and curvilinear design belonged to the first half of the 13th century. Cat Nos 1360/A8002 and 3047/A8334, with lozenges, hatching, shields and curvilinear design, were found in layers dating to the second half of the 13th century. Cat Nos 5220/A03–0130, 3875/A03–0118, 3717/A03–0160a, 3869/A03–0070 and 5395/A3192 came from early to mid-14th-century contexts; their principal decorative motifs included shields, lozenges, spirals, fleurs-de-lys and birds. Cat Nos 5868/A03–0004a and 5770/A12573 were unstratified.

Sheaths with similar construction and decoration have been found in London, Coventry, York, King's Lynn, Oxford, Southampton and Waterford (Tatton-Brown 1975, 163–4; *LMMC*, 185–199; Cowgill et al 1987, 54; Chatwin 1934, 60; Richardson 1959, 102–5; Mould et al 2003, 3369–89; Goodfellow and Thornton 1972, 96–7; Clarke and Carter 1977,

Sheaths (decorated) (Illus 155–6).

Cat/Accession	Area	Rig	Feature	Phase
South Sector				
570/A9120	4	V	M10	IId–IIg
1224/A8183	4	V	MC120a	IIh–IVa
1360/A8002	4	V	MC143	IVaa
3047/A8334	3	VI	M1.4d	IVb,IVc
3717/A03–0160a	7	VI	B34, Courtyard	Va
3869/A03–0070	7	VI, VII	M1.5b	Vaa
3875/A03–0118	7	VI, VII	M1.5b	Vaa
5220/A03–0130	7	VII	M8a, T7193	Va,Vaa
5395/A3192	4	VI	P1a	Vd
5770/A12573	3/4	V, VI	Unstratified	u/s
5868/A03–0004a	7–10	VI–VIII	Unstratified	u/s

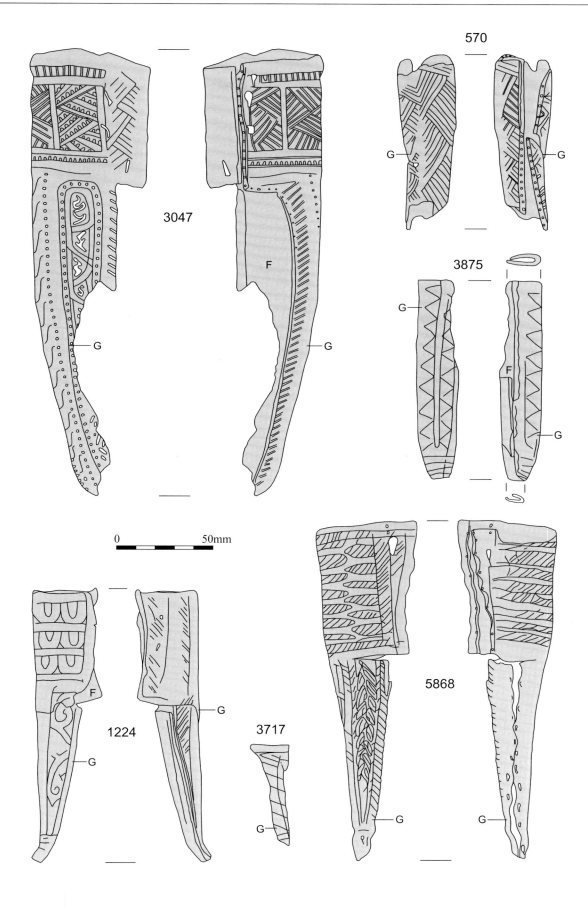

Illus 155 *Decorated sheaths.*

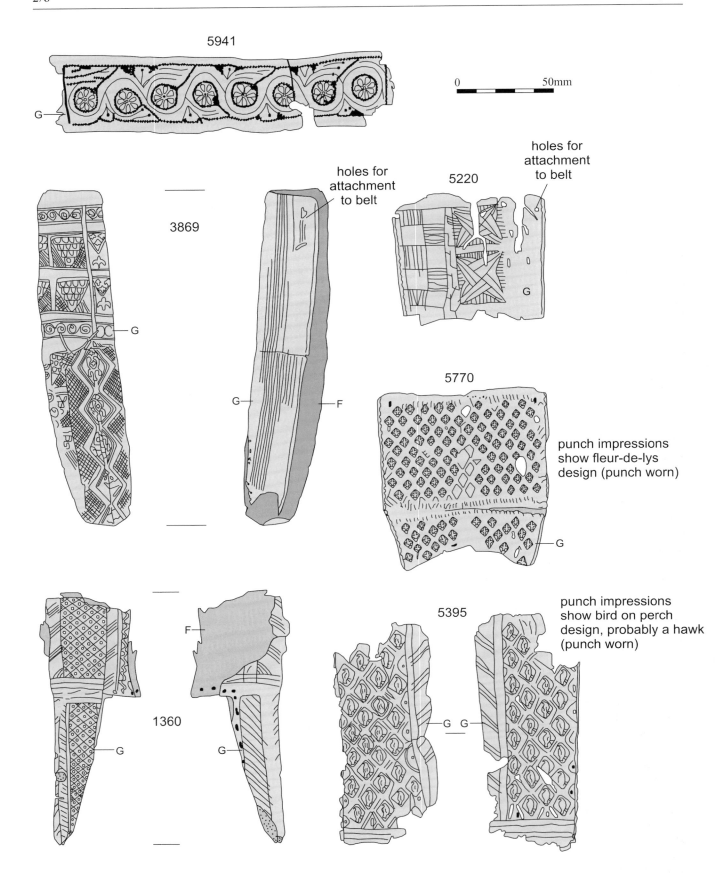

Illus 156 *Strap with rosettes and decorated sheaths.*

364–6; Hassall 1976, 294–5; Platt and Coleman-Smith 1975, 296, 299; Hurley 1997, 736–42). Parallels also exist in Scandinavia, whither they appear to have been exported from England (Blomqvist 1938, 189–219, quoted in *LMMC*, 157, 189, 190). Diagonal hatching was frequently used on sheaths, particularly as background. Examples of all-over use of diagonal hatching have been found at the Hungate and Coppergate (10th–14th centuries) sites, York; Custom House site, London; and King's Lynn (Richardson 1959, 103–4, Fig 29, no 3 [13th–14th centuries]; Mould et al 2003, 3369–89; Tatton-Brown 1975, 162–3, Fig 29, no 116 [early–mid-14th century]; Clarke and Carter 1977, 364–6, Fig 169, no 92 [c1250–1350]). Short zigzags were commonly used to fill in the space on either side of a decorated panel but were less often employed on their own as major motifs. Two examples do survive, nevertheless, in the Museum of London, as well as from Coppergate, York (*LMMC*, 191–2, Fig 59, A2351 [15th century]; Cowgill et al 1987, 162, no 483 [unstratified]; Mould et al 2003, 3369–89). The simple curvilinear designs on Cat Nos 1224/A8183 and 3047/A8334 probably represent attempts at reproducing acanthus scroll. Debased acanthus scroll was often used to enclose motifs such as the imaginary beasts on sheath no 1 from the Hungate, York (Richardson 1959, 102–103, Fig 29 no 1). Two examples of extremely simple designs, similar to those on Cat Nos 1224/A8183 and 3047/A8334, occur on another sheath from the Hungate, dated to late 12th–13th centuries (Richardson 1959, 103–4, Fig 29, no 2) and on a sheath in the British Museum (No 1903.6.23.72), on a larger scale than on Cat No 1224/A8183. More elaborate curvilinear motifs include interlaced and plaited designs, such as the rope pattern mentioned above. Several examples of rope pattern have been found in London (late 12th century, early–mid-14th century); Hull and Gloucester (12th–early 13th centuries) (Cowgill et al 1987, 115–16, no 372, 132–4, nos 405 and 409; Tatton-Brown 1975, 162–3, Fig 29, no 113; British Museum, No 1903.6.23.71, 56.7.1; Watkin 1987, Fig 131, no 435; Watkin 1983).

The use of conventionalised heraldic devices such as shields, lozenges and fleurs-de-lys as decorative motifs on these sheaths does not imply that the owners were entitled to wear such emblems, but rather that they wished to imitate the nobility (Richardson 1959, 106). Sheaths with elaborate shields are known from Coventry and London (Chatwin 1934, 60, nos 1, 2, 4, 11, 12; *LMMC*, 190, Plate XL, A3664 [13th century?]). Simpler shield patterns more similar to those from this site have been found at Kirk Close, Perth (13th–14th centuries); Hull; King's Lynn (c1350–1500); Custom House site, London (early–mid-14th century) and the Barbican ditch, Oxford (13th–15th centuries) (Thomas 1987, 182; Watkin 1987, Fig 131, no 433; Clarke and Carter 1977, 364–5, Fig 169, nos 39 and 90; Tatton-Brown 1975, 162–3, Fig 29, no 110, no 115, small holder for a ?bottle; Hassall 1976, 295–6, Fig 25, nos 6, 8, part of belt?). Lozenges or diamonds were commonly used on sheaths to enclose punched or stamped motifs, as demonstrated by examples from London (early–mid-14th century); Oxford (13th–15th century); Southampton (late 13th century); King's Lynn (c1250–1500); and Coventry (Tatton-Brown 1975, 163–4, Fig 30, 119; *LMMC*, 191, Plate XLII, no 1, British Museum no 1903.6.23.70; Hassall 1976, 294–5, no 1; Platt and Coleman Smith 1975, 296, 299, Fig 262, no 2157; Clarke and Carter 1977, 364–5, Fig 169, nos 89 and 91; Chatwin 1934, 60, nos 1, 2, 7, 11).

Cat No 1360/A8002, with lozenges enclosing dots, is almost identical to a sheath in the British Museum (No 1903.23.70); the latter is slightly larger, but the proportions of the sheath and the layout of its decoration are strikingly similar. The Museum of London possesses another parallel, larger again (M. IV 85 4650). The same form of decoration also survives on sheaths from Kirk Close, Perth (13th–14th centuries); London (early–mid-13th century); King's Lynn (c1250–1350); Newcastle (mid-13th century–mid-14th century) and Bristol Bridge, Bristol (13th–14th centuries) (Thomas 1987, 182, no 25; Cowgill et al 1987, 115–16, no 373, 156, no 465 [unstratified]; Dixon 1988, 102, Fig 42; Thomas forthcoming a). Fleurs-de-lys were very common decorative motifs; examples of them enclosed within lozenges survive from London (late 13th century–mid-14th century); Oxford (13th–15th centuries); Southampton (late 13th century); King's Lynn (c1250–1500); Bristol Bridge, Bristol; and Hull (*LMMC*, 191, Plate XLII, no 1–A3683; Tatton-Brown 1975, 162–3, Fig 29, nos 114 and 119; Cowgill et al 1987, nos 391 and 392; Hassall 1976, 294–5, Fig 25, no 1; Platt and Coleman Smith 1975, II, 296, Fig 262, no 2157; Clarke and Carter 1977, 364–5, Fig 169, no 89; Thomas forthcoming a; Watkin 1987, Fig 131). Cat No 3869/A03–0070, with its opposing zigzags enclosing fleurs-de-lys, is paralleled by two sheaths, from the Barbican Ditch, Oxford (13th–15th centuries) and the Custom House site, London (early–mid-14th century) (Hassall 1976, 294–5, Fig 25, no 1, on top front and lower back; Tatton-Brown 1975, 162–3, Fig 30, no 119, lower part).

Discussion

The parallels described above demonstrate that the decorated sheaths from this site were of a very common type. The main motifs (hatching, zigzags, curvilinear designs, shields, lozenges and fleurs-de-lys) were used frequently on leather, and especially on sheaths. The dating of the Perth High Street sheaths corresponds to that suggested by parallels, with all but one of the nine dated sheaths probably belonging to the 13th to mid 14th centuries. This group of 11 sheaths is perhaps best paralleled in decoration and date by those from the Custom House site, London. The decoration is very similar in both groups and not as elaborate as that on the majority of the sheaths in the Museum of London and the British Museum (personal observation). All 14 of the Custom House sheaths are of early to mid-14th-century date, while the High Street examples, as discussed above, are mainly of 13th- to early 14th-century date.

The striking similarity between Cat No 1360/A8002 and the British Museum's No 1903.6.23.70 suggests that decorated sheaths might have been imported to Perth from London. This hypothesis is strengthened by Blomqvist's belief that the Lund sheaths were imports from London (Blomqvist 1938, in *LMMC*, 187, 190). However, the motifs used, especially the diamonds and dots on Cat No 1360/A8002, were very common and were easily imitated. The crude nature of the attachment holes indicates that they were used locally. Therefore the possibility of their being made for export should be discounted.

Although, as discussed above, decorated knife sheaths occur regularly in medieval leather assemblages, they are not as common as footwear, and could accordingly be considered as an indicator of wealth and status. It is vital, on the other hand, to remember that the heraldic devices were used as imitative motifs, not as genuine symbols of nobility. As with the decorated uppers, engraved and stamped designs involved expertise and time, and thus would have made the finished product more expensive than an unadorned version.

Waste material: offcuts and scraps

The waste material includes not only the cut fragments of soles and uppers referred to above but also offcuts and other scraps. At least 3323 offcuts and 700 scraps survive. There were also 30 fragments that could have been either offcuts or scraps. Offcuts have been defined

as having at least one cut edge, while scraps have no cut edges, only torn ones. The offcuts consist of triangles, short, thin strips, rectangles, ovals and trapeziums, as well as many irregular shapes. The offcuts and scraps include both unworn and worn leather.

Many of the more irregular offcuts and scraps are skin offcuts or edges of skins, ie the primary offcuts identified by van Driel-Murray (1985, 45–51). These show that the High Street leather-workers started with whole skins, which they first trimmed. Some offcuts have several parallel short slits; these are possibly identification marks, made when the skins were pegged out to dry, as for example Cat Nos 5878/A03–0040b (Illus 159) and 5019/A03–0209 (Illus 159) (Biddle 1990, 245–8, Fig 53b; Ayers and Murphy 1983, Fig 21, nos 1 and 2). One triangular offcut has two converging rows of shallow depressions (Cat No 421/A03.0015d (Illus 159); these may be tooth-marks, suggesting that the leather-worker used his mouth as an extra hand (I Carlisle pers comm).

The rectangular, triangular and trapezoidal shapes are secondary offcuts, from cutting out soles, uppers and other objects. The thick triangles, usually with curved edges, are still unworn and are particularly indicative of cutting out soles from new leather. The thin strips, both long and short, are trimmings; these include many tiny snippets. They represent a third stage in the cutting-out process. Other more worn offcuts are probably fragments of objects cut up for reuse. This includes some larger objects.

Following van Driel-Murray's discussion of the three principal types of offcut, primary, secondary and trimming, an attempt was made to identify these in the High Street assemblage. Unfortunately, most of the

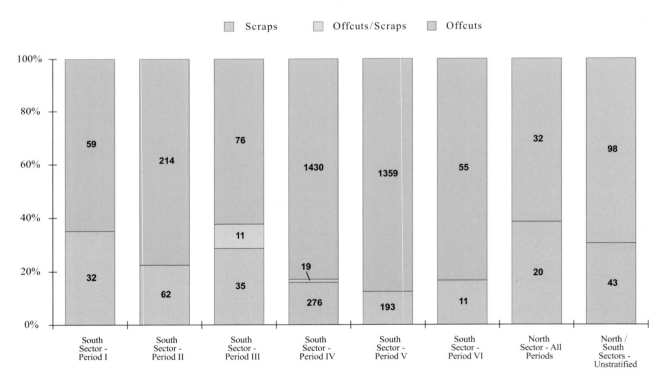

Illus 157 *Number and percentage of waste material categories arranged by period.*

offcuts were not conserved and are therefore no longer available for study. Accordingly, only 285 could be examined.

The three types recognised by van Driel-Murray were all identified, as well as a fourth, offcuts resulting from reuse. Primary offcuts accounted for 29% of the sample (82). Thirty of these had loosely oversewn edges, perhaps to prevent the hides from splitting; four had several parallel slits, possibly identification marks. Another offcut had a large oval hole, which is probably a peg-hole (Cat No 5259/A03–0053). The greater proportion of the sample proved to be secondary offcuts (132 fragments; 46%). These included triangles (42), wide strips (26), oblongs (13), trapeziums (10), semi-circles (3) and one square. Of particular interest were two double triangles and one double trapezium. The triangles are almost certainly from either side of a sole, while the double trapezium is possibly the negative left behind by cutting-out a leg-flap or side-piece of an upper. At least 56 trimmings were recognised, as well as 15 offcuts cut from used leather.

Primary and secondary offcuts in this sample occurred in Periods I–V, trimmings in Periods I, IV and V and reuse offcuts in Periods IV and V. However, as this sample forms such a small part of the original assemblage, no significance should be placed on the proportions surviving from each Period. In the South Sector, the quantities of waste material increases with each medieval period, from 91 (2%) items in Period I to 276 (7%) in Period II, 122 (3%) in Period III, 1725 (42%) in Period IV, 1552 (39%) in Period V; 66 (2%) were either unstratified or from Period VI. This suggests that by 1250–1350, leather-working, especially shoe making and repairing, was a flourishing and growing trade.

Miscellaneous fragments
(Illus 158–164)

The leather also included over 100 miscellaneous fragments, about a third of which are too insubstantial to merit discussion. Most of these were from contexts dated 1250–1350 (Periods IV and V).

Four of the miscellaneous fragments have been decorated. The earliest, Cat No 481/A10503 (Illus 158), is a trapezoidal fragment with engraved slits and punched dots. It was recovered from a backland midden in Rig VI which had been laid down late in the 12th century. Cat No 2272/A03–0426b (Illus 158), a triangular piece decorated with punched circles 3mm in diameter, was recovered from a pit in Rig VII which probably dated from the third quarter of the 13th century. Cat No 2819/A03–0273c (Illus 158) has been folded to form a rectangular container, possibly a comb case, which was probably stitched together. It has been decorated with rows of slits and a simple curvilinear motif, marked by slits. It was found in a midden in Rig VIII which dated from the late 13th century. Cat No 5767/A6203 (Illus 158) is a square fragment with

engraved rectangles, one of which is marked by a band of impressed or stamped gilt decoration, consisting of repeated candelabra and a stylised floral motif. The leather has possibly been folded. It does not appear to have been glued to anything. It came from an unstratified context and could even be post-medieval.

Miscellaneous fragments: ?clothing
(Illus 158–164)

Thirty-nine fragments are probably parts of clothing. Several large pieces appear to belong to jerkins, as, for example, Cat No 2883/A9361 (Illus 160), which has a row of 17 lace holes, as well as stitching for darts. Cat Nos 3961–3964/A03–0142b–e (Illus 163) are probably from the back of a jerkin, while Cat No 1827/A03–0376b (Illus 161) is possibly a rear shoulder piece. Cat No 194/ A13004c (Illus 164) is a long strip, with a v-shape cut out of it, which might mark the side of a garment. Parallel rows of stitching are common on some of these fragments, for instance, Cat Nos 1431/A6187f (Illus 164), 2274/A03–0411a (Illus 162), 2535/A03–0409b (Illus 161) and 3888/A03–0125c (Illus 160).

Paired stitch holes and signs of gathering are another characteristic, as on Cat Nos 1897/A03–0357m and 2307/A03–0279d (Illus 160). Some smaller fragments, which are mainly triangular or trapezoidal in shape, are probably inserts or gussets, as, for example Cat Nos 91/ A8688c (Illus 159), 1805/A03–0367b (Illus 159), 1826/ A03–0376a (Illus 161) and 3510/A03–0220 (Illus 159). Another triangular insert, Cat No 2769/A03–0113e (Illus 161), has a small rectangle of dense grain to flesh stitching, which was probably used to attach a strap or buckle.

Cat Nos 3569–3572/A7688e–h consist of four joining pieces, linked by thongs, one of which ends in a toggle (Illus 159). These bear a striking similarity to the thongs and toggles found on Upper Type K. However, the fourth piece, beneath the thongs, which would be part of the vamp/vamp throat if this were part of a shoe, is too insubstantial and has too many stitched edges. Four other fragments, Cat Nos 1568–1571/A03– 0423a–d (Cat Nos 1568 and 1569, Illus 160; Cat No 1570, Illus 163), have been folded and stitched to form substantial hems, while Cat No 26/A10499 (Illus 158) appears to be part of an elaborate, decorative binding.

The majority (31; 80%) of these fragments of clothing came from Period IV (the second half of the 13th century) and Period V (the first half of the 14th century). Six fragments were found in MC130 and Pit 7402 (MC126), five in M1.5b and four in M1.4e. The concentration of these items in Period IV and the earliest phases of Period V (during the second half of the 13th century and early 14th century), combined with the increased evidence for cobbling during these Periods, suggests that by then clothing fragments may have been stored for reuse. Perhaps significantly 15 (48%) of these clothing fragments came from just one property, Rig VII, with another five in M1.5b when Rigs VI and VII seem to have been combined.

Miscellaneous fragments (overall) (Illus 158–64).

Cat/Accession	Area	Rig	Feature	Phase
South Sector				
26/A10499	1	VI	MC006, T3852	Ib
91/A8688c	1/2	V	B10, South Room–Occupation (2b)	Icc
184/A7598	2	VI	M14b(b)	Ie
194/A13004c	2	VI	M14b(b)	Ie
195/A13004d	2	VI	M14b(b)	Ie
254/A7801b	2	V	M14b(a), Pit 3686	Id
335/A12301	3	VI	MC054a, Pit 5267, MW5265	(IIa)IIb
350/A6772j	2	VI	MC061	IIb
351/A6772k	2	VI	MC061	IIb
480/A10502	3	VI	M1.1d	IId,IIe
481/A10503	3	VI	M1.1d	IId,IIe
485/A10504a	3	VI	M1.1a	IId,IIe
486/A10504b	3	VI	M1.1a	IId,IIe
490/A10797	3	VI	MC085, WW5208	IId,IIe
559/A9552a	3	V	B23, Construction	IIb–IIff
560/A9552b	3	V	B23, Construction	IIb–IIff
727/A11643b	4	V	M10, Pit 4554	IId–IIg
728/A11643c	4	V	M10, Pit 4554	IId–IIg
803/A10775b	3	VI	M1.2, Pit 2648	<IIg(IIh)
828/A12279	3	VI	M1.2, Pit 2648, MW5166	<IIg(IIh)
830/A8105	4	V, VI	M11	IIh
867/A8634b	3	VI	M1.3	IIi
881/A8666c	3	VI	M1.3	IIi
905/A9366	3	VI	M1.3	IIi
958/A8813b	4	V	MC116	IIe–IIIc
969/A11252g	4	V	MC116	IIe–IIIc
1009/A8008	4	VI	M1.4a(a)	IIIa–IIIc
1086/A03–0278a	9	VII	B19 (Phase 2b), North Room–Floor (2b)	IIIc
1214/A9104	3	V	M6b	IIg–IIId
1228/A8687a	4	V	MC120a	IIh–IVa
1430/A6187e	4	V	MC156	IVaa
1431/A6187f	4	V	MC156	IVaa
1443/A8692a	4	V	MC158a, Pit 2228	IVaa
1507/A03–0410b	7	VII	MC130	<IIIc–IVaa
1508/A03–0410c	7	VII	MC130	<IIIc–IVaa
1568/A03–0423a	7	VII	MC130	<IIIc–IVaa
1569/A03–0423b	7	VII	MC130	<IIIc–IVaa
1570/A03–0425c	7	VII	MC130	<IIIc–IVaa
1571/A03–0425d	7	VII	MC130	<IIIc–IVaa
1572/A03–0423e	7	VII	MC130	<IIIc–IVaa
1639/A8537	3	VI	B2, Floor/Foundation (1)	IVa,IVaa
1692/A5124	3	V	B3 (South), Pit 2529	IVa,IVaa
1805/A03–0367b	7	VII	MC126, Pit 7402	IVaa,IVb
1826/A03–0376a	7	VII	MC126, Pit 7402	IVaa,IVb
1827/A03–0376b	7	VII	MC126, Pit 7402	IVaa,IVb
1882/A03–0353e	7	VII	MC126, Pit 7402	IVaa,IVb
1883/A03–0353f	7	VII	MC126, Pit 7402	IVaa,IVb
1884/A03–0353g	7	VII	MC126, Pit 7402	IVaa,IVb
1897/A03–0357m	7	VII	MC126, Pit 7402	IVaa,IVb
1992/A03–0362b	7	VII	MC126, Pit 7402	IVaa,IVb
2113/A03–0377b	7	VII	MC126, Pit 7402	IVaa,IVb
2272/A03–0426b	7	VII	MC126, Pit 7402	IVaa,IVb
2274/A03–0411a	7	VII	MC146, Pit 7339	<IVb
2307/A03–0279d	7	VI	M1.4f	IVc

(continued)

Cat/Accession	Area	Rig	Feature	Phase
2534/A03–0409a	7	VII	P8.2b	IVb
2535/A03–0409b	7	VII	P8.2b	IVb
2543/A03–0375b	7	VII	P8.2b	IVb
2544/A03–0375c	7	VII	P8.2b	IVb
2684/A03–0202e	9	VII	B18 (Phase 1/2), Pit 9301	IVaa,IVb
2695/A03–0182b	9	VII	B18 (Phase 1/2), Pit 9301	IVaa,IVb
2700/A03–0292a	7	VII	B18 (Phase 1/2), MF 7307	IVaa,IVb
2701/A03–0292b	7	VII	B18 (Phase 1/2), MF 7307	IVaa,IVb
2702/A03–0292c	7	VII	B18 (Phase 1/2), MF 7307	IVaa,IVb
2703/A03–0292d	7	VII	B18 (Phase 1/2), MF 7307	IVaa,IVb
2724/A03–0383	7	VII	B18 (Phases 2a & 2b), T7385	IVb
2769/A03–0113e	9	VII	B18 (Phase 2b), North Room, Hall & Hall South–Occupation (10)	IVb
2819/A03–0273c	10	VIII	M9b(a)	IVc
2820/A03–0273d	10	VIII	M9b(a)	IVc
2821/A03–0273e	10	VIII	M9b(a)	IVc
2883/A9361	3	V	MC155, Pit 2691	IVb,IVc
2996/A10777	3	V	MC155, Pit 2691	IVb,IVc
3120/A8694	3	VI	M1.4d, Pit 2566	IVb,IVc
3166/A3452	2	V	M1.4g, Pit 2800	IVb,IVc
3221/A6228c	3	V, VI	M1.4c	IIIa–IVcc
3360/A03–0241a	7	VII	M9a	IVc,IVcc
3403/A04–0079b	9	VII	M9a	IVc,IVcc
3510/A03–0220	10	VIII	M9b(b), PW6166	IVc,IVcc
3569/A7688e	3	VI	M1.4e	IVcc(Va)(VI)
3570/A7688f	3	VI	M1.4e	IVcc(Va)(VI)
3571/A7688g	3	VI	M1.4e	IVcc(Va)(VI)
3572/A7688h	3	VI	M1.4e	IVcc(Va)(VI)
3585/A7795b	3	VI	M1.4e	IVcc(Va)(VI)
3586/A7795c	3	VI	M1.4e	IVcc(Va)(VI)
3884/A03–0121c	7	VI, VII	M1.5b	Vaa
3888/A03–0125c	7	VI, VII	M1.5b	Vaa
3927/A03–0136c	7	VI, VII	M1.5b	Vaa
3928/A03–0136d	7	VI, VII	M1.5b	Vaa
3929/A03–0136e	7	VI, VII	M1.5b	Vaa
3961/A03–0142b	7	VI, VII	M1.5b	Vaa
3962/A03–0142c	7	VI, VII	M1.5b	Vaa
3963/A03–0142d	7	VI, VII	M1.5b	Vaa
3964/A03–0142e	7	VI, VII	M1.5b	Vaa
4014/A03–0165b	7	VII	P8.4	Va
4015/A03–0165c	7	VII	P8.4	Va
4151/A04–0088c	9	VII	P8.4	Va
4220/A6234b	2	V	B1(a), Construction–Levelling	IVcc,Va
4223/A6074b	3	V	B1(a), T2477	IVcc,Va
4250/A4491a	2	V	B1(b), Demolition	Va
4251/A4491b	2	V	B1(b), Demolition	Va
4252/A4491c	2	V	B1(b), Demolition	Va
4254/A6410b	2	V	B1(b), Demolition	Va
4256/A4909	2	V	B1(b), Demolition, Tumble	Va
4496/A4289d	3	V, VI	M1.5a	Va,Vaa(VI)
4820/A6237f	3	V, VI	M1.5a	Va,Vaa
4845/A03–0175r	7	VII	M8a	Va,Vaa
4884/A03–0114a	7	VII	M8a	Va,Vaa
4885/A03–0114b	7	VII	M8a	Va,Vaa
4938/A03–0162kk	7	VII	M8a	Va,Vaa
4980/A03–0174t	7	VII	M8a	Va,Vaa
4981/A03–0174u	7	VII	M8a	Va,Vaa
4982/A03–0174v	7	VII	M8a	Va,Vaa

(continued)

Cat/Accession	Area	Rig	Feature	Phase
5362/A5894g	4	VI	M3b	Vd
5621/A1229a	2	VI	M4c	Vd,Vdd
5762/A9914	2	V, VI	Unstratified	u/s
5767/A6203	3/4	V, VI	Unstratified	u/s
5788/A0800j	3/4	V, VI	Unstratified	u/s
5823/A03–0080	7/9	VII	Modern, T7014, D7014	VI
5870/A03–0007	7–10	VI–VIII	Unstratified	u/s
5873/A03–0028	7–10	VI–VIII	Unstratified	u/s
South/North Sectors				
5985/L2766a	–	–	Unstratified	u/s
5986/L2766b	–	–	Unstratified	u/s

Miscellaneous fragments:decorated (Illus 158).

Cat/Accession	Area	Rig	Feature	Phase
South Sector				
481/A10503	3	VI	M1.1d	IId,IIe
2272/A03–0426b	7	VII	MC126, Pit 7402	IVaa,IVb
2819/A03–0273c	10	VIII	M9b(a)	IVc
5767/A6203	3/4	V, VI	Unstratified	u/s

Possible clothing from Kirk Close, Perth included two pieces with L- or T-shaped loops, as well as two matching facings; another fragment had two parallel rows of tunnel stitching (13th–14th centuries; Thomas 1987, 184–5, 189–90). Fragments of a jacket were found at Leicester, but these had buttonholes with stitched edges (14th century; Allin 1981a, 165–7). Examples from Exeter included part of a jacket with an armhole facing and a triangular gusset (Friendship-Taylor 1984, 331–3, Fig 187, 60, 61, 65). A jacket sleeve from York had a concave shaping at one end, while an elaborate binding had slots for three rows of thonging (Tweddle 1986, 255–6, 265, Fig 117, no 859, Fig 118, no 862).

Miscellaneous fragments: ?containers

Seven fragments are probably parts of purses or containers of some form. Cat Nos 485/A10504a and 486/A10504b (Illus 158), for example, have been folded and stitched, one forming a small, square case or wallet, the other a simple rectangular sheath. Cat No 5762/A9914 (Illus 159), on the other hand, resembles an oddly shaped sole; it is possibly the base of a container, whose walls were attached by a butted edge–flesh seam. Cat No 5788/A0800j (Illus 159) may be part of a similar item. Cat No 350/A6772j (Illus 159) appears to have been a purse. Cat Nos 350/A6772j, 485/A10504a, 486/A10504b and 828/A12279 all came from deposits that had been laid down in Rig VI during Period II, the second half of the 12th century. Two others (Cat Nos 5762/A9914 and 5788/A0800j) were recovered from unstratified contexts. Cat No 2819/A03–0273c was recovered from a midden, M9b(a), that had been deposited in the backland area of Rig VIII late in the 13th century.

Cases similar to Cat Nos 485/A10504a, 486/A10504b and 2819/A03–0273c, were found at Novgorod (Brisbane 1992, 181–3, Fig V, 8, nos 1–3; mostly 13th–14th centuries). Simple purses formed out of a folded piece of leather are known from London (12th–early 14th centuries); Bayham Abbey, Sussex (late 15th–early 16th centuries) and Lübeck (late 12th–mid-13th centuries) (Egan and Pritchard 1991, 342–57; Jones and Thornton 1983, 124–5, Fig 55, 26, 27; Groenman-van Waateringe and Guiran 1978, Fig 71, 1 and 2).

Miscellaneous fragments: oval (Illus 158)

Three oval fragments, Cat Nos 803/A10755b (Illus 158), 2724/A03–0383 (Illus 158) and 2996/A10777, with each narrow end rolled to form a tab, have been slashed horizontally. One was from Period II, the others came from Period IV. Other examples are known from Parliament Street and Coppergate, York (c10th century–1300); Newcastle (mid-13th–14th centuries); Chapel Lane Staith, Hull (mid–late 14th century); Dublin (late 12th century); Waterford (early 13th century) and Haithabu (Tweddle 1986, 254, Fig 117, no 885; Mould et al 2003, 3409–10; Dixon 1988, 103, Fig 36, no 280; Jackson 1979; Ard Mhúsaen na H-Eireann 1973, 188–E 71.15193; O'Rourke 1997, 726, 730, Fig 18.9.13; Groenman-van Waateringe 1984, Taf 28).

Their function is unknown. The slashing might not be decorative, but to allow the fragment to stretch. It has been suggested that these objects might be that part of a slingshot that holds the stone or metal bullet (I Carlisle pers comm). Another possibility is that they are tongues of shoes; however, none of the High Street uppers appear to have had suitable stitching to attach such uppers.

Miscellaneous fragments: ?clothing (Illus 158–64).

Cat/Accession	Area	Rig	Feature	Phase
South Sector				
26/A10499	1	VI	MC006, T3852	Ib
91/A8688c	1/2	V	B10, South Room–Occupation (2b)	Icc
194/A13004c	2	VI	M14b(b)	Ie
254/A7801b	2	V	M14b(a), Pit 3686	Id
351/A6772k	2	VI	MC061	IIb
905/A9366	3	VI	M1.3	IIi
958/A8813b	4	V	MC116	IIe–IIIc
1009/A8008	4	VI	M1.4a(a)	IIIa–IIIc
1430/A6187e	4	V	MC156	IVaa
1431/A6187f	4	V	MC156	IVaa
1507/A03–0410b	7	VII	MC130	<IIIc–IVaa
1508/A03–0410c	7	VII	MC130	<IIIc–IVaa
1568/A03–0423a	7	VII	MC130	<IIIc–IVaa
1569/A03–0423b	7	VII	MC130	<IIIc–IVaa
1570/A03–0425c	7	VII	MC130	<IIIc–IVaa
1571/A03–0425d	7	VII	MC130	<IIIc–IVaa
1805/A03–0367b	7	VII	MC126, Pit 7402	IVaa,IVb
1826/A03–0376a	7	VII	MC126, Pit 7402	IVaa,IVb
1827/A03–0376b	7	VII	MC126, Pit 7402	IVaa,IVb
1882/A03–0353e	7	VII	MC126, Pit 7402	IVaa,IVb
1883/A03–0353f	7	VII	MC126, Pit 7402	IVaa,IVb
1897/A03–0357m	7	VII	MC126, Pit 7402	IVaa,IVb
2274/A03–0411a	7	VII	MC146, Pit 7339	<IVb
2307/A03–0279d	7	VI	M1.4f	IVc
2535/A03–0409b	7	VII	P8.2b	IVb
2769/A03–0113e	9	VII	B18 (Phase 2b), North Room, Hall & Hall South–Occupation (10)	IVb
2821/A03–0273e	10	VIII	M9b(a)	IVc
2883/A9361	3	V	MC155, Pit 2691	IVb,IVc
3510/A03–0220	10	VIII	M9b(b), PW6166	IVc,IVcc
3569/A7688e	3	VI	M1.4e	IVcc(Va)(VI)
3570/A7688f	3	VI	M1.4e	IVcc(Va)(VI)
3571/A7688g	3	VI	M1.4e	IVcc(Va)(VI)
3572/A7688h	3	VI	M1.4e	IVcc(Va)(VI)
3888/A03–0125c	7	VI, VII	M1.5b	Vaa
3961/A03–0142b	7	VI, VII	M1.5b	Vaa
3962/A03–0142c	7	VI, VII	M1.5b	Vaa
3963/A03–0142d	7	VI, VII	M1.5b	Vaa
3964/A03–0142e	7	VI, VII	M1.5b	Vaa
5362/A5894g	4	VI	M3b	Vd

Miscellaneous fragments: ?containers (Illus 158–9).

Cat/Accession	Area	Rig	Feature	Phase
South Sector				
350/A6772j	2	VI	MC061	IIb
485/A10504a	3	VI	M1.1a	IId.IIe
486/A10504b	3	VI	M1.1a	IId.IIe
828/A12279	3	VI	M1.2, Pit 2648, MW5166	<IIg(IIh)
2819/A03–0273c	10	VIII	M9b(a)	IVc
5762/A9914	2	V, VI	Unstratified	u/s
5788/A0800j	3/4	V, VI	Unstratified	u/s

Miscellaneous fragments: oval (Illus 158).

Cat/Accession	Area	Rig	Feature	Phase
South Sector				
803/A10775b	3	VI	M1.2, Pit 2648	<IIg(IIh)
2724/A03–0383	7	VII	B18 (Phases 2a & 2b), T7385	IVb
2996/A10777	3	V	MC155, Pit 2691	IVb,IVc

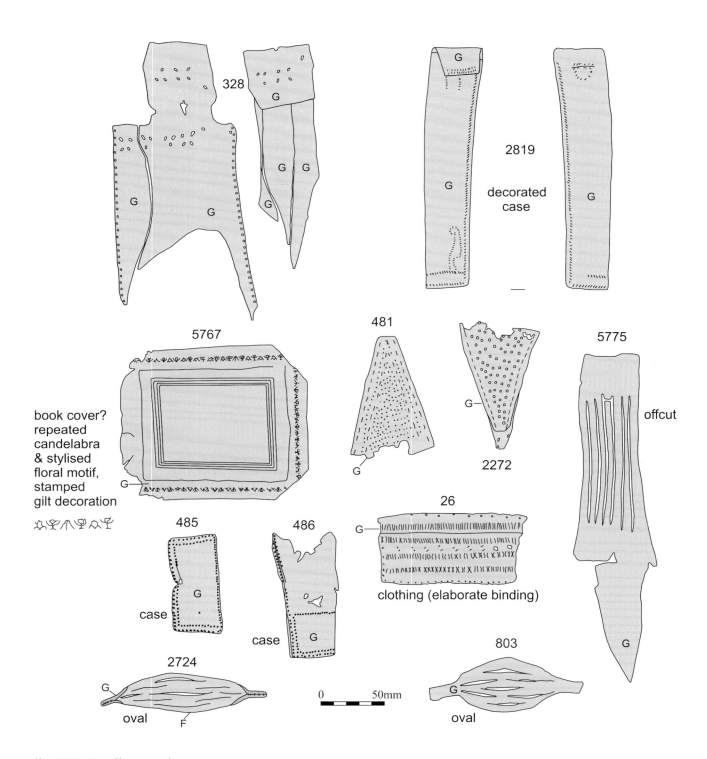

Illus 158 *Miscellaneous fragments.*

Miscellaneous fragments: edges loosely oversewn
(Illus 164)

Eleven pieces have one or more edges loosely oversewn; similar fragments were found at Kirk Close, Perth (Thomas 1987, 183). Their function is not understood; they are possibly primary offcuts (see Waste material).

Leather fragments with metalwork attached
(Illus 159)

Of the 15 fragments of leatherwork that had metalwork attached, 12 are classified as miscellaneous fragments

(see also Fascicule 2, The metalwork). Three pieces have bronze rivets. Cat No 1692/A5124 is an irregular strip that has been folded once, with grain surfaces exposed on both sides. Fragments of seven rivets survive in situ, as well as the holes for another 28. Cat No 1228/A8687a (Illus 164) is a rectangular fragment with two short edges folded and fastened by short rivets or nails. Cat No 1214/A9104 is a strip of leather perforated by two parallel rows of holes for 71 rivets, 23 of which survive. The rivets have heads of gold or copper on a lead base, while the shafts are of iron. Two straps from Mill Street, Perth, had iron rivets with domed heads, while impressions of rivets were found on 12 fragments from 45–75 Gallowgate, Aberdeen (Thomas and Walsh 1995; Thomas 2001a, 251).

Miscellaneous fragments: edges loosely oversewn (Illus 164).

Cat/Accession	Area	Rig	Feature	Phase
South Sector				
728/A11643c	4	V	M10, Pit 4554	IId–IIg
1992/A03–0362b	7	VII	MC126, Pit 7402	IVaa,IVb
2543/A03–0375b	7	VII	P8.2b	IVb
2544/A03–0375c	7	VII	P8.2b	IVb
3585/A7795b	3	VI	M1.4e	IVcc(Va)(VI)
3586/A7795c	3	VI	M1.4e	IVcc(Va)(VI)
4223/A6074b	3	V	B1(a), T2477	IVcc,Va
4256/A4909	2	V	B1(b), Demolition, Tumble	Va
4820/A6237f	3	V, VI	M1.5a	Va,Vaa
4980/A03–0174t	7	VII	M8a	Va,Vaa

Leather fragments with metalwork attached (Illus 159).

Cat/Accession	Leather type	Area	Rig	Feature	Phase
South Sector					
153/A12312b	Strap/belt (folded twice)	3	VI	MC037a, Pit 5157	Ia–Ie
342/A6772b	Strap (single thickness)	2	VI	MC061	IIb
828/A12279	Miscellaneous fragment	3	VI	M1.2, Pit 2648, MW5166	<IIg(IIh)
830/A8105	Miscellaneous fragment	4	V, VI	M11	IIh
1086/A03–0278a	Miscellaneous fragment	9	VII	B19 (Phase 2b), North Room–Floor (2b)	IIIc
1214/A9104	Miscellaneous fragment	3	V	M6b	IIg–IIId
1228/A8687a	Miscellaneous fragment	4	V	MC120a	IIh–IVa
1692/A5124	Miscellaneous fragment	3	V	B3 (South), Pit 2529	IVa,IVaa
2554/A04–0430	Strap (single thickness)	9	VII	P8.2b	IVb
3403/A04–0079b	Miscellaneous fragment	8	VII	M9a	IVc,IVcc
4151/A04–0088	Miscellaneous fragment	9	VII	P8.4	Va
4252/A4491c	Miscellaneous fragment	2	V	B1(b), Demolition	Va
5032/A03–0212m	Upper, rand	7	VII	M8a	Va,Vaa
5749/A5898i	Toggle	2	V, VI	Unstratified	u/s

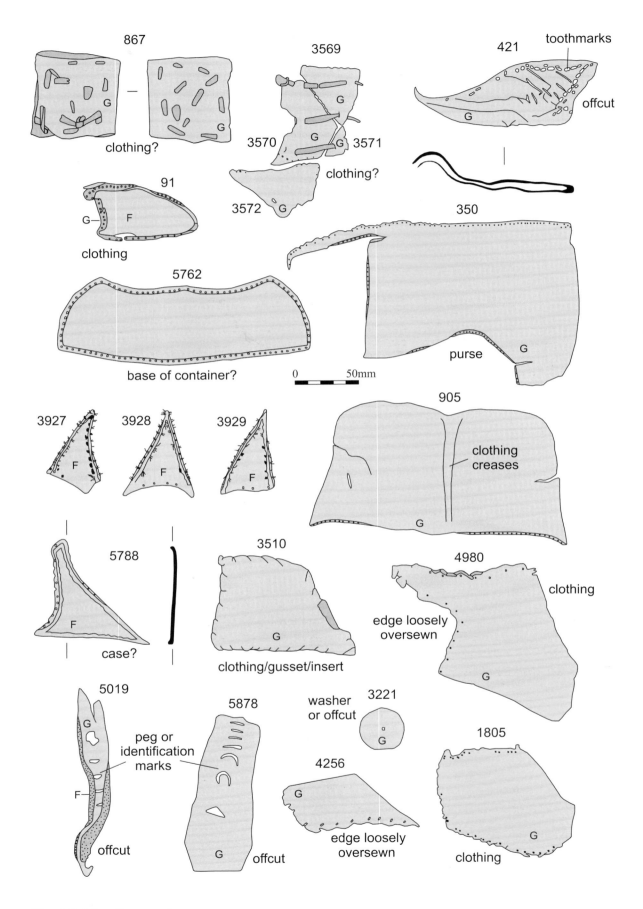

Illus 159 *Miscellaneous fragments.*

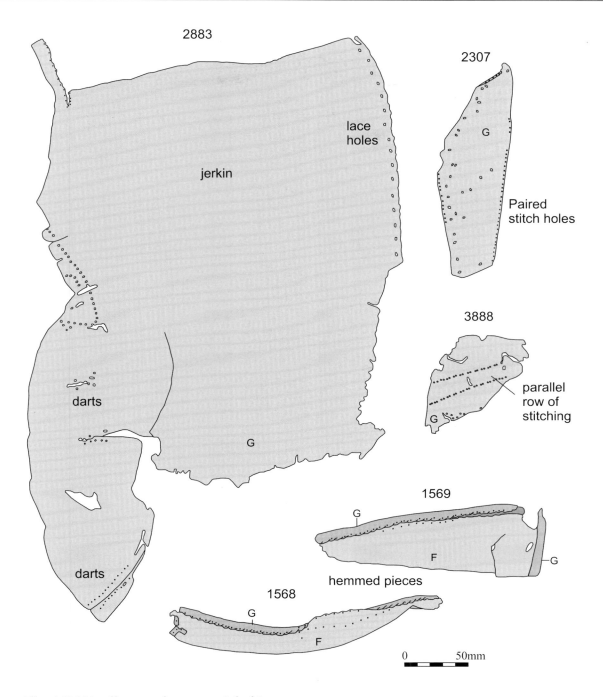

Illus 160 *Miscellaneous fragments: ?clothing.*

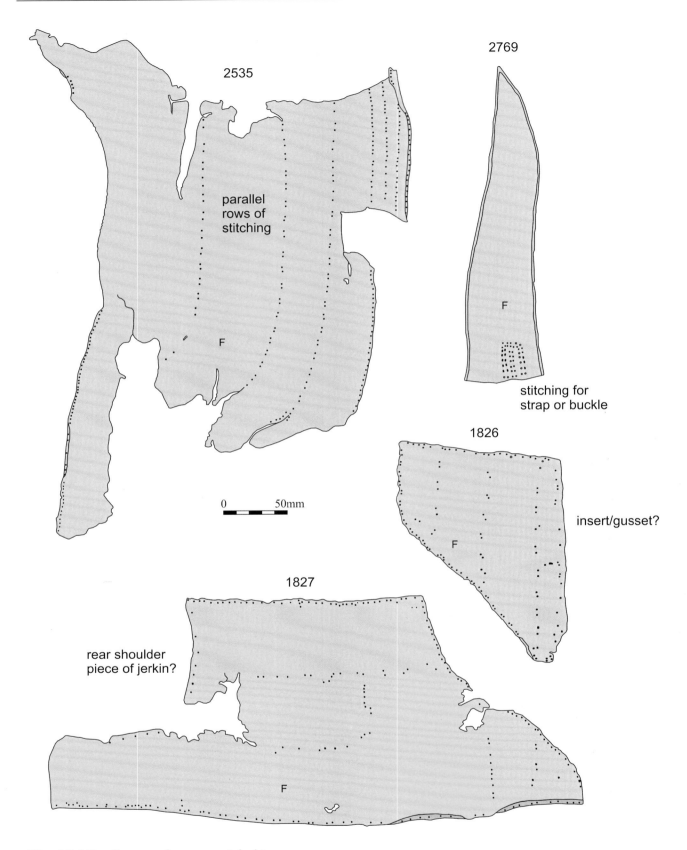

2535

2769

parallel
rows of
stitching

F

F

stitching for
strap or buckle

0   50mm

1826

insert/gusset?

F

1827

rear shoulder
piece of jerkin?

F

Illus 161 *Miscellaneous fragments: ?clothing.*

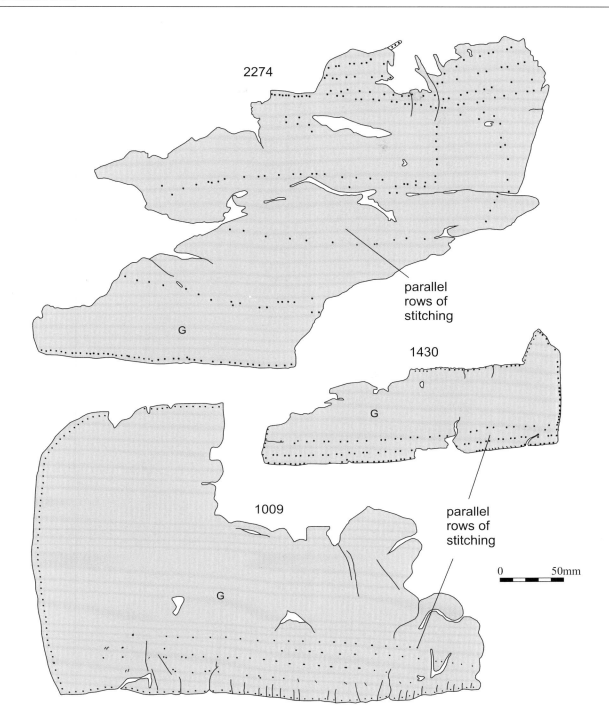

Illus 162 *Miscellaneous fragments: ?clothing.*

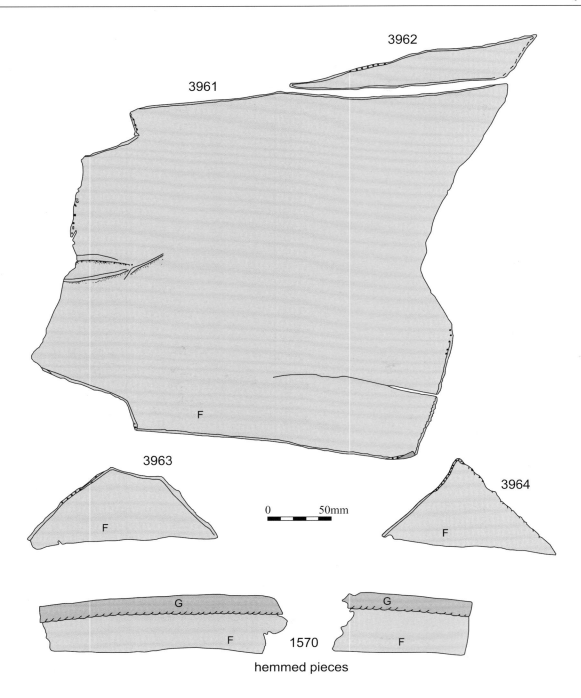

Illus 163 *Miscellaneous fragments: ?clothing.*

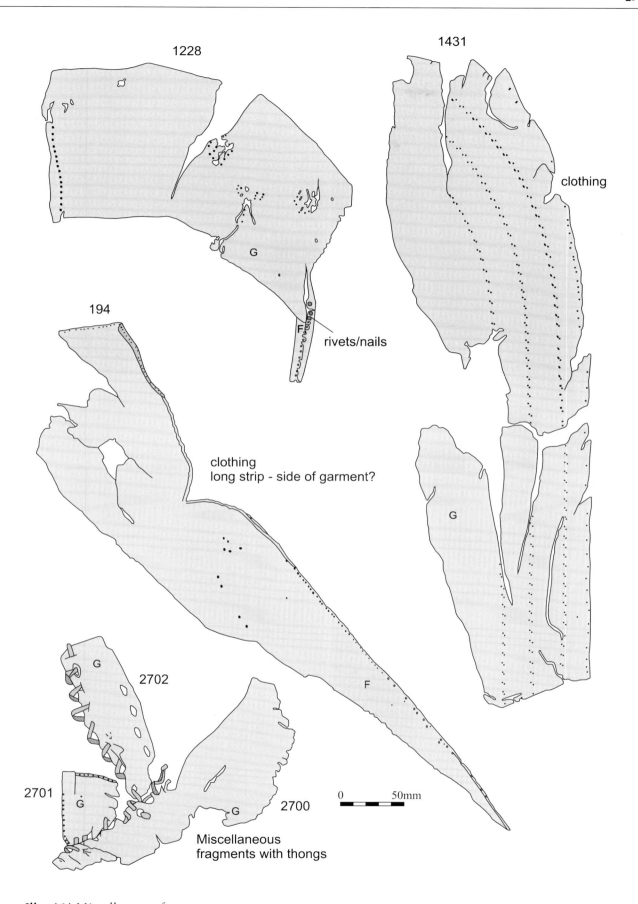

1228

1431

clothing

194

rivets/nails

clothing
long strip - side of garment?

G

F

2702

2701

2700

Miscellaneous
fragments with thongs

0   50mm

Illus 164 *Miscellaneous fragments.*

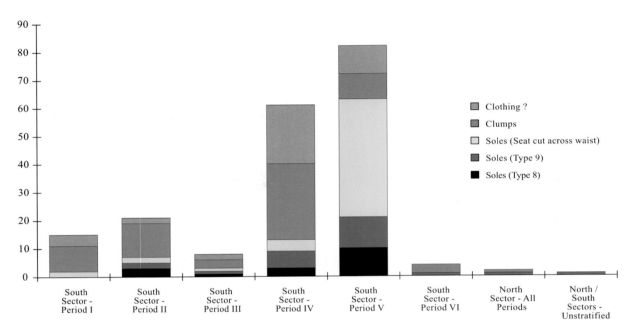

Illus 165 *Reusable material.*

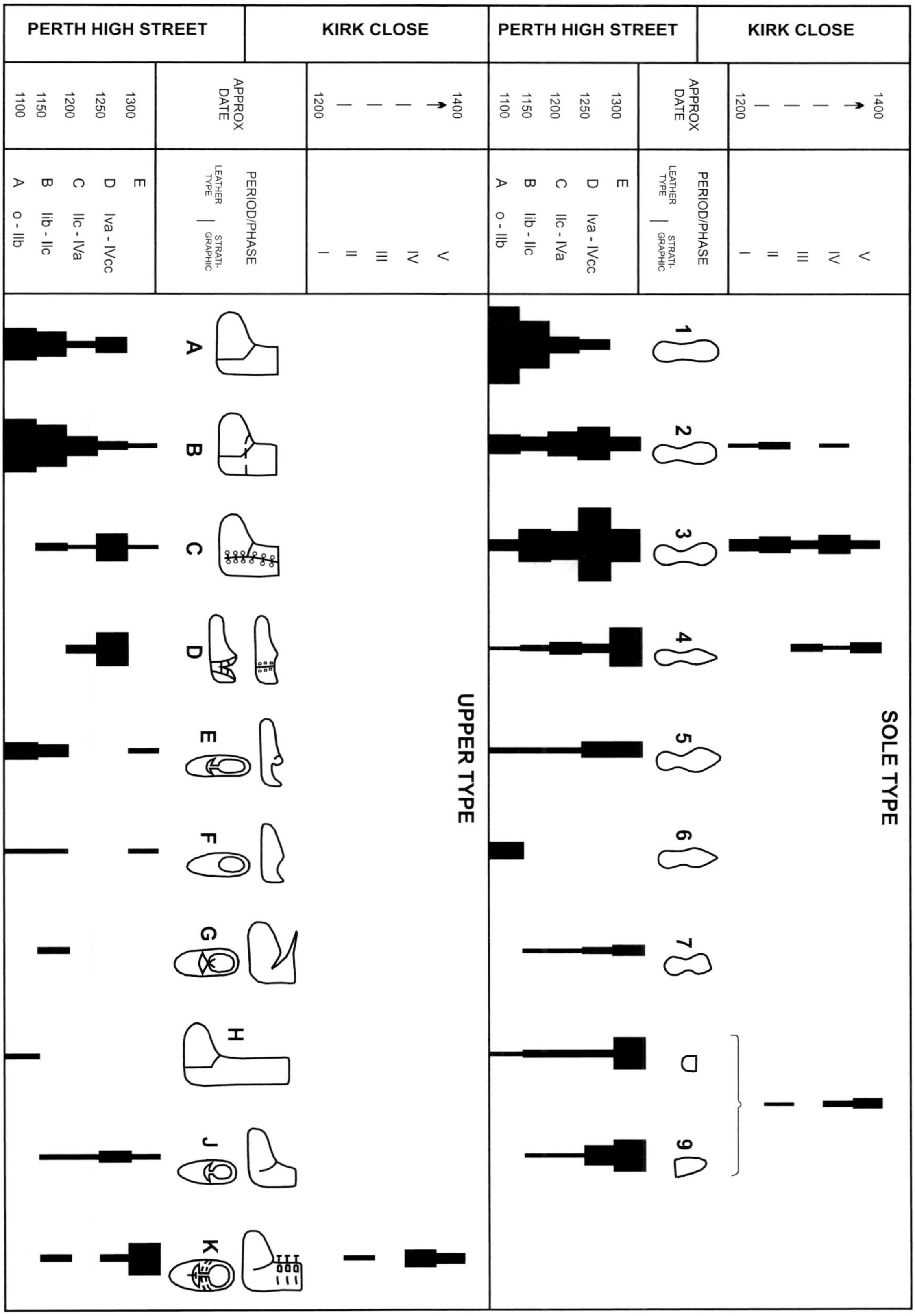

Illus 166 *Sole and upper types.*

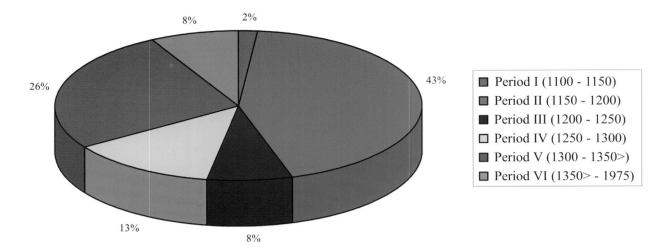

Illus 167 *Percentage of 'wool' yarns arranged by South Sector period.*

Illus 168 *Shoemakers' candelabra and detail (right). (Perth Museum and Art Gallery)*

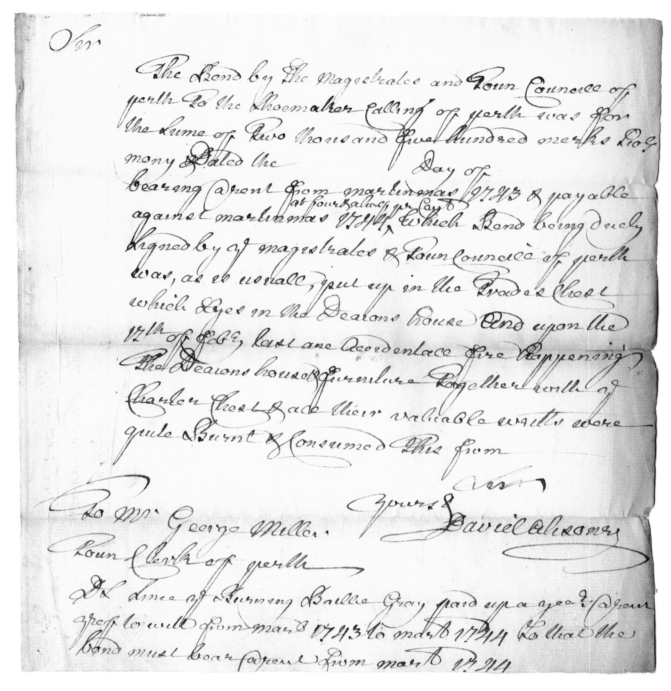

Illus 169 *Letter to George Miller, Town Clerk of Perth, dated 1745, about the fire in Deacon's house and the destruction of 'the Trades Chest'. (Perth and Kinross Council Archive, AK Bell Library, B59/29/84)*

Conclusions

The shoes, straps, sheaths, waste material and miscellanea discussed above comprise an important assemblage of worked leather, most of it closely dated to a period of little more than 250 years, c1100–1350. Shoes form the most impressive category, with details of manufacture and variations in style well represented. The sheaths comprise a smaller but still significant group, with their shape and decoration paralleled at various sites in England, Ireland and Scandinavia. The straps are more mundane but nevertheless important, while the sheer quantities of waste material (see Offcuts and Scraps) provide valuable evidence about leather-working in medieval Scotland, and Perth in particular.

When considering any explanation for the occurrence of this assemblage, it is important to remember that in a Scottish medieval burgh, firstly, rich and poor lived close together, thus producing a mixture of domestic refuse from different economic groups, and secondly, local industries often existed behind the frontages of burghal tofts, thus occasioning a further mixture of domestic and commercial waste. It is also significant that on other sites deposits of leather had been brought from elsewhere for infill. Thus excavations in Bristol have shown that an assemblage of leather had been used to backfill two doorways (Thomas forthcoming a and b). Of further relevance is Perth's record of flooding. Leather which was being worked on, or which was being stored for future reuse, might have been ruined by events similar to those of January 1993, and which are well recorded, for instance, for 1209, when ships sailed through the streets of Perth (Duncan 1974, 39–40). After such a flood, a great deal of leather might have been discarded in pits and middens.

Domestic repairs might account for some of the repaired shoes but not the large concentrations in pits and middens of cut fragments and offcuts. The presence of thick unworn offcuts and of primary offcuts suggest that shoe making and repairing were carried out on a commercial basis, perhaps as several small concerns since the material was recovered from a number of adjoining properties. The argument in favour of commercial shoe making is supported by the evidence from the animal bones (see Fascicule 4, The environmental remains) which were found in such quantities as to imply large-scale butchery as well as the existence of an extensive horn-working industry.

Thus, there appear to have been several adjacent industries: butchery, preparation of hides (both for local use and for export), horn-working and leather working, as well as other related activities. On the other hand, it is important to remember the ubiquity of leather in the medieval period, serving as it did a multitude of purposes: straps and fastenings of many kinds, including harnesses, belts, attachments for weapons; clothing, footwear and armour; saddles; containers, such as purses, bags, satchels and saddle bags, for 'dry' goods, and bottles and costrels for 'wet' goods. It is only the offcuts, scraps and cut-up objects that should be regarded as evidence for leatherworking and repairing on the High Street site itself.

In the South Sector of the High Street excavation the numbers of leather fragments increase from 294 (5%) in Period I (the first half of the 12th century) to 643 (10%) in Period II (the second half of the 12th century), dipping to 220 (4%) in Period III (the first half of the 13th century), but then increasing to 2441 (39%) in Period IV (the second half of the 13th century) and 2147 (35%) in Period V (the first half of the 14th century). Only 178 (3%) items, most of which were recovered from unstratified deposits, came from Period VI (1350–1975) contexts. In addition 248 (4%) pieces were detected in Area 5/Trench A (North Sector) or became detached from their context labels during conservation. These may have come from either the North or South Sectors of the excavation. These overall figures, particularly when viewed with those for waste material (see above, Waste material: offcuts and scraps), indicate that leatherworking expanded in each period (except Period III–the first half of the 13th century), culminating in Periods IV and V, 1250–1350>.

The evidence for two-part soles, seats cut across the waist, clumps, waste material and clothing fragments points to a flourishing trade in cobbling and shoe repairing by Period IV (the second half of the 13th century). The evidence for the increase in leatherworking is supported further by a study of the distribution of the leather over the High Street site. In Period I the leather only appears in small groups, the largest consisting of 57 fragments from M14b(b) (including Pit 3625), a Rig VI midden that had been laid down slightly before 1150. More substantial clusters appear during Period II (the second half of the 12th century), notably 65 items from M1.3 (a late 12th-century Rig VI backland midden), 93 from M1.2 (a stratigraphically slightly earlier division of what was essentially the same Rig VI backland midden, which included Pit 2648) and 163 from M10 (another late 12th-century backland midden, in this case from Rig V. It included Pits 2330, 4552 and 4554). The Period III assemblages, however, are no bigger, if not smaller, as, for example, 43 from B26 (a series of layers to the south of B3), 75 from an associated midden M6b (both Rig V context groups) and 106 from MC130 (a mid 13th-century Rig VII context group). During Period IV (the second half of the 13th century), on the other hand, numbers increase significantly, with 220 from M1.4f, 169 from B18 (Phase 2a), 163 from MC155 (including Pit 2691) and 544 from MC126 (including Pit 7402).

Seven groups of between 73 and 107 fragments were also recorded from this period: MC143, B18 (Phase 2b), M1.4d, P8.3, M9a, M9b and M1.4e. By Period V (1300–1350>) the concentrations have risen markedly with 535 from M1.5a and 406 from M8a, as well as 187 from P8.4 (including Pit 7216), 157 from M1.5b, 134 from B34–Courtyard, 121 from M3c and 103 from P1a.

The size of the various assemblages can also be used as an indication of the nature of their production. Thus, the very small clusters from Period I can most probably be equated with domestic refuse, or possibly with very small-scale leatherworking. Similarly, the larger groups from Period II reflect either the beginnings of commercial leather-working or an increase in production, while the enormous quantities from Periods IV and V represent either a large scale enterprise or, more probably, many separate craftsmen working closely together. Perhaps significantly an adjoining street is still called the Skinnergate or Skinners' Street (Duncan 1974, 36–37; Stavert 1991, 18; Fascicule 1, Historical introduction).

A study of the composition of the main deposits of leather also reveals the increasing importance of leatherworking. In Period I, footwear made up 74% of the largest group, waste material only accounting for 12%. By Period II, however, waste material pre-dominated (61.4%), with footwear playing a much smaller role (33%). This trend continues in Periods III, IV and V, with assemblages chiefly composed of waste material (87.5%, 79.3% and 75.5%), with much smaller quantities of footwear (8.5%, 17.5% and 22.4%). Moreover, the footwear consists mainly of cut-up fragments, with fewer identifiable sole and upper types.

The presence of cut-up footwear suggests that shoes were being repaired; however, the large number of offcuts from new leather, from the same assemblages, also implies that new shoes were being made as well, presumably by the same craftsmen. Thus, these craftsmen would appear to have been cordwainers. Documentary evidence from England, particularly from London, demonstrates restrictions that prevented shoemakers, or cordwainers, from repairing shoes and cobblers from making new shoes; however, these regulations date from 1409. Such restrictions are a feature of later medieval crafts, as different groups tried to protect their own interests (Salzmann 1923, 254–255; Tatton-Brown 1975, 166). It should also be remembered that the existence of this type of regulation implies that what was being forbidden did in fact happen. Such distinctions prevailed in late 18th-century Perth, as shown by the records of a trial of cobblers in 1771–2 (see Appendix 5, below). However, it should not automatically be assumed that they were observed in Perth between AD 1100 and 1350. Conversely, the evidence from the High Street strongly suggests that the same craftsmen were both making new shoes and repairing old ones.

As well as providing evidence for leather working in Perth, the leather reflects certain aspects of the lives of the medieval population of Perth. As discussed under shoes and sheaths, the leather assemblage gives a few limited indicators of the wealth and status of the medieval population of Perth, at least between 1100 and 1350. Shoes were being made in large numbers, and thus worn by at least some, if not, most of the population, including very small children, one of whom wore decorated shoes. The presence of silk demonstrates wealth and trade links abroad. Further evidence for wealth is provided by the uppers with vamp stripes and linings, and by the decorated sheaths and the rosette strap.

The parallels with leather from elsewhere in Scotland, England, Ireland and Scandinavia are striking. The similarities, for instance, in shoe design, could be explained by imitation or by movement of craftsmen or by separate development of what was the most convenient form. Thus, the Type H boot could be seen as an extension of a Type A one, or more probably, given the parallels in Scandinavia and Eastern Europe, either an imitation, or else of foreign manufacture, discarded by a trader or merchant. The decorated sheaths suggest both imitation and the spread of stamps with conventional motifs.

This assemblage also to a certain extent provides evidence for the local economy. Firstly, the hides were from beasts raised in the agricultural hinterland, which, because of the privileges given to Scottish burghs, could only be sold in the burgh (Duncan 1974, 44). The revenues from exported hides went to the Crown, while the income from shoe manufacture stayed locally. The evidence from the High Street shows that from the first half of the 12th century the population of Perth, or at least some of it, was well-shod, even enjoying luxuries such as silk stitching on their shoes. From the mid-12th century onwards there was a growing shoemaking and repairing trade. This trade may have experienced a recession in the first half of the 13th century, but thereafter it flourished, although the emphasis may have been on shoe-repair and reuse, rather than on the manufacture of new shoes. There is no obvious sign of recession caused by the wars and sieges of the late 13th and early 14th centuries, unless these events might explain the possible preponderance of repair and reuse rather than manufacture of new shoes.

Without doubt even now more than 30 years after it was excavated, the leather work from the High Street remains the most comprehensive collection to have been dug up in Scotland, and a major collection even by European standards. Although no longer the largest medieval leather assemblage from Scotland, it still includes a much greater range of shoe styles, sheaths, straps and miscellanea than has subsequently been found on other Scottish sites, such as, for instance, Aberdeen and Whithorn. (Stones 1982; Thomas 2001a; Thomas forthcoming d; Nicholson 1997, 499–509). Indeed, there are few English sites with as many upper styles, apart from some, such as Baynard's Castle, in the City of London (Grew and de Neergaard 1988). Perhaps the best parallel assemblages for the High Street material, which it should be remembered comes from just one site, are those from Coppergate, York and from the Schild site in Schleswig, with its essentially contemporary range of sole and upper types (Mould et al 2003; Schnack 1992b). The High Street assemblage is of major importance, providing closely dated examples of soles, uppers, straps and sheaths covering a period of little more than 250 years, from c1100 to c1350. As such it will probably be seen, together with Coppergate, York, to provide a link between earlier Anglo–Scandinavian sites in York and Dublin and the predominantly later sites which have been excavated in towns such as London and Newcastle Upon Tyne.

The leather catalogue
Clare Thomas with the late N Q Bogdan and P Z Dransart

With few exceptions only the illustrated leather fragments appear in this catalogue. Exceptions are fragments associated with illustrated pieces, for example conjoining uppers and soles, those associated with other materials eg metal, those *which retain impressions of other materials or those from which a radiocarbon (^{14}C) date was obtained. The catalogue numbering system follows the original leather catalogue, which is preserved in the site archive.*

South Sector

1 Sole (Type 6) Leather
Left sole with wide seat, wider waist and broad forepart ending in pointed toe, bent over. Delaminated and worn. Edge–flesh stitching channel; stitch length 3.5mm. Length 250.5mm; maximum width of forepart 97mm; width of waist 82mm; width of seat 80mm; thickness 3mm. Conserved. 11th–12th centuries.
A12303a; L0066; C3868–1; MC002; Phase Ia; Rigs V and VI
Illus 122

5 Sole (Type 1) Leather
Delaminated sole of either foot with most of seat and centre forepart, probably rounded toe. Stitching channels of edge-flesh seam; hole diameter 1 mm; stitch length 4-4.5mm. Surviving length 142mm; maximum width of seat 64mm; maximum width of forepart 75mm; width of waist 60mm; thickness 0.5mm. Conserved. 12th–13th centuries.
Radiocarbon date of 1060±35 BP (calibrated at 95 per cent probability to AD 890–1030) obtained.
A12300a; C3869–1; MC002; Phase Ia; Rigs V and VI
Not illustrated

6 Sole (Type 6) Leather
Delaminated fragment of very worn right sole, with slight narrowing for waist; broad forepart ending in pointed extension, tip of which is missing. Large hole in centre forepart, smaller hole at great toe area. Outer part of seat missing. Edge–flesh stitching channel; stitch length 3–4mm. Length 203mm; maximum width of forepart 78mm; width of waist 50mm; thickness 2mm (outer edge of forepart), 1mm (hole in centre of forepart). Pointed area probably extends c25mm beyond great toe area. Conserved. No closely similar published parallels. 11th–12th centuries.
A12300b; C3869–1; MC002; Phase Ia; Rigs V and VI
Illus 122

8 Offcut Leather
Offcut, delaminated; rectangular c70mm by 90mm by 1mm. Conserved.
Radiocarbon date of 910±35 BP (calibrated at 95 per cent probability to AD 1030–1210) obtained.
A12300d; C3869–1; MC002; Phase Ia; Rigs V and VI
Not illustrated

26 Miscellaneous fragment Leather
Approximately rectangular fragment, about a quarter of which has evidently been folded over; loosely oversewn along long folded-over edge. Tightly oversewn along other long edge, and along one short edge. Other short edge torn. Fragment is perforated by four horizontal bands of short vertical cuts. Leather in top band (on folded-over part) lies flat; in other three bands alternate strips of leather stand up, others depressed as if thong or lace had been passed through them. On flesh side is a row of seven (and traces of another two) tunnel stitches between second or third rows– for attachment to something. Decorative top band for boot? or binding of clothing. Conserved.
cf York (Tweddle 1986, 255–256, Fig 117 no 859)
A10499; L1698; C3822–1; MC006, T3852; Phase Ib; Rig VI
Illus 158

27 Strap (folded once) Leather (cattle hide)
Top band for matching upper Cat No 30/A10800d. Length 285 mm; width 6 mm (folded); thickness 3 mm (folded). Conserved.
A10800a; L0073; C3774-1; MC008' T3774; Phase Ib; Rig V
Not illustrated

28 Sole (Type 6) Leather
Left sole with only very slight narrowing for waist, and with broad and straight forepart, ending in point. Very worn and delaminated. Both seat and forepart have been repaired with clump soles. Edge–flesh stitching channel; stitch length 3.5–4.5mm. Length 240mm; maximum width of forepart 84mm; width of waist 68mm; maximum width of seat 69mm; thickness 3mm. Matches Upper (Type Bi) Cat No 30/A10800d, and Strap Cat No 27/A10800a. Conserved.
11th–12th centuries
A10800b; L0073; C3774–1; MC008; T3774; Phase Ib; Rig V
Illus 122

30 Upper (Type Bi) Leather
Fragment of upper of ankle boot with tunnel hole and single hole for one horizontal thong. Comprises vamp, vamp wing, vamp throat, quarters and leg flap. Not clear whether quarters and vamp wing join. Round hole in vamp wing– probably for thong; also tunnel hole in quarters. Lasting margin with stitching channel of grain–flesh holes; stitch length 4.5–5mm.

Edge–flesh stitching channels on vamp wing, vamp throat and quarters; stitch length 3–4mm. Top edge of quarters and leg flap and vertical edge of leg flap oversewn. Matches Sole (Type 6) Cat No 28/A10800b, and Strap Cat No 27/A10800a. Conserved. 12th–13th centuries
A10800d; L0073; C3774–1; MC008, T3774; Phase Ib; Rig V
Illus 129

43 Sole (Type 6) Leather
Left, very broad and squat with pointed toe, now bent over. Large hole in centre forepart, smaller hole in great toe area, slight crack towards rear of seat. Clump soles added to seat, centre forepart and front of forepart. Very delaminated. Edge–flesh stitching channel; stitch length 3.5–4mm. Length 208mm; maximum width of forepart 85mm; width of waist 61mm; maximum width of seat 62mm; thickness 2–3mm. Conserved. 11th–12th centuries.
Radiocarbon date of 840±35 BP (calibrated at 95 per cent probability to AD 1150–1270) obtained.
A8525; C3742–1/2; M2.1b; Phase Ic; Rigs V and VI
Illus 122

54 Sole (Type 1)? Leather
Fragment, left, with seat, waist and some of forepart, delaminated and worn, with very large hole in seat. Edge-flesh stitching channel; stitch length 5–7 mm; maximum surviving length c255mm; maximum width of forepart c115mm; width of waist 72mm; maximum width of seat 85mm. Thickness not measured because of delamination. Conserved.
Radiocarbon date of 975±35 BP (calibrated at 95 per cent probability to AD 990–1160) obtained.
A9886a; C3767–1/2; M2.1b; Phase Ic; Rigs V and VI
Not illustrated

55 Upper Leather: cattle hide and wool
Fragment of upper with vamp with oval toe, vamp wing and with part of quarters. Lasting margin with grain–flesh stitching channel: stitch length 4–6.5mm. Edge–flesh stitching channels; stitch length 3.5–4mm on vamp wings and quarters. Wool survives in some stitch holes. Conserved.
A9886b; L0074; C3767–1/2; M2.1b; Phase Ic; Rigs V and VI
Illus 144

60 Strap/belt (folded twice) Leather (cattle hide)
Fragment of strap or belt formed by folding one piece of leather twice; edges have been joined where they meet in centre of reverse with butted edge–grain seam; stitch length 6mm, 8mm, 7.5mm, 6.5mm. At one end, belt has been cut across diagonally. At other end pierced by holes, for buckle? Surviving length 238mm; width 42–46mm; single thickness 3mm. Conserved.
A8636a; L1677; C3737–1/2; M2.1b and B10, South Room–Floor/ Occupation (1); Phase Ic,Icc; Rigs V and VI
Illus 150

62 Sole (Type 1) Leather
Child's left sole with rounded toe, worn at rear of seat and at great toe area, where there are traces of holes for clump sole. Cracked at outside waist. Delaminated. Length 167.5mm; maximum width of forepart 66mm; width of waist none;

maximum width of seat 54mm; thickness 3mm. Conserved. 12th–13th centuries.
A8704a; C3737–1/2; M2.1b and B10, South Room–Floor/ Occupation (1); Phase Ic,Icc; Rigs V and VI
Illus 124

63 Strap (folded once) Leather
At one end, round hole diameter c1mm; at other end, two round holes diameter c1mm. Length c240mm; width 5–6mm; thickness 2mm. Top band of upper? Conserved.
A8704b; C3737–1/2; M2.1b and B10, South Room–Floor/ Occupation (1); Phase Ic,Icc; Rigs V and VI
Illus 148

65 Upper (Type E) Leather
Large fragment of upper of low cut shoe, consisting of vamp, vamp wing and throat, quarters and two small latchets. Almost complete upper, side-piece missing between vamp wing and quarters. Rounded toe, low throat with two latchets which do not meet. Rear of quarters slightly domed forming a peak. Lasting margin with stitching channel with grain–flesh holes; stitch length 4.5–5.5mm. Edge–flesh stitching channels on vamp wing, on vertical edge of quarters, and on lowest part of vamp throat; stitch length 3–4mm. Top edges of throat, vamp wing and quarters oversewn. On interior of quarters, tunnel holes mark position of approximately semi-circular stiffener, which survives separately. Conserved. Early–mid 12th century.
A8808; L0075; C3737–1/2; M2.1b and B10, South Room– Floor/Occupation (1); Phase Ic,Icc; Rigs V and VI
Illus 138

67 Upper (Type Aii) Leather (cattle hide)
Two large fragments and stiffener of upper of low ankle boot, with no thongs or holes for thongs. Larger fragment comprises rounded vamp, vamp wing, vamp throat, quarters and leg flap. On flesh side of quarters are stitch holes for small semi-circular stiffener, which survives separately. Smaller fragment is second leg flap. Lasting margin with grain–flesh stitching channel; stitch length 3.5–4mm. Edge–flesh stitching channels on vamp wing, throat, quarters and leg flaps; stitch length 2.5–3.5mm. Top edges of quarters and leg flaps oversewn. Conserved. 12th–14th centuries.
A8809b; C3737–1/2; M2.1b and B10, South Room–Floor/ Occupation (1); Phase Ic,Icc; Rigs V and VI
Illus 128

68 Sole (Type 1) Leather (cattle hide)
Left sole with wide seat and waist, broad straight-sided forepart, outer front partly bent over (because unnecessary space), broad rounded toe. Edge–flesh stitching channel; stitch length 3.5–5mm. Worn, cracked and delaminated. Very large hole in seat, small hole and big crack in centre forepart, and large hole in great toe area. Only very slight indications of tunnel stitches for repair clumps on underneath of side of sole. Conserved. 12th–13th centuries.
A8809c; L0076; C3737–1/2; M2.1b and B10, South Room– Floor/Occupation (1); Phase Ic,Icc; Rigs V and VI
Illus 117

91 Miscellaneous fragment Leather (cattle hide)
Approximately triangular fragment, with stitched edges turned
inwards; stitching channels of grain–flesh holes; hole diameter
c1mm; stitch length 2.5–4mm. Possibly fragment of clothing,
insert or gusset. Conserved.
A8688c; L1645; C3722–1/2; B10, South Room–Occupation (2b);
Phase Icc; Rig V
Illus 159

103 Sole (Type 1) Leather
Large left sole, almost straight-sided, with no waist; forepart
wide with very broad rounded toe. Very worn with large hole
in rear of seat and crack to inner edge; also very large hole
in inner front half of forepart. Very delaminated. Edge–flesh
stitching channel; stitch length 4.5–7mm. Length 263mm;
maximum width of forepart 104mm; width of waist 85mm.
Conserved. 12th–13th centuries
A03–0001; L0402; C4781–4; MC017; Phase Ia–Icc>; Rig V/VI
Illus 116

105 Upper (vamp) Leather (cattle hide)
Vamp with oval toe, vamp wing and rounded throat. Lasting
margin with stitching channel of grain–flesh holes; stitch length,
5mm, 6mm, 6.5mm, 7mm. Edge–flesh stitching channels on
vamp wing and throat; stitch length 4.5mm, 5mm. Very worn
and delaminated, most of grain layer missing. Conserved.
A10798b; L0037; C2399–4; MC018, Pit 2398; Phase Ib–Id;
Rig VI

117 Upper (Type Bi) Leather (cattle hide)
Fragment of almost complete upper of ankle boot, of typical
one piece wrap-around style, with tunnel-hole for one horizontal
thong. Comprises vamp, vamp throat, vamp wings, quarters
and leg flap. Tunnel hole for horizontal thong on closed side of
upper. Lasting margin with grain–flesh stitching holes; stitch
length c7mm; dimensions of holes c3mm by 1.5mm. Edge–flesh
stitching channels on vamp wing, quarters, throat and leg flap.
Top edges oversewn. Conserved. 12th–13th centuries.
A03–0002b; C4752–4; MC023; Phase Icc,Id; Rigs V and VI
Illus 129

125 Sole (Type 1) Leather
Right sole with rounded forepart, complete but worn at both
seat and forepart. Edge–flesh stitching channel; stitch length
3.5–5mm; diameter of holes c1mm. Length 186mm; maximum
width of forepart 82mm; maximum width of seat 61mm; width of
waist 60mm; thickness, outer edge of waist 4mm, inner edge of
forepart 4.5mm, outer rear edge of seat 5mm. Probably matches
Upper (Type Bi) Cat No 126/A12297b. Conserved. 12th–13th
centuries.
A12297a; L0056; C5097–3; MC025, Pit 5337; Phase (Ia–)Id;
Rig V
Illus 116

126 Upper (Type Bi) Leather
Large fragment, plus stiffener, of upper of child's ankle boot,
with tunnel holes for one horizontal thong on each side of boot.
Comprises vamp, vamp wing, quarters and leg flap. Complete
except for second leg flap. Impression of stiffener on flesh
side of quarters and vamp wing. Small triangular stiffener, with

lasting margin and with stitch holes for attachment to upper,
survives separately. Lasting margin with grain–flesh stitching
channel; stitch length 4–5mm. Edge–flesh stitching channels on
vamp wing, vamp, throat and quarters. Vertical and top edges of
leg flap oversewn. Matching Sole (Type 1) Cat No 125/A12297a.
Conserved. 12th–14th centuries.
A12297b; L0056; C5097–3; MC025, Pit 5337; Phase (Ia–)Id;
Rig V
Illus 129

127 Upper (Type Aii) Leather
Fragment of upper of low ankle boot comprising part of vamp,
vamp throat, vamp wing, quarters and one leg flap. Vamp wing
and quarters join, ie basically one-piece boot, missing second
leg flap. Lasting margin with grain–flesh stitching channel;
stitch length 4.5–6mm. Edge–flesh stitching channel on vamp
throat; vamp wing and vertical edge of quarters; stitch length
2–3.5mm. Short tear in vamp wing has been repaired with
butted grain-flesh stitching channel; stitch length 3–4mm. Top
edges of quarters, leg flap and vamp wing have been oversewn.
Small hole (diameter 1.5mm) may be for thong. On flesh side
of quarters, tunnel stitching for long low semi-circular stiffener.
Worn with much of lasting margin missing. Thickness c1mm.
Conserved. 12th–14th centuries.
A12306; L2478; C5097–3; MC025, Pit 5337; Phase (Ia–)Id;
Rig V
Illus 128

130 Sole (seat) Leather
Cut across middle; edge–flesh stitching channel; stitch length
5.5mm, 6.5mm, 7 mm. Very worn. Surviving length 60mm;
maximum width 88mm; thickness, centre cut across middle
of seat 2mm; crack in seat 1.5mm; stitching channel seam.
Conserved.
Radiocarbon date of 700±35 BP (calibrated at 95 per cent
probability to AD 1250–1320) obtained.
A12308c; L1695; C5097–3; MC025, Pit 5337; Phase (Ia–)Id;
Rig V
Not illustrated

142 Strap (folded once) Leather
Edges oversewn. Probably top band of low boot, Upper (Type
Aii) Cat No 144/A7789c. Worn and delaminated. Length
c280mm; width, folded once, 7–8mm. Conserved.
A7789a; L1713; C3639-2; P5.2a; Phase Ie; Rig VI
Not illustrated

143 Sole (Type 1) Leather
Straight, wide right sole with short seat, only very slight
narrowing for waist, and long broad forepart, both sides only
very slightly curved; front very broad and rounded. Sole is
almost symmetrical and is only identified as right foot by hole
in front forepart and by wear pattern on reverse. Also hole
in centre of seat. Edge–flesh stitching channel; stitch length
4.5–7.5mm. Length 197.5mm; maximum width of forepart
81mm; width of waist 61.5mm; maximum width of seat 67mm.
Thickness: outer edge of waist and forepart, inner edge of waist
3.5mm; upturned edge of rear seat 5.5mm; inner edge of seat
3mm; outer edge of seat and inner edge of forepart 4mm; worn
edges of holes 0.5–0.75mm. Conserved. 12th–13th centuries.

A7789b; L1713; C3639–2; P5.2a; Phase Ie; Rig VI
Illus 117

144 Upper (Type Aii) Leather
Fragment of low ankle boot, with no thongs, comprising
vamp and quarters. Lasting margin with stitching channel
of grain–flesh holes; stitch length 5mm and 5.5mm. Vertical
edge of quarter with edge–flesh seam; stitch length 3.5mm;
vertical edge of surviving short leg flap and top edge of
quarters oversewn, probably for top band Cat No 142/
A7789a (see Straps, folded once). Small semi-circular
stiffener survives separately, some of the stitch holes for it
just visible on flesh side of quarters. Grain side of stiffener
against flesh side of quarters. Very worn and delaminated.
Thickness c1mm. Conserved. 12th–14th centuries.
Radiocarbon date of 780±35 BP (calibrated at 95 per
cent probability to AD 1185–1285) obtained.
A7789c; L1713; C3639–2; P5.2a; Phase Ie; Rig VI
Not illustrated

146 Toggle Leather
Short thong rolled into toggle at one end with grain–flesh
holes at the other end, for attachment to shoe/garment/
article. Length of thong 22mm; thickness 1–2mm. Length
of toggle 17.5mm; thickness 6mm. Conserved.
A11658; C5158–3; MC037a, Pit 5157; Phase Ia–Ie; Rig VI
Illus 150

153 Strap/belt (folded twice) Leather and Cu alloy
Fragment formed of one piece folded twice and stitched
up centre of reverse in butted edge–grain seam. Both
sides of strap perforated by line of short diagonal strokes
parallel with each folded edge. Centre of both sides also
perforated by round holes c1.5–2mm in diameter, and
18mm, 15mm, 17.5mm, 16.5mm, 15.5mm, 16mm apart.
Fourteen holes survive. In one hole is copper alloy stud with
domed head on reverse and pin or shank of shaft almost
appearing on obverse. Area around hole on obverse marked
by impression of concentric circle and square. Belt torn/
cracked at both ends; diagonal slits end c40mm before
one end. Length 365mm; width 19–23mm; thickness 4mm.
Conserved.
A12312b; C5158–3; MC037a, Pit 5157; Phase Ia–Ie; Rig VI
Illus 149

156 Sole (Type 3) Leather (cattle hide)
Left sole with rounded seat, narrow waist and slender
forepart with oval toe. Very worn; portion of front of forepart
is missing; large hole in seat. Edge–flesh stitching channel,
stitch length 4–7mm; close concentration of stitch holes at
inside waist. Length 223.5mm; maximum width of forepart
83mm; width of waist 44mm; maximum width of seat 65mm.
Thickness, front of outer and inner edges of forepart 4mm;
inside waist, rear of inner edge of forepart, outside edge of
seat, waist and rear of forepart 4.5mm; inner edge of seat
5mm. Matches Upper (Type H) 163/A7787j. Conserved.
13th–14th centuries.
A7787c; L1762; C3672–1/2; B6 (Phase 1), South Room–
Floor (1); Phase Ie; Rig VI
Illus 141

161 Upper (Type Biii) Leather
Three fragments of upper of boot, with vertical thonging
and impression of horizontal thong. Largest fragment
comprises vamp, vamp wing, vamp throat, leg flap and
part of quarters, with tunnel stitch holes for semi-circular
stiffener, on flesh side. Vertical thong on closed side of
quarter; two short stretches on grain surface; length of
stretches of thong on grain side 5.5mm; thickness 1mm;
width 7mm; distance between the two stretches 18mm.
Second fragment, tall, thin, approximately trapezoidal,
joins quarters of largest fragment. Short stretch of thong,
total length 23mm; only one short stretch on grain side,
length 7mm. Above, two irregular vertical slits forming
horizontal tunnel, possibly caused by pressure from
vertical thong on flesh side. Third fragment is second leg
flap. Lasting margin with grain–flesh stitching channel;
stitch length 4–5mm, most of the lasting margin missing.
Edge–flesh stitching channels at vamp wing, vamp throat,
vertical edge of leg flap, on two edges of third fragment.
Vertical edges of quarters and leg flaps oversewn. Parts
of quarters and vamp very worn. Thickness 2–2.5mm.
Conserved. 12th–13th centuries.
A7787h; L1761; C3672–1/2; B6 (Phase 1), South Room–
Floor (1); Phase Ie; Rig VI
Illus 132

162 Upper (Type E) Leather
Large fragment of upper of low shoe, comprising vamp,
vamp throat, vamp wing, latchet and quarters. Quarters
and vamp wing probably join; second latchet missing.
Vamp has been decorated with three approximately
parallel lines cut from vamp throat to toe. Lasting margin
with stitching channel of grain–flesh holes; stitch length
4.5–5mm. Edge–flesh stitching channels on vamp wing,
vamp throat, vertical edge of quarters and vertical edge of
latchet; stitch length 3.5mm. Quarters very worn and torn.
Thickness 2mm. Conserved. 12th century.
A7787i; L1761; C3672–1/2; B6 (Phase 1), South Room–
Floor (1); Phase Ie; Rig VI
Illus 138

163 Upper (Type H) Leather
Two fragments of upper of high calf boot, with vamp
separate from quarters and leg. Vamp is in one piece,
with rounded toe, lasting margin with stitching channel
of grain–flesh holes; stitch length 5mm, 6mm, 7mm.
Edge–flesh stitching channels at vamp throat and on
both sides of vamp wing; stitch length 3mm. Thickness
1mm. Very worn. On flesh side are tunnel stitches
c15mm above lasting margin, matching tunnel stitching
on quarters–repair of lasting margin, but from inside
(see below). Larger fragment comprises quarters and
leg. Lasting margin with grain–flesh stitching channel;
stitch length 5–6mm; very worn. On flesh side are tunnel
stitches above lasting margin, as on vamp, as well as
for a triangular stiffener. Tunnel stitches above lasting
margin do not appear to cross zone of stiffener. Unlikely
to be repair, from inside; possibly for lining, whose top
edge would have been secured by hem stitch at top
edge: otherwise, possibly stiffener or strengthening strip

reinforcing lasting margin-like rand, but on inside of upper; unusual. Leg of boot much higher than on other examples; maximum height from lasting margin c350mm. Edge–flesh stitching channels where quarters join vamp wings and where leg flaps join vamp throat; edge–flesh stitching channels on vertical edges of leg show that these were joined together; stitch length 3–4.5mm. About two-thirds of top edge oversewn, the rest has edge–flesh stitching channel; stitch length 3–4mm; indicating that small, probably triangular, fragment of leg is missing. Fragment is very worn. Thickness c1mm. Matching Sole (Type 3) Cat No 156/A7787c. Conserved. 12th–14th centuries; sole: 13th–14th centuries.
A7787j; L1762; C3672–1/2; B6 (Phase 1), South Room–Floor (1); Phase Ie; Rig VI
Illus 141

165 Sole (Type 1) Leather (cattle hide)
Wide seat, waist, broad forepart, sides of whole sole very straight; toe very broad and rounded. Holes at great toe area and at rear of seat. Delaminated. Edge–flesh stitching channel; stitch length 3.5–5mm. Length 256.5mm; maximum width of forepart 109mm; width of waist 85mm; maximum width of seat 88.5mm. Conserved. 12th–13th centuries.
A7256a; L0084; C3622–2; M14b(b); Phase Ie; Rig VI
Illus 116

172 Strap (folded once) Leather and silk
Strap with silk thread on one side; two rows of very light brown stitching with a row of pink stitching sandwiched between. Thread does not penetrate to the other side of strap, though some of it is partially sewn through other side, hence sealing off fold of strap. Two cut edges of strap were stitched. Strap is approximately same length as top edge of Upper (Type Aii), Cat No 174/A7580c, therefore most probably was top band of this shoe. Length c290mm; width (folded) 10–12mm; width of stitched area 6mm; thickness (folded) 3mm. Conserved. Upper: 12th–14th centuries.
A7580a; L0085; C3622–2; M14b(b); Phase Ie; Rig VI
Illus 148

173 Sole (Type 2) Leather (cattle hide)
For right foot, with short narrow seat, wide waist and long broad forepart, ending in oval toe. Partially delaminated; slight wear on underside of seat. Edge–flesh stitching channel; stitch length 4–6mm. Length 221.5mm; maximum width of forepart 90mm; width of waist 54mm; maximum width of seat 59mm. Matches Upper (Type Aii) 174/A7580c. Conserved. 12th–13th centuries.
A7580b; L0085; C3622–2; M14b(b); Phase Ie; Rig VI
Not illustrated

174 Upper (Type Aii) Leather
Three fragments of almost complete low ankle boot with no trace of thongs. Largest fragment consists of vamp, vamp wing, vamp throat, quarters and leg flap. Second fragment, side-piece, linking vamp wing and quarters. Third fragment, leg flap. Lasting margin with stitching channel of grain–flesh holes; stitch length 4.5–6mm. Edge–flesh stitching channels on vamp wing, vamp throat, quarters, side-piece and leg flaps;

stitch length 3–4.5mm. Top edges of quarters and leg flaps oversewn. Matching Sole (Type 2) Cat No 173/A7580b, and Strap (folded once) Cat No 172/A7580a. 12th–14th centuries.
A7580c; L0085; C3622–2; M14b(b); Phase Ie; Rig VI
Illus 126

179 Upper (Type Bii)? Leather
Large fragment of upper of low boot with tunnel holes for four horizontal rows of thongs, with two thongs surviving. Comprises vamp, vamp wing, vamp throat, quarters and leg flap. Very worn, cracked in several places, front of vamp missing. Vamp wing and quarters do not join. On flesh side of quarters are tunnel stitch holes for triangular stiffener. On leg flap are four horizontal tunnel holes, one above the other; thongs pass through two of these. End of one thong split in order to fasten over toggle on second (missing) leg flap? If so, not Upper (Type Bii), but Upper (Type K). Near top of vamp wing are a pair of small holes, probably for thong, suggesting wrap-around thong, therefore type Bii. Lasting margin with grain–flesh stitching channel; stitch length 5mm. Edge–flesh stitching channels on vamp wing, vamp throat and vertical edge of quarters; stitch length 3mm. Vertical edge of leg flap cut. Side-piece and second leg flap missing. Conserved. 12th–14th centuries.
A7589e; L1723; C3622–2; M14b(b); Phase Ie; Rig VI
Illus 131

182 Sole Leather
Two fragments of child's sole consisting of worn seat and waist and thin strip joining at waist. Edge-flesh stitching channel; stitch length 4–6mm. Delaminated. Probably matches Upper (Type Bi) Cat No 183/A7579b. Conserved.
A7597a; L1656; C3622–2; M14b(b); Phase Ie; Rig VI
Not illustrated

183 Upper (Type Bi) Leather (cattle hide)
Two fragments of upper of child's ankle boot with tunnel hole on either side of quarters for one horizontal thong. Larger fragment comprises vamp, vamp throat, vamp wing, quarters and leg flap; smaller is leg flap. Lasting margin with grain–flesh stitching channel; stitch length 4–5mm. Edge–flesh stitching channels on vamp wing, vamp throat, quarters and leg flaps; stitch length 3.5mm. Top edges of quarters and leg flap oversewn. Thong?, thin irregular strip survives, top band. Matching Sole Cat No 182/A7597a. Conserved. 12th–14th centuries.
A7597b; L1656; C3622–2; M14b(b); Phase Ie; Rig VI
Illus 146 (does not show Cat No183)

185 Sole (Type 1) Leather (cattle hide)
Very straight and long, with no waist; broad round toe, probably left foot, judging from fold at front of forepart. Very worn and delaminated, most of grain layer missing. Edge–flesh stitching channel; stitch length 4–5.5mm. Length 257mm; width of waist 71mm; maximum width 89mm. Thickness: outer edge 3mm; rear of seat 4mm; folded over edge of front forepart. 2.5mm. Conserved. 12th–13th centuries.
A7600a; L0030; C3622–2; M14b(b); Phase Ie; Rig VI
Illus 117

186 Upper (Type G) Leather
Large fragment of upper of shoe with central fastening,
comprising vamp, vamp wing, low throat, quarters and latchet
ending in thong. Vamp wing and quarters join. Tunnel stitching
for rounded stiffener which survives separately. Rounded throat;
cut with no stitching channels, decorated with thin strip and
three approximately oval holes. Top edge cut. Probably missing
a second latchet which would have had either a thong or a hole
for a thong on surviving latchet. Lasting margin with grain–flesh
stitching channel; stitch length 3.5–5mm. Edge–flesh stitching
channel on vamp wing and quarters; stitch length 2–3mm.
Thickness 1–2mm. Conserved.
A7600b; L0030; C3622–2; M14b(b); Phase Ie; Rig VI
Illus 140

192 Upper (Type Bii) Leather (cattle hide)
Three fragments plus stiffener of high boot with tunnel holes
for two horizontal rows of thongs and unused tunnel hole for
third thong. Largest fragment comprises vamp, vamp throat,
vamp wing and leg flap. Tunnel holes for two horizontal thongs
on leg flap, above them a pair of slits form a third tunnel, which
seems never to have been used. On flesh side of vamp wing is a
diagonal row of tunnel stitching for stiffener. Second fragment is
trapezoidal side-piece joining vamp wing and probably quarters.
Tunnel stitching on flesh side for stiffener matching that on
vamp wing. Stiffener semi-circular with oversewn edges, no
surviving lasting margin. Third fragment joins rear of leg flap.
Lasting margin with grain–flesh stitching channel; stitch length
6mm. Edge–flesh stitching channels on vamp wing, vamp throat
and second fragment; stitch length 4mm. Vertical edge of vamp
wing very worn, original stitching channel replaced by a second
one by folding grain surface to form an edge. Similar stitching
channel on third fragment. Top and vertical edges of leg flap
and top edge of side-piece oversewn. Conserved. 12th–14th
centuries.
A13004a; L1676; C3622–2; M14b(b); Phase Ie; Rig VI
Illus 131

194 Miscellaneous fragment Leather
One long partly curved edge slightly folded (as with lasting
margin) and pierced by pairs of stitch holes (holes c4mm apart),
edge indented at one point forming a V. One end torn, the
other at right angles to short straight edge, again with pairs of
holes but edge not folded. All other edges torn. Very worn, and
pierced by four pairs of holes. Part of same object as Cat No
195/13004d? Clothing? Conserved.
A13004c; L1676; C3622–2; M14b(b); Phase Ie; Rig VI
Illus 164

195 Miscellaneous fragment Leather
Very tattered with folded-over curved edge with pairs of
holes. Part of same object as Cat No 194/A13004c? Clothing?
Conserved.
A13004d; L1676; C3622–2; M14b(b); Phase Ie; Rig VI
Not illustrated

208 Sole (Type 1) Leather
Right sole with wide seat and waist, broad forepart, rounded toe.
Very worn and delaminated. Edge–flesh stitching channel; stitch
length 5.5–8.8mm. Length 207mm; maximum width of forepart

84mm; width of waist 63mm; maximum width of seat 65mm.
Conserved. 12th–13th centuries.
A7434; L0083; C3625–2; M14b(b), Pit 3625; Phase Ie; Rig VI
Illus 117

218 Upper (Type Aii) Leather
Two fragments plus stiffener of low boot with no trace of thongs.
Larger fragment comprises vamp, vamp wing, vamp throat,
quarters and leg flap. Quarters and vamp wing join in butted
edge–flesh seam; stitch holes on flesh side of quarters indicate
position of stiffener. Smaller fragment is leg flap. Top right hand
corner cut and stitched: deliberate design or repair? Broad
triangular stiffener. Lasting margin with grain–flesh stitching
channel; stitch length 4–6mm. Edge–flesh stitching channels;
stitch length 3–5mm, on quarters, vamp wing and leg flaps. All
fragments very worn and delaminated. Conserved. 12th–13th
centuries.
A7648b; L0079; C3697–2; M14b(b), Pit 3625; Phase Ie; Rig VI
Illus 127

222 Sole (Type 1), Upper, Clump and Thong
Leather (cattle hide)
Held together by thong. Left sole with oval forepart. Edge–flesh
stitching channel; stitch length 5mm, 6mm. Forepart and seat
very worn; large part of former missing. Fragment of clump
attached to rear of seat, with thong, which passes through
sole, clump and upper. Thong knotted at rear of clump, which
extends beyond seat, where it is turned up slightly. Holes for
clump vary in size, suggesting an earlier repair with wool/thread.
Thong holes on upper extend as far as beginning of vamp but
no further. Upper consists of part of vamp and thin strip above
lasting margin which has grain–flesh stitching channel; stitch
length c5mm. Close concentrations of stitch holes suggest
repair. Upper type not definable. Sole, clump and upper dry,
crumbly and delaminated. Length of sole c280mm (excluding
rear of clump); maximum width of forepart 102mm; width of
waist 76mm; thickness 4mm. Rest of upper cut away for reuse?
Conserved. Sole: 12th–13th centuries.
A7436a; L0082; C3629–2; P5.2b; Phase Ie; Rig VI
Illus 104

229 Upper (Type G) Leather and silk
Fragment of upper of low shoe with latchets ending in thongs
and with silk thread. Comprises vamp, vamp wing, low cut vamp
throat, part of very tattered quarters, and two latchets ending in
thongs, now knotted together. Lasting margin with grain–flesh
stitching channel; stitch length 4mm. Edge–flesh stitching
channel on vamp wing; stitch length 2.5mm. Edges of throat,
latchets and quarters oversewn. Top edge of quarters oversewn
with brown silk thread. Fragment is very worn and delaminated.
Conserved. Fibre identification L5436. 13th–14th centuries
(nearest, but not exact parallel).
A7588c; L1745 and L5436; C3631–2; M14b(c); Phase Ie,If; Rig V
Illus 140

230 Upper (Type Kv) Leather
Fragment of upper, probably with central fastening, of high
shoe or low boot, comprising vamp, vamp throat, vamp wing,
part of quarters, and latchet, apparently split in two. Faint
trace of stiffener on flesh side of quarters. Lasting margin with

grain–flesh stitching channel; stitch length c5mm. Edge–flesh stitching channels on vamp wing, vamp throat and latchet. Top edge of quarters and of latchet oversewn. Latchet, now incomplete, split in two; designed as two separate flaps, or result of accidental split? Conserved. 13th–14th centuries (no exact parallel).
A7588d; L1745; C3631–2; M14b(c); Phase Ie,If; Rig V
Illus 142

239 Upper (Type Biii) Leather
Three fragments of upper of boot with vertical and horizontal thonging. Largest fragment, very worn, comprises vamp, vamp wings, vamp throat, leg flap and quarters. Second fragment joins quarters and vamp wing. Third fragment is second leg flap. Vertical thonging on closed side of quarters; second row of vertical thonging on open side of boot, on both vamp wing and second fragment. Short fragment of horizontal thong held in place by vertical thong on vamp wing. Lasting margin with grain–flesh stitching channel; stitch length 5mm. Edge–flesh stitching channels on vamp wing, vamp throat, quarters, second fragment, and on second leg flap; stitch length 3–4mm. Top edges of quarters and side-piece (second fragment), and top and vertical edges of leg flap oversewn: front of boot open. Lasting margin of quarters forms a small inverted 'V', suggesting that the sole might have had a pointed seat. Thickness 1.5mm. Conserved. 12th–13th centuries.
A7072b; L1667; C3601–2; M14b(c); Phase Ie,If; Rig V
Illus 132

255 Upper (Type Bi) Leather (cattle hide)
Large fragment of upper of child's ankle boot, with tunnel for hole for one horizontal thong on each side of quarters. Comprises vamp, vamp wings, vamp throat, leg flap and quarters/strengthener of peculiar construction. Part of quarters folded inwards and stitched to flesh side of quarters where stitch holes survive. Edge formed by this fold stitched through, equivalent of edge–flesh stitching channel for attachment to vamp wing. Bottom of inturned fragment has lasting margin matching that of quarters. Lasting margin has unusually small, neat round holes, diameter c1mm, stitch length 3–3.5mm. Other stitch holes on flesh side suggest semi-circular stiffener– but not central–and lining for leg flap? Fragment is worn and cracked. Crack at vamp throat, which has been repaired. Line of crack curves irregularly, most probably torn accidentally, not deliberately. Approximate length of boot c215mm; thickness 1.5–2mm. Conserved. 12th–14th centuries.
A12287a; L1771; C5145–3; MC034a; Phase Ie(If); Rig V
Illus 130

262 Sole (Type 1) Leather
Complete right sole with rounded toe, broad forepart, waist and seat. Edge–flesh stitching channel; stitch length c5mm. Worn, with hole in front of forepart. Tunnel stitch holes on reverse indicate that both seat and forepart have been repaired with clump soles, possibly more than once. Length 211mm; maximum width of forepart 85mm; width of waist 65mm; maximum width of seat 70mm. Thickness: inner edge of waist, rear of outer edge of forepart, front of inner edge of forepart, rear of seat 4mm; outer edge of waist, front of outer edge of forepart 5mm. Conserved. 12th–13th centuries.

A7044Bb; L1770; C3604–2; MC044b; Phase If; Rig VI
Illus 117

267 Upper (Type Bi) Leather (cattle hide)
Large fragment of very worn upper of boot, comprising vamp, vamp throat, vamp wing, part of quarters and leg flap. Tunnel holes for one horizontal thong on each side of quarters/vamp wing. Lasting margin with grain–flesh stitching channel; stitch length 5–6mm, and with edge–flesh stitching channels on vamp wing, vamp throat, and on part of top edge of quarters; stitch length 3–3.5mm. Vertical edge of leg flap and rest of top edge of quarters oversewn. Toe to vamp round. Toe of vamp and one side of vamp have been repaired with patches–tunnel stitches on grain side. Quarters very worn. Thickness c2mm. Conserved. 12th–13th centuries.
A7044Bg; L1770; C3604–2; MC044b; Phase If; Rig VI
Illus 130

277 Upper (Type Aii) Leather
Two joining fragments of upper of low ankle boot, comprising vamp, vamp wing, vamp throat, quarters, one leg flap, and side-piece linking quarters and vamp. Small leg flap missing. On flesh side of quarters, a few remaining stitch holes indicate position of semi-circular stiffener. Lasting margin with stitching channel of grain–flesh holes; stitch length 4–5mm. Edge–flesh stitching channels on vamp wing, vamp throat, vertical edges of side-piece, vertical edge of leg flap, and on vertical edge of quarters; stitch length 3mm. Worn and partially delaminated. Top edges of quarter and side-piece oversewn. Conserved. 12th–14th century.
A7074d; L1733; C3604–2; MC044b; Phase If; Rig VI
Illus 128

284 Clump Leather
Seat clump, with tunnel stitching holes. Length 118mm; maximum width 88mm; thickness 1.5–2.5mm. Conserved.
A9556a; L0057; C5089–3; MC053c; Phase If; Rig VI
Illus 104

286 Sole (Type 1) Leather (cattle hide)
Left sole with short seat, only slight narrowing for waist, broad forepart with rounded toe. Forepart very worn with large hole; repaired with a clump sole (now missing), attached by a thong which remains in situ. Also several small stitch holes round edge of hole–earlier repair, or tacking hole to clump? Seat worn and cracked, with holes in centre and rear, but no signs of repair. Edge–flesh stitching channel; stitch length 5.5–8mm; diameter of holes c1.5–1.75mm. Length 263mm; maximum width of forepart 93mm; width of waist 71.5mm; maximum width of seat 76mm. Thickness: outer edge of waist and forepart 3.5mm; inner edge of waist and forepart 4.5mm. Matches Upper (Vamp) Cat No 287/A03–0017b and Rand 290/A03–0017e. Conserved. 12th–13th centuries.
A03–0017a; C5306–3; MC053a; If; Rig V
Illus 104

287 Upper (vamp) Leather

Vamp with pointed toe. Lasting margin with stitching channel of grain–flesh holes; stitch length 4–5.5mm; and with low throat with edge–flesh seam; stitch length 4.5mm. Trace of edge–flesh seam on vamp wing; stitch length 4mm. Front of vamp worn and split from lasting margin, also wear along one side; worn and cut at throat. Matches Sole (Type 1) Cat No 286/A03–0017a and Rand Cat No 290/A03–0017e. Conserved. Sole: 12th–13th centuries.

A03–0017b; C5306–3; MC053a; Phase If; Rig V

290 Rand Leather (cattle hide)

Three fragments; stitch length 5–6.5mm. Belonging to Sole (Type 1) Cat No 286/A03–0017a and Upper (vamp) Cat No 287/ A03–0017b. Conserved. Sole: 12th–13th centuries.

A03–0017e; C5306–3; MC053a; Phase If; Rig V

Not illustrated

296 Upper (Type Bi) Leather (cattle hide)

Large fragment of upper of high ankle boot with tunnel hole for one horizontal thong, and with quarters/strengthener of peculiar construction. Comprises vamp, vamp throat, vamp wing, quarters and one leg flap. Tunnel hole for horizontal thong on closed side of quarters, clear impression of thong on quarters. Part of quarters has been turned back on itself, forming a small right-angled triangular strengthener, height 50mm, stitched along vertical arm of right angle with an edge–flesh stitching channel, using the fold in the leather as an edge; base of triangle–grain–flesh stitching channel; stitch length 4mm–shorter than that of lasting margin. Hypotenuse of strengthener has been attached to quarters with hem stitch. Lasting margin with grain–flesh stitching channel; stitch length 5–6.5mm. Edge–flesh stitching channels on vamp wing and vamp throat; stitch length 4mm. Vertical edge of leg flap cut, top edge of quarters oversewn. Quarters very worn; long crack down middle of vamp. Crack is fairly straight, with clearly cut edges; possibly cut deliberately, to relieve pressure. Small oval hole near top of leg, 4.5mm by 1.5mm, possibly for attachment to last. Rest of leg has been cut away–for reuse? Conserved. 12th–13th centuries.

A12632b; L0052; C4727–4; B16b, Pit 4726; Phase Id–IIa; Rig V

Illus 130

306 Sole (Type 2) Leather

Child's right sole with broad rounded toe. Edge–flesh stitching channel; stitch length 4.5–5.5mm. Worn and partially delaminated, with holes in rear of seat and inner front of forepart. Length 184mm; maximum width of forepart 70mm; width of waist 51mm; maximum width of seat 54mm. Thickness: outer edge of waist 2.5mm; front of forepart 4.5mm. Matching Upper (Type Bi) Cat No 307/A12635c. Conserved. 12th–13th centuries.

A12635b; C4727–4; B16b, Pit 4726; Phase Id–IIa; Rig V

Illus 146

307 Upper (Type Bi) Leather

Two fragments of upper of child's ankle boot, with two tunnel holes for one horizontal thong. Larger fragment comprises vamp, vamp wings, vamp throat, quarters and leg flap. Vamp and quarters join. Tunnel hole for horizontal thong on either side of quarters/vamp wing. Very worn and delaminated, particularly at throat and leg flap, where stitching channels are missing. Smaller fragment is second leg flap. Lasting margin with grain–flesh stitching channel; stitch length 4–5mm. Edge–flesh stitching channels on vamp wings, vamp throat and second leg flap; stitch length 3mm. Top edges of quarters and leg flaps and vertical edge of second leg flap oversewn, indicating that the two leg flaps were not sewn together. Matching Sole (Type 2) Cat No 306/A12635b. Conserved. 12th–14th centuries.

A12635c; C4727–4; B16b, Pit 4726; Phase Id–IIa; Rig V

Illus 146

313 Sole (Type 1), Rand, Clump and Upper (Type Biii) Leather (cattle hide)

Almost complete upper of boot in two fragments, with top band, stiffener and rand; fragments of sole with clump, survive separately. Upper: larger fragment comprises vamp, vamp wings, vamp throat, leg flap and quarters, with vertical thonging; smaller fragment consists of side-piece and leg flap, with top band attached to top edge. Triangular stiffener, flesh side facing flesh side of quarters, survives in situ. Both fragments of upper and stiffener have lasting margin with grain–flesh stitching channel; stitch length 4–5mm. Edge–flesh stitching channels on vamp wings, vamp throat, side-piece, quarters and bottom edges of leg flaps; stitch length 3mm. Top edges of quarters and leg flaps, and vertical edges of leg flaps oversewn, for attachment of top band. Edge–flesh stitching channel on outer leg flap indicates that small fragment of upper missing. Three fragments of rand still attached to quarters and one vamp wing; fourth fragment survives separately. Sole: three very worn and tattered fragments, almost certainly matching upper. Largest comprises waist, front of seat and rear forepart; tunnel holes for clumps survive on both. Second is most probably forepart with clump sole still attached, but too tattered to join accurately to middle fragment. Fragment of rand attached to front of forepart. Third is stitching channel of seat, but not possible to join to first fragment. Edge–flesh stitching channel on all three fragments; stitch length 4–5mm. Thickness (outer edge of forepart) 5mm; thickness elsewhere, and length and width not measurable. Both sole and upper are covered with thick hard mud containing small stones. Conserved. Sole: 12th–13th centuries; upper: 12th–13th centuries.

A12310; C5061–3; MC039, Pit 2609; Phase If,IIa; Rig V

Illus 145

314 Sole (Type 6) Leather (cattle hide)

Right sole with pointed toe turned outwards. Toe may have been stuffed with moss; it is noticeably unworn. Hole in centre of seat, rear of which is now bent over. Cracks in centre forepart, hole at great toe area. Maximum length c256mm; length of pointed toe (from great toe area) c30mm; maximum width of forepart 92.5mm; width of waist 57.5mm; maximum width of seat 75mm. Thickness: inner edge of waist 4mm; outer edge of waist 2mm; forepart 3.5–4mm. Edge–flesh stitching channel; stitch length 4.5–5mm. Possibly matches Upper (Type F) Cat No 315/A10365b. Conserved. 11th–12th centuries.

A10365a; C4477–3; MC049; Phase IIa; Rig V

Illus 122

315 Upper (Type F) Leather (cattle hide)
Upper of shoe with no latchets. Toe end of vamp rounded, but wear, cracks at toe and crack from vamp throat to toe, suggest that it might have been gathered to a point. Top edge deliberately cut, original top edge; a few remaining stitch holes indicate presence of a top band. Lasting margin with grain–flesh stitching channel; stitch length 4–5mm. Edge–flesh stitching channels on ends of both sides of upper; not clear whether these ends meet, or if a side-piece is missing. A straight slip-on shoe, with no fastenings. Possibly matches Sole (Type 6) Cat No 314/A10365a. Conserved. Mid 10th–mid 14th centuries (sole–12th century).
A10365b; C4477–3; MC049; Phase IIa; Rig V
Illus 139

325 Sole (Type 4) Leather
Left sole with pointed toe. Small hole in centre forepart. Rear of seat is cracked, worn and turned over. Edge–flesh stitching channel; stitch length 4.5–6mm. length c230mm; maximum width of forepart 79mm; width of waist 40mm; maximum width of seat 62mm. Thickness: outer edge of waist, outer edge of forepart 2.5mm, inner edge of seat, inner edge of forepart and waist 3mm. Conserved. 13th–14th centuries.
A03–0009b; C5255–3; MC049, Pit 5259; Phase IIa; Rig V
Illus 121

328 Strap (folded twice) Leather (cattle hide)
Folded twice, two edges stitched together with butted edge–flesh seam; stitch length 6mm, 5.5mm, 5mm, 6.5mm, 7mm; hole diameter c2mm. End folded over and stitched or nailed together, presumably to hold a buckle. Grain is on inside. Conserved.
A03–0009e; C5255–3; MC049, Pit 5259; Phase IIa; Rig V
Illus 158

334 Sole (Type 1) Leather (cattle hide)
Very large and broad left sole, with wide seat, waist and forepart, and very broad toe. Worn, with holes in rear of seat and front of forepart, and with crack towards rear of forepart. Stitch holes on underneath indicate that both forepart and seat have been repaired with clump soles, and that forepart has probably been repaired at least twice. Edge–flesh stitching channel; stitch length 4.5–6.5mm. Length 274mm; maximum width of forepart 112mm; width of waist 81.5mm; maximum width of seat 93mm. Thickness: rear of outer edge of forepart 2.5mm; inner edge of waist 4mm; outer edge of waist 2mm; rear and middle of inner edge of forepart, outer edge of seat 5.5mm; outer front of forepart, inner edge of seat 5mm; inner front of forepart 4.5mm; worn edges of holes 1mm. Conserved. 12th–13th centuries.
A03–0011; L0409; C5266–3; MC054a, Pit 5267; Phase (IIa)IIb; Rig VI
Illus 116

341 and 342 Linked straps (2) Leather and Fe?
Two, each of single thickness. No 341 length 325mm, width 8–11mm, thickness 3mm; stitched through on both edges, stitch length c2mm. Slit, c40mm long, near wider end; second strap passes through this slit. Near narrower end, short slit,

6mm long with small thin piece of leather through it. No 342 length 260mm, width 9–10mm, thickness 3mm; stitched through on both edges; stitch length 2mm. Slit near one end with first strap passing through. Other end, with metal rivet attached passed through slit in first strap. Probably too delicate for harness. Hawking equipment? Conserved.
A6772a, b; C3589–2; MC061; Phase IIb; Rig VI
Illus 151

343 Sole (Type 1), Rand and Upper
Leather (cattle hide) and wool
Right sole, rand and upper, still attached. Sole, straight with broad waist but narrow oval toe, which is beyond great toe area. Worn at rear of seat, slightly worn and cracked at outer edge of forepart. Length 263mm; maximum width of forepart 85mm; width of waist 76mm; maximum width of seat 72mm; thickness 4–5mm. Rand, thin strip 2mm thick, partially delaminated, perforated with oval holes, stitch length 5–6mm. Upper has been deliberately cut across front of vamp, with a sharp knife, probably for reuse; front of vamp left because worn. Lasting margin with grain–flesh stitching channel; stitch length 5–6mm. Wool survives in some holes. Upper type not definable. Conserved. 12th–13th centuries.
A6772c; C3589–2; MC061; Phase IIb; Rig VI
Illus 145

350 Miscellaneous fragment Leather
Fragment with one oversewn edge, stitch length 3–4mm, one straight and one curved edge with edge–flesh stitching channel; stitch length 2.5–3.5mm. Fourth edge cut. Thickness c2mm. Purse? Conserved
A6772j; C3589–2; MC061; Phase IIb; Rig VI
Illus 159

353 Sole (Type 1) Leather (cattle hide)
Child's left, with short round seat, wide waist, broad forepart, gently curved, narrowing to oval toe. Edge–flesh stitching channel; stitch length 4.5–6mm. length 156.5mm; maximum width of forepart 68.5mm; width of waist 52mm; maximum width of seat 57mm. Thickness: inner edge of waist and forepart and outer edge of seat, waist and forepart 3mm. Matches Upper (Type Bi) Cat No 357/A6773f. Conserved. 12th–13th centuries.
A6773b; L1661; C3589–2; MC061; Phase IIb; Rig VI
Not illustrated

357 Upper (Type Bi) Leather
Three fragments of upper of child's boot with tunnel hole for one horizontal thong on each side of quarters. Large fragment comprises vamp, vamp throat, vamp wing, quarters and leg flap. Impression of small triangular stiffener on flesh side of quarters. Quarters and vamp wing join second and third fragments–thin strips–which probably join top edge of quarters. Lasting margin with grain–flesh stitching channel; stitch length 5–6.5mm. Edge–flesh stitching channels on vamp throat, vamp wing, top and vertical edges of quarters, and on second and third fragments; stitch length 3.5–4mm. Matches Sole (Type 1) Cat No 353/A6773b. Conserved. 12th–13th centuries.
A6773f; L1661; C3589–2; MC061; Phase IIb; Rig VI
Not illustrated

358 Upper (Type Bii) Leather (cattle hide) and wool
Four fragments, plus top band, of upper of boot with tunnel holes for two horizontal rows of thong. Largest fragment comprises vamp, vamp throat, vamp wing, quarters and two leg flaps. On flesh side of quarters are stitch holes for low triangular stiffener, which does not survive. Single hole at vamp throat, with short stretch of thong threaded through it and knotted on flesh side. On closed side of quarters, two tunnel holes for horizontal thong(s), one above the other. On open side of quarters is tunnel hole with thong through it, knotted at one end. Second fragment, a long narrow triangle, joins leg flap and quarters (to first fragment) forming top corner of leg flap. Oval hole–for thong? Third fragment, a very small triangle, joins top of other leg flap, completing top corner. Fourth fragment is small triangle with fragment of rand attached by wool to its lasting margin; joins first fragment beneath junction of vamp wing and quarters, thus filling small gap. Top band, strap folded once; length 580mm, width (folded) 85mm, thickness (single) 1mm: length and bends show that band was originally attached to vertical and top edges of leg flaps and quarters. Front of boot open. Lasting margin with grain–flesh stitching channel; stitch length 4.5–8mm, on first and fourth fragments. Edge–flesh stitching channels on vamp wing, vamp throat, part of top edge of quarters, diagonal edges of leg flaps, one edge on each of second and third fragments, and on two edges of fourth fragment; stitch length 2.5–4mm. Vertical edges of leg flaps, part of top edge of quarters, and two edges on each of second and third fragments oversewn, for attachment of top band. Matches Sole (Type 2) Cat No 352/A6773a. 12th–14th centuries.
A6773g; L1661; C3589–2; MC061; Phase IIb; Rig VI
Illus 131 (reconstruction)

363 Sole (Type 1) with bunion? Leather
Left sole with wide seat, no waist, broad forepart with bulge, probably caused by bunion. Very worn and delaminated, with holes and cracks in both seat and forepart. Edge–flesh stitching channel; stitch length 4–5mm. Length 213.5mm; maximum width of forepart 109mm. Thickness: front of forepart 4mm; seat and outer edge of forepart 5mm. Matches Upper (Type Aii) Cat No 364/A2296b, even though the upper has shrunk considerably more than the sole; vamp matches very well, especially over the bunion bulge. Conserved. 12th–13th centuries.
A2296a; L0049; C3095–1; M14a, Pit 3040; Phase Id–IIc; Rig V
Illus 145

364 Upper (Type Aii) with bunion? Leather
Three fragments, plus stiffener, of upper of low ankle boot with no trace of thongs. Largest fragment comprises vamp, vamp wings, vamp throat, quarters and leg flap. Second fragment, side-piece, now torn in two, linking quarters and vamp wing. Third fragment, leg flap. On flesh side of quarters and of side-piece, stitch holes for stiffener, which survives separately. Lasting margin with grain–flesh stitching channels; stitch length 4–5.5mm. Edge–flesh stitching channels on vamp wing, vamp throat, quarters, leg flaps and side-piece; stitch length 2.5–3.5mm. Matching Sole (Type 1) Cat No 363/A2296a. Conserved. 12th–14th centuries.
A2296b; C3095–1; M14a, Pit 3040; Phase Id–IIc; Rig V
Illus 145

372 Upper with fastening? Leather
Two fragments of uppers with fastening? First fragment, quarters; stitch holes for semi-circular stiffener which survives separately. Thong passes through slit; second slit, forming tunnel, never used. One end of thong spade-like stitched to flesh side. Second fragment, leg flap, vamp throat, part of vamp. Thong through single slit, one end spade-like stitched to flesh side. Lasting margin with grain–flesh stitching channel; stitch length 3.5–4.5mm. Lasting margin is very neat. Edge–flesh stitching channels on vertical edge of quarters, vamp throat, vertical edge of leg and vertical edge of vamp wing; stitch length 3–4mm. Top edge oversewn. These two fragments almost certainly join to form quarters of low boot/ankle shoe. The two thongs probably met at the side of the foot. The thong in the second fragment is wider and might have had a buckle attached to it. Thickness c2mm. Conserved.
A4936; C3141–1; MC059, Pit 3142; Phase Id–IIc; Rig V
Illus 143

386 Strap (folded once)? Leather (cattle hide)
Short fragment of strap 116mm long, 38–44mm wide, and 2.5 thick. Short slashes on either edge, and approximately parallel pairs of lines of short slashes down the middle, suggesting strap was folded once, and stitched face to face. On either side of pair of short slashes, longer slashes. Length of short slashes 3–4mm; length of long slashes c15mm. Conserved.
A12377; C3903–1; MC065, T3907; Phase IIa–IIc; Rig VI
Illus 148

389 Sole (Type 1) Leather (cattle hide)
Child's left sole, with rounded toe. Edge–flesh stitching channel; stitch length 6–6.5mm. Length 142mm; maximum width of forepart 58mm; width of waist 44mm; maximum width of seat 44mm; thickness 2–3mm. Probably matches Upper (Type Bi) Cat No 390/A12296b. Conserved. 12th–13th centuries.
A12296a; C3886–1; MC065; Phase IIa–IIc; Rig VI
Illus 124

390 Upper (Type Bi) Leather
Fragment of child's ankle boot, with tunnel holes on closed side of quarter and on vamp wing, for one horizontal thong, fragment of which survives on vamp wing. Comprises vamp, vamp wing, vamp throat, and quarters. Lasting margin with grain–flesh stitching channel; stitch length 6–7mm. Edge–flesh stitching channels; stitch length 4–5mm, on vamp throat, vamp wing, vertical edge of quarters, and on inner part of top edge of quarters. Rest of top edge of quarters oversewn. Quarters cracked and worn. Matching Sole (Type 1) Cat No 389/A12296a. Conserved. 12th–14th centuries.
A12296b; C3886–1; MC065; Phase IIa–IIc; Rig VI
Illus 124

399 Strap (folded once) Leather
Edges oversewn; stitch length 4–5mm. One end broken; other end cut, with round hole in middle of width penetrating both thicknesses; diameter of hole 1.75mm. Length c340mm; width 7mm. Each edge 1mm thick, total width 2–3mm. Conserved.
A12293a; C5156–3; MC056, Pit 5155; Phase Ia–IIc; Rig VI
Illus 148

400 Sole (Type 1) Leather
Most of right sole, almost straight sided, with a rounded toe, large part of seat missing and very worn at front of forepart, which shows signs of repair. Edge–flesh stitching channel; stitch length 4mm. Maximum length 228mm; maximum width of forepart 77mm; width of waist 60mm. Thickness: inner forepart 3mm; inner waist 3–3.5mm; outer waist, outer forepart and seat 4mm. Conserved. 12th–13th centuries.
A12293b; C5156–3; MC056, Pit 5155; Phase Ia–IIc; Rig VI
Illus 117

402 Thong Leather
Thin strip with one broken end and one pointed end. Width: 4–4.5mm for c60mm, 6–6.5mm for c125mm: thickness c1mm. Conserved.
A12293d; C5156–3; MC056, Pit 5155; Phase Ia–IIc; Rig VI
Illus 152

404 Upper (Type Biii) Leather (cattle hide)
Very worn fragment of upper of boot with vertical thonging. Comprises vamp, vamp throat, quarters and leg flap. Quarters and vamp wing join. Missing second leg flap. Faint trace of stitching for low semi-circular stiffener on flesh side of quarters. Short stretches of vertical thonging on quarters and vamp wing. Lasting margin with grain–flesh stitching channel; stitch length 5.5mm; much of lasting margin missing. Edge–flesh stitching channels on vamp, wing, throat and quarters. Top edge of quarters and top and vertical edges of leg flap oversewn. Thickness 1–1.5mm. Conserved. 12th–13th centuries.
A12298a; L1750; C5156–3; MC056, Pit 5155; Phase Ia–IIc; Rig VI
Illus 133

406 Sole (Type 1) with bunion? Leather (cattle hide)
Right sole, with wide seat and waist and broad and fairly straight forepart, ending in wide rounded toe. Forepart and seat both worn, hole and cracks in seat and small part of stitching channel separated from rest of sole; large hole in centre forepart, smaller hole in great toe area, where stitching channel has cracked. On inner edge of forepart, slight bulge suggests a bunion. Edge–flesh stitching channel; stitch length 4–5mm. Length: 277mm; maximum width of forepart 114.5mm; width of waist 75.5mm; maximum width of seat 80mm. Thickness: outer edge of waist 3.5mm; inner edge of waist 4.5mm. Conserved. 12th–13th centuries.
A12493a; L0054; C5182–3; MC056, Pit 5155; Phase Ia–IIc; Rig VI
Illus 116

411 Upper (Type Biii) Leather (cattle hide)
Large fragment of upper of ankle boot, with vertical thonging. Comprises vamp with rounded toe, vamp throat, vamp wing, quarters and leg flap. Quarters and vamp wing probably meet. Second leg flap missing. Traces of triangular stiffener on flesh side of quarters. Vertical line of thonging on quarters, with three short fragments (width c4–4.5mm, length 3.5mm, 6.5mm and 4mm) on grain side and four (length c6.5mm, 7.5mm, 8.5mm and 7mm) on flesh side. Thong hole near edge of vamp throat–for horizontal thong? Also small hole or slit–for thong?–near top edge of boot. Lasting margin with grain–flesh stitching channel; stitch length 4–5mm. Edge–flesh stitching channel; stitch length 3–4mm. Top edge of quarters oversewn. Conserved. 12th–13th centuries.
A12493f; C5182–3; MC056, Pit 5155; Phase Ia–IIc; Rig VI
Illus 133

421 Offcut? Leather
Approximately triangular fragment, apparently folded in two, one side definitely grain, but the other looks more like flesh, yet definite fold, natural edge at one end. Grain surface is marked by short impressions–like those of tunnel stitches–and by irregular lines–natural marks from animal? Most probably offcut. Conserved.
A03–0015d; C5223–3; B4, Construction; Phase IIc; Rig VI
Illus 159

447 Soles (Types 8, 9) and Upper Leather (cattle hide)
Very tattered fragments of shoe, consisting of separate seat and forepart, sewn together across waist, and fragment of vamp, now attached to forepart by thong. Short, wide seat, worn, with edge–flesh stitching channel; stitch length 5–7.5mm. Short length of thong threaded through hole next to waist; also three other thong holes parallel to edge. Length 67mm; maximum width 60mm; width at waist 55mm. Forepart, almost symmetrical, long and fairly broad, but with pointed toe. Very worn and delaminated. Edge–flesh stitching channel; stitch length 5–6mm. Part of stitching channel replaced by thong. Length 84mm; width of waist 48mm; width at rear of waist 53mm. Very worn and delaminated fragment of vamp, with straw adhering to flesh layer. Lasting margin with grain–flesh stitching channel; stitch length 4.5–7mm, replaced by thong, knotted on flesh side of vamp. Also several very tattered fragments, some with straw attached, probably part of upper. Conserved.
A6722; L1648; C3570–2; B4, 'Byre'–Occupation; Phase IIc; Rig VI
Illus 145

452 Sole (Type 1) Leather and wool
Straight seat, no waist, fairly straight forepart, rounded toe. Edge–flesh stitching channel, stitch length 5.5mm, 6mm, 7.5mm. Very worn, with a hole in seat and two small holes and one large crack in centre forepart. Tunnel stitch holes on underneath indicate that both seat and forepart have been repaired with clump soles. Second horizontal row of stitches across forepart suggests that clump fastened more firmly or possibly second layer of clump added. Length: 228.5mm; maximum width of forepart 88mm; width of waist 70mm; maximum width of seat 75mm. Thickness: inner edge of waist 2.5mm; outer edge of waist 3.5mm; rear of seat 4mm; front of forepart, outer edge of forepart 5.5mm; front of inner edge of forepart 5mm; measurements of thickness suggest right sole but wear pattern at front of forepart and way outer edge of forepart is turned over and style of vamp, suggests left sole. Wool survives in a few stitch holes. Matching Upper (Type J) Cat No 456/A10048e. Conserved. 12th–13th centuries.
A10048a; L0002; C2384–4; M1.1f, Pit 2383; Phase IIb,IIc; Rig VI
Illus 147

453 Sole (Type 2) Leather

Right sole with short wide seat, slight narrowing for waist, long and broad gently curved forepart with broad rounded toe. Worn at rear of seat, part of which is missing, and at forepart, where there are two cracks. On underside, tunnel stitch holes indicate that seat and forepart have been repaired. Some of forepart clump stitch holes cross and run along line of one hole and crack, demonstrating that further damage has been caused by the clump itself, which was very small in relation to the whole forepart. Also partially delaminated. Edge–flesh stitching channel; stitch length 4–6mm. Stitch holes on inner edge of forepart and on corresponding edge of upper indicate that this stretch has been repaired. Surviving length 242mm; maximum width of forepart 106mm; width of waist 74mm; maximum surviving width of seat 91mm. Thickness: worn edge of seat 1mm; outer edge of waist 4.5mm; inner edge of forepart, turned up 5.5mm; outer edge of forepart, turned up 6mm. Matching Upper (Type Aii) of low boot Cat No 455/A10048d. Conserved. 12th–14th centuries.

A10048b; L0002; C2384–4; M1.1f, Pit 2383; Phase IIb,IIc; Rig VI

Illus 147

455 Upper (Type Aii) Leather

Fragment of upper of low ankle boot, with no trace of thongs, but with vamp, vamp throat, vamp wing and front of leg flap. Lasting margin with stitching channel of grain–flesh holes; stitch length 4mm, 5mm, 5mm, 5mm, 4.5mm, 3mm–mainly 4.5–5.5mm. Edge–flesh stitching channels on vamp wing, throat and vertical edge of leg flap; stitch length 2–4mm. Top edge of leg flap oversewn. Worn, particularly at front of vamp and along lasting margin; rest of quarters/leg flap missing. Thickness: stitched edges 2mm; worn edges c1mm. Matching Sole (Type 2) Cat No 453/A10048b. Conserved. 12th–14th centuries.

A10048d; L0002; C2384–4; M1.1f, Pit 2383; Phase IIb,IIc; Rig VI

Illus 147

456 Upper (Type J) Leather (cattle hide)

Vamp with vamp wing and throat in one edge–flesh stitching channel; stitch length 3–4mm, extending across foot from one side of lasting margin to the other. Lasting margin with stitching channel of grain–flesh holes; stitch length 5.5–7mm. Worn with two cracks, one of which, on inner edge, has been repaired with a patch. Thickness 2.5mm. Matching Sole (Type 1) Cat No 452/A10048a. Conserved.

A10048e; L0002; C2384–4; M1.1f, Pit 2383; Phase Ib,IIc; Rig VI

Illus 147

459 Strap (folded twice) Leather (cattle hide)

Two pieces, one folded twice with its edges joined by a butted edge to grain seam where they meet on the reverse. Edges of strap, on both sides, marked by short slashes 3–4mm long, 2–3mm apart. Centre of obverse also marked by irregular slashes, 4–5mm long, 10–12mm apart. At one end of strap is a slit 26mm long. The other fragment, a thin strip contained within the first fragment, is also pierced by the stitches on the main fragment. Folded strap: length 222mm, width 16mm, thickness 2mm. Single strip: length as folded strap, width

12.5mm, thickness 1mm. Conserved.

A10506a; C4470–3; M1.1c, Pit 5005; Phase IId; Rig VI

Illus 149

461 Upper (Type Bi) Leather (cattle hide)

Two joining fragments (originally one) of low ankle boot, with holes for one horizontal thong. Comprises vamp, vamp throat, vamp wing, quarters, and two leg flaps. Vamp wing and quarters join. On closed side of quarters, tunnel hole for horizontal thong, with creases left by thong on either side. On corner of one leg flap, round hole with thong passing through it, and anchored on flesh side with a knot. No corresponding hole on opposite leg flap, therefore wrap-around thong. Small hole penetrated leather– for attachment to last (?)– close to top edge of quarters. Near top corner of vamp wing; small horizontal tunnel-like depression–possibly too small to have been made by a thong; mark caused by bracing boot to last? Edge–flesh stitching channels on vamp throat, vamp wing, and vertical edges of quarters; stitch length 3–4mm. Top and vertical edges of leg flaps and top edges of quarters oversewn. Lasting margin does not survive. Conserved. 12th–14th centuries.

A10511; C4470–3; M1.1c, Pit 5005; Phase IId; Rig VI

Illus 129

469 Sole (Type 1) Leather and wool

Probably for right foot; almost straight sides; very slightly narrowing for waist; gently curved broad forepart, ending in broad oval toe. Worn at rear of seat, which is missing, and at front of forepart, where stitching channel is worn, and where there are several short cracks and one small hole. Edge–flesh stitching channel; stitch length 4.5–6.5mm. Wool survives in some stitch holes. Surviving length 237mm; maximum width of forepart 91.5mm; width of waist 71.5mm; maximum width of seat 75mm. Thickness: outer edge of waist, rear of outer edge of seat 3.5mm; inner edge of waist, forepart and seat, and front of outer edge of seat 4.5mm; outer edge of forepart 5mm. Conserved. 12th–13th centuries.

A12285a; L0059; C4470–3; M1.1c, Pit 5005; Phase IId; Rig VI

Illus 117

470 Sole (Type 1) Leather and wool

Probably left foot; rear of seat rounded, slight narrowing of waist, very straight forepart with squarish front. Forepart worn, with large hole. Edge–flesh stitching channel; stitch length 4–6mm. Wool survives in some stitch holes. Length 244mm; maximum width of forepart 9mm; width of waist 64mm; maximum width of seat 75mm. Thickness: outer edge of forepart 3.5mm; inner and outer edge of waist, front of forepart 4mm; inner edge of forepart and seat 5mm. Conserved. 12th–13th centuries.

A12285b; L0059; C4470–3; M1.1c, Pit 5005; Phase IId; Rig VI

Illus 116

475 Sole (Type 1) Leather and wool

Left sole with straight-sided seat, wide waist and broad forepart, very slightly curved, ending in oval toe. Hole at front of forepart and great toe area; outer side of front of forepart pushed inwards; shape probably due to wear. Worn at rear of seat where crack between stitching channel and seat.

Edge–flesh stitching channel; stitch length 4.5–7.5mm. Wool survives in most of the stitch holes. Length 244mm; maximum width of seat 70mm; maximum width of forepart 97mm; width of waist 65.5mm. Thickness: inner edge of waist 3.5mm; inner edge of seat, turned up, 5mm; inner edge of forepart 4mm; outer edge of waist and rear of forepart 3mm; outer edge of seat 4.5mm; front of outer edge of forepart 6.5mm; edge of hole 0.5mm. Matches Upper (Type E) Cat No 476/A12302b. Conserved. 12th–13th centuries.
A12302a; L0050; C4470–3; M1.1c, Pit 5005; Phase IId; Rig VI
Illus 139

476 Upper (Type E) Leather
Large fragment of low shoe comprising vamp, vamp wing, vamp throat, quarters, and latchet. Vamp wing and quarters do not join. Some tunnel stitches and impression of semi-circular stiffener on flesh side of quarters. Lasting margin with grain–flesh stitching channel; stitch length 4mm, 5mm. Edge–flesh stitching channels on vamp wing, throat, vertical edge of latchet, and quarters; stitch length 2.5–3.5mm. Top edge of latchet and quarters oversewn. Stiffener has lasting margin with stitching channel of grain–flesh holes; stitch length 4.5mm, 5mm, 5.5mm, 3.5mm; semi-circular with curved top-stitch holes for attachment to quarters. Matches left Sole (Type 1) Cat No 475/A12302a. Unusual in having vamp, side-piece, quarters join on outside of foot. Conserved. 12th century.
A12302b; L0050; C4470–3; M1.1c, Pit 5005; Phase IId; Rig VI
Illus 139

477 Strap (folded once) Leather (cattle hide)
Now flat, originally folded once. Tunnel stitching on fold, penetrating only one thickness–decorative. Edges stitched. Strap stitched together, with grain–flesh stitching at both ends. Length 350mm; width 21–37mm (unfolded); thickness 1mm (unfolded). Probably top band of upper. Conserved.
A12309a; C4470–3; M1.1c, Pit 5005; Phase IId; Rig VI
Illus 148

478 Upper (Type Aii) Leather (cattle hide)
Two joining fragments, plus stiffener, of high ankle boot with no thongs or holes for thongs. Larger fragment comprises vamp with rounded throat and wing, quarters and leg flap. Vamp wing joins quarters and leg flap. Lasting margin with grain–flesh stitching channel; stitch length 4.5–5.5mm. Smaller fragment, leg flap joining first leg flap and possibly vamp throat, but there might have been an inset over the instep– 'bellows tongue' (J Swann pers comm). Edge–flesh stitching channels on wing, throat, leg flaps and quarters; stitch length 2–3mm; hole diameter c 0.5mm. Top edges of quarters and leg flaps oversewn. Top edge of quarters has short vertical slit 23mm long, which has been stitched with a butted edge–flesh seam; stitch length 2–2.5mm; hole diameter c75mm–probably decorative seam. Vamp worn, with front missing, and with crack. Short slit on quarters probably crack not tie-hole. Tunnel stitch holes on flesh side of quarters mark position of semi-circular stiffener, which survives separately. Lasting margin with grain–flesh stitching channel corresponding to that on quarters; oversewn rounded edge for attachment to quarters. Vertical crack c45mm long, from

apex of semicircle; this crack stitched together with butted edge–flesh seam; stitch length 8–9mm; hole diameter c0.75mm. This was possibly an already cracked piece of leather repaired for use as stiffener. It would have been virtually impossible to stitch once stiffener was attached to inside of quarters. It might have been split to allow for curvature, but this is unlikely and probably unnecessary. Its irregular nature suggests a crack rather than a deliberate cut. Grain side of stiffener faces flesh side of quarters, which is unusual with stiffeners (J H Thornton pers comm). Upper almost complete, lacking only front end of vamp and a small side-piece, which would have filled in the oddly-shaped gap between quarters and leg flap. Stitching, especially on the butted edge–flesh, very neat. Conserved. 12th–14th centuries.
A12309b; C4470–3; M1.1c, Pit 5005; Phase IId; Rig VI
Illus 126

481 Miscellaneous fragment Leather
Approximately trapezoidal, with cut edges; one edge torn. Parallel to two long edges are two rows of short slits; inner rows meeting in a point. Between each pair of rows of slits is a row of dots. Space between inner rows also filled with shallow dots (on grain side). Slits penetrate to flesh side, but dots do not. Slits engraved, dots punched. Delaminated. Thickness c2mm. Conserved.
A10503; L1693; C4468–3; M1.1d; Phase IId, IIe; Rig VI
Illus 158

485 Miscellaneous fragment Leather
Rectangular; folded once. Perforated along one long side by stitching channel of grain–flesh holes, stitch length 2mm; along outer edges by two parallel stitching channels of grain–flesh holes, stitch length 2–2.5mm. Delaminated. Length 2–2.5mm; width 38mm; thickness c0.25mm. Case? Conserved.
A10504a; L1699; C4492–3; M1.1a; Phase IId,IIe; Rig VI
Illus 158

486 Miscellaneous fragment Leather
Very worn and crumbly, folded once, making a sheath-like shape. Along bottom edge, two parallel stitching channels with grain–flesh holes perforating both layers; stitch length 2.5–4mm. About 19mm above top row, single horizontal stitching channel with grain–flesh holes; stitch length 2.5mm. Up vertical edge, two parallel stitching channels with grain–flesh holes; stitch length 2.5–4mm for first 56mm, then single row, overstitched (?) rib along edge. Leather below single horizontal row dark and in good condition, above it is paler and very fragmentary and crumbly. Surviving length 102mm; minimum width 35mm; maximum width 50mm; thickness 0.75mm. Case? Conserved.
A10504b; L1699; C4492–3; M1.1a; Phase IId,IIe; Rig VI
Illus 158

503 Upper (Type C) Leather
Three fragments of low ankle boot with holes for side-lacing. Largest comprises vamp, vamp wing, vamp throat and quarters. Second is trapezoidal side-piece, linking quarters and vamp wing. Smallest is probably part of this upper.

Largest has five thong holes on vertical edge of vamp wing, edge parallel to holes oversewn, with five matching tie-holes on side-piece approximately 3mm by 2mm and 15.5mm, 12mm, 15mm and 14.5mm apart. Lasting margin with grain–flesh stitching channel; stitch length 5.5–6.5mm on largest and second fragments. Edge–flesh stitching channels; stitch length 2.5–3.5mm, on lower part of vamp wing, vamp throat, vertical edge of leg flap, vertical edge of quarters, part of edge with holes, and two other edges of side-piece, and two edges of third fragment. Conserved. 14th–15th centuries.
A03–0003b; C4433–3; P2.1a; Phase IIb–IIf; Rig V
Illus 135

505 Sole (Type 1) Leather (cattle hide)
Child's right sole with short seat, wide waist and long gently curved forepart with rounded front. Edge–flesh stitching channel; stitch length 4–7mm. Length 166.5mm; maximum width of forepart 45mm; maximum width of seat 48mm. Thickness: outside edge of waist and forepart 2.5mm, inner edge of waist, front of forepart 3mm; inner edge of forepart 3.5mm, rear of seat 4mm. Matches Upper (Type Bi) Cat No 508/A3447e. Conserved. 12th–13th centuries.
A3447b; L1671; C3582–2; M1.1d and M1.1e; Phase IId–IIf; Rig VI
Illus 124

508 Upper (Type Bi) Leather
Three fragments of child's boot, with tunnel holes for one horizontal thong. Large fragment comprises vamp, vamp wing, vamp throat and quarters. Second fragment, trapezoidal, joins vamp wing. Third fragment, also trapezoidal, possibly fits between quarters and second fragment. Tunnel hole with thong near top of second fragment; tunnel hole on closed side of quarters. Lasting margin with grain–flesh stitching channel; stitch length 4.5–6mm. Edge–flesh stitching channel; stitch length 3mm, on vamp wing, vamp throat and on second and third fragments. Thickness 1mm. Matches Sole (Type 1) Cat No 505/A3447b (Illus 124). Conserved. 12th–14th centuries.
A3447e; L1671; C3582–2; M1.1d and M1.1e; Phase IId–IIf; Rig VI
Not illustrated

524 Strap/belt (folded twice) Leather
Fragment, consisting of two pieces, one folded twice, with edges meeting on reverse, where stitched together with a butted edge to grain seam; stitch length 8–8.5mm; the other, placed inside the first, is a thin strip c1mm thick. Slashes at irregular intervals down the middle of the belt–decoration? One end appears torn, the other is cut and has several holes penetrating it–attachment for buckle? Length c330mm; maximum width 29mm; minimum width 17mm; total thickness 5mm. Conserved.
A9369; L0011; C2643–3; B5, WW3566; Phase IIa–IIff; Rig V
Illus 149

527 Upper (Type Bi) Leather (cattle hide)
Large fragment of child's ankle boot, with tunnel hole on closed side of quarters, and single hole at vamp throat for one horizontal thong. Comprises vamp, vamp wings, vamp throat, quarters and two leg flaps. Complete except for small low side-piece linking quarters and vamp wing. Lasting margin with grain–flesh stitching channel; stitch length 5mm. Edge–flesh stitching channels on vamp wing, vamp throat and on lower edges of leg flaps; stitch length 3–4mm. Top edges of quarters and top and vertical edges of leg flaps oversewn. Thickness 2mm. Conserved. 12th–14th centuries.
A6803; L1672; C3596–1/2; B5, South Room–Floor/Occupation (3); Phase IIa–IIff; Rig V
Illus 130

537 Upper (Type Bii) Leather
Three fragments, plus stiffener, of boot; very worn and partially delaminated; thong wrapped twice round boot, with tunnel holes enabling it to be wrapped twice more. Good example of boot with wrap-around thong. Two fragments, originally one, comprise vamp, vamp wings, vamp throat, quarters and leg flap. Third fragment is second leg flap, which is now loosely held in place by thong wrapped round boot twice. One end of thong secured to second leg flap by knots on both grain and flesh side of tunnel hole; thong passes to vamp wing, through tunnel hole bridging vamp wing and quarters, round rear of quarters and through tunnel hole on closed side of quarters, through tunnel hole on vamp wing, past throat, back to second leg flap, through single hole, round quarters again, through tunnel hole on closed side (above first one), then ends torn. At rear of quarters is trace of tunnel holes through which thongs once passed. On closed side of quarters are two more tunnel holes, above first two, suggesting that they could have been wrapped round boot twice more. Also another tunnel hole on leg flap. Lasting margin with grain–flesh stitching channel; stitch length 5mm. Edge–flesh stitching channels on vamp wing, vamp throat, quarters and leg flaps; stitch length 3mm. Top edges of quarters and leg flaps cut. Trace of stitch holes on flesh side of quarters, for semi-circular stiffener with survives separately. Conserved. 12th–13th centuries.
A6416a; L1774; C3569–1/2; B5, North Room–Floor/Occupation (1); Phase IIa–IIff; Rig V
Not illustrated

570 Sheath (decorated) Leather (cattle hide)
Fragment, in one piece, folded twice; edges meet in middle of reverse, where joined by butted edge to grain seam; stitch length 3.5–5mm. Part of top edge of reverse also has edge to grain holes. Front and rear of sheath are decorated with bands of diagonal hatching. Surviving length 97mm; maximum width 30mm; minimum width 21mm. Thickness: edge to grain stitching channel 3.5mm; elsewhere 1.5mm. Conserved. 13th–14th centuries.
cf Custom House site, London, similar cross-hatching, early to mid-14th century (Tatton-Brown 1975, 162–3, figs 29, 116).
A9120; C2279–4; M10; Phase IId–IIg; Rig V
Illus 155

590 Strap (single thickness) Leather
Fragment of single thickness with row of short slits parallel to each long edge, one row 2.5–3mm from edge, the other 5–7mm; slits approximately 5–6mm apart (centre to centre). One end torn, the other cut, though slightly irregular, with two irregular rows of slits parallel to it. In centre of strap are two round holes, diameter 5mm, and edge of third. Length 130mm;

width 27–29mm; thickness 2mm; Conserved.
A11250a; L1898; C2304–4; M10; Phase IId–IIg; Rig V
Illus 152

625 Sole (Type 1) Leather
Short wide left sole, with rounded toe. Very worn and
delaminated; holes towards rear of seat and in centre forepart,
and front inner portion of forepart missing. Tunnel holes on
underside indicate that both seat and forepart repaired with
clump soles at least twice. Forepart cracked along outer line
of stitching. Edge–flesh stitching channel; stitch length 5mm.
Length 264mm; maximum width of forepart 110mm; width of
waist 77mm; maximum width of seat 87mm; thickness 4–6mm.
Matches Upper Cat No 626/A9885b. Conserved. 12th–13th
centuries.
A9885a; C2333–4; M10; Phase IId–IIg; Rig V
Illus 104

626 Upper Leather (cattle hide)
Two fragments, with repair patch. Larger fragment comprises
toe end of vamp, vamp wing and quarters. Lasting margin
with grain–flesh stitching channel; stitch length 4–5mm. Two
edge–flesh stitching channels; stitch length 2.5–3mm. Part of
lasting margin missing, replaced by a long thin patch, attached
with tunnel stitching. Lasting margin on patch irregular. Quarter
has also been repaired, on grain side with a semicircular
fragment, attached by tunnel stitching, now missing. Smaller
fragment, vamp wing, joins front of vamp. Rest of upper cut
away. Probably matches Sole (Type 1) Cat No 625/A9885a
(12th–13th centuries). Conserved.
A9885b; C2333–4; M10; Phase IId–IIg; Rig V
Illus 104

631 Upper (Type Biii) Leather
Fragment of boot, with vertical thonging, comprises vamp with
oval toe, vamp throat, vamp wing, leg flap and part of quarters,
with three stretches of vertical thong on grain side. Thong
doubled before being threaded through tunnel holes. Lasting
margin with grain–flesh stitching channel; stitch length 5.5–
6.5mm. Edge–flesh stitching channels on vamp throat, vamp
wing and top edge of quarters; stitch length 3–4mm. Vertical
edge of leg flap oversewn, front of boot open. Conserved.
12th–13th centuries.
A10047a; C2462B–3; M10; Phase IId–IIg; Rig V
Illus 132

739 Long dagger sheath Leather (cattle hide)
Formed of one strip, folded twice and probably meeting and
joined in middle of reverse, with butted edge to grain seam;
stitch length 3.5mm. For c360mm from top 50–53mm wide,
narrowing to c20mm, but not complete. Large oval hole, c14mm
by 8.5mm, at 25mm from top, presumably for attachment to
belt, with twelve smaller holes, diameter 3.5mm, six above six
below. Stitching channel of short slits parallel with each edge,
c9–11mm from each edge–on both sides–slits not very wide
and no thread–possibly just decoration. Worn, with most of
reverse missing. Length c630mm. Conserved.
A9143; L0007; C2611–3; M1.2, Pit 2648; Phase <IIg(IIh); Rig VI
Illus 154

740 Sole (Type 3) Leather (cattle hide)
Left, with rounded seat, very narrow waist; forepart wide at
rear, then turned inwards to oval toe. Edge–flesh stitching
channel; stitch length 3.5–4.5mm. Partially delaminated; worn on
underneath of centre seat and of centre forepart. Length 243mm;
maximum width of forepart 83mm; width of waist 33mm; maximum
width of seat 64mm; thickness 3.5mm. Probably partner of right
Sole (Type 3) 774/A9365. Conserved. 13th–14th centuries.
A9144; L0069; C2611–3; M1.2, Pit 2648; Phase <IIg(IIh); Rig VI
Illus 120

774 Sole (Type 3) Leather
Right, two joining fragments. Seat and forepart worn and
delaminated. Edge-flesh stitching channel; stitch length 5-6mm.
Maximum length 243mm; maximum width of forepart 75mm; width
of waist 36mm; maximum width of seat 70mm; thickness 4-5mm.
Same shape as and probably partner of Sole (Type 3) 740/A9144.
Conserved. 13th–14th centuries.
A9365; C2611-3; M1.2, Pit 2648; Phase <IIg(IIh); Rig VI
Not illustrated

776 Sole (Type 2) with bunion Leather
Right, with rounded seat, wide waist, broad forepart, gently curved
and with bunion extension. Very worn and delaminated, with two
cracks in seat, one of which has had the effect of widening it. Grain
layer also very worn at front and centre forepart. Edge–flesh
stitching channel; stitch length 5mm, 6mm. Length 232.5mm;
maximum width of forepart 99mm; width of waist 63mm; width
of seat 83mm; thickness 5mm. Conserved. 12th–13th centuries.
A9371b; L0009; C2611–3; M1.2, Pit 2648; Phase <IIg(IIh); Rig VI
Illus 118

779 Upper (Type E) Leather (cattle hide)
Fragment of low shoe, comprising rear of vamp, throat, vamp
wing, quarters and latchet. Vamp and quarter wings joined in
butted edge–flesh seam; stitch length c2.5mm. Edge–flesh seam
also at throat. Top edges of quarters and vamp wing oversewn.
Second latchet missing. Front of vamp cut away. Crack in
remaining part of vamp. Lasting margin with stitching channel
of grain–flesh holes; stitch length 5.5mm, 5mm, 4mm, mainly
5–5.5mm. Also three holes 3mm apart–probably one is repair
hole. Thickness 3mm. Conserved.
A9371e; L0009; C2611–3; M1.2, Pit 2648; Phase <IIg(IIh); Rig VI
Illus 138

783 Sole (Type 3) Leather and wool
Right, with rounded seat, narrow waist and wide gently curved
forepart with broad oval toe. Fragment of rand still attached to
outer edge of forepart; wool survives there and in stitch holes
on inside waist and at front of forepart. Worn, especially at
rear of seat and front of forepart, where cracked. Edge–flesh
stitching channel; stitch length 4–9mm, chiefly 5–7mm. Close
concentration of holes along inner edge of seat, waist and rear
of forepart. Length 242mm; maximum width of forepart 89mm;
width of waist 45.5mm; maximum width of seat 70mm. Thickness:
outer edge of waist and seat 2.75mm; inner edge of waist 3.5mm;
outer and inner edges of forepart 4mm; inner edge of seat 5mm.
Conserved. 13th–14th centuries.
A9372a; L0045; C2611–3; M1.2, Pit 2648; Phase <IIg(IIh); Rig VI
Illus 120

798 Sole (Type 1) Leather
Right, with rounded toe. Worn and partially delaminated, with a hole in seat and two cracks in centre forepart. Tunnel stitch holes on reverse indicate that clumps were added to seat and forepart. Edge–flesh stitching channel; stitch length 4–6mm. Length 179mm; maximum width of forepart 73mm; width of waist 63mm; maximum width of seat 63mm; thickness 4mm. Conserved. 12th–13th centuries.
A10366; L0071; C2611–3; M1.2, Pit 2648; Phase <IIg(IIh);
Rig VI
Illus 104

803 Miscellaneous fragment Leather (cattle hide)
Oval, with protruding tabs at each end and with several cuts or slashes through central part. All edges cut but irregular. No trace of stitching. Tongue? Length 122mm; maximum width 45mm; thickness 3mm. Conserved.
A10775b; L1685; C2611–3; M1.2, Pit 2648; Phase <IIg(IIh);
Rig VI
Illus 158

810 Upper (Type F) Leather
Large fragment; comprises pointed vamp, vamp throat, vamp wing, and quarters with domed top edge. Faint trace of stiffener. Lasting margin with grain–flesh stitching channel; stitch length 4–5mm. Edge–flesh stitching channels on vamp wing and adjoining edge of quarters; stitch length 3mm; leather is so thin on part of quarters that holes are, in fact, grain–flesh. Vamp throat very worn, no stitching channel survives. Top edge of quarters also very worn, probably oversewn. Thickness: vamp wing 1mm; vertical edge of quarters 0.5mm. Matches Sole (Type 4) Cat No 811/A11219b. Conserved. Mid-10th–mid-14th centuries.
A11219a; C2611–3; M1.2, Pit 2648; Phase <IIg(IIh); Rig VI
Illus 139

811 Sole (Type 4) Leather (cattle hide)
Right, with short rounded seat, narrow waist, and long slender forepart, gently curved, with central point. Edge–flesh stitching channel; stitch length 4–5mm. Length 215mm; maximum width of forepart 79mm; width of waist 36mm; maximum width of seat 59mm. Thickness: outer edge of waist, outer, and rear and middle of inner edges of forepart, inner, outer and rear edges of seat 3mm; inner edge of waist, front of inner edge of forepart 3.5mm. Matches Upper (Type F) Cat No 810/A11219a. Conserved. 13th–14th centuries.
A11219b; C2611–3; M1.2, Pit 2648; Phase <IIg(IIh); Rig VI
Illus 139

821 Sole (Type 4) Leather (cattle hide) and wool
Left, long and slender, seat tapering towards rear, narrow forepart, almost symmetrical; pointed toe. Edge–flesh seam; stitch length 5–7.5mm. Wool survives in most of stitch holes. Holes towards rear of seat, repaired with clump sole, stitch holes visible on underneath. Also tunnel stitches on underneath of forepart, marking position of clump sole. However, forepart not visibly worn, except at one corner of clump area, where surface is slightly pitted. Length 237.5mm; maximum width of forepart 73.5mm; width of waist 51mm;

maximum width of seat 59mm. Thickness: inner edge of waist and forepart 4.5mm; inner edge of seat 5.5mm; outer edge of waist and forepart 4mm. Probably matches Rand Cat No 822/A11221b and Upper (Type Ai) Cat No 823/A11221c. Conserved. Sole: 13th–14th centuries; upper: 12th–14th centuries.
A11221a; L0068; C2611–3; M1.2, Pit 2648; Phase <IIg(IIh);
Rig VI
Illus 121

822 Rand Leather (cattle hide) and wool
Three fragments, stitch length 5.5mm, 7mm. Wool survives in all three fragments. Probably belongs to Sole (Type 4) Cat No 821/A11221a. Conserved.
A11221b; L0068; C2611-3; M1.2, Pit 2648; Phase <IIg(IIh);
Rig VI
Not illustrated

823 Upper (Type Ai) Leather (cattle hide)
Fragment of high ankle boot with no thongs or holes for them. Comprises vamp, vamp wing, vamp throat, quarters and leg flap. Second leg flap missing. Lasting margin with grain–flesh stitching channel; stitch length 4.5–7mm. Edge–flesh stitching channels on vamp wing, vamp throat, quarters and leg flap; stitch length 3–6mm. Top edge of quarters oversewn. Front of vamp worn, with stitching channel separated from vamp and with crack almost completely detaching front of vamp from rest of upper; also crack in vamp wing. Thickness approximately 1–3mm. Probably matches Sole (Type 4) Cat No 821/A11221a. Conserved. Sole: 13th–14th centuries; upper–12th–14th centuries.
A11221c; L0068; C2611–3; M1.2, Pit 2648; Phase <IIg(IIh);
Rig VI
Illus 127

828 Miscellaneous fragment Leather and Cu alloy
Fragment, with decorated copper alloy plate (see Fascicule 2, The non-ferrous metalwork, Cat No 42) attached to grain side, and with two thin copper alloy strips attached to flesh side. Fragment of leather is approximately trapezoidal in shape, slightly tapered, with cut edges on one short and two long sides; fourth side torn. Maximum surviving length 75mm; width at torn end c30mm, other short end 22mm. Thickness 1mm. Not apparently delaminated. Trapezoidal plate of copper alloy attached to grain side by four rivets. One end of plate broken (matching torn end of fragment). Approximately mushroom-shaped hole has been cut in the centre of the plate and in leather, probably for a key. Two thin strips of copper alloy on flesh side, originally attached to leather by the same rivets which hold the plate on the grain side– ie strengtheners for decorated plate. Most probably strap or latchet of object with lock, eg purse, wallet, satchel, trunk? One of the strips is still held in place by the rivets, but the other is now only attached at one end. Conserved.
A12279; C5166–3; M1.2, Pit 2648, MW5166; Phase <IIg(IIh);
Rig VI
Not illustrated

830 Miscellaneous fragment with metalwork Leather and Fe

Small, approximately triangular, fragment, very worn and partially delaminated. Thickness 1.5 mm. Nail with rectangular head through fragment. Conserved.
A8105; C2239-4; M11; Phase IIh; Rigs V and VI
Not illustrated

867 Miscellaneous fragment Leather (cattle hide)

Approximately square, c63mm by 73mm, consisting of a piece of leather, c1mm thick, 125mm wide and 140mm long, folded twice, resulting in a small square, with grain surface on outside, front and back, and on inside. Fragment held together by one thong, which passes repeatedly through all four thicknesses. Ends of thong are knotted together. All edges folded or cut–none stitched–part of sheath?/belt? Conserved.
A8634b; L0038; C2462C-3; M1.3; Phase IIi; Rig VI
Illus 159

875 Sole Leather

Fragment of left sole, with rounded forepart and front of waist. Edge-flesh stitching channel; stitch length 5mm 5.5mm, 6mm, 6.5mm. Very worn, with large hole. Surviving length 155mm; maximum width90 mm. Thickness: worn edge of forepart 0.75mm; worn edge at waist 1.5mm; outer edge of waist, rear of outer edge of forepart 3.5mm; inner edge of waist, rear of inner edge of forepart, middle of outer edge of forepart 4mm; middle and front of inner edge of forepart, front of outer edge of forepart 5mm. Matches Upper (Type Kiv) Cat No 878/A8665e. Conserved.
A8665b; L1692; C2462C-3; M1.3; Phase IIi; Rig VI
Not illustrated

878 Upper (Type Kiv) Leather (cattle hide)

Two fragments child's boot with central fastening. Larger comprises vamp, high vamp wing, vamp throat with no stitching, part of quarters, and latchet with cut edges and with horizontal slit. Smaller comprises small latchet attached to high vamp wing by butted edge–flesh stitching channel and with three cut edges. Tunnel hole and single hole, with thong end of toggle threaded through and thus anchored. Head of toggle through slit in first latchet. Lasting margin with grain–flesh stitching channel; stitch length 5–6.5mm. Edge–flesh stitching channel; stitch length 2.5–3.5mm, on vamp wing, second latchet, and on vertical edge of quarters. Thickness 2.5mm. Matching Sole Cat No 875/A8665b. Conserved. 13th–14th centuries.
A8665e; L1692; C2462C-3; M1.3; Phase IIi; Rig VI
Illus 143

897 Sole (Type 2) Leather (cattle hide)

Child's right sole with short wide seat, broad waist and forepart, fairly straight inner edge and gently curved outer edge, narrowing to a rounded toe. Worn, with crack in forepart and hole in centre of seat, and torn stitching channel at rear of seat. Edge–flesh stitching channel; stitch length 5mm, 4mm, 6mm, 6.5mm. Length 155mm; maximum width of forepart 70mm; width of waist 47mm; maximum width of seat 54mm. Thickness: outer and inner edges of waist and

rear of seat 2.5mm; outer edge of forepart 4.5mm; inner edge of forepart 3mm; worn edge of hole in seat 1mm. Matches Upper (Type Ai) Cat No 898/A11260b. Conserved. 12th–13th centuries.
A11260a; L0019; C2462C-3; M1.3; Phase IIi; Rig VI
Illus 124

898 Upper (Type Ai) Leather (cattle hide)

Fragments of child's high ankle boot with decorated vamp. Comprises vamp, vamp throat, vamp wing and quarters. Vamp wing and quarters do not appear to join; small fragment missing. Lasting margin with stitching channel of grain–flesh holes; stitch length 4–6.5mm. Edge–flesh stitching channels on vamp wing, throat, and vertical edge of quarters; stitch length 3–4mm. Rest of vamp throat, and vertical edge of leg flap, cut. Top edge of quarters oversewn, with very faint impression of top band. Vamp decorated with engraved line from throat to toe, and with two at right angles, across middle of vamp; scored with a blunt tool. Thickness 1mm. Conserved. 12th–13th centuries.
A11260b; L0019; C2642C-3; M1.3; Phase IIi; Rig VI
Illus 124

905 Miscellaneous fragment Leather (cattle hide)

Edge–flesh stitching channel; stitch length 3.5–4mm; hole diameter c1mm; other sides cut; approximately symmetrical; line down middle suggests it might have been folded, but with grain surfaces inwards. Slightly cracked and partially delaminated. Purpose– clothing? Length 204mm; height/width 106mm; thickness 2mm. Conserved.
A9366; L0077; C2597-3; M1.3; Phase IIi; Rig VI
Illus 159

916 Sole (Type 8) Leather

Seat, sewn across waist, with edge–flesh stitching channel; stitch length 3mm, 5mm, 5.5 mm. Edge–flesh stitching channel round rest of seat; stitch length 4–6.5 mm. Length 71mm; maximum width 70mm; width of waist seam 58mm. Thickness: waist seam 3mm; sides 3–4mm; rear 4–5mm. Joins Sole (Type 9) Cat No 917/A12490b, and both match Upper (Type Aii) 918/A12490c. Conserved. Upper: 12th–13th centuries.
A12490a; C4650-4; M1.3; Phase IIi; Rig VI
Not illustrated

917 Sole (Type 9) Leather (cattle hide)

Left forepart, sewn across waist, and with oval toe. Edge–flesh stitching stitch length 3.5–6.75mm. Partially delaminated. Length 171mm; maximum width 84mm; width at waist seam 49.5mm. Thickness 3–4mm. Matches Sole (Type 8) Cat No 916/A12490a and Upper (Type Aii) Cat No 918/A12490c. Conserved. Upper: 12th–13th centuries.
A12490b; C4650-4; M1.3; Phase IIi; Rig VI
Illus 123

918 Upper (Type Aii) Leather

Fragment of low ankle boot, with no trace of thongs. Comprises vamp, vamp throat, vamp wings and quarters, in one piece. Lasting margin has stitching channel of grain–flesh holes; stitch length 5–7mm. Edge–flesh stitching

channels on vamp throat, vamp wings and quarters; stitch length c3mm. Top edge of quarters oversewn. Slit on one side of quarters, possibly a deliberate cut for thong or lace. Cracked at front of vamp. Wide flap on each side, folded in to meet waist of sole. Matches Sole (Type 8) Cat No 916/A12490a and Sole (Type 9) Cat No 917/A12490b sewn together at waist. Conserved. 12th–13th centuries.
A12490c; C4650–4; M1.3; Phase IIi; Rig VI
Not illustrated

919 Sole (Type 2) Leather

Left, with long seat, wide waist and broad forepart, gently curved on both sides and ending in oval toe. Cracked across waist and across middle of forepart. Stitch holes indicate forepart repaired with clump sole. Edge–flesh stitching channel; stitch length 4–7.5mm. length 240mm; maximum width of forepart 95mm; width of waist 55mm; maximum width of seat 73mm. Thickness: inner edge of waist 2.5mm; outer edge of waist 2mm; rear and front of inner edge of forepart, front of outer edge of forepart 3.5mm; rear of outer edge of forepart 3mm; middle of outer edge of forepart and edge of seat 4mm; cracked edges of forepart and waist 1.5mm. Conserved. 13th–14th centuries.
A12536a; L2462; C4655–4; M1.3; Phase IIi; Rig VI
Illus 118

931 Upper (Type Biii) Leather (cattle hide)

Two fragments of boot with vertical and horizontal thonging. Larger consists of vamp with square hole near throat, vamp wing, vamp throat, quarters and leg flap. Hole may have been cut to relieve pressure on instep, or to hold decorative feature. Edges of hole are not sharply cut, but rounded, as if it had been rubbed. Smaller is side-piece linking quarters and vamp wing; no evidence for stiffener. Vertical thonging on closed side of upper with three short stretches of thong on grain side c7mm long, 5mm wide and 9mm apart. Five short fragments on flesh side, four in vertical line, bottom and top fragments horizontal, bottom fragment pointing towards vamp throat, top fragment towards quarters. Small round hole near top edge of quarters c60mm above uppermost fragment of thong on grain side. On smaller fragment; short piece of vertical thong with one stretch on grain side, length 4mm, width 5mm, three stretches on flesh side with upper horizontal line towards quarters and lower horizontal line towards vamp, probably connecting with horizontal thong on vamp wing–vamp throat, which passes along flesh side, emerging onto grain side through two small holes c37mm apart; thong is knotted on flesh side. Lasting margin with grain–flesh stitching channel; stitch length 5–6mm. Edge–flesh stitching channels; stitch length 2–6mm, on vamp wing, throat and quarters. Top edge of quarters and vertical top edges of leg flap oversewn. Conserved. 12th–13th centuries.
A12305; L0061; C3898–1; MC111; Phase IIb–IIIb; Rig VI
Illus 134

933 Sole (Type 2)? Leather

Right, large, with long seat, very slight narrowing for waist, and broad gently curved forepart ending in oval toe. Edge-flesh stitching channel; stitch length 5 - 6mm. Very worn and delaminated, with hole in seat and cracks in forepart.

Length 267mm; maximum width of forepart 100mm; width of waist 67mm; maximum width of seat 74mm. Thickness: inner edge of waist 5mm, elsewhere not measurable because of delamination. Matches Upper (Type Biii) Cat No 934/A03-0327b. Conserved.
A03-0327a; L2492; C9488-9; P8.0; Phase IIIa,IIIb; Rig VII
Not illustrated

934 Upper (Type Biii) Leather (cattle hide)

Two joining fragments of boot with one row of horizontal and three of vertical thonging. Larger fragment comprises vamp, vamp throat, vamp wing, quarters and leg flap. Quarters and vamp wing appear to join. Smaller fragment is second leg flap. Lasting margin with stitching channel of grain–flesh holes; stitch length 5–6mm. Edge–flesh stitching channels on vamp throat, wing, quarters and leg flaps; stitch length 5–6mm. Vertical stitching channel on quarters unusual in that along part of it grain has been folded inwards, forming an edge, with c5mm of grain folded inside. On flesh side of quarters, slight impression of semicircular stiffener. Top edges of quarters and leg flaps oversewn. The two fragments are linked by a horizontal thong and both have tunnel holes for vertical thonging with vertical thong surviving on larger fragment. Row of vertical thonging on closed side of quarters, with five short stretches of thong exposed on grain side– single oval hole beside thong– between top stretch and top of quarters. Two vertical rows of tunnel holes for thongs on smaller fragment– two tunnel holes with single hole at each end; second row continues on to vamp throat with one tunnel hole spanning join– suggesting holes made after shoe stitched together. Long horizontal thong emerging from flesh side of smaller fragment, where knotted– evidently once secured by lowest stretch of vertical thong, and still secured by lowest stretch of vertical thong on quarters, passes behind quarters, knotted to another fragment of thong. Matches Sole (Type 2) Cat No 933/A03–0327a. Conserved. 12th–13th centuries.
A03–0327b; L2492; C9488–9; P8.0; Phase IIIa,IIIb; Rig VII
Illus 134

970 Sole (Type 8) Leather (cattle hide)

Seat, with edge–flesh stitching channel across waist. Holes on underneath suggest repair clump was added. Delaminated. Edge–flesh stitching channel; stitch length 3.5–4.75mm, very neat; maximum length 79.5mm; maximum width 66mm; width at waist seam 57mm; thickness c4mm, but delaminated. Probably matches Sole (Type 9) Cat No 971/A11261b. Conserved.
A11261a; C2265–4; MC116; Phase IIe–IIIc; Rig V
Illus 123

971 Sole (Type 9) Leather

Left forepart with rounded toe, and trace of stitching channel across waist. Very delaminated. Edge–flesh stitching channel 4.5–6mm. Length 158.5mm; maximum width 78mm; width at waist seam 52mm (possibly c55mm before worn); thickness 5.5mm. Probably matches Sole (Type 8) Cat No 970/A11261a. Conserved.
A11261b; C2265–4; MC116; Phase IIe–IIIc; Rig V
Illus 123

1009 Miscellaneous fragment Leather
Approximately rectangular, 340mm by 235mm, 1mm thick, with stitching channel of very small grain–flesh holes on the three surviving straight edges; stitch length 4.5–5mm. On longest side, five other rows of stitching, parallel to edge: first row c15mm from edge, second 12mm from first, third c5mm from second, fourth c10mm from third and fifth c6mm from fourth. Thread and leather appear to have been gathered along these six rows of stitching. Leather cracked and delaminated, with large part of rectangle missing. Fragment of clothing? Conserved.
A8008; L0044; C2234–4; M1.4a(a); Phase IIIa–IIIc; Rig VI
Illus 162

1035 Sole (Type 3) Leather
Left, long with slender seat and waist and wider forepart, ending in oval toe. Very worn and delaminated, missing part of stitching channel and with holes in forepart. Edge–flesh stitching channel; stitch length 5.5–7mm. Maximum surviving length 259mm; maximum width of forepart 88mm; width of waist 42mm; maximum width of seat 68mm. Thickness: rear of inner edge of forepart 4mm; rear of inner edge of seat 4.5mm. The rest too delaminated. Conserved. 13th–14th centuries.
A8009a; L1726; C2527B–3;MC117, Pit 4695; Phase IIe–IIIc; Rig V
Illus 119

1042 Sole (Type 4) Leather (cattle hide)
Left, with pointed forepart. Worn with crack separating rear of seat from rest of sole. Crack in centre forepart and two at great toe area. Part of stitching channel missing. Edge–flesh stitching channel; stitch length 5–7.5mm, 5mm being most common. Maximum length 240mm; maximum width of forepart 82mm; width of waist 51mm; maximum width of seat 66mm. Thickness: inner edge of forepart 2.5mm; elsewhere 3mm. Conserved. 13th–14th centuries.
A8546; C2527B-3; MC117, Pit 4695; Phase IIe–IIIc; Rig V
Illus 121

1057 Strap (folded twice) Leather
Long, folded twice, edges joined with butted edge to grain stitching channel; stitch length 6–7mm. Length 1075mm; maximum width 58mm, tapering towards both ends. One end cut, with smooth rounded edges, width 20mm; the other, width 27mm, has edge–flesh stitching channel; stitch length 3–4mm, suggesting it was joined to another fragment before being folded. Wide part of strap decorated with two parallel stitching channels of short grain–flesh slits; stitch length 2–3mm. These stitching channels form two ovals and appear on both sides of fragment. No thread survives but probably stitched for decorative effect. Strap pierced at cut end by four round holes, diameter c3mm and c60mm, 100mm and 40mm apart for pin of buckle. Irregular spacing of holes suggests that these were made when they were required. Part of harness? Support for weaponry? Possibly part of horse tack, eg girth, but edge–flesh stitching channel would have been a weak point. Perhaps elaborate belt. Conserved.
A10623; C4544–4; MC117, Pit 4695; Phase IIe–IIIc; Rig V
Illus 153

1061 Strap/belt (single thickness) Leather (cattle hide)
Fragment, 210mm long, 18–25.5mm wide, formed of single thickness of leather (2mm). Perforated by five round holes, diameter c5mm and 37mm, 36.5mm, 38mm, and 32.5mm apart (edge to edge). Also perforated by channels of short slits, c3mm long and 4–5mm apart (edge to edge). Channels not exactly parallel with edges; at thinner end converging on and encircling last hole: at wider end perforated by channel of smaller slits or holes c1mm long and 2.5mm, 3.5mm and 4mm apart. Short cracks radiate from each of the five holes, suggesting wear from pin of buckle. Probably complete. Conserved.
A9554a; L1719; C4564–4; MC117, Pit 4695; Phase IIe–IIIc; Rig V
Illus 151

1062 Strap/belt (single thickness) Leather
Fragment, of single thickness, c117mm long, 30mm wide and 1mm thick. Very cracked, perforated by two round holes, diameter 5mm, 34mm apart, and by two channels of short (2mm) slashes c5mm apart. Conserved.
A9554b; L1719; C4564–4; MC117, Pit 4695; Phase IIe–IIIc; Rig V
Illus 151

1086 Miscellaneous fragment with metalwork Leather and Fe
Very small scrap with small iron buckle still attached; see Fascicule 2, The metalwork, Iron Cat No 17 (322). Conserved.
A03-0278a; L1061; C9439-9; B19 (Phase 2b), North Room–Floor (2b); Phase IIIc; Rig VII
Not illustrated

1089 Upper Leather (cattle hide)
Irregularly shaped fragment. Lasting margin with stitching channel of grain–flesh holes; stitch length 7.5mm. Three edge–flesh stitching channels; stitch length 4.5–6mm. One edge with grain–flesh holes, apparently hem stitch; thread remains in two holes. Unusual vertical stitching channel, central rib with grain–flesh holes on either side–implies leather folded tightly inwards and stitched through both layers, forming stiff rib–decorative effect for quarters? Thickness 2mm.
A03–0278d; L1369; C9439–9; B19 (Phase 2b), North Room–Floor (2b); Phase IIIc; Rig VII
Illus 144

1103 Sole (Type 2) Leather (cattle hide)
Left, with wide straight seat, part of which now folded over, wide waist, long forepart with oval toe. Worn, especially forepart with crack in front and large hole in centre; stitch holes indicate crack, but not central hole, repaired with clump sole, ie central hole indicates secondary wear. Partially delaminated. Edge–flesh stitching channel; stitch length 6.5–10mm. Length 256.5mm; maximum width of forepart 86.5mm; width of waist 60.5mm; appropriate maximum width of seat 76mm. Thickness: inner and outer edges of waist 3.5mm; inner edge of forepart 4.5mm; outer edge of forepart 4mm. Matches two fragments of Upper (Type Dii) Cat No 1105/A03–0287c and Rand Cat No 1104/A03–0287b. Conserved. 12th–14th centuries (upper: 13th–15th centuries).
A03–0287a; L1377; C9447–9; P8.1c; Phase IIIc; Rig VII
Illus 137

1104 Rand Leather
Fragment, stitch length 8mm, 9mm, 11 mm. Probably
matches Sole (Type 2) Cat No 1103/A03-0287a. Conserved.
A03-0287b; L1377; C9447-9; P8.1c; Phase IIIc; Rig VII
Not illustrated

1105 Upper (Type Dii) Leather (cattle hide)
Two fragments, almost certainly from same shoe. One
fragment consists of side-piece, joining sole on inner side,
at waist and front of seat, oblique split for side lacing,
each edge oversewn, four tie holes on each side, tunnel
stitching for facing or strengthener parallel to holes. The
other fragment is also side-piece, joining sole at outer waist.
Lasting margin on both fragments; grain–flesh stitching
channels; stitch length 6.5–9.5mm. Edge–flesh stitching
channels on second vertical edge of both fragments; stitch
length 2.5–5mm. Top edges of both cut. Thickness 3mm.
Matches Sole (Type 2) Cat No 1103/A03–0287a. Conserved.
13th–14th centuries
A03–0287c; L1377; C9447–9; P8.1c; Phase IIIc; Rig VII
Illus 137

1116 Sheath Leather (cattle hide)
Plain, constructed from single fragment of leather folded
once and sewn with a thong c4.5mm wide and c1mm thick.
Upper part is wider and is sewn with second, thinner, thong.
Worn, cracked and delaminated. Length 198mm; maximum
width 47mm; thickness, single, c0.75mm. Conserved.
A9889; L1710; C2606–3; M6a; Phase IIg–IIId; Rig VI
Illus 154

1145 Upper (Type Ai) Leather (cattle hide)
Almost complete upper, in three fragments, of high ankle
boot with no thongs or holes for thongs. First fragment
comprises vamp, vamp throat, vamp wing, quarters and part
of leg flap; vamp wing and quarters possibly join. Second
fragment, approximately triangular, joins top of quarter. Third
fragment is second leg flap. Lasting margin with grain–flesh
stitching channel; stitch length c5mm. Edge–flesh stitching
channel on vamp wing, vamp throat and vertical edges of
quarters and leg flap; stitch length 2.5–3.5mm. Top edge of
quarters oversewn. Thickness c0.5–1.5mm; leg flap 1.5mm;
second leg flap 1.5–2mm. Impression of stiffener on flesh
side of quarters. Conserved. 12th–14th centuries.
A4817b; C3549–1; M12; Phase IIg–IIIc(–IVa); Rig V
Illus 127 (reconstruction)

1214 Miscellaneous fragment with metalwork
Leather and Cu alloy
Strip, folded once, grain side outwards; both ends torn, one
long edge cut, other possibly torn (but this edge incomplete).
Part of larger object? Perforated by two parallel rows of
holes, c1.5 mm diameter, and 4.5, 5, 5.5mm apart; holes for
metal rivets of which 23 out of a possible 71 survive. Rivets
have heads of Cu alloy (see Fascicule 2, The metalwork,
Non-ferrous Cat No 83). Length c175mm; width (single/
folded) 15–18mm; thickness (single) 2mm. Conserved.
A9104; C2583-3; M6b; Phase IIg–IIId; Rig V
Not illustrated

1224 Sheath (decorated) Leather (cattle hide)
Small, decorated, with projecting upper part. Now in two
parts, joined together. Almost complete. Constructed from
a single piece of leather; upper part, height 60mm, folded
once, edges stitched together from reverse; lower part tapers,
folded twice, with edges meeting in middle of reverse, where
joined with butted edge to grain seam; stitch length c5mm.
Sheath ends in a narrow point, 6mm wide, 4mm thick, held
together by the stitching of the middle seam. Top end cut,
with no stitch holes. On upper part of reverse, pair of holes
for attachment to belt or other article. Decoration: front, upper
part, three horizontal rows, each with two shield or U-shaped
motif, all enclosed within a rectangle. Front, lower part, simple
curvilinear design– debased acanthus scroll– enclosed in
long narrow oblong. Reverse, upper part, two approximately
vertical lines with diagonal scorings. All decorations marked
out with shallow lines, c0.75mm wide, made with a blunt tool.
Length 149mm; width at top 33.5mm; width at base 6mm;
thickness at top 3mm. Conserved. 13th century.
A8183; C2247–4; MC120a; Phase IIh–IVa; Rig V
Illus 155

1228 Miscellaneous fragment with metalwork
Leather and metal (unspecified)
Approximately rectangular; each short edge folded once
and fastened with short nails, c9mm long, with domed
head, diameter c5mm; three nails survive, two broken, one
appears to be complete. The heads are on the grain side of
the article. Nail holes are c4–5mm apart; where nails are
missing, impressions of them are visible. One half of fragment
perforated repeatedly in three, possibly four, places–hard
to distinguish between deliberate perforation and wear–
decoration? Fragment very frail and worn, turned edges cut,
long tear down middle, long edges torn. Thickness 1.5mm.
Conserved.
A8687a; C2247–4; MC120a; Phase IIh–IVa/39–51; Rig V
Illus 164

1287 and 1288 Upper (Type Di) Leather (cattle hide)
Two fragments of shoe with side lacing. Larger (No 1287)
comprises vamp, vamp wings, vamp throat, latchets and
quarters; on closed side of quarters/vamp wing vertical row
of very neat tunnel stitching, tunnels only 3–3.5mm apart,
forming slight rib–to hold lining? Smaller (No 1288) is
approximately rectangular side-piece, linking quarters and
vamp wing. Two matching vertical rows of thong holes on
vertical edges of vamp wing and side-piece. Four or five
holes on vamp wing, adjacent edge oversewn, faint trace of
tunnel stitching for strengthener on flesh side, three holes
on side-piece, adjacent edge oversewn, tunnel stitching for
strengthener on flesh side. Lasting margin with grain–flesh
stitching channel; stitch length 6mm. Edge–flesh stitching
channels on vamp throat, diagonal edge of quarters, vertical
edge of latchet and on side-piece; stitch length 3–4mm.
Top edges of latchet, vamp wing, quarters and side-piece
oversewn. Thong links the two fragments: threaded through
holes, loosely knotted on grain side, passes to slit on larger
fragment, higher up, and c20–25mm from edge, knotted on
flesh side. Clumsy repair. Shoe very worn, particularly vamp,
with irregular slits. However, these may have originally been

part of openwork decoration. Side-piece is minus lasting margin. Thickness 1.5mm. Conserved. 13th–14th centuries.
A6415c, d; L1732; C2528–3; P2.2b; Phase IVa; Rig V
Illus 136

1310 Upper (Type J) Leather
Vamp of shoe, with rounded throat, and edge–flesh stitching channels on both sides of vamp wing and at throat; stitch length 2.3mm. Lasting margin with stitching channel of grain–flesh holes; stitch length 3.5–4mm. Very worn and partially delaminated. Thickness c2mm. Conserved.
A6377; L1688; C2536–3; P2.2b; IVa; Rig V
Illus 140

1314 Sole (Type 3) Leather (cattle hide)
Left, with seat which is straight on outer edge, slightly curved on inner and rear edges, slight narrowing for waist, wide forepart, almost straight on inner edge, curved on outer edge. Rounded toe. Edge–flesh stitching channel; stitch length 5mm. Stitch holes on underside indicate both seat and forepart repaired with clump soles. Hole up centre of sole. Length of hole 183mm; maximum width 23mm, pointed at each end. Edge–flesh stitching channel up each edge; stitch length 3–4mm. Sole made up of two pieces? Repair? Forepart worn and thin, particularly on left side of stitched hole, with three holes. Length 239mm; maximum width of forepart 98.4mm; width of waist 61.5mm; maximum width of seat 65mm. Thickness: inner edge of waist, seat, rear of inner edge of forepart 4mm; outer edge of waist and seat, rear and front of outer edge of forepart 3.5mm; middle of outer edge of forepart 4.25mm; middle of both edges of stitched hole 2mm; worn edge of forepart 0.25mm. Conserved. 13th–14th centuries.
A7989a; L1751; C2203–4; MC143; Phase IVa; Rig V
Illus 120

1360 Sheath (decorated) Leather (cattle hide)
Fragment, engraved with a blunt tool and punched with a hollow tool. Construction: made from single fragment of leather folded once, edges probably joined with grain–flesh seam, of which only a few stitches remain, as most of outer edge is missing, worn and cracked. Projecting upper part approximately rectangular when complete, lower part tapers to a point. A few stitch holes remain on projecting edge of rectangular section: stitch length c6mm. A few stitch holes also survive on lower section: stitch length 9–10mm. Decoration: upper and lower sections of front decorated with diamond pattern, each diamond filled with a round hole, apparently punched with a hollow tool. Diamonds c4mm by 4mm, holes diameter c1.5mm. The sections of diamond patterns are bordered by engraved straight lines, and between the upper and lower sections are two horizontal lines. On either side of upper section are panels with bands of four diagonal strokes with c1.5mm between each stroke and 7–9mm between each band; each panel c6mm wide. To right of right-hand panel of upper section is zone with continuous zigzag and edge of second zigzag pattern. At top of lower section, edge of three horizontal lines to right of diamond pattern. Lower section of reverse decorated with vertical panel of oblique strokes c2.5–3.5mm apart,

on left hand side; right hand side plain except for a few oblique strokes, continuation of chevrons on left hand side of diamond pattern on front. Most of grain side missing from reverse, but some remains with decoration; three horizontal lines, continuation of those bordering and beneath upper section of diamond pattern on front. Above this are another two vertical lines, whose impression also visible on flesh layer. To right of vertical lines, three bands of four slightly concave oblique lines c1.5mm between lines and 5–8mm between bands. Very worn, cracked and delaminated. Length 137.5mm; maximum width 46mm. Conserved. 13th–14th centuries.
cf Kings Lynn, diamonds enclosing punched holes, mid-13th to mid-14th century (Clarke and Carter 1977, 364–6, fig 169, 91)
A8002; L1772; C2237–4; MC143; Phase IVaa; Rig V
Illus 156

1361 Sole (Type 5) Leather (cattle hide)
Right, with long slender seat, very narrow waist, wide forepart ending in point. Edge–flesh stitching channel; stitch length 4mm. Length 213.5mm; width of forepart 79mm; width of waist 20mm; maximum width of seat 49mm. Thickness: outer and inner edges of waist, outer edge of seat, outer edge of forepart 2.5mm; inner edge of forepart and seat 3mm. Conserved. 13th–15th centuries.
A8007a; L1772; C2237–4; MC143; IVaa; Rig V
Illus 122

1362 Upper (Type Di/J) Leather (cattle hide)
Vamp of low shoe, lasting margin missing, separate from quarters, and with row of five tie holes on one vamp wing– hence types Di and J. Diameter of holes 1.5mm, and 7mm, 10mm, 9mm, 9mm apart. Edge parallel to holes oversewn. On flesh side, tunnel stitching for strengthener. Edge–flesh stitching channels on second vamp wing, vamp throat and vertical edge of latchet; stitch length 2.5mm. Top edge of latchet oversewn. Thickness 1.5mm. Conserved. 13th–14th centuries.
A8007b; L1772; C2237–4; MC143; Phase IVaa; Rig V
Illus 136

1430 Miscellaneous fragment Leather
Very tattered and torn, with hem stitching along four edges and two parallel rows of tunnel stitch holes. Similar to Miscellaneous fragment Cat No 1431/A6187f. Very worn. Thickness 0.75mm. Clothing? Conserved.
A6187e; L1655; C2215–4; MC156; IVaa; Rig V
Illus 162

1431 Miscellaneous fragment Leather
Two joining fragments with five rows of stitches, very torn and tattered, partially delaminated. Clothing? Conserved.
A6187f; L1655; C2215–4; MC156; IVaa; Rig V
Illus 164

1568 Miscellaneous fragment Leather
Short, with one long edge folded over and stitched down with hem stitch, other edges torn. Length 104mm; width 45–48mm; width of hem 13mm; thickness c1.5mm. Clothing?

Conserved.
A03–0423a; L2328; C7363–7; MC130; Phase <IIIc–IVaa;
Rig VII
Illus 160

1569 Miscellaneous fragment Leather
Short, with one long edge folded over and stitched down with
hem stitch, other edges torn. Length 190mm; width 37–47mm;
width of hem 13–15mm; thickness 1.5mm. Clothing? Conserved.
A03–0423b; L2328; C7363–7; MC130; Phase <IIIc–IVaa;
Rig VII
Illus 160

1570 Miscellaneous fragments (2) Leather
Two, with narrow hems. A03–0423c) Long strip, with one long
edge folded over and stitched down with hem stitch, leaving
scalloped impression on flesh side. One short edge also folded
over and stitched down. Second long edge cut. Second short
edge torn. Length 215mm; maximum width 25mm; width of hems
6–7mm; thickness 1mm. A03–0425d) Worn and delaminated,
with one long and one short edge folded over and stitched down
with hem stitch. Second long edge cut, second short edge torn.
Length 181mm; maximum width 60mm; width of folded edge
6–8mm; thickness 1mm. Clothing? Conserved.
A03–0423c,d; L2328; C7363–7; MC130; Phase <IIIc–IVaa;
Rig VII
Illus 163

1692 Miscellaneous fragment with metalwork
Leather, wood and Cu alloy
Irregular, folded once, with grain surfaces exposed on both sides.
Row of nine copper alloy rivets parallel with folded edge and
c3mm from it. Heads of six rivets and shaft of one survive in
situ, a seventh head and a shaft survive separately. Rivets pass
through small, approximately round, grain–flesh holes c4–5mm
apart. A further 26 holes are now without their rivets (originally 35
rivets). Fragment incomplete; is nailed to wooden object and was
folded in order to give neat edge. Leather on underneath side
cut leaving a regular edge–probably in order not to waste leather
which could have been used elsewhere. Thickness c1.5mm. Conserved. (see Fascicule 2, The metalwork, Non-ferrous Cat No 84).
A5124; C2510–3; B3(South), Pit 2529; Phase IVa,IVaa; Rig V
Not illustrated

1752 Sole (Type 2) Leather
Two joining fragments, very worn, probably right foot, with broad
seat, waist and forepart, ending in oval toe. Particularly worn at
rear of seat, outer edge of waist and forepart, and in centre of
forepart, where large hole now separates sole into two fragments.
Stitch holes on underside indicate forepart repaired with clump
sole. Slight delamination at rear of seat. Edge–flesh stitching
channel; stitch length 5–6.5mm. Length 246.5mm; maximum
width of forepart 103mm; width of waist 61mm; maximum width
of seat 73mm. Thickness: outer edge of waist 3mm; rear and
outer edge of forepart 4mm; front of outer edge of forepart
4.5mm; rear and front of inner edge of forepart, seat 5mm;
torn edge of forepart 1.5mm. Conserved. 12th–14th centuries.
A03–0350a; C7336–7; MC126, Pit 7402; Phase IVaa,IVb; Rig VII
Illus 118

1754 Sole (Type 3) Leather
Right, very worn, with wide seat, slightly narrower waist and
long gently curved forepart, with oval toe. Hole in seat and
three holes in forepart, partially delaminated. Stitch holes on
underside indicate seat repaired with clump sole. Edge–flesh
stitching channel; stitch length 4.5–7mm. Length 254mm;
maximum width of forepart 89mm; width of waist 52mm;
maximum width of seat 74mm. Thickness: outer edge of waist
3.5mm; inner edge of waist, inner edge of seat 4mm. Rest
delaminated. Conserved. 13th–14th centuries.
A03–0350c; C7336–7; MC126, Pit 7402; Phase IVaa,IVb; Rig VII
Illus 119

1804 Sole (Type 4), upper (Type Di) and thong
Leather (cattle hide)
Left sole with long thin seat; narrow waist and slender gently
curved forepart, ending in pointed toe; upper now attached by
thong. Edge–flesh stitching channel; stitch length 4–5mm. Seat
very worn, with large hole; part of stitching channel missing. Inner
front of forepart worn very thin, stitching channel replaced by
two holes and thong. Length 230mm; maximum width of forepart
82mm; width of waist 36.5mm; maximum surviving width of seat
54mm. Thickness inner edge of waist, outer edge of seat, rear
of outer edge of forepart 2.5mm; outer edge of waist 2mm; inner
edge of seat, rear of inner edge of forepart 3mm; middle of outer
edge of forepart 3.5mm; front of outer edge of forepart 4mm;
middle of inner edge of forepart 1.5mm; front of inner edge of
forepart 1mm; worn edge of seat 0.25mm. Upper comprises
vamp, vamp wing and quarters; side-piece c30mm wide missing.
Lasting margin with grain–flesh stitching channel; stitch length
4–5mm. Mostly cut away above lasting margin possibly for reuse.
Quarters with stitch holes for small triangular stiffener; long
diagonal edge, oversewn, with five tie-holes, row of tunnel stitch
holes on flesh side for facing or strengthener. Edge–flesh
stitching channels on quarters and vamp wing; stitch length
2.5–3mm. Inner edge of vamp attached to forepart of sole by
8mm wide thong, which passes through a slit in vamp and one
in forepart; knotted by being passed through a slit in itself.
Another slit in forepart, two more in vamp. Repair/replacement
of worn edge–flesh stitching channel. Conserved. 13th–14th
centuries.
A03–0367a; L2323; C7336–7; MC126, Pit 7402; Phase IVaa,IVb;
Rig VII
Illus 145

1805 Miscellaneous fragment Leather
Approximately oblong, with three oversewn edges, and one
cut or cracked edge. Maximum length 103mm; maximum width
96mm; thickness c1.5–2mm. Clothing? Conserved.
A03–0367b; L2323; C7336–7; MC126, Pit 7402; Phase
IVaa,IVb; Rig VII
Illus 159

1826 Miscellaneous fragment Leather
Small, approximately triangular. One short straight edge
c125mm long, stitched with pairs of holes 5mm apart, holes
6mm apart. Slightly curved edge also stitched with pairs of
holes 6mm apart, slightly gathered, holes 3–4mm apart. Third
edge slightly irregular and probably rand; parallel to it, four
rows of stitching 18mm, 41mm, 35mm apart, with pairs of holes

c15mm apart, holes 2mm apart. Thickness c1.5mm. Clothing?
Conserved.
A03–0376a; L2337; C7336–7; MC126, Pit 7402; Phase
IVaa,IVb; Rig VII
Illus 161

1827 Miscellaneous fragment Leather
Large, irregular in shape. One long edge, 415mm, has pairs
of grain–flesh stitch holes c8–10mm apart, holes 6mm apart,
parts of edge now folded over. Parallel to and c180mm from
this edge is an edge 183mm long also stitched with pairs
of holes 6mm apart, holes 4mm apart, thread has been
pulled, gathering leather together. Parallel edges joined on
one side by curved edge, again stitched with pairs of holes
c5mm apart, holes c6mm apart. Fourth, irregular, edge torn
or cut? Between the two parallel edges is a line of pairs of
holes 14–16mm apart, holes 3–5mm apart, parallel to shorter
edge and c65mm from it. Another line of stitching occurs
parallel with long edge, then curves up to join other line of
stitching–pairs of holes, but irregular and holes very small. A
line of pairs of holes c7mm apart, holes c4mm apart, at right
angles to long edge, probably joins curved edge which is
torn. A line of three pairs of holes c18mm apart, holes c2mm
apart, occurs in angle between long edge and curved edge.
Thickness c1.5mm. Clothing? Conserved.
A03–0376b; L2237; C7336–7; MC126, Pit 7402; Phase
IVaa,IVb; Rig VII
Illus 161

1991 Sole (Type 3) Leather
Right, slender, with pointed oval toe. Edge–flesh stitching
channel; stitch length 5–6mm. Worn and partially
delaminated, with holes in seat. Length 248mm; maximum
width of forepart 87mm; width of waist 38mm; maximum width
of seat 69mm. Thickness: inner edge of forepart 2.5mm;
outer edge of forepart 4mm; rear of seat 4.5mm. Conserved.
13th–14th centuries.
A03–0362a; L2489; C7342–7; MC126, Pit 7402; Phase
IVaa,IVb; Rig VII
Illus 119

2181 Sole (Type 7) Leather
Left, fragment with long rounded seat, very narrow waist and
gently curved forepart, turned inwards slightly. Cut across
front of tread, with worn stitching channel of edge–flesh
holes; stitch length 4.5mm, 6.5mm: possibly a repair seam.
Edge–flesh stitching channel round rest of sole; stitch length
4mm, 5mm, 6.5,mm 6mm, 7mm. Slight delamination at outer
edge of waist. Crack across middle of seat, thin strip missing.
Short crack on inside edge of forepart. Rear and front of
outer edge of forepart worn. Several shallow cuts in centre of
waist and forepart, and on either side of missing slit in seat.
A few holes on underside suggest seat repaired with clump
sole. Maximum surviving length 226mm; maximum width
of forepart 88mm; width of waist 34mm; maximum width of
seat 68mm. Thickness: inner edge of waist and rear of inner
edge of forepart, outer edge of seat, rear and middle of outer
edge of forepart 4mm; inner edge of seat, rear and middle of
outer edge of forepart 4mm; inner edge of seat, front of inner
edge of forepart 3.5mm; sewn edge across tread and front

of outer edge of forepart 2mm; worn edge of seat 1.5mm.
Conserved.
A03–0385a; L2334; C7342–7; MC126, Pit 7402; Phase
IVaa,IVb; Rig VII
Illus 123

2272 Miscellaneous fragment Leather (cattle hide)
Worn and completely delaminated triangular fragment
(grain and flesh layers completely separate) with two long
cut edges meeting in a point. Third edge torn, but part of
it may be cut. Grain–flesh slits parallel with long edges,
perforating both layers; slits c4–5mm from edge, and
4mm long and c3mm apart end to end, 5–6mm centre to
centre. Grain layer decorated with small circles, diameter
3mm, made with a hollow punch. Maximum length 105mm;
maximum width 64mm. Thickness: flesh layer 2.5mm;
grain layer 1mm. Conserved.
A03–0426b; L2499; C7342–7; MC126, Pit 7402; Phase
IVaa,IVb; Rig VII
Illus 158

2274 Miscellaneous fragment Leather (sheepskin)
Large, irregular, c280mm by 350mm, one straight edge
with grain–flesh stitching holes, but scalloped edge
suggests it has been oversewn. Stitching channel shiny–
like lasting margin–covered by binding? Another, irregular,
edge with stitching, part of it folded over, as if for hem.
Between these stitched edges are widely spaced rows
of stitching channels of grain–flesh holes; stitch length
c10–20mm; five such rows parallel with regular stitched
edge c50–60mm apart; two short rows at right angles to
these. Also three other rows, approximately parallel with
first five, but closer together, c11–13mm apart. Fragment
very worn and torn, c1mm thick. Possibly two tunnel holes.
Clothing? Conserved.
A03–0411a; L2319; C7338–7; MC146, Pit 7339; Phase
<IVb; Rig VII
Illus 162

2303 Upper (Type Di) Leather (cattle hide)
Fragment of shoe with part of vamp, vamp throat with
small latchet, low quarters, ending in diagonal edge with
row of five tie holes. Edge itself has been oversewn.
Interior very worn, no trace of tunnel holes for stiffener or
facing. Lasting margin with stitching channel of grain–flesh
holes; stitch length 6mm, 6.5mm, 7mm, 7.5mm. Top
edge oversewn. Edge–flesh stitching channel at vamp
throat; stitch length 3.5mm. Thickness 1mm. Conserved.
13th–14th centuries.
A03–0276d; L1367; C7294–7; M1.4f; Phase IVc; Rig VI
Illus 136

2307 Miscellaneous fragment Leather
Long and narrow, with approximately vertical row of 21
holes, mostly in pairs. Single hole and two pairs in middle
of fragment. Edge parallel to holes probably oversewn.
Two edge–flesh stitching channels; stitch length 3mm.
Thickness 1mm. Clothing? Conserved.
A03–0279d; L1370; C7294–7; M1.4f; Phase IVc; Rig VI
Illus 160

2312 Strap (folded twice) Leather (cattle hide)
Fragment, formed of strip of leather folded twice, edges meeting in centre of reverse at one end and stitched together in a butted edge to grain seam; stitch length c4.5mm. Join of edges slants towards one edge, and at other end the two edges are face to face. Several holes in centre of front of strap, through some of which a thong, c5mm wide and c2mm thick, passes. Row of slits parallel to each edge of strap, on both sides. Length 223mm; width, folded, 20mm; thickness, unfolded, 3mm. Very worn and cracked. Conserved.
A03–0280; L1371; C7294–7; M1.4f; Phase IVc; Rig VI
Illus 150

2333 Sole (Type 3) Leather
Right, with rounded seat, fairly narrow waist and wide forepart ending in oval toe. Very worn, with holes in seat and forepart, both of which repaired with clump soles. Edge–flesh stitching channel; stitch length 4.5–6mm. Length 257mm; maximum width of forepart 98mm; width of waist 46mm; maximum width of seat 73mm. Thickness: outer edge of waist 2mm; inner edge of waist 2.5mm; rear of outer edge of forepart 3mm; rear of seat 5.5mm; front of inner edge of forepart 6mm. Matches Upper Cat No 2337/A03–0291e. Conserved. 13th–14th centuries.
A03–0291a; L1738; C7294–7; M1.4f; Phase IVc; Rig VI
Illus 147

2337 Upper Leather (cattle hide)
Large fragment, comprising vamp, vamp wing and quarters. Lasting margin with stitching channels of grain–flesh holes; stitch length 4.5–6.5mm. Vamp wing and quarters joined with butted edge–flesh stitching channel; stitch length 2.5mm. Upper very worn and patched in three places, remainder appears to have been cut away, probably for re-use. Thickness 1.5–3mm. Matches Sole (Type 3) Cat No 2333/A03–0291a. Conserved. Sole: 13th–14th centuries.
A03–0291e; L1738; C7294–7; M1.4f; Phase IVc; Rig VI
Illus 147

2338 Sole (Type 3)? Leather
Left, long with seat, narrow waist and slender forepart, gently curved. Probably oval toe but end missing. Worn, especially on inner side of forepart and at rear of seat, partially delaminated. Surviving length 262mm; maximum width of forepart 89mm; width of waist 46mm; maximum width of seat 73mm. Thickness: worn edges 0.75mm; inner edge of forepart 2.5mm; inner edge of seat, outer edge of forepart 3.5mm; rear and outer edge of seat 4mm. Underside bears faint impression of checked pattern. Conserved. 13th–14th centuries.
A03–0308a; L1392; C7326–7; M1.4f; Phase IVc; Rig VI
Not illustrated

2361 Sole (Type 2)? rand and upper Leather and wool
Left sole with two fragments of rand and large fragment of upper still attached. Sole with seat tapering towards rear, wide waist and broad rounded forepart, narrowing to an oval toe. Edge–flesh stitching channel; stitch length 5–6.5mm. Worn, particularly centre forepart; wool survives in many stitch holes. Two fragments of rand still attached to waist and to rear of inner edge of forepart and to front of forepart, second fragment is bent over front of vamp, thus protecting it. Upper

comprises vamp, vamp wing and quarters joined. Lasting margin with grain–flesh stitching channel; stitch length 5–6.5mm. Edge–flesh stitching channels on vertical edge of quarters and vamp wing; stitch length 2–3mm. Top edges of quarters and vamp wing oversewn–high shoe, not boot. Stitch holes mark position of triangular stiffener. Length of sole 240mm; maximum width of forepart 90mm; width of waist 62mm; maximum width of seat 68mm. Conserved. 12th–13th centuries?
A03–0331a; L2326; C7326–7; M1.4f; Phase IVc; Rig VI
Illus 146

2486–2488 Upper (Type Ai) Leather (cattle hide)
Three fragments of high ankle boot, probably a child's, with no thongs or holes for thongs. No 2486/A03–0392h, large fragment comprises vamp, vamp wing, vamp throat, quarters and leg flap. On flesh side of quarters, impression of triangular stiffener, with trace of stitch holes. No 2487/A03–0392i, lower side-piece, fitting between vamp wing and quarters. No 2488/A03–0392j, side-piece fitting above Cat No 2487/A03–0392i, lasting margin with grain–flesh stitching channel; stitch length 5–7.5mm. Edge–flesh stitching channels on vamp wing, vamp throat, diagonal edge of quarters, on part of top edge of quarters and on both side-pieces; stitch length 3.5–4.5mm. Part of top edge of quarters oversewn. Probably missing higher fragment(s). Small triangular stiffener with lasting margin and two oversewn edges. Conserved. 12th–13th centuries.
A03–0392h-j; L2332; C7335–7; M1.4f; Phase IVc; Rig VI
Illus 128

2514 Belt/strap (single thickness) Leather (cattle hide)
Three fragments of belt of single thickness (2mm). Two join, combined length 490mm; width 45–50mm, two lines of short diagonal slits parallel to each edge; row of seven round holes in centre, hole diameter c5mm, and c35mm, 40mm, 55mm apart (centre to centre). One end of one fragment is perforated by oval holes–for attachment of buckle or other belt fitting? Third fragment, length 165mm; width 42–48mm, perforated by irregular pattern of oval holes–for belt fitting? Conserved.
A03–0401a; L2317; C7350–7; P8.2b; Phase IVb; Rig VII
Illus 152

2535 Miscellaneous fragment Leather
Large and very tattered but with stitching along two long edges and with parallel rows between. One long edge has been partially folded and stitched along fold– one part of edge now folded, other has opened out. Adjacent and almost parallel to still folded edge are three parallel rows of tunnel stitching c10mm apart, pairs of holes c3mm apart with c5mm between them. Parallel to these rows and to edge now opened out are three rows of tunnel stitching c27mm from first three rows and 40mm and 65mm apart, pairs of holes are c5mm apart with c10–12mm between pairs. Both ends of other long edge of fragment have been folded over and stitched along fold–now partially folded and partially opened out, middle part of edge oversewn, leaving scalloped edge. c415mm by 300mm. Clothing? Conserved.
A03–0409b; L2322; C7350–7; P8.2b; Phase IVb; Rig VII
Illus 161

2554 Strap (single thickness) with metalwork
Leather and Fe

Short fragment, of single thickness, length 53mm, width 7mm, thickness 3.5mm. Ring of iron buckle attached to one end of strap. Pin of buckle passes through grain–flesh hole in leather (see Fascicule 2, The metalwork, Iron Cat No 18 (599)). Other end of strap cracked, one slit 4.5mm long survives, also top edge of another beneath it. Two small round holes 5mm apart (centre to centre), and c1.5mm in diameter. Conserved.
A04-0430; C9245-9; P8.2b; Phase IVb; Rig VII
Not illustrated

2636 Strap (single thickness)? Leather
Of single thickness, with cut edge and two groups of four slits– for fastening? Length 261mm; maximum width 38.5mm; thickness 3mm. Conserved.
A03-0176; L1267; C9277-9; B18 (Phase 1/2); Phase IVaa,IVb; Rig VII
Illus 152

2652 Sole (Type 1) Leather
Child's left sole with long narrow seat, wide waist, long slender forepart with oval toe. Front of forepart bent over. Worn, with hole towards rear of seat; two small holes in centre forepart. Edge–flesh stitching channel; stitch length 4–7mm. Maximum length 165.5mm; maximum width of forepart 55.5mm; width of waist 42mm; maximum width of seat 47.5mm. Thickness: inner and outer edges of waist, outer edge of seat 3mm; inner edge of forepart 2.5mm; bent-over edge of outer forepart 4mm; inner edge and rear of seat 3.5mm; worn edge of hole in seat 0.25mm. Matches Upper (Type Bii) Cat No 2653/A03–0316c. Conserved. 12th–13th centuries.
A03-0316b; L1734; C7325-7; B18 (Phase 1/2), Pit 7324; Phase IVaa,IVb; Rig VII
Illus 146

2653 Upper (Type Bii) Leather
Large fragment of child's boot, with tunnel holes for two horizontal rows of thonging. Comprises vamp, vamp throat, vamp wing, quarters and leg flap. Two tunnel holes, one above the other, on each side of quarters. Tunnel stitch holes on flesh side of quarters indicate position of semi-circular stiffener. Lasting margin with grain–flesh stitching channel; stitch length 3.5–6mm (mainly 5mm). Edge–flesh stitching channels on vamp wing, vamp throat, vertical edge of quarters and leg flap and on part of top edge of quarters; stitch length 2.5–5mm. Rest of top edge of quarters and leg flap oversewn. Matches Sole (Type 1) Cat No 2652/A03–0316b. Conserved. 12th–13th centuries.
A03-0316c; L1734; C7325-7; B18 (Phase 1/2), Pit 7324; Phase IVaa,IVb; Rig VII
Illus 146

2700–2703 Miscellaneous fragments (4)
Leather (cattle hide)

Three fragments joined together by a thong. No 2700, long, with one very tattered edge and edge–flesh stitching channel; stitch length 3.5–4.5mm along half of second edge, rest of edge cut, with holes with thongs threaded through them; thong also passes through small, approximately oblong, fragment (No 2701) with two edge–flesh stitching channels; stitch length 3–4mm; fourth edge torn; No 2702 loosely connected to No 2700 by thong, edge with thong also has trace of edge–flesh stitching channel, opposite is cut and has four oval holes c9mm by 4mm and c17mm apart (centre to centre)– fragment of lasting margin? sandwiched between thong and c). Thong which connects Nos 2700 and 2702 is separate from that which links Nos 2700 and 2701. No 2703 comprises two thongs knotted together–probably part of same article. Conserved.
A03-0292a-d; L1381; C7307-7; B18 (Phase 1/2), MF 7307; Phase IVaa,IVb; Rig VII
Illus 164

2724 Miscellaneous fragment Leather
Approximately oval, narrowing at each end, with leather rolled together on flesh side forming a tab at each end, stitched with butted grain–flesh seam. Centre cut by several irregular lines. Maximum length 131mm; maximum width 31mm; thickness 2mm; width of tab 4–5mm; thickness of tabs 5mm. Tongue? Conserved.
A03-0383; C7384-7; B18 (Phases 2a and 2b), T7385; Phase IVb; Rig VII
Illus 158

2725 Sole (Type 3)?, rand and upper (Type C)
Leather and wool

Right sole, six fragments of rand, and two fragments of upper of boot; all sewn together with wool. Right sole with rounded seat, narrow waist, wide gently curved forepart, probably oval toe but point missing. Edge–flesh stitching channel; stitch length 5–6mm. Worn on outer edge of forepart where stitch holes perforate grain layer, not edge. Six fragments of rand, stitch length 5–6mm. Rand is wider at inside and outside waist, extending 7mm and 9.5mm respectively beyond stitching channel, thus improving water tightness of sole–upper seam. Two fragments of boot with tie holes for side lacing; larger comprises vamp, (missing front), vamp wing, vamp throat, quarters, and leg flap; smaller is leg flap. Lasting margin with grain–flesh stitching channels; stitch length 5–6mm. Edge–flesh stitching channel on top edge of quarters, vertical edges of leg flap and on vamp throat, and on lower part (20mm) of join between quarters and vamp wing/leg flap. Rest of top edge cut, not oversewn. Parallel to oversewn higher parts of those edges are tie holes. On vamp wing are six holes 20mm apart. On adjacent edge of quarters are eight holes 17–23.5mm apart. Holes not directly opposite each other, ie not paired. Parallel to tie holes are tunnel stitch holes on flesh side, for facing or strengthener. No stitch holes for stiffener survive. Boot complete but for toe of sole and upper, and small part of upper which would have joined top edge of quarters. Surviving length of sole 230mm; maximum width of forepart 85mm; width of waist 40mm; maximum width of seat 70mm; maximum height of quarters c145mm. Conserved. 13th–15th centuries?
A03-0413a; C7384-7; B18 (Phases 2a and 2b), T7385; Phase IVb; Rig VII
Illus 135

2745 Upper (Type C) Leather (cattle hide)

Three fragments of high boot with side lacing. Largest fragment is part of leg, with vertical row of nine thong holes c13mm, 15mm, 16mm, 17mm, 16mm, 15mm, 15mm, 17mm apart (measuring upwards). Edge parallel to holes oversewn. To left of holes, on flesh side, is tunnel stitching for facing or strengthener. Middle fragment is rectangular, probably leg flap, with vertical row of five thong holes, parallel to oversewn edge. Tunnel stitching on flesh side for facing or strengthener, to right of holes. Smallest, triangular fragment joins largest fragment. Edge–flesh stitching channels; stitch length 3–4mm; on second vertical edge and on part of bottom edge of largest fragment, on second vertical edge of middle fragment, and on two edges of smallest fragment. Hem stitch on rest of top edge of largest fragment, on top edge of middle fragment, and on third edge of smallest fragment. Rest of upper cut away. Thickness 2–3mm. Conserved. 14th–15th centuries.
A03–0294a; L1383; C7306–7; B18 (Phase 2b), North Room and Hall–Construction (1); Phase IVb; Rig VII
Illus 135

2747 Sole (Type 2) Leather (cattle hide)

Child's left sole with broad seat and waist and forepart, rounded toe. Underneath of seat and forepart slightly worn. Slight delamination at front of forepart. Edge–flesh stitching channel; stitch length 3–6mm. Length 141.5mm; maximum width of forepart 57mm; width of waist 38mm; maximum width of seat 49mm. Thickness: inner edge of waist, inner edge of forepart, middle of outer edge of forepart 3.5mm; outer edge of waist, rear of seat, rear of outer edge of forepart 3mm; inner edge of seat, front of outer edge of forepart 4.5mm. Conserved. 12th–14th centuries.
A03–0297a; L1386; C7306–7; B18 (Phase 2b), North Room and Hall–Construction (1); Phase IVb; Rig VII
Illus 124

2750 Sole (Type 3) Leather

Left, long with oval seat, moderately narrow waist and fairly wide forepart, bent inwards. Edge–flesh stitching channel; stitch length 4mm, 4.5mm, 5.5mm, 6mm, 8mm, 6.5mm. Very worn and delaminated, with holes in seat and forepart. Maximum length 259mm; maximum width of forepart 91mm; width of waist 49mm; maximum width of seat 71.5mm. Thickness: rear of inner edge of forepart 1.5mm; front of inner edge of forepart, outer edge of forepart 3mm; rear of seat 3.5mm. Conserved. 13th–14th centuries.
A03–0293; L1382; C7304–7; B18 (Phase 2b), North Room and Hall–Construction (2); Phase IVb; Rig VII
Illus 119

2754 Sole (Type 2) Leather

Right, with long narrow seat, slender waist, wide forepart, fairly straight on inner edge, gently curved outer edge. Very worn, with large hole in centre forepart and smaller one in seat. Edge–flesh stitching channel; stitch length 5–6.5mm. Surviving length 255.5mm; maximum width of forepart 95mm; width of waist 45.5mm; maximum width of seat 67.5mm. Thickness: outer edge of forepart 3mm; inner edge of waist and seat, front of outer edge of forepart 3.5mm; inner edge of forepart 4mm; worn middle outer edge of forepart 1.5mm.

Matches Upper (Type Dii) Cat No 2759/A03–0288f. Conserved. 12th–13th centuries.
A03–0288a; L1378; C7299–7; B18 (Phase 2b), North Room, Hall and Hall South–Occupation (10); Phase IVb; Rig VII
Illus 137

2759 Upper (Type Dii) Leather

Two fragments of low shoe with side-pieces slit for side lacing; larger comprises vamp, vamp wing, vamp throat, small latchet and quarters; slit or crack in quarter with thong or offcut emerging from it: smaller is side-piece, linking vamp wing and quarters. Vertical distance between holes: left 8.5mm, 10.5mm, 14.5mm, 11mm, 6.5mm; right 11.5mm, 11mm, 10.5mm, 12.5mm, 8mm (from bottom upwards). Horizontal distance between holes 12mm, 15mm, 17mm, 12.5mm, 13.5mm and 16mm. Lasting margin on both fragments, grain–flesh stitching channel, stitch length 5mm, 6mm. Edge–flesh stitching channels on vamp wing, vamp throat, vertical edge of quarters and on both vertical edges of side-piece; stitch length 2.5–3mm. Top edges of quarters, leg flap and side-piece oversewn. Larger fragment worn, cracked and delaminated. Smaller fragment in good condition. Second leg flap missing. Matches Sole (Type 2) 2754/A03–0288a. Conserved. 13th–14th centuries.
A03–0288f; L1378; C7299–7; B18 (Phase 2b), North Room, Hall and Hall South–Occupation (10); Phase IVb; Rig VII
Illus 137

2762 Sole (Type 9) Leather

Right forepart, slender, gently curved with oval toe now bent over. Very narrow waist with edge–flesh stitching channel. Two tunnel holes in rear of forepart, only one of which reaches grain layer, with short length of thong threaded through them: reuse of leg of upper of boot? Sole very worn and delaminated. Edge–flesh stitching channel; stitch length 6–7mm. Length 142mm; maximum width 73mm; width of waist 27.5mm; width of waist seam 29mm. Thickness not measured because of delamination. Conserved.
A03–0104b; L0462; C9132–9; B18 (Phase 2b), North Room, Hall and Hall South–Occupation (10); Phase IVb; Rig VII
Illus 123

2769 Miscellaneous fragment Leather (cattle hide)

Long triangular fragment with two edge–flesh stitching channels meeting in a point; stitch length 1.5–2.5mm. Third edge cut. At the end, grain–flesh stitch holes form and fill a rectangle for attachment of other article or for decoration? Thickness 2mm. Clothing or part of leg of upper of boot? Conserved.
A03–0113e; L0468; C9132–9; B18 (Phase 2b), North Room, Hall and Hall South–Occupation (10); Phase IVb; Rig VII
Illus 161

2771 Upper (Type C) Leather (cattle hide)

Small fragment of low boot with side lacing, probably leg flap. Parallel to vertical oversewn edge are four thong holes, diameter c2mm and 14.5mm, 13.5mm, 15.5mm apart. Tunnel stitching for facing or strengtheners. Top edge oversewn. Edge–flesh stitching channel on third edge; stitch length 3–3.5mm. Fourth edge torn. Worn and delaminated. Thickness

1.5mm. Conserved. 14th–15th centuries.
A03–0123a; L0476; C9132–9; B18 (Phase 2b), North Room,
Hall and Hall South–Occupation (10); Phase IVb; Rig VII
Illus 135

2775 Sole (Type 2) and rand Leather
Fragment of right forepart with oval toe. Edge–flesh stitching
channel; stitch length 5–7.5mm. Very worn, much of stitching
channel missing. Surviving length 82.5mm. Thickness rear
of outer edge 3.5mm; rear of inner edge 4mm; front of inner
edge 4.5mm; middle and front of outer edge 5mm; worn edge
at rear of forepart 3mm; worn edges, centre forepart 1.5mm.
Rand, stitch length 5–7.5mm, not attached but matches shape
of forepart. Forepart matches Upper Cat No 2777/A03–0124c.
Conserved. 12th–14th centuries.
A03–0124a, b; L0477; C9132–9; B18 (Phase 2b), North Room,
Hall and Hall South–Occupation (10); Phase IVb; Rig VII
Illus 146

2777 Upper Leather (cattle hide)
Fragment of vamp with rounded toe. Lasting margin with
grain–flesh stitching channel; stitch length 5–7mm. Edge–flesh
stitching channels on vamp wing; stitch length 3–4.5mm.
Thong 15–18mm wide threaded through slit in vamp, knotted
or anchored by being passed through itself, then threaded
through second slit in vamp. Rough repair? Very worn and
cracked. Matches Sole (Type 2) Cat No 2775/A03–0124a.
Conserved.
A03–0124c; L0477; C9132–9; B18 (Phase 2b), North Room,
Hall and Hall South–Occupation (10); Phase IVb; Rig VII
Illus 146

2784 Upper (Type C) Leather (cattle hide)
Very fragile fragment of low boot with side lacing, comprising
quarters, leg flap and vamp throat, with vertical row of seven
thong holes. Diameter of holes 1.5–2mm, and 14mm, 13mm,
15mm, 13.5mm, 14.5mm, 17.5mm apart (measuring upwards).
Edge parallel to holes is oversewn. Lasting margin with
grain–flesh stitching channel; stitch length 5.5–6mm. Edge–
flesh stitching channels on vertical edge of leg flap and on
vamp throat; stitch length 2.5mm. Top edge oversewn. On flesh
side of quarters, tunnel stitching marks position of triangular
stiffener, which survives separately. Conserved. 14th–15th
centuries.
A03–0245e; L1336; C9132–9; B18 (Phase 2b), North Room,
Hall and Hall South–Occupation (10); Phase IVb; Rig VII
Illus 135

2801 Upper (Type Di) Leather
Large fragment of low shoe with side lacing, comprising vamp,
vamp throat, vamp wing, small leg flap or latchet, and quarters.
Left foot. Two matching vertical rows of thong holes, three
on vamp wing and five on quarters. Top corner of vamp wing
missing. On flesh side, trace of tunnel holes for attachment of
facings or strengtheners. Edge adjacent to holes oversewn.
Lasting margin with grain–flesh stitching channel; stitch length
5, 6, 8mm. Edge–flesh stitching channels; stitch length 3,
4.5, 5.5, at vamp throat and on lower parts of vamp wing and
vertical edge of quarters below tie holes. Top edges of quarters
and leg flap oversewn. Crack at vamp throat. Lasting margin

worn, particularly at front of vamp and at quarters. Length
of shoe c240mm; thickness 2.5mm. Conserved. 13th–14th
centuries.
A03–0078; C9095–9; B18 (Phase 2b), Hall and Hall South–
Occupation (12a); Phase IVb; Rig VII
Illus 136

2818 Toggle Leather
Two long thin thongs emerging from double toggle. Constructed
from single piece of leather split into two thongs after first 3mm.
Parallel with split are two short slits through which the thongs
pass, thus forming a thick toggle. Thongs: length 147mm;
width 6–9mm; thickness c0.5mm. Toggle: length 15mm;
width 6–7mm; thickness 4mm. Four very small holes at loose
end of longer thong–for attachment to article to be fastened.
Conserved.
A03–0273b; L1364; C6146–10; M9b(a); Phase IVc; Rig VIII
Illus 150

2819 Miscellaneous fragment Leather (cattle hide)
Approximately rectangular, folded once lengthways. One side
has a projecting flap folded over second side; clear impression
on leather suggests that it was intended to be folded over, not
tucked in or otherwise used. Row of short diagonal grain–flesh
stitches parallel to cut edges of article, the holes on each side
matching exactly; probably stitched. At end of projecting flap
is a double row of slits. Other end of article bears second row
of slits parallel to and 7.5–9mm from first row. On side without
flap is a decorative motif at this end, marked out with a single
row of slits, starting and ending at this second row. At other
end of this side are two vertical rows of slits in centre. On other
side of article at same end as above mentioned slits is a small
triangular shape marked out with slits; at base of triangle a slit,
16.5mm long, perforates this side, its other edge also marked
with slits. For end of strap? Length, including flap, 223mm;
length of flap 24mm; minimum width, excluding flap, 34mm;
minimum width of flap 29mm; single thickness 1mm. Case?
Conserved.
A03–0273c; L1364; C6146–10; M9b(a); Phase IVc; Rig VIII
Illus 158

2820 Miscellaneous fragment Leather (cattle hide)
Small, consisting of strip folded once. Three rows of short
diagonal grain–flesh slits or stitch holes on one side, and one
row on the other, which is narrower. In present state, the ends
do not meet and rows of stitching at each end do not meet, but
possibly did originally. Stitched together or to belt of clothing or
other article? Another two rows of holes on first side could be
purely decorative. Length, folded, 43.5mm; maximum width
(side with three rows) 12mm; minimum width (side with one
row) 9mm. Single thickness c0.5mm. Conserved.
A03–0273d; L1364; C6146–10; M9b(a); Phase IVc; Rig VIII
Illus 152

2821 Miscellaneous fragment Leather (cattle hide)
Small, consisting of strip folded once. Diagonal slits parallel
to all edges, except on one side of fold. Ends and edges
match–could have been stitched together if edges also, then
not loop. Decorative stitching? Not oversewn, as edges do not
appear pulled. Length, folded, 35mm; maximum width 13.5mm;

thickness, single c0.75mm. Conserved.
A03–0273e; L1364; C6146–10; M9b(a); Phase IVc; Rig VIII
Illus 152

2872 Sole (Type 2) Leather (cattle hide)
Child's left sole with slender seat, only very slightly narrowing
for waist; forepart with almost straight inner edge, curved
outer edge, rounded toe. Slightly delaminated. Edge–flesh
stitching channel; stitch length 6–9mm, mostly 6–7mm. Length
168mm; maximum width of forepart 64mm; width of waist
45mm; maximum width of seat 46mm. Thickness: inner edge
of forepart 4.5mm; outer edge of seat 4mm; outer edge of waist
5mm; front outer edge of forepart 3.5mm. Conserved. 12th–13th
centuries.
A4894; L0020; C2483–3; MC155; Phase IVb,IVc; Rig V
Illus 124

2875 Strap/belt (single thickness) Leather (cattle hide)
Fragment of single thickness, c83mm by 31mm, delaminated,
grain side only remaining, thickness not measured. Irregular
stitching of grain–flesh holes or slits along each edge,
converging to meet in middle of width at cut end of strap. Also
six other holes, one in corner between stitching channel and
edges, five between the rows of stitches–three small, one large
and cracked around edges, one large and round, the two large
ones probably worn by pin or buckle. Conserved.
A9357a; L0001; C2530–3; MC155; Pit 2691; Phase IVb,IVc;
Rig V
Not illustrated

2876 Strap (single thickness) Leather (cattle hide)
Two fragments, of single thickness, very delaminated, probably
originally one. Stitching channel of grain–flesh slits along
each long edge; stitch length c6–8mm. Length 126mm; width
17–22mm. Conserved.
A9357b; L0001; C2530–3; MC155; Pit 2691; Phase IVb,IVc; Rig V
Illus 152

2883 Miscellaneous fragment Leather
Large and irregular c410mm by 280mm by 2mm. Along one
hem stitched edge is a row, c190mm long, of seventeen tie
holes c2mm by 1mm and 13mm, 11mm, 13.5mm, 11.5mm,
13.5mm, 12mm, 12.5mm, 10mm, 11mm, 11.5mm, 9mm, 10mm,
11.5mm, 9mm apart. Two rows of grain–flesh stitching secure
a fold– dart? On flesh side, several small circular impressions,
diameter 3–5mm. Clothing? Conserved.
A9361; L0027; C2530–3; MC155; Pit 2691; Phase IVb,IVc; Rig V
Illus 160

2985 Sole (Type 3) with bunion? Leather (cattle hide)
Right, with rounded seat, rear of which has curled up and
over, narrow waist, wide forepart ending in oval toe. Bulge
on inside of forepart, probably caused by bunion, hole next
to the bulge; also hole at rear of seat. Edge–flesh stitching
channel; stitch length 4.5–8mm–mainly 6mm, 8mm occurs
only twice, on either side of waist, stitching noticeably closer
at front of forepart. Length 227.5mm; maximum width of
forepart 96mm; width of waist 44mm; maximum width of seat
74mm. Thickness: outer and inner edges of waist, inner edge
of forepart 3mm; front of outer edge of seat 3.5mm; inner edge

of seat and rear of outer and curled up outer edge of forepart
4.5mm; worn edge of hole 0.5mm. Conserved. 13th–14th
centuries.
A10521; L0008; C2530–3; MC155; Pit 2691; Phase IVb,IVc;
Rig V
Illus 145

3033 Sole (Type 3) Leather
Left, with long seat, narrow waist and slender forepart,
tapering inwards to an oval toe. Worn, with part of front of
forepart missing, a hole in centre forepart, and stitching
channel separated from rear of seat. Edge–flesh stitching
channel; stitch length 3.5–5.5mm, mostly 4.5–5mm. Surviving
length 200mm; maximum width of forepart 75mm; width
of waist 31mm; maximum width of seat 57mm. Thickness:
outer edge of forepart 2.5mm; inner edge of forepart 3mm;
inner edge of waist, inner edge of seat 3.5mm. Conserved.
13th–14th centuries.
A3459; C2476–3; M1.4d; Phase IVb,IVc; Rig VI
Illus 120

3047 Sheath (decorated) Leather
Decorated fragment formed of one thickness of leather folded
twice and stitched up middle of reverse in a butted edge to
grain seam; stitch length 4mm, 4.5mm, 5mm. Upper part
projects. Reverse of upper part has three holes for attachment
to belt; three of these holes also penetrate front of sheath. Top
edge has been cut and folded inwards but not stitched. Bottom
end does not survive. Much of bottom section is missing.
Front and reverse engraved with a blunt tool and possibly with
a punch, for series of slots. Decoration was engraved before
leather was folded. Top part: front of projection decorated
with zone of alternating diagonal lines–rather faint. Rear of
projection plain. Front and rear of rest of upper part divided
into three panels. Panels on reverse and on fold decorated
with zones of alternating diagonal lines–neater and tighter
than those on projecting part. Panel on front also filled with
zones of alternating diagonal lines, but every second line
consists of shield or toothed pattern. Panels are bordered and
separated by plain bands. At top, above plain band, horizontal
band filled with short vertical strokes. At bottom, similar
band, but strokes are smaller and, particularly on reverse,
these form a shield or toothed pattern. Lower part: front has
been decorated with long thin panel, outside edge of which is
marked by band containing shallow dots c1.5mm diameter and
c4mm apart. Interior of panel has been filled with a curvilinear
design. Fold decorated with a band with shallow dots (more
rectangular than round, c1.5mm by 1mm and 3.5–4mm apart);
the two rows are c7mm apart. Area between them filled with
stylised elongated 'S'. Surviving part of reverse, adjacent to
edge to grain stitching channel decorated with short diagonal
strokes. Surviving length 242mm; maximum width of upper
part 63mm; maximum width of lower part 43.5mm thickness
3mm. Shield pattern–imitation of armorial bearings?–13th
century; cross-hatching 13th century or later? curvilinear
design–meaningless–debased acanthus scroll or debased
mythical beasts?–13th century. Conserved. 13th century or
later?
A8334; C2476–3; M1.4d; Phase IVb,IVc; Rig VI
Illus 155

3068 Sole (Type 7) Leather and wool
Left, with rounded seat, narrow waist and gently curved forepart
with an edge–flesh stitching channel across tread. Very worn,
partially delaminated. Edge–flesh stitching channel; stitch
length 4–7.5mm. Wool survives in one hole. Surviving length
217mm; maximum width of forepart 95mm; width of waist 46mm;
maximum width of seat 52mm. Thickness: inner edge of waist
and forepart 4mm; outer edge of waist 3mm; inner edge of
seat 5.5mm; outer edge of forepart 4.5mm; seam across tread
2.5mm. Conserved.
A8668c; L0016; C2476–3; M1.4d; Phase IVb,IVc; Rig VI
Not illustrated

3070 Sole Leather
Small fragment with edge-flesh stitching channel; stitch length
6.5mm, 7 mm. Conserved.
Radiocarbon date of 720±35 BP (calibrated at 95 per cent
probability to AD 720–1310) obtained.
A8668e; L0016; C2476–3; M1.4d; Phase IVb,IVc; Rig VI
Not illustrated

3072 Upper Leather
Fragment of front of vamp with lasting margin with stitching
channel of grain–flesh holes; stitch length 5.5–7.5mm. Rounded
toe. Small hole next to lasting margin with short piece of thong
passing through it–probably repair. Thickness 2.5mm.
A8668g; L0016; C2476–3; M1.4d; Phase IVb,IVc; Rig VI
Illus 144

3090 Strap/belt (folded once) Leather (cattle hide)
Fragment, folded once and stitched together where edges
meet–face to face, not oversewn–with diagonal grain–flesh
slits; stitch length c4mm. One end torn or cracked, with trace of
central hole. Stitching stops c40mm from other end, where five
round and oval holes penetrate both thicknesses–attachment
for buckle? End cut or torn but irregular and one thickness
extends slightly beyond the other. Length c290mm; width
27–28.5mm; single thickness c3–4mm. Conserved.
A5900a; L1700; C2790–2; M1.4d; Phase IVb,IVc; Rig VI
Illus 148

3108 Upper? Leather (cattle hide)
Fragment, with edge–flesh stitching channel along one short
edge; stitch length 5.5mm, 6.5mm, and along long edge edge–
flesh and grain–flesh, with grain folded to form flesh; stitch
length 4.5–5.5mm. Area above long edge has had long pointed
ovals cut out, and edges of three more? Decoration? Open
sandal? Ovals not very regular. Thickness 2mm. Conserved.
A8000a; L1729; C2567–3; M1.4d; Pit 2566; Phase IVb,IVc;
Rig VI
Not illustrated

3221 Miscellaneous fragment Leather (cattle hide)
Approximately round, diameter c35mm, with central hole,
diameter c2mm. Delaminated, two separate layers, c2.5mm and
0.25mm thick. Conserved.
A6228c; L0017; C2462A-3; M1.4c; Phase IIIa–IVcc; Rigs V
and VI
Illus 159

3246 Sole (Type 3) Leather
Left, long with slender rounded seat, narrow waist,
proportionately wider forepart, almost straight along inner
edge, more curved along outer edge, turning inwards slightly,
to broad slightly pointed toe. Edge–flesh stitching channel;
stitch length 4–5mm. Very worn, with outer part of seat missing,
forepart thin, cracked in centre. Stitching channel along outer
edge replaced by six, possibly seven, slits (as far as seat and
therefore possibly more) and thong, three fragments of which
survive. Maximum surviving length 253mm; maximum width
of forepart 93mm; width of waist 39mm; maximum surviving
width of seat 60mm. Thickness: inner edge of waist and seat,
rear of inner edge of forepart 3.5mm; front and middle of inner
edge of forepart 3mm; outer edge of waist, worn edge of seat
1mm; front of outer edge of seat 2.25mm; rear–middle of outer
edge of forepart 2.5mm; middle–front of outer edge of forepart
2.75–3mm. Thong: width 7.5–8mm; thickness 1mm. Conserved.
13th–14th centuries.
A6195; L1674; C2190A-4; M1.4b; Phase IVb–IVcc; Rigs V
and VI
Illus 120

3281 Strap (single thickness) Leather
Irregular strip of single thickness, c200 by 15–17 by 1.5–5mm,
delaminated. With traces of cracks or holes? edges cut.
Fragment of strap or belt? Conserved.
A03–0227a; L1318; C7233–7; P8.3/256; Phase IVc,IVcc; Rig VII
Not illustrated

3283 Upper (Type Kiii) Leather
Fragment of latchet? with one row of vertical thonging and
three rows of horizontal thonging, but not type Biii–central
fastening. Oversewn top edge, second edge torn, third and
fourth cut. Row of vertical thonging with four tunnel holes and
three short stretches of thong surviving on grain side. Three
rows of horizontal thonging, with tunnel hole and single hole in
each row. Thong survives on grain side between the holes in
upper and lower rows and through tunnel hole in middle row.
Horizontal rows lie along line of vertical tunnel holes; horizontal
thongs could only have been connected to vertical thong on
flesh side. Vertical thonging purely decorative? Thickness
1–3mm. Conserved. 13th–14th centuries.
A03–0227d; L1318; C7233–7; P8.3; Phase IVc,IVcc; Rig VII
Illus 144

3304 Strap/belt (single thickness) Leather (cattle hide)
Four delaminated fragments of short belt of single thickness,
perforated on each long edge by grain–flesh holes, diameter
c3mm and c15–20mm apart. Both ends cut, one stitched with
edge–flesh seam, traces of which remain, other end perforated
by round holes. Conserved.
A03–0250a; L1341; C7233–7; P8.3; Phase IVc,IVcc; Rig VII
Illus 152

3335 Sole (Type 2) Leather (cattle hide)
Child's left sole with short seat and longer forepart. Cracked at
front of seat and at inner and outer edges of front of forepart.
Edge–flesh stitching channel; stitch length 6mm, 5mm, 6.5mm.
Length 138mm; maximum width of forepart 64mm; width of
waist 40mm; maximum width of seat 43mm. Thickness: outer

and inner edges of waist, rear of seat and front of forepart
3.5mm. Conserved. 12th–13th centuries.
A03–0261a; L1352; C7271–7; P8.3 and M9a, PW7267; Phase
IVc,IVcc; Rig VII
Illus 124

3364 Upper (Type Di) Leather
Fragment, plus stiffener, of shoe with side lacing. Comprises
vamp, vamp wing, vamp throat, latchet and low quarters.
Side-piece missing. Parallel to oversewn edge of quarters
are six tie holes; on flesh side, tunnel stitching for attachment
of strengthener. Upper very worn, front of vamp and part
of quarters missing, no lasting margin survives. Irregular
oval hole cut in vamp– for decoration? Edge–flesh stitching
channels on vamp wing and vamp throat; stitch length 2mm–
very neat stitching. Top edge oversewn. Triangular stiffener
with lasting margin with grain–flesh stitching channel; stitch
length 6mm; and with stitch holes for attachment to quarters;
probably belongs to this upper. Conserved. 13th–14th
centuries.
A03–0223b; L1314; C7231–7; M9a; Phase IVc,IVcc; Rig VII
Illus 136

3382 Sole (Type 3) Leather
Right, with narrow seat and waist, slender forepart, turned
inwards slightly, oval toe. Short cracks at inner edge of centre
forepart and at outer edge of waist. Rear of seat missing.
Edge–flesh stitching channel; stitch length 6mm, 7mm,
8mm. Surviving length 215.5mm; maximum width of forepart
80mm; width of waist 39.5mm; maximum width of seat 59mm.
Thickness: outer edge of waist 2.5mm; outer and inner edges
of forepart 3mm; inner edge of seat 4mm; outer edge of
seat, inner edge of waist 4.5mm; worn edge of seat 0.75mm.
Conserved. 13th–14th centuries.
A03–0249a; L1340; C7238–7; M9a; Phase IVc,IVcc; Rig VII
Illus 120

3385 Upper (Type Dii) Leather (cattle hide)
Approximately rectangular fragment of shoe: side-piece split for
side lacing. Lasting margin with grain–flesh stitching channel;
stitch length 5.5–8mm. Edge–flesh stitching channels, stitch
length 3–4mm, on vertical edge and on part of top edge. Rest
of
top edge oversewn. Diagonal edge oversewn; parallel to it are
four or five tie holes c2mm by 4mm and c10mm apart. Tunnel
stitching for facing or strengthener on flesh side. Also, part of
second diagonal edge. Maximum height 47mm; thickness
2mm. Conserved. 13th–14th centuries.
A03–0233b; L1324; C7247–7; M9a; Phase IVc,IVcc; Rig VII
Illus 137

3403 Miscellaneous fragment with metalwork
Leather and metal
Irregular strip, length 57 mm, width 5–8 mm, thickness c1 mm;
apparently found in association with a cylindrical hollow lace-
end into which it is too thick to fit (see Fascicule 2, The
metalwork, Non-ferrous Cat 50). Conserved.
A04–0079a, b; L4917; C9001-8; M9a; Phase IVc,IVcc; Rig VII
Not illustrated

3412 Strap (single thickness) Leather (cattle hide)
Fragment of single thickness, 3.5mm thick, with cut on long
edges, with stitching channel of grain–flesh slits; stitch length
5–6mm, parallel to each long edge; one short edge cut or
cracked, other worn/torn. Strap has evidently worn or cracked
along line of stitching channel, towards cut end, for strap narrows
and remains of original stitching channel visible along edge,
second stitching channel replacing it overlaps slightly end of
stitching channel on wider portion. Length 176mm; original/
maximum width 24mm; minimum width of narrowest part 16mm.
Conserved.
A03–0081a; L0450; C9085–9; M9a; Phase IVc,IVcc; Rig VII
Illus 151

3413 Strap (single thickness) Leather (cattle hide)
Short, delaminated, fragment of strap of single thickness, with
edges cut along stitching channel of grain–flesh holes; stitch
length 4.5–5mm, parallel to each cut edge. Short edges torn.
Length 80mm; width 22mm. Conserved.
A03–0081b; L0450; C9085–9; M9a; Phase IVc,IVcc; Rig VII
Illus 151

3510 Miscellaneous fragment Leather (cattle hide)
Approximately trapezoidal fragment with three long and one
very short straight edges, and one slightly curved edge, all
oversewn; stitch length c10–12mm. Short edge and curved edge
slightly worn, slight delamination. Maximum dimensions: 114mm
by
78mm by 2mm. Conserved.
A03–0220; L1311; C6166–10; M9b(b), PW6166; Phase IVc,IVcc;
Rig VIII
Illus 159

3511 Clump Leather
Seat, with waist, stitch holes for attachment to sole. Length
86mm; maximum width 70mm; width at waist 45mm. Thickness
c1–2mm. Conserved.
A03–0251; L1342; C6131–10; M9b(b), Pit 6127; Phase IVc,IVcc;
Rig VIII
Illus 104

3569–3572 Miscellaneous fragments (4) Leather
Four fragments, two joined together, with oversewn edges and
with thongs and tunnel holes. Nos 3569/A7688e (triangular) and
3570/A7688f (trapezoidal) joined together by two thongs, one
of which is knotted, to form a toggle. No 3571/A7688g small,
with traces of two oversewn edges and with thong through
tunnel hole. No 3572/A7688h approximately triangular, with
one oversewn edge and two edge–flesh stitching channels;
stitch length 1–5mm; and single oval thong hole. Clothing?
Conserved.
A7688e–h; C2540–3; M1.4e; Phase IVcc(Va)(VI); Rig VI
Illus 159

3594 Sole (Type 5) Leather
Left, fragment with narrow waist, gently curved forepart, pointed
toe. Part of seat missing. Edge–flesh stitching channel; stitch
length 5.5–7mm. Stitching channel on inner edge of forepart
worn very thin, replaced by five thong holes 24mm, 12mm,
27mm, 19mm apart. Surviving length 215mm; maximum width of

forepart 82mm; width of waist 44mm. Thickness: worn edge of forepart 1mm; inner edge of seat 4mm; inner and outer edges of waist 3mm; rear of outer edge of forepart 3.5mm; upturned outer edge of front of forepart 4.5mm. Conserved. 13th–15th centuries.
A6220b; L0022; C2447–3; M1.4e; Phase IVcc(Va); Rig VI
Illus 122

3602 Upper (Type Ki) Leather (cattle hide)
Two joining fragments (originally one) of high shoe or low boot with central fastening, comprising rear of vamp, vamp throat, vamp wing, part of quarters and two latchets, one pierced by two long horizontal slits, the other by three horizontal slits and one round hole. Toggle emerges from centre of vamp throat, directly under end of latchet, thong of toggle knotted over edge of throat, long pointed tail on flesh side. Lasting margin with grain–flesh stitching channel; stitch length 5–6.5mm. Edge–flesh stitching channels on vamp throat, vamp wing and quarters; stitch length 4mm. Also three other fragments, very worn, probably part of same upper. Conserved.
A4329e; L1697; C2456–3; M1.4e; Phase IVcc(Va); Rig VI
Illus 142

3621 Upper (Type Bii) Leather (cattle hide)
Fragment of boot with tunnel holes for three horizontal rows of thonging. Comprises vamp, vamp wing, vamp throat and quarters. Three tunnel holes for horizontal thongs on closed side of quarter, only middle hole seems to have been used. Lasting margin with grain–flesh stitching channel; stitch length 5.5–7.5mm. Edge–flesh stitching channels on vamp wing, vamp throat and quarters; stitch length 4mm. Very cracked and frail, front of vamp worn, lasting margin missing. Thickness 2mm. Conserved. 12th–13th centuries.
A4914; L0023; C2456–3; M1.4e; Phase IVcc(Va); Rig VI
Illus 131

3670 Upper (Type F) Leather (cattle hide?)
Fragment of shoe comprising vamp, vamp wings, high vamp throat and very low quarters, no latchets. Side-piece linking vamp wing and quarters missing. Probably also missing piece of vamp throat, to give continuous oversewn edge. Lasting margin with grain–flesh stitching channel; stitch length 5.5–6.5mm. Edge–flesh stitching channels on vamp wings and vertical edge of quarters; stitch length 2.5mm. Top edge of throat, quarters and vamp wing oversewn. Tunnel stitching for triangular stiffener on flesh side of quarters. Adjacent to vertical edge of quarters, on flesh side, is a faint diagonal row of tunnel stitching and a well-defined vertical row on closed side at junction of vamp/quarters. On flesh side, therefore not decorative–attachment of lining, for quarters only? Worn, especially at front of vamp. Thickness 1.5mm. Conserved. Mid-10th–14th centuries.
A7791; L1744; C2544–3; P6; Phase IVcc,Va; Rig VI
Illus 140

3705 Strap/belt (folded twice) Leather (cattle hide)
Fragment, formed by folding leather twice; edges joined in a butted edge–grain seam; stitch length 5.5–6.5mm. Belt pierced by grain–flesh holes parallel with folded edges and by oval holes or slits up centre. Length c135mm; width, folded,

c3.5mm; single thickness 3.5mm. Conserved.
A03–0172a; L1263; C7187–7; B34, Floor; Phase Va; Rig VI
Illus 150

3717 Sheath Leather (cattle hide)
Small fragment of decorated sheath? with cut edge, with curve of fold remaining, other edges torn. Decorated with irregular lines, mostly diagonal, also part of two vertical lines forming rough lattice; near bottom edge are two parallel horizontal lines–frame of panel? Surviving length c55mm; thickness 2mm. Conserved.
A03–0160a; L0693; C7191–7; B34–Courtyard; Phase Va; Rig VI
Illus 155

3859 Sole (Type 8) Leather
Fairly long seat, sewn across waist, edge–flesh stitching channel; stitch length 5.5mm, 7mm (waist), 4.5mm, 6mm (perimeter), plus 7.5mm, 9mm, 10mm, 10.5mm; duplicate holes on sides and rear on grain, not edge–probably repair. Length 81.5mm; maximum width 63.5mm; width at waist 41mm. Thickness: sides and waist 3.5mm; upturned edge at rear of seat 2.5mm. Probably matches Sole (Type 9) Cat No 3860/A03–0048b. Conserved.
A03–0048a; L0427; C7079–7; M1.5b; Phase Vaa; Rigs VI and VII
Illus 123

3860 Sole (Type 9) Leather
Right forepart, wide almost straight inner edge, curved outer edge, oval toe. Narrow waist with edge–flesh stitching channel. Very worn and delaminated, especially along inner edge. Edge–flesh stitching channel; stitch length 4.5mm; at waist 6.5mm, 6mm, 7mm. Maximum width 78mm; width of waist 39mm. Thickness: outer edge 4mm. Probably matches Sole (Type 8) Cat No 3859/A03–0048a. Conserved.
A03–0048b; L0427; C7079–7; M1.5b; Phase Vaa; Rigs VI and VII
Illus 123

3863 Sole (Type 4) Leather
Left, with long slender seat, narrow waist and wide gently curved forepart with pointed toe. Seat worn, with crack, hole in centre, and with part of stitching channel detached. Delaminated, stitch holes indicate seat repaired with clump sole. Edge–flesh stitching channel; stitch length 5.5–8.5mm. Length 238.5mm; maximum width of forepart 85mm; width of waist 37.5mm; maximum width of seat 56mm. Thickness: front of forepart 3mm; rear outer edge of forepart 3.5mm; outer edge of waist, middle of outer edge of forepart, front of inner edge of forepart 4mm; inner edge of waist 4.5mm. Conserved. 13th–14th centuries.
A03–0067a; L1096; C7079–7; M1.5b; Phase Vaa; Rigs VI and VII
Illus 121

3865 Clump Leather and wool
Right forepart clump with pointed toe and with tunnel holes for attachment to original sole. Delaminated. Wool remains

in some holes. Length 101.5mm; maximum width 73mm.
Thickness 2mm. Conserved.
A03–0068; L1094; C7079–7; M1.5b; Phase Vaa; Rigs VI and VII
Illus 104

3866 Upper (Type Ki) Leather (cattle hide)
Latchet? of upper with central fastening? Oblong, fragment,
two edge–flesh stitching channels; stitch length 2–2.5mm; two
edges with tunnel stitching on flesh side, fifth edge cut; thin strip
with edge–flesh stitching channel–vamp throat? Shorter edge
with tunnel stitching perforated by one T-shaped slit and by
two tunnel holes with thongs of toggles passed through them.
Conserved. 13th–14th centuries.
A03–0069a; L1098; C7079–7; M1.5b; Phase Vaa; Rigs VI
and VII
Illus 142

3869 Knife sheath Leather (cattle hide)
Decorated, formed of one piece of leather, probably folded
twice, with edges sewn together with butted grain to edge seam.
One folded edge and one edge with grain to edge holes survive.
Top edge cut. Decoration: front plain band near top, beneath
it horizontal band with six spirals within; plain band; horizontal
band with one whole rectangle and two halves of rectangles.
Whole rectangle contains shield, which has been sub-divided
into four rows: top row, four shields; second row, three shields;
third row, two shields; fourth row, one shield; background
between shield and rectangle filled with very neatly stamped
chequered pattern; one of the half rectangle appears to contain
the same design, the other has a small shield in top left corner
containing two, possibly three, debased *fleurs-de-lys*, and
beneath shield larger *fleur-de-lys*. Same pattern of rectangles
and shields repeated in next row, followed by plain band, then
horizontal band with six spirals. Lower part of sheath divided
vertically, larger part of front filled with 4½ lozenges, formed
by two parallel pairs of zigzag lines. Lozenges appear to be
filled with a *fleur-de-lys* just recognisable in top lozenges, less
distinct in others, because of cracks. *Fleurs-de-lys* probably
stamped. Triangular spaces between zigzags and side of panel
filled with neat stamped chequered pattern. Outer edge of lower
part of shield decorated with shields and spirals. Decoration:
reverse; undecorated except for very fine and regular vertical
lines. Near top, two holes one above the other, for attachment
to belt or other article. Length 183.5mm; maximum width
38mm; single thickness 2mm. Shield pattern and *fleurs-de-lys*
copying of armorial bearings?; spirals debased acanthus scroll?
Conserved. 13th century.
A03–0070; L1089; C7079–7; M1.5b; Phase Vaa; Rigs VI and VII
Illus 156 (appears as no 3984 – illus needs to be altered)

3870 Upper (Type Kii) Leather
Latchet? of upper with central fastening? One cut edge, one
with edge–flesh stitching channel, two oversewn. Three parallel
slits or cracks. Length c62.4mm; width 65mm; thickness 2mm.
Conserved.
A03–0098a; L1756; C7079–7; M1.5b; Phase Vaa; Rigs VI
and VII
Illus 142

3875 Knife sheath Leather (cattle hide)
Small, formed of thin strip of leather folded twice, edges meeting
on reverse, not centrally, by butted edge to grain seam; stitch
length c5mm. Decorated with vertical zones of zigzag, two on
front, one on reverse, engraved with a blunt tool. Bottom marked
with four roughly parallel horizontal lines c3mm apart. Top
edge cut. Part of one folded edge missing. Length (probably
complete) 108.5mm; width, folded, 22mm; thickness, single,
1.5mm. Conserved 12th–13th centuries.
cf Dyer and Wenham 1972, 96–8, no 1, rear decorated
with similar zigzag lines, 12th–13th centuries (pottery);
Richardson 1959, 103, engraved lines round point imitating
metal reinforcing bands?
A03–0118; L0471; C7082–7; M1.5b; Phase Vaa; Rigs VI and VII
Illus 155

3876 Strap/belt (single thickness) Leather (cattle hide)
Fragment of single thickness, 300mm long, 29mm wide,
4.5mm thick, with row of short diagonal slits parallel to each
long edge but probably not stitched; decorative. Pierced by
two approximately oval holes 4mm by 6mm and 2.5mm by
4mm. Cut at each end to form a point. Conserved.
A03–0120a; L0473; C7082–7; M1.5b; Phase Vaa; Rigs VI and VII
Illus 151

3877 Sole (Type 2) Leather
Right, complete, with long fairly narrow seat, only slightly thinner
at waist, and long broad forepart, gently curved, with oval toe.
Edge–flesh stitching channel; stitch length 6–8.5mm, except
for one of 4mm. Worn, especially at rear of seat, and crack
across front of seat. Maximum length 253mm; maximum width
of forepart 90mm; width of waist 52mm; maximum width of seat
64mm. Thickness: inner edge of waist and seat, rear of inner
edge of forepart 4.5mm; middle of inner edge of forepart, rear
of outer edge of forepart 3.5mm; outer edge of seat and waist,
front of outer edge of forepart 4mm. Conserved. 12th–14th
centuries.
A03–0120b; L0473; C7082–7; M1.5b; Phase Vaa; Rigs VI and VII
Illus 118

3878 Sole (Type 9) Leather
Pointed left forepart, very worn and delaminated, faint traces of
stitching across waist, long and narrow with very narrow waist;
similar to Sole (Type 4) foreparts. Worn, particularly along inner
edge. Edge–flesh stitching channel; stitch length 4.5–6mm.
Maximum length 157mm; maximum width 63mm; width of waist
29mm. Thickness: inner edge c 0.75mm; rear of outer edge,
front of outer edge 3.5mm; middle of outer edge 4.5mm; waist
2.5mm. Conserved.
A03–0120c; L0473; C7082–7; M1.5b; Phase Vaa; Rigs VI
and VII
Illus 121

3888 Miscellaneous fragment Leather
Irregular, very worn, with three approximately parallel stitching
channels of grain–flesh holes; holes, 2.5mm apart, are in pairs
and pairs are 4.5mm apart. Fragment of clothing? Conserved.
A03–0125c; L0478; C7082–7; M1.5b; Phase Vaa; Rigs VI and VII
Illus 160

3927 Miscellaneous fragment Leather and wool
Triangular, with two edge–flesh stitching channels forming a
point; stitch length 4.5–6mm. Wool survives in stitch holes.
Third edge cut; tunnel stitch holes across this edge. Length
62mm, width 41mm. Thickness: edge–flesh stitching channels
4–4.5mm; cut edge 2.5mm. Repaired front of forepart of sole?
Conserved.
A03–0136c; L0489; C7169–7; M1.5b; Phase Vaa; Rigs VI
       and VII
Illus 159

3928 Miscellaneous fragment Leather and wool
Triangular, with two edge–flesh stitching channels forming a
point; stitch length 4.5–6mm. Wool survives in stitch holes.
Third edge cut; tunnel stitch holes across this edge. Length
71mm, width 57mm. Thickness: edge–flesh stitching channels
4–4.5mm; cut edges 2.5mm. Repaired front of forepart of soles?
Conserved.
A03–0136d; L0489; C7169–7; M1.5b; Phase Vaa; Rigs VI
and VII
Illus 159

3929 Miscellaneous fragment Leather and wool
Triangular, with two edge–flesh stitching channels forming a
point; stitch length 4.5–6mm. Wool survives in stitch holes.
Third edge cut; round hole and trace of tunnel stitch holes
on flesh side. Length 70.5mm, width 41mm; thickness: edge–
flesh stitching channels 4–4.5mm; cut edges 2.5mm. Repaired
front of forepart of sole? Conserved.
A03–0136c–e; L0489; C7169–7; M1.5b; Phase Vaa; Rigs VI
and VII
Illus 159

3961–3964 Miscellaneous fragments (4)
Leather (cattle hide)
Four, with edge–flesh stitching channels, possibly clothing.
No 3961/A03–0142b approximately oblong, with two long edge–
flesh stitching channels; stitch length 3–4.5mm; both edges
indented at one end–armhole? Edge between indentations
irregular but with trace of grain–flesh stitching channel. In centre
of fragment, grain–flesh stitch holes suggest a dart. Fourth
edge irregular, partly oversewn, partly edge–flesh stitching
channel. Thickness: edge–flesh stitching channel 2mm; worn
edge 0.75mm. Conserved.
No 3962/A03–0142c long thin triangular fragment with two long
edge–flesh stitching channels; stitch length 3–4.5mm; third
edge possibly oversewn, might join one of long edges of No
3961. Thickness: edge–flesh stitching channel 2mm; oversewn
edge 1mm. Conserved.
No 3963/A03–0142d approximately trapezoidal fragment with
three edge–flesh stitching channels; stitch length 3.5–6mm.
Fourth edge torn. Part of No 3961? Thickness: edge–flesh
stitching channel 2mm; worn edge c 0.5mm. Conserved.
No 3964 triangular fragment, with one edge–flesh stitching
channel; stitch length 3.5–4.5mm, one oversewn edge and third
edge worn. Part of b)? Thickness: edge–flesh stitching channel
1.75mm, worn edge c 0.5mm. Conserved.
A03–0142b–e; L0494; C7169–7; M1.5b; Phase Vaa; Rigs VI
and VII
Illus 163

3985 Sole (Type 5) Leather
Right, fragment with rounded seat, narrow waist, fairly narrow
forepart. Worn, front missing but probably pointed. Edge–flesh
stitching channel; stitch length 5–7mm. Surviving length
240mm; maximum width of forepart 82mm; width of waist
34mm; maximum width of seat 64mm. Thickness: outer edge of
waist, rear of outer edge of forepart, inner edge of waist 3mm;
front of outer edge of forepart 2.5mm; rear of inner edge of
forepart, outer edge of seat, rear of seat 4mm; worn edges of
forepart c1mm. Conserved. 13th–15th centuries.
A03–0170b; L1261; C7169–7; M1.5b; Phase Vaa; Rigs VI
and VII
Illus 122

3988 Upper (Type Kii) Leather (cattle hide)
Very worn irregular fragment with central fastening, vamp, vamp
throat, quarters and latchet, which is pierced by three
slits c19mm by 2mm. Lasting margin with grain–flesh stitching
channel; stitch length 4mm. Two edge–flesh stitching channels;
stitch length 2.5mm on quarters. Top edges of latchet, quarters
and throat oversewn. Small oval hole for thong at vamp throat.
Thickness 1mm. Conserved. 13th–15th centuries.
A03–0170e; L1261; C7169–7; M1.5b; Phase Vaa; Rigs VI
and VII
Illus 142

3989 Upper (Type Kiii) Leather (cattle hide)
Fragment with central fastening, most probably part of quarters
and leg flap, with three horizontal thongs, each threaded
through a single hole and tunnel hole; two thongs end in loops,
third broken. Short grain–flesh stitching channel at throat.
Vertical edge of latchet cut. Top edge oversewn. Thickness
1.5–2mm. Conserved. 13th–15th centuries.
A03–0170f; L1261; C7169–7; M1.5b; Phase Vaa; Rigs VI
and VII
Illus 142

4030 and 4031 Upper (Type Ki) Leather (cattle hide)
Two fragments with central fastening. No 4030, larger fragment
comprises vamp throat and latchet; No 4031 is second latchet.
On latchet of No 4030, parallel to oversewn vertical edge, are
two horizontal slits, ending in eyelets. Single hole at middle
of vamp throat, with toggle threaded through it; edge of thong
cut or torn on grain side. On latchet of No 4031, parallel to
oversewn vertical edge, is a long horizontal slit ending in eyelet;
above it, tunnel hole and single hole, with thong end of toggle
threaded through it. Top edges of both latchets oversewn.
Edge–flesh stitching channels at vamp throat of No 4030 and on
second vertical edge of No 4031; stitch length 4mm. Conserved.
13th–14th centuries.
A03–0156c,d; L1894; C7185–7; P8.4; Phase Va; Rig VII
Illus 142

4048 Upper Leather
Small fragment, approximately trapezoidal, almost triangular,
with two opposite and converting edges oversewn, one edge
cut, one worn. Part latchet? Thickness 1.5mm. Conserved.
A03–0159h; L0168; C7185–7; P8.4; Phase Va; Rig VII
Illus 143

4123 Sole (Type 3) and rand Leather and wool
Right, with rounded seat, narrow waist, long forepart with straight inner edge and bulging outer edge, turned inwards, oval toe. Edge–flesh stitching channel; stitch length 4–8mm. Worn, with cracks in centre of seat and forepart. Wool survives in a few stitch holes. Maximum length 239mm; maximum width of forepart 86mm; width of waist 38mm; maximum width of seat 65.5mm. Thickness: outer edge of waist, inner and outer edges of seat 2.5mm; rear outer edge of forepart, middle of inner edge of forepart 4mm; inner edge of waist, front of outer and inner edges of forepart 3.5mm; middle of outer edge of forepart, rear of inner edge of forepart, rear of seat 5mm. Matching Upper Cat No 4131/A03–0214i. Also fragment of rand still attached to rear of seat. Conserved. 13th–14th centuries.
A03–0214a; L1305; C7208–7; P8.4; Phase Va; Rig VII
Illus 120

4124 Sole (Type 4) Leather
Left, with long narrow seat, slender waist, gently curved forepart, almost symmetrical; pointed toe. Worn, with part of seat missing and with two cracks in centre of forepart. A few tunnel stitches on underside suggest forepart repaired with clump sole. Edge–flesh stitching channel; stitch length 6–9mm. Surviving length 240.5mm; maximum width of forepart 80mm; width of waist 38mm; maximum width of seat 53mm. Thickness: inner edge of waist and seat, rear of inner edge of forepart 4mm; middle of inner edge of forepart 3.5mm; front of inner edge of forepart, outer edge of seat and waist, rear of outer edge of forepart 3mm; rear of outer edges of seat 2mm. Conserved. 13th–14th centuries.
A03–0214b; L1305; C7208–7; P8.4; Va; Rig VII
Illus 121

4131 Upper Leather (cattle hide)
Fragment of vamp, with lasting margin, stitch length 5 - 6 mm. Matches Sole (Type 3) Cat No 4123/A03–0214a. Conserved. Sole: 13th–14th centuries.
A03–0214i; L1305; C7208–7; P8.4; Phase Va; Rig VII
Not illustrated

4151 Miscellaneous fragment with metalwork
Leather and Cu alloy
Three pieces, two joining hollow copper alloy strap, possibly with leather passing through it and with piece of leather attached to corrosion on one fragment: strapend or chape (see Fascicule 2, The metalwork, Non-ferrous Cat No 51). Conserved.
A04–0088; L3968; C9010–9; P8.4; Phase Va; Rig VII
Not illustrated

4153 Upper (Type Kii) with bunion? Leather (cattle hide)
Large fragment with central fastening, comprising vamp, vamp throat, vamp wing, quarters and latchet or leg flap with four long horizontal slits, probably left foot. Lasting margin with grain–flesh stitching channel; stitch length 6–9mm. Edge–flesh stitching channels at vamp throat, vamp wing and vertical edge of quarters; stitch length 3.5–4.5mm. Top edge of quarters and vertical edge of leg flap and part of vertical edge of vamp wing oversewn. No traces of tunnel stitching for any facing.

Long crack down vamp; torn not cut, accordingly accidental, not deliberate. Front of vamp fairly pointed. Considerable wear towards front of vamp, but behind toe, suggests that either the shoe was too narrow or that the wearer had a bunion. It is also possible that the shoe was too long, with the toe extending beyond foot. Probable length of boot c220mm. Very worn and fragile. Conserved.
A03–0198b; L1289; C7215–7; P8.4, Pit 7216; Phase Va; Rig VII
Illus 142

4248 Sole (Type 3) Leather
Right, with long narrow seat, waist and wide rounded forepart with oval toe. Very worn, thin and cracked, several short cuts in seat–possibly remains of stitching for clump sole. Edge–flesh stitching channel; stitch length 4mm. Length 259.5mm; maximum width of forepart 92.5mm; width of waist 36.5mm; maximum width of seat 64mm. Thickness: outer edge of waist, rear of outer edge of forepart 1mm; inner edge of waist, outer, inner and rear edges of seat 2mm; outer edge of front of forepart 3mm; middle of outer and inner edges of forepart 3.5mm. Conserved. 13th–14th centuries.
A4943c; L0015; C2746–2; B1(b), Demolition; Phase Va; Rig V
Illus 119

4250–4252 Miscellaneous fragments with metalwork (3)
Leather and Cu alloy
Three fragments: one offcut and one scrap from shoe? Traces of stitching, no apparent connection with metal. Third fragment found inside one bent piece of three pieces of bronze/copper, but possibly not associated (see Fascicule 2, The metalwork, Non-ferrous Cat 187). Conserved.
A4491a–c; L3591; C2748–2; B1(b), Demolition; Phase Va; Rig V
Not illustrated

4256 Miscellaneous fragment Leather (cattle hide)
Fragment with two cut and two oversewn edges, c0.5mm thick. Conserved.
A4909; L1648; C2775–2; B1(b), Demolition, Tumble; Phase Va; Rig V
Illus 159

4287 Upper Leather
Two torn fragments (adjoining, originally one) of vamp decorated with three ribs/four grooves from throat to toe. Very worn and torn and partially delaminated. Lasting margin with stitching channel of grain–flesh holes; stitch length 3–4.5mm. Edge–flesh stitching channel at vamp throat and wing; stitch length 3–3.5mm. A third fragment is torn part of upper with lasting margin; stitch length 4–5mm; and two edge–flesh stitching channels. Thickness c1mm. Conserved.
A6398; L1665; C3534–1; M5a, Pit 3540; Phase IVb–Vc; Rigs V and VI
Illus 144

4307 Upper (Type E) Leather
Fragment of low shoe, comprising vamp, part of vamp throat and quarters with stitch holes for tall triangular stiffener. Lasting margin with grain–flesh stitching channel; stitch length 4.5–8mm. Edge–flesh stitching channels on vamp throat and

vertical edge of quarters; stitch length: quarters 3–3.5mm, throat 4.5–5mm. Top edge oversewn. Very worn and cracked. Conserved. 12th century.
A1223b; L0031; C2404–3; M1.5a; Phase Va,Vb(VI); Rigs V and VI
Illus 138

4493 Sole (Type 2) Leather (cattle hide)
Child's right sole, complete but worn, with holes in rear of seat and in centre forepart. Rounded toe. Edge–flesh stitching channel; stitch length 5mm, 6mm, 7mm, 6.5mm, 7.5mm. Length 127mm; maximum width of forepart 51mm; width of waist 33.5mm; maximum width of seat 44.5mm. Thickness: worn edge of holes 0.5mm; seam edge 3.5mm. Conserved. 12th–14th centuries.
A4289a; L0036; C2404–3; M1.5a; Phase Va,Vb(VI); Rigs V and VI
Illus 124

4495 Toggle Leather
Thong, c110mm long, thick end of which has been rolled and threaded through itself to form a toggle. Conserved.
A4289c; L0036; C2404–3; M1.5a; Phase Va,Vb(VI); Rigs V and VI
Illus 150

4530 Sole (Type 4) Leather
Right, with pointed toe. Worn across forepart, with hole in great toe area, large hole in centre forepart and crack from large hole to outer edge of forepart; also worn at rear of seat, with stitching channel missing and small crack through centre of seat. Edge–flesh stitching channel; stitch length 4.5–8mm, mostly 6–7mm, fairly regular but slightly long and coarse. Maximum surviving length 226mm; maximum width of forepart 80.5mm; width of waist 43mm; maximum width of seat 58mm. Thickness: outer edge of seat, outer edge of forepart 5mm; outer edge of waist 3mm; outer and inner edges of forepart, turned up, inner edge of waist 4mm; inner edge of forepart, by hole and inner edge of seat 3.5mm. Conserved. 13th–14th centuries.
A6245a; C2404–3; M1.5a; Phase Va,Vb(VI); Rigs V and VI
Illus 121

4533 Sole (Type 3) Leather
Part of right sole, front of forepart and rear of seat missing, with two triangles cut out of centre forepart and one triangle cut out of seat. Remains of edge–flesh stitching channel; stitch length 5–6mm; most of stitching channel on the outer edge appears to have been cut away. The triangles have been well cut from underneath with a very sharp knife, probably by a cobbler or shoemaker; the triangles on the forepart were overcut in three places, that on the seat twice. The triangles would have been very thin, as they were cut from the weakest and most worn part of the shoe, the centre forepart. The purpose of these cut-outs is not clear. In its present condition, with front of forepart and rear of seat missing, the sole almost resembles a simple face mask, but this is probably purely coincidental. Maximum surviving length 180mm; maximum width of forepart 79mm; width of waist 38mm; maximum surviving width of seat 58mm. Thickness, delaminated,

c3.5mm. Conserved. 13th–14th centuries.
A6400; C2404–3; M1.5a; Phase Va,Vb(VI); Rigs V and VI
Illus 120

4815 Sole (Type 2) Leather
Right, with broad straight seat, narrower waist and wide forepart with rounded toe. Very worn, part of rear of seat missing and with cracks at waist and centre forepart. Edge–flesh stitching channel; stitch length 4–9mm, mainly 5–7.5mm. Surviving length 206mm; maximum width of forepart 86mm; width of waist 50mm; maximum width of seat 64mm. Thickness: outer edge of waist and forepart 3mm; inner edge of forepart 4mm; inner edge of waist 5mm. Conserved. 12th–14th centuries.
A6237a; L0024; C2405–3; M1.5a; Phase Va,Vb; Rigs V and VI
Illus 118

4844 Upper Leather
Very thin and worn triangular fragment with two oversewn edges and one edge–flesh stitching channel; stitch length 2.5mm. At narrow end of triangle, eyelet, edges of which have been oversewn. Thickness c1mm. Latchet with fastening? Conserved.
A03–0175q; L2491; C7140–7; M8a; Phase Va,Vaa; Rig VII
Illus 143

4887 Sole (Type 3) Leather
Right, with rounded seat, narrow waist and forepart, turned inwards, ending in oval toe. Edge–flesh stitching channel; stitch length 4.5–7mm. Centre forepart very worn, with large hole. Length 257mm; maximum width of forepart 88mm; width of waist 38mm; maximum width of seat 66.5mm. Thickness: outer edge of waist, centre of inner edge 2.5mm; inner edge of waist 3mm; rear of outer edge of forepart 2mm; centre of outer edge of forepart and front and rear of inner edge of forepart 3.5mm; front of outer edge of forepart 4mm. Conserved. 12th–13th centuries.
A03–0128b; L1309; C7168–7; M8a; Phase Va,Vaa; Rig VII
Illus 119

4979 Toggle Leather
Formed by rolling up wider end of thong and threading it through itself. Length of thong, excluding toggle, 100mm; width of thong, excluding toggle, 1.5–5mm; thickness of thong, excluding toggle 1mm. Length of toggle 52mm; width of toggle 10mm; thickness of toggle 5mm. Conserved.
A03–0174s; L1265; C7201–7; M8a; Phase Va,Vaa; Rig VII
Illus 150

4980 Miscellaneous fragment Leather (cattle hide)
Worn and partially delaminated, with three loosely oversewn edges. Thickness c0.75mm. Conserved.
A03–0174t; L1265; C7201–7; M8a; Phase Va,Vaa; Rig VII
Illus 159

5019 Offcut Leather (cattle hide)
Thin strip with cut edges and vertical row of four oval holes, with fifth, larger, hole at top. Edges folded over towards narrower end. Conserved.
A03–0209; L1301; C7204–7; M8a; Phase Va,Vaa; Rig VII
Illus 159

5032 Upper, rand with metalwork (nails?) Leather and Fe
Fragment from quarters of shoe or boot, with rand, lasting
margin of quarters and lasting margin of stiffener? all held
together by nails? Conserved.
A03-0212m; C7205-7; M8a; Phase Va,Vaa; Rig VII
Not illustrated

5101 Upper? with fastening Leather (cattle hide)
Fragment with hem stitching at each edge at wider end,
becoming tunnel stitching as the two rows converge,
surrounding slit in narrower end. Probably latchet. Slit is big
enough to go over a toggle. Hem stitching was probably for
attachment to upper. Conserved.
A03-0046; L1091; C9012-9; M8a; Phase Va,Vaa; Rig VII
Illus 144

5220 Sheath (decorated)? Leather (cattle hide)
Fragment of leather, probably part of decorated sheath, folded
once, edges meeting and stitched together with edge–flesh
stitching channel; stitch length 5mm. Decorated with engraved
lines made with a blunt tool. Decoration on one side of front
consists of rectangles, vertical strokes alternating with plain
rectangles– in column adjacent to edge, three panels with
vertical strokes, two plain; in next, three plain and two with
horizontal strokes. Rest of this side and part of reverse-fold
decorated with a star pattern, formed by two interlocking pointed
ovals; areas to side of stars filled in with horizontal strokes.
Decorated before folded. Rest of reverse undecorated, but
pierced by three pairs of oval holes c5mm by 2mm, c15–16mm
between pairs; holes of lower two pairs c11mm apart, those of
top pair c18mm apart. Leather between the holes is split. Whole
fragment is very worn, torn, cracked and delaminated and both
top and bottom edges are worn, not cut or finished. Surviving
length 71mm; width, unfolded 80mm; width, folded 40mm.
Rectangles with hatching–imitation of armorial bearings?
Star pattern–also part of armorial bearings? 13th century?
A03-0130; L0483; C7172-7; M8a, T7193; Phase Va,Vaa;
Rig VII
Illus 156

5221 Sole (Type 7) Leather
Long, left, with slender seat and waist, and wide gently curved
forepart, turned inwards, with edge–flesh stitching channel
across front; stitch length 5mm, 9mm. Stitch holes indicate both
seat and forepart repaired with clump soles. Worn, with hole in
outer part of seat and with outer edge of forepart partially worn
away. Length 254mm; maximum width of forepart 88mm; width
of waist 41mm; maximum surviving width of seat 59.5mm; width
of front of forepart 54mm. Thickness: inner edge of waist and
rear of inner edge of forepart 4.5mm; inner edge of seat 5mm;
outer edge of waist, front of outer edge of seat and front of outer
edge of forepart 3.5mm; rear of outer edge of forepart 3mm;
front of inner edge of forepart 4mm; middle/rear of outer edge
of seat 1.5mm; front of forepart, worn middle of outer edge of
forepart and worn edges of hole in seat 0.75mm. Conserved.
A03-0138a; L0490; C7172-7; M8a, T7193; Phase Va,Vaa;
Rig VII
Illus 123

5240 Sole (Type 4) Leather
Right, with long narrow seat, waist and slender forepart,
gently curved with pointed toe. Very worn, with holes in seat
and forepart. Slits indicate position of tunnel holes used in
attachment of clump sole to seat, waist and rear of forepart.
Edge–flesh stitching channel; stitch length 6–8mm. Length
273.5mm; maximum width of forepart 85mm; width of waist
48mm; maximum width of seat 69mm. Thickness: inner
and outer edges of waist 1mm; outer edge of forepart, inner
edge of forepart, outer edge of seat 3mm; inner edge of seat
2.5mm. Conserved. 13th–14th centuries.
A03-0090; L0457; C7141-7; B53 (Phase 1), Central Area–
Occupation (3c); Phase Vb; Rig VII
Illus 121

5241 Sole (Type 2)? upper and rand
Leather upper (cattle hide) and wool
Left sole and upper in three fragments, still joined together,
with wool surviving. Sole is complete, with wide seat, slight
narrowing for waist and wide forepart, oval toe. Edge–flesh
stitching channel; stitch length c5–7.5mm. Length 262.5mm;
maximum width of forepart 100mm; width of waist 61.5mm;
maximum width of seat 75.5mm. Thickness: outer edge of
waist, rear of outer edge of forepart 3mm; front and middle of
outer edge of forepart and rear of seat 6mm. Rand between
sole and upper almost complete. Extends beyond sole for
c9mm at inside waist and at front of forepart. At front of
forepart, two fragments of rand, forming double thickness
protecting front of vamp. Grain–flesh holes, round and oval,
stitch length as edge–flesh stitching channel. Upper in three
parts, quarters, from outside waist towards front of inside
edge of seat; quarters have been cut away just above lasting
margin for reuse. Second fragment, side-piece, bridges gap
on inside edge between quarter and vamp wing; again cut
away above lasting margin. Vamp, with vamp wing on each
side, from inside waist to outside waist. Vamp has also been
cut away above lasting margin, except for front, where more
survives. All three fragments have lasting margin with stitching
channel of grain–flesh holes; stitch length 5–6mm, 6.5mm,
8mm. Edge–flesh stitching channels on vertical edges; stitch
length 2mm. Wool survives in sole–rand–upper seam but not
edge–flesh seams of upper. Vamp is torn at lasting margin on
inside edge, stitch holes indicate repair. Conserved. 12th–14th
centuries?
A03-0216; L1307; C7129-7; B53 (Phase 1), Central
Area–T7152; Phase Vb; Rig VII
Illus 146

5299 Sole (Type 9) Leather
Left forepart sewn across rear of waist; very narrow waist,
wide forepart narrowing to a slightly out-turned point. Worn,
particularly in centre and part of stitching channel on inner
edge missing. Edge–flesh stitching channel; stitch length
5mm, 6.5mm, mainly 5.5–6mm. Length 149mm; maximum
width 73mm; width of waist 32mm. Thickness: inner edge
of waist, front of outer edge of forepart 3mm; inner edge of
forepart, rear of outer edge of forepart 2.5mm; middle of outer
edge of forepart 1.5mm. Conserved.
A6247; L1711; C2750-4; M4a; Phase Va–Vc; Rigs V and VI
Illus 123

5395 Sheath (decorated) Leather (cattle hide)
Four fragments, decorated, comprising front and back grain layers and front and back flesh layers. Sheath made with one piece of leather, folded once and joined where edges meet with grain to edge stitching; stitch length 6.5mm. Sheath is not complete; top edge may survive on one fragment; at its other end, stitching channel curves inwards slightly– bottom of sheath? Both front and back of sheath decorated with lozenges or rhomboids containing a bird, probably a hawk, on a perch. Pattern stamped, probably with an old stamp. Fold decorated with bands of three diagonal lines, engraved with a blunt tool on wet leather. Diagonal lines are on either side of fold, forming a chevron, suggesting that sheath was decorated before leather was folded. Edge of folded area marked on both sides by wide engraved line. Maximum surviving length 130mm; maximum surviving width 55mm; thickness: delaminated. Conserved. 14th–15th centuries ?
cf sheath from York with stamped eagles, with 14th to 15th century parallels from London and from Lund in Sweden (Richardson 1959, 103–4, Fig 29, 4).
A3192; C2159–4; P1a; Phase Vd; Rig VI
Illus 156

5555 Sole (Type 9) Leather
Pointed left forepart with narrow waist and wide tread, sewn across waist. Edge–flesh stitching channel; stitch length 4.5–7mm. Worn in centre where slightly cracked. Length 126.5mm; maximum width 72mm; width of waist 31mm. Thickness: middle and rear of outer edge of forepart 4mm; front of outer edge of forepart, front of inner edge of forepart and waist 3.5mm; rear of inner edge of forepart 4.5mm; middle of inner edge of forepart 3mm. Conserved.
A6242a; C2153–4; M3c; Phase Vd; Rig V
Illus 123

5599 Sole (Type 7) Leather
Right, with edge–flesh stitching channels across middle of seat and across front of forepart; stitch lengths 5–6.5mm. Edge–flesh stitching channel round rest of sole; stitch length 5–9mm; coarse. Worn, with hole in centre of forepart; delaminated sole. Scratch marks at waist, could be animal growth marks, or else could have been deliberately made with a blunt tool; very unlikely to be a trademark. Length 185mm; maximum width of forepart 80mm; width of seam across forepart 57mm; width of waist 38mm; width of seam across seat 54mm. Conserved.
A4352a; C2171–4; M3c; Phase Vd; Rig V
Illus 123

5606 Upper (Type J) Leather (cattle hide)
Large fragment of high boot, comprising quarters and leg, separate from vamp. Lasting margin with grain–flesh holes; stitch length 4–5mm. Edge–flesh stitching channels; stitch length 2.5–4mm. Top edge oversewn. Also, stitch holes for small triangular stiffener. Worn. Maximum height of leg c230mm; thickness 1–2mm. Conserved.
A03–0254; L1345; C6012–10; MC174, Pit 7013; Phase (Va–)Vd (Vdd); Rig VIII
Illus 143

5608 Sole (Type 4) Leather
Child's right sole, with long seat and slender waist and forepart, with pointed toe; worn, especially at front of forepart and rear of seat. Edge–flesh stitching channel; stitch length 5.5mm, 6.5mm, 7mm; at outer edge of seat, close concentration of holes (repair). Length 165mm; maximum width of forepart 55mm; width of waist 28mm; maximum width of seat 41mm. Thickness: outer edge of waist and forepart 3.5mm; inner edge of waist 4mm; inner edge of forepart 4.5mm; rear of inner edge of seat 2.5mm; front of forepart 1.5mm; rear of seat 2mm. Conserved. 13th–14th centuries.
A03–0065; L1095; C7013–10; MC174, Pit 7013; Phase (Va–) Vd (Vdd); Rig VIII
Illus 124

5637 Strap (folded once) Leather (cattle hide)
Fragment of belt or strap, approximately 270mm long, 17-40 mm wide, with pointed oval hole, 45mm by 16mm at wide end and at narrow end ten small holes, diameter c2–3 mm in two clusters (for attachment of buckle or other fastening?). Formed of two separate pieces of leather, placed together with grain on either side. One fragment is folded once, thus forming a double thickness. Both fragments stitched together along edges and around large oval hole, except that there is no stitching at end with small holes, where edges cut, original edge or not? Thickness of each layer 2–2.5 mm; overall thickness 6mm. Conserved.
A1241; L1663; C2137–4; M3e, Pit 2111; Phase Vdd; Rig VI
Illus 152

5638 Upper (Type Ki) Leather (cattle hide)
Small fragment, possibly latchet, with one edge–flesh stitching channel; stitch length 3.5mm, and with three oversewn edges. Parallel to vertical oversewn edge are three holes with ends of toggles threaded through two of them; both thongs (of toggles) pass through tunnel hole on flesh side; one thong also passes through second thong also passed through second tunnel hole. No thong survives through third hole which ends in long split-hole for toggle from second latchet? Maximum dimensions 75mm by 50mm by 2mm. Probably latchet attached to quarters by edge–flesh stitching channel. Conserved. 13th–14th centuries.
A1249a; L1764; C2137–4; M3e, Pit 2111; Phase Vdd>; Rig VI
Illus 142

5739 Sole (Type 4) Leather (cattle hide)
Almost symmetrical with curled over pointed toe. Probably for right foot. Crack in seat, worn at front of forepart and underneath of centre forepart, partial delamination. Edge–flesh stitching channel; stitch length 4–6mm. Length 223mm; maximum width of forepart 77mm; width of waist 44mm; maximum width of seat 64.5mm. Thickness: outer edge of waist 3.5mm; outer edge of seat 4mm; inner edge of waist 2.5mm. Conserved. 13th–14th centuries.
A12307c; L0064; C3870–1; Unstratified; Rigs VI and VII
Illus 121

5740 Upper (Type Biii) Leather
Two fragments of ankle boot with vertical thonging. Larger
fragment comprises vamp with oval toe, vamp wing, vamp
throat, part of quarters and leg flap; smaller fragment is rest
of quarters–originally one fragment, now torn. Quarters and
vamp wing join. Line of vertical thonging on closed side of
quarters, spanning join between the two fragments. Three
tunnel holes, c11mm long, on larger fragment, three on
smaller fragment, two being 6.5mm long and the other 9mm
long. Short length, 32mm, of thong threaded through these
tunnel holes; width of thong 5mm. Small hole, c2.4mm by
1mm, on larger fragment near vamp throat (for thin pointed
end of thong?). Lasting margin with grain–flesh stitching
channel; stitch length 5.5–6.5mm. Edge–flesh stitching
channel on vamp wing, vamp throat, bottom edge of leg
flap and vertical edge of quarters; stitch length 3–6.5mm.
Top edge of quarters and top and vertical edges of leg flap
oversewn. Conserved. 12th–13th centuries.
A12307d; L0064; C3870–1; Unstratified; Rigs VI and VII
Illus 132

5749 Toggle, with metalwork Leather (cattle hide) and
metal
Strip of leather c350mm long, 8–9mm wide and 4mm thick,
no stitching. Three lumps of metal and mud? attached.
Conserved.
A5898i; L1758; C2716–2; Unstratified; Rigs V and VI
Illus 152

5762 Miscellaneous fragment Leather
Edges slightly bent and perforated all round by grain–
flesh holes of c1mm diameter; stitch length 4.5–5.5mm.
Symmetrical in shape, could have been folded but now no
signs of fold. Thickness 2–2.5mm. Conserved.
A9914; L0070; C2716–2; Unstratified; Rigs V and VI
Illus 159

5767 Miscellaneous fragment Leather
Approximately square, 124mm by 145mm, and c0.25–
0.5mm thick. Three edges cut, fourth worn; all corners worn.
A central box is marked out by two engraved lines forming
rectangles, one inside the other. Lines possibly stamped.
Rectangles, 99mm by 73–76mm and 85mm by 65–66mm.
Outer line 2mm wide, inner 1mm. Third line, c10mm out
from larger rectangle, forming another rectangle–faint and
irregular. Fourth rectangle marked by band of impressed
or stamped decoration infilled with gilt/gold coloured
substance; fourth side of this rectangle does not survive
on torn side of fragment. Stamped decoration consists
of repeated candelabrum motif and stylised floral motif.
Fragment folded once if not twice but not permanently.
Cover for flat article but no sign of glue on flesh side: boot
cover? Conserved. Post- medieval?
A6203; L1654; C2001–3/4; Unstratified; Rigs V and VI
Illus 158

5768 Sole (Type 2) and 5769 rand and upper (Type J)
Leather (cattle hide) and wool
Complete sole (No 5768/A9821a), rand and nearly
complete upper (No 5769/A9821b) of left ankle boot with

woollen thread and part of felt lining surviving (see also this
Fascicule, The textiles, Cat No 406). Sole has short rounded
seat, fairly broad waist and gently curved forepart with central
oval toe. Edge–flesh stitching channel; stitch length 5.5–
7mm. Wool survives in this seam, all round but visible only at
rear of outer forepart, outer rear of seat, and inner waist. Sole
is worn, with large hole in centre of seat, large hole in centre
of tread of forepart, and small hole in outer rear of forepart.
Trace of stitch holes for seat and forepart clumps. Length
229mm; maximum width of forepart 90mm; width of waist
55.5mm; maximum width of seat 61mm; thickness 5–16mm.
Short fragment of rand at outer waist and another at front of
forepart/vamp: providing protection for front of vamp? Upper
consisting of three fragments with probably a fourth missing.
Largest comprises vamp, vamp throat, both vamp wings each
reaching far back. Outer vamp wing incorporates complete
outer leg flap, inner vamp wing has only rear of inner leg flap,
ie front of inner leg flap was a separate piece and is now
missing. Second largest, approximately trapezoidal in shape,
consists of quarters joined to outer vamp wing/leg flap and
to inner vamp wing/leg flap and to small third fragment of
upper. Quarters also attached on flesh side to stiffener. Third
fragment of upper is very small and triangular and is attached
to sole, vamp and quarters. Approximately trapezoidal
stiffener, still in position, attached to sole and lasting margin
of quarters by wool, but thread stitching its upper edges to
flesh side of quarters does not survive. Lasting margin with
stitching channel of grain–flesh holes on all three fragments
of upper and on stiffener; stitch length 5.5–7mm. Edge–flesh
stitching channels on vamp throat, vertical edges of leg flaps
and vamp wings and of quarters; stitch length 2.5–3.5mm.
Upper is worn, with cracks and holes, especially along both
outer and inner edges of vamp and along vertical edge of
outer vamp wing. At rear of seat, small fragment of felt lining
survives. Trace of felt all over inside of boot. Construction
unusual, with separate quarters and with third fragment of
upper which suggests cobbler miscalculated in cutting out
vamp and quarters and had to insert another fragment to fill
a gap. Approximate height of vamp throat 40mm; maximum
height of quarters 90mm; thickness of upper 2mm. Upper:
approximate height of vamp throat above sole 40mm.
Conserved. 12th–13th centuries.
A9821a,b; C2001–3/4; Unstratified; Rigs V and VI
Illus 140

5770 Sheath (decorated) Leather (cattle hide)
Fragment decorated with *fleurs-de-lys*. Formed of one piece
of leather, folded once, edges joined by grain to edge seam;
stitch length 3–4mm. Upper part of sheath is approximately
rectangular, lower part pointed (but upper part does not
project). Upper part pierced by two holes, adjacent to seam
–holes pierce both back and front– for attachment to belt or
other article. Lower part has two holes on one side, one on
the other, otherwise no difference between the two sides.
Decoration identical, except that on side with two holes
on lower part it is less distinct (more worn by contact and
therefore reverse?). Fragment, now unfolded, was decorated
with stamped diamonds containing *fleurs-de-lys* before being
folded. Upper margin of sheath marked by a row of short
vertical lines engraved with a sharp tool. Upper part of sheath

filled with diamonds with *fleurs-de-lys* in 19 vertical rows (front and back) with four, five in alternating rows. Upper rectangular part and lower tapering part divided by double row of short vertical lines engraved with a sharp tool. Area beneath this again filled by diamonds with *fleurs-de-lys*. Surviving length 97mm; maximum width 39mm; thickness c2–3mm, but delaminated. Conserved.
A12573; C2001–3/4; Unstratified; Rigs V and VI
Illus 156

5774 Upper? Leather (cattle hide)
Fragment with fastening, with two thongs threaded through four tunnel holes, probably tongue or latchet rather than shoe. Both thongs knotted/anchored at one end of fragment. At other end, on flesh side, c140mm of one thong extends beyond tunnel holes; second thong broken. Between the two rows of tunnel holes is a line of short slashes. One short end of fragment has very neat grain–flesh stitching channel, edge bent (substitute for edge–flesh stitching channel?). Thickness 1mm. Conserved.
A12754d; C2001–3/4; Unstratified; Rigs V and VI
Illus 143

5775 Offcut Leather (cattle hide)
Length 265mm; maximum width c60mm; thickness 1.5–2mm; an area c120mm long and 60mm wide has been cut six times, leaving seven strips c6–7mm wide. Conserved.
A12574e; L0048; C2001–3/4; Unstratified; Rigs V and VI
Illus 158

5779 Sole (Type 2) Leather
Right, with rounded toe, worn at centre forepart, with hole and with long tunnel stitches, indicating that repair clump was added. Similarly, hole in centre of seat surrounded by a few tunnel stitches. Edge–flesh stitching channel; stitch length 5–10mm, mostly 7–9mm, very coarse, holes diameter 3mm; very close stitching at inner waist, hole diameter 1mm, seven holes close together, stitch length 2mm, 4mm, 3.5mm, 2.5mm– repair? Length 239mm; maximum width of forepart 83mm; width of waist 51mm; maximum width of seat 62mm. Thickness: outer edge of waist 4mm; inner edge of forepart and waist 5mm; outer forepart 6mm; rear of seat 6.5mm. Conserved. 12th–14th centuries.
A0800a; C2006–3/4; Unstratified; Rigs V and VI
Illus 118

5780 Clump/upper repair patch? Leather
Clump or repair patch? Edge–flesh stitching channel on one edge; stitch length 6mm; tunnel stitch holes on other edges. Length 103mm; width 25mm; thickness 4–5mm. Conserved.
A0800b; C2006–3/4; Unstratified; Rigs V and VI
Illus 104

5788 Miscellaneous fragment Leather
Triangular, 2.5–4.5mm thick, ?case, with edge–flesh stitching on all edges, hole diameter c2.25mm, stitch long but very regular, length 6–7mm. Conserved.
A0800j; C2006–3/4; Unstratified; Rigs V and VI
Illus 159

5793 Sole (welted) Leather
Seat and waist fragment of outer sole of welted shoe. Parallel to edges of waist is a stitching channel of grain–flesh slits; stitch length 2.5mm. Parallel to this row on left side and parallel to right edge, towards front, is a row of grain–flesh holes (nails or stitching?); stitch length 6.5mm, 5.5mm. Edge–flesh stitching channel across front of fragment; stitch length 6.5mm, 7.5mm. Grain–flesh holes (nails or stitching ?) round edge of seat; stitch length 6.5mm, 7mm, 9mm, 8mm, 10mm. Across front of seat is a row of grain–flesh holes, from grain side, only just piercing flesh side, probably nail holes. Centre of seat is perforated by seven holes (for nails?) probably flesh side up but hard to tell. Length 130mm; width at front of seam 63mm; width of waist 55mm; maximum width of seat 70mm. Thickness: right side of waist 2mm; left side of waist 2.5mm; seam across front 5mm; seat 4mm. Conserved.
A0817b; L1746; C2006–3/4; Unstratified; Rigs V and VI
Illus 145

5823 Miscellaneous fragment Leather (cattle hide)
Cut. Pointed slit at wide end, length 30.5mm, maximum width 3.5mm. Traces of edge–flesh stitching channel on long edges, towards narrow end. All edges cut. Loop? Shoe or other fastening? Length 101mm; width at one end 11mm; at other end 20mm; thickness 1–2mm. Conserved.
A03–0080; L1093; C7014–7; Modern, T7014, D7014; Phase VI; Rig VII
Illus 152

5824 Sole (Type 9) Leather (cattle hide)
Pointed left forepart, long and slender, stitched across rear of waist. Edge–flesh stitching channel; stitch length 2.5–5mm. Length 177mm; maximum width 76mm; width of waist 46mm; width at seam at rear of waist 62mm. Thickness: inner edge of waist, rear of inner edge of forepart, front edge of forepart, front of outer edge of forepart, stitched edge across rear of waist 3mm; middle and rear of outer edge of forepart and outer edge of waist 3.5mm; middle and front of inner edge of forepart 2.5mm. Conserved.
A03–0127a; L0480; C7164–7; Unstratified; Rigs VI and VII
Illus 123

5855 Clump Leather and wool
Seat, formed of two fragments joined with butted edge–flesh stitching channel; stitch length 4.5–7.5mm, with wool surviving. Reused fragments of soles? Tunnel stitches round perimeter for attachment to original sole. Unusual clump, very economical but probably neither very practical nor strong. Length 100mm; maximum width 75mm; thickness 1–3.5mm. Conserved.
A03–0133f; L0486; C7164–7; Unstratified; Rig VI and VII
Illus 104

5868 Sheath (decorated) Leather
Decoration: bands of hatching and rope pattern.
Construction: of one piece of leather, originally approximately triangular. Lower part pointed, folded twice, edges meeting in middle of reverse side. Upper part is rectangular and projecting, meeting very close to projecting side with butted

edge to grain stitching channel; stitch length 11mm. Bottom
end of sheath cut and turned in slightly, top edge cut.
Pointed hole near top right hand corner of front of sheath
with two very small holes above it; large and small holes
in corresponding positions on reverse for attachment to
belt or other article. Top edge of reverse slightly lower than
that of front. Cracks at junction of lower and upper parts of
sheath. Decoration: front, upper part– rectangular panel
of irregular diagonal hatching divided by pairs or bands of
horizontal lines: seven bands on right hand side, enclosing
six zones of hatching: pairs of bands join in middle of panel
to form six bands which continue across rest of front and
whole of reverse, with hatching enclosed. To right of this
large rectangular panel is a narrow strip of diagonal hatching
and a small zone of hatching which contains the pointed
hole described above. Also, horizontal zones of hatching
at top and bottom of rectangular panel. Decoration: front,
lower part– triangular panel with plaited or rope pattern
enclosed by diagonal hatching. No decoration on reverse.
Length 183mm; width of upper part 52mm; maximum width
of lower part 30mm; minimum width of lower part 2mm;
single thickness 1.5mm; folded thickness, bottom end 4mm.
Conserved. 13th–14th centuries.
cf Richardson 1959, 103 for hatching 13th century or later,
Tatton-Brown 1975, 162–3, figs 29, 113 (Custom House site,
London) for rope pattern early to mid 14th century.
A03–0004a; C7000–7–10; Unstratified; Rigs VI-VIII
Illus 155

5872 Sheath (long, plain) Leather (cattle hide)
Long strip of leather slightly curved towards the bottom,
folded twice, edges meeting up middle of reverse where
stitched together in a butted edge to grain seam; stitch length
3–4mm. No decoration. Bottom end of sheath tapered,
ending in gently rounded curve, not sharp point. Top edge of
sheath cut, not in a straight line (original top?). Fragile and
very delaminated. Length, straight, 353mm, curved c360mm;
maximum width 56mm; single thickness 2.5mm. Conserved.
A03–0019; C7000–7–10; Unstratified; Rigs VI–VIII
Illus 154

5873 Miscellaneous fragment Leather (cattle hide)
Approximately triangular, with rounded apex in which a
small central and a larger concentric circle are partially
cut; 13mm towards broad end a short loop? is cut out (part
of fastening?). Maximum length 112.5mm; minimum width
10mm; maximum width 64mm; thickness 2mm. Conserved.
A03–0028; L0414; C7000–7–10; Unstratified; Rigs VI–VIII
Illus 152

5875 Sheath (short, plain) Leather
Very worn fragment of plain sheath, formed by one piece of
leather folded once and stitched where edges meet. Tattered
and partially delaminated. Maximum surviving length
206.5mm; width 35.5mm. Conserved.
A03–0037a; L1099; C7000–7–10; Unstratified; Rigs VI–VIII
Illus 154

5878 Offcut Leather (cattle hide)
Irregular, with seven cuts in a row. Dimensions c131mm by
51mm by 1.5mm. Conserved.
A03–0040b; L0420; C7000–7–10; Unstratified; Rigs VI–VIII
Illus 159

5880 Strap (folded once) Leather (cattle hide)
Fragment, folded once, with, on one side, two rows of short
grain–flesh slits 5.5mm long and 2.5–4mm (end to end) apart.
The rows are parallel to edges of strap except where one side
of strap widens by c10–14mm. Edge to grain stitching channel
parallel to edge of wider part; stitch length 5.5–7mm. Parallel
to stitching channel is a row of grain–flesh slits 3–4mm long
and 3–4mm apart. Long edges of strap are cut on unwidened
and on widened sides to extension, and long edge on widened
side is torn after c90mm of edge to grain stitching channel. At
that end, which is torn, at c20mm from end, slits cease on both
sides. Other end is also torn. Length 347mm; maximum width,
folded, 33mm; minimum width, with cut edges, 17mm; single
thickness 2mm.
A03–0425b; L2485; C7000–7–10; Unstratified; Rigs VI–VIII
Illus 148

North Sector (Area 5)

5889 Upper (Type Biv) Leather
Two joining fragments, originally one, of upper of boot with
short stretch of thong through slit in vamp wing, knotted on
flesh side. Comprises vamp, high vamp wing, vamp throat,
quarters with stitch holes for semi-circular stiffener and leg flap.
Quarters and vamp wing join. Complete but for second leg flap.
Lasting margin with grain–flesh stitching channel; stitch length
5–5.6mm. Edge–flesh stitching channels on vamp throat, vamp
wing, vertical edge of leg flap and on vertical edge of quarters;
stitch length 3mm. Top edges of quarters and leg flap oversewn.
Quarters and front of vamp worn and cracked. Stitch holes
on flesh side around crack in side of vamp and around part of
vamp, lasting margin missing suggests that these areas have
been repaired. Stitch holes on flesh side of quarters, beneath
those for stiffener, also suggest repair. Conserved. 12th–14th
centuries.
A7805c; L1748; C0435–5; CG005; Phase 4(5)
Illus 134

5924 Strap (single thickness) Leather
Piece, of single thickness with pointed end with roughly oval
hole and with five short slashes, for decoration? Partially
delaminated. Surviving length 233mm; width 23–24mm;
thickness 0.35mm. Conserved.
A0115; C0062–5&A; Lade (4); Phase 6–12(b–e)
Illus 152

5929 Sole (Type 9) Leather
Left forepart with oval toe. Edge–flesh stitching channel across
waist, and round perimeter; stitch length, waist 4mm, rest 7mm.
Length 145mm; maximum width 75mm; width of waist 29mm.
Thickness: at waist 2mm, at toe end of forepart 3mm, on inside
and outside edges 4mm. Conserved.
A0110a; C0063–5&A; Lade (4); Phase 6–12(b–e)
Illus 123

5941 Strap/belt (single thickness), decorated Leather
Short fragment of single thickness, one long edge cut but
apparently not stitched. One long edge cut, with stitching
channel of grain to edge holes; stitch length c6mm. One short
edge torn the other cut and apparently stitched, trace of grain–
flesh stitching channel. Decoration: eight rosettes set within
spirals or whorls, all within a long rectangular frame. The frame
and innermost ring of spirals marked out by small punched dots,
each of c1mm diameter. Some additional lines and triangular
patches also marked out with three dots. Outer rings of whorls
or spirals marked by narrow lines engraved with blunt tool on
wet leather. Rosettes stamped, almost certainly with same
stamp. Each rosette has seven petals. Rosette diameter
11.5mm each. Surviving length 181mm; maximum width 42mm;
thickness c1mm, delaminated? Conserved.
A0802; C0100–5&A; Lade (4); Phase 6–12(b–e)
Illus 156

5942 Sole (Type 2) Leather (cattle hide)
Child's right, with almost straight inner edge, curved outer edge,
of forepart, rounded toe. Edge–flesh stitching channel; stitch
length 5mm, 6mm. Crack at waist. Length 118.5mm; maximum
width of forepart 48mm; width of waist 34mm; maximum width of
seat 41mm. Thickness: outer edge of waist, front of outer edge
of forepart, rear of seat, 3mm; inner edge of waist and seat,
middle of outer edge of forepart, inner edge of seat, 3.5mm;
front of inner edge of forepart 2mm. Conserved. 12th–13th
centuries.
A0807a; L1715; C0100–5&A; Lade (4); Phase 6–12(b–e)
Illus 124

5958 Strap/belt (single thickness) Leather (cattle hide)
Fragment of single thickness, greyish-blue, worn, with two
rounded corners. Decorated with two parallel rows of short
diagonal cuts next to edge, two round holes, diameter c5.5–
6mm and 23mm apart; in centre is trace of third hole on worn
torn edge. Signs of wear (pin or buckle?) around edges of both
surviving holes. Length 113mm; width 45.5mm; thickness 2mm.
Conserved.
A0100; L0043; C0026–5&A; CG024; Phase 14–16
Illus 151

South/North Sectors

5978 Upper (Type Biii) Leather (cattle hide)
Two fragments of very worn and tattered boot with two rows
of vertical thonging. Larger fragment comprises vamp, vamp
throat, quarters and leg flap. Smaller fragment joins diagonal
edge of quarters. On both sides of quarters is a vertical row of
tunnel holes with thongs. On closed side of quarters are four
short stretches of thong (on grain side), and on open side are
three short stretches of thong (on grain side). Upper end of each
thong is pointed (on flesh side). Lasting margin with grain–flesh
stitching channel; stitch length 4.5–6.5mm. Edge–flesh stitching
channels on vamp wing, vamp throat, vertical and diagonal
edges of quarters, and on second fragment; stitch length
4–5mm. No stitching survives on vertical edge of leg flap.
Quarters very worn. Conserved. 12th–13th centuries.
A?; L1694e; C?; Unstratified
Illus 133

5979 and 5980 Uppers? (2) Leather
Two fragments. No 5979/L1694f with lasting margin with
stitching channel of irregularly spaced oval holes; stitch length
13.5mm, 11mm, 11.5mm, 5.5mm, 6mm. One edge has part
edge-flesh, part grain–flesh, ie grain folded to form edge.
Similarly, on third edge, stitch length 3mm, 3.5mm, 2mm
(vertical edge), 4mm, 4.5mm, 5.5mm, 5mm (horizontal edge).
No 5980/L1694g similar, stitch length 4.5mm, 5mm, 6mm,
3.5mm, 7mm, 8mm, 14mm; other two edges both compare,
stitch length 2.5-3.5mm (vertical), 3-4mm (horizontal). These
two fragments appear to join along their vertical edges (repair
fragments for upper?). Thickness 2.5-3mm. Conserved.
A?; L1694f,g; C?; Unstratified
Illus 104

5983 Sole (welted) Leather
Fragment of seat, welted, with stitching channel of grain–flesh
holes c5.5mm in from the edge; stitch length c3.5mm, 6mm,
2mm, 3mm, 5mm, very irregular. Five small round holes in
centre, which just penetrate from flesh to grain. Worn, not easy
to distinguish between grain and flesh sides. See also No 5984.
Conserved.
A?; L2766b; C?; Unstratified
Illus 145

5984 Sole (welted) Leather
Seat, welted, with stitching channel of grain–flesh holes c7.5mm
in from edge; stitch length c3–4mm. Seat appears to have
grain side up. Centre is perforated by about twelve oval holes
(one large, seven medium, four small). Irregular groove across
seat to rear of waist, cracked at front, worn and very dry and
brittle, most of stitching channel missing, only outline survives.
Thickness c4–5mm. See also No 5983. Conserved.
A?; L2766c; C?; Unstratified
Illus 145

APPENDICES

Leatherwork including silk

Cat/Accession	Leather type	Area	Rig	Feature	Phase
South Sector					
172/A7580a	Strap (folded once)	2	VI	M14b(b)	Ie
229/A7588c	Upper (Type G)	2	V	M14b(c)	Ie,If

Leatherwork including wool

Cat/Accession	Leather type	Area	Rig	Feature	Phase
South Sector					
55/A9886b	Upper	1/2	V, VI	M2.1b	Ic
312/A12378b	Upper	3	VI	P5.3b	If,IIa
343/A6772c	Rand, sole (Type 1), upper	2	VI	MC061	IIb
352/A6773a	Sole (Type 2)	2	VI	MC061	IIb
356/A6773e	Rand	2	VI	MC061	IIb
358/A6773g	Upper (Type Bii)	2	VI	MC061	IIb
452/A10048a	Sole (Type 1)	4	VI	M1.1f, Pit 2383	IIb,IIc
462/A10599a	Sole (Type 1)	3	VI	M1.1c, Pit 5005	IId
464/A10599c	Upper	3	VI	M1.1c, Pit 5005	IId
469/A12285a	Sole (Type 1)	3	VI	M1.1c, Pit 5005	IId
470/A12285b	Sole (Type 1)	3	VI	M1.1c, Pit 5005	IId
471/A12285c	Sole (Type 1)	3	VI	M1.1c, Pit 5005	IId
473/A12285e	Upper (Type Biv)	3	VI	M1.1c, Pit 5005	IId
475/A12302a	Sole (Type 1)	3	VI	M1.1c, Pit 5005	IId
504/A3447a	Sole (Type 1)	2	VI	M1.1d & M1.1e	IId–IIf
548/A6412	Upper (stiffener)	2	V	B5, North Room–Floor/Occupation (2)	IIa–IIff
783/A9372a	Sole (Type 3)	3	VI	M1.2, Pit 2648	<IIg(IIh)
789/A9546b	Sole	3	VI	M1.2, Pit 2648	<IIg(IIh)
792/A9546e	Rand	3	VI	M1.2, Pit 2648	<IIg(IIh)
813/A11220b	Rand, sole, upper	3	VI	M1.2, Pit 2648	<IIg(IIh)
821/A11221a	Sole (Type 4)	3	VI	M1.2, Pit 2648	<IIg(IIh)
822/A11221b	Rand	3	VI	M1.2, Pit 2648	<IIg(IIh)
857/A8527a	Sole (Type 3)	4	VI	M1.3	IIi
876/A8665c*	Rand	3	VI	M1.3	IIi
1003/A8011a	Sole (rounded forepart)	4	VI	M1.4a(a)	IIIa–IIIc
1026/A03–0317a	Sole (Type 1)	9	VII	P8.1b	IIIc
1028/A03–0317c	Grain–flesh stitching channel	9	VII	P8.1b	IIIc
1130/A03–0263a	Sole (Type 2)	9	VII	M15	IIId
2361/A03–0331a	Rand, sole (Type 2), upper	7	VI	M1.4f	IVc
2651/A03–0316a	Sole (Type 1)	7	VII	B18(Phase 1/2), Pit 7324	IVaa,IVb
2719/A03–0314c	Rand	7	VII	B18(Phase 2a), External (1)–Pit 7314	IVb
2725/A03–0413a	Rand, sole (Type 3), upper (Type C)	7	VII	B18 (Phases 2a & 2b), T7385	IVb
3068/A8668c	Sole (Type 7)	3	VI	M1.4d	IVb,IVc
3343/A03–0183a	Sole, upper	7	VII	M9a	IVc,IVcc
3427/A03–0051a	Upper, sole, rand	9	VII	M9a, Pit 9026	IVc,IVcc
3721/A03–0160e	Sole (forepart)	7	VI	B34, Courtyard	Va
3726/A03–0160j	Upper	7	VI	B34, Courtyard	Va

(continued)

1 The yarns used in the leatherwork

H Bennett and the late N Q Bogdan

While examining the leatherwork from the High Street, 55 pieces were found to have retained the yarn used in their construction or repair (see Illus 167). In two cases, both of which came from deposits that had been laid down shortly before 1150, silk thread survived. One, a band of leather (Cat No 172/A7580a), perhaps a binding for a garment or shoe, has lines of decorative surface stitching in pink and white silk; the other was a Type G upper (Cat No 229/A7588c). In the other 53 cases, the yarn appeared to be wool or animal hair.

Although examples were recovered from all six South Sector Periods, the chronological distribution appears to be significant. Twenty-three (43%) of these examples of 'wool' yarn came from contexts that dated from Period II, the second half of the 12th century, and another 14 (26%) from layers that dated from the first few decades of the 14th century, Phases Va to Vbb in Period V. Curiously in the light of the relatively large number of Period II examples, only one (2%) certainly came from Period I (the first half of the 12th century) and four (8%) from Period III (the first half of the 13th century). Low as the Period III figure is, it is perhaps pertinent to remember that the Period III leatherwork formed only 4% of the total recovered during the excavation. Of all the results, perhaps the most interesting is that from Period IV. 39% of all the leatherwork from the site came from deposits that

were laid down during this Period, the second half of the thirteenth century; and yet, only seven (13%) items with yarns formed from animal hair were recovered from Period IV contexts.

The state of preservation of the yarns is extremely variable: from tiny degraded remnants in stitch holes to considerable lengths which have retained some strength and resilience and still perform the function of holding together sections of shoe. Eight of the yarns, all plyed, are sufficiently well preserved to allow examination of their structure, although in some cases it is not clear whether one or more thicknesses of yarn are present. The yarns are listed above. All the yarns are in shades of brown, although one (Cat No 3343/A03–183a) contains blue fibres visible under a microscope.

The normal material for sewing leather shoes is thread of linen or hemp but, as the Perth yarns have an unusual appearance, it was decided to take a group of samples, from both poorly preserved and well preserved specimens for microscopic examination. The results of this analysis also appear in the lists above. Of the constructional yarns, seven proved to be wool, varying in type from hairy to generalised medium, one to be cow hair, and one cow or goat hair; a tenth sample proved on closer inspection to be extraneous plant matter and not in fact part of a yarn.

Cat/Accession	Leather type	Area	Rig	Feature	Phase
3819/A03–0164c	Upper (lasting margin)	7	VI	B34, Courtyard	Va
3820/A03–0164d	Sole (edge–flesh stitching channel)	7	VI	B34, Courtyard	Va
3865/A03–0068	Clump	7	VI, VII	M1.5b	Vaa
3906/A03–0132k	Upper	7	VI, VII	M1.5b	Vaa
3926/A03–0136b	Sole	7	VI, VII	M1.5b	Vaa
3927/A03–0136c	Miscellaneous fragment	7	VI, VII	M1.5b	Vaa
4041/A03–0159a	Sole (seat cut across waist)	7	VII	P8.4	Va
4088/A03–0210b	Sole (rounded forepart)	7	VII	P8.4	Va
4123/A03–0214a	Rand, sole (Type 3)	7	VII	P8.4	Va
4152/A03–0198a	Sole (seat cut across waist)	7	VII	P8.4, Pit 7216	Va
4816/A6237b	Sole (Type 9)	3	V, VI	M1.5a	Va, Vaa
5241/A03–0216	Rand, sole (Type 2), upper	7	VII	B53 (Phase 1), Central Area–T7152	Vb
5768/A9821a & b 5769/A9821b	Rand, sole (Type 2), upper (Type J)	3/4	V, VI	Unstratified	u/s
5851/A03–0133b	Sole	7	VI, VII	Unstratified	u/s
5854/A03–0133e	Sole (pointed forepart)	7	VI, VII	Unstratified	u/s
5855/A03–0133f	Clump	7	VI, VII	Unstratified	u/s

Discussion

That all the constructional yarns examined should be animal hair is most unexpected. Linen thread would not necessarily be preserved by the damp environment of the site and it is possible that the many leather fragments which lack any trace of yarn in the stitch holes were sewn with linen which has not survived. The finding of leather shoes sewn with animal hair, and in particular wool, which is much softer and less durable as a yarn than linen, is highly unusual. As far as is known, the only recorded parallel is a pair of shoes sewn with 3-ply woollen thread from the Dungiven (Ulster) costume, an outfit of the late 16th or early 17th century (Henshall and Seaby 1962, 119, 129, 135). The possibility has been considered that only lightweight indoor shoes were sewn in this manner, but at least two of the finds (Cat Nos 2725/A03–0413a and 5241/A03–0216) are substantial pieces of footwear with soles up to 2mm thick, which were presumably intended for general use.

It should be noted that the ancient practice of constructing shoes with leather thongs, which was being replaced in Britain by sewing with thread by the end of the first millennium AD, but which nonetheless continued in more remote areas, including parts of Scotland, to the end of the 19th century (Swann 1973, 17; Mackay and Carmichael 1894, 141–2), is not represented here (although thongs were used to repair some of the Perth shoes, eg Cat Nos 222/7436a, Illus 104; 286/A03–0017a, Illus 104; and 1804/A03–0367a, Illus 145). In other respects than the choice of yarn, the shoes from Perth represent construction methods normal in Britain in the late Middle Ages. The use of yarn made from animal hair may, therefore, represent a response to a sudden or unusual shortage of flax. It is perhaps pertinent to remember that 14 instances of the use of yarn made from animal hair dated from a period during which Perth is known to have been besieged (see Fascicule 1, Historical introduction, for further details).

2 Conservation of leatherwork
Tom Bryce

The preservation of wet/waterlogged leather (shoes, belts, straps, etc) from the High Street can, on the whole, be regarded as being very good. Treatment methods for this type of object generally involve cleaning, careful removal of water, applying various oils, fats and wax mixtures and manipulation of the specimens to their correct shape. After some experimental work, the great majority of the leather was treated by washing with 2% V/V Lissapol NBD, in water, to remove soil and dirt; soaked for one hour in 2% V/V Hydrochloric Acid;

thoroughly washed free of chemicals; immersed in two acetone baths of 30 minutes duration each; removed from Acetone and partly air-dried before applying one or two coats of a leather dressing. This was composed of anhydrous lanolin and Bavon (ASAK ABP) in Genklene, incorporating 1% fungicide. The leather was manipulated at intervals around the time that the lubricant was being applied.

Several repairs were carried out, using the leather consolidant Pliantex (in ethyl acetate).

3 Shrinkage during conservation
Clare Thomas

An attempt has been made to determine the rate of shrinkage of the leather during conservation, by comparing measurements taken from the original drawings with those made after conservation. This exercise was restricted to soles, sheaths and a few straps with easily comparable lengths; uppers were excluded as their irregular nature makes comparison of drawings by different hands unwise. Rates of shrinkage ranged between 0%

and 29% but mainly varied between 6% and 13%, with an average of 9%.

As noted in Appendix 2 above, the leather from the High Street was dried with acetone. Research in London has shown that leather conserved in this manner tends to shrink more (up to 16%) than leather which has been freeze-dried (up to 8%) (Grew and de Neergaard 1988, 138–9). For a discussion of shrinkage during burial, see Shoe sizes, above.

Table 14 *Shrinkage during conservation.*

Cat/Accession	Leather type	Phase	Pre-conservation length (mm)	Post-conservation length (mm)	Difference	%
South Sector						
28/A10800b	Sole (Type 6)	Ib	249	240	9	3.6
43/A8525	Sole (Type 6)	Ic	238	208	30	13
54/A9886a	Sole (Type 1)	Ic	282	255	27	10
58/A8635a	Sole (Type 1)	Ic,Icc	228	212.5	15.5	7
62/A8704a	Sole (Type 1)	Ic,Icc	194	167.5	26.5	14
68/A8809c	Sole (Type 1)	Ic,Icc	310–315	287	23	7
103/A03–0001	Sole (Type 1)	Ia–Icc>	292	263	29	10
104/A10798a	Sole (Type 1)	Ib–Id	205	193	12	6
120/A03–0005	Sole (Type 1)	Icc,Id	msl 267	250	17	6
121/A03–0006	Sole (Type 1)	Icc,Id	msl 291	266	25	9
125/A12297a	Sole (Type 1)	(Ia–)Id	205	186	19	9
136/A12291	Sole (Type 1)	(Ia–)Id	200	182	18	9
173/A7580b	Sole (Type 2)	Ie	245	221.5	23.5	10
175/A7589a	Sole (Type 2)	Ie	280	275 5	2	
185/A7600a	Sole (Type 1)	Ie	278	257	21	7.5
208/A7434	Sole (Type 1)	Ie	243	207	36	15
286/A03–0017a	Sole (Type 1)	If	284	263	21 7	
314/A10365a	Sole (Type 6)	IIa	296	256	40	14
323/A10600	Sole (Type 1)	IIa	281 (toe folded over)	255	26	9
331/A6774a	Sole (Type 1)	IIb	307–315	271	36/44	12
334/A03–0011	Sole (Type 1)	(IIa)IIb	313	274	39	12
385/A12304	Sole (Type 1)	IIa–IIc	270	227	43	16
403/A12295	Sole (Type 5)	Ia–IIc	281	240	41	15
406/A12493a	Sole (Type 1)	Ia–IIc	300	277	23	8
462/A10599a	Sole (Type 1)	IId	msl 194	184	10	5
475/A12302a	Sole (Type 1)	IId	268	244	24	9
491/A12290a	Sole (Type 1)	IIb–IIf	261	231	30	11.5
570/A9120	Sheath (decorated)	IId–IIg	msl 97	97	–	0
611/A9879a	Sole (Type 2)	IId–IIg	231	212	19	8
625/A9885a	Sole (Type 1)	IId–IIg	294	264	30	10
733/A9887	Sole	IIe–IIg	msl 224	159.5	64.5	29
740/A9144	Sole (Type 3)	<IIg(IIh)	270	243	27	10
774/A9365	Sole (Type 3)	<IIg(IIh)	279	243	36	13
783/A9372a	Sole (Type 3)	<IIg(IIh)	258	242	16	6
788/A9546a	Sole (Type 3)	<IIg(IIh)	285	259.5	25.5	9
795/A9884a	Sole (Type 3)	<IIg(IIh)	237	212.5	24.5	10
798/A10366	Sole (Type 1)	<IIg(IIh)	198	179	19	10
821/A11221a	Sole (Type 4)	<IIg(IIh)	247	237.5	9.5	4
831/A8518a	Sole (Type 3)	IIh	268	251.5	16.5	6
846/A8544	Sole (Type 1)	IIIa–IIIc	280	240	40	14
919/A12536a	Sole (Type 2)	IIi	252	240	12	5
922/A11639a	Sole (Type 1)	IIb–IIIb	242	219	23	9.5
933/A03–0327a	Sole (Type 2)	IIIa,IIIb	285	267	18	6
937/A11644	Sole (Type 3)	IIIb	msl 238	213.5	24.5	10
970/A11261a	Sole (Type 8)	IIe–IIIc	86	79.5	6.5	8
971/A11261b	Sole (Type 9)	IIe–IIIc	178	158.5	19.5	11
1042/A8546	Sole (Type 4)	IIe–IIIc	266	240	26	10
1087/A03–0278b	Strap (folded	IIIc	345	280	55	16

(continued)

Cat/Accession	Leather type	Phase	Pre-conservation length (mm)	Post-conservation length (mm)	Difference	%
	once)					
1095/A03–0270a	Sole (Type 3)	IIIc	265	252	13	5
1103/A03–0287a	Sole (Type 2)	IIIc	278	256.3	21.5	8
1106/A03–0304a	Sole (Type 3)	IIIc	300	267	33	11
1144/A4817a	Sole (Type 2)	IIg–IIIc(–IVa)	266	233	33	12
1195/A9883	Sole (Type 3)	IIg–IIId	287	271	16	6
1206/A8680a	Sole (Type 4)	IIg–IIId	272	253	19	7
1215/A9373a	Sole (Type 3)	IIg–IIId	233	214.5	18.5	8
1224/A8183	Sheath (decorated)	IIh–IVa	151	149	2	1
1426/A6187a	Sole (Type 3)	IVaa	244	228.5	15.5	6
1504/A03–0405	Sole (Type 5)	<IIIc–IVaa	msl 261	255	6	2
1553/A03–0422a	Sole (Type 4)	<IIIc–IVaa	msl 238	215	23	10
1659/A03–0417a	Sole (Type 2)	IVa–IVb	msl 250	235	15	6
1743/A03–0347a	Sole (Type 2)	IVaa,IVb	msl 285	247	38	13
1804/A03–0367a	Sole (Type 4), upper (Type Di), thong	IVaa,IVb	234	230	4	2
1809/A03–0374a	Sole (Type 2)	IVaa,IVb	msl 283	267.5	15.5	5.5
1991/A03–0362a	Sole (Type 3)	IVaa,IVb	267	248	19	7
2181/A03–0385a	Sole (Type 7)	IVaa,IVb	240	226	14	6
2300/A03–0276a	Sole (Type 8)	IVc	98	88	10	10
2312/A03–0280	Strap (folded twice)	IVc	(excluding projecting thong) 240	223	7	3
2333/A03–0291a	Sole (Type 3)	IVc	286	257	29	10
2361/A03–0331a	Sole (Type 2), upper, rand	IVc	268	240	28	10
2651/A03–0316a	Sole (Type 1)	IVaa,IVb	190	165.5	24.5	13
2713/A03–0299	Sole (Type 3)	IVb	278	261	17	6
2714/A03–0311a	Sole (Type 2)	IVb	161	144	17	10.5
2722/A03–0307a	Sole (Type 3)	IVb	276	245	31	11
2728/A03–0295a	Sole (Type 4)	IVb	278	254	24	9
2747/A03–0297a	Sole (Type 2)	IVb	156	141.5	14.5	9
2750/A03–0293	Sole (Type 3)	IVb	280	259	21	7.5
2754/A03–0288a	Sole (Type 2)	IVb	msl 281	255.5	25.5	9
2779/A03–0232	Sole (Type 4)	IVb	287	254.5	32.5	11
2819/A03–0273c	Miscellaneous fragment	IVc	245	223	22	9
2872/A4894	Sole (Type 2)	IVb,IVc	183	168	15	8
2985/A10521	Sole (Type 3), bunion	IVb,IVc	251	227.5	23.5	9
3033/A3459	Sole (Type 3)	IVb,IVc	225	200	25	11
3047/A8334	Sheath (decorated)	IVb,IVc	msl 268	242	26	10
3048/A8335	Sole (Type 3)	IVb,IVc	184	161.5	22.5	12
3068/A8668c	Sole (Type 7)	IVb,IVc	225	217	8	4
3117/A8681a	Sole (Type 5)	IVb,IVc	246	226	20	8
3246/A6195	Sole (Type 3)	IVb–IVcc	270	253	17	6
3321/A03–0066a	Sole (Type 3)	IVc,IVcc	msl 242	226.5	15.5	6
3335/A03–0261a	Sole (Type 2)	IVc,IVcc	159	138	21	13
3352/A03–0246a	Sole	IVc,IVcc	msl 227	200	27	12
3376/A03–0240a	Sole (seat cut	IVc,IVcc	113	102	11	10

(continued)

Cat/Accession	Leather type	Phase	Pre-conservation length (mm)	Post-conservation length (mm)	Difference	%
	across waist)					
3382/A03–0249a	Sole (Type 3)	IVc,IVcc	msl 230	215.5	14.5	6
3384/A03–0233a	Sole	IVc,IVcc	msl 235	221	14	6
3396/A03–0268a	Sole	IVc,IVcc	-	-	-	-
3405/A03–0052a	Sole (Type 3)	IVc,IVcc	msl 249	233	16	6
3501/A03–0186a	Sole (Type 3)	IVc,IVcc	msl 245	235	10	4
3508/A03–0221	Clump	IVc,IVcc	138	120	18	13
3511/A03–0251	Clump	IVc,IVcc	102	86	16	16
3624/A6077c	Sole (Type 7)	IVcc(Va)	218	202	16	7
3707/A03–0134a	Sole (Type 3)	Va	278	260	18	7
3857/A03–0044	Sole (Type 5)	Vaa	msl 225	215	10	4
3858/A03–0047	Sole (Type 4)	Vaa	msl 221	206.5	14.5	7
3863/A03–0067a	Sole (Type 4)	Vaa	msl 266	238.5	27.5	10
3869/A03–0070	Sheath (decorated)	Vaa	209	183.5	25.5	12
3873/A03–0116b	Sole (Type 3)	Vaa	141	135.5	5.5	4
3875/A03–0118	Sheath (decorated)	Vaa	120	108.5	11.5	10
3877/A03–0120b	Sole (Type 2)	Vaa	275	253	22	8
3947/A03–0140a	Sole (Type 9)	Vaa	160	147	13	8
3985/A03–0170b	Sole (Type 5)	Vaa	262	240	22	8
4228/A6419	Sole (Type 3)	IVcc,Va	msl 278	244	34	12
4229/A6373	Sole (Type 3)	IVcc,Va	271	236	35	13
4283/A4901a	Sole (Type 5)	IVb–Vc	235	212.5	22.5	10
4493/A4289a	Sole (Type 2)	Va,Vaa(VI)	137	127	10	7
4533/A6400	Sole (Type 3)	Va,Vaa(VI)	msl 198	180	18	9
4811/A6189	Sole (Type 4)	Va,Vaa	265	241	24	9
4815/A6237a	Sole (Type 2)	Va,Vaa	226	206	20	9
4827/A03–0106	Sole (Type 4)	Va,Vaa	242	222.5	19.5	8
5240/A03–0090	Sole (Type 4)	Vb	291	273.5	17.5	5
5241/A03–0216	Sole (Type 2), upper, rand	Vb	(incl vamp) 288	262.5	25.5	9
5329/A6399a	Sole (Type 5)	Vb–Vc	270	238	32	12
5599/A4352a	Sole (Type 7)	Vd	202–205	185	17	8
5608/A03–0065	Sole (Type 4)	(Va–)Vd(Vdd)	msl 177	165	12	7
5768/A9821a & 5769/A9821b	Sole (Type 2), rand, upper (Type J)	u/s	260	229	31	12
5779/A0800a	Sole (Type 2)	u/s	268	239	29	11
5824/A03–0127a	Sole (Type 9)	u/s	195	177	18	9
5868/A03–0004a	Sheath (decorated)	u/s	200	183	17	8.5
5871/A03–0008	Sole (Type 3)	u/s	258	235.5	22.5	9
North Sector						
5908/A0113	Sole (Type 5)	4–11	msl 155	133	22	14
5924/A0115	Strap (single thickness)	6–12(b–e)	267	233	34	13
5929/A0110a	Sole (Type 9)	6–12(b–e)	164	145	19	12
5958/A0100	Strap/belt (single thickness)	14–16	msl 138	113	25	18

4 Identification of animal species

Clare Thomas

The hair follicle pattern on the leather was examined, in order to determine the animal species. Only the conserved leather was included. A large proportion of the leather was too worn, or particularly in the case of uppers, too stretched and distorted, for the pattern to be identified. Most of the soles proved too worn; however, in some cases, the pattern was clear on the upturned edge of edge–flesh stitching channels. All the identified soles were made of cattlehide.The follicle pattern survived better on uppers, where it was usually cattlehide. Some instances of goatskin were observed but unfortunately this information appears to have been lost in the interval between the original identification and final work on the report, and is thus not recorded in the catalogue, as the instances of cattlehide are.

The preponderance of cattlehide is perhaps surprising, given the evidence from the mammal bone (see Fascicule 4, The mammal bone) which indicated that goats were being slaughtered in large numbers, presumably for cheap meat. The use of cattlehide for soles is however to be expected, as it is thicker. The use of cattlehide for uppers may indicate a preference for tough, practical footwear.

5 The history of leatherworking in Perth

Clare Thomas

The evidence from the High Street site demonstrates that leather was being worked and made into shoes, boots, straps, sheaths and clothing from the early 12th century onwards. The history of this trade is further illuminated by documentary references, but unfortunately these are almost all later in date than the stratified deposits from the site. Despite this, they have been studied in the hope of finding information which might be applicable to the period 1100–1350. Relevant sources include the *Perth Guildry Book*, royal charters, minutes of the Shoemakers' Incorporation and Glovers' Incorporation, and sundry burgh records.

Early references

Early references to leatherworking include a mention in 1362 of 'vico sellatorum' ('Saddlers' Street') in a charter of David II (Fittis 1875, 525). Even earlier, monastic records name Baldwin the Lorimer, originally from the Low Countries. Baldwin made harness, one terret and two horse-collars being the annual rent for his toft (Stavert 1991, 15). David I allowed Scone Abbey to have its own shoemaker and tanner, who together with the abbey's third servant, a smith, enjoyed the 'same privileges in Perth as the king's burgesses' (ibid).

Perth Guildry Book

Further evidence for leatherworkers can be found in the *Perth Guildry Book* which recorded entries of new members as well as other guild business, from 1452 to 1601 (Stavert 1993). Skinners, for example, are mentioned regularly. Soutars (souters) or cordinars occur less frequently, and fall into three chronological periods. Thus, the book records the entry of six soutars between 1461 and 1494, but only two from 1528 until 1558. During this period, however, 'David Nicol Decane of the Cordinaris' is mentioned in a letter of the Guild, dated to 1545, showing that the shoemakers, along with other crafts, were becoming more involved with the Guild. Eleven years later, in 1556, 'David Roberstone cordonar' is reproved for breaking Guild rules.

However, from 1567 to 1594, entries appear to become more regular, with eight souters or cordinars admitted to the guild (Stavert 1993, 29, 72, 76, 77, 87, 123, 126, 169–70, 237–8, 256, 269, 273, 288, 297, 358, 367, 392).

Only one harness-maker, John Richardsone, is mentioned. His date of entry, 30 September 1575, sits between those of eight saddlers who joined the guild between 1561 and 1589. It is interesting that there are no earlier instances of saddlers. The date range for their admittance is similar to that for the last phase of entries of soutars (Stavert 1993, 246, 252, 260, 284, 289, 294, 313–14, 343, 348, 364).

In the earlier years, membership of the guild was restricted to merchants and their heirs. Conflict between the guild and the crafts led to an agreement in 1555, after which the number of craftsmen admitted to the guild increased markedly. Thus the large number of entries of soutars and saddlers in the second half of the sixteenth century reflects the growing power and importance of the craft incorporations (Stavert 1993, vii).

The Shoemakers' Incorporation

In 1927 Peter Baxter, a Perth journalist and amateur local historian, published a history of the Shoemakers' Incorporation of Perth, based on their minute books, which dated from 1545 onwards. It is not always possible to distinguish between the substance of the original entries and Baxter's comments (Baxter 1927). Unfortunately, the present location of the original minute books dating to before 1793 is not known; unlike those of the Glovers' Incorporation, they are not in Perth and Kinross Council Archive. Nevertheless, Baxter's commentary, although it must be treated with caution, does provide considerable information on the organisation and activities of the Incorporation, especially as regards its existence before 1545, control of entry to the craft, guardianship of its monopoly, financial dealings, property transactions and welfare. Minutes of the Shoemaker Incorporation of Perth (1793–2000) are held in Perth and Kinross Council Archive, A K Bell Library (MS 156).

Evidence for the Shoemakers' Incorporation prior to 1545

Although the minute books examined by Baxter only begin on 14 July 1545, evidence suggests that the Incorporation existed earlier, at least as some form of craft body. According to Baxter, the records of King James VI Hospital, Perth, refer to 'St Duthan, the patron saint of the shoemaker craft'. Baxter also mentions 'an agreement between the Town of Perth and the Cordiners (Shoemakers), anent St Duthan's altar, of date 26th January 1496' (ie, probably 1497), but unfortunately he does not quote his source (Baxter 1927, 1). However, the calling's connection with the altar is substantiated by the first minute (14/7/1545) and by an entry of 1696: 'the calling's papers concerning the altarage of St Duthan ... had been put in the Trade chest' (Baxter 1927, 19).

The altar is also mentioned in other sources, though with slightly different dedications. Thus, on 23 November 1514, 'Sir Robert Keillor, Chaplain of the altar of St Duchay' gave up a tenement in the Southgate (Fittis 1885, 307–308). The *Perth Guildry Book* also names the altar twice. On 9th March 1548, the persons concerned were instructed to attend on the following day at 'Saint Duthas altar, within the paroch kirk'. Similarly, on 14 May 1548, the parties involved were told to meet 'in sainct John's kirk at Saint Duthis altar the morn' (Stavert 1993, 191, 194). Later, in 1738, a piece of land is described as bounded by the 'Aiker of St Crispian, founded within the Church of Perth' (Fittis 1885, 307–8). Fittis also talks of an altar dedicated to 'SS. Duchane, Crispin and Crispinian. To these three saints an altar was founded by the shoemakers. Of St Duchane we know nothing' (ibid).

Crispin and Crispinian were 3rd-century AD martyrs, who were popularly believed to have 'exercised their trade of shoemaking so as to avoid living from the alms of the faithful and thus became the patron saints of cobblers, shoemakers and leatherworkers' (Farmer 2004, 124–5). St Duchane or Duthas is possibly Duthac, an 11th-century Scottish bishop, who worked mainly in Ross–shire (ibid, 153–4).

Furthermore, the earlier existence of the Shoemakers' Incorporation is also suggested by a brass candelabra (Illus 168), which was bought in 1812 by the Perth Literary and Antiquarian Society, 'lately belonging to the Shoemaker Incorporation of this place' (Perth Museum – extract from Minute Book 22/12/1812). Baxter refers to it as 'the brass candelabra of St Duthan's altar', while according to a note in the museum, it 'originally is said to have hung in the Shoemakers' Incorporation Gallery and belonged to them' (Baxter 1927; Perth Museum – Note 8/4/1926). The candelabra, which once again hangs in St John's Kirk, is probably Flemish, possibly dating to the mid-15th-century (Hunter 1932, 32). If it originally belonged to the Shoemakers, then it implies that they were already a wealthy body in the 15th century. However it should be noted that there were frequent rearrangements of the use of St John's Church in the post-Reformation years. Thus the association of the candelabra with the Shoemakers may be accidental.

Further evidence for the existence of a formal body of shoemakers before 1545 is provided by their ownership of the 'Soutarland', between Coupar Angus and Burrelton. According to Baxter, it had been given to them by Coupar Angus Abbey, in return for the provision of shoes for the monks. Again, Baxter does not explain his source, but the Souterland is mentioned at least four times in the minutes, in 1693, 1694, 1696 and finally in 1752, when it was sold (Baxter 1927, 14, 16, 19, 83).

Thus, the reference to the altar of St Duthan and its candelabrum, and to the Souterland, imply the existence of an organised craft body of shoemakers

prior to 1545. The absence of early charters or other documents is almost certainly explained by the destruction by fire in February 1745 of the Incorporation's Charter chest. The fire at Deacon Buchan's house and the loss of the chest are recorded in the Minute Book and in a letter to the Town Clerk of Perth, informing him that the town's bond of 2500 merks, due to the Incorporation, had been destroyed (Baxter 1927, 70; PKCA, B59/29/84).

The other information to be gleaned from Baxter all dates to after 1545. Some of the regulations may have existed earlier, but their relevance to the period 1100–1350 is dubious. Hence, they have been summarised very briefly. Firstly, entry to the craft was carefully controlled, and was restricted to burgesses of the town. Secondly, the Incorporation was very careful to protect its privileges. Non-freemen who attempted to sell shoes had their wares seized, and were taken to court, as, for example, James Moor, who in 1762 or 1763 was accused of making faulty shoes and of not paying the required dues. Similarly, in November–December 1771, David Miller, Joseph Scott and others were fined for 'encroaching on the liberties of the trade'. On payment of five shillings sterling yearly, they were allowed to mend shoes in the future (Baxter 1927, 32). Similarly, c1707–10 the Incorporation opposed a proposal to introduce a 'Public Shoemarket' at which non-freemen might sell their wares, including, to the horror of the Incorporation 'high and raised-heel shoes'.

The welfare of members and their dependants was one of the Incorporation's concerns. Thus in 1698, at the instigation of the Town Council, the calling agreed 'to pay various sums monthly to six poor members' (ibid, 20). The Incorporation also possessed mortcloths, which were draped over coffins at funerals; one of these survives in Perth Museum, along with the charter chest which replaced the one burnt in 1745. It still bears the Incorporation's coat-of-arms and the date 1745. The Museum also retains the money box and the deacon's chair.

Other evidence for the Shoemakers' Incorporation in the Perth Archives

Documents in Perth and Kinross Council Archive reflect the Burgh's involvement with the Shoemakers' Incorporation. For instance, a late 17th-century letter to the Town Council, by an unknown author, complains of a lack of service to the town by the Shoemakers (Illus 169). No mention of this letter is made in the Incorporation's minutes. It is possible that this letter is somehow linked to the attempt in 1709–10 to hold a public shoe market (PKCA, B59/29/29).

The Archive also records the Burgh's part in the formal life of the Incorporation, as, for example, in numerous 18th-century Indentures of Apprenticeship, and in the official account of the 1771–72 trial of unfreemen shoemakers David Millar, Joseph Scott, James Simson and others (see above). The minutes of the Shoemaker Incorporation, 1793–2000, are now deposited in the Archive. However there is nothing of relevance to the medieval period.

The Glovers' or Skinners Incorporation

Various records of the Glovers' or Skinners' Incorporation survive in Perth and Kinross Council Archive. These include three volumes, which comprise the minutes from 1593 to 1726, a 17th–18th-century index to the minutes, and extracts from the minutes, ranging from 1593 to 1904. Other documents consist of a ratification of the craft's customs, dating from 1485, a letter of James VI prohibiting the export of skins, and numerous title deeds. The minutes are similar to those of the Shoemakers, with detailed

regulations on behaviour of members, apprentices, entry of new members, purchase of mortcloth, etc. Of particular interest is the prohibition on attempts to sell sheepskin or dog leather as if it were goat skin.

Conclusion

The surviving documentary references to Perth leatherworkers date to post-1545, with very few exceptions. Our information on the Shoemakers' Incorporation for the period 1545–1793 is restricted to Baxter's account and interpretation, apart from the records of indentures and of the 1771–2 trial. However, despite this, it is possible to say that from 1545 there was an organized body of shoemakers, and that it might have existed earlier.

6 Glossary of textile terms used in this fascicule

P Z Dansart

bast fibres Fibres extracted from the stems of some dicotyleonous plants (eg, nettle, flax or hemp) or from the inner bark of certain trees and shrubs.

binding warp A warp which is secondary to the main warp (see below); it serves to bind the weft floats in a compound weave.

chevron twill In a 2/1 twill or 2/2 twill (see *twill weaves* below), if the direction of the diagonal lines formed by the weave is reversed in one system, the effect produced is that of a chevron.

comber unit A section of a textile (or a pattern repeat in a textile), the warp ends of which are controlled by the comber board. In a drawloom, the comber board is threaded with pulleys which control the warp ends belonging to each pattern repeat.

compound weaves A weave with two functionally differentiated warp sets (known respectively as the main warp and the binding warp), and two or more different weft series. Such textiles, usually of silk or silk and some other fibre, such as linen, were woven on a drawloom. Many of them were produced in Persia, Byzantium, Syria, Egypt, Islamic Spain, Italy and Sicily. One of the most common forms of compound weave is known as weft-faced compound twill, also termed 'samitum' or 'samite', in which the weft follows an under one, over two order of interlacing (that is, 1/2) with the binding warp threads. Other weave possibilities include an under one, over three order of interlacing (1/3). Compound weaves may also be executed in tabby or plain weave.

diamond twill In a 2/1 twill or 2/2 twill (see *twill weaves* below), the direction of the diagonal formed by the weave may be reversed in both warp and weft. The effect achieved is that of a diamond or lozenge shape.

extended weave A weave in which the threads of one system or both systems are paired or grouped, so that two or more threads follow the same course. Four of the PHSAE textiles (tabby and 2/1 twill) are extended by pairing threads in one system (probably the weft).

four shed twill A twill formed from units of four threads in both warp and weft; many authors use term to refer to 2/2 twill (see *twill weaves* below).

freis Old Scots spelling of frieze, a coarse woollen cloth with a nap, usually on one surface only; from the French *friser*, 'to curl'.

gore 1 A locally inserted weft which serves to level the fell of a textile where unequal warp tension prevents the weft from being perpendicular to the warp (Hoffman 1964, Figures 146 and 147). In warp-weighted looms, the warp elements may sag and pull the weft into a curve, which may be corrected by inserting extra weft passes in order to even up the weaving. Similar problems may also occur in horizontal looms, for example if the breast and end beams are not of a consistent diameter, or if warp yarns with different diameters are used. In European medieval textiles, this feature is usually associated with the warp-weighted loom. **2** A triangular insert of cloth in the side, front or back seams of a garment such as a tunic.

grège Reeled silk thread from which the gum sericin has not been removed.

heddle A device for lifting and lowering selected warp threads (eg, alternate threads in the case of a loom set up for tabby weave) in order to open a shed, prior to entering the weft.

knitting the heddles This is the term employed by Hoffman (1964, 133–5) for the process of forming heddles (see *heddle* above) using a continuous yarn, which is passed round selected threads and a rod. The heddle rod may then be lifted in order to open the shed (see *shed* below). Möller-Wiering (2011, 62) employed the phrase 'knotting of heddles'.

lozenge twill See *diamond twill* above.

main warp The ground or principal warp of a textile. In many cases, it is the only warp employed in a textile. However, in some compound weaves there are two sets of warp, the main warp (which is often obscured by the weft floats) and a binding warp (see above).

nap A term which refers to the surface of a textile. A nap may be produced as part of the finishing process whereby some of the fibres are 'raised' from the surface of the fabric. It involves loosening fibres from the yarns which constitute the cloth by means of teasles or mechanical processes. Note that the term nap was formerly used to denote a rough surface on a cloth which was sheared and smoothed, in other words, to a surface which was subject to finishing (Emery 1980, 173–4). However, the term is used here generally to refer to the process of producing (or the effect of) a raised surface.

pick An individual weft thread, or group of weft threads, which passes through one shed.

pin-beater A small, pointed, slightly curved tool of bone or wood. It was used for beating the weft into the fell of the cloth, in an upward motion, on the warp-weighted loom. It is assumed that it was employed for weaving cloth with a fairly high warp density (Hoffman 1964, 320–1). In an experiment of the 1950s to weave wadmal (see *wadmal* below) twenty ells long, the pin beater was used to push up the weft first with the shed open, and again after it had been closed (ibid, 135–6). In contrast, the sword-beater was only employed when the shed was closed.

reeled silk Untwisted yarn formed by reeling together the paired filaments from cocoons of the silkmoth. The silkmoth secretes a pair of silk filaments known as a bave, one of which is too fine to be used alone. Accordingly, a group of baves (three to ten) are combined (Emery 1980, 8). See *grège* and *thrown silk*.

samitum A medieval term for a weft-faced compound twill. The term samite is also employed.

satin A weave which is formed from units of at least five threads in the warp and weft. Each end passes over four (or more) threads and under one thread or each end passes under four (or more threads) and over one.

selvedge A closed edge on a textile. In this work it refers to the edge formed by turns of the weft as it passes round the outermost warp thread(s).

shed An opening formed by raising selected warp threads. The weft is passed through this space. Various devices may be employed for opening the warp, eg leashes, shafts or tablets.

sprang A form of interlinking ('plaiting'), oblique interlacing ('braiding') or oblique twining executed on a frame. One set of threads is employed and no weft. The interworking of the threads at the top of the frame duplicates the movements, in a simultaneous fashion, at the bottom. Where the working of the two ends coincides at the transversal median line, a distinctive structure holds the final interworking to prevent the piece from unravelling (Emery 1980, 66, 69).

SS A textile in which both the warp (or system 1) and the weft (or system 2) are of S spun yarn.

starting edge (or **starting border**) A transversal closed edge which forms the top of a cloth as woven on a warp-weighted loom (Hoffman 1964, 151–83). This border is produced in the process of warping and setting up such a loom; it may be woven or twined (ibid, Figure 70).

tabby A weave in which each weft thread passes over and under successive warp threads. The over one, under one interlacing in the first passage of the weft, is followed by an under one, over one order in the second. The unit of weave is constituted by two warp and two weft threads. It is also known as plain weave. The term tabby derives from cloth made in the quarter known as *attābī* in Baghdad (May 1957, 67).

tablet weaving A form of warp twining in which the warp threads spiral round each other and enclose the weft within each twist. The shed is produced by a series of tablets (cards) which are square and flat in shape; the warp is threaded through perforations in the corners of each. In order to change shed, the weaver turns the tablets.

three shed twill A twill formed from units of three warp and three weft threads. Many authors employ the term to refer to a 2/1 twill (see *twill weaves* below).

thrown silk Yarn produced by twisting reeled filaments of silk.

twill weaves Twill weaves are formed from units of at least three threads in warp and weft. In a 2/1 twill, the weft passes over two warp threads and under one, and for each subsequent passage of the weft, the warp grouping is stepped one warp thread to the right or left. In a 2/2 twill, the weft passes over two warp threads and under two, producing warp and weft floats of equal span. If the shift is always to the right or left, continuous diagonals are formed on both faces of the fabric, but the direction of the diagonal on one surface is the reverse of that on the other (Emery 1980, 92).

vaðmál A Norse term for a measure of cloth, used both as a value and to make payments (Østergård 2009, 62). The cloth was made in Scandinavian countries, including Shetland, Orkney and Greenland, but it was particularly associated with Iceland. It was woven on a warp-weighted loom often in a 2/2 twill (see *twill weaves* above), and also in other weaves, including tabby and 2/1 twill.

velvet A textile with a pile in the warp. During weaving, a supplementary warp passes over a series of rods in order to raise loops above the ground weave. Subsequently the loops may be shorn, or they may be left as loops.

wadmal See *vaðmál*.

warp A set of longitudinal threads held under tension on the loom.

warp end A single warp thread.

warp-weighted loom A vertical loom consisting of supports and an upper horizontal beam; the warp is kept under tension by a number of free-hanging weights to which groups of warp threads are tied (Hoffman 1964, 5).

weft Threads which interlace with the warp in a transversal direction; during weaving the weft is passed through the sheds.

woollen A soft, somewhat fuzzy yarn spun from wool which has been carded, so that the fibres lie at right angles to the yarn after it has been spun (Leadbeater 1976, 91).

worsted A smooth, firm yarn spun from wool which has been prepared by combing. The process of combing means that the fibres lie parallel to each other, and that they tend to follow the direction of the yarn when spun (ibid, 90).

ZI In this fascicule, this term is employed in reference to silk tabbies in which the warp (or system 1) is composed of Z twisted yarn and the weft (or system 2) of untwisted yarn.

ZS A textile in which the warp (or system 1) is composed of Z spun yarn and the weft (or system 2) of S spun yarn.

ZZ A textile in which both the warp (or system 1) and weft (or system 2) are composed of Z spun yarn.

7 Glossary of leatherworking terms used in this fascicule

butted seams The edges of adjoining upper sections are butted together and joined by a seam, often an edge–flesh one (qv), invisible on the reverse side (Thornton 1973b, 44).

clump (or **clump sole**) A half-sole added to a shoe, usually as a repair (Thornton 1973b, 45).

delamination The condition of leather which has separated during burial into grain and flesh layers, due to the incomplete penetration of the tan liquor when it was made (Thornton 1973b, 45).

eared shoe In the 16th century, following a long period of pointed shoes, toes became very square and wide; for a short time, 1535–55, the corners of the toe were extended sideways resembling ears (Thornton 1973b, 45).

edge–flesh seams The stitching holes are pierced from the edge of the section (usually the sole) to the flesh side; commonly used in the majority of medieval shoes (qv) (Thornton 1973b, 45). Also used to link fragments of uppers.

facing A strip of leather or other material used to strengthen tie-holes.

flesh The inner surface of a piece of leather originally next to the animal's body; the loose fibres are usually prominent (Thornton 1973b, 45).

follicle pattern The distinctive pattern left on the grain side of the leather by the animal's hairs.

forepart The front of the shoe (or sole or insole).

grain The outer surface of a piece of leather originally bearing the hair, fur, wool etc. Each animal has a characteristic grain pattern and the surface is normally smooth. Soles usually have the grain side downwards resting on the ground; insoles usually have the grain side upwards so that the foot rests on it. Uppers normally have the grain side outwards except for suedes (Thornton 1973b, 45).

heel A component added to the rear (or seat) end of the sole, originally for utility but then as fashion. May consist of separate 'lifts' ('built heel') or be a block of wood covered with leather or other material. In either case the bottom section which rests on the ground is called the 'top piece' (Thornton 1973b, 45).

insole The inside bottom part of a shoe on which the foot rests, sometimes referred to as 'the foundation of

the shoe'. In a turnshoe (qv) there is no separate insole, the foot resting on the inner surface of the sole which also acts as an insole (Thornton 1973b, 45).

instep A rather imprecise area on top of the foot between the rear of the toes and the ankle joint. The name is also incorrectly used for the arch or waist of the foot underneath (Thornton 1973b, 45).

lasting margin The lower edge of the shoe upper which is turned under and fixed to the insole (or sole) during lasting (Thornton 1973b, 46).

latchets The top fronts of the quarters (qv) are extended into straps which pass over the instep of the foot, sometimes resting on the tongue of the shoe vamp. These straps or latchets may not quite touch each other, in which case they may be joined by a buckle (Thornton 1973b, 46). Also used in this report to describe the low flaps found on shoes of Types D and E, but which do not appear to have been fastened in any way other than by possibly being stitched to each other.

leg flap Used in this report to describe the top fronts of quarters of boots, of Types A, Bi–iii, C and H. None of these leg flaps show any signs of central fastening, eg toggles. Some pairs may have been bound, either with stitching or with a top band, and thus the front of the boot was left open.

quarters The sides of a shoe upper joining on to the vamp at the front and meeting each other at the back of the heel. If there is a seam here it is called a 'backseam'. The term 'quarters' is derived from the fact that if there is a join at the back, then a pair of shoes has four of them. Medieval shoes do not usually have a backseam, the inside and outside quarters forming a continuous section (Thornton 1973b, 46).

rand A long narrow strip of leather of roughly triangular cross-section included in an upper/bottom seam (or elsewhere) to make it more waterproof or decorative. Some early turnshoes have such a rand and if this is wide enough, an additional sole (possibly a repair one) can be stitched to it (see **Turn-welt**) (Thornton 1973b, 46).

seat (**heel seat**) The rear end of the insole or sole on which the heel of the foot rests (Thornton 1973b, 46).

sole The part of the shoe which is in contact with the ground. If the shoe has a separate heel (qv) the bottom section of this next to the ground is called the 'top-piece'. (Thornton 1973b, 47).

stiffener (or **heel stiffener**) A reinforcement placed inside the back of the quarters. In early shoes the top edge is often stitched to the quarters by a type of hem stitch (or overseam or whipped seam) which produces a scalloped effect along this edge; the bottom edge is lasted in with the upper (Thornton 1973b, 47).

stitching channel A row of stitch holes, sometimes set in a groove.

stitch length The distance between the centres of the stitches or stitch holes in a row (Thornton 1973b, 47).

throat The central position of the rear end of the vamp resting on the instep of the foot. (Thornton 1973b, 47).

tie holes The holes in quarters, latchets or tongues through which a string, ribbon or thong is passed to hold the shoe on the foot (Thornton 1973b, 47). In shoes or boots with side lacing, tie holes are also found on the side-pieces.

tongue A backwards extension from the vamp throat (qv) resting on the instep of the foot. Latchet ties (qv) may pass over or under it and sometimes there is a pair of holes through which the tie string passes (Thornton 1973b, 47).

top band A narrow strip of leather or other material stitched to the top edge of the quarters (or legs of a boot) for decorative purposes. (Thornton 1973b, 47).

tread The widest part of the sole forepart in closest contact with the ground (Thornton 1973b, 47).

tunnel holes Pairs of slits forming tunnels through which thongs of Type B boots have been threaded.

tunnel stitch A seam used in repairing to attach a new piece of leather, eg a clump sole (qv), on top of an old one. The holes enter the surface of each piece, pass for a short distance through the substance (between grain and flesh) and then reappear on the same side. Sometimes called a 'caterpillar stitch' (Thornton 1973b, 47). Also used in this report to describe the stitches used to attach facings and top edges of quarters to the flesh side of the shoe, without perforating the leather.

turnshoe construction The shoe is made inside out (normally with the flesh side outwards) by sewing the lasting margin (qv) of the upper to the edge of a single sole, which also acts as an insole. The shoe is then turned the right way round so that the grain side of the leather is on the outside of the shoe and the upper/sole seam is now inside. It was apparently introduced to this country by the Saxons (Thornton 1973b, 47).

turn-welt A turnshoe which has an extra wide rand (qv) included in the seam so that this becomes a welt to which a first sole, and later a repair one, can be stitched. It is the intermediate stage between a turnshoe and a welted shoe appearing 1500 (Thornton 1973b, 48).

vamp The front section of a shoe upper covering the toes and part of the instep (Thornton 1973b, 48).

vamp wings The sides of the vamp extending backwards either side of the throat to join the quarters (Thornton 1973b, 48).

waist The narrow part of a shoe sole or insole under the arch of the foot (also called the waist) (Thornton 1973b, 48).

welt A narrow strip of leather sewn round the lasting margin (qv) of the upper and joining it either to the insole edge or to a 'rib' raised on the flesh side of the insole near the edge. The sole is attached to this welt by a second seam. It appears to have been developed from the rand (qv) and the two names are sometimes confused with each other (Thornton 1973b, 48).

welted construction A method of shoe construction introduced to this country about 1500 and still used (although mechanised). It takes place in three stages:
  i The upper is lasted and held in position by nails or bracing thread.
  ii The lasted upper is sewn together with a welt (qv) to the edge of the insole (early examples use the actual edge itself with an edge–flesh seam (qv) but later ones used an upstanding rib set in a short distance from the edge).
  iii The sole is then stitched to this welt (Thornton 1973b, 48).

8 Glossary of archaeological terms used in this fascicule

A Accession number given to artefacts.

Area The excavation was divided into ten areas, each of which was administered by a supervisor. Areas 1–6 were excavated during the 1975–6 Season; 7–10 during the following season. Area 1 lay on the High Street frontage, Areas 5 and 6 on the Mill Street frontage.

Building (with letter) Standing structures, ie those standing and surveyed in 1975 (see CD insert in Fascicule 1); (with number) excavated timber and stone buildings (see Fascicule 1, The buildings).

byre Scottish term for a cow shed.

c circa; about/approximately.

C Context number, a reference number assigned to every feature and layer during the excavation.

close Scottish term for a lane/path between buildings.

Context/Feature index Index of the Context Numbers (arranged numerically) and including the following fields of information:
  i Context/Feature Number
  ii Rig(s)
  iii Area(s)
  iv Context Group Designation
  v Context Group Sequence Number
  vi Feature Designation and Reference Number
  vii Phase(s)
  viii Matrix Level(s)
  ix Figure Numbers
  x Page Numbers of description/discussion
Deposited in site archive.

Context Group (CG) One or more contexts grouped together on the basis of interpretation, eg Buildings, Paths etc, and/or their relationship to other context groups (indicated by the prefix CG).

Context Group Designation The Context Groups were divided on the basis of interpretation into twenty-one categories.

Context Number Reference number (indicated by the prefix C) assigned to every feature and layer during the excavation; see Context Index in archive for full list.

D Drain; a Feature Category.

Drains Feature Category (indicated by the prefix D).

ft feet (Imperial measurement).

Gully (Gullies) Feature Category (indicated by the prefix T).

H Hearth; a Feature Category.

HBF Highland Boundary Fault

Hearths Feature Category (indicated by the prefix H)

Lade The Town Ditch/Moat; Context Group Designation within North Sector.

Layers Those Context Numbers which were not designated as Features.

MC Miscellaneous Context Group; Context Group Designation within the South Sector.

MF Miscellaneous Feature; a Feature Category

Midden Context Group Designation (indicated by the prefix M).

Miscellaneous Context Group(s) Context Group Designation (indicated by the prefix MC).

Miscellaneous Features Feature Category (indicated by the prefix MF).

Miscellaneous Wood Feature Category (indicated by the prefix MW).

mm Millimetre(s).

MW Miscellaneous Wood; a Feature Category.

Natural Context Group Designation (Undisturbed fluvio-glacial sand).

North Sector That part of the site containing Areas 5 and 6 and Trenches A and B.

occ Occupation layer(s).

OPH Old Parliament House.

ORS Old Red Sandstone.

Oven Context Group Designation within Area 5.

PA Post Alignment(s); a Feature Category.

Path(s) Context Group Designation (indicated by the prefix P).

Period Chronological division.

Period I Pre-1150.

Period II 1150–c1200

Period III c1200–c1250.

Period IV c1250–c1300.

Period V c1300–1350>.

Period VI Post-medieval and/or modern.

Phase 1 Chronological division; sub-division of a Period reflecting a variation in the site's structure/path pattern. **2** Phases of buildings.

PH Post Hole(s); a Feature Category.

PHSAE Perth High Street Archaeological Excavation.

PHSAEC Perth High Street Archaeological Excavation Committee.

Pit(s) Feature Category.

Post Alignment(s) Feature Category (indicated by the prefix PA).

Post Hole(s) Feature Category (indicated by the prefix PH). This category includes post pits and robbed postholes.

Post Pits Pits dug to insert a post/stake; see *PW* below.

Post(s) Feature Category (indicated by the prefix PP).

PP Post(s)/stake(s); Feature Category.

PW Post Pits with timber in situ; Feature Category.

RCAHMS Royal Commission on the Ancient and Historical Monuments of Scotland.

Rig(s) Property (division).

SA Stake Alignment(s); a Feature Category.

SDD Scottish Development Department (of Scottish Office).

Sondage Machine-cut pit.

South Sector That part of the site containing Areas 1–4 and 7–10.

Stake Alignment Feature Category (indicated by the prefix SA).

SUAT Scottish Urban Archaeological Trust.

T Trench/Gully; Feature Category.

TS Tree Stump; Feature Category within the South Sector.

Trench(es) Feature Category (indicated by the prefix T).

U/S Unstratified.

Vennel(s) Scottish term for a Lane/Path.

Wall Stone Wall(s); Feature Category.

Wattle Wall(s) Feature Category (indicated by the prefix WW) within the South Sector.

WW Wattle Wall(s); Feature Category.

Wynd Scottish term for a Lane/Path.

yd yard (Imperial measurement).

References

Note The fascicules referred to in the text are PHSAE Fascicules 1, 2 and 4 as listed below.

Adorno, R 1981 'On pictorial language and the typology of culture in a New World chronicle', *Semiotica* 36, Parts 1 and 2, 51–106.

Albers, A 1965 *On Weaving*. Middletown, Connecticut.

Alexander, D, Bogdan, N Q and Grounsell, J 1998 'A late medieval hall-house at Uttershill Castle, Penicuik', *Proc Soc Antiq Scot* 128, 1017–46.

Allen, J R 1903 'Part III, Archaeological survey and descriptive list, with illustrations', in Allen, J R and Anderson, J *The Early Christian Monuments of Scotland*. Edinburgh.

Allin, C E 1981a 'The leather', in Mellor, J and Pearce, T *The Austin Friars, Leicester*, 145–67. Leicester (=CBA Research Report, 35).

Allin, C E 1981b *The Medieval Leather Industry in Leicester*. Leicester (=Leicestershire Museums, Art Galleries and Records Service Archaeological Report 3).

Amt, E 1993 *Women's Lives in Medieval Europe: a Sourcebook*. New York and London.

Ancient Burgh Laws 1868 *Ancient Laws and Customs of the Burghs of Scotland 1124–1424*, Innes, C (ed). Edinburgh (=Scottish Burgh Record Society).

Anderson, A O 1908 *Scottish Annals from English Chronicles A.D. 500 to 1286*. London.

Ard Mhu'saem na H-Eireann 1973 *Viking and Medieval Dublin: Catalogue of Exhibition, National Museum Excavations 1962–73*. Dublin.

Armitage, P L 1976 'Seven sheep skulls and inferences from them', in Schofield 1976, 239.

Armstrong, P 1977 'Excavations in Sewer Lane, Hull, 1974', *East Riding Archaeologist* 3 (=Hull Old Town Report Series No 1), 51–60.

Armstrong, P 1980 'Excavations in Scale Lane/Lowgate 1974', *East Riding Archaeologist* 6, (=Hull Old Town Report Series No 4), 68.

Armstrong, S J 1987 'Leather', in Armstrong and Tomlinson 1987, 42–44.

Armstrong, P and Tomlinson, D 1987 *Excavations at the Dominican Priory, Beverley, 1960–1983*. Hull (=Humberside Heritage Publication 13).

Ayers, B and Murphy, P 1983 'A waterfront excavation at Whitefriars Street Car Park, Norwich 1979', in Wade-Martins, P *Waterfront Excavation and Thetford Ware Production*, 1–60. Norwich (=East Anglian Archaeol Rep, 17).

Baart, J et al 1977 *Opgravingen in Amsterdam*. Amsterdam (Amsterdams Historisch Museum).

Ballin Smith, B 1999 'Other small finds of ceramic, glass, metal and stone', in Crawford, B E and Ballin Smith, B (eds), 168–82.

Barber, E 1992 *Prehistoric Textiles*. Princeton.

Barrow, G W S 1973 *The Kingdom of the Scots*. London.

Barrow, G W S 1988 *Robert Bruce and the Community of the Realm of Scotland*. Edinburgh.

Battiscombe, C F (ed) 1956 *The Relics of Saint Cuthbert*. Oxford.

Batzer, A and Dokkedal, L 1992 'The warp-weighted loom: some new experimental notes', *Tidans Tand* 5, 231–4.

Baxter, P 1927 *The Shoemaker Incorporation of Perth*. Perth.

Baxter, P 1928 *Perth: Past and Present*. Perth.

Baxter, P 1930 *Perth's Old-time Trades and Trading*. Perth.

Beaudry M C 2006 *Findings: The Material Culture of Needlework and Sewing*. New Haven and London.

Beaulieu, M 1989 'Le costume Français, Miroir de la Sensibilité (1350–1500)', in Pastoureau 1989, 255–86.

Bender Jørgensen, L 1979 'Middelaldertextilerne fra Svendborg', *Arbog for Svendborg and Omegns Museum* 1, 1–7.

Bender Jørgensen, L 1987 'The textile remains', in Welender, R D E, Batey, C and Cowie, T G 'A Viking burial from Kneep, Uig, Isle of Lewis', *Proc Soc Antiq Scot* 117, 149–74.

Bender Jørgensen, L and Tidow, K (eds) 1982 *Archäologische Textilfunde: Textilsymposium Neumünster, 6.5.–8.5.1981*. Neumünster (=North European Symposium for Archaeological Textiles Monogr 1).

Bender Jørgensen, L, Magnus, B and Munksgaard, E (eds) 1988 *Archaeological Textiles: Report from the Second NESAT Symposium*. Copenhagen (=Arkæologiske Skrifter, 2).

Bennett, H M 1975 'A murder victim discovered: clothing and other finds from an early eighteenth century grave on Arnish Moor, Lewis', *Proc Soc Antiq Scot* 106, 172–82.

Bennett, H M 1982 'Textiles', in Murray 1982, 197–200.

Bennett, H M 1987 'Textiles', in Holdsworth 1987, 159–74.

Bennett, H 1995 'Textiles', in Bowler et al 1995, 971.

Bennett, H M nd (a) 'Textile Fragments from Elgin, 1976', in Lindsay, W J *Excavations in Elgin, 1976–1981*. Unpublished archive report.

Bennett, H M nd (b) 'Textiles from Threave Castle, 1975', Scottish Development Department (Ancient Monuments), unpublished report.

Bennett, H M nd (c) 'Textiles from Papa Stour, Shetland, 1978', University of St Andrews, unpublished report.

Bennett, H M and Habib, V 1985 'Textiles', in Holmes, N M McQ, 'Excavations south of Bernard Street, Leith, 1980', *Proc Soc Antiq Scot* 115, 423.

Bersu, G and Wilson, D M 1966 *Three Viking Graves in the Isle of Man*. London (=Soc Medieval Archaeol Monogr Ser, 1).

Biddle, M 1990 *Object and Economy in Medieval Winchester: artefacts from medieval Winchester*. Oxford (=Winchester Studies 7, ii).

Biddle, M and Keene, S 1990 'Leather working', in Biddle 1990, 245–7.

Biddle, M and Elmhirst, L 1990 'Sewing equipment', in Biddle 1990, 804–17.

BL, British Library, Add Ms 42130, Luttrell Psalter (begun before 1340).

Blanc, O 1989 'Vêtement Féminin, Vêtement Masculin à la Fin du Moyen Age. Le Point de Vue des Moralistes', in Pastoureau 1989, 243–53.

Blomqvist, R 1938 'Medeltida skor i Lunk', *Kulturen*, 189–219. (Translation no 152, December 1954, Ministry of Works Library, Lambeth Bridge House).

Blomqvist, R 1945 'En Medeltida skotyp', *Kulturen*, 138–56. (Translation 146, December 1954, Ministry of Works Library, Lambeth Bridge House).

Bogdan, N Q and Wordsworth, J W 1978 *The Mediaeval Excavations at the High Street, Perth, 1975–76*. Perth (Perth High Street Archaeological Committee).

Bond, J M and Hunter, J R 1987 'Flax-growing in Orkney from the Norse period to the 18th century', *Proc Soc Antiq Scot* 117, 175–81.

Bowler, D Cox, A and Smith, C 1995 'Four excavations in Perth, 1979–84', *Proc Soc Antiq Scot* 125, 917–99.

Brett, G 1956 'The "Rider" silk', in Battiscombe 1956, 470–83.

Brisbane, Mark 1992 *The archaeology of Novgorod, Russia*. London (=Soc Medieval Archaeol Monogr Ser, 13).

Brunello, F 1973 *The Art of Dyeing in the History of Mankind*. Vicenza.

Brydall, R 1895 'The monumental effigies of Scotland, from the thirteenth to the fifteenth centuries', *Proc Soc Antiq Scot* 29 (1894–1895), 329–410.

Burkett, M E 1979 *The Art of the Felt Maker*. Kendal.

Burnham, D K 1980 *A Textile Terminology: Warp and Weft*. London.

Butt, B and Ponting, K (eds) 1987 *Scottish Textile History*. Aberdeen.

Caldwell, D H 1981 'Metalwork', in Good and Tabraham 1981, 90–140.

Cameron, A S and Stones, J A (eds) 2001 *Aberdeen: An In-depth View of the City's Past*. Edinburgh (=Soc Antiq Scot Monogr Ser, 19).

'Carita' (Mrs I A Simpson) 1909 *Lacis: Practical Instructions in Filet Brodé or Darning on Net*. London.

Carlisle, I 1998 'The leather from Swinegate, York'. (Unpublished archive report).

Carus-Wilson, E M 1954 *Mediaeval Merchant Venturers*. London.

Carus-Wilson, E M 1957 'The significance of the secular sculptures in the Lane Chapel, Cullompton', *Medieval Archaeol* 1, 104–17.

Carver, M O H 1979 'Three Saxo–Norman tenements in Durham City', *Medieval Archaeol* 23, 26–35.

Caulfield, S F A P and Saward, B C 1882 *Dictionary of Needlework*. London.

Cavers, K 1993 *A Vision of Scotland: The Nation Observed by John Slezer 1671–1717*. Edinburgh.

CDS *Calendar of Documents relating to Scotland Preserved in Her Majesty's Public Record Office, London*, Bain, J (ed). Edinburgh, 4 vols, 1881–8.

Chaplin, R E and Barnetson, L 1976 'The animal bones', in Schofield 1976, 229–39.

Chatwin, P B 1934 'Knife and dagger sheaths from Coventry', *Trans and Proc Birmingham Archaeol Soc* 58, 60.

Chron Fordun 1993 *John of Fordun's Chronicle of The Scottish Nation*, Skene, W F (ed). Llanerch, 2 vols (facsimile reprint of 1872 edition).

Ciaraldi M 2009 'The plant macroremains. Evidence of domestic and industrial activities at Edgbaston Street, Moor Street, Park Street and the Row, Birmingham', in Rátkai, S (ed) *The Bull Ring Uncovered: Excavations at Edgbaston Street, Moor Street, Park Street and The Row, Birmingham, 1997–2001*, 239–58. Oxford.

CIETA 1964 *Centre International d'Étude des Textiles Anciens. International Vocabulary of Technical Terms*. Lyons.

Collingwood, P 1974 *The Techniques of Sprang*. London.

Cowan, I B and Easson, D E 1976 *Medieval Religious Houses Scotland*. London and New York.

Coupar Angus Chrs 1947 *Charters of the Abbey of Coupar Angus*, Easson, D E (ed). Edinburgh (=Scottish History Society, 2 vols).

Cowgill, J, de Neergaard, M and Griffiths, N 1987 *Knives and Scabbards*. London (=Medieval Finds from Excavations in London, 1).

Cox, A 1996 'Backland activities in medieval Perth: excavations at Meal Vennel and Scott Street', *Proc Soc Antiq Scot* 126, 733–821.

Craigie, W A 1925 'Earliest records of the Scots Tongue', *Scot Hist Rev* 22, 61–7.

Crawford, B E and Ballin Smith, B (eds) 1999 *The Biggins, Papa Stour, Shetland. The History and Excavation of a Royal Norwegian Farm*. Edinburgh (=Soc Antiq Scot Monogr Ser, 15).

Crowfoot, E 1975 'The textiles', in Platt and Coleman-Smith 1975, 334–9.

Crowfoot, E 1977 'Textiles', in Clarke, H and Carter, A (eds), *Excavations in King's Lynn 1963–1970*, 374–7. London (=Soc Medieval Archaeol Monogr Ser, 7).

Crowfoot, E 1979b 'Textiles', in Carver, M O H, 'Three Saxo–Norman tenements in Durham City', *Medieval Archaeol* 23, 36–9.

Crowfoot, E 1980 'The Textiles', in Hill, C, Millet, M and Blagg, T (eds), *The Roman Riverside Wall and Monumental Arch in London: excavations at Baynard's Castle, Upper Thames Street, London, 1974–76*, 112–15. London.

Crowfoot, E 1990 'Textiles', in Biddle 1990, 467–88.

Crowfoot, G M 1939 'The tablet-woven braids from the vestments of St Cuthbert at Durham', *Antiquaries J* 19, 57–80.

Cruikshank, P 2011 'Flax in Croatia: traditional production methods, the use and care of linen in folk costumes and implications for museum conservation', *Textile History* 42 (2), 239–60.

Cunnington, C W and Cunnington, P 1952 *Handbook of English Medieval Costume*. London.

Curle, C L 1982 *Pictish and Norse Finds from the Brough of Birsay 1934–1974*. Edinburgh (=Soc Antiq Scot Monogr Ser, 1).

Dedekam, H 1925 *To tekstilfund fra folkevandringstiden*, (Bergens Museums Årbok 1924–25, Hist-antikv. række Nr 3), np.

De Neergaard, M 1985 'Children's shoes in the thirteenth to sixteenth centuries', *Costume* 19, 14–20.

Depping, G-B (ed) 1837 *Réglemens sur les arts et métiers de Paris, rédigés au XIIIe siècle et connus sous le nom du livre des Métiers d'Etienne Boileau*. Paris.

Desrosiers, S, Vial, G and de Jonghe, D 1989 'Cloth of Aresta. A preliminary study of its definition, classification, and method of weaving', *Textile History* 20, Part 2, 199–233.

Desrosiers, S 1999 'Draps d'Areste (II). Extension de la classification, comparaisons et lieux de fabrication', *Techniques et Culture* 34, 89–119.

Ditchburn, D 1988 'Trade with Northern Europe, 1297–1540', in Lynch et al 1988, 161–79.

Dixon, E 1895 'Craftswomen in the Livre des Métiers', *Economic J* 5 (18), 209–28.

Dixon, S 1988 'The leather', in O'Brien et al 1988, 93–103.

Dixon, S 1989 'The leather work', in O'Brien, C et al 1989 'Excavations at Newcastle Quayside: The Crown Court Site', *Archaeol Aeliana*, 5th series 17, 177–9.

Donelly, J 1980 'Thomas of Coldingham, merchant and burgess of Berwick upon Tweed (died 1316)', *Scot Hist Rev* 59 Part 2, 105–25.

Dransart, P 2001 'Charred yarn and textile remains', in Alvey, R C, Britnell, W J, Courtney, P and Dransart, P 'Finds and building materials from Ty ^-mawr, Castle Caereinion', *Montgomeryshire Collections* 89, 109–12.

Dransart, P Z 2002 *Earth, Water, Fleece and Fabric: an Ethnography and Archaeology of Andean Camelid Herding*. London.

Dransart, P 2007 'Mysteries of the cloaked body: analogy and metaphor in concepts of weaving and body tissues', in Mitchell P (ed) *Trivium 37. The Nature and Culture of the Human Body*, 161–87.

Dransart, P 2012 'Representing gender and homo-sociality: hierarchy and clerical investments in medieval Scotland', in Harlow, M (ed) *Dress and Identity in the Past*. Oxford.

Dransart, P and Bogdan, N Q 2004 'The material culture of recusancy at Fetternear: kin and religion in post-Reformation Scotland', *Proc Soc Antiq Scot* 134, 457–70.

Dunbar, J G 1963 'Excavations at Skirling Castle, Peebleshire and James' Fort, Stirling', *Proc Soc Antiq Scot*, 96 (1962–3), 244–5.

Dunbar, J T 1989 *The Costume of Scotland*. London.

Duncan, A A M 1950 'The dress of the Scots', *Scot Hist Rev* 29, 210–12.

Duncan, A A M 1974 'Perth: the first century of the burgh', *Trans Perthshire Soc Natur Sci*, (Special Issue), 30–50.

Duncan, A A M 1975 *Scotland: the Making of the Kingdom*. Edinburgh.

Dyer, J and Wenham, P 1958 'Excavations and discoveries in a cellar in Messrs Chas Hart's premises, Feasegate, York, 1956', *Yorkshire Archaeol J* 39, 419–25.

East, K 1983 'The shoes', in Bruce-Mitford, R *The Sutton-Hoo Ship Burial,* 3ii, 792–5. London.

Eckhel, N 1988 'Raising and production of raw materials for weaving', in Radauš Ribarić and Rihtman Aguštin 1988, 59–65.

Egan, G and Pritchard, F 1991 *Dress Accessories c1150–c1450*. London (=Medieval Finds from Excavations in London, 3).

Emery, I 1980 *The Primary Structures of Fabrics*. Washington DC.

Endrei, W 1968 *L'évolution des techniques du filage et du tissu du Moyen Age à la Révolution Industrielle*. Paris.

Endrei, W and Egan, G 1982 'The sealing of cloth in Europe, with special reference to the English evidence', *Textile History* 13 Part 1, 47–75.

ERS 1878–1908 *The Exchequer Rolls of Scotland*, Stuart, J, Burnett, G, Mackay, A J G and MacNeill, G P (eds). Edinburgh, 23 vols, 1264–1600.

Espinas, G and Pirenne, H 1920 *Recueil de documents relatifs á l'histoire drapière en Flandre*. Brussels, Part 1, Volume III.

Evans, J 1952 *Dress in Medieval France*. Oxford.

Farmer, D H 2004 *Oxford Dictionary of Saints*. Oxford.

Fawcett, R 1986 *Inchmahome Priory*. Edinburgh.

Ferdière, A 1984 'Le travail du textile en Région Centre de l'Age du Fer au Haut Moyen-Age', *Revue archéologique du Centre de la France* 23 (2), 209–75.

Fittis, R S 1875 *The Perthshire Antiquarian Miscellany*. Perth.

Fittis, R S 1885 *Ecclesiastical Annals of Perth to the Period of the Reformation*. Edinburgh and Perth.

Flanagan, J F 1956 'The figured-silks', in Battiscombe 1956, 484–525.

Fothergill, R (ed) 1979 *What's in a Name: a Survey of Perth Street Names*. Perth.

Fothergill, R (nd) *The Inches of Perth*. Perth.

Fraser, M and Dickson, J H 1982 'Plant remains', in Murray 1982, 239–43.

Friendship-Taylor, D 1984 'The leather', in Allan, J P *Medieval and Post-medieval Finds from Exeter 1971–80*, 323–33. Exeter.

Froissart, J 1979 *Chronicles*, translated by G Brereton. Harmondsworth.

Gabra-Sanders, T 1997 'An important collection of archaeological textiles from Sillerholes, West Lothian:
a preliminary report', *Proc Soc Antiq Scot* 127, 965–6.

Gabra-Sanders, T 2001a 'Textiles', in Cameron and Stones 2001, 222–32.

Gabra-Sanders, T 2001b 'Thimbles', in Mitchell et al 2001, 92.

Gabra-Sanders, T 2001c 'The Orkney hood, re-dated and re-considered', in Walton Rogers, P, Jorgensen, L B, and Rast-Eicher, A (eds) *The Roman Textile Industry and its Influence*. Oxford.

Gabra-Sanders, T and Ryder, M L, 2001 'Textiles and associated objects', in Mitchell et al 2001, 125–37.

Galbreath, D L 1949 'An early mention of Scottish dress', *Scot Hist Rev* 28, 198–9.

Gaskell-Brown, C 1986 'The medieval waterfront: Woolster Street. The finds', *Plymouth Museum Archaeol Ser* 3, 53–8.

Gathercole, P W 1958 'Excavations at Oakham Castle, Rutland', *Trans Leicester Archaeol and Hist Soc* 34, 17–38.

Geijer, A 1938 *Birka III: Die Textilfunde aus den Gräbern*. Uppsala.

Geijer, A 1979 *A History of Textile Art*. London.

Geijer, A 1980 'The textile finds from Birka', *Acta Archaeologia* 50 (1979–1980), 209–22.

Gómez-Moreno, M 1946 *El Panteón Real de las Huelgas de Burgos*. Madrid.

Good, G L and Tabraham, C J 1981 'Excavations at Threave Castle, Galloway 1974–1978', *Medieval Archaeol* 25, 90–140.

Goodall, I H 1990 'Tanning, currying and leather-working tools', in Biddle 1990, 247–50.

Goodfellow, A V and Thornton, J V 1972 'Leather shoe parts from excavations in Low Petergate, York 1957–8', *Yorkshire Archaeol J* 44, 97–105.

Goubitz, 0 1983 'Die ledervondsten', *Rijksdienst voor het oudheidkundig Bodemonderzoek*, Overdrukken 198, 274–83.

Goudge, C E 1979 'The leather', in Heighway, C M, Garrod, A P and Vince, A G 1979 'Excavations at 1 Westgate Street, Gloucester', *Medieval Archaeol* 23, 193–6.

Gould, J and Thornton, J H 1973 'Mediaeval leather and pottery found near Minster Pool, Lichfield', *Trans South Staffordshire Archaeol and Hist Soc* 14 (1972–3), 57–60.

Grant, I F 1961 *Highland Folk Ways*. London.

Grew, F and de Neergaard, M 1988 *Shoes and Pattens*. London (=Medieval Finds from Excavations in London, 2).

Grierson, S 1985 *Whorl and Wheel: the Story of Handspinning in Scotland*. Perth.

Groenman-van Waateringe, W 1975 'Society ... rests on leather', in Renaud, J G N (ed) 1968–1975 *Rotterd am Papers. A Contribution to Medieval Archaeology*. Rotterdam, vols 1 and 2, 23–34.

Groenman-van Waateringe, W and Guiran, A J 1978 'Das Leder von Lübeck', *Grabung Konigsti; 59, Lübecker Schriften zur Archäologie und Kulturgeschichte*, 1, 161–73.

Groenman-van Waateringe, W 1984 'Die Lederfunds von Haithabu', in Schietzel, K (ed) *Berichte uber Ausgrabungen in Haithabu*, 21, Neumünster (Schleswig-Holsteinisches Landesmuseum für Vor- und Frühgeschichte).

Groenman-van Waateringe, W and Krauwer, M 1987 'Das Leder von Lübeck, Grabungen Schüsseibuden 16/Fischstrasse 1–3', *Lübecker Schriften zur Archäologie und Kulturgeschichte*, 10, 75–84.

Groenman-van Waateringe, W and Velt, L M 1975 'Schuhmode im Späten Mittelatter, Funde und Abbildungen,' *Zeitschrift für Archäologie des Mittelalters*, 3, 95–119.

Gulvin, C 1973 *The Tweedmakers: a History of the Scottish Fancy Woollen Industry, 1600–1914*. Newton Abbot.

Guðjónsson, E E 1962 'Forn Röggvarvefnadur', *Árbók Hins Íslenzka Fornleifafélags 1962*, 12–71.

Guðjónsson, E E 1979 'Icelandic loop-braided bands: krilud bond', *Bulletin de Liaison du Centre International d'Étude des Textiles Anciens* 49, 65–7.

Hald, M 1950 *Olddanske Tekstiler*. Copenhagen.

Hald, M 1980 *Ancient Danish Textiles from Bogs and Burials. A Comparative Study of Costume and Iron Age Textiles*. Copenhagen (=Publications of the National Museum, Archaeological–Historical Series, 21).

Halyburton's Ledger 1867 *Ledger of Andrew Halyburton, 1492–1503*, Innes, C (ed). Edinburgh.

Harrison, P and Janaway, R 1997 'Textiles', in Moloney, C and Coleman, R 'The development of a medieval street frontage: the evidence from excavations at 80–86 High Street, Perth', *Proc Soc Antiq Scot* 127, 757–8.

Hassall, T 1976 'Excavations at Oxford Castle', *Oxoniensa* 41, 276–96.

Heckett, E 1990 'Some silk and wool head-coverings from Viking Dublin: uses and origins – an enquiry', in Walton and Wild 1990, 85–96.

Heckett, E W 1992 'An Irish "shaggy pile" fabric of the 16th century – an insular survival?', *Tidens Tand* 5, 158–68.

Hedges, J W 1982 'Textiles', in MacGregor 1982, 102–29.

Heinemeyer, E 1966 'Zwei gotische Frauenhaarnetze', *Waffen- und Kostümkunde* 8, 13–22.

Henderson, I 1998 '*Primus inter pares*: the St Andrews sarcophagus in Pictish sculpture', in Foster, S M (ed) *The St Andrews Sarcophagus: A Pictish Masterpiece and its International Connections*, 97–167. Dublin.

Henry, F 1970 *Irish Art in the Romanesque Period 1020–1170 AD*. London.

Henshall, A S 1950 'Textile and weaving appliances in prehistoric Britain', *Proc Prehist Soc*, New Series, 16 (1950), 130–62.

Henshall, A S 1952 'Early textiles found in Scotland. Part I – locally made', *Proc Soc Antiq Scot* 86 (1951–1952), 1–29.

Henshall, A S 1964 'Five tablet-woven seal tags', *Archaeol J* 121, 154–62.

Henshall, A S, Crowfoot, G M and Becwith, J 1956 'Early textiles found in Scotland. Part II– medieval imports', *Proc Soc Antiq Scot* 88 (1954–1956), 22–39.

Henshall, A S and Maxwell, S 1952 'Clothing and other articles from a late 17th-century grave at Gunnister, Shetland', *Proc Soc Antiq Scot* 86 (1951–1952), 30–42.

Henshall, A S and Seaby, W A 1962 'The Dungiven Costume', *Ulster J Archaeol* 24–25 (1961–2), 119–42.

Higham, M C 1989 'Some evidence for the 12th- and 13th-century linen and woollen textile processing', *Medieval Archaeol* 33, 38–52.

Hochberg, B 1980 *Handspinning*. Santa Cruz, California.

Hoffmann, M 1964 *The Warp-Weighted Loom*. Oslo.

Hogarth, S 1987 'Ecclesiastical vestments at York Minster before the Reformation', in Ingram, E (ed) *Thread of Gold*, 8–14. York.

Holdsworth, P (ed) 1987 *Excavations in the Medieval Burgh of Perth, 1979–1981*. Edinburgh (=Soc Antiq Scot Monogr Ser, 5).

Holmes, U T Jr (trans) 1952 *Daily Living in the Twelfth Century. Based on the observations of Alexander Neckam in London and Paris*. Madison (University of Wisconsin).

Hunter, T 1932 *St John's Kirk, Perth. A History*. Perth.

Hurley, M F 1997 'The sheaths from Waterford', in Hurley et al 1997, pp**.

Hurley, M F, Scully, O M B and McCutcheon, C (eds) 1997 *Late Medieval Age and Viking Waterford: Excavations 1986–1992*. Waterford.

Hutchings, P 1983 'The leather artefacts', in McNeil, R 'Two 12th-century Wich Houses in Nantwich', *Medieval Archaeol* 27,78–82.

Jackson, S 1979 'The leather', in Ayers, B 'Excavations at Chapel Lane Staith, 1978', *East Riding Archaeologist 5* (=Hull Old Town Report Series No 3), 47–57.

Jackson, S 1983 'The leather', in Sanders, G B and Armstrong, P 'A watching brief on the Beverley High Level Sewer Scheme 1980/81', *East Riding Archaeologist* 7, 66–9.

Jackson, S 1987 'Objects of leather', in Young, G A B 'Excavations at Southgate, Hartlepool, Cleveland, 1981–82', *Durham Archaeol J* 3, 47–8.

Johnson, S 1785 *A Dictionary of the English Language in which the Words are Deduced from their Originals*, vol 2. London, 6th ed.

Jones, A R and Stallybrass, P 2000 *Renaissance Clothing and the Materials of Memory*. Cambridge.

Jones, J and Thornton, J H 1983 'Leather', in Streeten, A D F 1983 *Bayham Abbey – recent research including a report of excavations1973–76 directed by the late Helen Sutermeister*, 124–5. Lewes (=Sussex Archaeol Soc Monogr 2).

Kamínska, J and Nahlik, A 1960 'Études sur l'industrie textile du haut Moyen Age en Pologne', *Archaeologia Polona* 3, 89–119.

Keene, D 1990 'Tanning', in Biddle 1990, 243–5.

Kenward, H and Hall, A 2001 'Plants, intestinal parasites and insects', in Cameron and Stones 2001, 280–95.

Kerridge, E 1985 *Textile Manufacturers in Early Modern England*. Manchester.

King, D 1968 'Two mediaeval textile terms: "Draps d'Ache", "Draps de l'Arrest"', *Bulletin de Liaison du Centre International d'Étude des Textiles Anciens* 27, 27–9.

Kjellberg, A 1979 'Tekstilmaterialet fra "Oslogate 7"', *De arkeologiske utgravninger i Gamlebyen, Oslo 2*, 83–104.

Kjellberg, A 1982 'Medieval textiles from the excavations of the old town of Oslo', in Bender Jørgensen and Tidow 1982, 136–50.

Kostelníková, M 1990 'Eine kurzgefaßte Übersicht über die Textilforschung in Mähren (Tschechoslowakei)', in Walton and Wild 1990, 113–18.

Lacey, K. 1987 'The production of "Narrow Ware" by silkwomen in fourteenth and fifteenth century England', *Textile History* 18 (2), 187–204.

Laing, H 1866 *Supplemental Descriptive Catalogue of Ancient Scottish Seals, Royal, Baronial, Ecclesiastical, and Municipal embracing the period from A.D. 1150 to the Eighteenth Century*. Edinburgh.

Larsen, A J 1992 'Footwear from the Gullskoen area of Bryggen', *Bryggen Papers*. Bergen.

Leadbeater, E 1976 *Handspinning*. London.

Lindsay, W J 'Excavations in Elgin, 1976–1981'. Unpublished archive report.

Lindström, M 1982 'Medieval textile finds in Lund', in Bender Jørgensen and Tidow 1982, 179–92.

LMMC 1940 *London MuseumMediaeval Catalogue*. London.

Lynch M, Spearman M and Stell G (eds) 1988 *The Scottish Mediaeval Town*. Edinburgh.

McClintock, H F 1936 'The mantle of St Brigid at Bruges', *J Royal Soc Antiq Ireland* 6, 32–40.

MacElvaney, M 1993 'The leather', in Ellison, M, McCombie, G, MacElvaney, M, Newman, A, Williams, A, Taverner, N, O'Brien, C 'Excavations at the Newcastle Quayside waterfront development at the Swirle', *Archaeol Aeliana*, 5th Ser, 21, 213–14.

MacGregor, A (ed) 1982 *Anglo–Scandinavian Finds from Lloyds Bank, Pavement, and Other Sites*. London (=Archaeology of York, The Small Finds, Fascicule 17/3, 136–45, 154).

Mackay, J G and Carmichael, A 1894 'Notes on a pair of pampooties, or shoes of raw hide, from Aran More, Galway Bay and on cuaran and other varieties of shoes used in the Highlands and Islands of Scotland', *Proc Soc Antiq Scot* 28 (1893–4), 136–50.

McRoberts, D 1956 'The Fetternear Banner', *Innes Review* 7, 69–86.

May, F L 1957 *Silk Textiles of Spain: Eighth to Fifteenth Centuries*. New York.

MED 1954 *Middle English Dictionary*, Kurath, H and Lewis, R E (eds). Michigan.

Mitchell, A 1880 *The Past in the Present: the Rhind Lectures for 1876 and 1878*. Edinburgh.

Mitchell, K L, Murdoch, K R and Ward, J R 2001 *Fast Castle: Excavations 1971–86*. Edinburgh (=Edinburgh Archaeological Field Soc).

Moireau, F 1993 'Deux silos médiévaux à Suèvres (Loir-et-Cher)', *Revue archéologique du Centre de la France* 32, 179–85.

Möller-Wiering, S 2011 *War and Worship. Textiles from 3rd to 4th-century AD Weapon Deposits in Denmark and Northern Germany*. Oxford.

Morris, C A 2000 *Craft, Industry and Everyday Life: Wood and Woodworking in Anglo–Scandinavian and Medieval York*. York (=Archaeology of York: The Small finds, Fascicule 17/13).

Mould, Q, Carlisle, I and Cameron, E 2003 *Craft, Industry and Everyday Life. Leather and Leatherworking in Anglo–Scandinavian and Medieval York*. York (=Archaeology of York: The Small Finds, Fascicule17/16).

Müller-Christensen 1960 *Das Grab des Papstes Clemens II. im Dom zu Bamberg*. Munich.

Munro, J H 1978 'Wool-price schedules and the qualities of English wools in the later Middle Ages c.1270–1499', *Textile History* 9, 118–69.

Munro, J 2009 'Three centuries of luxury textile consumption in the Low Countries and England, 1330–1570: trends and comparisons of real values of woollen broadcloth (then and now)', in Nosch, M-L and Vestergard, K (eds) *The Medieval Broadcloth: Changing Trends in Fashions, Manufacturing and Consumption*, 1–73. Oxford.

Murray, J C (ed) 1982 *Excavations in the Medieval Burgh of Aberdeen, 1973–1981*. Edinburgh (=Soc Antiq Scot Monogr Ser, 2).

Muthesius, A 1974 'De Zijden Stoffen in de Schatkamer van de Sint Servaaskerk te Maastricht', *Publications de la Société Historique et Archéologique dans le Duché de Limburg* 110, 325–60.

Muthesius, A 1982a 'The silk fragment from 5 Coppergate', in MacGregor 1982, 132–6.

Muthesius, A 1982b 'The Silks from the tomb', in Coldstream, N and Draper, P (eds) *Medieval Art and Architecture at Canterbury before 1220*, 80–7. London.

Muthesius, A 1987 'Silk', in Holdsworth 1987, 167–71.

Mynard, D C 1969 'Excavations at Dover Castle', *J Brit Archaeol Assoc*, 3rd Ser 32, 101–4.

NED 1888–1933 *A New English Dictionary on Historical Principles*, Murray, J A H (ed). Oxford.

Neill, M 1991 'A Lost Last', *Archaeology Ireland* 5 (2), 14–15.

Nicholson, A 1997 'The leather', in Hill, P *Whithorn and St. Ninian. The Excavation of a Monastic Town 1984–91*, 499–509. Stroud.

NMAS 1892 *Catalogue of the National Museum of Antiquities of Scotland*. Edinburgh.

Nockert, M. 1982 'Some new observations about the Bocksten costume', in Bender Jørgensen and Tidow 1982, 277–82.

Nørlund, P 1924 'Buried Norsemen at Herjolfsnes', *Meddelelser om Grønland* 67, 1–270.

Noss, A 1966 'Bandlaging', *By og bygd* 19, 111–42.

O'Brien, C, Brown, L, Nicholson, R and Dixon, S 1988 *The Origins of the Newcastle Quayside. Excavations at Queen Street and Dog Bank*. Newcastle upon Tyne (=Soc Antiq Newcastle-upon-Tyne Monogr Ser, 3).

Okasha, E 1992 'Anglo–Saxon inscribed sheaths from Aachen, Dublin and Trondheim', *Medieval Archaeol* 36, 59–66.

O'Rourke, D 1997 'Leather artefacts', in Hurley et al 1997, 702–22.

OSA 1791-9 Low, G 'United Parishes of Birsay and Harray', in *Statistical Account of Scotland*, vol xiv, Sinclair, J (ed), Edinburgh (available online at http://stat-acc-scot.edina.ac.uk/link/1791-99/Orkney/Birsay%20and%20Harray).

Østergård, E 1982 'The medieval everyday costumes of the Norsemen in Greenland', in Bender Jørgensen and Tidow 1982, 267–76.

Østergård, E 2009 *Woven Into the Earth: Textiles from Norse Greenland*. Aarhus.

Oswald, A 1963 'Excavation of a thirteenth century wooden building at Weoley Castle, Birmingham, 1960–61', *Medieval Archaeol* 6–7 (1962–3), 132.

Ottaway, P 1982 'A burial from the South Aisle of Winchester Cathedral', *Archaeol J* 139, 124–37.

Øye, I 1988 *The Bryggen Papers. Main Series Vol 2: Textile Equipment and its Working Environment in Bergen c1150–1500*. Oslo.

Palliser, Mrs B 1910 *History of Lace*. London (rev ed by Jourdain, M and Dryden, A).

Pastoureau, M (ed) 1989 *Le vêtement – histoire, archéologie et symbolique vestimentaires au Moyen Age*. Paris (Cahiers du Léopard d'or, 1).

Paterson, J W 1950 *Inchcolm Abbey*. Edinburgh.

Pedersen, I R 1992 'Silk threads on leather objects from the Middle Ages', *Tidens Tand* 5, 141–50.

Perry, D R 'The excavation', in *PHSAE Fascicule 1*, 27–126.

Perth Museum and Art Gallery *St John's Kirk File*. Extract from Minute Book of Perth Literary and Antiquarian Society, 22 Dec 1812.

PHSAE Fascicule 1 2010 Perry, D R, Murray, H, Beaumont James, T and Bogdan, the late N Q *Perth High Street Archaeological Excavation 1975–1977. The excavations at 75–95 High Street and 5–10 Mill Street, Perth*. Perth (= Tayside Fife Archaeol Comm Monogr).

PHSAE Fascicule 2 2012 Haggarty, G, Hall, D W and Vince, the late A G et al *Perth High Street Archaeological Excavation 1975–1977. The ceramics, the metalwork, and the wood.* Perth (= Tayside Fife Archaeol Comm Monogr).

PHSAE Fascicule 4 2011 Hodgson, the late G W I et al *Perth High Street Archaeological Excavation 1975–1977. Living and working in a medieval Scottish burgh. Environmental remains and miscellaneous finds.* Perth (= Tayside Fife Archaeol Comm Monogr).

Piponnier, F 1989 'Une révolution dans le costume masculin au XIVe siècle', in Pastoureau 1989, 225–42.

Piponnier, F and Mane, P 1995 *Se vêtir au Moyen Âge.* Paris.

Platt C and Coleman-Smith R 1975 *Excavations in Mediaeval Southampton 1953–1969, vol 2. The Finds.* Leicester.

Ponting, K 1987 'The Scottish contribution to wool textile design in the nineteenth century', in Butt and Ponting 1987, 78–94.

Pritchard, F 1982 'Textiles from recent excavations in the City of London', in Bender Jørgensen and Tidow 1982, 193–208.

Pritchard, F 1984 'Late Saxon textiles from the City of London', *Medieval Archaeol* 28, 46–76

Pritchard, F 1988 'Silk braids and textiles of the Viking Age from Dublin', in Bender Jørgensen et al 1988, 149–61.

Pritchard, F 1991 'Small finds', in Vince, A G *Aspects of Saxon and Medieval London, 2. Finds and Environmental Evidence*, 120–278. London (=London Middlesex Archaeol Soc, Special Paper 12).

Radauš Ribarić, J and Rihtman Aguštin, D (eds) 1988 *Čarolija niti. Vještina narodnog tkanja u Jugoslaviji. The Wonder of Weaving: Folk-weaving Skills in Yugoslavia.* Zagreb.

Raknes Pedersen, I 1982 'The analyses of the textiles from Evebø/Eide, Gloppen, Norway', in Bender Jørgensen and Tidow 1982, 75–84.

Reed, R 1966 *Science for Students of Leather Technology.* Oxford

Richardson, J S 1907 'Notice of portion of stone mould for casting pilgrims' signacula and ring brooches', in 'Notice of kitchen-midden deposits on North Berwick Law, and other antiquities in the vicinity of North Berwick; with a note of an undescribed sculptured stone, with symbols, in the island of Raasay', *Proc Soc Antiq Scot* 41 (1906–7), 431.

Richardson, K M 1959 'Excavations in Hungate, York', *Archaeol J* 116, 51–114.

Robbert, L B 1983 'Twelfth-century Italian prices: food and clothing in Pisa and Venice', *Social Science History* 7 (4), 381–403.

Robinson, D 1987 'Botanical remains', in Holdsworth 1987, 199–209.

Robinson, J 2004 *British Museum Objects in Focus: The Lewis Chessmen.* London.

Roch, D 1876 *Textile Fabrics.* London.

Ross, A 1895 *Scottish Home Industries.* Glasgow (reprinted 1976).

RRS 1971 *Regesta Regum Scottorum: the Acts of William I, King of Scots 1165–1214*, Barrow, G W S (ed). Edinburgh.

Russell, J 1939 'English medieval leatherwork', *Archaeol J* 96, 132–41.

Ryder, M L 1968 'The evolution of Scottish breeds of sheep', *Scottish Studies* 12, 127–67.

Ryder, M L 1970 'Structure and seasonal change in the coat of Scottish wild goats', *J Zoological Soc London* 161, 355–61.

Ryder, M l 1981 'British medieval sheep and their wool types', in Crossley, D W (ed) *Medieval Industry.* London (=CBA Research Report 40).

Ryder, M L 1983a *Sheep and Man.* London.

Ryder, M L 1983b 'The hair and wool from the Perth High Street Excavation', in Proudfoot, B (ed) 1983 *Site, Environment and Economy*, 33–41. Oxford (=BAR Int Ser, 173).

Ryder, M L 1987 'Evolution of the fleece', *Scientific American* 255, No 1, 112–19.

Ryder, M L 1992 'The interaction between biological and technological change during the development of different fleece types in sheep', *Anthropozoologica* 16, 131–40.

Ryder, M L and Gabra-Sanders, T 1992 'Textiles from Fast Castle, Berwickshire, Scotland', *Textile History* 23, Part 1, 5–21.

Salzman, L F 1923 *English Industries in the Middle Ages.* Oxford.

Scarlett, J 1987 'Tartan: the Highland cloth and Highland art form', in Butt and Ponting 1987, 65–77.

Schia 1977 (in leather report)

Schjølberg, E 1984 'The hair products', *The Bryggen Papers*, Supplementary Series No 1, 73–91. Bergen.

Schjølberg, E 1998 '12th century twills from Bergen, Norway', in Bender Jørgensen, L and Rinaldo, C (eds), *Textiles in European Archaeology. Report from the 6th NESAT Symposium, 7–11th May 1996 in Borås*, 209–13. Göteborg (=GOTARC Series A, Vol 1).

Schmedding, B 1978 *Mittelalterliche Textilien in Kirchen und Klöstern der Schweiz.* Bern (=Schriften der Abegg Stiftung, 3).

Schnack, C 1992a 'Schuhe aus dem mittelalterlichen Konstanz', *Schriften des Vereins für Geschichte des Bodensees und seiner Umgebung* 110, 95–102.

Schnack, C 1992b *Die mittelalterlichen schuhe aus Schleswig.* Ausgrabung Schild 1971–1975, Ausgrabungen in Schleswig, Berichte und Studien, 10, Neumunster.

Schnack, C 1993 'Lederfunde von der Schlachte in Bremen', *Bremer Archäologische Blätter*, NF2, (1992–3), 61–70.

Schnack, C 1994 'Mittelatterliche Lederfunde aus Konstanz (Grabung Fischmarkt)', *Materialhefte zur Archäologie in Baden-Würtemmberg* 26.

Schofield, J 1976 'Excavations South of Edinburgh High Street, 1973–4', *Proc Soc Antiq Scot* 107 (1975–1976), 155–241.

Schuette, M 1956 'Tablet Weaving', *CIBA Review* 117 (Nov 1956), 2–28.

Schuette, M and Müller-Christensen, S 1963 *La Broderie*. Paris.

Shaw, F J 1979 'Sumptuary legislation in Scotland', *Juridical Review*, New Series 24, 81–115.

Simpson, W D 1959 *A Short History of St John's Kirk, Perth*. Perth.

SND 1931–1976 *The Scottish National Dictionary*, Grant, W and Murison, D D (eds). Edinburgh.

Sortor, M 1993 'Saint-Omer and its textile trades in the Late Middle Ages', *American Hist Rev* 98 (5), 1475–99.

Spearman, R M 1988b 'Workshops, materials and debris – evidence of early industries', in Lynch et al 1988, 134–47.

Spencer, B 1975 'The ampullae from Cuckoo Lane', in Platt and Coleman-Smith 1975, 242–9.

Staniland, K 1978 'Clothing and textiles in the Court of Edward III', in Bird, J, Chapman, H and Clark, J (eds) 1978 *Collectanea Londiniensia: Studies in London Archaeology and History presented to Ralph Merrifield*, 223–34. London (=London Middlesex Archaeol Soc, Special Paper No 2).

Staniland, K 1991 *Medieval Craftsmen: Embroiderers*. London.

Stauffer, A 1992 *Die mittelalterlichen Textilien von St Servatius in Maastricht*. Bern (=Schriften der Abegg Stiftung, 8).

Stavert, M L 1991 *Perth: a Short History*. Perth, 2nd ed.

Stavert, M L 1993 *The Perth Guildry Book 1452–1601*. Edinburgh (=Scottish Record Society, New Series 19).

Stewart, M E C and Thoms, L 1976 *It Will Soon be Too Late*. Perth

Stones, J 1982 'Leather objects', in Murray 1982, 191–7.

Sturdy, D 1958 'The Clarendon Hotel, Oxford – Shoemaking', *Oxoniensa* 23, 75–7.

Swallow, A W 1973 'Interpretations of wear marks seen in footwear', *Trans of the Museum Assistants' Group* 12, 28–32.

Swann, J M 1973 'Shoe fashions to 1600', *Trans of the Museum Assistants' Group* 12, 14.

Tatton-Brown, T 1974 'Excavations at the Custom House Site, City of London 1973. Part I', *Trans London and Middlesex Archaeol Soc* 25, 197, 199–200.

Tatton-Brown, T 1975 'Excavations at the Custom House Site, City of London, 1973. Part II', *Trans London and Middlesex Archaeol Soc* 26, 154–167.

Taylor, M 1978 *The Lewis Chessmen*. London.

Thomas, M C 1981 'The leather', in Good and Tabraham 1981, 123–6.

Thomas, C 1982 'The leather', in McGavin, N 'Excavations at Kirkwall, Orkney', *Proc Soc Antiq Scot* 112, 413–6.

Thomas, C 1987 'Leather', in Holdsworth 1987, 174–90.

Thomas, C 1991 'The leather shoes and leggings', in Hodder, M A 'Excavations at Sandwell Priory and Hall, 1982–88', *South Staffordshire Archaeol Soc Trans* 31 (1989–90), 102–11.

Thomas, C and Walsh, A 1995 'Leather', in Bowler et al 1995, 971 and 978–9.

Thomas, C 1995 'Leather', in Lewis, J and Ewart, G *Jedburgh Abbey.The Archaeology of a Border Abbey*, 114. Edinburgh (=Soc Antiq Scot Monogr Ser, 10).

Thomas, C 2001a 'The leather', in Cameron and Stones 2001, 241–58.

Thomas, C 2001b 'Leather', in Mitchell et al 2001, 138–42.

Thomas, C 2002 'Leather', in Lewis, J and Pringle, D *Spynie Palace and the Bishops of Moray. History, Architecture and Archaeology*, 144–6. Edinburgh (=Soc Antiq Scot Monogr Ser, 21).

Thomas, C forthcoming a 'Leather from Bristol Bridge, Bristol 48/81', in Williams, B *Excavations at Bristol Bridge, Bristol*. Bristol and Region Archaeological Services, Bristol City Museums and Art Gallery. Unpublished excavation report.

Thomas, C forthcoming b 'Leather from Bristol, Redcliffe Street, 107/80 CLK', in Williams, B *Excavations at Redcliffe Street, Bristol*. Bristol and Region Archaeological Services, Bristol City Museum and Art Gallery. Unpublished excavation report.

Thomas, C forthcoming c 'The leather from Brooks Wharf, Upper Thames Street, London', in Bruce, G and Stevens, T 'Archaeological investigations at Brooks Wharf, 48 Upper Thames Street', AOC Archaeology Group.Unpublished archive report.

Thomas,C forthcoming d 'The leather from Bon Accord, Aberdeen'.

Thomas, S 1980 *Mediaeval footwear from Coventry. A catalogue of the collection of Coventry Museum*. Coventry.

Thompson, M W 1956 'A group of mounds on Seasalter Level near Whitstable', *Archaeologia Cantiana* 70, 55–57.

Thompson, M W 1967 *Novgorod the Great*. London.

Thompson, M W 1968 'The horizontal loom at Novgorod', *Medieval Archaeol* 12, 146–7.

Thornton, J H 1959 'Shoes from Clare Castle, Suffolk', *Proc Suffolk Institute Archaeol* 28.2, 146–52.

Thornton, J H 1961 'Shoe fragments from excavations on the Town Wall, Roushill, Shrewsbury', *Medieval Archaeol* 5, 187–206.

Thornton, J H 1969a 'The mediaeval shoes from the Lich Street site, Worcester', *Trans Worcestershire Archaeol Soc*, 3rd Ser, 2 (1968–9), 56–62.

Thornton, J H 1969b 'Leather', in Addyman, P V 1969 'Late Saxon settlement in the St. Neots Area', *Proc Cambridge Antiq Soc* 62, 91.

Thornton, J H 1973a 'The examination of early shoes up to 1600', *Transactions of the Museum Assistants' Group* 12, 2–13.

Thornton, J H 1973b 'A glossary of shoe terms', *Transactions of the Museum Assistants' Group* 12, 44–48.

Thornton, J H 1974 'Leather', in Beresford, G 'The Medieval Manor of Penhallan, Cornwall', *Medieval Archaeol* 18, 141–2.

Thornton, J H 1977 'Leatherwork', in Durham, B 1977 'Archaeological investigations in St Aldates, Oxford', *Oxoniensia* 42, 155–60.

Thornton, J H 1990a 'A leather belt', in Biddle 1990, 545–6.

Thornton, J H 1990b 'Shoes, boots and shoe repairs', in Biddle 1990, 591–617.

Thornton, J H 1990c 'Leather balls', in Biddle 1990, 707–8.

Thornton, J H 1990d 'Knife sheaths', in Biddle 1990, 862–3.

Thurlby, M 1981 'A 12th-century figure from Jedburgh Abbey', *Proc Soc Antiq Scot* 111, 381–7.

Tidow, K and Schmid, P 1979 'Frühmittelalterliche Textilfunde aus der Wurt Hessens (Stadt Wilhelmshaven) und dem Gräberfeld von Dunum (Kr. Friesland) und ihre archäologische Bedeutung', *Probleme der Küstenforschung im südlichen Nordseegebiet* 13, 123–52.

Tweddle, D 1986 'Finds from Parliament Street and other sites in the city centre', in Addyman, P V (ed) *The Archaeology of York*. (= Archaeology of York: Fascicule 17/4, 237–56).

van Driel-Murray, C 1985

van Driel-Murray, C 1987 'A note on shrinkage', *Archaeological Leather Group Newsletter*, no 2 (1986–7).

van Uytven, R 1983 'Cloth in medieval literature of Western Europe', in Harte, N B and Ponting, K G (eds), *Cloth and Clothing in Medieval Europe*, 151–83. London (=Pasold Studies in Textile History, 2).

Vetterli, W A 1951 'The history of indigo', *CIBA Review*, 85 (April 1951), 3066–71.

Vogt, C 2010 'Episcopal self-fashioning: the Thomas Becket mitres', in Wetter, E (ed) *Iconography of Liturgical Textiles in the Middle Ages*, 117–28. Riggisberg.

Vons-Comis, S Y 1982a 'Medieval textile finds from the Netherlands', in Bender Jørgensen and Tidow 1982, 151–62.

Vons-Comis, S Y 1982b 'Das Leder von Lübeck, Grabung Heiligen-Geist-Hospital, Koberg 9–11', *Lübecker Schriften zur Archäologie und Kulturgeschichte* 6, 239–50.

Wahlgren, E 1986 *The Vikings and America*. London.

Walton, P 1981 'The textiles', in Harbottle, B and Ellison, M, 'An excavation in the Castle Ditch, Newcastle upon Tyne, 1974–6', *Archaeol Aeliana*, 5th Ser 9, 75–250.

Walton, P 1988 'Caulking, cordage and textiles', in O'Brien et al 1988, 78–85.

Walton, P 1989 *Textiles, Cordage and Raw Fibre from 16–22 Coppergate*. London (= Archaeology of York:The Small Finds, Fascicule17/5).

Walton, P 1990 'Textile production at Coppergate, York: Anglo–Saxon or Viking?', in Walton and Wild 1990, 61–72.

Walton, P 1992a 'The dyes', in Crowfoot, E, Pritchard, F and Staniland, K *Textiles and Clothing c1150–c1450*, 199–201. London (=Medieval Finds from Excavations in London, 4).

Walton, P 1992b 'The textiles', in Evans, D H and Tomlinson, D G *Excavations at 33–35 Eastgate, Beverley 1983–86*, 188. Sheffield (=Sheffield Excavation Reports No 3).

Walton, P and Wild, J-P (eds) 1990 *Textiles in Northern Archaeology. NESAT III: Textile Symposium in York, 6–9 May 1987*. London (=North European Symposium for Archaeological Textiles Monogr 3).

Walton Rogers, P 1997 *Textile Production at 16–22 Coppergate*. York (=Archaeology of York: The Small Finds Fascicule 17/11).

Walton Rogers, P 1999 'Textile, yarn and fibre from the Biggings', in Crawford and Ballin Smith 1999, 194–202.

Walton Rogers, P 2001 'Dyes', in Cameron and Stones 2001, 238–40.

Watkin, J 1987 'The leather', in Armstrong, P and Ayers, B 'Excavations in High Street and Blackfriargate', *East Riding Archaeologist* 8 (=Hull Old Town Report Series No 5), 219–26.

Watkins, J G and Williams, R A H 1983 'An excavation in Highgate, Beverley, 1977', *East Riding Archaeologist* 7, 71–84.

Watkins, M J 1983 'Finds from minor sites', in Heighway, C *The East and North Gates of Gloucester and Associated Sites: Excavations 1974–81*, 178–85. Bristol (=Western Archaeological Trust Monogr, 4).

Wiesner, M 1986 'Spinsters and seamstresses: women in cloth and clothing production', in Ferguson, M W, Quilligan, M and Vickers, N J (eds) *Rewriting the Renaissance: The Discourses of Sexual Difference in Early Modern Europe*, 191–205. Chicago and London.

Wild, J P and Bender Jørgensen, L 1988 'Clothes from the Roman Empire. Barbarians and Romans', in Bender Jørgensen et al 1988, 65–98.

Wilmott, T 1982 'Excavations at Queen Street, City of London, 1953 and 1960, and Roman timber-lined wells in London', *Trans London Middlesex Archaeol Soc* 33, 1–78.

Wilson, G 1905 *The Annals of the Glover Incorporation 1300–1905*. Perth.

Woodward, F 1994 *The Scottish Pearl in its World Context*. Edinburgh.

Zarnecki, G 1971 *Romanesque Art*. London.

Acknowledgements

Textiles

The scope and scale of the finds of textiles from Perth High Street by far exceeded the most optimistic expectations and the three main authors have been fortunate that, in the course of preparing this report, so many people have readily given help and advice. To all of these they offer their thanks with gratitude.

The report was begun while Dr Bennett was on the staff of the then National Museum of Antiquities of Scotland (now National Museums Scotland) and she wishes to acknowledge the contribution of her colleagues there, particularly Helen Dalrymple and Dr Jim Tait of the Research Laboratory, Charles Burnett, Dr David Caldwell, and Doreen Moyes who prepared the photographic plates of the textiles. The conservation of the examples of lacis was the work of M Findlay and K Hunter (PHSAE). Apart from their main reports, Dr Michael Ryder and Professor M C Whiting also gave help on special points, as did Dr Caldwell.

In addition, the following specialists provided opinions and information: C L Curle; E Crowfoot; Dr Leonie von Wilckens of the Germanisches National-museum; Audrey Henshall; Dr Marta Hoffmann; Frances Pritchard, K Staniland and Michael Rhodes of the Museum of London; June Swann of Northampton Museums; Naomi Tarrant of the then Royal Scottish Museum (now National Museums Scotland); Santina Levey and colleagues in the Department of Textiles and Dress, Victoria and Albert Museum; Sandra Vons-Comis; Penelope Walton Rogers, Dr Anna Muthesius and Thea Gabra-Sanders. Dr Dransart began to work on the textile report in 1992. In addition to the above named people (and in particular, Thea Gabra-Sanders), she wishes to thank Prof Janet Burton, Mark Hall, Uto Hogerzeil, Sylvia Hogerzeil-Kien, Dr William Marx and Prof Richard Oram. She is also indebted to Derek Hall, Catherine Smith, David Perry and Lisbeth M Thoms for their constant support and vigilance during the editorial process. Responsibility for any errors or infelicities, however, remains with the main authors of this fascicule.

Special appreciation is due to Rose Smith, administrator to PHSAE, without whose unfailing efficiency and support the initial work could not have been completed, and to the staff of Perth Museum and Art Gallery. Without their help and, in particular, that of Michael King, the updating and revision of this fascicule would have been impossible. Similar sentiments should also be expressed about the role of Olwyn Owen of Historic Scotland. It is in no small measure due to her tactful help and enthusiastic support that it has been finally possible to update and complete this fascicule.

Leather

Many people have helped with the leather report over the last 35 years. Particular thanks are due to June Swann, formerly Keeper of the Shoe Collection at Northampton Museum, and the late John Thornton, of Northampton College of Technology, for their advice and guidance. Alison Reid, Mike King and Mark Hall at Perth Museum were very patient in allowing access to the leather at various times. Conservation was carried out at the laboratories of the National Museum of Antiquities (now National Museums Scotland). Additional conservation was carried out at Dundee Museum (Camperdown House). Others who provided assistance include Steve Connelly at Perth Archives, Dr Christiane Schnack, who sent copies of her reports on leather from Schleswig, Bremen and Konstanz; the staff of the British Museum, Museum of London and the York Archaeological Trust; David Ogston, minister of St John's Kirk; Ian Carlisle; David Caldwell; The Antiquaries Library, London; Rose Smith, Olwyn Owen, Derek Hall; Catherine Smith, David Perry and Lisbeth Thoms. Information on bagpipes was provided by Mr Duncan McDiarmid, Castle Menzies Farm, Aberfeldy.

The excavation and the publication

For information regarding the excavation and its history, readers are referred to the Acknowledgements section of Fascicule 1, where we extend grateful thanks to all those who contributed to the PHSAE project from inception to publication.

The post-excavation process was managed by Derek Hall from 2004 onwards and he also indexed this Fascicule. Lisbeth Thoms in her role as TAFAC editor copy-edited and oversaw the process. This fascicule was collated and prepared for publication by Catherine Smith and David Perry who gratefully acknowledge the help of their colleagues at Alder Archaeology and at SUAT Ltd, in particular David Bowler.

Illustration credits

The figures in the textile report were drawn by Dr Helen Bennett (Illus 2, 6–14); Sylvia Mackiewicz (Illus 15, 52, 56–7, 59–60, 62, 65, 67, 71); Dr P Z Dransart (Illus 23, 45–6, 85, 88–9, 93); Susan Mitford (Illus 91, 95); Alice Curteis (Illus 87); Roger Dennis (90) and were redrawn and digitised by David Munro and Tamlin Barton. Tamlin Barton digitised the plates, bar charts and lists in the text.

Leather illustrations from Illus 102 onwards were drawn by Clare Thomas with corrections and

digitisation by Dave Munro and Tamlin Barton. The
front cover painting is by Maureen Rooney Mitchell.

   Photographic illustrations are reproduced by courtesy
of the following institutions: Illus 3, Bridgman Art
Library; Illus 4, 5 and 73, the British Library; Illus 80–
4, National Museums Scotland; Illus 54, 63, Victoria
and Albert Museum (Crown Copyright); Illus 64,
Germanisches Nationalmuseum; Illus 86, Historic
Scotland; Illus 92, Bibliothèque Municipale de Tours;
Illus 100, Robert Gordon University; Illus 55 and 168–9,
copyright Perth Museum and Art Gallery.

Index to Perth High Street Archaeological Excavations 3

Note Entries in capital letters indicate chapter headings